The Politics of Irish Literature

The Politics of Irish Literature

From Thomas Davis to W. B. Yeats

BY MALCOLM BROWN

UNIVERSITY OF WASHINGTON PRESS
SEATTLE

First published in Great Britain in 1972
© Malcolm Brown 1972
University of Washington Press edition first published in 1972

Library of Congress Catalog Card Number 72–152328

ISBN 0–295–95170–2

Printed in Great Britain

I laugh at those Irish gentlemen who talk as if they were the representatives of something higher than their native land. . . . Let me tell those gentlemen, if they are not Irishmen, they are nothing.

HENRY GRATTAN
September 6, 1785

Politics are, indeed, the forge in which nations are made, and the smith has been so long busy making Ireland according to His will that she may well have some important destiny.

W. B. YEATS
"The Literary Movement in Ireland" (1901)

PREFACE

Modern Ireland provides us with the classic case of an impressive literature brought to birth by politics. My purpose here is to set that literature back into place in its original historical context. In my opinion, this operation lights up in a startling cross-illumination both the literature and the historical narrative associated with it. It is professionally hazardous, though, for it is "interdisciplinary," involving both history and literature, two separate, autonomous, and boundary-conscious academic establishments that are not commonly at ease in one another's company. Still, my task sounds as if it ought to be easy to bring off. Given: the familiar corpus of Irish literature. What could be simpler than interleaving into it the supposedly simple chronicle of Irish history?

It is not really quite so simple. Frustration begins with our discovery that the old reliable mechanisms of literary annotation cannot be domesticated in the Irish environment. An illustration of this problem is found in a popular anthology which quotes Yeats's "Under Ben Bulben," and for the lines

> You that Mitchel's prayer have heard,
> "Send war in our time, O Lord!"

gives the following annotation: "John Mitchel, an Irish patriot imprisoned for his activities, wrote in his *Jail Journal:* 'Give us war in our time, O Lord!'" The gloss is approximately accurate but very bare. We sympathize, but we can only say of this editor's friendly foray against our ignorance:

> You throw the sand against the wind,
> And the wind blows it back again.

Yeats despised historians and ordered them to get off the earth. They disrupted the market where he brought his intuitions. For ourselves, we cannot be so rash. We need to stay with the gloss on Mitchel until it surrenders its pertinent meaning. The inquiry cannot be pursued by halves, and it will grow at last into a full-length account of the life and times of nineteenth-century Ireland. This by necessity, since Irish history, like the old-time religion, gives true baptism only through total immersion.

II

The scenario of Irish history that answers our special needs does not come ready-made, though large fragments are at hand. Since the Second World War, Irish historians have published a dozen or more very incisive and important monographs dealing with the period of my inquiry. Naturally, we must begin with these to assemble the parts of our story; and insofar as they could serve a purpose, I have exploited them without stint. Since the random reader outside Ireland probably knows as little about Daniel O'Connell as about Edward the Confessor, one need hardly fear any danger of offering a twice-told tale.

Unfortunately, the monographs supply no connective tissue, for the epic impulse of the great nineteenth-century ideological historians is at this moment dead. Moreover, they are oriented almost exclusively toward parliamentary history, with an occasional side expedition into episodes of clerical intrigue. Since Irish history is sometimes parliamentary or clerical, they will sometimes tell us all we will ever want to know about a given episode—about the case of Isaac Butt, for example. About other important Irish figures who never made it to Westminster, they will tell us less. And about the most important single figure in the history of Irish cultural nationalism, Thomas Davis, the postwar historians seem almost bound by a conspiracy of silence. A scholar's only recourse is to Gavan Duffy's three ancient biographies of Davis, even though Duffy is supposed to be an inelegant citation in a bibliography. His treatment of Davis is said to be unhistorical, but who would know?

Irish historical monographs almost never touch, even lightly, upon Irish literature, and it is hard to see how they ever could. Except for the Home Rule episode, the floor of the House of Commons was totally separated from the structure of popular social affections that Thomas Davis called "felt history." And yet the poets and the parliamentarians did live in the same country at the same moment; hence there must necessarily be some perspective that can project their parallel unfolding chronicles without causing eyestrain in the beholder. I have found such a matrix in the Irish nationalist press, the only source known to me that undertook to treat—as elements of a single consecutive thread—the concurrent political and cultural history of the country. I have therefore depended upon it for providing continuity and common bond, and also the proper historical chiaroscuro appropriate to "felt history." Much of the narrative I have to relate is therefore drawn from ballads and popular sarcasms, from the passionate topical responses of hustings and newspaper office, from old wives' tales, from the savory style of chance episodes, and from the color of local personalities, especially of type specimens like William Keogh, Pierce Nagle, John Kenyon, or A. M. Sullivan, all of them insignificant in formal history, but extremely important carriers of true meanings and genuine affections in "felt history".

III

Amid the din of the voices of "felt history," no ear is so avid and no voice so piercing as that of the great poet. We will overhear many historical *aperçus* of our Irish writers as they offer us poetic footnotes upon the Irish nation, past, present, and future. At the close of our narrative they will even become historical exhibits in their own right. But while our historical reconstruction is going forward, poets must be held mostly under constraint. To take one's Irish history from an uncritical reading of Yeats, Joyce, O'Casey, and O'Faolain is, though convenient, a reckless procedure in any case; and as a base for comparative inquiry—for judging the perspicuity of a poetic vision by reference to historical assumptions drawn from precisely the same source—it is altogether pointless. But to assemble the history elsewhere and then to set it against the poetic version is a productive and enlightening exercise.

IV

The nationalist issues dealt with here are charged with a terrible immediacy. In the same week these words were written, Irishmen died in the streets battling under the familiar banners of our story. I am afraid that I must anticipate wrathful responses, set off by who knows what. I ought therefore to present my personal credentials and declare that I am myself neither Irish nor English. If I cannot pretend to be neutral toward the issues, at least I am innocent of inherited partisanship and sectarianism, a predilection so insidious that the world's costliest education often affords but superficial immunity against it. In recompense for any virtue that an overseas perspective might bring, a price is exacted. A foreigner can never possess more than a partial mastery of any historical idiom into which he was not born, and he must expect to commit an occasional solecism that will hover about his text like a gnat. We do not usually think of a gnat as a deadly insect. Yet a distinguished Irish historian once undertook to exterminate an American upstart for asserting (among other things) that the Plan of Campaign was first published on October 25, 1886, when in fact it had appeared on October 23.

I have no intention to imply that Americans are entitled to the least self-praise in philosophizing upon the story of Irish troubles. There is clearly no moral advance in the application of modern napalm to reinforce the old-fashioned outlook of "Buckshot" Forster, whose cure for dissidence was well described by his brother-in-law Matthew Arnold, partisan of sweetness and light: fling the ringleaders from the Tarpeian Rock and flog the rank and file. On the other side of the colonialist dispute, American readers of populist persuasion cannot properly feel much superiority to their Irish counterparts. Irish nationalists' interminable wrestling with their frustrations undoubtedly generated much lost motion, but also served to build up a set of paradigms to define every imaginable contingency likely to be met by an enthusiastic mass disaffection. American critics, and even poets, may with a little effort likewise learn humility from the painful and rather incomplete education of their great Irish models.

v

It is useful to look upon the round century of Irish nationalism falling between 1840 and 1940 as a unity of sorts, with a convenient break in the middle. As history, the first half opens with the rise of Young Ireland in 1842 and closes in the great Irish catastrophe of 1893, the death of parliamentary Home Rule, or in its subsequent burial under the Tory election landslide of 1895. On the literary front, it opens with Thomas Davis' first self-conscious experiment in the poetics of nationalism and ends with Lady Gregory taking young Yeats by the hand to Coole Park for convalescence and private talks about the creation of an Irish national theater. The modern half-century following 1895 can undoubtedly be better grasped after the preceding period has been mastered. I have therefore put the first half first and made it my subject. I commend the exploration of the second half to my colleagues in Irish studies. It is usually thought to be the more exciting, both in historical drama and in literary accomplishment. No doubt—but I have found the earlier half quite rich enough for the blood.

VI

I wish to express my particular gratitude to colleagues who read this work in manuscript: Professors E. H. Eby, Giovanni Costigan, and John Pearson, all of the University of Washington; Professor Maurice Harmon of University College, Dublin, and the School of Irish Studies; Professors Meredith Cary and William Keep of Western Washington State College; and Mr. Paul Hunter. Naturally, none of these scholars is to be held guilty for my sins. I wish to acknowledge also that the University of Washington Research Fund allocated to me grants for books, microfilms, and expert stenographic help.

I gratefully acknowledge permission to quote from copyrighted material as follows: *The Variorum Edition of the Poems of William Butler Yeats*, *The Variorum Edition of the Plays of William Butler Yeats*, and *The Letters of William Butler Yeats*, by permission of Michael Butler Yeats, The Macmillan Company, New York, Macmillan Company of Canada Limited, and A. P. Watt & Son, London; *Ulysses* by James Joyce by permission of Random House, Inc., New York, and The Bodley Head, London.

Seattle, Washington   M. B.
September 1971

CONTENTS

CONTENTS

PART I

The Peculiar Irish Setting

CHAPTER 1

History and Poetry: Some Irish Paradoxes

I

Let us make a list of four names: G. B. Shaw, W. B. Yeats, James Joyce, and D. H. Lawrence. If we asserted that these were the most distinguished writers in the British Isles during the first half of the twentieth century, we would probably not provoke much argument. But what a queer list it is, for three of the four were born in Dublin. A solitary, provincial city, noted in the commercial almanac chiefly as a shipping port for cattle on the hoof—why should it have been called upon to supply most of a great nation's prime literary talent? A tentative answer that insinuates itself into our thought is that culture must breed most where most is going on, where the most profound and excruciating issues drive toward resolution. For, if Dublin in the last hundred years was the least opulent city in the British Isles, it was at the same time the most exciting.

Out of what is civic excitement generated, if not out of history? From Norman times to the nineteenth century, the history of Dublin was mostly the history of the Anglo-Irish wars. Norman, Plantagenet, Brucite, Marian, Elizabethan, Jacobean, Cromwellian, Williamite, French Revolutionary, and Napoleonic—all the wars were reducible to one simple, transparent motif: Irish misfortune under foreign conquest. After Waterloo the wars recessed while Britain became the workshop of the world; and amid the celebrated advance of Victorian times, Ireland was the retarded child. There used to be a commonplace saying that Warsaw's slums were the foulest in all Europe; but an Irish poet demonstrated statistically that by comparison with tsarist Poland, Victorian Ireland had got much the worst of it.[1] Out of the mountain of sociological data that describes the unhappy condition of Ireland, a single bit can serve for a summary, if the neo-Malthusians will allow it: in the eighty years between Young Ireland (1842) and the Treaty (1922)—roughly in the life span of Yeats's father—the population of England

3

and Wales multiplied two and one-half times, but the population of Ireland shrank to one-half its original size.

Through the centuries of dominion, English statesmen found little occasion to exhibit toward Ireland the spirit of reciprocity that had successfully cemented their union with Scotland. Irishmen they regarded as just another of the lesser breeds, a prostrate enemy always behind in the indemnity payments. They adventured into Ireland, one historian has said, "as men visit a wreck on a neighbouring coast."[2] Gladstone freely confessed that the English record in Ireland was the darkest stain upon the history of a splendid people. His testimony is informed, and we must underscore it. It is the *pons asinorum* leading into every phase of Irish cultural insight, and woe to the inquirer who cannot cross it, whether from sentimentality toward the *ancien régime* or from an obsession for irony, a "Paradox Lust" in Joycese. Cecil Woodham-Smith has noted that the study of Irish history requires a temporary conversion of the greatest English heroes into villains, and that Elizabeth I, Cromwell, William III, and (one might add) the younger Pitt and Lord John Russell will appear in Irish history in a special characterization quite distinct from their English or perhaps even their absolute stature. This conversion is not just optional, it is essential.

Indignity, chronic wretchedness, and occasional episodes of the most acute agony made up the permanent norm of Irish life. The corollary was perpetual Irish disaffection, alternately flaring defiantly or sputtering in impotence, but never quite dying away. One hundred years ago Ireland was a minor agrarian nation, poor and defenseless, while England was the most formidable power the world had ever known. There were Irishmen who refused to be overawed. They fell into the habit of defying English authority whenever they believed themselves able. When not, they cried shame in a loud voice upon the political Union binding them to Great Britain and employed the deadly Irish asperity in desecrating the imperial ideal which trueborn Englishmen understood to be ordained of God. One hundred years ago this dispute showed no sign of resolution or self-exhaustion, and it was ordinarily classified as "insoluble."

All English statesmen since the Wars of the Roses understood that the Irish tie was not secure. As realists they recognized the weight of Irish hatred and the probable embarrassments of statecraft that the amputation of Ireland would impose upon a dismembered kingdom. They knew the danger of adverse precedent and looked for guidance in the truism that so long as any first defection from the empire could be prevented, additional ones could by definition never occur. These truths they both "knew" and "embodied," to use the Yeatsian discrimination. They never questioned the wisdom of their fixed policy of crushing at convenience all Irish national ambitions, and neither moral argument nor physical threat altered their resolve in the slightest. "The Repeal of the Union we regard as fatal to the Empire," Lord Macaulay proclaimed in Parliament, "and we will never consent to it—never . . . never . . . never . . . never till the four quarters of the world had been convulsed by the last struggle of the great English people for their place among the nations."[3] In defiance of Macaulay's resolve, the Irish nationalists could bring no arms or likelihood of arms. Yet they posted up the reply: "If Irishmen are ever to enjoy the rights of human beings, the British Empire must perish."[4]

Time after time the nineteenth-century Irish rebels marched against the might of the empire, and always they were beaten back. Time and again they regrouped, shifted strategy, and prepared to march again. Ireland became the prototype of colonial unrest, an advance model for a great deal of subsequent world history. Most of the standard stratagems by which a small nation may defy a great one are Irish improvisations—among them, the very powerful (if often insufficient) weapon of nonviolent "moral force," the technique of the boycott (named for the astonished Connaught land agent who was its first victim), parliamentary obstruction, and urban guerrilla harassment against an army of occupation.

Beleaguered English authority in Ireland replied with imaginative countermoves. It updated ancient methods of divide and rule and made an Irish Sudetenland of Orange Ulster. It blanketed the land with old-fashioned constabulary and modern secret police. It set up numerous reform commissions and instituted a bold but tardy scheme of land redistribution. Most auspicious experiment of all, it found the good sense, when all seemed clearly lost, to order the British garrison to march up the gangplanks of waiting troopships and sail away. In 1921 that day did come at last; the compulsive word "impossible" dropped out of the discussion of Irish affairs and Ireland became, as foretold in Thomas Davis' old fighting song, "a Nation once again." Frank O'Connor remembered the hot summer morning in 1921 when the gates of Cork barracks swung open and the departing British troops in full war kit filed out. Cork men wept happily as "seven hundred years filled with more anguish than a world beside could show" were brought to a close.[5]

On that July day the English statesmen who had always found strength in "the integrity of the empire" suddenly had to live with the fact that the integrity was broken. Their magic verbalism now worked its magic for the opposition. A provincial dispute had thereby blown up one of the great storms of modern history. Using Irish methods, India and Burma in their own good time detached themselves from English domination. After them came a stampede of new nations, as decolonialization around the world re-enacted the Irish pattern.

Afterward, the practical benefits of Irish liberation proved to be less than overwhelming. The new nation was "partitioned," that is, decapitated. Liberated Irishmen were disappointed to find that the burdens inherited from centuries of deprivation were not to be cast off overnight and that their aggressive nationalist instruments, born of adaptation to long English rule, were not demobilized easily, even after they had become a nuisance. Having pushed ahead of the times in escorting colonialism out the front door, Irishmen were also the first to discover that neocolonialism had slipped back through the kitchen window, as was said of God in Kant's metaphysics. Some Irish patriots confessed to a dead sensation of anticlimax in their hard-won victory. Ironists, especially of literary bent, have had a field day here. This phase of Irish history is not my story, but I might in passing give warning that in Irish matters, irony is often unsafe for the user. For example, Oliver St. John Gogarty once proclaimed that the Free State (the vessel of all the ironies and anticlimaxes) could never have survived except for W. B. Yeats. And nobody has ever proposed that independence ought to be called off as a bad job. Its long mission realized, Ireland subsided into repose, well earned and of uncertain duration. The ancient melodrama faded from Irish history and the foreign correspondents checked out of the Shelbourne Hotel. With lower blood pressure, Irishmen turned to confront the unheroic tensions and tasks of the new day.

II

One hundred years ago Irish political initiative flowed from the Irish Republican Brotherhood (IRB), called the Fenians, an elite conspiratorial band of militant and battle-hardened nationalist partisans. For sixty years afterward the Fenians were to pursue their single goal—full separation of Ireland from the Union with Great Britain. They scheduled an insurrection for 1865, the year of Yeats's birth. They tried again in 1867, and twice they attempted a naval invasion of Canada. Their jail rescues were among the most sensational episodes of the century, as *Ulysses* reminds us. Later, some of them turned to capricious violence. Later still, standing in the shadows, they formed an intransigent cadre inside the respectable cultural and political organs of the constitutional nationalists. From first to last they harried the tired Irish moderates, warning that all the comfortable half measures must finally fail and that, in the words of James Clarence Mangan's bloody poem of 1846, "gun-peal and slogan-cry" must echo through the Irish mountain glens and "flames wrap hill and wood" before independence could be won.

In the dock and on the gallows the Fenians' demeanor was typically so proud and ferocious that sometimes their very enemies were converted. Their recklessness caught the Irish imagination. An exciting aura surrounded their raids, their escapes, their deaths, their colossal funerals, their colorful minor mechanisms of conspiracy—their disguises, codes, and secret movements "on the hillside" or "in their own keeping," as they put it. One of their secret codes inevitably made its way into *Finnegans Wake.*

All Fenians were war-oriented. But here agreement ceased and factionalism took over, accompanied by a hearty barrage of uncomradely abuse. As the original brotherhood fell apart, the dominant faction to emerge was the Clan-na-Gael, with headquarters in New York and led by an exile, John Devoy, a humorless Irish Cato. Devoy believed that Irish nationalists ought to make use of every weapon, not even excluding the legal. Curious to learn what a constitutional program could accomplish, he poured Irish–American money into Charles Stewart Parnell's Home Rule campaign and Michael Davitt's mobilization of land-hungry peasants in the Irish Land League. Devoy's spasmodic moderation outraged a rival Fenian faction, the "Dynamitards," led by Jeremiah O'Donovan Rossa, another exile hiding in New York. Rossa thought Parnell and Davitt "impure" and contemptible; and while waiting for the great war of liberation, he proposed to fill out the time with interim acts of terrorism in the Bakhuninist style. One of the Rossa group's degenerate splinters, the "Invincibles," carried out the notorious Phoenix Park murders in 1882, the year of James Joyce's birth. An illustration both of the Dynamitard mentality and of the extraordinary reach of cultural lag may be found in the opening pages of Brendan Behan's *Borstal Boy,* which tell how a sixteen-year-old Irish boy found himself in a Liverpool hotel in 1939 determined (as we learn from Behan's biographer) to blow up the British battleships anchored in the Mersey with a package of sugar and some saltpeter.

Another Fenian fragment gathered around John O'Leary. Like all the rest, he waited hopefully for war against England; but he strenuously opposed Rossa's dynamite, Parnell's parliamentary campaign, and Davitt's peasant agitation, three equally damnable heresies in his opinion. Yet O'Leary's political differences had not fully isolated him from the two dominant wings, and in 1885 he was the most distinguished Irish revolutionary still alive, unbroken, out of jail, and at his Dublin post of duty.

Those who suppose that O'Leary was some sort of a boy scout in Irish history have misjudged their man. His purpose in life was to hasten the Irish revolution, not to impede it. In his old age all his reflexes from forty years of political work were intact. Shortly before he died and went down to his celebrated grave, he spoke at the dedication of a memorial erected in Dublin to honor James Stephens, the Fenian leader. He said: "This is not a time for making speeches. There is work to be done in Ireland, and every one of you knows what it is. Go home and make ready."[6] Young Joyce, watching O'Leary make his myopic course through the Dublin bookstalls, saw in him the living reminder of the Fenian principle of "physical force," the persuasion that it was wasted time to broach the Irish issue to an Englishman without a gun in hand. O'Leary had carried one himself in James Fintan Lalor's brief insurrection of 1849. Sixteen years later he was chairman of the council of war that had prepared the first attempted Fenian rising. He was editor of the seditious newspaper *Irish People*, and his efforts to use the paper to call Irishmen to arms had led to his arrest, trial, and conviction for treason felony. On behalf of the idea of physical force, he spent five years in English prisons and another fifteen years in exile.

III

In the long interlude of quiet between insurrection, O'Leary practiced patience, struggled to calm his hotheaded comrades, and took up the methodical tasks of organizing for the next insurrection to come. He liked to proselytize, when he could, among the Irish youth, specializing in those he might by luck steal from the ranks of the enemy, the "Ascendancy"—the Protestant landed gentry and their satellites, who made up the resident corps of English rule in Ireland.

O'Leary's second passion was belles-lettres. He had a poetess in his own household, his sister Ellen, author of "To God and Ireland True." Another lady poet, called "Eva of the *Nation*," and the novelist Charles J. Kickham were his particular friends. His rooms were stacked to the ceiling with books, and he owned the best Anglo-Irish library of his time. He knew Turgenev, du Maurier, Whistler, and Swinburne personally. His brother Fenians were puzzled when he tried to hold them accountable for familiarity with the world's literary masterpieces as well as for revolutionary virtue, but he felt his two passions were inseparable. He believed that Irish poetry must be national, and Irish nationalism poetic.

In the mid-1880s O'Leary felt more than ordinary delight when he made a convert of young William Butler Yeats, something of a defector from the enemy and, a bigger prize, a poet of great promise. This fact O'Leary was among the first to recognize as he estimated the value of his recruit. "It is one of the many misfortunes of Ireland that she has never yet produced a great poet," said O'Leary in 1886. But he added confidently, "Let us trust that God has in store for us that great gift."[7] For Yeats the meeting with O'Leary was the fateful encounter of his life, placing "the poet in the presence of his theme," a favor Yeats repaid by giving O'Leary the affection of a son and the place of highest honor in his poems and memoirs. Under O'Leary's tutelage Yeats began the apprentice study required of the new Irish–Ireland convert. He planned first to soak himself in

Irish literature, lore, folkways, and history. Next he would write Irish literature. Then, in emulation of O'Leary's instinct for political organization, he too would organize. He would make a literary movement for Ireland.

There exists a record of Yeats's first appearance at the London branch of the Irish Literary Society, where he had come one stormy night to lecture "in an eerie voice" on the fairies. From that start he moved in on all the Irish cultural clubs, stirring a membership of giggling girls to beautiful lofty thoughts. He collected other Irishmen into patriotic claques, book subscription schemes, debating societies, commemoration committees, and much later, as his crowning organizational achievement, into a national theater. Later on he sponsored a press, a modest patronage system, and an academy. Except for the Abbey Theatre, the results of most of this frenzied committee work were not very important. But apart from the committees, Yeats was a prodigy of joyful literary incitement. We have many descriptions of his persuasiveness, from George Moore's at the outset to Frank O'Connor's at the finish. For half a century Yeats kept Dublin in a pitch of literary excitement from which there was no immunity except in flight, if then. When his work was finished, he had proved beyond doubt that, however delicate and impalpable the materials of his art might be, the literary imagination can be summoned forth and organized rather easily when all the conditions are ready.

Year after year the roster of Irish writers lengthened: Douglas Hyde, George Moore, George Russell, Edward Martyn, Lady Gregory, John Synge, Padraic Colum, James Stephens, Oliver St. John Gogarty, Daniel Corkery, Sean O'Casey. Ireland, said Yeats, had rocked the cradle of genius; "nobody could have hoped for so much genius."[8] The celebrated literary formulations accumulated and cohered into an imaginative cosmos. The "terrible beauty" and the "terrible state of chassis," the "clean burial in the far north," and the snow "falling into the dark mutinous Shannon waves" became familiar catch phrases wherever books were taken seriously; and Ben Bulben and the Aran Islands were soon features of the literary landscape as common as Walden Pond and Egdon Heath. The beggar "rolling a blind pearl eye" and the Tailor of Garrynapeaka, Oisin and Angus Og, MacDonagh's bony thumb and the guests of the nation, Gypo Nolan and the man who invented sin, Mrs. Casside and Minnie O'Donovan, Sean Keogh and the Countess Cathleen—these and a thousand other creatures poured forth, jostling each other like Cruikshank's people on a Dickens title page. The cornucopia was the Irish literary movement, a loose fraternity of Dublin and Cork writers who hoped to put their careers in step with Irish history, marching, as it seemed, in full exultant surge into a resplendent future.

9

IV

Now we must move into a minor key, for here the fine harmony between
Irish poetry and Irish nationalism begins to jar. For all its splendors, the
history of the literary movement was also a history of troubles. In the first
years of the movement Yeats had come to know well the squalls of Dublin
public life, but he had ridden them out expertly. He had the support of
O'Leary's wing of the nationalists, and he could safely count on the friendliness, or at worst the neutrality, of most other Irishmen. They applauded
when he wrote of Irish topography, wedding race to "hill and wood." When
he wrote "The Tables of the Law," they did not applaud and neither did
they complain, but amiably acquiesced in his explanation that there must
be an art for the few as well as for the many. In 1899 Cardinal Logue, who
had not read *Countess Cathleen* but thought it probably heretical, was routed
in public combat and silenced, and by a Protestant poet. Yeats did not even
have to accept Arthur Griffith's offer to send out his strong-arm patriots,
who stood by anxious for a chance to silence the pious hecklers.

Somewhere along the way Yeats's Fenian support was alienated and his
working platform knocked from under him. He drifted free of the course
O'Leary first set for him. O'Leary now had new disciples who looked
toward 1916. Yeats challenged them for possession of the patriot's magic
name; for while they had distinctly heard the old man say, "Go home and
make ready," Yeats had only heard him say, "There are things no man
should do, even to save a nation." Old comrades became irreconcilable
enemies. Griffith's boyos now came to the Abbey Theatre as disrupters
instead of cohorts. The collaboration of poet and people turned sour, and
a paralyzing sense of futility settled over the writers, deadening the joy with
which they had first launched their busy Irish projects.

Yeats's own poetic voice fell long silent. His often-quoted tribute to
O'Leary as the origin of "all I have set my hand to" shifted into reverse
in the next sentence: "I read with excitement books I should find unreadable to-day, and found romance in lives that had neither wit nor adventure."[9]
His attitudes veered about and grew embittered against his "fool-driven"
land. Brooding hopefully on Armageddon, he began to spin out his cycles
of history, tinkering among his wheels within wheels with a fervor reminiscent of a retired British colonel caught up in the Shakespeare–Bacon
theory. Moore began saving up his spleen for *Hail and Farewell*, composed
for five years in secret like an infernal machine assembled in the basement;
then he went into exile, if voluntary expatriation may be so called. Synge
died hounded and rejected. Next came a generation of writers specializing
in antipatriotism. Systole, diastole—the idealist gave place to the "born
sneerer." Irish writing passed into the hands of James Joyce, Liam

O'Flaherty, Sean O'Faolain, Frank O'Connor, Patrick Kavanagh, and Austin Clarke. Yeats's indignation against Ireland arrived at the insult-sexual ("On Those That Hated the *Playboy*"). Joyce pushed on to the insult-carminative in the close of the "Sirens" chapter of *Ulysses*, and stands as champion of the literary method that guaranteed a tavern brawl.

The insolence of poets, shouted from afar, from Zurich or Belgravia, or ventured under the license allowed a dying man, answered a blow with a blow. To be rejected in Dublin was not just an ordinary rebuff. Shelley, Byron, and Walter Savage Landor had embarked, too, on political adventure, and William Morris even saw the inside of a jail. But their disputes were always free and fair, merely a grave difference among English gentlemen. For reasons easy to discover, Irish debate did not honor such rules of war. Dublin's verbal warfare was pitiless and deadly—whence arose her aesthetic causes célèbres. Not counting the lesser skirmishes, five poetical disputes expanded into engagements known the world around. (1) During the week of 1907 in which Synge's *Playboy of the Western World* opened at the Abbey Theatre, riots occurred each night protesting unpatriotic aspersions against Irish chastity and loving-kindness. (2) Dublin's city fathers rejected with insolence the offer made by Lady Gregory's nephew, Sir Hugh Lane, to give a collection of paintings to the city, conditional upon the erection of an art gallery astride the Liffey to house them. (3) Joyce's failure to publish *Dubliners* in Ireland proved the respectable Dublin literary publishers to be liars and cowards. (4) The Dublin popular press, supported by the cackle of bigotry and ignorance, subjected the Irish writers to a cross fire of sarcasms and mean conjecture for two decades. (5) Ireland celebrated her independence by inaugurating in 1929 a literary censorship whose zeal in the cause of old-maidish prudery achieved laughable, unimaginable, Platonic perfection.[10]

Time hardly healed these wounds. After public derision of the poets had wearied itself, a massive, glacial indifference settled in. Said Yeats: "We and all the Muses are things of no account." Today the edifice of Irish literature is best known to Irishmen by hearsay, as another of those "attractions"—like Bunratty Castle, though less remunerative—which, for reasons that remain mysterious to the native, draw strangers from afar and sustain tourism. Foreign pilgrims used to lament that Yeats's Galway tower, Thoor Ballylee, which had once enshrined a lonely poet in communion with mysterious wisdom, had been repossessed by the milch cow, Ireland's other tribal totem older than Yeats's Anglo–Irish horse. Recently the cows were driven out and the tower was restored; not by popular demand, though, but by the Irish tourist board.

V

Meanwhile, as if through the mechanics of Yeats's interlocking cones, the literary slump in Ireland was balanced off by boom times abroad, where Irish writers were finding a very friendly welcome. Fastidious journalists in London declared Moore to be one of the most accomplished stylists of our language. An Englishwoman, Miss A. E. F. Horniman, who was also a Unionist, came forward to subsidize the Abbey Theatre. Yeats went often to dazzle the American lecture circuit, was considered for a British peerage, and won the Nobel Prize. Synge's box office in London was a sellout; some of the Abbey actors were called to opulence in Beverly Hills; and O'Casey reported that the Yankee dollar made up nine-tenths of his royalties. Joyce's fame, emanating out of Paris, shot up in dazzling splendor, and he became the most talked-about writer in Europe.

Yeats and Joyce both died at the opening of the Second World War, and at its close, as the Cold War commenced, a reassessment began in earnest. An enormous Yeats-Joyce-Irish scholarly and critical corpus accumulated, to which seemingly everybody, including the present writer, contributed his mite. The academic channels of belles-lettres filled with encomiums. Such a mass of posthumous laudation gathered about the great Irishmen that James Stephens' old-fashioned praise of Yeats in 1948—"perhaps the greatest since Tennyson"—sounded like another case of Dublin spite. American appreciations traveled overseas to the desks of Dublin newspaper book-page editors who, unlike many of their countrymen, often knew their Irish literature expertly. They courteously reviewed them all, patiently pointing out the foreigner's inevitable errors—that Standish O'Grady was the name of two different men, that the naval bombardment of the General Post Office and the shelling of the Four Courts were not the same historical transaction, and so on. Now and then they betrayed a humorous wonderment at the commotion, like Synge's old Aranman who concluded that Irish studies must be the chief occupation of the outside world.

VI

The reverberations of acclaim won by Irish writers abroad among strangers and, on the other hand, the chilly reception accorded them by their fellow Irishmen make a cultural anomaly that has no parallel. Other great international writers one thinks of—Goethe, say, or Victor Hugo or Mark Twain—were indigenous above all and found their esteem abroad only a mildly pleasant echo of their esteem at home. The Irish writers' formally declared purpose was even more explicitly national. Yeats was to be at "one with Davis, Mangan, Ferguson" (an ambition criticized as immodest by the

Dublin press). Lady Gregory wrote "to give dignity to Ireland," George Moore to record "what Paddy Durkin and Father Pat would say to me by the roadside." Even Joyce, as every undergraduate knows, aimed to "forge in the smithy of my soul the uncreated conscience of my race." These were the ideals; in actuality they had to find all their friends in Paris, in Sweden, in Naini Tal, in New Haven, in Sassenach England, while Paddy Durkin and Father Pat passed by on the other side.

Playing over a familiar score, we have now reached the page where the popular disenchantment-with-Ireland motif is usually sounded. According to the customary interpretation, O'Leary was a type of the tempter who leads poets down the political road to artistic suicide. Better the Irish writers should have taken Ezra Pound's advice to "swill out these national movements"; then they might have been spared their victimization by the Irish multitude, which spurned and soiled their generous high gifts. Have the writers not themselves cried out in pain that Ireland is "the old sow that eats her farrow," a land of "stupid, boorish, and dispirited people," "maimed at the start" by "great hatred" in "little room," where nothing could thrive but the "convent, the public-house, and the racing meet," or in another of George Moore's triads, where nothing could thrive but the celibate: the nun, the priest, and the bullock? Has it not been written that the Irish informer is "indispensable" to Ireland's "hurley-stick rebellions" and that "all that was sung, all that was said in Ireland is a lie"? Irish literature sometimes seemed to know no other subject than the vulgarity and greed of the party politicians, the life-denying bigotry of the clergy, the ignobility of the Irish rabblement. Second thoughts on this conclusion would seem to be not merely gratuitous, but actually perverse.

But what fickle haters the writers were. Irish ignobility, Irish grandeur, these contraries flashed on and off with such a wayward impulse that the Irish do seem surely a queer sort of people at the latter end of the Western world.

> A Muse by these is like a mistress used,
> This hour she's idolized, the next abused.

Yeats's "indomitable Irishry" of today were his 'rats" yesterday, and Joyce's lousy Irish cur mutated occasionally into a noble wolfhound. Literary commentators are more consistent. They do not forgive Dublin the trouble she gave her writers. Their outlook is somewhat myopic, for when all is said, Dublin's bounty was infinitely more generous than Sweden's. "Strife is better than loneliness," said Yeats's favorite Gaelic proverb. To understand what he meant, one must try to imagine the Irish writers transported to Belfast, or Sheffield, to keep the comparison to English-speaking cities of Dublin's size, or to the author's own city, Seattle, where theater riots are naturally quite unknown.

Whatever the charms of the disenchantment-with-Ireland motif, the Irish historical place and time were in fact necessities to the poets. At the height of the movement Yeats and Moore liked to quote Turgenev: "Russia can do without every one of us, but not one of us can do without her—Woe to him who thinks he can, and woe two-fold to him who actually does without her! The cosmopolitan is a nonentity—worse than a nonentity; without nationality is no art, nor truth, nor life, nor anything."[11] If the Irish theme were deleted from the work of Synge, Colum, Lady Gregory, Stephens, O'Casey, Joyce, O'Flaherty, O'Faolain, O'Connor, or Kavanagh, nothing at all would be left. If it were deleted from the work of Yeats, most of the best would be gone. The least Irish of the writers in the movement, Lionel Johnson, still did his best work in Ireland. "The green shadow of a Ferrara wall" or some other distant haven for the imagination often tempted the Irish writers. Sometimes temptation won and some alternative path was chosen. All did lead as predicted to nonentity. It is undoubtedly the case that had it not been for Yeats, John O'Leary's name would not be known outside of Ireland. But this proposition can also be turned around without absurdity. Or at least the point has been argued by one formidable witness, Frank O'Connor, who thought that "but for an accidental meeting with the old Fenian leader John O'Leary, Yeats might easily have ended as a fine minor poet like Walter De La Mare."[12]

In a more elegant variant, the disenchantment motif concedes this dependence and grants that O'Leary's meeting with Yeats was a necessary first step in the operation of the "fortunate fall." Ireland made the bed where one could carry out the symbolist directive, *se coucher dans la merde*, and participated in the creativity of her writers in the sense that John Wilkes Booth might be said to have made a contribution to "When Lilacs Last in the Dooryard Bloom'd." Irish experience is thought to be an agon and Irish literature a transfiguration of Irish ignobility into the exaltation of art. The Lane art gallery affair had put Lady Gregory through one of these transfigurations, the subject of a poem by Yeats, "To a Friend Whose Work Has Come to Nothing." This poem was later paraphrased in W. H. Auden's familiar line on Yeats which fixes the attitude handily: "Mad Ireland hurt you into poetry."

VII

But was Ireland really mad? To look skeptically on Auden's infectious epithet discloses that it has been hiding one of those large intellectual vacuums that curiosity must eventually find disconcerting. What precisely was the relationship of the Irish literary movement to Ireland itself? The answer to the question calls for a bit of digging.

Our inquiry opens with a fact: in 1886 Yeats received from O'Leary certain Irish books that were to initiate his career. What were the books and what did they say? We can answer these questions by consulting a reading guide for patriots published by O'Leary in that year. This little pamphlet, *What Irishmen Should Know*, is interesting for its anticipation of several of Yeats's own opinions: that learning the Irish language was beyond the capabilities of the human brain, but that the Gaelic legends and poems were just as good in translation anyhow; that Irish folklore and mythology were precious national possessions, though lacking any imaginable applicability; that James Clarence Mangan was a better poet than Thomas Davis, but that neither one was the poet Ireland really deserved. As the pamphlet shows, O'Leary started his pupils out with a very inclusive course in Irish literature, not forgetting such fringe claimants as George Farquhar and George Berkeley. Upon this base he envisioned that a more intense fire would be lighted by the deeds and words of a group of literary revolutionists of the 1840s called Young Ireland, and by their mouthpiece, the *Nation*, the most important Irish nationalist newspaper in nineteenth-century history. That extraordinary journal had voiced decade after decade the unrehearsed responses of embattled, eloquent, and intelligent men to each week's new crop of Irish errors, lessons, small victories, and large frustrations, and it made a prime vehicle for the "felt history" of nineteenth-century Ireland.

Three members of the *Nation*'s staff formed the core of O'Leary's reading program. The first figure of Young Ireland and the foremost cultural theorist of Irish separatism was Thomas Davis, dead forty years. His life work was the *Nation* itself; he published nothing else. Second to Davis, O'Leary placed John Mitchel, then some ten years dead, a Tom Paine turned Jeremiah, Young Ireland's wildest temperament, who later turned his great energies to proslavery journalism in Virginia. Yeats read his *History of Ireland* and also an earlier work, *Jail Journal*, a record of hatreds so intense that it has earned a sort of special immortality for the incandescence of its language. The third was Sir Charles Gavan Duffy, whom Yeats would soon engage in literary combat, cofounder of the *Nation*, a last survivor of Homeric days in Irish history during the 1840s. In 1880 he had been called into service as a polemical historian in order to answer a slanderous and tendentious history of Ireland that had recently been published by Thomas Carlyle's disciple, J. A. Froude. Many Irish rebuttals to Froude appeared, but O'Leary gave the prize to Duffy's memoirs, *Young Ireland*.

O'Leary's three Young Irelanders were all exceptional human beings in their separate ways. Their writings are impassioned, lucid, fearless, and in the English view, often criminal. They made up a powerful exhibit for

O'Leary to offer a respectable young student like Yeats, who had to take his nationality mostly out of books. Yet the sum of their writings still left the Irish story only partially and obliquely told.

O'Leary's books were, in fact, secondary. The oral tradition was the main channel through which Irish nationalist sentiment flowed, and its chief expressions were folk proverbs, slogans, hero and villain symbols, ballads recited and songs sung, and the arguments and ruminations of the agrarian organizer, the parish priest, the publican, or some other village Nestor. Living Irishmen could remember when the peasants were universally illiterate, there were no popular books at all, and the oral tradition was the sole medium of communication:

> By the fireside on a winter night, at fairs and markets, the old legends and traditions were a favorite recreation. The wandering harpers and pipers kept them alive; the itinerant school-master taught them with more unction than the rudiments. Nurses and seamstresses, the tailor who carried his lapboard and shears from house to house, and from district to district, the pedlar who came from the capital with shawls and ribbons, the tinker who paid for his supper with a song and a story, were always ready with tales of the wars and the persecution.[13]

In Thomas Davis' time three-fourths of the Irish peasants were still illiterate, and in Yeats's time the oral folk channels remained vigorous. Illiteracy constituted one of the charms of the country for the literary.

Beyond question, Yeats established genuine Irish connections when he took up a stance receptive to O'Leary's Ireland. But neither of O'Leary's sources communicated perfectly to his understanding. In the popular oral tradition even O'Leary himself was never quite at home, as he sometimes lamented. Yeats's line of informants from "the indomitable Irishry" was also perhaps rather thin. Uncle George Pollexfen's cook out in Sligo; Katherine Tynan's prize folk specimen, Pat Gogarty, the cobbler of Clondalkin; and Lady Gregory's Gaelic-speaking paupers, always conveniently available for interview, hovering like "flies in winter" in the Gort workhouse (a scene which O'Faolain sketched sardonically in his story "The End of the Record")—these could not easily bear the great weight of aesthetic responsibility Yeats's theories made them liable for. Here we find in embryo one meaning of his lifelong struggle with the problem of "abstraction," a problem little known to John Synge, "that rooted man," and even less to such indigenous and well-manured garden specimens as Joyce, O'Casey, or Kavanagh.

While Yeats's grasp of O'Leary's nationalism was often incisive, it was also somewhat blurred by willfulness and impatience. The *Nation* itself, the indispensable record, he did not know. A witticism disposed of his fellow patriots who went "daily" to "some public library" to pore over Thomas Davis' "old newspaper."[14] Irish historians he held in the loftiest contempt. For a pure lyricist, his offhand opinionation would have been inconsequential. But in a poet who was rather aggressive in asserting his private historical insights, any failure of discernment would have to be noted, if only to highlight his areas of clear-sightedness. The function of a seer, etymologically speaking, is to see.

When Joyce came on the scene a generation later, he required no reading course in Irish history, having actually lived in it with an intimacy and depth denied to Yeats. As everybody knows, his Irish experience was extraordinarily compelling. It was somewhat circumscribed, though, by the selective absorption of the Irish past into the popular Catholic tradition. The "age of Burke and of Grattan" did not impinge at all upon his imagination, nor Young Ireland either, except for snatches of its songs; but he was passionately immersed in the Fenian and Home Rule episodes. His chief limitation as an Irish witness derives from the timing of his exile. He left Ireland in 1904 at the bottom of a dreary political downswing, and he tended to view the condition of Ireland as an infinite stasis prolonging that one miserable moment. As time passed and Irish history moved on, his exile necessarily rendered him increasingly remote and ignorant, but without any compensating adjustment of his self-assurance. The presumption of Ezra Pound to speak dogmatically on American affairs after a lifetime of absence is a parallel case. Still, insofar as Arthur Balfour's Ireland was once upon a time reality, Joyce was without rival in his mastery of its taste and flavor, its "felt history." His strength was Yeats's weakness.

Yeats was a witness more than once to the excesses of Irish *ressentiment*. When hatreds burst into frenzied spasms of futile destruction, it made an ugly sight, impossible to overlook, easy to deplore. But why was it that angry Irishmen stayed always at that simmer? One cannot discover whether he ever earnestly asked himself the question. And yet the question must be asked.

CHAPTER 2

Thomas Davis' Ireland

I

Nineteenth-century Irish colonial discontent focused its animus against the Act of Union of 1800. In form the Union was a novel Irish institution, but in substance it was a wearing and tiresome old story—more English misrule.

One of the areas of Irish grievance was commercial. English ambition proposed to hold Irish trade under those same famous disabilities that made history in colonial Boston and Philadelphia. Irish merchants resented the degraded economic status allotted to them, and awaited their chance for revenge. There is nobody who does not know the old adage, "England's extremity is Ireland's opportunity," and that opportunity came when the English army bogged down in Virginia and New Jersey after 1776. With Henry Grattan at their head, the Irish Protestants quickly organized their own army, called the Volunteers, a militia nominally for defense against the French flank, but actually for asserting a military argument to free Irish commerce from English interference. Emulating the American example, the Volunteers met in convention at Dungannon in 1782 and pronounced the Dublin Parliament, "Grattan's Parliament," to be independent of Westminster. The bold act of 1782 ushered in a brief season of Irish mercantile prosperity, leaving a symbolic mark upon the landscape in James Gandon's stately Palladian Dublin buildings, the Four Courts, the Custom House, and the remodeled Parliament House.

But a second economic misfortune even more grave was the condition of Irish agriculture. About a hundred years before the Union, William III's armies had won crushing victories over the Irish Catholics at the Boyne and Aughrim. The Williamite wars then closed in 1691 with the Treaty of Limerick, a Carthaginian peace by which a small minority, the Protestant Ascendancy, seized exclusive possession of all the Irish civic and economic rights. With an acquisitive eye fixed upon the remaining Catholic assets, Dublin's Protestant Parliament enacted anti-Catholic laws of the most imaginative brutality, resuscitating all the religious hatreds of the English Reformation as though the Spanish Armada, Guy Fawkes, and the burning

18

of Latimer and Ridley were contemporary episodes. Thus began the infamous century of the Penal Laws, demeaning Irishmen into "slaves that were spat on," in Yeats's cruel taunt.

A long history of conquests, plantations, and confiscations, topped off by the Penal Laws, built an intolerable rack-rent land system, combining the most morbid features of feudal and laissez faire exploitation. In this sector of the Irish economy, the Protestants were no longer the oppressed, but the oppressors. Bishop Berkeley looked at the gentry of Penal Law times and said: "vultures with iron bowels." A contemporary fellow dignitary of the Irish Anglican church, outraged by the same ruthlessness in the countryside, composed a little pamphlet we usually think of as the most scathing satire of all the literature of the world. It was entitled "A Modest Proposal for Preventing the Children of poor People in Ireland, from being a Burden to their Parents or Country."

Agrarian abuses built up a potentially explosive anger among the peasants. And since the Protestant Ascendancy felt keenly the personal dangers of vengeance to which the top-heavy structure exposed them, they welcomed the security provided by a sturdy English connection. On this front they were impelled toward imperial loyalty.

The violent and seemingly insoluble contradiction in the ambitions of the Irish Protestants—alienated from England, yet suffering the indignity of the English connection in order to allay the nightmares of an Irish jacquerie—supplies us with one of the essential keys to modern Irish history and literature. The shouting of the Volunteers had hardly died away at Dungannon before the dilemma began to blight the great victory just achieved. For, while the 1782 declaration asserted Irish independence, it also reaffirmed Irish loyalty to England through the crown. England departed from Parliament House, good-bye; but England was still in possession of Dublin Castle and maintained there a disruptive dual government, ultimately fatal.

When Grattan's Parliament turned to confront the agrarian crisis (or its equivalent form, the religious crisis), it found itself virtually paralyzed. It was a fabulously unrepresentative legislature, three-fourths of the members representing pocket or rotten boroughs. The Irish pension list for bribing the members was even larger than the English; and Grattan's historical luster is based in good part on his strange honesty, his refusal to sell the nation for personal advantage. Even so, his conscience was not quite clean, and much of the Dublin parliament's forensic talent was spent in debates between the Grattan and Ponsonby Whigs and the Fitzgibbon and Beresford Tories on the question whether the Protestant Ascendancy could best perpetuate itself by moderating or by solidifying the civil disabilities of the Catholics. The permanent unfinished business of the House was self-reform, and it remained unfinished business at the end.

Militant republicans from the old disbanded Volunteers looked upon the arrogance of Irish political corruption with growing anger, and some of them concluded that revolution itself would not be so difficult as parliamentary reform. Among these was Wolfe Tone, a Protestant who had been awakened by the American Revolution and set afire by the French. He rose to public prominence as the secretary of the Catholic Convention, organized to gather whatever benefits it might from William Pitt's fear of the rising crescendo of the French Revolution. There had been two partial remissions of the Penal Laws, one in 1778, the second in the intoxicating times after Dungannon; and in 1792–93, with Tone playing an important part in the negotiations, a third installment of remission was petitioned by the Catholic Convention. In a sudden burst of generosity in that regicide year, Pitt extended the voting franchise to the Irish Catholics, not only to the respectability but to the mass of the peasantry, to the so-called forty-shilling freeholders. But returning quickly to sobriety, he still withheld the right of Catholics to sit in Parliament. The hordes of new voters were thus privileged to vote for the same Protestant oligarchy that already held the parliamentary seats. The comedy in College Green was unrelieved until the pool of blood gathered at the end of the story.

Tone saw in the Irish peasants a natural revolutionary force that might sweep away at a blow both the English connection and Grattan's Parliament, which he labeled "bungling," "unworthy," treacherous, and despicable. Since there is a good deal of modern confusion on this first principle, Tone's critique deserves a passing notice. He wrote a pamphlet in 1791 called "An Argument on Behalf of the Catholics of Ireland," the Irish equivalent of the American firebrand, *Common Sense*, by his friend Tom Paine:

> The Revolution of 1782 was a Revolution which enabled Irishmen to sell at a much higher price their honor, their integrity, and the interests of their country; it was a Revolution which, while at one stroke it doubled the value of every boroughmonger in the kingdom, left three-fourths of our countrymen slaves as it found them, and the government of Ireland in the base and wicked, and contemptible hands who had spent their lives in degrading and plundering her; nay, some of whom had given their last vote decidedly, though hopelessly, against this, our famous Revolution. Who of the veteran enemies of the country lost his place or his pension? Who was called forth to station or to office from the ranks of the opposition? Not one. The power remained in the hands of our enemies, again to be exerted for our ruin, with this difference, that formerly we had our distresses, our injuries, and our insults gratis at the hands of England; but now we pay very dearly to receive the same with aggravation, through the hands of Irishmen—yet this we boast of and call a Revolution![1]

While Tone was still working for the Catholic Convention, he joined with a coterie of Belfast and Dublin republicans to organize a revolutionary center called the United Irishmen. The purpose was to arouse the country to take up arms for the principles of the rights of man in the manner of George Washington. Forced to flee the country, he journeyed via America to France to secure military aid. The decisive trial of arms came in 1798 (a date fully memorialized in Irish song), with uncoordinated insurrections in Ulster, Mayo, and at Vinegar Hill in Wexford. The French ships moving to the rebels' aid were delayed, and the troops that finally landed at Killala could not give the support promised. Tone himself was captured at sea aboard a French warship. The rebels were defeated (as is told in Yeats's *Cathleen ni Houlihan*), their leaders were hanged, and thousands of the rank and file were slaughtered. Irishmen never forgot the ghastly details of the pitch caps, mobile gibbets, disembowelings, and garrotings at the hands of the roving Protestant yeoman terrorists; and Parnell brooded all his life upon the tale of a '98 rebel on the family estate in Wicklow who was beaten to death across the belly while tied to the cart's tail.

The Dublin Parliament's pretense to independence was now rudely over-ridden as a matter of course. In an intensified atmosphere of greed and jobbery, Grattan's Parliament passed Pitt's Act of Union with Great Britain and expired. Grattan protested in an outburst of passionate oratory, and voted against the Union. His vote was of no value. The Union became a fact on the first day of the nineteenth century, terminating the age "of Burke and of Grattan," among whose notable acts were its pusillanimous assertion and then corrupt surrender of the Irish nationality. Grattan's subdued eulogy over the corpse of his Parliament confessed that something was amiss from the start, and that the members never were really happy "to stand in the sphere of their own infamy."

II

After the Act of Union there was one final bloody spasm of resistance. Robert Emmet, a young Protestant friend of Tone's and Tom Moore's, was led by wishful hopes of a Napoleonic invasion of England in the summer of 1803 to organize a supporting Irish diversion. Even the warmest friend of Ireland must confess that its revolutionary staff work throughout history was never better than slovenly. The bungling of the mobilization dates forestalled the rising in the countryside, while in Dublin the mob pushed Emmet aside and roved leaderless through the streets. After murdering a couple of citizens, including the lord chief justice, they scattered at the first appearance of the English troops. Emmet fled into Wicklow and could have escaped to America, but he came back to town to visit his sweetheart and was captured. He was tried before Lord Norbury, the "hanging judge" of the new "bloody assizes." Understanding that his life was already lost, he took pains to turn the courtroom into a tragic stage. Upon being sentenced, he addressed the court with an astounding piece of prose that immediately won the same currency in Ireland that the Gettysburg Address enjoys in America. Readers of *Ulysses* will recall Mr. Bloom's fixation on its last two sentences, though the recitation as a whole runs to a couple of hundred words:

> My lords you are impatient for the sacrifice. The blood which you seek is not congealed by the artificial terrors which surround your victim—it circulates warmly and unruffled through the channels which God created for noble purposes, but which you are now bent to destroy, for purposes so grievous that they cry to heaven. But yet be patient! I have but a few more words to say— I am going to my cold and silent grave—my lamp of life is nearly extinguished —my race is run—the grave opens to receive me, and I sink into its bosom. I have but one request to make at my departure from this world, it is—the charity of its silence. Let no man write my epitaph; for as no man, who knows my motives, dare now vindicate them, let not prejudice or ignorance asperse them. Let them rest in obscurity and peace! Let my memory be left in oblivion, and my tomb remain uninscribed, until other times and other men can do justice to my character. When my country takes her place among the nations of the earth, then, and not till then, let my epitaph be written. I have done.

By Norbury's sentence the prisoner was to be hanged and his head severed from his body; the orders were carried out by the executioner in faithful detail before a large Dublin crowd, standing petrified in terror. The scene recurred in Irish nightmares for three generations.

III

With the Dublin capital out of business, the scene of Irish political activity shifted to London, but with the same old Ascendancy cast of actors from College Green. Pitt's campaign for the Union had given the Catholic bishops to understand that their support would be thoughtfully rewarded by the full repeal of all remaining Penal Laws. Lured by that half-promise, they had given his enterprise their blessing. But when the Union had passed, they were informed that Emancipation would cause His Majesty George III to suffer personal pain, so that it was therefore out of the question. Thus, Catholics still could not sit in the House of Commons, though they did have the right to vote.

The moral bankruptcy of the old leadership being plain to all, the people groped for some scheme to pool their voting strength in their own rather than in the landlords' interest. They chose for leader a young Catholic lawyer, Daniel O'Connell, a modern breed of politician with an extraordinary populist flair. In 1826 he backed an opponent of the reigning Beresford family in Waterford and won. In 1828 he directly challenged the Protestant monopoly of parliamentary seats by offering himself as a candidate in Clare. Defying the threat of eviction—for the ballot was not secret— peasant voters to the last man mustered at his call. In a happy frenzy of agitation, O'Connell got himself elected, and shortly afterward forced the Duke of Wellington and Sir Robert Peel to surrender full religious emancipation. The Ascendancy never forgave the upstart. He had insinuated himself between them and "their" peasants, and was that not plain larceny?

Once aroused, the peasants proved difficult to pacify. While still hot from the Emancipation campaign they turned to make war upon the Anglican tithes, the most baroque insolence of English rule. Although most of the Irish population was Catholic, the Anglican Church of Ireland was the established church, solely endowed with the right to tithe. Catholic peasants could not understand why they should support a church to which they did not belong and to which, in most of the country, nobody belonged at all. Spontaneously and without much support from O'Connell, peasants began to resist tithe payment. Some nameless rebel hit upon a new weapon he called "exclusive dealing," later to be called "moral Coventry" by Parnell and "boycott" by Michael Davitt. There were clashes with the constabulary and several dozen deaths. Spreading over Ireland, the tithe war was very troublesome to eradicate, and it forced the English to call the first of their partial, stubborn, and oblique retreats.

When O'Connell, "the Liberator," took his seat in the House of Commons at the head of an Irish delegation, he found his followers too few to exert prime force, but numerous enough to make the balance between Whig and Tory. In 1835 he formed a coalition with Viscount Melbourne and the Whigs, the "Litchfield House compact," by which he won modest Irish concessions and patronage in exchange for Irish votes. Whenever he could, he said, he always liked "to get a little something for Ireland." As the Whigs' power waned, he foresaw a Tory ministry and the end of his Whig alliance. Recalling his famous successes on the Clare hustings, he turned his thoughts once more to peasant agitation and announced the founding of the Loyal Irish Association for the Repeal of the Union. This was the cue that brought the Young Irelanders in 1842 onto the stage of Irish history, Thomas Davis in the lead.

IV

While O'Connell was playing his friendly parliamentary game with the English Whigs, the condition of Ireland was rapidly worsening. The burden

23

of Irish troubles always fell heaviest upon the peasants, since they were not just the bottom of the heap but the substance of the nation, the primary source of Irish wealth. Viewed from afar, from above, from Dublin or London, the peasantry seemed a vast, teeming, roiling mass of faceless humanity, repulsive and frightening. The spell of this terror was very persistent. Even a casual reader of W. E. H. Lecky's Irish histories will sense that this civilized and learned Unionist gentleman looked upon the Irish mass of Victorian times with uncontrollable hatred and terror. It also survived into modern Irish literature, where it can be clearly traced through Joyce's work, and it informs much of Yeats's poetry, including "The Second Coming." Looking at itself in its own mirror, the peasantry saw its facelessness disappear; but its savage vitality still showed, broken into a puzzle of contradictory potentials. William Carleton, one of the rare Irish writers who "knew the peasant," depicted him as a creature compounded of ignorance, affection, wild poetry, anger, hospitality, terror, superstition, drunkenness, piety, orgiastic pugnacity, and cutting wit, a blood brother to the muzhik of Tolstoy and Turgenev.[2] The common base for both the outside and the inside views was a brutal, brutalizing poverty, matched with a volcanic but spasmodic human energy.

During the Napoleonic Wars the value of Irish corn had risen abnormally, inflated by scarcity and Corn Law bounties. Irish landlords found profit in adding variable units of labor to their fixed units of land, intensifying tillage to the limit. The Irish peasantry had cooperated with this great economic law by taking up smaller and smaller parcels of poorer and poorer land, paying ever higher rent, and meanwhile mutliplying merrily to replenish the earth. At the time of O'Connell's Emancipation campaign, the boom in small grains was already passing. Suddenly economic law forbade tillage and smiled upon the grazing of cattle. Units of labor had now to be subtracted from the land. The glib Malthusian word "overpopulation" was uttered with increasing vigor, together with the wisdom that "Irishmen breed like rabbits."

In Thomas Davis' Ireland, the countryside recognized three dominant classes of peasants—graziers, small peasants, and cottiers—all competing fiercely against one another for the land. The graziers, the "strong farmers" of Yeats's poetry, were the top of the heap. They were tenants, but tenants on the grand scale, men of substance owning great cattle herds that fed on the rich lime-fed Irish grass until ready to be shipped to England for fattening and slaughter. In 1842 graziers anticipated a happy future, with the prospect of continually expanding pasturage at the expense of the tillage of their distressed neighbors.

Next below the graziers lay the huge mass of small peasants. The typical Irishman of 1842 was a subsistence farmer living entirely on the produce of a few rented acres. It is well known that the potato was his staple food. Next to the potato patch was a little plot of pasture that fed the family cow. Since potatoes and buttermilk made up his diet, the peasant had little to buy but salt meat for biennial protein orgies at Easter and Christmas. If there were common lands on the hillside for grazing a sheep or two, the family clothing was homespun and handwoven. But while self-sufficient in one sense, the Irish peasant was also entangled in the whims of world trade. In addition, he required a sizable lump of hard cash for the land-lord: he planted half of his holding to small grains, which the family re-served for cash sale and dared not touch for its own use. The butter each week and the calf each year went to market to raise cash for the landlord. If there were leftover potatoes, they fed a pig, which was also turned into cash for rent; English cartoons symbolized the Irish peasant as an idiot bumpkin off to the fair with this same rent-paying pig held by a string tied to one hind leg.

This economy was highly precarious. The impounding or the accidental death of a cow might destroy a family. Any fall in the price of oats, any rise in the rent upset the delicate balance between cash and subsistence, requiring the oats to encroach on the potato patch and bringing tightened belts all winter. Yet the small peasant lived in relative opulence. Below him lay the still more precarious world of the cottiers, about one-fourth of the Irish population, landless, cowless, pigless agricultural laborers. With a couple of pounds scraped together out of haphazard wages at one-fourth the English farm-labor pay scale, they rented a spare quarter-acre of potato ground from some small peasant and starved along through the year on the crop it produced. Often, when deprived even of shelter, they took to the roads as itinerant beggars. Peasants slipping down the social ladder came at last to this ultimate bottom where they were confronted each day by Malthus' well-known "positive checks" and stood face to face with death, from "disease occasioned by squalid poverty, by damp and wretched cabins, by bad and insufficient clothing, by the filth of their persons, and occasional want"—Malthus' own words on Ireland.

To compound the chaos in the countryside, there had grown up a class of rural "middlemen"—land agents, rent collectors, tithe proctors, and other overseers—whose function was to urge along the upward flow of money so that the much-handled pound note the peasant surrendered out of the safe-keeping of his tall hat could make its ultimate way into the hands of the gentility. Feared and hated by their business contacts both above and below, and generally disdained as parasites, these functionaries made natural villains for the novels about the Irish agrarian scene. Only O'Connell would spare them a kind word: as the organizers of the yeoman terror of 1798 they had saved the country from revolution, he said.

The landlords in Thomas Davis' Ireland were absorbed in a frantic search for some method to rid their lands of small tenants. Rural depopulation had already begun as scattered tenancies vanished, some through the attrition of chronic rural poverty, others in the recurrent localized famines. But this process was too leisurely to give satisfaction. To speed things up, "clearings" or "exterminations"—that is, massive evictions—had been experimentally undertaken with partial success. They had so inflamed the peasantry, however, that caution and postponement seemed wise. In 1842 the Irish agrarian issue rested upon this surly and unstable truce.

Those charged with maintaining the tranquillity of Ireland were not to be envied. The peasants were observed to be moving toward some great crisis, and the gathering fear of the "trefoil stained with blood" could not be eased. Ireland had inherited a long tradition of anarchic land war waged by the "Ribbon" societies (referring to the ribbon given the new member during the secret ritual of initiation as a private token of membership), secret terrorist lodges which fought evictions by "moonlighting" vengeance. Ribbon fervor was amalgamated into O'Connell's disciplined new mass organizations, producing a lockstep stride more frightening than the old-fashioned moonlight outrages. A few hamstrung jackasses or a murder here and there had raised no issue affecting general landlord survival; but when the peasantry began to stir en masse, the distant rumble of revolution was unmistakable.

One could never predict, though, whether a random stimulus would produce agrarian frenzy or catalepsy. The peasantry found great difficulty in keeping up momentum, in integrating a self-shaping force, or in developing leaders out of their own ranks. Between 1798 and Young Ireland no leader of consequence had appeared among them, and in the whole of the nineteenth century they would show only two: the agrarian Michael Davitt at the bottom of the social scale; and at the opposite end Cardinal Cullen, of "strong-farmer" stock, who employed his close peasant realism with equal effect in Vatican intrigue on behalf of papal infallibility or in the throttling of Irish insurgence. Leaderless, the peasantry lay a tempting instrument for some other hand to wield. According to one Gray Porter, a Protestant landlord of county Fermanagh, when revolutionary Ireland finally took the field, it would consist of "dashing and splendid" Protestant officers like himself on horseback followed into battle by the "Catholic multitudes."[3] Naturally the other social classes nominated themselves for the same role.

V

Next to the peasantry, the stunted Irish commercial classes had been most severely thwarted by the English connection. Nineteenth-century Ireland was no place for speculators who hoped to strike it rich. Woe to the vanquished, Ireland was assigned after Limerick its approximate economic limits for all time: it was to be a reserve larder when summoned, but was to withhold food shipments when so instructed; it was to be a remitter of rent, an army barracks, and a naval base. In 1691 and again in 1800, England crippled Irish shipping and industry (Ulster textile manufacture excepted), following a policy that had led Swift to offer the ruined Dublin businessmen the advice: burn everything English except English coals. The native mercantile channels were as effectively choked up under the Union as the silted harbors of the decaying Irish seaport towns. A self-perpetuating economic stagnation set in, and three hundred years after Limerick the Republic of Ireland is still struggling to extricate itself from the ancient vicious cycle. Hardly anybody other than Guinness the brewer and Murphy the biscuit baker could ever make money in Catholic Ireland. Yet the dream of a Gaelic Manchester persisted, and England's most tenacious enemies were the Irish leaders who came forward in response to the dream.

After Dublin lost its function as a capital, the legal and administrative professions became largely surplus. Doctors and teachers were pinched, when not actually impoverished, by the stagnation of the country. The paltry level of Irish education hindered the normal flow of educated Irish youth into the careers that nurture respectability.* In 1842 these irritations had created on the one hand a pervasive torpor and on the other hand a small hard stratum of discontented men possessed with pride, ambition, and ability, but with no prospects and no cause to love England. These lawyers, doctors, journalists, teachers, poets, engineers, clerks, recusant pastors, and other professional men of the middle class made a permanent knot of leaders for Irish nationalism.

VI

Even the Protestant Ascendancy, the gentry at the apex of the Irish pyramid, the partners, resident agents, and presumed beneficiaries of English rule, were not unanimously happy about the Union with Great Britain. All of them remembered better days and with good reason dreaded the future. During the Napoleonic boom in wheat many had gone into debt up to the limit of their war-inflated incomes, and with the deflation that followed Waterloo they found themselves fighting a perpetual rearguard skirmish against bankruptcy. The very first Irish agrarian "reform" adopted by

* The bafflement of the Irish professional man is memorably described in Sean O'Faolain's account of his feelings when he found himself competing against self-assured young Oxonians: "I thought back to Ballinasloe and Ennis. . . ." See *Vive Moi* (Boston: Little, Brown and Co., 1964), p. 262.

Parliament was an Encumbered Estates Commission. Like the Irish work-houses it enjoyed bureaucratic prosperity in the midst of universal de-pression.*

Mutual distrust eventually put a strain upon the Ascendancy partner-ship with the English. The spirit of *Castle Rackrent* and "The Rakes of Mallow" troubled the English evangelicals and left doubts about the recti-tude of the Irish partners:

> Spending faster than it comes,
> Beating waiters, bailiffs, duns.

Apart from morality, the Ascendancy's incompetence was beyond dispute. Its assignment under the Union was to keep Ireland pacified. As the task grew increasingly beyond its power, it not only had to worry for its safety and solvency, but it also had to listen to the English partners deliver ser-mons upon failure. Pitt had warned the Irish Protestants to rule or be de-stroyed, and Carlyle and his protégé Froude were as brutal toward them for failing to overmaster Irish disaffection as toward the canaille itself.

The Irish Protestants sent out constant cries for help, but England lis-tened with a half-deaf ear and responded in its own good time. Convinced that they had been fleeced and betrayed by the Union, some of the Irish landlords threatened heroic redress: they would go over to the enemy, put themselves at the head of the peasants, and seize their destiny in the role of Irish Lafayettes. A genteel menace; still, a few of the gentry in 1842 were sufficiently angry, compassionate, or desperate to be potential converts to Irish separatism.

VII

The English defense against any Irish threat was to hold fast if possible, to concede nothing gratis, but to give ground amiably when concession was inescapable, and if general retreat was called, to prepare immediately for counterattack. The first line of defense was the constabulary, assisted by plainclothesmen, spies, dossier clerks, and enthusiastic semiprofessionals who left a trail of perjury, forgery, and provocation across the pages of Irish history. The courts, too, were imperial instruments as required. In important trials jury rigging was taken for granted. A tally made by

---

* In Irish literature this deflationary squeeze is a familiar story. Later phases of the prolonged fall of rents were to wipe out the family fortunes of the Yeatses and the Joyces. Simon Dedalus undertook his famous journey to Cork to cash in the last of his inherited real estate, a symbolic act which severed his son forever from the respectable class who sent their sons to Clongowes Wood and played charades with the Sheehy girls on Sunday evening. John Butler Yeats's six hundred Kildare acres went the same way. The same contraction also injured the Moores, the O'Gradys, and the Synges. All of these families happened to be gravid with literary talent, but the entire educated class in Ireland was no less afflicted.

Michael Davitt showed that during the nineteenth century the House of Commons passed on the average one Irish coercion act per year, each permitting the suspension of some part of the regular processes of English law. "Which is the palladium of English liberty," John Mitchel asked; "is it habeas corpus or the suspension of habeas corpus?" Force of arms was naturally the ultimate base of English rule. Foreign travelers observed that while soldiers were seldom seen in England or Scotland, in Ireland they were as common as hussars in light opera. Behind all stood the British army, ready when needed against open insurrection. These final field exercises occurred normally at about half-century intervals with one exception: the mid-eighteenth-century insurrection date, falling due in Penal Law times, was skipped.

Imperial force was never squandered needlessly. Nor were concessions hasty. Expert use of the tactics of delay wore out the disaffected. The Emancipation of the Catholics in 1829 belatedly honored a promise made nearly a century and a half earlier. A second promise—to fulfill the first one—had been allowed to mellow for three decades and to generate an incipient rebellion before the gracious event became actual. English rule from day to day rested mainly on the parsimonious arts of authority, especially upon the ability to make capital of Irish inertia and division. Just as Ireland was a model of political insurgency, it also became a clinical case study of political impotence and debasement.

Following any major military or political defeat, Irishmen sank readily into mass bewitchment, a normal enough reaction to be sure. After a disaster like Limerick or Emmet's rising, Irish prostration was so hopeless that the very machinery of law and order seemed gratuitous or ornamental. The victim appeared to be addicted to his victimage, the author of his own affliction, and deserving of no better than he had got. In the swing of Irish experience from one upsurge to the next, the nadir phase of paralysis gave place to a cringing defeatism of the tearful variety, still abject but suggesting convalescence. Sean O'Faolain found the essence of pure servility in the Gaelic poets of Penal Law times; and Young Ireland located the maudlin phase in Tom Moore's *Irish Melodies*: "Oh, forget not the field where they perished!" Irish literature is packed with specimens of both, eliciting a range of critical responses: they are ugly, embarrassing, and so on. But considered as ethnic traits, they were merely another of Ireland's many colonial misfortunes. If one were speaking of Yorkshiremen, let us say, what conceivable sense could there be in the concept of their "ignobility" or "*hysterica passio*"?

Internecine feuds sprouted like fungi out of Irish demoralization. Factionalism, sectarianism, xenophobia, *ressentiment*, and other forms of meanness rose up constantly between one dispossessed Irishman and another.

The perpetual turmoil inside the Irish national family gives us the word "Donnybrook," whose spirit Joyce caught with a passage in *Ulysses* telling how every Irishman fights against some other Irishman, or if no other is at hand, against one whom Yeatsists will quickly identify as the "Antiself":

> Dublin's burning! Dublin's burning! On fire, on fire!
> (Brimstone fires spring up. Dense clouds roll past. Heavy Gatling guns boom. Pandemonium. Troops deploy. Gallop of hoofs. Artillery. Hoarse commands. Bells clang. Backers shout. Drunkards bawl. Whores screech. Foghorns hoot. . . . It rains dragon's teeth. Armed heroes spring up from furrows. They exchange in amity the pass of knights of the red cross and fight duels with cavalry sabres: Wolfe Tone against Henry Grattan, Smith O'Brien against Daniel O'Connell, Michael Davitt against Isaac Butt, Justin M'Carthy against Parnell, Arthur Griffith against John Redmond, John O'Leary against Lear O'Johnny, Lord Edward Fitzgerald against Lord Gerald Fitzedward, The O'Donoghue of the Glens against The Glens of The Donoghue. . . .)[4]

The wear and tear of cyclic defeat accounts for much of this querulousness, while the conflicting ambitions of the various Irish social strata generated further friction. But, as everybody knows, the universal maxim of empire is, divide and rule; and a striking feature of Irish divisiveness was that it was invariably timed to burst open at the apex of the recurrent nationalist upsurges. One of the regular tasks of Dublin Castle through the centuries was to discover and exploit Irish disagreements, or if native spontaneity were lagging, to lend a helping hand. Two time-tried incubators for hatching feuds are race and religion. Race was much talked about, but not very useful; in the absence of any salient difference in pigmentation or facial contour, the Irishmen and the Englishmen seemed to belong to the same breed. The stylized English caricature of "Paddy," modeled after O'Connell's long upper lip and button nose, was quite unreliable for racial identification of the long-nosed Eamon de Valera or of Gavan Duffy, described by Mrs. Carlyle as "horse-faced." A better hope for division lay in religion. Since sectarianism is the special happiness of sect, this source of division was all but self-generating.

VIII

Ireland is by tradition mostly, though not unanimously, Catholic. The highest Catholic ratio occurred just at the time of Young Ireland with a proportion of about seven out of eight; afterward the proportion fell because of the heavier population loss among the Catholics. At present Catholics make up about three out of four in the Republic of Ireland and Northern Ireland combined. The Protestant minority belonged to two sects: the Church of Ireland Anglicans, scattered thinly throughout most of the country but numerous in Ulster; and the dissenters, a solid block of Presbyterians concentrated in lowland and coastal Ulster. In the south and west virtually everyone was Catholic; there were almost no dissenters at all and the Anglicans were outnumbered by as much as fifty to one. But in parts of Ulster, if one gerrymandered cleverly, Catholics were only a large minority among a Protestant population of Anglicans and Presbyterians.

The Irish Catholic, especially the peasant, was renowned throughout Europe for the intensity of his religious passion. In Ireland, said A. M. Sullivan, even the men go to Mass. The peculiar fervor is not mysterious to the historian. By 1530 Ireland had already sufficient national consciousness to resist the English Reformation, and it remained still basically Catholic in 1691. The Penal Laws were contrived to strip the Irish native bare, and, for good measure, to convert him to Protestantism; but the success of the first aim could only be achieved in the failure of the second. The Penal Laws fixed absolute Protestant dominance over Catholic Ireland, but the conversion of the "papists" had to be confessed a total failure. Strengthened by persecution, Catholicism became the Irishman's solace and badge.

Irish Catholicism in 1842 had emerged as a prime power. It held the affection of most of the population. It enjoyed near-perfect intimacy with the people. The priests and curates were recruited out of the countryside and not, like the Anglican clergy, from the upper classes; and the bishops were always Irishmen and not, like the eighteenth-century Anglican bishops, English placemen. From this base the Church stood in a position to sway Irish thought and enforce Irish morals, to elect and defeat political candidates, and to open up its store of wisdom on the sovereign problems of land tenure or English dominion. Frederick Lucas, an English Tractarian convert to Catholicism, described the special position of the Irish clergy in this way:

> In Ireland the priests have a peculiar function to perform. . . . Between them and the people religion is not a gulf of separation, but a bond of the tenderest union. They belong to the same race as the people, and feel for all their sufferings, temporal as well as spiritual. At the same time, the sacerdotal character, the higher views of life, the greater experience of the world, the more cultivated intellect, raise them above the rank in which they were born; and as they form the *only* educated class which truly sympathizes with the people, they necessarily form the only class to whom, in those temporal matters in which the poor Catholic farmer requires an adviser better educated than himself, he can have recourse, and from whom he can receive guidance.[5]

But Irish Catholicism was not one happy family. It had a private social pyramid of its own. While most of the Irish poor were Catholics, some of the Irish Catholics were not at all poor. Catholics were numerous among the

31

"middlemen," and many more were to be found in the substantial middle class and even in the gentry. The Penal Laws had not put any special disabilities on Catholics engaged in trade. Some had amassed large mercantile fortunes, and as soon as the persecution began to slacken, they often liked to buy landed estates and set themselves up in country elegance. For example, George Moore's Catholic great-grandfather, made wealthy by the Spanish wine trade, came home after Dungannon, bought a large area of marginal land in Mayo, and there built Moore Hall. In this way he erased the double stain of trade and Catholicism and became a member of the Irish gentry, but naturally with a second-class status. Class stratification presented the clergy and bishops with a need to weigh carefully the precise degree of importance attaching to each of the conflicting interests within their flocks; and it can safely be said that they were not inclined to impugn out of hand the special class objectives of their well-to-do parishioners. But on occasions the clergy's opinions harmonized with the views that arose from the very bottom of Irish society out of the daily experiences of the poorest laity. At such times, as in the Wexford insurrection of 1798, the tangible physical power of armed and marshaled Irish Catholicism moving through the boreens of Enniscorthy, the priests at the head, gave all observers food for somber thought.

In a moment of ebullience the Irish historian P. S. O'Hegarty once estimated that the Irish Church was "ninety-nine percent national." This was plainly an overstatement, for the nationalist clergy confronted a powerful antinational opposite, called "ultramontanism," which yearned toward Rome. The hierarchy, while Irish to the core, was not merely Irish. It had also to take into account the mission of the Church from global and eternal perspectives. In reaching its decisions on Irish nationalism it had to weigh such a question as this: would the Church be apostolically stronger with a solid minority of eighty-five Irish Catholics sitting at Westminster in the center of world power, or with a majority of seven out of eight in a third-class independent Dáil in College Green? The question gave its own answer contradicting the answer reached independently by some of the laity.

Beginning in O'Connell's day, a good deal of Irish history was to be made in the bishops' palaces, where a great agonizing would try to reconcile all these conflicts. If reconcilement could not be made, the conservative decision was to be expected, if not always actually forthcoming. Those who cherish the ironies of history will note this as an example: the Irish hierarchy upon its emergence from English persecution, became one of the chief obstacles to Irish revolt against England, its erstwhile persecutor. But the cynical Pitt saw no anomaly here. Doctrinaire anti-Catholicism seemed to him very stupid, and his reply to the no-popery fanatics of his day was to advocate not only Catholic Emancipation but subvention of the Irish clergy as well—a hasty tender perhaps, but not a philanthropic one. The thought Pitt had in mind was candidly endorsed by the empire-minded English prelate Henry Cardinal Manning when he said, "Show me an Irishman who has lost his faith and I will show you a Fenian."

On principle the Irish clergy condemned the idea of forthright separation, though an unconsciously humorous proviso was added—except by free English assent. A theological rule held that rebellion was sinful unless it was just, Christian, and further, unless it was likely to succeed. As an antidote to fatuous vain-glory this doctrine made good sense. But in genuine crises it threw the weight of the Church always on the side of the established order. Unfortunately for all rebels, no one can exactly measure beforehand the likelihood of success. Church doctrine therefore in substance informed the Irish radicals that if, in spite of the opposition of the clergy, they ever did win, their success would prove their right to be duly blessed. Meanwhile, cross-purposes between the clergy and the laity could be guaranteed. Somebody would charge somebody else with "godlessness" and a split would follow as a matter of course, isolating the more radical Catholics and abandoning them to the methodical grindings of English power.

In its interfaith relations the peasant Catholicism of the south and west confronted the Church of Ireland at the time of Young Ireland with little to fear. The Anglicans were dominant in wealth and power, being the sect of the Ascendancy and an official arm of English rule. But they were so few that the Church of Ireland was almost the null sect. Nineteenth-century efforts to expand their numbers by offering small bribes to potential converts had ended in fiasco. "Proselytizing" became an ugly word, and "soupers," hungry Catholics who went over to the Anglicans for a bowl of soup, were cast out of the community. As late as 1908 Lady Gregory had to threaten litigation against George Moore to force him to delete a passage from *Hail and Farewell* describing her girlhood "proselytizing" ventures with her sisters. Such embroilment was persistent, yet it seldom became rabid in Catholic Ireland, partly because the Anglican clergy had learned Christian humility in their lonely isolation and were little inclined to militancy, and partly because the sect was too small in the south and west to serve for splitting the Irish from within.*

IX

In the north of Ireland, in Ulster, the religious climate was very different. In the seventeenth century the rich bottom lands of Ulster had been seized

---

* The gentle demeanor of Yeats's father and county Down grandfather is sometimes traced to their Irish Anglican-rectory upbringing; and Douglas Hyde, Robert Graves's father, and Isaac Butt were said to have derived their gentleness out of the same source. But the fanatical Standish O'Grady was an Irish Anglican rector's son, too.

33

from defeated Irishmen and settled with imported Scottish Presbyterian farmers, the so-called Scotch-Irish, while the displaced Catholics took up the worthless hillside farms nearby. Where spoiler and despoiled remained neighbors, trouble was bound to arise. But the Presbyterians remembered "Bloody Claverhouse" and their own persecution. They despised the established church no less than the Catholics did and harbored warlike anti-English sentiments of their own. It was the Ulster dissenters who had put the backbone into Grattan's Volunteers at Dungannon. Wolfe Tone's prime political strategy was to weld Protestant and Catholic together for struggle against England, hence the name of his organization, United Irishmen. He all but succeeded. "The language and bent of the conduct of these Dissenters," wrote Lord Westmoreland from Ulster in 1791, "is to unite with the Catholics, and their union would be very formidable. That union is not yet made, and I believe and hope it never could be."[6] He was correct: Ulster's nonsectarian impulse did not survive into the nineteenth century.

After 1798 Ulster took off on a course of development different from that of Catholic Ireland. The Ulster peasants had succeeded in establishing the "Ulster tenant right," which recognized their equity in the improvements they made on rented holdings. They enjoyed more security than the southern Catholics, and they became better farmers for the improvements encouraged by the tenant right. They thus felt less of the desperate necessity that kept the south and west in continuous unrest throughout the century. In the northern towns the Ulster linen industry had survived the general destruction of Irish manufactures, and now it prospered and expanded. Belfast alone among large Irish cities showed signs of life, even before its great shipyards were founded. In 1842 Ulster was already tied more closely to Liverpool and Manchester than to industrially defunct Dublin, Cork, and Limerick.

As the differentiation between the north and south widened, the ancient religious wounds were found to be reopened easily. Ulster Protestants, who had long held the best jobs as well as the choicest farms in the province, with the remnants left to the Ulster Catholics, were soon persuaded that in an independent Ireland the tables would be turned, since Catholics were preponderant in Ireland as a whole, and that they would then be the victims instead of the beneficiaries of the long-established Ulster custom of discrimination. In 1795 the Orange Order was founded to break up Tone's coalition of dissenter and Catholic and to "maintain the Protestant constitution" by methods and beliefs familiar to Americans through its stepchild of a later time, the Ku Klux Klan. This sinister strong-arm society, whose bigotry enjoyed the sponsorship of members of the royal family and the acquiescence of most of Protestant Ulster, made harassment of Catholicism its purpose in life. In a Catholic country it could only breed violent disorder.

34

Dublin Castle henceforth had no more occasion for Lord Westmoreland's fears. To keep the north and south split apart required only that an Orangeman appear at the proper moment to shout: "To hell with the Pope!" The Catholics responded with their own terrorist counterpart, the Ancient Order of Hibernians, which aped all of the Orange Order's vices, so that there was no lack of provocation from either side. A blood feud feeding on its own insanity and bursting occasionally into wholesale carnage had become a normal institution in Ulster and constituted another serious internal obstacle to Irish unity.[7]

X

Such were the frustrations of Irish nationalist ambitions. To these another must be added—Irish inexperience. Irish nationalists won their political education slowly and in the most painful way possible, through the skin and by the neck. Lacking omniscience, they could only apply to each new crisis the lessons of the crisis preceding, and they were therefore always preparing for the previous battle rather than for the next one. And yet they did learn.

The nationalists learned, or at least they came to believe, that the very survival of Ireland required nothing less than an absolute separation from England. They learned that this objective was not going to be accomplished easily. Irish history they studied minutely, assessing again and again its errors and successes. They learned to range imaginatively over the full palette of possible ways of resistance, according to the four dominant historical precedents: (1) the method of 1798, open insurrection; (2) the method of 1782, the threat of military force against an imperiled England; (3) the method of the tithe war of 1832, broad economic warfare—openly illegal, occasionally violent, but not military; and (4) the method of the Clare elections of 1828, legal, nonviolent mass agitation.

They learned that two could play the splitting game. In 1842 Irish nationalists were well trained by history to exploit England's external difficulties. Grattan and Tone had shown great skill in capitalizing on the American and French Revolutions, out of which they had extracted the Irish Volunteers, the Dungannon Convention, and the first relaxations of the Penal Laws. Outcries of Irish pain had already shown promise for alienating Americans from England, and they would grow increasingly effective. Close rapport between rebel Ireland and all shades and complexions of French politics was axiomatic policy on both sides.

The internal balance of English affairs was scrutinized closely. O'Connell not only played Tory against Whig, but also made noisy threats to join forces with the Chartists (though not seriously, for he despised them as

35

much as the Tories did).[8] A more subtle task was to disturb the ordinary Englishman's complacency on what was called "the Irish problem," so that in the next crisis to come, English opinion would suffer its own frustrating moral doubts and cross-purposes. An attack was opened against the contemptuous cliché of the "stage Irishman," of Paddy with his shillelagh, his jug of poteen, and a pig in the parlor. English good opinion was courted through the invention of a specialized mode of indirect address which presumed to be a high-minded dialogue on Ireland between Irishmen, but was really designed to be overheard abroad by hesitant English well-wishers. One is constantly surprised in reading even such fervent nationalists as Duffy or O'Leary to find that in their minds they are addressing an English reader. This stylistic manner governed most of the corpus of Irish literature and serious political commentary (though not its oratory or popular ballads). It stayed strictly on its good behavior, for few Irish thinkers were pure Anglophobes. They understood the power of England too well to suppose that a disorganized hysterical rage could ever prevail against it. When they set out to build a counterforce that might command equal respect, their urge to self-indulgence in the pleasure of hatefulness for its own sake was, when possible, muted in public and transformed into a secret understanding that Irishmen shared quietly among themselves.

At home the nationalists probed every fissure in the Catholic hierarchy, hoping to set a more nationalist priest or bishop against one more loyalist. They wooed each generation of the Protestant Ascendancy, winning over many distinguished personalities, but without ever softening the mass itself. The list of illustrious nationalists drawn from Protestant Ireland was impressive—Jonathan Swift, Henry Grattan, John Philpot Curran, Richard Brinsley Sheridan, Wolfe Tone, Henry Joy McCracken, Lord Edward Fitzgerald, Robert Emmet, and more to come.

Solidarity, so very hard to build and so fragile when built, they set above all other ideals, even excessively, as Michael Davitt once charged when he complained that Irishmen were "unity-mad." Very slowly they learned how the ranks must be closed. The betrayer was stigmatized ferociously as a matter of course; and after him the bigot, the absolute necessity for nonsectarianism having been discovered as early as the time of the Volunteers. In 1842 Irish nationalists understood that only a scoundrel would attack another man's sect as such. And if the other sect attacked first? Human frailty in the heat of dispute often overwhelmed the best arguments for nonsectarianism, especially in a deteriorating political atmosphere. The first malignant symptom of *ressentiment*, foretelling the end of an advancing phase of Irish history, was the recurrence of religious bigotry.

Argument, tact, and cleverness, it was learned, could carry Irish national unity just so far, and beyond that more moving persuasions were required.

In the task of building a power symbology, Irish nationalists learned to operate with finesse and telling effect. In 1842 the Irish mystique in all its murky and amorphous majesty was not quite yet fully perfected, but its moment was at hand.

A final lesson: the Irish nationalists learned that their opportunities had to be made as well as waited for, unless one could afford to wait forever. Flaming words, redemptive symbology—these were essential, granted; and Irish modes in religion, language, and cultural tradition had to be collected, arrayed, and made battle-ready. But the brother-nationalists of Wales and Scotland had done all that, and still they remained mere dilettantes. They lacked the advanced Irishman's professional respect for the deed. In 1842 Irishmen remembered that O'Connell's campaign in Clare had proved what audacity could do and had demonstrated that for combating defeatism and restoring self-respect to Irishmen who still cowered in servility and misery, no cure was as magical as a bold dramatic action with brass bands at the head of the parade.

PART II

Young Ireland

CHAPTER 3

O'Connell and Davis
in Partnership

I

A momentous episode in Irish literature was a public quarrel that took place
in 1845 between Thomas Davis, a poet, and Daniel O'Connell, the political
leader of Ireland. The tacit partnership of these two, which preceded their
quarrel, was still more momentous. When the two great nationalists were
working in amity, they generated a force so explosive that they frightened
everybody, themselves not least.

The O'Connells were ancient Catholic landowners who had by an oversight escaped dispossession under the English plantations and the Penal
Laws.[1] Their vast lands at Darrynane were infertile but picturesque, boun-
ded by the Atlantic cliffs of Kerry that mark the extreme western limits of
Europe. Daniel was the son of a mere shopkeeper, a fact from which his
aristocratic enemies derived some satisfaction. But thanks to boundless
energy and a precocious wit, he was singled out for favorite by a wealthy
uncle called "Old Hunting Cap," the captain of the clan, a landowner and
smuggler. He inherited his uncle's great property, and along with it, a
certain complacency toward the Providence by which worldly favors are
bestowed. In later years a foreign journalist who was invited to stay for
dinner at Darrynane sat down at table with more than one hundred
cousins, menials, and guests, with the old man presiding loquaciously at the
head like a Scots Highland chief (but less bibulous, says Lecky). Another
journalist visitor, a spy from the *Times*, found the Darrynane medieval
tenantry living in up-to-date squalor.

O'Connell was among the first Catholics to be called to the Irish bar
after the second relaxation of the Penal Laws in 1793. While still a youth, he
established himself as the most brilliant Irish advocate of the age, displaying
an expert command of law and a skill in swaying juries that Irishmen came
to think supernatural. Where the Englishman's law was the hereditary

enemy and the crown prosecutor a stock villain, his sensational acquittals for the defendant made him automatically a folk hero. The next step from law into politics was natural. Ireland demanded a fighter, and now his pugnacity came to the fore. The O'Connell political headquarters was kept busy negotiating affairs of honor with numerous dignitaries whom he had insulted, among them Benjamin Disraeli and Sir Robert Peel; and one of his challengers, a Protestant alderman named D'Esterre, was killed by O'Connell's bullet. His detractors have made much of the scurrility of his tongue, and Yeats once blamed it for all the sorrows of Ireland. Without doubt he was guilty of verbal intemperance, but his angriest and most vituperative words could not match the vilification to which his enemies subjected him every day of his life for half a century.

One of his political talents was a humorous, palavering manner, a habit for which his somber contemporaries used the term "undue levity." The Irish word game was his special pleasure. He invented the nickname "Orange Peel" to deflate the redoubtable Sir Robert. It was his opinion that the lord chancellor, Sir Edward Sugden, bore a name that one must hesitate "to give to a pig." Here again Yeats blushed at the vulgarity, quite unnecessarily. Behind the plain, stark tragedy of insurgence there lurks a more intimate comic face, arising from enthusiastic social motion uninhibited by guidelines. In a later time Frank O'Connor and Peadar O'Donnell would catch the comic energy of a political resurgence, though the richest formulation belongs to O'Casey's reminiscences and constitutes his particular glory. O'Connell's subversive horseplay did set him apart from Irishmen who wore the long face, from Davis, Smith O'Brien, Parnell, Devoy, Arthur Griffith, de Valera, and, surprisingly, from James Joyce, whose depiction of this special flavor in Irish history is uniformly sour and unimaginative. But it put him in the happy company of Swift, Wolfe Tone, "Big Jim" Larkin, Michael Collins, and the rest of the Irish pantheon who were not born humorless, including W. B. Yeats himself.

The stenographic reports of O'Connell's Irish speeches often had to use the parenthesis "prolonged laughter." More often the notation was "hear, hear." As an orator he was demonstrably one of the most effective in world history. His voice was said to have had an extraordinarily arresting quality, pleasing to the ear and capable of both sweet nuance and a rasping, bellowing roar which could penetrate to the fringes of an assembly of a million people. His oratorical rhetoric was not florid, but was blunt, lucid, sarcastic, and devoid of genteel ornament. "Mr. O'Connell advanced to the front of the platform and thanked his listeners for their applause"—this was the newspapers' ritual introduction to the verbatim reports of his speeches. He then proceeded in careless ease, circling discursively about the topic of the day, rather like an ordinary citizen thinking out loud:

The enemies of Repeal talked about agitation, forsooth, preventing the influx of English capital. A more absurd idea never entered the mind of man (hear, hear). But he denied that any rational dispassionate man could entertain it for a moment. It was a mere miserable pretence, the fallacy of which must be evident even to those who use it. He asserted distinctly that not one shilling of English capital was kept out of this country by agitation. If English capital was to be kept out of countries where agitation existed, how did it come that it had found its way in such enormous quantities to the States of South America, where not only agitation but actual revolution might be said to be the order of the day (hear, hear)? It was well known that in Buenos Ayres alone, where bloodshed and confusion prevailed to a frightful extent, English capital was invested to the amount of several millions (hear, hear). It was all a mockery therefore to pretend that English capitalists would not come over here, because the Irish people peaceably and constitutionally agitated to have their wrongs redressed. Why did they not come when we were tranquil and noiseless (hear, hear)?[2]

This style does not sound very intoxicating, yet multitudes of listeners found it so. Often it touched the Irish throng with warmth and immediacy, voicing their deepest and most passionate longings. O'Connell spoke to Irishmen, said Sean O'Faolain, in "the secret language of fellowship in helotry."[3] After a century and a half of stupefaction, his countrymen roused to life to cheer their vindicator, the pure Celt who defied the Protestant Ascendancy in its inner sanctum, disdaining its rage against his "ruffian," "blackguard" impudence. The intimacy and authority of his rapport with the Irish people became the ideal of all subsequent Irish leaders—political or cultural—though none ever recaptured the old Liberator's magic touch.

O'Connell's purposes required more than air passing through the larynx. He also had a rare talent for organization. Tirelessly experimental, he formed and dissolved an intricate procession of clubs, committees, councils, and associations, ranging up and down the scale of the Irish social classes in order to seek out dormant attitudes at each level. The list seemed almost endless, but one of his ideas, conceived during the Emancipation campaign, turned out to have special value. This was the "Catholic rent," a tiny weekly sum collected from all the people responsive to his appeal. Out of an insignificant farthing a week rose not only a war chest, but also a formidable machinery for bringing about contact between membership and leadership and generating a feeling of *participation mystique* among all the countless sprawling atoms.

O'Connell found the perfect organizational cadre for his agitations already at hand in the Catholic clergy. "It is a blessed consolation," he said, "patriotism and religion run in the same channel."[4] The rent was ordinarily collected at the church door after Mass, often by the parish priest, though if the treasury was quite full, paid officials took charge. What an organization

43

it was: a full-time agitator and dues collector, armed with supernatural authority, promoting a popular cause, working in intimate contact with the people in every townland of Ireland. O'Connell freely granted that the Church had organized his victories by legwork at the parish level: "the Catholic clergy . . . here is the secret of my success."[5] It was not an organization to be taken lightly. His first rent scheme had forced Emancipation upon the Duke of Wellington, that dreadful Irish peer whose Dublin birth O'Connell said was like "a tiger cub dropped in a fold." In the pride of his power for political organization, he had the pleasure of calling Wellington a "screaming coward" and a "stunted sergeant"; and he was one of the few mortals ever to feel the Iron Duke bend under his pressure. A peaceable agitation had done such damage to a haughty opposition. What then might be its potential?

These were the glories of O'Connell's organizations. But there were problems, too. His success aroused an equally close-marshaled Orange opposition, for the Belfast Calvinists were themselves not amateurs in the political craft. More serious, an organization built upon the clergy was necessarily bound in by the political outlook of the Church. Most of the priests were happy to go along with the excitement day by day, yet disapproved the logic latent in the forces O'Connell stirred into motion. And his own outlook was not different from theirs. The clergy, he said, "entered unreservedly into my views"; and it could have been added, he also into theirs, from necessity as well as free choice.

Of all the things he hated, he hated revolution the most. He had all the normal reflexes of any landlord. He remembered with detestation the revolutionary French peasantry, *ces féroces soldats*, marching against landed property and the Church, a scene he witnessed as a seminarian at Douay in 1793. He had fled back across the Channel from France on the same day that Louis XVI was guillotined.* Though he owed his law career to Wolfe Tone, he hated the man's work and his memory nonetheless. He had joined the loyal Dublin militia in the Emmet disturbances of 1803 in fear of a peasant rising, observing that if the "miscreants" won, "they would rob and they would murder." He praised the Protestant yeoman terror in 1798, but he read its warning to Catholics clearly, too. There was also the merest touch of the toady in his make-up. The word "Loyal" was not prefixed to the title of his Repeal Association for comic effect. It was long remembered with embarrassment that he had presented Caesar's crown of laurel to George IV, that besotted monarch who disgusted everybody, and Irishmen most of all. At Victoria's coronation, his excessive gestures of deference, his smirkings and bowings, made him the second most conspicuous person

---

* Lecky informs us that Tone's friends the Sheares brothers crossed on the same day in a contrasting mood, bearing as a treasure a handkerchief dipped in the beheaded king's blood.

present, much like Yeats performing his singular crab dance in the Swedish court as recounted in "The Bounty of Sweden."

O'Connell's political object was to arouse the Irish peasantry just so much and no more—a touchy proceeding, for once set in motion they might stampede. Against the contingency of a runaway he took three precautions beyond his dalliance with the clergy. First, he kept all phases of his agitations under his personal surveillance, delegating no responsibility, not even the most trivial. Second, he took pains to isolate his followers from radical movements abroad, above all from French republicans and English Chartists. His ideological quarantine was a prime specimen of Irish particularism, which asserted that Irishmen possessed a unique spirituality likely to be contaminated by any foreign influence other than, of course, the Roman. O'Connell's third precaution against Irish militance was to limit all political action to "moral force," or as it is now called, "nonviolence," his foremost lasting contribution to the political arts. As long as his followers stopped short of fisticuffs, he let them run on as boisterous as you please; but upon the text "Shed thou no blood" he stood as immovable as Portia: "Not for all the universe contains would I, in the struggle for what I conceive my country's cause, consent to the effusion of a single drop of blood, except my own."[6]

In taking all these precautions to hold his followers in check, O'Connell faced the danger that they might not budge at all. His political program was often less than exciting, and there were anticlimaxes from past exploits to live down, too. His great Emancipation victory had brought neither instantaneous nor delayed miracles. In exchange for the right of Catholics to sit in Parliament, the forty-shilling franchise was now withdrawn. The new property qualifications, to which O'Connell assented, had disenfranchised the very men who carried Emancipation for him in Clare; and the poor Irish, who had hitherto been forced to vote for somebody they did not want, were now unable to vote at all and hence were politically as impotent after Emancipation as before.

After 1829, while *nouveau riche* Catholic merchants and gentry went to sit at Westminster, the Irish peasants found their life still unchanged. Ribbon disturbances flared again in Munster, and pauperism spread in the towns. Having made Melbourne the prime minister, O'Connell's lieutenants were able to bask in the Whig sunshine. Stephen Woulfe became first baron of the exchequer and Richard Lalor Sheil the master of the mint. But still the peasants waited; "the lash went on." And so when O'Connell at the age of sixty-five announced his plan for a new association to agitate for the Repeal of the Union, he was answered by an embarrassing silence. For many months he struggled to bring in members, but only a random person here and there responded.

II

O'Connell's most notable early recruit was Thomas Davis, a Protestant barrister, then only twenty-six years old and fated to die young five years later. He was the precise antithesis of the loud and hearty O'Connell. Shyness and introversion gave him a false air of arrogance. In a public setting he was not noticed, and fellow students at Trinity College could not place him in later years. Abstinent and too frail for rigorous exercise, he was cut off from all convivial pastimes. But in his library or among friends he was transformed into a man of compelling social force, "the greatest and best of his generation," capable of massive intellectual labor. He resembled young William Ewart Gladstone or Arthur Henry Hallam in his evangelical lust for work, as well as in a solemnity uncommon in one so youthful. He belonged to a familiar nineteenth-century type, a generous and talented young man of the middle class, armed with a strong sense of rectitude and purpose and driven by a conviction, not unfounded, of limitless personal capability.

Davis left Trinity College a materialist, a utilitarian, a believer in progress through universal education—that is to say, a Benthamite. To the end of his life he remained one, with one important adjustment. Like John Stuart Mill, he found a lack of emotional sustenance in the doctrinaire Benthamite diet and fell into an adolescent mental crisis. Like Mill, he made the same saving discovery of poetry. His awakening came not through Wordsworth, however, but through another romantic call with a different message, Irish nationalism. Soon after college, probably on a trip to the Continent he is known to have made, he read the post-Napoleonic French historians. Jules Michelet could hardly have been overlooked by any intellectual of the times, and Davis read and emulated him as a matter of course. Those stiff saffron-robed pre-Conquest Gaels with their charming barbarisms of geasa and fosterage, stock figures in the future Irish literary movement, came ultimately through Davis out of Michelet's medieval pageantry. Passing beyond Michelet, Davis found his true guiding star in another distinguished French historian of the time, Augustin Thierry, whom he repeatedly exalted above "any other historian that ever lived." In Thierry the full splendor of Irish nationalism was revealed to him, not by analogy with France as in Michelet, but in its explicit Irish setting.

Thanks to the ancient national enmity of France toward England, Frenchmen had always watched Ireland from afar as a potential ally and they traditionally commiserated with the Irish people. In the course of writing a history of the Normans, Thierry became involved in a study of the English conquest of Ireland. His Gallic sympathy for the Irish against the Saxons, their "conquerors and oppressors," grew into an impassioned partisanship.

He came to the conclusion that the Irishman's "unconquerable obstinacy never to despair" in seeking to repossess his nationality "was perhaps the greatest example that a people had ever given," more glorious than even that of the Jews under the captivity.[7] The supreme statement of Irish history, past, present, and future, Thierry found to reside in—of all places —Irish songs "inspirés par la muse de l'indépendance. Ces chants retentissent encore dans les villages et sur les bords des lacs, accompagnés du son de la harpe, instrument révéré comme eux. C'est là que sont enregistrés les malheurs de l'Irlande et les crimes de ses oppresseurs" (". . . inspired by the muse of independence. These songs resound still in the villages and on the shores of the lakes, accompanied by the sound of the harp, instrument revered like them. There are recorded the sorrows of Ireland and the crimes of its oppressors").[8]

Thierry especially admired the songs of Tom Moore, several of which he translated into French, and he believed that "Forget Not the Field Where They Perished" was the quintessential utterance of the Irish soul. Davis himself knew well enough that Thierry's harps twanging on the shores of Irish lakes were a hallucination out of Alphonse de Lamartine. What Thierry believed already accomplished was in fact not even begun. But Davis resolved that it would be, immediately, and would correspond exactly to Thierry's specifications.

Instead of damping down Davis' Benthamite predilections in the normal romantic manner, Thierry set them afire. He decided that great utilitarian victories could be won if rational principles could be coupled to the force of passionate drives. Patrick Pearse, looking back on Davis' accomplishment three-quarters of a century afterward, saw it as a new definition of Irish patriotism: "nationality is a spirituality." Davis would have certainly assented, but only if the definition could include the full list of the good things of life—"science, industry, skill," plus "all the studies and accomplishments of peace and war."[9]

III

Returned to Dublin from his year abroad, Davis published in a Dublin newspaper in 1841 an important essay called "Udalism and Feudalism,"[10] an optimistic survey of Ireland's economic potential. Anticipating Carlyle's *Past and Present*, which appeared two years later, the essay began with an attack on the "scientific" English analysis of the Irish peasant economy. His awkward word "udalism" took for its ideal an agrarian society like "cold and rocky" but prosperous Norway. He envisioned Norway as a happy land, dominated by a thoughtful and busy middle class—somewhat more poetical, perhaps, than the actual burghers of Christiania—and resting upon a sturdy landowning peasantry; he had evidently read his Cobbett well. His thought thus ran into direct collision with laissez faire dogmatists, whom he correctly suspected of harboring intolerable schemes for the country's future. Was it not irrefutable that Irish lands must be cleared by eviction, amalgamation of tenancies, and emigration in order to relieve Irish "overpopulation"? But proper logic, as Davis argued, did not terminate at the *quod erat demonstrandum* that the Malthusian solution to the Irish agrarian problem must proceed forthwith, but rather started from the given that this solution was above all others unthinkable. Ireland had no redundant population, he said; and citing Switzerland and Denmark as evidence, he argued that Ireland could support twenty-five million, three times its 1840 population and seven times its population in the twentieth century.

O'Connell's agrarianism was a niggardly half-measure, stopping short with an apologetic plea to extend to Ulster tenant right. "Udalism and Feudalism" went well beyond O'Connell and advocated "peasant proprietorship" for Ireland. Davis cited France and Holland as models of prosperity built on peasant ownership of small farms, and he quoted from Herodotus: " 'Who was the happiest of men?' said Croesus to Solon. 'Tellos,' answered the sage; 'he was an Attic yeoman; he lived a good neighbor and a good farmer, till his children had grown up strong and comely, and honest, and then he died fighting for Athens.' "

The rudimentary good sense of Davis' agrarianism, which sounds so moderate today, was not appreciated in 1842, when peasant proprietorship was considered tantamount to bloody revolution. How could land that belonged to landlords suddenly belong to peasants, unless the peasants rose up and seized it? Davis' essay made no open call to arms, but it hinted of dangerous sympathies. He quoted Gustave de Beaumont's opinion that the Irish aristocracy "is nothing but an obstacle which men should hasten to remove." He praised the Comte de Mirabeau and Georges Danton for transforming the French peasantry into a landowning class and applauded Jean Sismondi's opinion that the Irish social order "must be changed from top to bottom." Even Ribbonism he found to have its desperate virtues. Listing the succession of Irish peasant guerrilla bands—the "levellers, and hearts of oak, right boys, white boys, terry aults, ribbonmen"—who had spontaneously taken up arms against the Irish landlords, he asked: "Who shall judge them?"

IV

Laissez faire had, in Davis' opinion, nothing to offer the Irish countryside, nor the Irish towns, either. He deplored the results of that policy in England: the blighted factory landscape; the reformed English poor law, that "prison for poverty"; the shoddy and poisonous merchandise poured out from the factories; the "sickly faces, the vicious and despairing looks" seen in the black Lancashire cities; the mill hands exiled from "the field, the hill, the corn, the lowing herd, the bleating lamb, the whistling plow-boy, the village church." He cried: "Oh, no! oh, no! ask us not to copy English vice, and darkness, and misery, and impiety; give us the worst wigwam in Ireland and a dry potato rather than Anglicize us."[11]

This plea sounded as though Davis were warming up to one of those sentimental sermons, compulsive among the later Irish patriots, about the superiority of the Irish spirit over the disgusting materialism of the Saxon. His point, however, was the opposite. While "Udalism and Feudalism" denounced the human suffering brought on by industrialization, Davis had no complaints whatever to offer against its attendant benefits. "Some invention which should bring the might of machinery in a wholesome and cheap form to the cabin" seemed to him the most sensible long-term industrial objective. To his taste, English political economy was not "too materialistic" for Ireland; it was not materialistic enough. He noted that the English factory owners had shown no mercy in reducing their own fellow countrymen to the beastly degradation he had seen in Lancashire. What misery would their factories not bring over to Ireland, then, to a people whom they despised as aliens inside their commonwealth? Irishmen must therefore beware the English aim to "assimilate Ireland to England." Here Davis departed from the usual conclusion: Ireland must not assimilate to England, he said; Ireland must assimilate to Ireland instead, that is, must be industrialized by Irish entrepreneurs. He surveyed this prospect in a dialogue with himself, one-half representing a visionary man of progress, the other a timid man of prudence. Suppose, he said, Irishmen should attempt to establish factories:

What will you make? Soft goods? Manchester is ready to sell them to all the world at three per cent profit on her capital, and cannot. Or hardware? Birmingham is canting her stores, and can hardly get bidders. Have you coals? No. Have you capital to pay wages? Have you hereditary skill, the shipping, the command of the markets that England has? No. What have you then? Cheap labor, water-power, harbors, and position for trade. All well and good; but are you serious in thinking water-power can compete with steam, and naked hands with the overflowing capital of England? Look, you say, to Germany competing with England. But how has Germany been able to do so? Thus: she had water-power and coals in abundance; she had labor as cheap as Ireland, and yet she long failed, and England gorged her markets. How then did she succeed? Come to the point! Thus, sir, thus; she had national government. She did as Ireland did when we had national government. She imposed duties or prohibitions on English goods. She was willing to pay a little dearer to her own manufacturer than to foreigners. The German farmer paid a little more for clothes, and furniture, and utensils; but he was saved twice as much, which he should have given in poor tax. And now comes the German's reward (if manufacturing success be desirable); Germany has trained artisans, great factories, the home market a monopoly, and she therefore begins to undersell England. Why not imitate her? you say.[12]

So: the secret gift of Thierry's *"muse de l'indépendance"* on the shores of Irish lakes is cheap labor and import duties? Davis' formula was almost too candid. As for import duties, the mere mention of them not only panicked Englishmen, but also failed to capture the imagination of Irishmen. Years later Arthur Griffith would also observe that nobody stood up to cheer when he announced in a scolding voice that patriotism enjoined the duty "to pay if necessary an enhanced price for Irish goods." Rationality alone was not the vehicle to carry this project. But suppose it were presented as an emotion, a passion, a mystique?

V

Such were Davis' thoughts when he made his move and presented himself at the Corn Exchange to enroll in O'Connell's Repeal Association. In keeping with the axiom that the Protestant opposition must be split, O'Connell welcomed him as a prize defector and immediately elevated him to the association's executive board. In keeping with the companion axiom, that religious sectarianism must be silenced, Davis carefully publicized his abhorrence of Orange bigotry, declared "a love for all sects," and asserted that the correct religious attitude for Ireland was a "haughty impartiality." For many months he silently studied O'Connell and the workings of his stalled Repeal mechanism. Then in the spring of 1842 he decided that he might carve out a place in the nationalist movement for his own ideas through an independent weekly journal, provided he could interest O'Connell in a venture outside his personal control.

He made a partnership with two young middle-class Catholics, Gavan Duffy, already a successful Belfast journalist although even younger than Davis, and John Blake Dillon, a barrister from Connaught. The three arranged to begin publication in the autumn of a new journal to be called the *Nation*. Around the editorial office they gathered a dozen-odd exceptional young men, the lawyers, doctors, and writers who are known to history as Young Ireland. Charles Trevelyan, a young British treasury official who was later to leave an ugly mark on Ireland's history, went over from London to see if the empire was endangered. He reported back that the Young Irelanders were analogous to *les jeunes gens de Paris*, and he credited them with supplying O'Connell's party with whatever taste, intellect, and philosophy it possessed. He suspected that the young men were merely sowing their radical wild oats, as many English elder statesmen had done when young and foolish.[13]

O'Connell's explicit assignment for Davis in the Repeal movement was to agitate the Protestants, especially the Protestant middle classes and the "cultivated classes." These groups were said to be essential to O'Connell's success but deaf to his appeals. The *Nation* was expected to seek them in the byways and the hedges and compel them to come in. Davis and Duffy accepted their assignment eagerly, understanding that it was their prime task. With youthful self-assurance Duffy guaranteed that the *Nation* would not just split the Protestants in the three provinces of the south and west, but actually sweep them into the movement for Repeal. He conceded, however, that another generation of work would be needed to dissolve the Ulster Orange opposition.

VI

Davis led off with a plea for industrialization, a shift of emphasis away from the agrarianism of "Udalism and Feudalism." Mercantile self-interest he now pressed forward emphatically. He sought out all occasions to commend Benjamin Franklin to Irishmen. He found Ireland's foremost need to be technical education. "Why are we so poor and paltry?" his catechism ran, and the answer was, "From want of industrial education."[14] A generation in advance of T. H. Huxley he attacked the Irish schools for teaching "classical frivolities" instead of "the nature, products, and history, first of their own, then of other countries." Fixing his gaze on Ireland's picturesque scenery, on the "cliffs vast and terrible," and on "dreamily beautiful Killarney," he naturally beheld the spirit whose dwelling is in the light of setting suns. He also saw a vision of future tourists coming in shiploads to help the trade balance of some future separatist Irish exchequer.

A scanty outcrop of coal in the green fields of Roscommon made him as euphoric as any American speculator, and as ready to dream of a vast iron and coal complex rising like mists out of a cow pasture. "Arigna must be pierced with shafts and Bonmahon flaming with smelting houses," he cried. "Our coal must move a thousand engines, our rivers ten thousand wheels."[15] He declared that "we must read books of statistics,"[16] startling advice from the grandfather of the Celtic twilight. Davis and his friends were aglow at the prospects, but their contemporaries were unmoved. Davis understood that they must be inoculated with enthusiasm—but how? Cultural nationalism was an answer.

The *Nation* approached the Protestant lower classes, too, in this business-like spirit, bearing the same economic arguments against the Union. It pleaded with the Anglican skilled workers of Dublin in the name of naked self-interest "to join our Presbyterian and Catholic countrymen in their holy and gallant efforts to abolish absenteeism, to keep Irish money in Ireland, to bring back trade, to fill our stomachs and clothe our backs, to make us united, rich, free, and honored." The Anglican skilled workers, in reply, commended the *Nation* for its courtesy. But, as they pointed out, Deuteronomy 28 had said apropos of Catholicism: "Cursed shalt thou be in the city and cursed shalt thou be in the field; cursed shall be thy basket and thy store." These words "clearly prove to us," they said, that Ireland's national suffering was a just visitation of the wrath of God, "incurred by the national prevalence of false religion." Therefore the question of Repeal or Union turned upon a prior question, "whether is true the Protestant or the Roman Catholic church? Thence another question arises . . . which shall prevail?"[17] Duffy's estimate that the *Nation*'s job would be easy began to sound overoptimistic. Against such monumental bigotry, what might prevail? Again, cultural nationalism was an answer.

VII

Davis' militant agrarianism as set out in "Udalism and Feudalism" was revived by the infant *Nation*, though only for a moment. The first issue set off a blast:

> We announce the new era—be this our first news—
> When the serf-grinding landlords shall shake in their shoes.[18]

A staff poet supplied indignant verses on the survival of the droit du seigneur among Irish landlords. A subsequent issue reported a Ribbon murder in Limerick. A Mr. Scully had been killed out in the marsh while duck hunting at the supper hour. The *Nation* reported the crime in detail and closed with editorial interpretation: the late Scully was an exterminator whose "conduct towards his tenantry was well calculated to excite those feelings of hatred with which he was universally regarded."[19] He need not have been surprised when he found retribution at hand; and the fact that he was a Catholic proved that agrarian grievance rather than religious acrimony lay at the source of all rural outrage. The next week the *Nation* was still on the subject, and the conclusion was drawn that "though the laws of man are against them [Ribbon terrorists], they are justified in the sight of God."

This sort of dangerous talk did not fit the role assigned to Davis in the Repeal movement, and he was soon put under pressure to moderate his opinions. His partner Duffy could not have been in accord with them, for he believed that the success of Irish nationalism required one of two conditions: either England must be in "mortal peril" or Irishmen must be united in a "combination of all classes." Since England was in no danger in 1842, Duffy's rule made the nationalist strategy wholly dependent upon winning the good will of the Irish landlords. In that case, the *Nation*'s affection for Ribbonmen and Danton would injure the movement. Another Young Irelander, Daniel Maddyn, warned Davis of the dangers of agrarian radicalism: "In a civil war, the fanatical and illiterate would at once swamp the party."[20] Davis was able to stand off both Duffy and Maddyn. But a warning that could not be ignored came from O'Connell himself. Through a speech delivered by his son John in the Repeal Association he advised the *Nation* to divorce itself from its French affections, France being synonymous with atheism, bloodshed, and confiscation.

Davis yielded to the pressure. He had shown a good theoretical grasp of the peasants' situation; yet he lacked any concrete tie with them, and he underestimated the urgency of their crisis. He was soon convinced that the combination of all classes might really be promising. He dreamed of Ireland's problems solved by the self-critical capability of the Protestant landlords:

> Fancy the aristocracy, placed by just laws, or by wise concessions, on terms of friendship with their tenants, securing to these tenants every farthing their industry entitled them to; living among them, promoting agriculture and education by example and instruction; sharing their joys, comforting their sorrows, and ready to stand at their head whenever their country called. Think well on it. Suppose it to exist in your own county, in your own barony and parish. See the life of such a landlord, and of such farmers—so busy, so thoughtful, so happy! How the villages would ring with pleasure and trade, and the fields laugh with contented and cheered labor. Imagine the poor supporting themselves on those waste lands, which our rents and taxes would reclaim, and the workhouse turned into a hospital or a district college. Education and art would prosper; every village [would be] like Italy with its painter of repute. . . .[21]

But John Blake Dillon, the third of the *Nation* partners, had grown up in Roscommon and was not so sanguine. "A Connaught landlord," he said on reading Davis' bucolic idyl, "sees but one object in Creation, and that is himself. . . ."[22]

The *Nation*'s agrarian militancy faded. The "serf-grinding landlords" were not heard of again; the Ribbonmen were no longer praised. Weekly counsels of patience prevailed. Peasant proprietorship was no longer stressed, and in its place appeared the unexciting phrase "prospective laws" and the planks of O'Connell's timid agrarian program. The old spirit of "Udalism and Feudalism" persisted in only one guise. In pursuing its campaign to bring in the Protestants, the *Nation* supplemented its other appeals with systematic scaremongering, hinting at the imminence of bloody outbursts "not dreamed of just now" unless nationalism prevailed. Armageddon, it warned, was avoidable only "if the aristocracy aid the People in getting manufactures" and in pursuing the rest of Davis' commercial program for Ireland.[23] These dire prognostications, printed in a public press, were no private message for the eyes of landlords alone, and the peasants who read them in the *Nation* must have found them fascinating. But otherwise, Davis no longer had much solid sustenance to offer them. Yet peasants too were essential in any combination of all classes. And how might they still be reached? If not substantially, then unsubstantially; and the answer was once again to be: cultural nationalism.

VIII

To give substance to the *Nation*'s program, Davis followed Thierry's lead and turned excitedly to explore the Irish cultural inheritance. He sent out an inquiry for professional advice about how to nationalize the aesthetic vision. A leading Irish painter, unnamed, sent back the warning: "you have lurking hopes that things can be forced." Davis must count painting out. Poetry, though, was another matter, and the painter added:

> You should give Ireland first a decided national school of poetry—that is song —and the other phases of national art will soon show themselves. . . . Some great passion—some earnest and unworldly feeling—some profound state of thought, something that, whilst making this material universe the scene, and its material offspring the actors, shall yet reach at what is far above and beyond it all—something of this kind alone will extricate the lightning flash "from the black cloud that bound it." And would you seek any less than the highest?[24]

This oracular call, at once urgent and obscure, harmonized with Davis' own bent. He turned to and saw the job done.

The vernacular language of Irish nationalism was not mystical. Its common denominator was plain truculence. Its symbology treasured such trifles as insolent nicknames (a Joycean specialty) or any random derision. O'Connell had raised sarcasm to a national voice, and his saucy epigrams, taunts, and rejoinders, along with those of Swift, Tone, and John Philpot Curran, were a sort of folk poetry recited at cabin hearths. A large repertoire of satiric street ballads expressed a political impudence shading into sedition.

Irish political objectives, too, were essentially utilitarian, worldly, optimistic. The ecstasies of the bursting larder form the lyrical burden of Samuel Ferguson's best-known song, praising "the fair hills of holy Ireland":

> Large and profitable are the stacks upon the ground,
> *Uileacán dubh O !*
> The butter and the cream do most wondrously abound,
> *Uileacán dubh O !*

Unhappily, "abound" they did not. They should abound, though, and must. Irishmen were propelled by real grievances and expected real relief. If separation from England were won, prosperity would descend upon them all and ravishments would be forthcoming. That they should have given first thought to such "materialistic" ambitions was hardly peculiar or in need of apology. What ought the homeless, the hungry, and the thwarted to dream about, if not of pigs and potatoes, tenant rights, custom duties, and vacant judgeships? These practical longings paired off appropriately with the militant impulse. Gavan Duffy, taking his words from *The Lady of the Lake*, thus urged the Irish to "spoil the spoiler" of his spoils and "from the robber rend his prey," or in Napoleon's ethics, *enrichez-vous* ! "Help yourself" might sound like an attractive battle cry, and O'Connell used it freely with a reference at once grandiose and vague. But in the raw it was not the perfect approach. *Enrichez-vous* ! was easily confused with its cousin, *chacun pour soi* !, which quickly degenerated in turn to *sauve qui peut* !

The separate elements of the potential Irish nation normally gravitated toward unity, though in a halting way. I have discriminated three strata existing in 1842 with nationalist leanings: the Catholic peasants; the ambitious segment of the middle class, both Catholic and Protestant; and a disaffected landlord here and there. The strata had not yet formed that would dominate Ireland in later times: Joyce's shabby-genteel Dubliners; James Connolly's dockers and Sean O'Casey's knights of the pick and shovel; and the newly propertied farmers, who have been made immortal in Somerville and Ross's story, "The Holy Island." Whether in the simple groupings of 1842 or the more complex groupings of 1904, these were all by circumstance anti-English. But each separate stratum had its own separate ambition, often conflicting with one another. In order to preserve unity and to hold to the strict nationalist objective, it was necessary to find the right bond.

In Davis' cultural nationalism an amorphous idealism provided the inclusive, nonspecific, emotive vessel for gathering all the miscellaneous Irish objectives into one broad nationalist sentiment. The landlord petitioning for a new coercion act and the Ribbonman terrorizing "land grabbers" could now fraternize as fellow patriots—theoretically, that is—to fight for "the old cause that never dies." In this function nebulosity was the first virtue of the symbology.

In its role as the unifier and intensifier of Irish nationalism, Davis' mystique generated an impressive power, even a grandeur, which it had borrowed back from the enormous social force it had itself polarized. If anyone is inclined to doubt this judgment, he is urged to consult the expert appraisals of Gladstone and Lloyd George. And whatever one might think of the bad manners of militant nationalism in general, one must hesitate to judge the Irish mystique harshly, on balance. Winston Churchill, another expert, was not misled into supposing that Irish nationalism shared with the malignant nationalist sarcomas of Europe and Asia any resemblance other than the most trifling. At the beginning of the Second World War his cable to de Valera opened with Davis' own greeting: "A Nation once again!"

IX

Yeats's judgment of Davis makes sport of his ideal of "the good citizen," whose vulgar, measured tread Yeats heard in the crude rhythms of Davis' patriotic verse.[25] The insight was undoubtedly apt. Davis was as engaging a specimen of pure, transparent *Bürgerlichkeit* as one will ever find, especially of its creative phase that commonly appears among backward or distressed peoples. What Yeats did not see was that this same good citizen was also the author of his own ghostly spiritual poetics. For a couple of decades Yeats tried to trace his source to the Irish peasant. But since it did not comfortably belong there, he was forced into a slow realization of error and an attendant painful disenchantment with old Paudeen. "To bring a soul to Ireland" was not a subconscious mission of peasants, but the self-assigned task of Young Ireland, a little group of ambitious and practical-minded intellectual leaders from the solid middle class. Davis was the Irish brother of those European patriots, his contemporaries—Adam Mickiewicz, Pierre Béranger, Giuseppe Mazzini (with whom he is most often coupled)—who etherealized and ignited nineteenth-century progressive longings wherever they found their fatherland. Did not Joyce categorize the ethereal Tom Moore himself as just a "shopkeeper"?

The most selfless Irish patriot would have to concede that Davis' mystique bore a strain of dissimulation that threatened eventual trouble. The militant wing of the Irish middle class—that is, O'Connell, Davis, Duffy, and, later, Mitchel, Stephens, A. M. Sullivan, Butt, and Parnell—proposed to seize possession of Ireland in the name of all the Irish people. Ordinarily their own private objectives were mapped out with some care. But the mechanisms through which their mystical Irish brothers were to share in spoils, as well as in glory, were left in vague outline. The national mystique hinted at universal rewards the leaders were not strictly prepared to deliver. In Davis' day, and even as late as Parnell's, the ambiguity was not crucial. Suppose the leaders could actually have broken England's grip—what then? *On s'engage et puis on voit* (you make your move and see what happens): that was Napoleon's best advice to any nineteenth-century adventurer who found himself face to face with this impasse. The Irish leaders accepted such a gentleman's gamble. They were not exactly candid with their junior comrades, but neither were they dishonest. If they could have won, their program from the day of independence onward actually could have improvised itself. Anybody at all in an independent Ireland could have conducted a more sensible government of the country than the actual government of Sir Robert Peel and Lord John Russell, Charles Trevelyan and Charles Wood, though perhaps none could have said explicitly in advance how it might be done.

As time passed, the authority of the middle-class leaders to act as trustees for the whole Irish nation was to become increasingly tainted. They seemed in the process of underripe decay that has been so scrupulously recorded in *Dubliners, Hail and Farewell,* and *Poems Written in Discouragement.* Militance gave way before prudent second thoughts, dissimulation grew more habitual, nerves more touchy. Shortly after the turn of the century James Connolly raised the question whether they should not step down and allow their leadership to pass to the rank and file. No chance of that. Eventually the day came when the mystification had to be cleared away, and with it came a murderous collision inside the Irish family. The ambiguity of Davis' mystique was paid for finally in the Civil War of 1921–23. By then, though, its charter pledge—to win independence first —had been fulfilled.

CHAPTER 4

The Nation's *First Year*

I

Thomas Davis was methodical to a fault. When he sat down to write a book he inscribed the epigraph first. Duffy found among his papers a fragment of a biography of Wolfe Tone with "*Nil desperandum*" neatly copied on page 1 and the rest in order up to the point where death stopped his relentless progress. To bring a soul to Ireland seemed a project amenable to method, and method begins with education: let education commence. The national schools were silent on Limerick and Dungannon: let the omission be remedied forthwith. Irishmen were ignorant of their history: let a popular library of Irish episodes and heroes be published instantly. Irishmen were losing the Irish language: let it be preserved. Davis was the first national leader to see the incendiary political potential of the native tongue, whose survival was of no concern to O'Connell, though unlike Davis he did actually speak it. "What! give up the tongue of Ollamh Fodhla?" Davis asked. "No! oh, no! . . . A nation should guard its language more than its territories."[1]

Turning to the arts, he pondered the degraded state of Irish sculpture, recommending that Trinity College acquire and display a plaster cast of every beautiful piece of sculpture in the world in order to inspire any patriot sculptors who might happen along. To the painters he sent a list of seventy-two patriotic scenes to be rendered in oil as soon as feasible, covering Irish history from the landing of the Milesians to O'Connell on the Clare hustings. He sketched a project to place a patriotic engraving on the wall of every peasant cabin, carrying out Goethe's theory that the organic soul ought to "see a fine picture" every day.[2]

II

A nationalist school of verse had a more substantial tradition to start from. The embryo of the Irish poetic mystique had already appeared a generation before Davis in the songs of Tom Moore. Responding to the gloom that settled over Dublin in the first years of the Union, *Irish Melodies* had

58

embraced defeat and made a good thing out of it, transforming it into the sweet habit-forming enticement that exudes out of "The Harp That Once through Tara's Halls" and "Let Erin Remember" and less winningly from some of the rest of the lyrics that Joyce called Tom Moore's "Irish Maladies." His characteristic tone is heard in the keening of the stragglers on a battlefield in a song called "After the Battle":

> The last sad hour of freedom's dream
> And valor's task mov'd slowly by,
> While mute they watch'd till morning's beam
> Should rise and give them light to die.
> There's yet a world where souls are free,
> Where tyrants taint not Nature's bliss:—
> If death that world's bright opening be,
> Oh! who would live a slave in this?

These verses would cure anybody's euphoria, but some might think them too dismal altogether. The trouble with Moore, Davis said, was that he "too much loves to weep."

By 1842 Moore's exhausted Irish muse had long since surrendered the Dublin cultural front to a new breed of youth. Ten years before the *Nation*, a little group of Tory juveniles at Trinity College had started a political-literary monthly called the *Dublin University Magazine*. Learned and lively, it caught on and established itself for a long happy life as a junior contemporary of *Blackwood's Magazine*, *Fraser's Magazine*, and the *Quarterly Review*. The new magazine attached itself to the Irish Protestant Ascendancy as an intellectual house organ, so to speak. The first article in the first issue, in January 1833, was entitled "The Present Crisis." And what crisis was it? It was the destruction of Irish civilization by the Clare election, the British Reform Act of 1832, and the tithe war. O'Connell haunted the contributors; they could not shake him off their minds. They also expressed a sullen but reserved distrust of England and produced a peppery assortment of Orange phobias, especially against the fertility, superstition, inveracity, slovenliness, greed, and vulgarity of the "papists."

For a garnish to dignify these Ascendancy attitudes, the magazine took great pains with its artistic and cultural pieces, following out the theory (later adopted by Yeats) that good taste is the foremost stigmata identifying a proper ruling caste. But at the end of its first year of publication, in December 1833, the magazine's literary department had not yet come up to expectations. It promised, though, that the flatness of its Horatian translations and Trinity sonneteering would soon be remedied by fresh native talent. After all, it said, Ireland was "the birthplace of song, where poetry is almost literally the *prose* of the Irish peasant, and the harp is the national designation." The editor responsible for the new tack was Isaac Butt of

Donegal, a name that will break into our historical narrative many times as he drifts from championship of the Orange Order into nationalism and at last into the top nationalist leadership. For poetry in the native Irish mode his advocate was Samuel Ferguson of Belfast, a friend and Trinity classmate of Davis. Three months after the new policy began, the readers had the rare pleasure one day in March 1834 of turning the page and finding a fresh addition to the immortal lyrics of the English language, Ferguson's "Fairy Thorn."

Ferguson emerged at the same time as the magazine's cultural ideologist. An essay called "A Dialogue between the Head and Heart" (1833) made a surprisingly candid confession of the way in which the Irish gentry's dual personality had responded to Emancipation—showing how their self-righteousness and presumption were unhappy "to stand in the sphere of their own infamy" as Grattan had said; and how their fear was actually inflamed by affection, since the heart felt the enemy was really right and therefore the head understood it to be the more dangerous. The head-and-heart essay was followed in April 1834 by a long, serialized critique of the chief Irish literary event of the times, the publication by James Hardiman, a pious Catholic linguist working with a team of assistants, of a two-volume collection of English translations of Irish poetry, called *Irish Minstrelsy* (1831). The gist of Ferguson's critique is contained in his opening question: "O ye fair hills of holy Ireland, who is he who ventures to stand between us and your Catholic sons' goodwill?" The answer could be only Hardiman, for he had attempted to duplicate in poetry O'Connell's success in isolating the Catholic masses politically from their former leaders in the Protestant Ascendancy.

But the poetic raid had failed, Ferguson thought, and he suggested that the Ascendancy could recoup some of its recent defeats at Hardiman's expense. Although he was only twenty-three and insecure in his knowledge of the Irish language, he felt no hesitancy in labeling the veteran scholar and his team as disloyal, fretful, querulous, malicious, rancorous, popish, puerile (twice), spurious, unclassical, and lamentably bad. (Long afterward Douglas Hyde added the general epithet "fearful" for the team, although he believed that several of Hardiman's own efforts were excellent.)

For example, there was a poem by a Catholic priest called "Roiseen dubh," literally, "Rosie the Brunette." It was unquestionably the priest's love song to a young parishioner, Ferguson said. One of the quatrains he translated thus:

> Oh, smooth rose, modest, of the round white breasts,
> You are she that left a thousand pains in the very center of my heart;
> Fly with me, oh first love, and leave the country;
> And if I could, would I not make a queen of you, my Roiseen dubh?

Now, Hardiman had declared the poem to be a political allegory exalting Irish nationalism, plainly in order to allay his embarrassment at the holy man's misbehavior, Ferguson said. "And why, in the name of holy nature, should the priest not be in love? and why in the name of sacred humanity should the priest not long to enjoy his love?" Anticipating George Moore's exploitation of this sensational theme three-quarters of a century later, he advised the lovesick cleric to "pitch his vows to the Pope, the Pope to purgatory, marry his black rose-bud, and take a curacy from the next Protestant rector."

Beneath Ferguson's raillery one soon perceives that he had himself fallen hopelessly under the spell of Hardiman's materials. Irish antiquarianism had caught him, and tumuli, assonances, and ogam inscriptions would hold him a devotee as long as he lived. His first service to the passion was to show Hardiman how to translate antique Irish poetry. At the end of his critique he appended an anthology of twenty of his own poetic renditions from the minstrelsy, proving beyond doubt that there was one arena where the Belfast Protestant could overmaster the O'Connellite.

By the time the *Nation* first went to press in 1842 the muddy waters of the old quarrel with Hardiman had settled. It was not really debatable that translations should be as accurate, as graceful, as unbigoted, and as impassioned as possible. So much on Ferguson's side. But against Ferguson, Davis had found in Hardiman one assumption that pleased him; and it was that the Irish minstrelsy was national, and unapologetically political.

III

There was a poet around town named James Clarence Mangan, a half-starved exotic given to odd dress and manners and a weakness first for alcohol and later for opium. From the beginning, Butt's magazine bought poems from him. They were not usually in the Irish mode but more conventional romantic fare, mostly German and Levantine translations and imitations. But in 1838 Mangan got a job on the Irish Ordnance Survey, one of the "little somethings" that the Litchfield House compact got for Ireland. Among his fellow surveyors were the foremost Irish antiquarians and linguists of the generation, George Petrie, Eugene O'Curry, and John O'Donovan. Mangan somehow amalgamated with these three to form a new team rather more potent than Hardiman's. The antiquarians supplied a translated and interpreted text, and Mangan put it into verse. The resulting poems the *Dublin University Magazine* did not buy, and they were published elsewhere just before the *Nation* began. One of them, "The Woman of Three Cows," was quaint and genial. Three others were firebrands: "Kathleen Ny-Houlahan," "Kincora," and a lament on the 1607 flight of the earls. Davis and Duffy decided to seize this talent and attach him to the *Nation*'s staff.

IV

A mass base for Davis' poetic project was discovered in Irish folk music and ballads, since, as Duffy observed, all Irishmen had for music "an appetite almost as imperious as hunger." Davis was as avid for music as any other Irishman, and one of the few surviving glimpses into his early youth depicts him listening in tears to the old airs played on a fiddle by "a common country fellow." The editor of the *Citizen*, the journal that had published several of his early essays, was Henry Hudson, one of the great line of Irish musicologists who opened for the public the treasure of Irish folk music, described by Sir Arnold Bax as "the most varied and beautiful folk music" to be found anywhere on earth.[3]* Tom Moore had made a mint exploiting it. Davis said that "music is the first faculty of the Irish, and scarcely anything has such power of good over them." It was therefore "the duty of every patriot" to make the fullest "use" of this charming national addiction, since a fine old tune could escort a good idea past barriers of indifference at any social level.[4]

With a bit of research Davis learned that four print shops in Ireland were exclusively engaged in publishing halfpenny ballads for sale in the streets and at fairs, economic proof of the Irish lust for verse. When he examined some of these broadsides, he found them often humorous or tender; but more often they were "coarse," bombastic, politically confused, and poorly printed. "A high class of ballads," he concluded, "would do immense good." He proposed two patriotic projects, a ballad history and a ballad topography. The history was to be built up as a mosaic of independent ballads treating isolated episodes such as he had listed for the patriotic painters. "A genuine ballad history," he said, "is the greatest book (religion apart) that a country can possess." The ballads of topography would celebrate the *genius loci* of the varied Irish landscape. He commended accuracy to the scenic balladeers and observed that their task required direct observation, poets who had "panted on our mountains" and "pierced our passes." He supplied a catalogue of the scenic possibilities.[5]

Before coming to Dublin, Duffy had already found that Irish readers were pleased by some ballads he had printed in his Belfast paper. When he was ready to make up the first issue of the *Nation*, he sent out a call for more verse of the same sort. Davis, who had never tried poetry before,

* The same ethnic sensibility was later exemplified in the fabulous scope of Joyce's active repertoire of Irish songs, four hundred of them quoted in *Ulysses* alone. See Mathew J. C. Hodgart and Mabel P. Worthington, *Song in the Works of James Joyce* (New York: Columbia University Press, 1959).

returned in a week or so with "The Lament for the Death of Owen Roe O'Neill," and Duffy's memoirs recalled that in the three remaining years of his life Davis composed poetry without cessation "as spontaneously as a bird."[6] Several Trinity College students, who would later become austere judges, doctors, and empire statesmen, mailed in dangerous verses to be printed anonymously. One of these was "O'Donnell Abu." Another was "The Memory of the Dead," which had such frightful seditious power that in due time it sent Duffy to jail; and the author, John Kells Ingram, a Dublin doctor, did not publicly acknowledge his brain child until fifty-seven years had passed. Copious unsolicited talent introduced itself through the mail, often in rough script on school scratch paper, a recurrent phenomenon of Irish letters of which Sean O'Casey provided the last notable instance.

v

Nothing is easier than to be arch or witty at the expense of the verse that resulted from Davis' program. A great deal of it was exceedingly inept. Even O'Connell, who had no taste at all, complained of the *Nation*'s "poor rhymed dullness." Most of the verse was so barren of individuality that the names of the authors could be scrambled without incongruity. Duffy, a gifted man but utterly prosaic, went to work with the rest and composed "Fág an Bealach" (Clear the Road!). Yeats heard crude echoes of Scott, Macaulay, and "Hohenlinden" in the verse, and Byron and Longfellow might be added: it was an unhappy chance that brought "The Skeleton in Armor" to the Dublin bookshops in 1842 just when the young men were tuning their fiddle. Mangan was unable to supply the *Nation* with a great poem on assignment, though his sense of humor did not desert him:

> O'Connell's a tremendous ass-
> aulter of tyranny and Tories
> And we the *Nation*, are his ass-
> istants and share—hurrah—his glories.[7]

The same mails that brought the editors new and unknown talent, like John Keegan's "Devil May Care," also brought a stream of verse so bad that, according to I. A. Richards' theory, inspiration must be invoked to account for it. Duffy conducted an amusing weekly column of biting reproof to discourage deluded amateur poets, but the principle on which he screened their work was itself unclear. He let pass this temperance poet's vision of a spree:

> From habit, and from choice, and some
> Will almost own from fate,
> They sought a Lethe midst their gloom,
> And wildly felt elate.[8]

63

Disappointment in the *Nation*'s poetry cannot be claimed as an original aesthetic insight. The "de-Davisation" of Irish literature, proposed by Yeats in 1894 and by John Eglinton (who coined the phrase) in 1906, has not encountered any strong recent opposition.

The strictures, however, are somewhat beside the point. Most of the verses were ephemera, of no serious concern to anybody:

> Accursed who brings to light of day
> The writings I have cast away![9]

Those that did survive cannot be judged as poems, for the genre to which they belong and in which they earned their hearing was not poetry but song in the strict musical sense. In two immensely popular compilations of verse published by the *Nation* in 1843 and 1844, about half the titles bore subscripts to indicate that they were to be sung, like Tom Moore's melodies, to specified traditional airs. Most of the remainder appeared in a third anthology in 1845 accompanied by anonymous musical scores and "arrangements for the voice and pianoforte." Since then, none of the lyrics has ever been known apart from its tune.

Yeats once reported that he could never hear "The West's Asleep," Davis' song, "without great excitement." In revision he deleted the sentence.[10] His indecision suggests perplexity in his effort to balance his own opinion against the judgment of the public. Because he was tone-deaf, he was never "present" at any performance of the song. He was in no position to challenge the esteem it enjoyed in Ireland, and he was in fact required in fairness to pay it humble deference, as an English-speaker cannot but defer to Russian opinions of Pushkin. At the same time, he knew that as a rigid model for poetry as such, it could only bring artistic disaster. Thus he complained of Tom Moore's melodies that "all but all" were "artificial and mechanical when separated from the music that gave them wings."[11] But except for the limited genre of "literary song"—"Down by the Sally Gardens" and the like—any song at all would naturally suffer the same deflation "separated from the music," just as a painting may be reduced to banality by black-and-white reproduction.

In song, when a dominant musical tempo takes command over poetic rhythm, poetic indelicacies can not only be permitted, but may actually be an enhancement. The song referred to by Yeats, "The West's Asleep," contains these lines:

> And fleet as deer the Norman ran
> Through Curlews Pass and Ardrahan,
> And later times saw deeds as brave;
> And glory guards Clanricarde's grave—

To the hasty reader the lines are brassy and raw, an artificial and mechanical manipulation of standard Irish emotional cues of heroic site, actor, and incident. But sung by a good tenor voice to the air of "The Brink of the White Rocks," they are indescribably moving. They realize Davis' aim to compose living symbols that would make the world listen. Perhaps twenty more of the *Nation*'s songs, equally potent, must also be taken seriously. They are not a symptom of the idiocy of the Irish throng nor of its vulgar taste for subliterature. Still resilient and winning after more than a century of opportunities for oblivion, they can be assumed to be a permanent fixture among Ireland's great cultural possessions.

VI

Davis proceeded to prose literature. "Have you ever tried dramatic writing?" he asked his friend Maddyn, in the spirit in which Yeats and George Russell would later approach literate young Dubliners. He added, "I wish to heaven someone would attempt Irish historical fiction." He laid down the principles on which historical novelists should work: the Irish historical novel must center on fictitious characters, since the historical figures who would appear could not "reach any decisive time"; that is, literal Irish history provided no agreeable dénouements. Gerald Griffin, recently dead, had once said that the future masterpiece of Irish history would "paint Ireland struggling incessantly and unsuccessfully, now beaming with hope, now crouching in despair, still never crushed and never quite triumphant." Davis agreed: "This *is* our history, and must be told." If this seemed to be despair, "say rather perseverance." He listened hopefully for an Irish Sir Walter Scott to announce himself.[12]

When no Irish Scott answered this summons, the *Nation* settled for a fair equivalent. Davis pronounced William Carleton to be a "historian" because he had preserved for future generations a record of vanishing Irish types, the Ribbonman, the poor scholar, the faction fighter, the matchmaker, the connoisseur of fairies (whose demise he predicted within twenty years), and other people drawn from his vehement recall of a demonic childhood in county Tyrone. But Carleton was attached to Butt's magazine. Duffy therefore opened up a public courtship to win him over from the Orange to the national organ. So Carleton, like Mangan, joined the staff and set to work on a massive novel about the agrarian crisis, called *Valentine M'Clutchy* after the name of its evil "middleman" villain. At the same time he sketched out several shorter novels of stern moralistic intention, one attacking Ribbonism, another deploring the universal manure pile beside the peasant cabin door. And in further line of patriotic duty he wrote a scurrilous denunciation of Charles Lever, another native novelist from Butt's ménage, and more recently the new editor of *Dublin University Magazine*, replacing

Butt. Lever's stage Irishmen, said Carleton, were the invention of a selfish and sordid pander and Judas, of a man who had sold himself and his nation's repute to English taste for English gold.*

VII

Such was the *Nation*'s cultural artillery, fired point-blank at all irrational resistance to Repeal. According to the plan, the Protestants were to be swept into an emotional fervor that would overwhelm their Ascendancy prejudices and transform them into selfless, supermundane Irishmen, avid to "reach at what is far above and beyond it all." Davis believed that the proper phrase set to the proper cadence would actually incite them to abdicate their privileges in some mad Irish *jeu de paume*. Nothing of the sort occurred. A group that had shown itself insensitive to Irish actuality was hardly to be reached through Irish symbols; and the Ascendancy proved equally as impervious to intoxication as to right reason. Failure to win a Protestant following damaged Davis' self-confidence, as he began to see that his agitation could hope at best merely to chip here and there from loyalist solidity. Hence, when one of the most distinguished aristocrats of the Ascendancy began to show signs of responding, there was great rejoicing in the *Nation*'s columns.

The response came from William Smith O'Brien, one of Irish history's most interesting actors, a brother of Lord Inchiquin, a lineal descendant of Brian Boru, and a great Irish landlord. He was about ten years older than Davis. As a student at Cambridge breathing its evangelical atmosphere, he had absorbed the same ethical sensitivity that Davis had acquired at Trinity College, so that the two spoke the same moral language. Then he had come home to make his political career in the normal manner as a loyalist M.P. for county Clare. In line of political duty he had once challenged O'Connell and had actually fought a duel with the Liberator's attendant buffoon, Tom Steele. Slowly he learned that a thin skin and loyalism made a miserable combination. He began to voice his tormented thoughts at Westminster and in letters to the press, all deliberate and ponderous, for even his small talk sounded like a page out of *Hansard*. For a long time he weighed the two sides of the matter. "Personal considerations" and "a lingering hope" of

---

* Lever was apparently touched by this critique, for he shortly afterward resigned from the editorship and began composition of a peace offering, a novel of his own on the agrarian crisis, called *Saint Patrick's Eve*. The novel is somewhat derivative from Carleton; yet it is excellent in its own right. It carries a narrative idea more imaginative than is common in Irish fiction: a peasant is given a permanent remission from rent payment for saving the life of the landlord's son in a brawl at a village fair. He builds his life on this unparalleled piece of good luck. Then after many years the old landlord dies and the "middleman" presents him with a bill not just for the current rent, but for the entire balance due. This wrecks the peasant's life until a happy ending makes everything right again.

English generosity were balanced in his mind against the actual record of "irritation and insult" to Ireland and coercion with "bayonets that menace our bosoms." Finally he decided to go abroad to study "whether, among the governments of central Europe, there are any so indifferent to the interests of their subjects as England."[13] Promising to take his stand one way or the other at his return, he set out for the Continent, leaving the *Nation* in suspense.

But Smith O'Brien was unique. For all the years of effort the *Nation* expended in courting influential Protestants, it captured only this one grand prize, so that in evaluating its accomplishment of O'Connell's primary assignment, one can only say that its failure was not quite total. In time Davis' patience with the "cultivated classes" was strained; and behind the stylistic courtesy the *Nation* had adopted to counteract O'Connell's scurrility, it began to betray exasperation. In one blistering leading article Davis termed them "a filthy mass of national treason . . . coward patriots and criminal dandies."[14]

VIII

If the cultivated one-eighth of Ireland was not waiting for the strains of "O'Donnell Abu," the other seven-eighths were. On October 15, 1842, when the first issue of the *Nation* appeared, the editors were pleased to find the entire issue sold out before noon. "The country people are delighted with us if their letters speak true," Davis wrote.[15] Dillon went home to county Roscommon, in the most distressed district of Ireland, and wrote back excitedly to his partners: "I am astonished at the success of the *Nation* in this poor place"—twenty-three subscriptions in hungry Ballaghaderreen.[16] The bottom of the Irish social pyramid, "to whom reading was not a necessity," felt the force of the journal each week "like electric shocks." After a few months of publication the *Nation* was able to report that it had become the largest weekly newspaper in the history of Ireland. With a circulation of twenty-five thousand and an estimated ten readers for each copy, it had a regular audience of a quarter of a million persons.

It could not be denied that the *Nation's* success was indebted to O'Connell's blessing. Davis might rightly claim that "journals, with all their means and appurtenances, were, and are to be for many a day, the stimulating power in Ireland."[17] But the prior virtues of organization were brought home to him as soon as O'Connell ordered the Repeal wardens to help build his circulation. Many wardens ordered bundles for distribution at weekly Repeal meetings; some read aloud each weekly issue to the membership, half of whom could not read. Davis developed the amateur's respect for a professional's political organization and wrote a panegyric on its workings:

The People are united under the greatest system of organisation ever attempted in any country. They send in, by their Collectors, Wardens, and Inspectors, to the central office of Ireland, the contributions needed to carry on the Registration of Voters, the public meetings, the publications, the law expenses, and the organisation of the Association; and that in turn carries on registries, holds meetings, opens reading rooms, sends newspapers, and books, and political instructions, back through the same channel; so that the Central Committee knows the state of every parish, and every parish receives the teaching and obeys the will of the Central Committee.[18]

In cheerful recognition of the debt this wonderful mechanism owed to the clergy, the *Nation* was ready to prove its gratitude. When some Connaught peasant agitators, in the spirit of the times, demanded a reduction in baptismal rates from two and six to one shilling, their campaign met with the sternest reproof: "Shame upon them! say we."[19]

IX

O'Connell's good will toward the *Nation* was not a charitable benevolence, for the journal had its uses to him, too. It filled four to eight columns each week with a stenographic report of his latest oratory, and it paid him unstinting praise in prose and verse. More important than the flattery, its message had got through where he had failed, and it set the spark to his Repeal agitation. It will be remembered that Repeal had been stagnating for two years before the *Nation* began publication. By generating nationalist emotions that O'Connell had never even imagined, it had suddenly galvanized Irish political sentiment. Though dour by instinct, John O'Leary remembered after half a century the ecstatic shock of the early *Nation* as the most intense experience of a lifetime. "Perhaps it may give some notion of the effect produced on me to say that I then went through a process analogous to what certain classes of Christians call 'conversion.' I can but vaguely remember my unregenerate state."[20] The Repeal Association came to life and began to move. The *Nation*'s success in reaching the ear of the people had brought it over into O'Connell's private sector, where he was not accustomed to sharing his leadership; but he made it welcome.

Heartened at last, O'Connell staged a public debate on Repeal in the Dublin Corporation, or city council. His eloquence routed his young Tory opponent, the amiable Isaac Butt, recently the editor of the *Dublin University Magazine*. The pitch of excitement rose and was further inflamed by the *Nation*. O'Connell had for some time been in the habit of going occasionally into the country to conduct Repeal meetings. Just after the Dublin Corporation debate he held one of his meetings in Trim, county Meath. To the surprise of all, thirty thousand people turned out. He held another in Mullingar. The crowd increased to a hundred thousand. Then he went to

Cork, and there his audience swelled to half a million. The Repeal Association published in the *Nation* each week the income from the Repeal rent, providing future historians with a rare measure of an excited public's true temperature. At the time of the *Nation*'s first issue, the rent income was 50 pounds a week. In the week of the meeting at Trim it was 500 pounds. After the Cork meeting it rose rapidly to 2,000 pounds.

O'Connell now drew the conclusion that his "monster meetings," speaking with so many millions of earnest voices, must necessarily overawe Sir Robert Peel and force him to sue for terms. Davis, too, was convinced of the power of O'Connell's mass meetings. He wrote to the skeptic Maddyn: "O'Connell prevailed in '29 by the *power* of fighting, not the *practice* of it; may he not do so again? You will say no, for England is dead against us. What's the proof of her being so?"[21] In the midst of the jubilation over the monster meetings, the *Nation* printed a chapter from the official *Repealer's Primer*, answering Maddyn's doubts in O'Connell's terms:

> ANTI-REPEALER: Then, granting that England is not in the condition to engage in a sanguinary struggle, and that the wisdom of the Repeal leaders will prevent rebellion, how do you propose to overcome the English parliament? how do you propose to gain a majority there?
>
> REPEALER: This history of that slowly matured fruit—Catholic emancipation—will answer that question. . . . And now, if you please, let us leave the impractibility question.[22]

Yet all the while the worry lingered: suppose Peel would not surrender? After all, the Repeal hordes could not even vote.

There was a troublesome Repealer named William Conner, a farmer and a wag rivaling the Liberator himself in the homely humor of his speeches. In the midst of the frenzy of the hour, he arose in the association to propose that the point of the monster meetings be sharpened through a general strike against rent. O'Connell's son, in the chair, was thrown into panic by the resolution, and after some commotion on the floor, he ruled the member out of order. Conner retired, grumbling at the chair's victory: "Humbugging has been going on long enough." The *Nation* next Saturday attacked Conner as vile, depraved, abhorrent, cowardly, and criminal. In the same paragraph it then turned upon the landlords, and without mitigating its tone, it declared that class to be profligate, a nuisance, and a curse.[23] These were hysterical hours in Young Ireland's career.

O'Connell was increasingly elated by the sensational effects of his oratory. After Cork he scheduled a rapid succession of mass meetings in all parts of Ireland for the summer and early autumn of 1843. Week by week he became more daring in his attacks upon the Union. When Sir Edward Sugden, the lord chancellor, dismissed a number of country justices of the peace for giving support to Repeal, O'Connell simply organized a dual judiciary made up of the ex-justices, who acted as arbitrators with the consent of the contending parties. He also began to assemble a dual legislature called the Council of Five Hundred. By midsummer his oratorical rhythms lent to the peaceful message of moral force an overtone that sounded almost like the eve of the Battle of Lexington. At Mallow four hundred thousand listeners were thrown into delirium by what seemed to be a declaration to meet English coercion with counterforce, although a sober reading of his text in the *Nation* next Saturday showed that his words were a lawyer's equivocation and not a revolutionary defiance. He said:

> The time is coming when we must be doing. Gentlemen you may learn the alternative to live as slaves or die as freemen. . . . I think I perceive a fixed disposition on the part of our Saxon traducers to put us to the test. . . . In the midst of peace and tranquillity they are covering our land with troops. . . . But gentlemen, as long as they leave us a rag of the Constitution we will stand on it. We will violate no law, we will assail no enemy, but you are much mistaken if you think others will not assail you. (A voice, We are ready to meet them.) To be sure you are. Do you think I suppose you to be cowards or fools.[24]

Three weeks later at Baltinglass, before three hundred thousand people, O'Connell said: "I am called Washington—he was driven into the field and obliged to take up arms," and again an equivocation was added, "I know a trick worth two of that."[25] That week the Repeal rent stood at 3,100 pounds.

Still the crescendo mounted. A monster meeting was held at Tara which surpassed anything yet seen in all of recorded history. Forty brass bands hailed the entry of the Liberator with triumphal patriotic music, and ten thousand Repealers mounted on horseback escorted him to the platform. People began arriving at dawn and continued to pour in over the choked roads all morning. One could not see the entire crowd from any point: the Hill of Tara was covered with Repealers, the plain around was covered, and on the Dublin road the multitude stretched solidly three miles back from the speaker's platform. No one knew the actual number of listeners present, but the *Nation*, after giving thought to its reputation for statistical restraint, settled on the convenient round number, one million persons. Duffy went out to Tara with his notebook and reported the meeting for the *Nation*:

> There were more men present than possessed Scotland when William Wallace raised the standard of independence; or in Athens in the days of world renown. The British Army at home and abroad, or the Armies with which Napoleon trod Europe under foot, did not muster as many grown men as gathered around O'Connell on that day.
>
> It was a sight, not grand alone, but appalling—not exciting merely pride, but *fear*.[26]

X

The 1843 series of monster meetings was to close on Sunday, October 8, at Clontarf, on the north shore of Dublin Bay, where Brian Boru had defeated the Danes in the eleventh century. The meeting promised to surpass Tara, and early in the week crowds of Repealers from the far parts of Ireland began moving toward Dublin. Saturday morning Peel finally made his move. He proscribed the meeting and dispatched cavalry to Clontarf, while Wellington looked forward to a good day's sport on Sunday, according to his sentiment:

> Pour la canaille
> Faut la mitraille [grapeshot].[27]

O'Connell's time for decision had come, and he did not hesitate for an instant: he retreated. He canceled the meeting and sent the mounted Repealers riding out on every road converging on Dublin to turn back the crowds. Saturday's *Nation* had time to insert the notice of Peel's proclamation, but not enough time to remove a poem entitled "March to Clontarf":

> Then where's the tyrant power on earth
> That would, or could, or dare resist us?[28]

On Monday O'Connell came to the Repeal headquarters and confessed that Saturday had been a "hideous" day; but now he felt much better, for he could see that Peel's proscription of the Clontarf mass meeting was without "a shred of legality." In refusing to be provoked, Repeal had won a great bloodless victory. The following Saturday was the *Nation*'s first birthday. Its editorial advice was: "Trust in O'Connell and fear not." But an ominous item appeared beside the first-anniversary leading article. It reported rumors that a grand jury had just returned secret indictments against the nationalist leaders and journalists and that grave developments were expected hourly. Later that afternoon O'Connell, his son John, his chief Repeal officials, a couple of priests, the editor of the *Freeman*, and Gavan Duffy of the *Nation* were arrested on a charge of sedition.

XI

On this same day, Smith O'Brien arrived home from the Continent to learn the news of the Repealers' arrest and to disclose his answer to the question he had taken abroad. It was no—there was no misrule in all continental Europe to equal England's misrule in Ireland. With the understanding that Repeal stood for the "combination of all classes," he took the plunge at last. He begged O'Connell's leave "to transmit herewith £5, my first subscription to the treasury of the Loyal Repeal Association of Ireland."[29] Needing a stand-in to take his place during the state trials now impending, and perhaps for the imprisonment to follow, O'Connell named Smith O'Brien.

XII

So ended the *Nation*'s first year. Its like would never be known again, for Clontarf was the death of the Repeal movement. Yet Irishmen never forgot the echoes of O'Connell's cheering host at Tara of the Kings. Whatever the old Liberator may have lacked, it was not every leader who could bring out a million men to his mass meetings. It wanted still but a Carnot, said Duffy, "to organize and direct that immense mass of physical and moral power," and "a new nation might that day have been born."[30] In a sense, imperial rule in Ireland was foredoomed henceforth, though what inexhaustible rearguard skill and resourcefulness it still held in reserve was yet to be painfully demonstrated.

Irish nationalists never forgot, either, that the *Nation* had been the spark that set off O'Connell's Repeal explosion. They sometimes did forget, however, that it was only a spark, a necessary cause perhaps, but very far from a sufficient one. Davis' songs came to be regarded overenthusiastically as pure wizardry. Irishmen in later time, especially when hard-pressed in retreat, listened for the new magician who, with only a verse or two and a couple of old airs, could turn the tide of their disasters. In storm and doldrum alike, the air was to be filled with warlike incantations in the hope of once again raising up the hordes of ready men who had gathered at Tara. The compulsive demand for ever more piercing exhortation was to cause much pain to Irish writers half a century afterward.

Irish writers, too, would long remember the happy phase of the O'Connell-Davis partnership before Clontarf. Mitchel recalled years later how "many an eager boy, from the Giant's Causeway to Cape Clear, cut open the weekly sheet with a hand shaken by excitement."[31] Duffy thought the *Nation*'s penetration into the hearts of the Irish people during its first year "a marvel," and after half a century it was still the most marvelous memory of a full and exciting life. "It is impossible at this time," he wrote, "to realize the amazement, the consternation swelling almost to panic, and the final enthusiasm and intoxication of joy with which the new teaching was received."[32] The intoxication of joy was felt no less by the performers than by the listeners, when the dark abstract void of rural Ireland suddenly filled with applause for their work, "the voice of the nation." Yeats's literary movement began in nostalgia for the sea of eager faces hanging upon Davis' words. Who could resist Duffy's promise of intoxication of joy as a happy exchange for an "out-worn heart, in a time out-worn?"

CHAPTER 5

The Retreat from Clontarf

I

After Clontarf the decay of O'Connell's Repeal movement spread uncontrolled. The state trials absorbed the full energies of all the leaders for nearly a year, leaving the agitation to peter out week by week. In leisurely time the defendants were tried and convicted by an all-Orange jury. Delay of sentencing killed several more months. Finally they were called up in June 1844 and sentenced to one year's imprisonment in Richmond jail, south Dublin. Three months later came a pleasant surprise: on appeal, the House of Lords reversed the jury's verdict and freed the prisoners. The news reaching Dublin in the evening, O'Connell and the rest went home that night and slept in their own beds. Next morning they returned to Richmond to lead one of those great Dublin street processionals that mark the stages of Irish history, moving back in triumph through the city, cheered by a multitude which filled the street from curb to curb and stretched six miles from front to rear. The prisoners' carriages were drawn by joyful Repealers who earnestly trusted that the Liberator, once more free, would now lead them out of the maze of their tribulations. It was not an exorbitant hope, yet it would be many a long day before Dublin would have another triumph to celebrate.

Politically, O'Connell had come to a dead end. He had pushed moral force to its limits and had failed. Beyond, he thought he saw the abyss of "Jacobinism"; therefore the need of the day was for ordered retreat. But retreat to what? He was suddenly timid and uncertain and could not say, but the revival of the old Whig alliance at some opportune time was plainly on his mind.

A view of the prison yard at Richmond revealed an incongruous scene of the great prisoner: "addressed by bishops; complimented by Americans; bored by deputations; serenaded by bands; comforted by ladies; half smothered with roses; half drowned in champagne"—a much-pampered convict. "In an elegant tent, with a green flag flying over it, O'Connell, with his green Mullaghmast cap on, received his deputations and made them gracious answers, not without a seasoning of merry jest. Through the trees, and amongst parterres of flowers, one might see 'the martyrs' and their friends sauntering about."[1] This sarcasm of John Mitchel's insinuated that O'Connell in Richmond jail had already betrayed Repeal. His speech on his release bore out the suspicion, for he spoke warmly of the Whigs and announced that the monster meetings would not be resumed. The meeting at Clontarf, he said, "was called legally, it was illegally prevented from meeting," hence "we are bound to vindicate a great principle." But vindication did not lie in actually holding that meeting; that was not at all necessary since "the principle has been sufficiently vindicated by the House of Lords."[2] So far from Tara of the Kings had the eleven months in criminal court taken him.

He was now seventy years old and failing. The anxieties of the state trials had deeply afflicted him, and the disease that Young Ireland later liked to call by the lurid name "softening of the brain" was already perceptible in the confusion of his behavior. He spent more and more time with his beagles at Darrynane, leaving the business of the Repeal movement to the care of his petty and treacherous son John. A sympathetic weariness overtook his followers. The skyrocketing of income from the Repeal rent was long past; now its steady fall was a weekly reminder of failure at hand.

II

The Repeal Association maintained a busy surface optimism, but under it lay the shameful fact that none could deny but few were bold enough to mention: O'Connell's ludicrous self-exposure. The Young Irelanders had mostly agreed with O'Connell's guess that Repeal was going to be won cheaply. They were perhaps not so euphoric as the Liberator, who grandly guaranteed at Roscommon that "the hour is approaching, the day is near, the period is fast coming when—believe me who never deceived you—your country shall be a nation once more."[3] The *Nation* was unclear how a monster meeting "could conquer a great army,"[4] yet it was as severely jolted as O'Connell himself when Wellington's cavalry rode out through the streets to Clontarf. The Young Irelanders might be said to have shared somewhat in the moral onus of the fiasco. But not holding any position of authority in the association, they had no actual responsibility and were free to dissociate themselves from it.

From the moment of O'Connell's surrender to Peel's proclamation, the Young Irelanders regarded him as an obstacle blocking the path of Irish nationalism. In the first hours following Clontarf, Davis' anger had flashed out in a ballad entitled "We Must Not Fail," with the chilling word "coward" plain to see:

74

We took the starving peasant's mite
To aid in winning back his right,
We took the priceless trust of youth;
Their freedom must redeem our truth.

· · · · · · · · · · · · · · · · · · · ·

Earth is not deep enough to hide
The coward slave who shrinks aside;
Hell is not hot enough to scathe
The ruffian wretch who breaks his faith.[5]

These verses did not say that O'Connell should have brought a regiment of
pikemen out to Clontarf, but they certainly did say that he should have held
fast, faced up to Wellington's dragoons, and let the consequences be what
they might.

Davis and the Young Irelanders watched the symptoms of O'Connell's
disintegration with the greatest alarm. Like Yeats's O'Rahilly, they had
helped to wind O'Connell's clock and now they wished to hear it strike.
They were forced, therefore, to try to seize the initiative of the movement for
themselves. But if the old man was no longer leading, he still tolerated no
insubordination. Hence they saw that they must act quickly to establish
their own lines of public communication.

Desperation, almost panic, showed plainly in Young Ireland's scramble
to find some popular foothold of their own, independent of O'Connell.
Their first adventure led them headlong into a youthful absurdity. Next to
O'Connell and Davis, the most memorable Irish historical figure of the
times was Father Theobald Mathew, who made war on drunkenness with
revivalist methods. He had produced one of those spectacular mass emotional
explosions that fascinate sociologists, as his teetotal crusade spread through
Ireland like a Missouri camp meeting afflatus. Though nonpartisan, he had
been essential to O'Connell's Repeal agitation. Had there been a million
drunks at Tara, O'Connell would undoubtedly have had difficulty in
carrying out his promise of nonviolence, and Peel's anxiety over the monster
meetings was based less on the numbers who came out than on their fearful sobriety. The Young Irelanders, too, greatly admired Father Mathew.
He had gathered a hundred thousand people into a single meeting to take
the pledge, had built a membership of two million, had cut the Irish con-
sumption of spirits in half, had eliminated nonagrarian crime from county
Cork. He had found what the Young Irelanders were seeking, a scheme to
generate a mass spiritual fervor for useful ends. They joined up and took the
pledge, and Duffy reported that the *Nation*'s editorial rooms never saw
anyone "gravely exceed in wine" or heard anyone "utter a coarsely licentious jest."[6] The *Nation*'s impulse was to harness the methods of Father
Mathew to its own program by stirring up an abstinence frenzy of its own.

75

It persuaded Carleton to write a temperance novel for the cause. Then one Saturday without warning it came forth with a great blast against another filthy and expensive Irish habit, the use of snuff. This campaign died the same week in which it was born, and one imagines that Dublin's laughter must have done its work.

Another tack was tried. If the shortest road out of Manchester was through the door of the nearest pub, after Father Mathew's crusade there was no road at all out of Ireland's misery. The *Nation* pondered this difficulty: "Teetotalism has taken from the people their *only* enjoyment. They are altogether without public amusement. They dare not meet for athletic sports, or they are denounced as illegal and riotous assemblies; they dare not go to 'night dances,' as their Clergy, knowing that intoxication has sometimes made them scenes of immorality, have forbidden it. . . . *They need some stimulant.*"[7] Has it not been said that Ireland sober is Ireland stiff? Father Mathew's own solution for the problem was to organize parish brass bands for teetotalers. The remedy the *Nation* prescribed without false modesty was itself, its program—get manufactures, improve trade, keep absentee rents in Ireland, and the rest of it—but especially its celebrated nationalist spirituality, which was offered to serve among its other useful purposes as a substitute for the *cruiskeen lawn*.

The *Nation* came forward next with a blueprint for the establishment of reading rooms to be sponsored by the Repeal Association—three thousand of them, one for every parish in the country, all devoted to the nurture of patriotism. It promised that these would make the association more businesslike, resuscitate the dying pressure of the agitation, and combat peasant sin. A reading list of nationalist books was drawn up for guidance. "The Association," said the *Nation*'s prospectus, "will supply the Repeal rooms with at least a few of the very best books. The People will be reading and learning them instead of drinking, smoking, or card-playing."[8] Davis took his proposal to O'Connell, who offered no open objection; but noting that it aimed to tap the sources of his own strength, he sabotaged it with silence.

Could the *Life of Henry Grattan* in four handsome volumes really draw Irish youth from tobacco, whisky, and pitch and toss? The *Nation* thought so. One Young Irelander, Thomas MacNevin, brought in a report of having captivated a rural audience of two hundred with nightly readings from Benjamin Franklin's *Autobiography*. He envisioned a nationwide program of public readings stressing the "biography of self-sustained energetic men." The *Nation* turned to exhortation: "Every parish has a school, a news room, a Repeal Reading-Room, or some one of them, or it has not. Where they are not they must be established—where they are they must be watched, nurtured, made productive."[9] But nothing much happened, and repeated frustration gave the young men an unfamiliar sensation of futility. "In nothing are we, Irish, more deficient than promptitude and exactness in business," they said, as their hopes for the three thousand reading rooms evaporated. In the end John O'Connell openly attacked the scheme and killed it, leading Davis to reply in a sentence pattern familiar to readers of Irish literature through its reiteration by John O'Leary and Yeats: "There are higher things than politics, and I will never sacrifice my self-respect to them."[10] The word "politics" was beginning to take on a specialized function here; and as O'Connell noted, the speaker himself, strictly considered, was not as innocent of political motive as his words implied.

Finally Young Ireland organized the Eighty-two Club. The *Nation* had not forgotten that its first duty was to win the cultivated classes for Repeal, but, as we have seen, the task had not been carried out. After the release of the prisoners from Richmond, it occurred to Davis that there should be a new association formed to catch the cultivated sympathizers who perhaps wished to belong to something, but avoided the Repeal clubs as too vulgar. So the *Nation* announced the formation of the Eighty-two Club, whose name commemorated the year of Dungannon. Its formal purpose was "to encourage Irish art and literature and to diffuse a national feeling through society."[11] It was rigorously nonsectarian, serving to bring O'Connell, who was honored with the presidency, into an unaccustomed friendly social rapport with some of the more elegant Protestants. Other well-to-do Catholics were naturally expected to crowd forward to mingle with their Protestant fellow countrymen. Except for O'Connell and the Catholic Young Irelanders, however, the club remained mostly liberal Protestant, and the *Nation* was forced to publish a rather embittered leading article castigating loyalism among the Catholic gentry, in theory a contradiction in terms, in actuality a painful fact.

To render itself exclusive, the Club required a costly tailored uniform, described by the *Nation* in full: "a green body coat with velvet collar, white skirt linings, and gilt buttons inscribed '1782,' in a wreath of shamrocks, white tabinet vest, green pantaloons, uniform with coat in winter, and white duck in summer, patent leather boots, white kid gloves, and black satin cravat."[12] As a further safeguard against popular contamination, it adopted what Duffy called "a strict ballot," that is, the blackball. As it turned out, the club solved none of Young Ireland's problems. Duffy thought it too exclusive. Denny Lane noted that it did not make Repeal any more palatable to Protestants, though it did inflame their nationalism in the literary and musical sectors. Dublin in its cynical way thought the club hilarious, and Lane especially warned against attempting to export it to Cork: "In Cork the people in general have a great hatred of uniforms. . . . This I think principally arises from the morbidly keen sense of the ludicrous which Cork men generally possess."[13]

The comic stumbling of Young Ireland in the immediate post-Clontarf phase bore all the marks of perennial Dublin farce. But *on s'engage et puis on voit*; and who is immune to error? Against the background of the tragic history that was then unfolding, with its million human lives at stake, Young Ireland's activity during those desperate months appeared in retrospect rather more pathetic and wistful than comic. Davis' teetotalism, reading rooms, and green uniforms aimed to strike a secular taproot into the mass of popular Ireland in emulation and rivalry of the organization of the Repeal Association, that is, ultimately, of the clergy itself. Following this thread of Davis' thought, a later generation tried again with Yeats's national theater and Douglas Hyde's Gaelic League, succeeding where the pioneer had failed.

III

After these organizational catastrophes Davis sometimes felt the world falling in on him.[14] Though normally active and optimistic, he began to ponder the true scope of Young Ireland's difficulties and the growing signs of Irish defeat. The more gloomy the prospect, the more transcendental his language. If Young Ireland had nothing else left, it had voice. It owned the *Nation* with its monopoly on literary taste and on "what is far above and beyond it all." A letter from Davis to a couple of hundred resigning London Repeal wardens showed him thinking that if worst came to worst and the Young Irelanders were cut adrift from O'Connell's association, they could still function from their private base, "the rising national literature of Ireland."[15] Above "politics," above mere organization, there was poetry and the poetic nation. Its "angel voice" was the *Nation*.

The finished form of Davis' more somber ideology, heavy with thoughts of impending defeat, was elaborated in a defensive letter to Maddyn, Young Ireland's croaking raven:

> The machinery at present working for Repeal could never, under the circumstances like the present, achieve it; but circumstances *must* change. Within ten or fifteen years England must be in peril. Assuming this much, I argue thus. Modern Anglicanism, i.e., Utilitarianism, the creed of Russell and Peel as well as of the Radicals, this thing, call it Yankeeism and Englishism, which measures prosperity by exchangeable value, measures duty by gain, and limits desire to clothes, food, and respectability; this damned thing has come into Ireland under the Whigs, and is equally the favorite of the *Peel* Tories. It is believed in the political assemblies in our cities, preached from our pulpits (always Utilitarian or persecuting); it is the very apostle's creed of the profession, and threatens to corrupt the lower classes, who are still faithful and romantic. To use every literary and political engine against this seems to me the first duty of the Irish patriot who can foresee consequences.[16]

78

Davis then weighed the chances for an Irish papal supremacy, a "Catholic Ascendancy" that would supplant the Protestant Ascendancy. He felt no alarm. Better Catholic Ascendancy than to be trapped in "the iron gates of that filthy dungeon" of Englishism or Yankeeism. Moreover, "even a few of us laymen" could, he thought, effect the certain ruin of papal supremacy in twenty years, "leaving the people mad it might be, but not sensual or mean." Finally, he weighed the virtues of insurrection, a subject which he had previously preferred to touch only poetically. His letter continued:

> Still more willingly would I (if Anglicanism, i.e., Sensualism, were the alternative) take the hazard of open war, sure that if we succeeded the military leaders would compel the bigots down, establish a thoroughly national Government, and one whose policy, somewhat arbitrary, would be anti-Anglican and anti-sensual; and if we failed it would be in our own power before dying to throw up huge barriers against English vices, and dying to leave example and a religion to the next age.[17]

Within this single expression of Davis' momentary despondency, Irishmen of poetic bent might find all the ideas and affections that seemed needed in the well-stocked sensitive mind for a long time to come. Davis' black thoughts authorized the brigade of Irish "anti-Sensualists" to follow. A very large part of Yeats's nationalist thought is referable to it: his Red Hanrahan, "faithful and romantic" and lower-class; his "Man Who Dreamed of Fairyland," defying the "exchange values" of Englishism and Yankeeism; his "somewhat arbitrary" militarist hero, Eoin O'Duffy; his Senate speeches against "papal aggression"; and in Davis' italicized qualification of the phrase "*Peel* Tories," even a forethought of his "Prayer for My Daughter." "To use every literary engine" against Utilitarianism, Yankeeism, Englishism—Davis' words seem a clear command precisely echoed in Yeats's famous phrase, the "war of the soul against the intellect."

But when Davis' thought was taken up by his posthumous literary disciples, its substance was lost. His grand and gloomy aestheticizing drew its entire meaning from the immediate concrete occasion—the cowardice of the Irish gentry, the impassive and sinister threats of English political economists, and Davis' own intuition of ruinous social cataclysm at hand. His tone of paroxysm sounded to a later literary generation as though it were directed exclusively against "Sensualist" philistinism and bad taste. That was only his way of speaking. He was lamenting instead his glimpse of the oncoming of naked barbarism.

IV

The *Nation*'s first year had built a nationalist symbology from two interlocking elements—a practical base and an "anti-Sensualist" overlay. At peak strength, the two halves operated as a single organism, complementing and enriching each other. The practical half gave point, force, and body to the ideal. The idealistic half gave perspective and reinforcement to the practical, lighting its own splendor with the dignity and exaltation it had abstracted from the success of the system as a whole. But in retreat the symbology would be subjected to fragmentation, the two halves tending to pull apart, with consequent damage to each. The practical half then drifted back toward a grubby, inglorious opportunism. The idealistic half, freed from the pull of gravity, took off toward a "pure" obscurantism, toward a mysticism that struck Yeats as having "never been entangled by reality"[18] and that persuaded George Russell it was the true substance of Ireland, requiring a body made up of lakes, hills, people, and so forth only because (like John MacCormack's "Little Bit of Heaven") it had to have some place to alight.

In bringing anti-Sensualism to Ireland, where it was already in redundant supply, was Davis not carrying coals to Newcastle, as the saying is? To hold its position Young Ireland was forced to declare itself more spiritual than not only the Yankee and Saxon, but even O'Connell himself. "The restoration of Irish independence has been advocated too exclusively by narrow appeals to economy," the *Nation* wrote in obvious reference to the Liberator. Its own first object, by contrast, was not to combat Irish poverty, nor even to secure for the people a domestic legislature, but most of all, it said, rising to crescendo, to "inflame and purify them with a lofty and heroic love of country—a Nationality of the spirit as well as of the letter."[19] To accuse O'Connell of being defective in this of all traits touched on the outrageous. True, he had no niche in his program for *les chants qui retentissent sur les bords des lacs*, and his view of Irish history was unromantic and crude. He merely said, "The English arrived in Ireland one fine morning about six hundred years since, and have done nothing but disturb and devastate it."[20] But after all, he was the crony of archbishops and marched beside a thousand priests and fifteen hundred curates, the official custodians of Ireland's world-famed spiritual assets. Well: if O'Connell's shoe fit the clergy, let them wear it, too—that was the *Nation*'s implied attitude. This was not the last time that Irish poets would betray annoyance in the discovery that when they brought spirituality to the Irish marketplace, they found a strong competitor already operating there. The rarefied mists that became the trademark of the Irish literary movement in later times traced from Davis' practical quandary, how to achieve a spirituality beyond pure ether.

V

We have no record of O'Connell's thoughts on the spirituality contest, but there were many signs of his growing impatience with Young Ireland on other matters. He proclaimed that his release from Richmond jail was a "miracle," the result not of English party politics but of divine intervention; and when the Young Irelanders laughed at his fancy, his feelings were hurt. His captive newspaper began to hint that the Young Irelanders were a war party, and innuendoes spread that they were also "godless." Even sex got into the quarrel eventually, in spite of the young men's aversion to licentious jest. John O'Connell "uttered a shout of triumph" upon discovering in the pages of a Young Ireland anthology these lines of verse:

> There was an Irish lad
> And he loved a cloistered nun.

"Could anything be plainer," said Duffy, paraphrasing the attack, "than that Young Ireland wanted the cloisters to be violated ?"[21]

There were disputes over literary taste. O'Connell was fond of Sam Lover,[22] but the *Nation* despised him as "one who pandered to English prejudice by taking the stage Irishman as his hero," and it saw nothing humorous in Handy Andy's scheme for icing the champagne. Davis, on the other hand, liked Carleton, William Maginn, and "Father Prout," but O'Connell thought of these either as vile Peelites or, worse still, Catholic renegades. Davis' self-assured reply to O'Connell's critical blustering was a model formulation of civilized literary self-defense, not bettered by Yeats's response in a parallel case years later. "Uniformity of taste in literary matters is not to be expected, and, perhaps not to be desired," he said, adding that literature "is a subject in which a mistake will do nobody any harm."[23] In defending the novelist John Banim he seems to have been thinking also of the *Nation*'s staff poet—poor, miserable, opium-eating James Clarence Mangan—and further, of all the *poètes maudits* of the world, "who have so strong a claim, not only on the forbearance, but the gratitude of the world." Who would be so cowardly, he asked, as to heap wanton injury "upon those whose gift, while it confers only delight and benefit to others, is a fatal one to themselves ?"[24]

VI

Soon bigotry intruded into the dispute, for demoralization was now out of control. Peel in early 1845 concluded that coercion had had its full inning in Ireland and that the time was ready for the shift to amelioration. "I sent a message of peace to Ireland," he told the House as he presented two Irish education bills. The first bill provided a threefold increase in the funds for Maynooth College, where Irish youth train for the priesthood. This offer had the double advantage to Peel of cooling the disloyal ardor of the Catholic clergy while at the same time inflaming the divisive passions of Orangemen, who went about for years afterward muttering against "the perfidy of the Maynooth grants."

Peel's second bill proposed to set up three nonsectarian Irish colleges for the benefit of the country in general. Davis found the proposal irresistible. As we have seen, his trust in the virtue of education was the foundation of all his thought, and long before Peel's bill he had happily envisioned a cluster of peaceful academic towers arising above the trees against the backdrop of the Dublin Mountains, where great minds might labor for Ireland's comfort and splendor. The Catholic hierarchy divided on the nonsectarian feature, some bishops stressing the urgency of improved Irish education regardless of the sponsorship, others believing that the Irishman's faith would be jeopardized if Catholics sat in the same classrooms with Protestants in what was called a "mixed" college. Archbishop MacHale joined with the latter group and denounced Peel's bill, so that the proposed colleges quickly got themselves stigmatized as "godless." O'Connell resoundingly attacked the bill in the hope of embarrassing Peel. Davis refused to agree with him, and put up a fight both in the *Nation* and in the association.

One afternoon at the end of May 1845 the mixed colleges issue was being warmly debated in Conciliation Hall, the Repeal Association's fine new headquarters. O'Connell gave a long speech against the bill. When he had finished, a Young Irelander named Michael Barry defended the mixed colleges, speaking ostentatiously as a Catholic. The next speaker was a man named Conway, who had applied for membership in the Eighty-two Club and been blackballed. He attacked Barry as an irreligious Catholic, invoking the authority of St. Patrick, who "was no friend or patron of masked infidelity—or mixed education (hear, hear)." He then extended his attack to Young Ireland collectively. Davis came heatedly to Barry's defense. He took the floor and was addressing Conway scornfully as "my old college friend—my Catholic friend—my very Catholic friend" when he was interrupted by O'Connell: "It is no crime to be a Catholic I hope? . . . The sneer with which you used the word would lead to the inference." Davis sensed a fight impending and pleaded for calm and unity. "Disunion, alas, has destroyed our country for centuries," he said; but he would not recant, and he finished his argument in favor of the bill. O'Connell then rose again to speak angry words which echoed harshly in the minds of Irishmen for a century afterward:

> The section of politicians styling themselves the Young Ireland party, anxious to rule the destinies of this country, start up and support the measure.

There is no such party as that styled "Young Ireland" (hear, hear). There may be a few individuals who take that designation on themselves (hear and cheers). I am for Old Ireland (loud applause). 'Tis time that this delusion should be put an end to (hear, hear, and cheers). Young Ireland may play what pranks they please. I do not envy them the name they rejoice in, I shall stand by Old Ireland (cheers). And I have some slight notion that Old Ireland will stand by me (loud cheers).[25]

When he finished, Davis was weeping and Dillon, sitting behind him, began to spit up blood. In the meeting all was excitement, shock, and anger. At last Smith O'Brien, the chairman, broke the spell with his sole recorded witticism: "I belong to Middle-aged Ireland." Then there were apologies and handshaking all around. But the damage was done. O'Connell's great organization, whose efficiency had so pleased Davis, had turned itself into an efficient nuisance, ready to spread slanders against Young Ireland with preternatural speed. O'Connell's taunt, "There is no such party as that styled 'Young Ireland,'" had touched the tender spot, precisely like Davis' epithet "coward" after Clontarf. Thanks to the cruel accuracy with which the two leaders had exposed one another's contradictions, Peel might now relax, for "the integrity of the empire" was to be safe for a long time to come.

O'Connell's angry questioning of who would "rule the destinies of this country" was strictly political in its immediate application, intended merely to force a clean split between the left and right wings in the Repeal Association. But in seeking to arm Young Ireland for combat, Davis had entangled the peripheral aesthetic issue in the main dispute. Poetic nationalism he claimed to be not merely an equal partner, but even the receiver in bankruptcy of the religious nationalism at the source of O'Connell's power. By accident O'Connell had broached this secondary issue, and his either-or dilemma forced a senseless choice between "godless" poetry (Young Ireland) and holy antipoetry (Old Ireland). The question thus became, Shall poets "rule the destinies of this country"? The popular answer was a vociferous no heard from the aroused sanctimonious Irish philistinism for which the two O'Connells set a miserable example, henceforth one of the fixed poles of Irish culture. But another possible answer suggested by the form of the question was yes. More than once in his career, Yeats was to have that answer in mind. In that case, any poet's detractors were not only vulgarians but traitors. The poet's activity carried its own guarantee of virtue, together with the temptation to grandiloquence seen occasionally even in the shy and gentle Davis. To such implied claims the philistines naturally responded with O'Connell's withering sarcasm to Davis: for whom do you speak and how many votes do you command?

VII

Then suddenly Davis was dead of scarlet fever, only three months after the fight over the mixed colleges bill. Duffy was awakened in the early morning and summoned to the house of Davis' mother in Baggot Street to behold "the most tragic sight my eyes had ever looked upon—the dead body of Thomas Davis." A servant told Duffy that through all his last hours Davis had complained of "interrupted work." The stricken *Nation* came out on Saturday with heavy black borders in mourning for its guiding spirit. It printed an account of the funeral. The Eighty-two Club had come, also the officials of the Repeal Association, the Dublin Corporation, and all the Irish learned societies and academies. O'Connell wrote in from Darrynane, "As I stand alone in the solitude of my mountains, many a tear shall I shed in memory of the noble youth."[26] A horde of nameless mourners appeared at the funeral, as told in Yeats's anecdote borrowed from Oscar Wilde's mother. She had seen the hearse and the great crowd pass and had asked, "Who is dead?" Someone said, "Thomas Davis." Though one of the "cultivated classes," she had to ask again: "And who was he?" And the reply was, "He was a poet."[27]

There is a curious fact about Davis' premature death that provides us —by subtraction, as it were—with a powerful insight into the moral energy of Irish nationalism. If we kept a tally of the prominent Irishmen in our narrative who were jailed or forced to flee the country, we would already have recorded in 1843 the names of the two O'Connells and Duffy (besides Isaac Butt, though he was jailed for debt rather than for his political beliefs). Eventually the list will grow to great length and include almost every Irish name mentioned in this volume. Missing from the jailer's roll call is only one leading historical personage: Thomas Davis, dead at thirty-one. John O'Connell once astonished Davis' friends with the accusation that a moral blight attached to the dead youth: what kind of a patriot was it who would dare to expire before he had ever matriculated in Green Street Courthouse?

CHAPTER 6

Black '47

I

Davis died on September 16, 1845. Three days earlier the British horticultural press had taken its first notice of the alarming appearance in Ireland of the "potato murrain" or potato rot. In a few weeks the blight had spread all over Ireland, destroying about half of the 1845 potato harvest. Potatoes were the only source of carbohydrates for the Irish small peasants and cottiers, and without them they would starve. Thus began the Irish famine, one of the major peacetime disasters of modern history. It found the native leadership weakened by the split between Old and Young Ireland; and worse troubles lay ahead.

Davis' sudden death was a staggering blow to the Young Irelanders. Their deference to his judgment was absolute and their affection for him pure adulation. Among them he had no rivals, only disciples. For a moment they were not sure they could carry on without him. But events in the three years after his death were to move at an even dizzier pace than in the three years preceding, and the survivors were not allowed much time for weeping. Young men unknown to Davis knocked to ask admission, and the living cast about to replace the dead. Three of Davis' lieutenants—Gavan Duffy, John Mitchel, and Smith O'Brien—were the presumptive heirs to his leadership, each representing a single facet of his own many-sided personality. With fine poise and sweetness of temper, Davis had made harmony among them. But his survivors could not. On top of all its other woes, Young Ireland had now to contend with its own internal disintegration.

Gavan Duffy took over the *Nation*. He represented the practical side of Davis' character, the voice that said, "Arigna must be pierced with shafts." He was clear-headed, efficient, and prudent; he kept his shop so that his shop might keep him. He made a financial success of every activity he undertook, including radicalism, as O'Connell sarcastically reminded him. These qualities permeated his prose style, which was forcible, lucid, and fair-minded. But he was more timid than Davis and more awed by respectability. His printer's style sheet required a deferential capital for "the

People," but as has been noted, he was one of the sources for the dilution of Davis' original agrarian radicalism. One of his poems, "The Muster of the North," contains the lines:

The Green alone shall stream above our native field and flood—
The spotless Green, save where its folds are gemmed with Saxon blood!

To this poem he appended a footnote for disclaimer: "The ballad here printed is not meant as an apology for these excesses." He often used the word "excess," and he shared all of O'Connell's fears of "democratic excess."

Duffy's prudential reflexes were made clear in a leading article he wrote immediately after Davis' funeral. Starting off from the familiar jacquerie threat, long used by Davis to penetrate the after-the-hunt drowsiness of the Protestant gentry, he diverged into a bold new idea of his own concerning the Young Irelanders' proper historical function: in the coming revolution they would be the referee. He had long been convinced that "Ireland will not be redeemed by the Aristocracy—it cannot be redeemed by the Peasantry,"[1] leaving the name of the redeemer an easy riddle to answer. Recently he had been studying Lamartine's *L'Histoire des Girondins*, a proper guide to sobriety "à la veille d'une révolution." According to the French analogy, either a peasant revolution or an aristocratic counterrevolution would shortly be attempted in Ireland. "Out of such a crisis," said Duffy, "sprung the great French Revolution." But there was a third way, by which both "excesses" could be avoided. Righteous and temperate young men might intercede as mediators. "Such fiery young men, disciplined in the strictest probity, as those who chastised the courtly tyranny with the one hand, and beat back the murderous mob tyranny of the Marats and Robespierres with the other, would stand between the lords and the tillers of the land, and arbitrate justice without violence."[2] Young Ireland, in short, should constitute itself the Irish Gironde, with Duffy for its Brissot.

In exact contrast to Duffy was John Mitchel, volcanic and irreconcilable, representing the angry Davis who had put the *Manual of Artillery* on his bookshelf beside his Thierry and Béranger. His father was an Ulster Presbyterian minister who had defected to Unitarianism, so that he had Calvinist nurture but no home in any of the three great Irish sectarian families. He was a newcomer to the *Nation*. While the early Young Irelanders were theorizing about Irish agrarian grievance, he was gaining a concrete intimacy with it in the legal defense of peasants charged with stealing the landlords' seaweeds and limestone. Of all the Young Irelanders, he had the best knowledge of the condition of Ireland when he came to join the *Nation* just before Davis' death. He had read Carlyle fervently, absorbing both his thought and his style. He considered *The French Revolution* "the profoundest book that English literature ever produced"; and after the two men became friends, Carlyle's talk seemed to him "like the speech of Paul or Chrysostom."[3] When he first began to write for Young Ireland, Davis had to order him to delete his distressing Carlylean mannerisms. Following this necessary stylistic surgery, he became the most incisive and fearless writer among the Young Irelanders.

Mitchel's private verbal impulses were, like Duffy's, released by Davis' death. A Tory newspaper had remarked that the Irish railways under construction would increase the mobile striking power of the British garrison, since troops could soon move to the most remote glen in Kerry or Donegal within six hours. Mitchel replied in an unsigned editorial known in Irish history as "the railway article." Since the domestic military attributes of railways had been broached, he said, the subject might profitably be pursued. There were two ways of looking at this matter. "The materials of railways, good hammered iron and wooden sleepers—need we point out that such things may be of use in other *lines* than assisting locomotion." He advised the Repeal wardens to study the interesting tactical possibilities of railway cuts. Andreas Hofer, the anti-Napoleonic Tyrolese patriot, could not have asked for a finer setting for ambush than a railway cut: "Imagine a few hundred men lying in wait upon such a spot with masses of rock and trunks of trees ready to roll down—and a train or two advancing with a regiment of infantry, and the engine panting near and nearer, till the polished studs of brass on its front are distinguishable and its name may be nearly read; 'Now—, in the name of the Father, and of the Son, and of the Holy Ghost!—now.' "[4] No doubt about it, Mitchel knew how to make himself heard. Pietists were horrified at this blasphemy, and Mitchel had to show that he had merely quoted good Catholic Hofer's own words. O'Connell was furious at the *Nation*'s presuming to instruct his wardens to flout the principle of moral force. Acting perhaps at O'Connell's instigation,[5] the government began legal action against the *Nation*; and Duffy, as editor, was forced to bear once again, as at the time of the state trials, the legal burdens of somebody else's incendiarism.

Smith O'Brien, the last of the three heirs, represented Davis' precious case of nationalism in the Protestant aristocracy. He had chosen the popular Irish side as a deliberate act of honor, "though free to refuse." He is thus the beau ideal of Yeatsian sociology and of Yeatsian mask-psychology, but no example of Yeatsian gaiety. One finds no other figure in Irish history quite so painfully torn by irreconcilable scruples. In going over to the Repeal Association, and in his more courageous affiliation with Young Ireland, he had not solved his dilemma or eased the pain of his stark public agonizing between caution and recklessness. Still, he had wealth, social position, a spartan fairness, and a seat in Parliament. He was the automatic first choice for leader in all of Young Ireland's political adventures.

Davis' cultural nationalism had no heir. Duffy, it is true, had made himself Young Ireland's foremost expert on folk balladry and had edited its semiofficial collection, which in time ran to fifty reprintings. He also carried forward Davis' literary spirituality. Here is a characteristic sentence out of the *Nation*: "Beside a library, how poor are all the greatest deeds of man— his constitution, brigade, factory, man-of-war, cathedral—how poor are all miracles in comparison."[6] These words resound like Davis' own, but appear actually in Duffy's book review of one of the posthumous Davis anthologies. Yet Duffy lacked Davis' prime enthusiasm, and he took over cultural nationalism as though it were merely another of the *Nation*'s assets, like the printing plant and the subscription list. The temperamental Mangan was reinforced by a poetry machine operated by Miss Jane Elgee—later to be Lady Wilde —a young patrician who signed herself "Speranza" and discovered a rhyme for the word "sunlight" (it was "dunlight"). Other literary activity was reduced to nostalgic reprintings from the grand year 1843, plus occasional genteel appreciations of classic English poets, always a safe enterprise. Davis' cultural campaign was dead with Davis. A succession of screaming practical crises swept down upon Young Ireland, and for a long time to come Irish nationalist literature was to be more in the seed than the flower. Apostolic literary zeal would not be known again in Ireland until John O'Leary took it up afresh forty years later.

II

The developing famine was the new excitement of the hour. Within two weeks of Davis' death, murmurs of alarm were heard in Conciliation Hall. An elderly nationalist told of his recollection of past Irish famines: " ' . . . there was no use in mincing the matter,' he said, 'they had famine at their door' (hear, hear). He knew that the poor would divide their last morsel with each other till they had nothing to divide. . . . The landlords saw all this, yet did not come forward."[7] O'Connell, always happy to embarrass Peel, gathered a committee of Dublin dignitaries and led them to the Castle to wait upon the Tory lord lieutenant, the "cold, curt, and monosyllabic" Lord Heytesbury. The delegation bore a memorial written by O'Connell respectfully beseeching the government to act quickly to forestall suffering and death, a last voice of sanity before madness overwhelmed the Irish scene. It pressed the government to take certain immediate steps: to halt the export of Irish grain and livestock and the distillation of spirits, to establish emergency food distribution centers, to organize public works projects, and to rescind the tariff on American cornmeal imports to Ireland. At the next meeting of the association, O'Connell in fine anecdotal form described the Castle audience and quoted the lord lieutenant's words, read from a prepared statement, as he dismissed the delegation: "My Lord Mayor and gentlemen—It can scarcely be necessary for me to assure you that the state of the potato crop has for some time occupied, and still occupies, the most anxious attention of the government." Said O'Connell, "Much obliged to him for nothing (laughter)."[8]

Peel winced at his old enemy's barbs, and his first reaction to the oncoming famine was naturally to introduce a fresh Irish coercion bill. After that, he prepared a relief program that followed in several respects O'Connell's proposals to Lord Heytesbury. The first demand, to halt Irish food exports, was unthinkable not only for Peel but for O'Connell as well, and soon afterward it was dropped. Peel met the second and third demands forthrightly. He organized foreign food purchases, food depots, and public works projects with all deliberate speed. For temporary relief of immediate hunger under only partial potato crop failure, this part of Peel's program was timely, and it saved many from death in the early months of 1846. Yet there were dangers in the scheme, too. The public works projects were "unproductive," that is, useless on principle. The finances were left to the voluntary impulses of landlord committees, whose private contributions formed the base for matching funds from the treasury. In making each district responsible for "its own" destitute peasants, Peel's relief measures, in giving every landlord fresh reason to pray that his tenants would depart from his sight forever, increased the pressure toward clearances. And by confusing emergency relief with charity, Peel guaranteed the insufficiency of response that accompanies any levy based on passing the hat, while at the same time inciting in the donors a maudlin self-congratulation by which they read their niggardliness as heroic benevolence, in the manner of Yeats's *Countess Cathleen*.

O'Connell's fourth demand, the emergency remission of the tariff on Irish food imports, brought a response from Peel violently disproportionate to the occasion. Contrary to all Tory morality, Peel shocked the country in December 1845 by announcing himself opposed to continuing the Corn Laws, the government bounty on agricultural produce. He explained his conversion as necessitated by the Irish potato failure, arguing that Irish hardship would be lessened if the price of American cornmeal imports could be reduced by the removal of the Corn Law customs duty. This is one of history's most inventive non sequiturs. Those Irish peasants in danger of starvation ordinarily bought no agricultural produce; they only sold it. Corn Law repeal could only bring about a general deflation of food prices on the English market. Ireland as an exporter of food would have found it disadvantageous at any time, but in the shadow of the famine it could prove disastrous. When Corn Law repeal was finally carried in mid-1846, the price of Irish grain and livestock fell, the peasant brought home less cash from the market, his resources for rent payment were diminished, and his likelihood of hunger and eviction was increased.

For a month or so the coming of the hunger brought the old prancing, fire-eating O'Connell back for one last performance. He poured out his scorn upon the Duke of Cambridge for his words of advice to the hungry Irish. If O'Connell's quotation is accurate, the royal duke had said that "rotten potatoes and sea weed, or even grass, properly mixed, afforded a very wholesome and nutritious food. They all knew that Irishmen could live upon anything, and there was plenty of grass in the field, even though the potato crop should fail."[9] O'Connell warned that it was not inconceivable for the English to attempt to "starve the Irish nation," for Edmund Spenser, "with his vividness of poetic imagination," had proposed just this policy for Ireland. "If it should be attempted," he added, "I do not hesitate to assert that it would be the duty of every man to die with arms in his hands." The stenographer then inserted a parenthesis: "The entire meeting here rose and cheered with utmost enthusiasm for several minutes." This was in January 1846. But as the winter deepened, he grew meek and confused and sounded increasingly senile.

In the spring of 1846 hunger began to find its first victims, and gusts of unrest stirred in the countryside. O'Connell's stock of impoverished oratorical effects poured out by rote: "My advice is tranquility and endurance amongst the people. . . . Let there be loud voices but unwilling arms." He reawakened the now-empty echoes of past glory: "Is there no remedy? Is there no hope? Must we then despair? Despair? No, no—a thousand times no—there shall be no despair. There is hope. There is a remedy. . . . Hurrah with us for the Repeal!"[10] In his country's agony, he had defaulted his leadership.

On the famine issues the *Nation* followed O'Connell's lead as long as it could. It applauded when he annihilated the Duke of Cambridge in the grand old style. But while he grew more bland and dissociated, its own language grew more harsh. It seized upon all of his militant leads, just when he was anxious that they should be forgotten. It was especially taken by the first demand of his Heytesbury memorandum—prohibition of Irish food exports during the emergency—and by his warning of a possible English attempt to starve the nation. By April 1846, when O'Connell's daily counsel was for tranquillity and endurance, the *Nation* had become extremely alarmed at the state of the country. There had been a few deaths already, and hunger was spreading from the cottiers into the mass of the small peasantry. It foresaw "thousands on thousands waiting for typhus." And as sinister as the growing death lists were the reports of numerous clearances by the landlords.

III

On the heel of the first frightening winter, Mangan's dormant poetic imagination suddenly came to life. One Saturday in April 1846 the *Nation* published his poem "Siberia." The solemn gloom of the verse took on added power from its setting among the accounts of "families in caves," "suicide to escape beggary," "mills and stores ransacked," "Limerick counting their deaths," and the terrifying prognostication, "worse is coming."[11]

Mangan then followed up with a series of lamentations: for Sir Maurice Fitzgerald, for Patrick Sarsfield, for Banba, for Innisfail, for Timoleague. In their midst appeared two poems derived from Ferguson's prose translations in the Hardiman critique twelve years earlier. One was "O'Hussey's Ode to the Maguire,"* which was rejected by both *Dublin University Magazine* and Duffy, presumably for the unchristian morality in its last four lines:

> Hugh marched forth to the fight—I grieved to see him so depart;
> And lo! to-night he wanders frozen, rain-drenched, sad, betrayed—
> *But the memory of the lime-white mansions his right hand hath laid*
> *In ashes warms the hero's heart!*

Mangan's second poem from Ferguson was based on the prose translation of the anonymous "Roiseen dubh." He had already written a couple of very flat and embarrassing versions based on Ferguson's interpretation. Now he dropped the lovesick priest, removed the breasts, and went for the nationalist allegory. The result was printed in the *Nation* on May 30, 1846. The last stanza said:

> O! the Erne shall run red
>   With redundance of blood,
> The earth shall rock beneath our tread,
>   And flames wrap hill and wood,
> And gun-peal, and slogan cry,
>   Wake many a glen serene,
> Ere you shall fade, ere you shall die,
>   My Dark Rosaleen!
>   My own Rosaleen!
> The Judgment Hour must first be nigh,
> Ere you can fade, ere you can die,
>   My Dark Rosaleen!

---

* Ferguson had admired O'Hussey for his "Homeric" quality. Half a century later James Joyce, more old-fashioned, admired him because there was no other passage in English literature "in which the spirit of revenge has been joined to such heights of melody," and because a poet like Mangan "sums up in himself the soul of a country and an era." Joyce, *Critical Writings*, ed. Ellsworth Mason and Richard Ellmann (New York: Viking Press, 1959), p. 184.

More than one cautious critic has ventured to call this a perfect lyric; and thus it must be said that an outcry of anger against a high season of perfidy, criminal folly, and mass death had created the highest poetic accomplishment of Young Ireland.

In that same infamous month, William Carleton began serial publication of a famine novel called *The Black Prophet*, based on his recollections of the 1817 famine in Ulster. Like his earlier story, "Tubber Derg," the novel concerned itself with the suffering that lay behind the mortality statistics. Carleton depicted the hunger in a series of powerful vignettes: one took place in an extortionist mealmonger's warehouse; another showed a conference among the members of a proud peasant's family where the awful choice to "go out" (that is, to beg on the roads) was finally made; and another occurred in a pestilential cabin where a neighbor burst open the door to discover the entire family dead or dying. But beyond communicating the raw feel of human pain, Carleton's peasant brain had trouble seizing the meaning of the catastrophe. His wisdom followed the outlines of O'Connell's intellectual bankruptcy, but also included a querulous assault against "politicians," meaning presumably O'Connell himself, but Young Ireland no less; for with this novel he had left the *Nation* and returned to his old home in *Dublin University Magazine*, whose special brand of economics he once again embraced without visible effort.

IV

Young and Old Ireland were now hopelessly divided and groping for some *casus belli*. It was found in the old issue of the Whig alliance. A section of the Tories under Disraeli split away from Peel, and as the spring of 1846 wore on, the Whigs sensed victory in the breeze. O'Connell then bethought himself once more of the joys of an alliance with Whigs in power. He began secret negotiations with the Whigs' leader, Lord John Russell, the celebrated author of the Reform Act of 1832 (and the grandfather of the famous English Russell of our own time).

The Young Irelanders read O'Connell's mind and set themselves the task of spoiling his dream of a new Whig love feast. They forced themselves to swallow their fears of the great man and to move into open battle. The *Nation* warned its readers to beware of "*pretended* Irishmen, luke-warm, milk-and-water, deaf small-beer lovers of their country. . . . They will buy you, and they will sell you at a small profit."[12] Each week came another leading article: "Beware of the Whigs," "Look Out for the Whigs." O'Brien sent in a letter advising the utmost caution against the Whigs. In mid-June 1846, with Peel's hours as prime minister near their end, the *Evening Mail* quoted O'Connell as saying privately to Lord John Russell: "All he

[O'Connell] ever wanted was a real Union—the same laws, the same franchises, etc." This was almost certainly an accurate quotation, and the *Nation* wrote with clever insolence that it had "no authority from Mr. O'Connell to contradict this; yet do we unhesitatingly pronounce it an audacious lie."[13] Thomas Meagher (pronounced "marr"), a post-Davis Young Ireland recruit with a knack for florid oratorical effects, came to the next association meeting and delivered a savage attack against Whig place hunting and by implication against O'Connell himself, whose backstairs politics he placed in contrast to those of Davis, "our guide and prophet." Attacked in his own fortress by a virtual stranger, a "juvenile," O'Connell could not allow Meagher to go unanswered.

A week later Peel's ministry fell and the Whigs came in. With his friend Russell now safely in power, O'Connell had leisure at last to chastise the juveniles, and he crossed over to Dublin to direct the association in cleansing itself. In a tense meeting he rose to speak high praise of the new prime minister. Lord John Russell had personally conveyed his sympathy with "the misery in which the people of Ireland are," and had made him a solemn promise of "the most comprehensive measures of relief."[14] He next turned to the attack upon Young Ireland. He moved a resolution to define the association's theoretical position against violence, denouncing violence at all times, in all places, under all conditions whatsoever. He then returned to Westminster, leaving the association to tear itself apart in snarling over the meaning of the word "nonviolence."

The resolution was senseless, and it could not have been accepted without humiliation. But it was so phrased that it could not be rejected either, without seeming to make an equally senseless call for an immediate '98 insurrection. The Young Irelanders' debate struggled unsuccessfully to escape from the trap. In due course the motion was put to a vote and carried, and then the bickering took up the scholastic question, Do we now condemn George Washington and the Belgians of 1830 ? This went on for a couple of weeks until Meagher, frenzied by his own oratory, proclaimed that he for one would never, never "stigmatize" the sword—"no, my lord, for at its blow a giant nation sprang from the waters of the Atlantic and by its redeeming magic the fettered colony became a daring, free republic." He was interrupted by John O'Connell, who ruled that such talk was offensive to the principle of nonviolence. Thereupon the Young Irelanders with Smith O'Brien at their head all stood up and walked out of Conciliation Hall.

v

During the week of the split the potato blight returned. This second attack of the blight in 1846 found the peasants' reserves spent under the hardships of the previous winter and spring, their few possessions sold for food, their bodies wasted by months of hunger while waiting for the new crop. This time the crop loss was total and absolute. It was not long before word spread that an unspeakable disaster was at hand. People were really dying all right (as Freud said in the autumn months of 1914) and not just one here and there, but in very large numbers.

The Repeal party did "get a little something" from its bargain with Russell, for O'Connell became the dispenser of Irish political patronage. But on important issues of statecraft his opinions were not solicited. Russell had no time for the complaints of the toothless Irish dragon. The Whigs' "most comprehensive measures of relief," the promise of which had been cited to overawe the juveniles, were now unveiled. Russell led off with the closure of the food depots and the stoppage of government food importations. "Private enterprise" would take over these functions. The instantaneous result was famine shortage and famine prices. Later, Russell reneged in part, setting up free soup kitchens and restoring some of the cornmeal depots, which then sold food at slightly more than open-market prices in order not to hamper the private enterprise of the mealmongers. After a brief pause Russell's next comprehensive relief measure was the closure of Peel's work projects. The three retrenchments, falling in the first weeks of the failure of the new potato crop, gave the countryside a foretaste of what the laws of political economy held in store.

After long delay Russell came forward with a new works projects scheme, even more useless than Peel's, to be financed through a new arrangement called the Labor Rate Act. Under the Tories the government had matched local funds. Under the more sound fiscal wisdom of the Whigs, landlords in the stricken districts were required to pay all, "in order to alleviate the exorbitant demands," according to Sir George Nicholls, commissioner of the Irish Poor Law. Half was to be raised by current local rates, half was advanced as a treasury loan to the district, to be repaid in ten years through taxation. This arrangement confronted many landlords with a choice between ruthless clearances—if they dared—or bankruptcy. A third choice, to defy the Labor Rate Act, was only theoretical, since the British army that stood behind the tax collector was the same that prevented agrarian uprisings. A final Whig relief measure was "taskwork." The busywork on Russell's superuseless relief projects was paid by the piece at less than the going wage in order to equalize the economic rewards with the peasants' actual expenditure of enthusiasm and calories. All these innovations were interesting as such, but by far the most arresting difference to be observed now that the Whigs were in, clear even to the nonexpert, was that people were dying faster than ever.

The enormity of the famine that now commenced has always been difficult to communicate. In struggling to illuminate the "mere data," eye-witnesses found themselves baffled by the inadequacies of ordinary language. "Indescribable," "unbelievable," "language would fail to give an adequate idea," "I defy anyone to exaggerate," "no coloring can deepen the black-ness of the truth," and so on—these frantic protestations appear in all first-hand accounts. Carleton himself protested, not quite accurately, that his own words were powerless to describe the famine terror. For the less gifted, the language by which ordinary experience is grasped and shared was inadequate. There was little dramatic heightening and no "tragic joy." But sheer iteration will in time reward the earnest searcher with a sort of com-prehension. Through three terrifying winters the killing processes never paused. Beginning in October 1846 the Dublin newspapers filled their "State of the Country" columns with a regular predictable quota of horrors clipped from the county weeklies, an interminable budget of black, swollen, and naked corpses, heightened now and then with the extra terrors of canni-balism, bodies devoured by dogs and crows, and whole villages given the last rites of the Church en masse. At the average rate of ten thousand deaths each week, less in summer and more in winter, the famine toll accumulated, last week, this week, next week, on and on, hopelessly and seemingly with-out possible end.

VI

In the face of disaster O'Connell's old-time pugnacity found only one tar-get, Young Ireland. The Repeal Association, dying as he was, revived for a few weeks after the split, as the pious hurried to pay their dues in gratitude for the Liberator's great casting-out of the godless juveniles. Thereafter it sank heavily, still cursing the ungrateful young men whose discomfiture O'Connell watched with as much glee as the times could allow. He called them "the literary Repeal Association, as it were," and predicted that they would meet with less success than their models, "Voltaire, Rousseau, and the other infidel French writers." Their isolation delighted him. "What chance has Young Ireland of getting a bishop?" he asked. "They boast of having two clergymen with them." Although Archbishop MacHale sympa-thized privately with the secessionists, other bishops let fall their blessings on O'Connell's holy war. Bishop Higgins sent in a letter which was read to the members: "The *Nation* . . . is in my mind the most dangerous publica-tion that has ever appeared in Ireland. . . . [it] appears to me, to my clergy, and to our flocks to tend directly to the overthrow of the Catholic faith and morals. . . . Do these persons already forget that all their importance, if any they possess, is entirely owing to your superhuman and unbounded influence?" O'Connell regaled his dwindling remnant with realistic de-

95

scriptions of the ingenious contrivances used by the Protestant yeomen to execute the 1798 insurrectionists taken prisoner: "Ah, these Young Irelanders have cruel hearts, to endeavor to excite the people to an insurrection of that kind."[15]

These little revenges were small help for his larger pain. He moved through the awful scene dazed and helpless. He interpreted the famine as "an act of God," hence he spent a good deal of time in prayer. He wore out his ebbing vitality in spasmodic charity drives, hoping to save a random life here and there, and to his closest friend he wrote that the times "are indeed more awful than you have any notion of. All our thoughts are engrossed with the two topics—endeavoring to keep the people from outbreaks, and endeavoring to get food for them."[16] The first endeavor was rather more successful than the second.

In December 1846 O'Connell's failing health forced him to withdraw from the association, leaving John O'Connell in command. Early in the new year, "the black '47," he made a last feeble, begging speech in the House of Commons. A few weeks later he left England for the Continent in a futile search for health, crawling off to die like the famine victims in Kerry. In May 1847 he died in Genoa en route to Rome, where his heart was sent for repose after removal from his body.

VII

In the jargon of our time, O'Connell was hypercharged with charisma, so that it is futile to try to appraise him without superlatives, good or bad. The historian Lecky thought him the most skilled political organizer in all history. Gladstone called him "the greatest popular leader the world has ever known." Remembering that this witness was a member of Peel's cabinet at the time of the monster meetings, one can grant that he might well say so. But remembering also that he was not a neutral observer—nor Lecky either—one will set his suspicions on the alert. Lecky's and Gladstone's unbridled language was undoubtedly compounded in part out of genuine gratitude to O'Connell for having said the word at Clontarf that dissolved his frightful thundercloud into the Sunday morning mists. From the Irish point of view, this same act would not necessarily be greatness but, in Davis' embittered language, cowardice, betrayal, and embezzlement of "the starving peasant's mite." Irishmen could hardly be expected to applaud the kind of world-shaking greatness that gave them the famine and the political catastrophes of the 1840s, and generally speaking they have not done so with any clear éclat. Prior to the destruction of Nelson's Pillar, they allowed O'Connell only the second-best monument in downtown Dublin. They do not celebrate his birthday, and in recent years they were hard-pressed to find money to preserve his old home in west Kerry. Ireland has an oversupply of shrines already, and what is Darrynane House but the emblem of an impostor Moses?

Stephen Dedalus fixed this view of O'Connell's niche in Irish history unforgettably: "Gone with the wind. Hosts at Mullaghmast and Tara of the kings. Miles of ears of porches.* The tribune's words howled and scattered to the four winds. A people sheltered within his voice. Dead noise. Akasic records of all that ever anywhere wherever was. Love and laud him: me no more."[17] This vignette fits into the mosaic of Joyce's "Aeolus," the god of winds, and the obvious purpose is to portray O'Connell as a wind-making machine of such "haystack- and roof-leveling" force that it left behind it a wasteland—in short, as the archetypal misleader and demagogue.

But Joyce's sketch is still not a satisfactory likeness, and if we turn to Balzac for a foreigner's impartial view, we find a judgment very much like Gladstone's. He called O'Connell the "embodiment of a people" and set him equal to Napoleon and Cuvier as one of the three giants of his age, suggesting that if O'Connell's wonderful mechanism came to nothing, it still made the model for another mobilization that might come to something. The "advanced men" of Irish nationalism often arrived at some such conclusion as that, and John Mitchel's last thoughtful words on the subject produced the arresting adjective string: "wonderful, mighty, jovial, and mean old man," the leader who, if he did nothing else, broke forever the spell of the long servility of the Irish people.

Yeats offers us a judgment different from all of these. "The Great Comedian" and "the old rascal" are the familiar phrases from the poems; and from the prose we derive "common," "vulgar," "bragging," and "loose-lipped." A caricature presents O'Connell as a "grin through a horse-collar." He serves Yeats as a stereotype of the ignoble, to be set for comparison against Emmet, then Davis, then Parnell. A Yeatsist disciple uses the killing phrase, "the so-called liberator." Back of all this acerbity hovers the thought of the demagogue, but with quite a different content than Joyce put into his portrait. Yeats's hatred of O'Connell was not stimulated by the same scenes that had goaded Young Ireland into fury, nor by O'Leary's contempt for moral force, not by Joyce's implied charge that he had twice deserted his battle post of duty, betraying those who "sheltered within his voice" into the hands of their enemy. Yeats's animus had a special source, and in an unguarded moment he told us what it was: "When at the Clare Election, he conquered the patriots of a previous generation by a slanderous rhetoric, he prepared for Committee Room No. 15 and all that followed."[18] In other words, O'Connell had turned the Catholic "multitudes" loose to

* " . . . in the porches of mine ear did pour / The leperous distilment." *Hamlet*, act 1, sc. 5, lines 63-64.

prey upon their Protestant betters; or more precisely, he had stolen the Catholic vote from its rightful owners and smashed the political hegemony of the descendants of James Fitzgerald and John Beresford, the "patriots of a previous generation," members of the oligarchy that Wolfe Tone thought necessary, even at the cost of his own life, "to strip of its plumage and its tinsel." But these acts of O'Connell's were just those that Balzac thought sublime, and somebody has to be wrong.

VIII

In the first months of the split the Young Irelanders were equally as demoralized as O'Connell. To discount their isolation they consoled themselves with the thought that whatever had been lost, they were still in possession of Davis' spiritual empire: "You have still the Press—you have still schools—you have the Repeal reading room—you have a literature half made—a growing intellect, and nascent machinery of thought. You have songs to melt or stir you—history to store your memory, and nerve your heart—and records, still unchronicled, but the more vivid to your imagination, of your own mighty outbursts in '43."[19] On its fourth anniversary, in October 1846, the *Nation* announced once again that "a soul has come to Ireland." Be that as it might, the Young Irelanders were now on the outside looking in, cut off from the mass of their suffering and dying fellow countrymen.

The nadir of Young Ireland's despair fell in the first weeks of 1847. The *Nation* could no longer hide the emptiness of its slogans, yet they flowed on, listlessly. Peasant proprietorship came back to feeble life for a few weeks, reclamation of the bogs had its turn, and like O'Connell when he had nothing to say, it occasionally demanded the instantaneous Repeal of the Union. As always, it waited expectantly for the patriotic conversion of the Protestant gentry. Its tone was alternately abject and hysterical as the ghastly reports from the country accumulated. "What is to be done?" it asked of the new year of 1847. "Such is the startling, the appalling question which every lover of his country asks himself, and which every thinker is striving to answer; and rapidly it is becoming still more appalling, still more startling. Scarcity has ripened into famine, and disease and crime are stalking in its footprints. Every day's account is big with misery, and scenes of woe at which the heart sickens are in thousands of habitations. What is to be done? Alas! alas! our greatest calamity is that we can do nothing."[20]

"We can do nothing"—this bewitchment was broken in a burst. As soon as the dying Liberator left the country, the secessionists set up a rival organization of their own called the Irish Confederation, and in the following months they were busy opening up its operations. As a matter of course

Smith O'Brien became its chairman, in order not to frighten away the landed gentry. It appeared to differ from O'Connell's association only in the vigor with which it castigated Whig place-hunting. A number of local Confederation clubs were chartered, named after national heroes—the St. Patrick Club, the Davis Club, and the like. Most of the clubs were located in Dublin and the larger towns, and great areas of Ireland had none at all. Next, the Confederation laid plans to contest elections in selected districts where its strength was concentrated. Its first campaign, a by-election in Galway in March 1847, was encouraging, losing to the incumbent attorney general by only six votes. When Russell dissolved Parliament in the late spring, the Confederates looked forward hopefully to establishing themselves as an Irish political fixture. Once again they were to learn painfully the price of political wisdom.

The issue of the *Nation* that carried the news of O'Connell's death was for the second time in the newspaper's history set up in heavy black rulings for mourning. Even after more than a century the reader may still be touched to see the doleful black borders framing the columns that reported the universal disaster. That same week at Skibbereen, the most malignant pesthole in Ireland, three thousand petty criminal cases awaited trial— mostly for theft of food—seventy persons there were sentenced to transportation, and sixty-five ejectments were ordered by the court. That same week at Cork, Father Mathew provided free interment for 277 corpses, not counting the ninety from the workhouse. And so on. But most of this issue was devoted to eulogy. Next week the black rulings remained and the eulogies continued. Among them was a note of discord, a letter from Father John Kenyon of Templederry, county Tipperary, one of Young Ireland's "two clergymen." He wished to dissent from the polite view of O'Connell's achievement: "O'Connell has boasted that he guided us, and his toadies have vouched every word he told us for fifty years. Well, then, let us look about and calculate our obligations for the service. . . . [We are brought] to such an abyss of physical and moral degradation, as no race of mankind were ever plunged in since the creation. We are a nation of beggars—mean, shameless, lying beggars."[21] Capitalizing quickly on this ill-timed breach of the etiquette of the wake, John O'Connell circulated the priest's letter as evidence that his father had been "murdered" by the ingratitude of the Irish Confederation. Meanwhile the funeral was postponed, and postponed again, and all the while the *Nation* stayed in journalistic crepe. Then the news came that there would be no funeral soon. John O'Connell had ordered the corpse placed in a preservative and kept overseas for three months until the general elections. Then a grand orgy of mourning would finish off Young Ireland.

As a result, when the Confederates ventured out into the country to seek votes, they were met everywhere with brickbats and clubs and by mobs shouting "Murderers!" and "Up Old Ireland!" The late Liberator's non-violence principle, it was noted grimly, applied only to the English. "We had not found the gentry antagonists half so angry and prejudiced as the populace," said Duffy. "They would have stoned us at Cork, butchered us at Belfast, and made a bonfire of a Confederate meeting at Kilkenny. We had won the intellectual artisans who read and thought, and the young men in the towns universally, but certainly not the peasantry." Duffy's list omitted the ugliest of the riots, in Limerick, when Smith O'Brien and Mitchel were almost murdered, an incident recorded in Thackeray's un-funny jingle, "The Battle of Limerick." A friendly letter from a rural reader sympathized with the Confederates' problem: "It is very hard to know the Irish peasantry. Citizens seldom do. The Confederates knew no more of Ireland than the Cockneys do. There is a great want of candor among us. Except the priests, every man's hand is against us. We have, therefore, acquired the habit of hiding our opinions even from each other. One fact is certain, we love Ireland and would serve her if we could see how."[22] All in all the general elections of 1847 were an unmitigated calamity for the Irish Confederation. O'Connell had spoken truly when he said, "There is no such party as that styled 'Young Ireland.'"

IX

After these humiliations, a last hope still remained: Would the wisdom and statesmanship of the landed gentry not save the day? An Irish council of peers and gentry was cajoled by Young Ireland into leaving behind "the rustle of their planted hills" to gather in Dublin, there to decide upon a patriotic program for the crisis. The *Nation* lived in suspense while the great landlords deliberated; for did the gathering not remind one of 1782 or even 1789? It repeatedly pointed out the glories latent in the first of these memories and the dangers in the second—unless the delegates came around to Repeal before the uprisings were scheduled to commence. The landlords actually did complain against England, and especially against the Labor Rate Act, which promised their financial ruin. Duffy said later without intended irony that the council at the outset had contemplated becoming Federalist and might have willingly been pushed into "something more," that is, Repeal, "if they could be protected against democracy and priests."[23] No such assurance being forthcoming, the sole accomplishment of the gentry's debates was a resolution demanding a new Irish coercion act.

X

This plea for coercion the prime minister heard and heeded. Lord John Russell had other plans too, new "comprehensive measures of relief." In mid-summer 1847 the work projects were abruptly abandoned altogether, leaving Ireland dotted to this day with roads that end unexpectedly in the middle of the bog. The emergency soup kitchens were locked up and dismantled. Famine relief was henceforth to be confined to breaking rocks in the workhouses. When the workhouses were full, together with their various emergency annexes, there would be outdoor relief on the local poor law rates. Since the local districts were bankrupt, a fact perfectly understood by everybody, the new measures guaranteed that the famine would continue.

The other novelty of the 1847 relief law was a stringent means test requiring applicants to divest themselves of all tenant holdings of more than one quarter-acre before admission to relief. This clause forced peasant clearances on a national rather than a piecemeal scale, and relieved the evicting landlords and "middlemen" from the hazards of assassination under the old-fashioned system of legal ejectment, cabin by cabin. The means test was named the "Gregory clause" after its author, member for Dublin, Sir William Gregory of Coole Park, county Galway—the future husband in his old age of a young neighbor girl, Augusta Persse, known to us as Lady Gregory. Sir William's autobiography, edited by Lady Gregory, devotes a page or two of comment to the incident, quoting with approval the opinion of the *Dublin University Magazine* that the Gregory clause had put an end to the two paramount hardships of the famine, namely, "the absorption by undeserving persons of a large portion of the public funds"* and a poor rate that "in many cases" had risen above "the yearly rent of the land." Sir William added that only nine of the hundred-odd Irish members had voted against the Gregory clause, and that O'Connell's son had voted for it. "Old Archbishop MacHale never forgave me on account of it," he said. "But it pulled up suddenly the country from falling into the open pit of pauperism on the verge of which it stood. Though I got an evil reputation in consequence, those who really understood the condition of the county have always regarded this clause as its salvation."[24] Sir William's imperturbability should be kept in mind when interpreting Yeats's acid lines about those ungrateful farmers who carried off the stonework of some great manor house to "patch the pig pen."

With unabated virulence the famine began its third year's run. There was a blessed respite from the potato rot but still nothing to eat. Over a

---

* This cornerstone of aristocratic sociology found its way into *The Countess Cathleen*, where Teigue is (1) actually starving, and (2) pretending to starve in order to cadge from the countess.

large part of Ireland no seed potatoes were to be had for planting. The government was aware of the shortage long in advance but had done nothing. The peasants had often been forced to boil up the seed potatoes for food, or else were occupied on the public works at planting time and dared not leave for fear of not being rehired afterward. Potato plantings in 1847 were one-fifth of the usual. Hunger was once again the prospect for the new year. Could such things be? They could. What next?

CHAPTER 7

'48 and Insurrection

I

As the Young Ireland Confederates were being pitilessly knocked about in furtherance of their political education, a strange new actor came on the scene: James Fintan Lalor. His collected writings, which can be read through in half an hour, included a dozen or so bold epigrams that made a great reverberation through Dublin's stagnant famine air. He was an original, a deformed, asthmatic recluse, boorish and impossible to work with. Still, he had generated a stock of fresh ideas about the condition of the country. The *Nation*'s nadir, the leading article quoted earlier—"Alas! alas! . . . we can do nothing"—had, he said, "made me *ill*"; and he had written a letter to Duffy setting forth a less defeatist view of the situation. *He* had never, he said, been enticed to go on board O'Connell's Repeal ship: "I knew her at once for a leaky collier-smack, with a craven crew to man her, and a sworn dastard and foresworn traitor at the helm." He considered the whole effort of the monster meetings misspent, for no matter how many Irishmen came to hear the oratory, they held no lever that could be applied against England. Besides, Repeal was a secondary issue; a "mightier question" lay in the possession of the land. Because Ireland was a nation of the landless, it was "rotting to a foetid ruin"; but "create the husbandman, and you create the mechanic, the artizan, the manufacturer, the merchant." Unless Ireland was to perish, it must locate some power to set against English power, not necessarily force of arms, but at least a capability to wound. Such a power existed, waiting, in the land-hungry peasantry. Therefore: "unmuzzle the wolf-dog. There is one at this moment in every cabin throughout the land, nearly fit already to be untied—and he will be savage by-and-by."[1]

Lalor's letter seemed too hot to publish, but it was handed around among the Young Irelanders and vigorously debated in private. Anxious like any other editor to publish a readable journal, Duffy was attracted to Lalor's style, but the ideas frightened him. Smith O'Brien agreed with Duffy that it would be wrong to unmuzzle the wolf dog. John Mitchel, on the other hand, liked Lalor's ideas very much. Under their impact he rethought the whole Irish quandary and reached some startling new conclusions. The shabby closing act of the Irish council now convinced him that the landlords' deliberations had perpetrated a fraud, making bogus militant talk to blackmail the English into a new coercion act. He concluded that the combination of all classes, Duffy's and Smith O'Brien's favorite guide to political life, must be scourged out of Young Ireland's program without a moment's delay. He explained his sudden enlightenment:

> I long thought that if only all "ranks and classes," as the phrase runs, could be banded together for the Repeal of the Union, the wrong and injustice would disappear; "Irish noblemen and gentlemen"—the thick-headed individuals before mentioned—would straightway treat their tenants like Christian men, and not like wild beasts, and the tillers of the soil would suddenly acquire a perpetuity in their lands, and sitting, every man of them, under his own vine and fig-tree, would consume the fruits of the earth in peace, with none to make them afraid. It was an agreeable delusion, and the fabulous glories of "Eighty-two" shed a glow over it for a while. But it was a dream: "Irish noblemen and gentlemen" no longer acknowledge Ireland for their country—they are "Britons;" their education, their feelings, and what is more important to them, their *interests*, are all British. British "laws" eject and distrain for them, British troops preserve "life and property," and chase their surplus tenants. For them judges charge—for them hangmen strangle.

The landlords were not tomorrow's comrades of the bivouac, but today's mortal enemy, inseparable from the other enemy, the English. The need of the moment was ruthless attack and the confiscation of the Irish land:

> Irish landlordism has grown so rotten and hideous a thing, that only its strict alliance, offensive and defensive, with British oligarchy saves it from going down to sudden perdition. So soon as this became clear to my mind, I, for one, desisted from the vain attempt of seducing the English landlord garrison in Ireland to fraternise with Irishmen, and turned upon the garrison itself. I determined to try how many men in Ireland would help me to lay the axe to the root of this rotten and hideous Irish landlordism; that we might see *how much would come down* along with it.[2]

Simultaneously, Mitchel arrived at a momentous new insight into the sources of the famine. He had been brooding for a long time on the gargantuan confusion in the administration of famine relief. He observed that the muddle went beyond random expectation and enjoyed such fullness of perfection that it seemed to be almost a work of art, a fulfillment of plan. A number of other Irishmen, including the Tory Isaac Butt, had drifted toward the same thought. "Can we wonder," asked Butt, "if the Irish people believe—*and believe it they do*—that the lives of those who have perished, and who will perish, have been sacrificed by a deliberate compact to the gain of English merchants ?" He quickly added, however, "Of any such compact we acquit the ministers."[3] Under the unbearable emotional stresses of late 1847, Mitchel refused to acquit the ministers. Suddenly he thought he saw the entire famine relief operation during the past twenty-four months as a calculated scheme on the part of both Peel and Russell to exterminate the Irish people, not figuratively as in the peasants' metaphor for eviction, but in the stark and literal sense. There was the "act of God," to be sure, the blight fungus. But the famine itself had features that set it apart from any other in all history. First, it had occurred not on the poor backward fringes of civilization, among Australian bushmen, but inside the imperial Union of Great Britain, the workshop of the world, the most advanced nation on earth. Second, it had occurred during years in which most Irish crops except potatoes were bountiful. Even O'Connell had seen the anomaly of ships laden with Irish grain sailing out of Dublin and Cork harbors while Irishmen were famishing; even he had said that Irishmen should die with arms in their hands if starvation should be attempted. Well, Mitchel concluded, such was in fact the case; or in the words of his famous indictment: "The Almighty, indeed, sent the potato blight, but the English created the Famine."[4]

The relief apparatus now came under the attack of Mitchel's very considerable satiric powers. He was the first to spotlight the role of Charles Trevelyan, "a Treasury clerk," as the architect of the catastrophe. Learning that it was Trevelyan who entreated the queen to appoint a day of almsgiving for the starving Irish, he wrote: "Keep your alms, ye canting robbers. We spit upon the benevolence that robs us of a *pound* and flings back a penny in *charity*; and if the English cared to show their compassion for the Irish, let them take their fangs from our throat."[5] In a later time, John O'Leary's sarcastic intonation of the words "philanthropy" and "humanitarianism"[6] seems more to echo Mitchel's special bitterness against English evangelicals than to sponsor his famous disciple's universal ethical abstraction, "cast a cold eye." The age-old dialogue between bureaucracy and starvation has never been delineated with more acid disdain than Mitchel's. One of his vignettes described how the lord lieutenant, Lord Clarendon, dispatched agricultural extension agents laden with scientific advice into the blighted area at Mullet. Too late: on arrival they found all their prospective pupils already dead. Another described how a traveler journeying through the dismal wastes of rock and bog in west Mayo came at last to the grandest building for fifty miles around, "rearing its accursed gables and pinnacles of Tudor barbarism, and staring boldly with its detestable mullioned windows, as if to mock those wretches who still cling to liberty and mud cabins— seeming to them, in their perennial half-starvation, like a Temple erected to the Fates, or like the fortress of Giant Despair, whereinto he draws them one by one and devours them there:—the Poor-house."[7] Another described the gala dedication of Dublin's model soup kitchen:

> There, in the esplanade before the "Royal Barracks," was erected the national model soup-kitchen, gaily bedizened, laurelled, and bannered, and fair to see; and in and out, and all around, sauntered parties of our supercilious second-hand "better classes" of the castle-offices, fed on superior rations at the people's expense, and bevies of fair dames, and military officers, braided with public braid, and padded with public padding; and there, too, were the pale and piteous ranks of model-paupers, broken tradesmen, ruined farmers, destitute sempstresses, ranged at a respectful distance till the genteel persons had duly inspected the arrangements—and then marched by policemen to the place allotted them, where they were to feed on the meagre diet with *chained spoons*—to show the "gentry" how pauper spirit can be broken, and pauper appetite can gulp down its bitter bread and its bitterer shame and wrath together;—and all this time the genteel persons chatted and simpered as pleasantly as if the clothes they wore, and the carriages they drove in, were their own—as if "Royal Barracks," castle, and soup-kitchen, were to last for ever.[8]

Frenzied, "maddened" as he said, Mitchel was driven to the logic of the French marshal of a later time: our position is lost, situation splendid!—we attack. Young Ireland was unarmed, isolated, demolished at the polls, trailed by Castle spies, threatened with imprisonment, and deserted by its allies. Therefore, said Mitchel, it must assault its twin adversaries at once; for since landlordism and the English connection were equivalent to one another, he could "see no way to put an end to either but by destroying both."[9] "A kind of sacred wrath" overwhelmed him and his few friends; and as he said later, "they could endure the horrible scene no longer and resolved to cross the path of the British car of conquest, though it should crush them to atoms."[10]

II

The original strategy proposed by Mitchel was that of the tithe war. Lalor had already begun to organize the peasantry along that line. In the fall of 1847 he had gathered four thousand peasants in a meeting at Holycross, county Tipperary, and pleaded with them to stand together on the principle that the first claims upon the produce of every Irish tenancy, prior to both rent and poor rates, should be food to maintain life in the farm family and beasts, and seed for the next planting. To enforce this claim he recommended a rent strike supported by intimidation of the buyers of distrained property and violent resistance to ejectment. Mitchel appropriated Lalor's scheme as it stood, adding two more objectives. First he proposed resistance to the collection of the poor rates and boycott of the workhouses as the only escape from the Gregory quarter-acre clause. Duffy thought this proposal insane, arguing that a million or so Irishmen were being kept alive by government relief, stingy though it might be, and that those who refused to take relief on principle would find that the price of their principle was instant starvation. But Mitchel had made a second proposal: to frustrate the export of Irish food by any efficient means—sabotage of grain convoys, destruction of rural bridges, or the rifling of warehouses. This campaign, he hoped, would feed the Irish peasantry, allowing the destruction of the relief system.

Mitchel understood that in carrying out such a program one could not avoid sporadic clashes, but that success would for a time depend upon minimizing violence rather than seeking it out as a paramount objective. However, he spoke a language increasingly inflammatory. He found that before any resistance at all could start, he must counteract the apathy resulting from hunger and from O'Connell's years of preachment against violence. Confederate clubmen out in the country sent in reports that the peasants were conditioned not only to submit, but to die. They said "God's will be done" and went away and died like wounded animals. If they could be awakened out of their "tranquillity," a progression of small fires might spread into a general conflagration, or so he hoped. Eventually he looked to "try the steel" at the head of an armed rebellion of the 1798 mode. He knew that thirty thousand British troops were stationed in Ireland, ten thouand in Dublin alone. But three-fourths of the rank and file of the British garrison consisted of Irish peasant boys, whose disloyalty to their English officers seemed a fair risk in the crisis, especially since these same Irish boys had proved to be the most enthusiastic consumers of his seditious journalism.

After Mitchel's mind was set in its new fixation, events moved very fast. In December 1847 Duffy was no longer able to breathe the brimstone fumes and dismissed him from the *Nation*'s staff—with sadness, one would suppose, since the journal's vitality proved to be as dependent upon Mitchel's pen in 1847 as upon Davis' in 1842. In January 1848 Smith O'Brien decided that Mitchel must also be purged from the Confederation. O'Connell's purification ritual was to be re-enacted in a new setting, but with courtesy.

Smith O'Brien's campaign against Mitchel opened with a resolution defining the Confederation position. It sought "legislative independence" by the sole means of "a combination of creeds and classes." Duffy seconded his thought, referring to the ghastly year just ended as "hopeful" because it brought "one light . . . the first real growth of nationality among the higher classes."[11] Mitchel, in reply, looked about the hall for converted landlords and found only Smith O'Brien and one other, his own brother-in-law, John Martin. The Confederates, it seemed, had as many landlords as O'Connell had said Young Ireland had priests, namely, two. Mitchel offered his own program for blocking food exports and boycotting relief, adding that the Confederation must also persuade the peasantry to arm in haste. Michael Doheny answered him with a somber appraisal of their predicament: "How many of them would take the advice? What need we conceal from ourselves the fact—if they were all armed this moment, guided by those they most trust, the great majority of them would use those very arms against us. But even if that were not so, where are your peasantry?—sicklied, hungry, wasted, exiled, or in their graves. If you want to arm, I tell you your best chance—go to Skibbereen, reanimate the corpses that are huddled there and bid them arm." Smith O'Brien's resolution passed, and Mitchel and his followers walked out. Meanwhile the famine raged on, and a priest wrote in from Mayo: "There is not a day that I do not meet hundreds of paupers, the squalor and wretchedness of whose appearance no person can depict."[11]

Taking his cénacle—Mangan the poet and John Kenyon the patriot priest—along with him, Mitchel moved down the street and started a rival weekly, the *United Irishman*, named in honor of Tone and '98. Tone's famous words appeared on the new journal's banner: "If the men of property will not help us they must fall: we will free ourselves by the aid of that large and respectable class of the community—the men of no property." Free for the first time, Mitchel set out to learn whether the force of his satiric pen could alter the drift of Irish history. He opened fire with a journalistic barrage against Lord Clarendon, the lord lieutenant: "I expect no justice, no courtesy, no indulgence from you; and if you get me within your power I entreat you to show me no mercy, as I, so help me God, would show none to you."[12] He scarified the government, the food exporters, the relief officials, the bigots, the moral force "humbug," the landlords, the English.

III

Mitchel was purged from the Confederation on February 5, 1848. Three weeks later he was back again. The martial ardor of Irish nationalist politics was suddenly reinvigorated by the arrival on February 23 of news of revolution in France. The people of Paris had merely reached a certain level of disgust and, *voilà*, Louis Philippe fled in disguise and the Hôtel de Ville was occupied by citizens, at their head Duffy's intellectual mentor, the aristocrat, romantic poet, and historian of the Gironde, Alphonse de Lamartine. In a few weeks Metternich had fled Vienna, and Germany and Italy were in conflagration. Everywhere prospects were looking up for spontaneous uprisings. Mitchel congratulated himself on his foresight. The Confederates sent a delegation to infidel Paris, though Lamartine, under English threat, soon chilled their fraternal advances. Even John O'Connell, passing through Paris in the February Days, was infected with republicanism and made himself available for Irish unity talks. The most extraordinary reaction, however, was Duffy's. The *Nation* dropped its timidity without transition and—outdistancing Mitchel altogether—it came out next Saturday with a mobilization call for an independent Irish army. "If we are not slaves and braggarts, unworthy of liberty," said Duffy's editorial, "Ireland will be free before the coming summer fades into winter."[13] In the full hearing of Dublin Castle he appointed autumn for the insurrection and briskly transacted other revolutionary military business. He designed a field uniform ("no fripperies"), fixed the size of the army units, and set up a program for systematic fraternizing with the constabulary.

Duffy seemed at first to have caught the revolutionary contagion in an especially virulent form. But a more consistent motive came to light in a frantic letter he hurried off to Limerick, pleading with Smith O'Brien to come back to Dublin to take charge of the headlong movement. The one way of safety ahead, he said, was for the middle classes to stay "in front" of the rising millions; then "a peaceful revolution" could follow from "watching and seizing our opportunity." He had decided for the 1782 modus, in the hope that he could confront Lord John Russell in the autumn, as Grattan had confronted England, with a showy national guard, and could then await like Grattan the delivery of the Renunciation Act by courier from Westminster. "It may be won without a shot being fired," he ventured. The danger he foresaw was the same that O'Connell had faced in all of his agitations, that is, the separation of the leadership from the main body of the peasantry, so often too far behind or too far ahead. "There will be an outburst sooner or later, be sure of that," he wrote Smith O'Brien. "But unless you provide against it, it will be a mere democratic one. . . ." If a rising were attempted and failed, he expected that the English terror of '98 would be repeated. But success would be even worse: "it will mean death and exile to the middle as well as the upper classes . . . [and] you and I will meet on a Jacobin scaffold, ordered for execution as enemies of some new Marat or Robespierre, Mr. James Lalor or Mr. Somebody else [i.e., Mitchel]."[14]

The chances of military success were hardly favorable when one of the three leading revolutionists believed that revolution would be the worst possible outcome of the crisis. But Duffy was not in full control either of events or of his own men. The younger Confederate clubmen talked gaily about the approaching battle, and Smith O'Brien was not at all frightened by Duffy's sans-culotte scare. The misery of his private quandary had long since led him stoically to prepare his neck for the noose: "Neither the scaffold on the one hand nor the infuriated mob on the other shall deter me from pursuing the course which I deem conducive to the interests of Ireland," he wrote Duffy.[15] Negotiations looking toward united military action went on continually, but winter passed into spring and still no common base could be found. The popular tide of defiance continued to rise.

In April 1848 the government made its first countermove, arresting Smith O'Brien, Meagher, and Mitchel on a charge of sedition. The first two came to trial in May. Since the state trials after Clontarf, the Whigs had lacked the nerve to draw up another all-Orange jury. As expected, then, the juries in the trial of Smith O'Brien and Meagher could not reach a verdict. The prisoners were released and charges against Mitchel were dropped. So far, the government was not faring the best, and Mitchel moved on to his next step. On May 13 he published an open call to arms, still with no time or place for the hosting named:

> You little know the history and sore trials and humiliations of this ancient Irish race; ground and trampled first for long ages into the very earth, and then taught—expressly *taught*—in solemn harangues, and even in sermons, that it was their duty to die, and see their children die before their faces, rather than resist their tyrants, as men ought. . . . But I tell you the light has at length come to them; the flowery spring of this year is the dawning of their day; and before the cornfields of Ireland are white for the reaper our eyes shall see the sun flashing gloriously, if the heavens be kind to us, on a hundred thousand pikes.[16]

IV

That same day, Castle detectives came to Mitchel's home at suppertime and arrested him once again. He was charged under newest coercion measures. There were patriots who were saying that Mitchel's "criminal folly" was advancing the English cause, but the government did not share that opinion. The prosecutor was privileged to challenge prospective jurors without limit, and in the end he found the twelve men who could be trusted to convict.

The Confederate clubmen of Dublin, now largely Mitchelite, soon saw that there would be no hung jury in this trial. They raised the question whether an attempt should not be made to rescue him, either from jail before the trial or in transport. The personal fate of Mitchel was their original concern; then a weightier issue arose. Rescue, it was thought, would "signal insurrection," and the debate turned on the issue of whether a rising should or should not commence "then and there." Meagher believed, like the rank and file in the clubs, that "the ship that carried him away should sail upon a sea of blood." Concluding that the Mitchelites were *provocateurs* in English pay, Smith O'Brien betook himself to Limerick to avoid the embarrassment of a decision. Duffy was opposed to rescue, arguing that England could crush the country in two weeks merely by blockading the cornmeal ships inbound from New Orleans, that the British garrison in Dublin was too strong to attack directly, that insurrection needed more time to prepare. Those favoring rescue replied that Mitchel was indispensable to the movement; that the rising should start first in Dublin where the clubs were more reliable, and spread later into the more doubtful countryside; that the British garrison in Dublin, however large, needed to be brought into action to test whether the Irishmen who made up its enlisted ranks would not mutiny. The final decision, in retrospect the most important Young Ireland ever made, was against rescue. The council visited Mitchel in jail to ask him to sign a letter requesting the clubs not to attempt a rescue. Said Mitchel later: "I refused utterly; and perhaps too bitterly."[17]

Mitchel was convicted and sentenced to fourteen years of transportation. When sentence was passed, he addressed the court: "The law has now done its part, and the Queen of England, her crown and government in Ireland are now secure, 'pursuant to Act of Parliament.' I have done my part also."[18] The next day at noon he was taken by prison van to the North Wall to be put on board a British naval ship, which was waiting with steam up. A crowd had gathered near the quay. They heard the clink of his chains as he passed. Someone shouted, "Farewell, Mitchel!" and he turned and made a formal bow. The crowd saw him stumble and fall as he went on deck, then the ship weighed anchor immediately and moved out of port. It was, all in all, said Mitchel, an interesting week:

> During the same week the poor-houses, hospitals, gaols, and many buildings, taken temporarily for the purpose, were overflowing with starving wretches; and fevered patients were occupying the same bed with famished corpses: but on every day of the same week large cargoes of grain and cattle were leaving every port for England. The Orangemen of the North were holding meetings to avow hostility to Repealers and to "Jezebel," and eagerly crying, "To hell with the Pope!" Thus British policy was in full and successful operation at every point, on the day when I left my country in the fetters of the enemy.[19]

V

The rest of the tale of '48 is quickly told. On the day Mitchel left his country in fetters, the Confederation resolved to act—not to make an insurrection "then and there," but to plan one then and there that would take place as soon as the harvest, such as it was, could be gathered. The air became charged with expectation. Smith O'Brien, Meagher, John O'Mahony, Kevin O'Dougherty, Doheny, and other Confederate leaders went out from Dublin into the country to test the ardor of the peasantry and the provincial townsmen. They were very favorably impressed. Even Cork, slow to form clubs, paraded seven thousand clubmen by moonlight in the city park for Smith O'Brien's review, and Doheny and Meagher found Kilkenny and

Tipperary on the point of explosion. A night meeting on the slopes of Slievenamon rivaled O'Connell's monster meetings. When Meagher came down off the mountain, he found the towns along the Suir in feverish turmoil: "It was the Revolution, if we had accepted it. Why it was not accepted, I fear I cannot with sufficient accuracy explain."[20]

The Confederate leaders still moved in confusion. They had no arms, no money, no staff, no council of war, no plan of campaign. The *Nation's* sedition intermingled hysteria with diffidence. Duffy had recently issued a moderate pronunciamento, "The Creed of the *Nation*," to counteract Mitchel's inflammatory influence; it was now reprinted. On the agrarian issue Duffy offered the unexciting thought that the "claims of labor" must be placed upon "some solid and satisfactory basis," though not in labor's self-interest, for all revolutions are "intrinsically unselfish."[21] On July 8 the *Nation's* first leading article bore the chilly title, "What If We Fail?" Yet when Lord Clarendon commenced systematic arrests of the Confederate leadership on July 9, Duffy was at the top of his list. As the police led the prisoner away, a large crowd gathered and someone asked Duffy if he cared to be rescued. He replied, "Certainly not!"

On July 21 Clarendon suspended habeas corpus, proclaimed Dublin and Cork, and ordered all persons therein to surrender their weapons. A young Kilkenny clubman named James Stephens made a speech recommending defiance of the proclamation: "Treasure your arms as you would the apples of your eyes, and bury your arms safely in the hope of a happy resurrection."[22] That was the day the rebels finally got around to electing a council of war and fixing on a battle plan: they would start the rising in Tipperary, where success was now thought certain, in order to lure the British garrison out from Dublin and allow the Dublin clubs to attack the Castle. The *Nation* since Duffy's arrest had fallen under the editorship of Speranza, who gave the signal for the rising in a manifesto called "*Jacta Alea Est*." Seized by the Ascendancy's old battle dream of the dashing Protestant aristocracy leading the Catholic hordes to glory, she wrote: "One instant to take breath, and then a rising; a rush, a charge from north, south, east, and west upon the English garrison, and *the land is ours*. . . . Who dares to say he will not follow, when O'BRIEN leads?"[23]

VI

In utter agony but dutiful to the end, Smith O'Brien went into Tipperary to raise an army and begin the war. In his pocket he carried a letter from Duffy which resembled a military order: "You will be the head of the movement, loyally obeyed, and the revolution will be conducted with order and clemency, or the mere anarchist will prevail with the people and our revolution will be a bloody chaos. You have at present Lafayette's place as painted by Lamartine. . . ."[24] His misadventures were so preposterously compounded that they occupy a special niche in military history. He was almost unknown in Tipperary and he made no agrarian appeals whatever. Yet his oratory did gather a large band of peasants and "thirty rust-eaten fowling pieces," besides some pikes. For fear of alienating the landed gentry, he forbade his starving troops to commandeer food and supplies. He also required them to observe the law of trespass in their maneuvers, a unique rule of war remembered in Percy French's great comic song, "Slattery's Mounted Fut." His military objective was to taunt the constabulary into arresting him, "to force the enemy to strike the first blow"; whereupon his troops would counterattack and the war would be on, or as Meagher liked to put it, "then, up with the barricades and invoke the God of battles!" At Killenaule the rebels made a roadblock. An officer of dragoons rode up and demanded to pass. James Stephens, who had followed Smith O'Brien into the field, fixed the officer in the sights of his carbine and was ready to open fire and begin the insurrection, but Dillon stayed his hand and the officer rode on through. More days were spent in wandering about the countryside trying to locate an enemy force that would perpetrate the necessary arrest. Lord Clarendon had ample leisure to prepare his military rebuttal.

Smith O'Brien's incompetence was so striking as to suggest provocation. *Agents provocateurs* were well known to be employed by the Castle. Carleton's *Rody the Rover*, published three years earlier, had made a sensational exposure of the device. Just before Smith O'Brien took the field, the Confederates were fascinated by the discovery of one of them in their midst, betrayed by police bumbling, a man named Kirwan who was arrested for inflammatory speeches and publicly brandishing a pike. When police raided his home they found a secret cache of Orange Lodge paraphernalia. Embarrassed, the government hastily recognized him as one of their own and released him. However, the employment of *provocateurs* and spies benefited the government by creating a widespread public fear that the agents must surely be concealed everywhere. (Joyce's phobia about informers originated in this fear.) Smith O'Brien himself, as we have seen, suspected that the militancy of the Mitchelites was a paid provocation.[25] In turn he fell victim to the hysteria himself. Duffy reported: "Authentic news came to us from without that many of the ignorant populace in Dublin whispered that Smith O'Brien had deliberately betrayed them to make a real insurrection impossible. The police were probably responsible for this invention; but Old Ireland welcomed it."[26]

This bit of historical byplay later took Yeats's fancy as a telling emblem of Irish ignobility. The Dublin mob, he said, had rewarded Smith O'Brien's generosity with the accusation "of being paid by the government to fail";

and it was this beastly ingratitude that had led Goethe to observe that "the Irish always seem to me like a pack of hounds dragging down some noble stag."[27] But remembering that the probable source of the rumor was the Castle, and remembering Smith O'Brien's truly singular behavior in the field (the government owed him a debt of gratitude for service rendered, said Peel, in "making rebellion ridiculous"),[28] and remembering too, Smith O'Brien's haste in making the accusation of paid provocation against Mitchel, one finds difficulty in responding fully to Yeats's invitation to wrath.*

If the generals in Young Ireland's army were inept, the peasant rank and file were hardly better. Enthusiasm they had in abundance, but discipline was beyond them. The troops cheered when Smith O'Brien made a speech, but then they ignored all his orders. One morning, inspection discovered several thousand troops to be without rations. Smith O'Brien sent them home to get some and they never came back. A couple of weeks earlier some of the priests had passed through the ranks blessing the rebels' arms. Dillon told Meagher, "Oh! if you had seen them when the old priest blessed them, you'd have thought they could have swept the country from sea to sea, and done the business with a blow." Then it was found that the priests had suddenly turned about and were ordering the troops to disband. New recruits were demobilized as fast as they were enlisted. Hannibal or Napoleon, said Dillon, could have done no better than Smith O'Brien had they tried to campaign with Tipperary peasants.[29] And where was Father Kenyon, the patriot priest who was to have led his flock directly from Mass into battle as soon as the insurrection began? Rebel leaders read in the newspaper that he had just made a submission to his bishop. A delegation hastened to Templederry to remind him of his pledged word. He greeted them "with irony" and explained that Smith O'Brien's courteous military methods could never succeed; that if they really wanted to fight, they ought to start by seizing hostages and the landlord's silver plate; and that it was unbecoming for a priest to engage in a "bootless struggle."

Whatever the cause, Smith O'Brien's insurrection was the final link of Young Ireland's long chain of disasters. On July 27, 1848, the rebels besieged a squad of constables in a farmhouse at Ballingarry. The constables opened fire and killed two peasants. Then the besiegers wandered away and the leaders scattered. Mass arrests followed quickly. Some of the leaders escaped to America, some to Paris; but most were captured. The war was over, and at a portentous moment, for just then the news broke of another

---

* Yeats's interpretation was enthusiastically endorsed by the liberal English historian, J. L. Hammond. Goethe's remark (made to Eckermann during the Emancipation crisis of 1829) is worth looking up as a curiosity. He thought the trouble in Ireland was that the Catholics were persecuting the Protestants; hence his stag was Protestantism and his dogs were the Irish Catholics. How this Orange Lodge sentiment got transmitted to Weimar is mysterious—through the English ambassador, perhaps?

total failure of the potato crop and the start of another year of the famine.

There was one afterglow following Ballingarry. In the autumn of 1849 Lalor gathered a few young friends and some peasants to make an attack on police barracks in Tipperary and Waterford. The main event never came off, but a skirmish on the flank killed several constables and attackers. Lalor was arrested and died shortly afterward. His young lieutenants were caught as they scattered on the hillside, but they were not brought to trial. One of them was Thomas C. Luby, later to become a leading Fenian. Another, more famous than Luby, was John O'Leary.

VII

After the police had rounded up the stragglers, a new series of state trials began. Duffy was brought to trial three times but never convicted. He was released in May 1849. Smith O'Brien was unsuccessfully defended by Isaac Butt. Convicted of high treason, he was sentenced to be hanged, drawn, and quartered according to the barbarous formula. When his sentence was commuted to life imprisonment, he declined to accept the commutation, raising an unprecedented legal problem. Once again he was on the losing side; the commutation was forced upon him, and he found himself transported to Van Diemen's Land, toward which Mitchel had earlier set out in fetters. Meagher also received a death sentence commuted to transportation for life, along with Terence Bellew MacManus and Kevin O'Dougherty, who would later achieve immortality in *Finnegans Wake* because of the happy accident that his middle name happened to be "Izod."

In due time Van Diemen's Land gathered an exclusive little club of Young Ireland felons. All of the convicts—except Smith O'Brien, who was too proud to give parole—were on ticket of leave to move about, live with their families, and occupy themselves as they pleased. They were forbidden to meet one another, but they did meet secretly, finding a picturesque spot to rendezvous at a shepherd's hut on Lake Sorel, high in the central Tasmanian mountains. There Mitchel once caught a baby kangaroo, which he took home in his arms, riding on horseback over the mountains, as a pet for his boys. He sent Dublin word of his order of preference for Tasmanians: "First, and best, he chose the women; second, the dogs; third, the horses; fourth, the kangaroos; fifth, the men; and sixth, the opossoms and wallabys."[30] But the charms of kangaroos and Tasmanian scenery were found to yield diminishing returns. Whenever the felons gathered at the lake, they had two engrossing topics to discuss. The first was how to escape. With the help of a network of Irish secret agents operating on British ships, all succeeded in slipping away one by one to San Francisco. The second subject was a post-mortem upon Ireland and especially upon their own failure.

CHAPTER 8

Beside the Sickbed: Carlyle, Duffy, Dr. Cullen

I

After Ballingarry the physical Irish nation lay ruined; politically, it was deader than dead. Seven of the top Confederate leaders were convicts in Van Diemen's Land. Most of the rest were hiding in Paris or New York. Further resistance was out of the question; only a fantastic like Lalor could think of insurrection in such an atmosphere. Young Ireland's seven-year struggle had apparently been swept away as though it had never been. The reading rooms were all gone, and the Irishmen who had been stirred by Davis' cultural nationalism were in the famine grave pits, in America, in the workhouse, in prison. Even temperance was defunct, and Irishmen with personal problems were once more free to drink themselves into stupefaction at pleasure. Bit by bit John O'Connell surrendered the assets of the dead Repeal Association to his creditors: first went the instruments of the brass band, then the library, finally Conciliation Hall itself. Once again Ireland found herself at the nadir of the cycle.

Famine mortality was already subsiding when Lalor's small military adventure took place in the autumn of 1849, though the suffering continued for another two years. A new visitation of the potato rot appeared in 1849, and 1850 brought still another. Then the worst was over, and the toll of the whole calamity could be reckoned in perspective. The precise number of the victims would never be known, but an estimate of the mortality was possible. By extrapolation from earlier censuses one could determine that Ireland had a population of eight and a half million in 1846. But in 1851 only six and a half million persons could be found. Roughly one million of this deficit represented those who had perished directly from starvation or hunger-induced fevers.[1] This phase was followed by a panic flight, "as if pursued by wild beasts," among the uprooted peasantry. The second million of the missing persons had emigrated, or at any rate they had left Ireland aboard ship—thousands of them, 10 to 12 percent by some estimates, died in passage to America or in quarantine. This exodus of the Irish, beginning with the "black '47," would continue without interruption for one hundred consecutive years.

The famine did not respect class lines, for the typhus, once it became epidemic, could not be contained. But the most savage effects, naturally, were suffered by the peasantry. The 1851 census showed that famine mortality, together with Gregory's quarter-acre clause plus a great new wave of legal ejectments— which grew bolder as peasant resistance collapsed —had eased the landlords' puzzlement over how to clear the land of "redundant population." By 1851 three-fourths of the cottiers' plots had disappeared off the face of the land. Three-fourths of the small tenancies of one to five acres had also disappeared, having been amalgamated into larger farms. About two million rural persons had been violently dislodged to make room for the grazier. Malthus' imperious primary check had undoubtedly made a great deal of solitude in Ireland, and the recurring image used by travelers to project the sensation of the postfamine countryside was its vast emptiness and silence:

> We and our bitterness have left no traces
> On Munster grass and Connemara skies.[2]

Not quite all the traces were gone, though, for Wilfred Blunt saw the outlines of the old hearths and potato patches all over western Ireland a half-century after the famine.

How was one to grasp so monstrous a calamity? How was one to interpret it? William Stokes, a doctor during the famine, observed that "nations, as well as individuals, must purchase experience, even though the cost is ruinous."[3] If the famine was the price of wisdom, what was the wisdom that it had purchased—supposing one to be content neither with banalities about the mysterious ways of Providence nor with the self-congratulations of the Malthusians, who saw their sagacity satisfactorily confirmed in the empty countryside?

II

In the summer of 1849 Thomas Carlyle came to Ireland to give this very question his closest attention. "Ireland really *is* my problem," he told himself, "the breaking point of the huge suppuration which all British and all European society now is."[4] As Young Ireland's most distinguished friend abroad, he was presumed likely—within his very peculiar limitations—to be sympathetic to the Irish outlook, if an Englishman could be. Ten years earlier he had declared his good will in *Chartism*: "England is guilty towards

Ireland and reaps at last, in full measure, the fruit of fifteen generations of wrongdoing." Carlyle arrived in Dublin with his benignity intact, for he declined Lord Clarendon's dinner invitation, preferring to put himself in the hands of Young Ireland instead. His warmest Dublin admirer, John Mitchel, was unfortunately some thousands of miles away; but Gavan Duffy had been released from jail just in time to offer him a guided tour of the country, a second-best but tolerable cicerone. The two set out tête-à-tête by train and Irish car to circle the country clockwise from Dublin, stopping along the way to talk with provincial clubmen who had been released from jail at the restoration of habeas corpus.

Carlyle's diary of his tour with Duffy recorded a graphic scene of universal devastation, though the wisdom he derived from it proved to be intertwined platitude and hysteria. Other than the clearances, nothing pleased him. When a crone offered him "the dainty of the country," the famous dyspeptic stomach was turned, for he had not been warned that this was the local name for goat's milk laced with poteen. One whole day was spoiled by an "ignorant" boatman singing "obscurely emblematic" songs about "Repale." His sarcasm was provoked by all Irish songs, whether rendered in Duffy's off-key voice to speed the miles through Connaught, or in M. J. Barry's lusty choruses while rowing across the Cove of Cork. He pronounced the Killarney echoes "not worth much" and the Giant's Causeway not "worth a mile to travel to see." Clew Bay, highly recommended to him, was for his taste altogether too "dim and shallow." The famine still gripped Ireland at the time of his tour, yet he was incurious about it and placed the word itself inside inverted commas. A funeral on the road annoyed him: "Funeral overtaken by us; the 'Irish howl'—totally disappointing, there was no sorrow whatever in the tone of it. A pack of idle women, mounted on the hearse as many as could, and the rest walking; were hoh-hoh-ing with a grief quite evidently hired and not worth hiring."[5]

Discreetly, the famished dead seldom crossed his line of vision, but beggars were everywhere, approaching him at every crossroads with clever simulations of hunger. He was not born yesterday, and divil a halfpenny their tricks ever got from him. Duty led him to inspect every workhouse along the route of the tour. He found them increasingly nauseating as he rode westward, and in Castlebar and Westport, county Mayo, their excesses broke his Caledonian reserve:

> Human swinery has here reached its *acme*, happily: 30,000 paupers in this union, population supposed to be about 60,000. Workhouse proper (I suppose) cannot hold above 3 or 4000 of them, subsidiary workhouses, and outdoor relief the others. Abomination of desolation; what *can* you make of it! Outdoor quasi-*work*: 3 or 400 big hulks of fellows tumbling about with shares, picks, and barrows, "levelling" the end of their workhouse hill; at first glance you

would think them all working; look nearer, in each shovel there is some ounce or two of mould, and it is all make-believe; 5 or 600 boys and lads, pretending to break stones. Can it be a *charity* to keep men alive on these terms? In face of all the twaddle of the earth, shoot a man rather than train him (with heavy expense to his neighbors) to be a deceptive human *swine*.[6]

Levity apart—if this was levity—Carlyle concluded sagely that there must be "a beginning in checking pauperism," but he knew not how. He wished that Peel were thirty again. It was not Repeal of the Union that Ireland needed, "but repeal from the Devil" instead. England was not opposed to Repeal, and was in fact "heartily desirous" of it, would embrace it "with both hands" were it not that England saw that it "had been forbidden by the laws of Nature." Concerning the new Irishmen, the product of O'Connell's agitations and the *Nation*'s songs, Carlyle expressed his opinion in the boldest image of the diary: "Kildare railway; big blockhead, sitting with his dirty feet on seat opposite, not stirring them for me, who wanted to sit there: 'One thing we're all agreed on,' said he 'we're very *ill governed*; Whig, Tory, Radical, Repealer, all admit we're very ill governed!' —I thought to myself 'Yes indeed: you govern yourself. He that would govern you well, would probably surprise you much my friend,—laying a hearty horsewhip over that back of yours.' "[7] Back home in Scotland, he was pleased to recall, one heard no noisy blackguard ignorance of this sort, but instead "silent intrepidity and valor" and a "constant submission to the Divine Will."[8]

Such was the judgment of Dr. Anti-Cant, Ireland's sometime friend, on Irish demos and Irish hunger, the wisdom bought at the cost of a million Irish lives. In brutality, the foremost enemy of English laissez faire could not be discriminated from its devotees, the political economists. Carlyle himself seems to have sensed some lack of penetration in his Irish thoughts. He never developed the notes of the Irish tour; and the publication of the diary itself we owe to Froude, who brought it out the year after Carlyle's death as a boost for Gladstone's 1881 Irish Coercion Bill. The peevishness of Carlyle's last judgment on Ireland did not break his habit of weeping briefly over evicted Irish peasants "dying there in the ditch" whenever he wished to make a piquant contrast against the "humanitarian cant" that insisted upon "pampering West-Indian niggers."

III

Duffy the cicerone and Carlyle the tourist sitting opposite him traded roles occasionally. In Westport Duffy gave way uncharacteristically to Carlyle's own vision and saw before him not "the People" of the *Nation*'s style sheet, but unclean pauperized beasts, "more debased than the Yahoos of Swift, creatures having only a distant and hideous resemblance to human beings." When some old beggarwoman in Westport *"shrieked"* at him for "a hep-ney," for one moment he "prayed to God" for a cleansing Noah's flood to inundate the county of Mayo.[9] But only for one moment; then his normal eager non-Carlylean good cheer resumed control.

What worried Duffy more than beggars and workhouse paupers was the silence of the countryside, everywhere "apathetic," "sick," "weary," and—anticipating Joyce's much-admired epithet—"paralyzed." Like all other Irish observers of the time, he found language inadequate to describe the actuality: "No words printed in a newspaper or elsewhere will give a man who had not seen it a conception of the fallen condition of the West and South."[10] Northward from Limerick he saw the true scope of the clearances. Clare was a wilderness, Lough Corrib another dead sea. He noted the in-numerable dead "stumps" of vanished farms, cabins unroofed and battered down to make sure they would never again be occupied. In Ulster, too, clearances were being pressed forward as audaciously as anywhere else, even in Cuchullain's "Gap of the North." Passing through Connaught, Duffy showed Carlyle the estate of Lord Lucan at Castlebar, hedged and plotted for the habitation of hundreds of peasant families, now all deserted. They met not one solitary soul for miles along the highway. Carlyle wrote in his diary that night: ". . .'cruel monster!' cry all people; but . . . Lord Lucan *is* moving, at least, if all others lie rotting."[11] Duffy could not agree. The root of the Irish disaster, he now concluded, lay in the cupidity of landlords: even "the Whigs were not so merciless." He understood for the first time why Mitchel had fought so passionately against the combination of all classes. The beginning of the wisdom he was to extract from the famine was the belief that to find "the lost path," one must start from this proposition: "the land question is to be got settled first, and forth-with."[12]

But what could be done? At first Duffy thought nothing could be done: "I confess that for a space I despaired of Irishmen in Ireland." Like many of his fleeing fellow countrymen, he was tempted to envision a new Ireland reborn in Boston. The seduction was put behind and he concluded, "In this land, or nowhere, the Irish nation must grow up."[13] One of Carlyle's thoughts on the famine was attractive to Duffy's common sense. The great thinker had written in a young Dublin admirer's autograph book: *"Fais ton fait!"* Irish paralysis had but one cure, the deed: "Do your deed!" Duffy was hardly three months out of jail before he began publication of the *Nation* again, new and improved. Speranza tuned up and supplied a poem praising the Doctrine of Work, beginning, "Close the starry dream portal." Duffy resurrected Davis' old fixation upon import duties and set up an agitation to "buy Irish," citing pins, toothbrushes, sealing wax, and sickles as proper commodities for home industry. He was himself once again.

While in jail Duffy and Thomas Meagher had been locked up together. Taking their daily exercise, the two pondered on their defeat and wondered where they might find a new lever to set Ireland in motion once more. One day Duffy had hit upon what seemed a brilliant idea. "You and I committed a blockhead blunder, my friend," he told Meagher. "We arrayed against us the most vital institution of Irish Ireland, by mere folly." The institution was the Catholic clergy. The clergy had built O'Connell's power, and in postfamine Ireland the clergy alone could "trumpet away the grave-yard sleep of the nation." Meagher was inclined to agree: the future nationalism of Ireland, he replied, would have to be "baptized in the Holy Well."[14] Duffy turned Meagher's phrase over in his mind approvingly. He concluded that henceforth Irish nationalism must avoid the "French tone" so painful to the clergy. Those Parisian verbalisms that Davis had brought into the movement from his reading of Thierry must be left behind in order to construct a holy nationalism. He suggested Hungary for the model, the same decision taken later out of a kindred motive by Arthur Griffith and Sinn Fein.

Duffy now questioned whether Davis' rigorous nonsectarianism had any merit at all. It had made the Catholics suspicious, and at the same time had brought in no Orangemen. What was really needed was more sectarian vigor, not less. Take land reform, for example. In the north the Protestant farmers were now up in arms over a bill in Parliament to equalize Irish tenant rights, not by extending the Ulster custom to the other three provinces, but by abolishing it altogether. Duffy thought a person ought to be able to prevail upon the Ulster preachers to preach land reform as Presbyterianism. Simultaneously, the priests in the south could organize it as a Catholic idea. The leaders of the two sects could then get together and make common cause "by committee."

According to the motto *Fais ton fait!* Duffy searched out his agrarian priests, his agrarian Orangemen, and two sectarian journalistic allies, Frederick Lucas of the Catholic *Tablet* and a Protestant, John Gray of the *Freeman's Journal*. Within one month after the revival of the *Nation*, Duffy allied himself with two agrarian priests at Callan, county Tipperary, and proclaimed excitedly that there soon would be tenant protective societies "from sea to sea." Blessed by Archbishop MacHale, a Dublin convention launched the Irish Tenant League in August 1850 and formulated the demands that governed the Irish agrarian movement for the next two generations, the so-called Three Fs: free sale of tenant equity (that is, the Ulster tenant right), fixity of tenure, and fair rent.[15]

Though hardly robust, the Tenant League had new sources of strength.

Through Duffy's fame it was heir to all the prestige of militant nationalism, and a few priests and preachers were now friendly for the first time. Duffy decided that the league ought to be able to win perhaps a dozen seats in the next parliamentary elections. It seemed unpromising that so insignificant a force could bend the unwieldy House of Commons to its will. It was observed, however, that the balance in the House was extremely delicate between the three great divisions, the Whigs, the Peelites, and the protectionist Tories. No ministry since 1845 had had more than the slimmest hold upon the government. In an impasse, a small bloc of independent members might command a very great price for its votes, provided it was tight-knit and incorruptible. Having watched the ruinous encroachment of place-seeking into O'Connell's empire, Duffy expected that it would reappear as a danger to any new Irish bloc. He and his friends therefore persuaded the Tenant League to require of all parliamentary candidates seeking its endorsement a written pledge to "withhold all support from any cabinet that will not advance [its] principles,"[16] that is, the enactment of the Three Fs into law.

IV

In Rome, no less than in Ireland, 1848 was not soon forgotten. A couple of years earlier Pius IX had opened his pontificate by abandoning the repressive policies of his predecessor, Gregory XVI, and had carried out a series of popular political gestures: amnesty for Gregory's political prisoners, a city council for Rome, a committee of lay advisers on the administration of the Papal States. These mild and well-intentioned reforms, pushed forward against the advice of the Gregorian cardinals, earned "Pio Nono" a warm popular reputation. When the 1848 Italian revolution first broke in the streets, he bowed before the liberal storm of the February Days and granted the Papal States a constitution.

But as the months of 1848 passed, the Italian revolution deepened. In the autumn, the papal prime minister was assassinated. During the insurrection that followed, Pius fled Rome, moving down the coast a few miles to Gaeta, under the protection of Naples. There he remained for a year and a half until the armies of Napoleon III restored him to St. Peter's. He was now positively disenchanted. The "Pope of Progress" lost his amiability, and at Gaeta he reverted with a vengeance to the illiberalism of Gregory XVI. To compensate for the forthcoming amputation of his temporal arm, he set about to strengthen the unity and discipline of the hierarchy and to nurture the Rome-oriented, or ultramontane, tendency of the Church. His post-1848 career was eventually crowned with the promulgation of the dogma of papal infallibility, and with the *Syllabus Errorum*, a point-by-point condemnation of sixty-three aspects of nineteenth-century "modernism." The syllabus of "errors and perversions" stood against all the heresies that gave him pain: Cavour's nationalism; Garibaldi's secret societies, the Carbonari and the Freemasons; and so on down the list—indifferentism, scientism, communism, and as a stinger for Mazzini and the poetic troublemakers, pantheism.

For all his sorrows, the pope in exile at Gaeta still had time to spare for his flock in distant Ireland. In December 1849 an important vacancy occurred with the death of the archbishop of Armagh. The local chapter, in due form, sent Rome and Gaeta three names from whom the new archbishop could be chosen. Passing over the nominees, the pope chose instead his good friend Paul Cullen, the rector of the Irish College in Rome.

Cullen was the son of a Westmeath peasant, origins which seem to have inspired Joyce's rendition of his name as "cardinal scullion." An uncle had been killed and his father's house burned for disloyalty during the rising of '98, but after the Union the family had prospered uncommonly and was no longer attracted to insurrection. The boy was so precocious in piety and learning that he was singled out first for holy orders, then, the height of dreams, for a Vatican career. In 1820 he arrived in Rome a lad of seventeen, in the last years of Pius VII, that well-known face in the middle foreground of the Jacques David painting of Napoleon's coronation. Four pontificates passed and a fifth had begun; and still Cullen was in Rome, seasoned by the Latin atmosphere until he was twice more Italian than Irish when measured by time exposure. Enjoying a growing prestige in the Vatican, he had been Gregory XVI's chief adviser on Irish affairs in the last years of O'Connell's leadership, and his authority grew with the elevation of Pius IX.

There exist a dozen formal biographies of John Cardinal Newman and three of Henry Cardinal Manning; but of Paul Cardinal Cullen, none. In outward appearance he was meek and prosaic; and when bystanders tried to reconcile his seeming lack of force with his obvious possession of very great force, the contradiction suggested some mystery hidden in the depths of personality. His enemies saw not so much mystery as deviousness. The meek demeanor, they concluded, was a façade to strengthen the social efficiency of a very clearheaded and obstinate cleric. Thus Gavan Duffy quoted a Maynooth professor who complained: "He is for narrow views, clandestine manoeuvres. . . ."[17] The Fenians called him "the Kalmuck fox," echoing the clandestine theme and referring also to an oriental cast of features not very visible in his portraits.[18] O'Leary thought "bull-dog" a more apt name. An unassailable authority, after summarizing the copious criticisms of Cullen's character, observed that the scrutiny of his personal papers would "offer comparatively little matter for an *apologia*."[19]

These traits in no way unfitted Cullen for carrying out the Vatican's post-1848 strategical objectives. Pius IX thought him the one man who could confidently be entrusted with the authority of the Church in times disturbed by Irish heresy and unrest. Armed with the title of primate, and doubly armed with the added title of papal legate, he went home to take command. In 1850, for the first time in thirty years, he set out for Ireland, bearing an assignment to pacify the country by making the most pious people of Europe more pious still.

Like every ambitious new administrator, Cullen naturally found much to deplore in his predecessor. The Irish bishops were inclined to go each his own way, especially the popular and politically adventuresome John Mac-Hale. Laxness of discipline had proved its dangers in the 1848 political crisis by the absence of any single, dominant, clear episcopal voice. The bishops had publicly split on the question of mixed education, an issue which found Cullen and MacHale by accident on the same side, both in strong opposition. But other bishops had cooperated with Peel's colleges, and one of them actually sat upon the "godless" college governing board. These divisions, Cullen thought, must cease.

Cullen found dangerous tendencies also at work among the laity. Gavan Duffy proclaimed his dutiful Catholicism in a clear voice and fathered a nun and two priests-to-be, besides seven more good Catholic offspring, but Cullen spotted him as an enemy of the faith, the most convenient symbol for the entire liberal-literary complex of Young Italy and Mazzini, of Young Ireland and its memory of Davis as "our guide and prophet," of the *Nation*'s songs, of Ballingarry and the other heresies that Pius IX's new political orientation detested. Duffy reported that His Grace always gave the appearance of friendliness toward him; but Cullen's private remarks show that he had despised Duffy from the start—"a wicked man, to act with whom, after his conduct in 1848, was impossible until he had fasted fifty years on bread and water."[20]

For Cullen to have harbored fears of Duffy's radicalism was not very discriminating, and his judgment was in general tinged with paranoia. Yet he had a point. While the *Nation* had cooled off noticeably since Speranza's bacchanal in the week of Ballingarry, it still carried unrepentant echoes of the old defiance. It followed all the doings of Meagher, Mitchel, Smith O'Brien, and the other felons in Van Diemen's Land, and reported their opinions as though it were still the year 1848. Meagher's ten-thousand-word letter from overseas describing his week in Tipperary during the insurrection was printed in installments. And when one of the American exiles, Dalton Williams, sent word that he had decided to settle down in Mobile and never return to Ireland, the *Nation* carried a reminiscence of his deeds of 1848 and reprinted one of his bloodthirsty ballads, once used as court evidence against the Repealers in the state trials:

Let the trumpets ring triumph! The tyrant is slain!
He reels o'er his charger deep-pierced through the brain;
And his myriads are flying, like leaves on the gale—
But who shall escape from our hills with the tale?

For the arrows of vengeance are showering like rain,
And choke the strong rivers with islands of slain,
Till thy waves, lordly Shannon, all crimsonly flow,
Like the billows of hell, with the blood of the foe.

Duffy might not be John Mitchel, but as Cullen could see, neither was he ready for fifty years of bread and water. It was distressing to note that the dangerous man was not only back in politics again but using priests for his vote canvassers.

V

Archbishop Cullen, like Duffy, was disinclined to languor. After he had been consecrated at Armagh, he sent out an immediate call to the Irish bishops to gather for the first time in six hundred years in synodical convocation. For meeting place he chose the cathedral of Thurles, in the nesting ground of the Tipperary insurrection of 1848 and of the new Tenant League. The synod went into session in the summer of 1850, just at the close of the first Tenant League convention. Newspapermen who journeyed down to Thurles to report the spectacle noted the contrast, soon to grow into an open hostility, between "the firm, vigorous energy of Dr. MacHale . . . and the calm, thoughtful, saintly suavity of Dr. Cullen." They observed that the keynote of the synod was "obey your prelates," and "act with Christian union"; and they learned that the primate would address himself particularly to the condemnation of mixed education.[21]

After the synod had been allowed to grow mellow for a month, Cullen rose to speak the authoritative word. He pointed out first that the Irishman's faith was beset by cunning satanic forces. He implored both the shepherds and their flocks to turn their fullest energy to unmasking these subtle enemies. A place where evil worked its mischief was in the Queen's Colleges set up by Peel. Cooperation with the Queen's Colleges must cease, he said, and debate upon the issue was no longer welcome. "All controversy is now at an end—the judge has spoken—THE QUESTION IS DECIDED."[22]

Next he took note of the "temporal afflictions of the People," of "their corporal wants and sufferings," and he enjoined the bishops to "treat them with all possible kindness and compassion." In one paragraph of his address he found strong words to condemn the extermination of the peasantry: "We behold our poor not only crushed and overwhelmed by the awful visitation of Heaven, but frequently the victims of the most ruthless oppression that ever disgraced the annals of humanity. . . . The desolating track of the exterminator is to be traced in too many parts of the country—in those levelled cottages and roofless abodes. . . ." He warned those who had enriched themselves by this inhuman practice that their greed endangered their chances for eternal salvation.

He wished not to be misunderstood, however. In scolding the exterminator he was not condoning vengeful thoughts in the exterminee. To those who had been injured, his best advice was to cherish the blessedness that accompanies the acceptance of the divine will: "Instead . . . of being impelled by the promptings of that sanguinary resentment, which, far from alleviating their sufferings, never fails to aggravate them with tenfold bitterness and intensity, let them [the exterminated peasants] treasure deep in their hearts, and constantly recall to their remembrance, those consoling promises of Jesus Christ, 'Blessed are ye poor, for yours is the kingdom of heaven. Blessed are ye that hunger now, for you shall be filled.' "[23]

His Grace turned next to the subject of literature, a vehicle of sin and infidelity he considered no less dangerous than the mixed colleges. It had, he said, set about to "unfix the principles" of believers, to spread "anti-Christian philosophy." It had "devoted all its reasoning and research to sapping the foundations of faith." It had gained entrance to the heart by Voltairian "flattering the pride of the intellect," and he was compelled to deplore what Yeats—an incongruous comrade—in a later time called:

> The ravens of unresting thought;
> Flying, crying, to and fro.

Cullen particularly warned the bishops of a new literary danger he had observed developing on the Continent, an effort to "taint the purity" of believers through the charms of poetic pleasure. The grossest sensualism was abroad, so depraved that it would have corrupted "even the society of the Pagan world." It had been translated into "your" (that is, into "his") language, he said; it closed in upon the innocent from every side; "and we bitterly lament to state, [it is] occasionally to be seen even in the precincts of the domestic circle, where nothing defiled should be permitted to enter, but whence the anxious vigilance of parental love, as well as its awful responsibility, ought to have been prompt in banishing, with indignation, everything calculated to taint the purity, or unfix the principles, of its youthful charge."

The reader will recognize in these remarks the definitive formulation of clerical puritanism, a celebrated Irish literary topic. Cullen's synodical warning against the literary assault upon Irish purity laid down the precedent that led in due time to Ireland's theater riots. It also gave us, through reaction, *The Wanderings of Oisin*, "The Fiddler of Dooney," "News for the Delphic Oracle," *Hail and Farewell*, *The Crock of Gold*, and "The Man Who Invented Sin," which somewhat even the score.* Cullen's literary puritanism had no conceivable application to nonreading Ireland in that year of *David Copperfield* and "In Memoriam." It was at most only a far-sighted investment in the distant future of literature, when the charge "Filthy!" could finally take its place beside the charge "Infidel!" as a magical weapon in the Irish critical vocabulary.

One is not sure that literature was foremost in Cullen's mind when he spoke. There is indirect evidence that Cullen's interests included the demographic, a well-recognized concern of the Church. One remembers that the etiology of the famine which traced it to overpopulation appealed overwhelmingly to all political quietists. What else could they say? Malthusianism, it should be remembered, was not devoted solely to the prediction of demographic cataclysm but was concerned also with a study of population checks. The preferred check was "moral restraint," a pure Malthusian category and also a theological one. It is sometimes thought to be a hypocrisy, though Cullen's heirs proved it otherwise. Ireland was to achieve the world's highest propensity to celibacy and to postponed marriage (together with an extremely low rate of illegitimacy), driving up the average age of marriage for Irish males until it stood at just under fifty years. Cullen's preachment was so efficacious that the fears of overpopulation were eventually replaced with Father John A. O'Brien's contrary anxiety over "the vanishing Irish."

A second demographic check was emigration, not a painless choice. Irish literature dwells often on the havoc it caused at home, and American literature from Thoreau onward takes note of the Irish immigrant's savage induction into the New World jungle. But certainly it was preferable to starvation, and Cullen found other agreeable things to say in its favor. The famine, he said later, was "a special dispensation of God to disperse the Irish people over every country of the globe" in order that they might everywhere "lift the standard of the Church."[24]

VI

In Ireland the hierarchy was administratively organized by geographical designation. Dr. Browne, for example, was not just a bishop but the bishop

---

* It gave us, further, the more complex reaction of *Ulysses*, in which Cullen's attitude appears in mirror inversion. With an inflamed sense of sexual sin that would be incomprehensible anywhere in Europe except in the British Isles, Joyce built a major theme of the loathsomeness of the "unclean female loins," surpassing Cullen, St. Kevin, and St. Augustine, whose anatomical discovery Yeats was "not too old" to borrow for his own momentary dip into Joycean matter with the showpiece, "Crazy Jane Talks with the Bishop."

of Elphin, "the Dove of Elphin," as O'Connell called him without any thought of constitutional impropriety. It seemed an inevitable arrangement, recommended by common sense. In England, however, the hierarchy was not so designated. Pius IX, trying to put his house in order, decided in 1850 that it should be, since the flooding of famine refugees into the Midlands had at last given the English Catholic prelates something to administer. A papal bull announced the reorganization. Just at the close of the Synod of Thurles, the English primate, Cardinal Wiseman, issued a pastoral letter under the enlarged title of "Archbishop of Westminster," using the phrase, "we govern and shall continue to govern the counties of Middlesex, Hertfordshire," and so on. The language was somewhat archaic and ritualistic, the timing not the happiest. Protestant militants in England were still brooding over Peel's Maynooth grants and were further irritated by the progress of the Oxford movement, which had won first Newman and now Manning over to Rome amid noisy publicity. The new papal bull stirred up a violent adverse Protestant reaction in England, with the *Times* leading the hue and cry in spite of the private opinion of the editor, who told Charles Greville he thought "the whole thing a gross humbug and a pack of nonsense."

The prime minister himself joined in. Lord John Russell was one of those who felt personally hurt by the Tractarian backsliders. In spite of their sound English upbringing in the Thirty-nine Articles, they had descended to the "mummeries of superstition." But a graver consideration for Russell was his disintegrating parliamentary majority. On Guy Fawkes Eve 1850 he sent a letter on "Papal Aggression" to the Anglican bishop of Durham expressing his "alarm" and "indignation" that the pope should assert "a pretension of supremacy over the realm of England, and a claim to sole and undivided sway, which is inconsistent with the Queen's supremacy." In deference to the bigoted mass hysteria he had himself engendered, he followed up with a legislative attack. In February 1851 he introduced into the House the Ecclesiastical Titles Bill, which would forbid the Catholic bishops from ornamenting themselves with geographical designations on pain of criminal penalties.

Across in Ireland Duffy and his friends in the Tenant League were properly frightened by the rising bigotry. Its effect upon their program to make a "league of the North and South" could only be disastrous. But the delights of Irish sectarianism were never easily resisted, so that Duffy's warnings were scarcely heard. When the Orangemen came into the streets with their big bass drums, hotheaded Catholics also rose to take Russell's bait. His insolence had been all but intolerable, and outrage against his astonishing bill was natural enough. As Duffy feared, the bill was as tempting to opportunist Catholics as to Orangemen.

VII

Rosencrantz and Guildenstern now came forward to the center of the post-famine Irish stage in the persons of a couple of alert adventurers, John Sadleir and William Keogh. They seized upon the opportunity that knocks but once, earning themselves a special ignominy in Irish history. Sadleir was a strong-farmer's son who had risen prodigiously, having organized a chain of savings banks in Tipperary and built a reputation for financial brilliance. A genteel brigand and plunger, he would have been more at home in the company of Jay Gould and Daniel Drew than in the stagnant back-waters of postfamine Ireland.* In 1847 he was elected Whig member for Carlow. Keogh went to the House in the same year, a Peelite member for Athlone, and as late as 1848 he was an unrepentant loyalist. He was a barrister with a knack for platform oratory and an urge to leadership, for he had often heard it said that he resembled Napoleon. He struggled under a hopeless load of debt. "Money is a great object with me," he told a colleague. Both men had discovered that a backbencher was a lonely figure at Westminster, but that anyone commanding a block of votes was somebody else again. Probing the Irish inane in search of some emerging power, Keogh attended the first convention of the Tenant League, while Sadleir made contact with it through his cousin, a Tipperary M.P. Cautious politicians, practicing the art of the possible, they then shied away from the league. They preferred to wait and see, and while they were waiting, the no-popery frenzy broke in England.

The first overt Irish reply to Russell's bill was parliamentary obstruction, as Duffy's scheme for a pledge-bound Irish bloc was put into immediate action in the House of Commons. The original Irish floor leader was George Henry Moore, a member for Mayo, whose ample gifts of astuteness and generosity were inherited only in fragments by his more famous son, the novelist. In spite of Yeats's aspersions on the quality of his blood line, he was one of the most distinguished Irishmen of the century, combining liberal nationalism, great oratorical power, an acid wit, impressive land-holdings in west Mayo, and, a not inconsequential item of Irish prestige, the famous racing stable immortalized in his son's novel, *Esther Waters*. Moore gathered a nucleus of angry Irish members and pledged them to vote against whatever ministry was in power, under all circumstances, in the hope of paralyzing the work of the House of Commons until the Irish demands were met. Twenty members were recruited to Moore's caucus, barely a fifth of the whole Irish delegation, but enough to be heard. There were interesting possibilities in the scheme, attractive to Sadleir and Keogh.

* The boldness of his swindles was captured for literature through Mr. Merdle in *Little Dorrit*, for whom he was the life model.

They joined up and were such vociferous nuisances in obstructing the House that they won for the little caucus the name, "The Pope's Brass Band."

Back home the pair teamed up with Cullen to organize Catholic indignation committees in the countryside. These coalesced in the summer of 1851 in a great Dublin aggregate mass meeting to establish the Catholic Defense Association, with Cullen in the chair, Keogh in command, and Sadleir on the flank giving support with an ambitious new Dublin weekly, the *Telegraph*, holier than Lucas' *Tablet*, more patriotic than Duffy's *Nation*, more respectable than either, and selling for half their price, for he was said to be a financial wizard.

The Ecclesiastical Titles Bill became law, but still Russell could not save his ministry, the same that had long ago promised O'Connell "comprehensive measures of relief." It collapsed in February 1851 and was succeeded by an interim government under Lord Derby pending general elections. The Tenant League organizers, priests in the south and preachers in Ulster, charged out into the country, determined to fight the election on the land question. Sadleir and Keogh now found the Tenant League's political organization attractive and they edged in, though without receiving a hospitable welcome. At a meeting in Cork a Tenant Leaguer accused Keogh to his face of being "not sincere." In excited denial he swore with the awful formula, "so help me God," twice repeated, that "so help me God, no matter who the Minister may be, no matter who the party in power may be, I will neither support that Minister nor that party unless he comes into power prepared to carry the measures which universal popular Ireland demands."[25]

The election was a triumph for the Tenant League. Virtually all the Irish Whigs were defeated. The strength of the Irish bloc doubled to forty, roughly the number with which Parnell would begin his work in 1880. Duffy himself was elected for New Ross, and on election night his jubilant backers lit bonfires on the hilltops to honor the new M.P. who only three years before had been fighting in the courts for his life. The celebration was premature, a situation not without parallels in other times and places.

The sectarian issue lost the Tenant League its foothold in Ulster. As Duffy had feared, every league candidate lost there. The Ulsterman Sharman Crawford, parliamentary leader of the Irish agrarians, had with a grand gesture given up his seat for Rochdale to stand for Orange Down, and lost. "Shame on the North," said Duffy's leading article. John Stuart Mill, whom Duffy and Lucas invited to come over and stand for election in Ulster as a Tenant Leaguer, was able to congratulate himself that he had stayed at home. In the south, on the other hand, the Tenant League had cashed in nicely on the revulsion against the Ecclesiastical Titles Act. Even if sectarianism had been an unwelcome ally, the tenant movement was now "baptized in the Holy Well."

When the House of Commons reconvened, Lord Derby's ministry was immediately toppled. Lord Aberdeen was called upon to form a new coalition, completed in the closing hours of 1852. The perennial Lord John Russell was back as one of the ministers, also Lord Palmerston. Gladstone was chancellor of the exchequer. But for surprised Irishmen, by far the most interesting names in the new government were those of William Keogh, solicitor general, and John Sadleir, junior lord of the treasury. Lord Aberdeen had let it be known privately that the Ecclesiastical Titles Act was to be henceforth a dead letter, and he had given the place-seekers the places they sought. Instantly the Tenant League's pledge-bound bloc was cut in half and left with nothing but its bold campaign promises for souvenir. And what of those peasants who had voted for the league in spite of threats of eviction? *Sauve qui peut!*

VIII

Next the Tenant League found itself deprived of its clerical organizers, for as Newman learned from the grapevine, Cullen was "thick with the Government."[26] The curate who had managed Duffy's election victory, Father Doyle of New Ross, was translated to an inferior parish up on the mountainside. Then Father O'Shea and Father Keefe of Callan, the founders of the Tenant League, were threatened with suspension and forbidden from further political activity. The National Council of Bishops meanwhile met to lay down the general guideline, "no priests in politics"—unless a bishop approved. If this interference continued, said Duffy, the game was finished, "for elections could no more be won without the help of the local priests than Charles Edward could have raised the Scottish Highlands without the help of their chiefs."[27]

Duffy concluded that the enigma of Cullen's behavior was not very profound after all. A friend wrote him an explanation that fitted all the parts together to his satisfaction: "Rome returns to her design of treating Ireland as an intrenched camp of Catholicity in the heart of the British Empire, capable of leavening the whole Empire—nay, the whole Anglo-Saxon race —and devotes every nerve to that end. But the first postulate is the pacification of Ireland. Ireland must be thoroughly imperialized, legalized, welded into England. Paul Cullen succeeded Castlereagh."[28] Duffy was ready to surrender. Serving on the House committee that set up home rule for Australia, he had made himself expert on the attractive new colony. He sold the *Nation*, resigned his seat in the House, and in the autumn of 1855 sailed for Sydney. In his last leading article as editor of the *Nation*, he squared all his accounts with Cullen and Keogh, leaving behind a blistering indictment. His peroration was long remembered for its piquancy: ". . . there seems to be no more hope for the Irish Cause than for the corpse on the dissecting-table."[29]

Duffy watched from the antipodes the fulfillment of his predictions. About the time of his departure, rumors circulated that Sadleir's banking empire was unsound, and in Duffy's last glimpse of him in the House, he "looked wild, haggard, and repulsive." To postpone disaster he began forging title deeds to use as collateral for loans from the London banks. When he could borrow no more, a run closed his central Tipperary bank. Auditors discovered that its assets were one-tenth its deposits. Sadleir's personal account had been two hundred thousand pounds overdrawn, apparently to buy votes and to subsidize the devout journalism of the *Telegraph*. Next morning he was found dead on Hampstead Heath, lying like James Steerforth with his head on his arm. Irish nationalists find relish in adding the detail that "a silver tankard smelling strongly of prussic acid was at his side." His brother, also an M.P., fled the country to escape prosecution; and his right bower, Edmund O'Flaherty, another M.P., who had gone into the Aberdeen government as commissioner of income tax and had been described by Keogh in the House as possessing "honor, veracity, and high character," also turned up missing, leaving fifteen thousand pounds of unpaid debts behind him. Keogh himself, however, sailed unharmed through the storm that wrecked his swindling intimates. He had already moved up from solicitor general to attorney general, and in the midst of the Sadleir scandal the government with striking coolness of nerve elevated him to the bench.

With Duffy's departure for Australia, the last of the 1848 leaders was gone. Ireland entered the limbo known to political science as a condition of political vacuum. In the vacuum, Cullen's ultramontane faction expanded comfortably. O'Connell's last regressive stratagem, the Whig alliance—"to get a little something for Ireland," as he used to say—became the pillar of Irish politics. The Whigs had come back into power in early 1855 under Lord Palmerston, a great Ascendancy landlord and therefore given to what Yeats called "sweet laughing eagle thought" and to an agrarian philosophy summed up in his simple proposition, "tenant right is landlord wrong." Palmerston unfortunately preferred Mazzini to Pio Nono, but he was otherwise sound, and Cullen became thicker than ever with the government.

Cullen valued religious pomp, so that new churches were rising all over Ireland as parish committees mobilized to attack two centuries of arrears in the ecclesiastical building program. Otherwise, not one of Catholic Ireland's deprivations had been even confronted, let alone cured. Cardinal Wiseman visited Ireland in 1858 and noted that "religious progress is far in advance of what is considered social improvement."[30] The country could not sustain its own people, so that year after year the tide of human beings moved out of the countryside down to the Galway, Cork, and Dublin docks and went on board ship, bound for other lands. They carried abroad Cullen's mission to the heathens, infidels, and Protestants, but also the deep sensation of having been unforgivably wronged that had stirred their generation of Irish history and made it "remembered forever."

CHAPTER 9

John Mitchel after '48

I

While Gavan Duffy was trying his hand in agrarianism, his old comrades were scrambling back on their feet. Archbishop Cullen instructed Dr. Newman to keep them out of the new Catholic university, recently opened to compete with the godless Queen's Colleges. But several of them got in all the same. Said Newman: "There was a knot of men who, in 1848, had been quasi-rebels. They were clever men and had cooled down, most of them. I did not care much for their political opinions. Dr. Moriarty introduced them to me and I made them professors."[1]

The felons and exiles overseas were not so easily accommodated. Around the world Young Irelanders turned up in odd places—in Brisbane, Calcutta, Ottawa, New York, Boston, even in Helena, Montana, where a burnished copper statue preserves to this day the memory of Thomas Meagher, the same who scorned to stigmatize the sword. All of these men had tasted defeat and watched the wreck of their careers; some had slipped quietly into the service of the British Empire, and some, like Darcy M'Gee, had turned venomously anti-Irish. But nobody wept and said "they went forth to the battle but they always fell," and nobody thought to make a public exhibition of himself as one who had been duped and made disenchanted. "It was well to have been young then," said John O'Leary, "and, now that I am growing old, my pulse beats quicker as memory brings back, imperfectly indeed but still vividly, the vision of how I felt and what I thought in that famous year."[2]

Soul-searching there was in plenty, some of it excruciating. Smith O'Brien brooded the rest of his life over his failure, which he was inclined to attribute less to his own inadequacies than to the refusal of the tormented Irish people to rise at his call. He was especially exasperated against the Tipperary and Kilkenny priests who had countermanded his call to insurrection: "The fact is recorded in our annals that the people preferred to die of starvation at home, or to flee as voluntary exiles to other lands, rather than to fight for their lives or liberties."[3] Among the 1848 leaders he was the most defeatist,

and his message for the coming Irish generations was that if they were thinking of armed resistance against English rule, they should forget it. Yet he
rebuffed with dignity all the government's hints that Her Majesty's pardon
awaited only a word or two of repentance. These words never came and in
time he was pardoned without them. His quixotic impulses never came to
rest, and shortly before he died he was last heard flashing a message of succor to the distant Poles: "Shall Poland be left unaided, shall she be deserted,
by Ireland? . . . I proudly answer, No! Ireland to the rescue! Ireland to
the rescue of Poland."[4] In the end the Irish repaid his memory with his own
brand of painful affection.

II

The most frenzied 1848 post-mortem was undoubtedly John Mitchel's.
Banishment shattered him: "An exile in my circumstances is a branch cut
from its tree; it is dead and has but an affectation of life."[5] The once-
fearless patriot suddenly found himself a lonely and terrified straggler,
Bricriu Poison-Tongue soured in the prison hulks and half-maddened by
doubts and despair. This new Mitchel unburdened himself eloquently in
the pages of his *Jail Journal*, something of a pioneer experiment in the expression of *ressentiment*, a work which Yeats commended for its "music and
personality"[6] and from which he borrowed those harsher Carlylean elements
of his own thought that are usually identified loosely as "Nietzschean."

Jail Journal opens in a fit of violent weeping, followed by a prolonged
deliberation on suicide. Mitchel was fascinated by the phenomenon of the
split personality. Thus Mangan he remembered as not one person but two,
"one well known to the Muses, the other to the police." Everybody, in fact,
was really double. "Every man," he said, "holds chained up within him a
madman."[7] An early section of *Jail Journal*, a dozen extraordinary pages,
describes a mind watching itself disintegrate through a *hic et ille* debate, on
one side a hysteric called "Ego" and on the other his timid adversary
"Doppelganger," representing the commonplace. "I do observe a singular
change in you of late days," says Doppelganger, "almost a tinge of atrocity,"
a mood "blacker than mere natural malignity." Welcoming the indictment,
Ego proclaims that "Death is Birth," unwitting endorsement for Baudelaire's "*Vive la mort!*" on the Paris barricades in that same eventful year.
Ego recommends barbarism as good medicine, declaring it to be the force
behind all the larger patterns of human advance. Kings and lords, he says,
are now obsolete, and will remain so, but only "until we shall have advanced
to them again via barbarism, in the cyclical progress of the species,"[8]
broaching an Irish literary theme made perhaps all too familiar in a later
time. When the conventional Doppelganger has been thoroughly cowed by

Ego's brilliance, the two drink together to the toast, "Artificial Drainage," a bloody pun on one of the public works proposals for the famine.

Isolated, confused in his bearings, Mitchel had little capability left but for dissociated anger. Lurid daydreams of violence whirled through his headlong thought: "I wish at times to be awake, long for a rattling, sky-rending, forest-crashing, earth-shaking thunder storm, and fancy that the lightning of heaven would shoot a sharper life into blood and brain."[9]

His blackest thoughts grew from the refusal of the Young Ireland leaders to try to rescue him from jail. It will be remembered that this issue was excitedly argued at the time, with the clubmen in favor and Gavan Duffy opposed. Citing the impersonal logic of strategy, Mitchel had urged, as I have already told, that his rescue should signal an insurrection "then and there." The alternative, the decision actually taken, had led to Ballingarry, whereas his own plan must surely have succeeded, he thought. When he asked himself why he who was so right was not listened to by his comrades, who were so wrong, he never failed to make generous allowance for their nobility of intent. And yet he had to confess to himself that they had been guided by a certain stupidity, too, and even cowardice, with perhaps a touch of personal malice; for he could not wholly avoid looking at the council's decision from a personal viewpoint, he being the goat. All these pusillanimous Girondist vices he charged up against one convenient source, the "dastard," Mr. "Give-in" Duffy, whom he thenceforth insulted incessantly, thus opening up one of those symptomatic feuds that always accompanied an Irish political downswing. This vendetta was so prolonged that forty years later Yeats was able to dip into it for a quick tactical gain.[10]

When the police delivered Mitchel aboard the armed steamer *Shearwater* at the North Wall, his chains were taken off and he was escorted to an officer's private cabin aft. He took his last look at Dublin Bay, and finding pen and paper, he wrote:

> After all, for what has this sacrifice been made? . . . What *have* I gained? Questions truly which it behoves me to ask and answer on this evening of my last day (it may be) of civil existence. Dublin City, with its bay and pleasant villas—city of bellowing slaves—villas of genteel dastards—lies now behind us, and the sun has set behind the blue peaks of Wicklow, as we steam past Bray Head, where the Vale of Shanganagh, sloping softly from the Golden Spears, sends its bright river murmuring to the sea. And I am on the first stage of my way, faring to what regions of unknown horror? And may never, never—never more, O, Ireland!—my mother and queen!—see vale, or hill, or murmuring stream of thine. And *why*?[11]

So soon had Timon risen up to guide the despairing patriot. His genteel dastards need no further gloss here, but the bellowing slaves were a harshness not expected. For six months past he had placed his hopes increasingly in the spontaneous militance of the Dublin clubs. Rank and filers had prepared the scheme for his jail rescue, then the council had forbidden them to act. But even against orders they were ready to proceed on their own. "Let no foul tongue spit its sarcasm upon the people," said Meagher in recalling the incident. "They were ready for the sacrifice, and had the word been given the stars would burn tonight above a thousand crimsoned graves." When the Confederate council came to his cell with a letter already prepared in his name and instructing the clubs not to attempt a rescue, Mitchel had refused to sign it. Just so. But still they had not risen. He waited and they never came, except to the North Wall to see him removed in fetters.

Honor forbade that he should press his suspicion of betrayal in his own name, but he found a quotation from Isaiah that he felt to be worth quoting: "I have trodden the winepress alone, and of the people there was none with me; for I will tread them in mine anger and trample them in my fury, and their blood shall be sprinkled upon my garments and I will stain all my raiment. For the day of vengeance is in my heart."[12] He could also transfer his hurt to the parallel case of Smith O'Brien, Meagher, and MacManus, under death sentence two months later, awaiting rescue themselves in Tipperary:

> A few daring spirits, headed by O'Mahony, once contemplated an attack and rescue; but the people had been too grievously frightened by the priests (on account of their miserable pauper souls), and too effectually starved by the government, to be equal to so dashing an exploit: and so that solemn and elaborate insult was once more put upon our name and nation; and the four men who had sought to save their people from so abject a condition lay undisturbed in Clonmel gaol, sentenced to death. Considering which humiliating picture, one might be tempted to repeat the bitter words of Don Juan D'Aguila—"Surely Christ never died for *this* people!"[13]

We catch here the harsh strains of a familiar Irish air. This theme, if Mitchel had chosen to embellish it, could have swelled to the familiar refrain of a later time: "Ireland is the old sow that eats her farrow." But at this point he abruptly turned back. So, Christ had not died for the Irish; then his next word was "yet" and his next sentence began: "Yet whosoever had studied even the imperfect sketch which I have given of the potent and minutely elaborate system of oppression . . . ," and so on, his forgiveness outpacing his anger. What checked him here is uncertain. Perhaps it was some instinct of pride that forbade him to dishonor the perfection of his curtain speech in Green Street Courthouse, when he arose in the dock to tell the sentencing judge: "I have done my part also." He possessed, too, a

137

strain of humility hidden by his public ferocity. After all, he was one who had seen a famine winter in Galway. He had caught pained glimpses, also, of Young Ireland's own shortcomings, which he had shared in part—its "rose colored puff-clouds," its "deleterious flatulent pabulum." The teakwood timbers of a prison ship were formidable stuff, he said, elements in a real world where "nobody seems to be sensible of the merits and fame of those fine young literary men, who, from their little coterie, breathed a new soul into Ireland." In the same chastened mood he reconsidered his past harshness toward O'Connell's memory and softened it somewhat, recognizing now an imperfect earthy strength not seen before.[14]

Whatever it was that held his latent animosity toward Ireland suspended, it was not benevolence. He had dropped that into the bay at the North Wall and had reverted to his earliest mentors, Jeremiah and Calvin, the prophets of his boyhood Presbyterianism, and especially to Carlyle, "the only man in these latter days who produces what can properly be termed books."[15] A newer guide he found in Joseph de Maistre, the eulogist of hangmen. Henceforth he saw mankind as one vast festering mass of depravity, Irishmen excepted.

III

Jail Journal is a sustained nausea. Mitchel could loathe as enthusiastically as "noster Thomas" himself. He hated capitalists and he hated socialists, those creatures "somewhat worse than wild beasts." He hated the English, as everybody knows, but he hated the Yankees no less. "I despise the civilization of the nineteenth century," he said, "and its two highest expressions and grandest hopes most especially."[16] He hated the strong, also the weak. He was against many things: "comfort" and "happiness," Teufelsdröckh's favorite abominations; "snivelling jackasses"; commerce; steam engines; "pudding and praise and profit"; Jews; the "stratified debris" of popular literature; Bacon, Macaulay, and also Mazzini; the naturalist von Humboldt, who had blasphemously constructed a "cyanometer" to measure the blueness of the very empyrean; thin-skinned penology, which "so richly rewards" criminals; sentimentalists who opposed strangulation. Oddly, he was against flogging, now that he had actually seen men flogged in the British penal colonies. But he soon corrected for this drift toward decadence: there would be no scourging in the army of the future Irish republic, he said; instead, all second offenders would be shot. Above all, he was against "cant," Carlyle's verbal tic for the extermination of the irksome.

And what was he not against? He discovered that he had a fondness for Negro slavery. When his prison ship dropped anchor at Pernambuco, he looked about him to locate the picturesque, like any tourist in Kerry. His eye fell upon the Brazilian slaves who had rowed out to the warship in small boats. He would not himself like to own slaves, yet they did have their charm, "fat and merry, obviously not overworked or underfed," and it pleased him to watch the "lazy rogues, lolling in their boats, sucking a piece of green sugar cane."[17] On reaching the United States in 1853 after having escaped from Van Diemen's Land, he found slavery still more attractive. His first American quarrel was with the antislavery faction in the Know-Nothing party, who combined abolition with a raucous no-popery agitation that sounded for his taste too much like the Orangemen back home in Newry. He extended his antipathy to abolitionists in general, whom he seems to have considered a subbranch of the Know-Nothing party. To make his opinion heard, he started a proslavery newspaper in New York, the *Citizen*.

Through the spring and summer of 1854 the *Citizen* moved in a whirl-wind of projects and excitements. There was a lengthy public feud with Gavan Duffy. There was a fight with Archbishop Hughes of New York, running in installments through many months, over the ethics of armed force in Irish nationalism. Riding high, Mitchel wrote to the archbishop: "The Constitution of America (which may God long preserve!) happily fixes a bit between the teeth of you all; and clips your claws and draws your fangs. . . . Although your Grace should wear a Hat as red as fire, you will hardly in our times preside at an *auto da fé* in the Park."[18] There was the war in the Crimea, where England would have been in mortal danger had it not been for the mix-up that placed France, Ireland's ally, on England's side. There was excited talk about a "Young America" to which Mitchel could not but be spiritually in tune. Young America came forward with a plan to occupy Cuba and Japan "ahead of the English," and Mitchel wanted to be there. There was a weekly crisis over the congressional fortunes of the Nebraska bill, which Mitchel followed as a southern partisan, for his interest had now fixed itself upon the defense of slavery.

There lived in Dublin at the time an elderly philanthropist named James Haughton, a wealthy merchant who had supported Repeal and Young Ireland, and beyond that, most of the humanitarian causes of the time, including abolition. When the escaped Irish felons reached America, he wrote them urging that they join him in abolition as he had joined them in Repeal. Mitchel replied in an insolent open letter, published in the *Citizen*, accusing Haughton, "an amiable monomaniac," of feeling indifferent to the famine but being seized "with a paroxysm of violent sympathy with the fat negroes of America."[19] He concluded: "We deny that it is a crime or a wrong, or even a peccadillo, to hold slaves, to sell slaves, to keep slaves to their work by flogging or other needful coercion; we only wish we had a good plantation well stocked with healthy negroes in Alabama."[20] Henry

Ward Beecher entered the dispute, crying "Fallen! Uprooted!" and pointing to Mitchel's inconsistency. In Ireland he was for freedom, but in America he was against it. Mitchel's reply to Beecher reminded that "most learned clerk" that Socrates, Christ, and Thomas Jefferson, not to mention Leonidas and Themistocles, had approved of slavery, or at least had not disapproved, and that Beecher's attitude could best be described by one word—cant.

No newspaper could long survive this manic pace, and before the year was out Mitchel was forced to sell the *Citizen* and move on. "The 'Alabama Plantation' swept off ten thousand readers at one blow," he said in farewell. "Archbishop Philo-Veritas [Hughes] with his pastoral crozier drew away a few thousand more. The Reverend Mr. Beecher rushed upon me with his tomahawk at one side: some Catholic priests cursed me from their altars at the other." But he had won good friends elsewhere. He was invited to visit Virginia, and there he saw the "luckiest, jolliest, and *freest* negroes on the face of the earth," and learned that "the cause of negro slavery is the cause of true philanthropy." From New Orleans he wrote: "How deeply and urgently this nation needs a good rattling war—a war with some nation that is fairly its match, to occupy its mind and give a career to its craving and impassioned youth. I tell you it is like Carleton's tailor, 'blue moulded for want of a *baytin*'; it will blow up, like any other high-pressure steam-boiler; and it is not insured."[21] He enjoyed such gracious southern hospitality that he flounced out of New York, clipped his Mosaic beard back to a goatee, and set up as editor of a proslavery paper, the *Southern Citizen*, in Knoxville.

When the Civil War began, he moved to Richmond as editor of the *Enquirer* and later the *Examiner*. Even after Grant opened his *coup de grâce* campaign around Petersburg in 1864, he still believed the South's prospects excellent, arguing that the North, like old England, was financially bankrupt if the truth were known—"the greenbacks support the war and the war supports the greenbacks." He sent his three sons into the Confederate army. Captain James survived three years with Lee; but Private Willy enlisted in Pickett's division and died at Gettysburg, and Captain John died of wounds at Fort Sumter at the close of the war. Immediately after Appomattox, Mitchel hastened north again. While all the northern newspapers were still in shock from Lincoln's assassination, he turned up in New York, witty and unreconstructed, to begin work as editor of the copperhead newspaper, the *Daily News*. "I never devoured my enemies, roast or boiled," he said. "I ask leave of nobody to come to this city." His plan, so the *Times* thought, was evidently to publish "another *Richmond Enquirer* adapted to a northern latitude."[22] He wrote his mother that "New York is the most Southern city in America," confidence that proved oversanguine. The Union army at that time held only two prisoners on general charges of war crimes, both confined at Fortress Monroe, Virginia. Best known was Jefferson Davis; the other was Senator Clay of Alabama. Then one day there was a third prisoner taking his exercise in the fortress yard: John Mitchel. He had been arrested at the *Daily News* office and taken aboard a Virginia-bound naval vessel before his friends could appear with a writ of habeas corpus.

Those friends who were powerless to save Mitchel from imprisonment were Irish-American patriots. Four months later, their pressure on Secretary of War Stanton secured his release on condition that he leave the United States. He went then to Paris, where he received a letter from his son, Captain James, asking him to sit down and compose a vindication of the defeated South. Mitchel had suddenly had enough of that lost cause: "I must admit that I grudge it what it cost us . . . the lives of our two sons in defence of a country which, after all, was not their own." He wrote his wife to stop James from making "a martyr of himself"—"it is quite a bad trade. . . . I had rather be a farmer."[23] Guided by this practical advice James underwent transfiguration, emerging as a successful New York politician. He rose to the rank of fire marshal and begot a son who, thanks to the warm memories of his grandfather's name on Third Avenue, was in the fullness of time elected an anti-Tammany mayor of New York City.

Mitchel's proslavery exploits delighted the English press, which spread the scandal around the world as proof of the general insanity of Irish nationalism. He had alienated many other good friends of the Irish besides Beecher and Haughton. To salvage an important Irish reputation needed a vigorous justification. Mitchel himself offered several apologies. We have already heard him say that every man is half mad, an invitation to value him for his worth and charitably to forget the rest. He also hinted that he was a Promethean man, born to defy all authority, James Joyce ahead of his time. The hint was eagerly followed up by his biographer, William Dillon, who observed of the Fortress Monroe episode: "It is to be remembered that there were others before John Mitchel who found it as hard as he did to get along peaceably with the powers that be, and whom, nevertheless, the judgment of succeeding ages has not condemned—notably Socrates, and a greater than Socrates."[24]

IV

Mitchel's proslavery persuasion was an especially crude expression of Irish particularism, the same subbranch of xenophobia that had led O'Connell to expel infidel Chartists and frenchified Young Irelanders from the Repeal Association. Irish apologists commonly defend Mitchel on the same grounds —when an Irish patriot went overseas and quarreled with the citizens there, necessarily he was right and they were wrong. Dillon assured us that Mitchel's satirical rejoinder to Beecher's "abolitionist cant" was, all in all, "equal to anything in Swift."[25] A fierce patriot of a later day, Arthur Griffith, explained Mitchel's American career in this way: "At the conclusion of the American Civil War he was imprisoned by the Yankee Government, which, under the guise of philanthropy and liberty had violated the States rights of the South. Mitchel's argument for the South could not be countered by the Northern logicians, but it was punished with imprisonment and attempted indignity."[26] As Yeats often warned us, Griffith was not a subtle adversary with whom one exchanged light rapier wit.

A philosophical self-defense is preserved in Mitchel's correspondence with Father Kenyon. In the original *Citizen*, Father Kenyon was cited as an ethical authority. He had declared that "Mr. Mitchel's published opinions about Negro slavery" were of such sort "as the truest lover of liberty and of the Catholic religion may lawfully adopt"; and he had expanded on the thought with whimsical humor: "We are all slaves."[27] When Mitchel started the *Southern Citizen* in Knoxville, he sent Father Kenyon a prospectus, expecting more genial wit. Instead he received a sharp rebuff, for constancy was not Father Kenyon's primary tincture: "Actively to promote the [slave] system for its own sake would be something monstrous."

Not so, replied Mitchel; in Dublin he had "specially hated the *British system*" and had fought it with "less devotion to truth and justice than raging wrath against cant and insolence." In Knoxville he was really doing the same brave work, for the British system was not confined to the British Isles: "Now I meet that evil power here also; he is everywhere, and nowhere more active and mischievous than in these United States," which had succumbed like Lord John Russell and Nassau Senior to the greedy lust for commerce, "obscenist of spirits."[28] Familiar words, reminiscent of Davis' attack on Englishism and Yankeeism in his defeatist phase and foretelling the poetical flood to come. To the alert, Mitchel's argument might have given warning that if beautiful, lofty words exalting spirit over matter could defend slavery, they could equally well justify any action whatsoever.

The Southern slaveowners were in Mitchel's opinion hostile to commerce and immune from cupidity. For a man whose lifelong pride was his ability to smell out cant, this myth of a nation of anticommercial slaveowners was rather insensitive. Mitchel's American fugue must always weigh in the judgment of his place in history, even in Irish history, for it gave a glimpse of what problems his followers would quickly have found in his leadership had the Irish cards in 1848 been dealt in his favor. His failure was not unique, however, but mirrored the aberrations that beset the typical provincial agrarian in the crises of the times. Mitchel resembled Cobbett in his mixture of rare good sense with fatuity; and he resembled Carlyle himself, whose downward path from *Chartism* to the *Latter Day Pamphlets* after the shocks of 1848 was an exact parallel to Mitchel's course from the *United*

Irishman to the *Southern Citizen.* Devin Reilly, Mitchel's closest disciple, had sensed the hazards of agrarianism pure and simple and had sent the master the oracular warning, unheeded, that Ireland was "the *avant garde* into Europe, or the Vendée." Mitchel attempted a violent fusion of both, creating the wild schizoid flair admired by Yeats as "personality." Except for literary purposes, personality at such a price hardly seemed worthwhile.

V

With the passing years, Mitchel's demoralization healed and the familiar patriot of the *United Irishman* came back to life. Assuming the role of a historian, he retraced all the steps leading to his 1848 downfall, reasserting and augmenting his original apologia. The fruit of this effort was a series of memoirs of the troubled times beginning with "An Apology for the British Government in Ireland," published serially in the *Nation* in 1858, recast in 1860 as *The Last Conquest of Ireland (Perhaps)*, and further rewritten twice afterward.

While Mitchel's shadow Ego was busy frisking in proslavery American politics in his extraordinary fashion, his stodgy friend Doppelganger was still brooding on the Irish issues of 1848. The world since then being manifestly too much for Mitchel to comprehend, he chose to go back and pick up the thread where he had lost it at the North Wall. He set about to dignify and monumentalize his thoughts and deeds at the pinnacle of his life, when his enemies were Irish landlords and English dragoons instead of Henry Ward Beecher and Abraham Lincoln. His affair of the heart with aristocratic Virginia planters had not tempered his low opinion of their Irish counterparts. Of Irish landlords he continued to believe as he had believed in the heat of the crisis, that the famine had proved them to be not only useless and "thick-headed" but cowards as well. His retrospective manner was confident and casual, sensing correctly that Irish opinion had settled the dispute in his favor with resounding finality. Everybody was now abusing the landlords. "They convicted us of guilt," said Yeats on behalf of the Sligo gentry. They did that, much thanks to John Mitchel.

Mitchel still insisted that English administrators had "sent the Famine." As we have seen, he attacked the act of God theory of the famine and substituted for it a theory of mass murder masked as charity. Merely on the face of it, his charge certainly sounded incredible; for did Lord John Russell not speak the tongue that Shakespeare spake? Even to those intimate with the hunger, Mitchel's accusation was not always self-evident truth;* but

---

* Roger MacHugh found that the famine experiences are "as real to the inhabitants today as are the events of last year." He also found that the act of God rather than mass murder is the more current folk explanation of the disaster. See MacHugh, "The Famine in Irish Oral Tradition," in *The Great Famine*, ed. Edwards and Williams, p. 391.

neither was it hard to believe. Michael Davitt, a standard case, thought the famine the crowning unforgivable sin of English rule in Ireland, and he put his anger in the strongest language he knew: "Nothing more inhumanly selfish and base is found to the disgrace of any class in any crisis in the history of civilized society."[29]

VI

After Carleton's time, the famine seldom penetrated the imagination of Irish writers. Neither the catastrophe nor the resulting anger impinged at all upon George Moore, a Catholic, or on Lady Gregory, an Anglican, though both were born into the Connaught gentry just as the hunger subsided; or on Sean O'Casey or James Stephens the poet, native Dubliners of the next generation. After all, the traditional apology, "words cannot describe," is unbecoming in a professional writer. Yet there exists a small genre of retrospective famine literature, and in it some sort of reaction to Mitchel's accusations is necessarily involved.

Liam O'Flaherty is a principal contributor to the genre with his impressive naturalistic novel, *Famine* (1937). Its debt to Mitchel is rather more to the *Jail Journal*'s "bellowing slaves" than to the *United Irishman*'s hundred thousand flashing pikes; for O'Flaherty envisioned the Irish peasantry as a "horde of ants" not unworthy to be candidates for extermination. The second chief exhibit is Yeats's *Countess Cathleen*. It too recalls Mitchel when one of the characters discovers the act of God theory to be a very poor recommendation for the Irishman's traditional worship:

> God and God's mother nod and sleep—at last
> They have grown weary of the prayers and candles,
> And Satan pours the famine from his bag,
> He does not nod, nor sleep, nor droop his eyelids;
> I am half mindful to go pray to him. . . .[30]

But the speaker is a revolting character, a "materialist," so that Yeats's own attitude remains enigmatical. His attention to Irish grievances was always slight and sustained only with difficulty. As soon as convenient his play turned to a more congenial theme, decidedly anti-Mitchelite, the exaltation of the supernatural benevolence of the Irish aristocracy toward the deserving poor. Later he abandoned Mitchel's stance altogether, complaining that it was "rancorous and devil possessed."

In *Ulysses* Mitchel's accusation is indignantly repelled. Born Anglophobe though he was, Joyce thought the charge of mass murder deranged, at least in the 1904 version he had heard repeated about Dublin, once too often, apparently. His satire on the gaseous patriotism of "the citizen" presents the famine legend as compounded cliché and imposture:

They were driven out of house and home in the black 47. Their mudcabins and their shielings by the roadside were laid low by the batteringram and the *Times* rubbed its hands and told the whitelivered Saxons there would soon be as few Irish in Ireland as redskins in America. Even the grand Turk sent us his piastres. But the Sassenach tried to starve the nation at home while the land was full of crops that the British hyenas bought and sold in Rio de Janeiro. Ay, they drove out the peasants in hordes. Twenty thousand of them died in the coffinships.[31]

Many readers have found pleasure in Joyce's refusal to traffic with such xenophobia. But recent historical scholarship has disturbed the mellow comforts of their sapience and tends to confirm Mitchel's most lurid accusations. The Irish historians who contributed to the volume of essays called *The Great Famine* (1957) reconnoitered Mitchel's ground and corrected his report somewhat, mostly in the details. Thomas P. O'Neill questioned whether Ireland actually exported during the famine sufficient grain to feed the country, pointing to a large net surplus of imported cornmeal and wheat over exported grain in 1846–47. But he concluded that it was "anomalous" that there should have been any Irish grain exports at all during those months. E. R. R. Green, another contributor to the same volume, cited statistics to show this accounting to be incomplete, inasmuch as the Irish export of beef and mutton actually increased during the famine. Moreover, while the export of pork did fall off sharply in 1847 (since the pigs like the people lived on potatoes), half a million pigs were exported under the policy of business as usual during the crucial months just before and after the failure of the 1846 potato harvest.[32]

But the heart of Mitchel's indictment lay elsewhere: he claimed that a famine at the center of the world's richest empire was a contradiction so monstrous that one could only assume somebody in power must have had some kind of will that a famine should be. This accusation has led historians into an examination of the motives of Lord John Russell and his ministry. A search was launched to discover if some Dracula lurked hidden in Whitehall. Charles Trevelyan, the administrator of the government's relief program, has been particularly scrutinized, and his attitude toward the life and death of Irish peasants closely canvassed. Professor O'Neill cited his rather too excited greeting to the catastrophe in October 1846: "This [problem] being altogether beyond the power of man, the cure has been applied by the direct stroke of an all-wise Providence in a manner as unexpected and as unthought of as it is likely to be effectual."[33] Trevelyan's Jehovah was clearly a student of Malthus. Cecil Woodham-Smith's widely read volume, *The Great Hunger* (1962), probed further into the motivation question. Fresh from her triumphant research into the murderous follies of English administrators during the Crimean War, she corroborated the work of her

Irish colleagues, stripping away from Trevelyan and his superiors their pious mask of famine charity and compassion. She disagreed with Mitchel in accepting the overpopulation premise, but overall her work was his vindication. Mitchel's most outrageous charge had said of the Whig relief policy initiated in 1847: "Steadily, but surely, the Government people were working out their calculation; and the product anticipated by 'political circles' was likely to come out about September in round numbers—*two million Irish corpses*." One of Mrs. Woodham-Smith's discoveries came very near to proving the incredible; for she found Nassau Senior, Russell's chief economic adviser, casting a cold eye on the same scene and complaining that he feared the famine toll would halt prematurely at a mere one million deaths, far short of the ideal objective demanded by the science of political economy.[34]

For all that, Trevelyan as the likeliest suspect did not appear to fit the specifications for the monster being sought by the historians. He was, after all, just another hard-working muscular Christian of the times, whose vanity was that he was so strong morally that he could make "courageous" decisions—at somebody else's cost. The search for motive therefore turned from the study of personality inside the Whig ministry to a second line of inquiry: an examination of the social philosophy behind the administration of famine relief. In the histories of the catastrophe, one senses a common tendency to rest when the chain of causation has been traced back to a kind of stupid ministerial infatuation with what is called the "sanctity of laissez faire." More scrupulously, Mitchel had pushed beyond that point (and at the same time disposed of the Dracula search) in asking himself what the motive would be for just that particular infatuation:

> If my *Apology*, then, shall help to convince my countrymen, and the world, that the English are not more sanguinary and atrocious than any other people would be in like case, and under like exigencies; that the disarmament, degradation, extermination and periodical destruction of the Irish people, are measures of policy dictated not by pure malignity, but by the imperious requirements of the system of empire administered in London; that they must go on, precisely as at present, while the British empire goes on; and that there is no remedy for them under heaven save the dismemberment of that empire; —then the object of my writing shall have been attained.[35]

One modern historian has recast Mitchel's outrageous thought with the maximum possible tact: "If the British chose not to consider Ireland part of Britain, when such an emergency arose, they could hardly complain if the Irish did likewise."[36]

VII

Mitchel conceded only one correction of the beliefs he had once held as editor of the *United Irishman*. Duffy having honored him by abandoning the combination of all the classes in favor of peasant agitation, Mitchel returned the courtesy by quietly allowing Duffy his own point: England, he now agreed, must be in mortal peril before the Irish could attack. The amended rule seemed to imply a confession that he had attempted to lead the Irish people into a pointless slaughter in 1848, since with England not in peril, his own insurrection scheme could have fared no better by the rule than that "poor extemporized abortion of a rising" at Ballingarry. In fact, however, he always held that the famine itself had made a unique exception to the rule. It had so cheapened human life that any number of battle casualties would have been inconsequential. Once more he brought out Jeremiah for his support: "They that be slain with the sword be better than they that be slain with hunger; for these pine away, stricken through for want of the fruits of the field."

The modern reader recognizes that in Mitchel's day the ninety-nine years of the *pax Britannica* between Waterloo and Ypres had two-thirds of its span still to run. In 1848, however, so extended a delay of Irish opportunity seemed inconceivable. Not comprehending that the Irish threat was in itself one prime cause for the lengthening years of peace, Mitchel confidently told himself each year that "bankrupt England" must surely come to disaster next year. This was the context of his outcry "Send war in our time, O Lord!" His wait did seem very long, and the seventy-year delay showed his rule to be potentially as quietistic as O'Connell's moral force and Duffy's Girondism. But only up to a point. Supposing that England should really be in peril, as in Flanders in 1916, what were Irish nationalists supposed to do by Mitchel's rule? Those who were caught off guard by Easter Week had not learned their Irish history very well.

Mitchel's phrase is embedded in Yeats's valedictory poem:

> You that Mitchel's prayer have heard,
> "Send war in our time, O Lord!"
> Know that when all words are said
> And a man is fighting mad,
> Something drops from eyes long blind. . . .[37]

Send war for what? Against whom? As it happened, Mitchel had a context, but Yeats gave us none. Still, we have to have a context. If one went about repeating the fine ringing line simply as concretizing an attractive inner state, he would be aping Mitchel, right enough, but it would be the other half, the crazy American who carried a derringer and prayed for "a good rattling war"—any war—"to occupy its mind and give a career to its craving and impassioned youth."

PART III

Fenianism

CHAPTER 10

Mr. Shook

I

"Like whipped schoolboys,"[1] most of the leaders of the crushed Young Ireland movement were well chastened by defeat. "Most of them," said John O'Leary, "had had enough of the fighting policy for the time being, and some for their natural lives."[2] But a remnant was not inclined either to surrender like Smith O'Brien or to wait with Mitchel for some "pure" opportunity by and by. Not long after Ballingarry these men began to turn over in their minds how to strike the next blow. All the mistakes leading to the late deplored military fiasco they analyzed soberly, hoping to turn in a better performance next time around. With no special acrimony against anyone they dissected the fall of O'Connell and the imperfections of their recent Young Ireland generals. They then turned their energies to steer an adjusted course, and thereby created the theory and practice of Fenianism and the potent structure of the Irish Republican Brotherhood (IRB).

The founder of Fenianism was James Stephens (not to be confused with his namesake, the poet). He was the young Kilkenny clubman we have already seen serving as Smith O'Brien's impatient aide in the field at Killenaule. After Ballingarry he escaped wounded through the police cordon in Tipperary and fled to France, arriving there in the turmoil of the short-lived Second Republic. Taking up the role that sociologists call "participant observer," he familiarized himself with the French brand of insurrection. Just when Gavan Duffy set out to disinfect the *Nation* of its French taint, Stephens was studying Blanquiste methods on the Parisian barricades. He stayed in Paris nearly a decade, supporting himself by giving English lessons and by literary work, writing feuilletons for the Paris newspapers and translating Dickens into the tongue he had just imperfectly acquired.

The multiple disasters suffered by Irish nationalism since the flood tide of O'Connell's Repeal movement had not deflated Stephens' enthusiasm. From headquarters in a Parisian boardinghouse* he began to assemble a

* By odd chance it was the same dingy establishment that Balzac had used for his model of *la maison Vauquer*.

nucleus for a new Irish movement. He found a disciple in John O'Mahony, the Young Irelander who had wanted to rescue Smith O'Brien and Terence Bellew MacManus from Clonmel jail. There too he recruited John O'Leary, a boyhood friend who had come to the old boardinghouse to visit a Tipperary cousin among the exiles.

In 1856 Stephens slipped back into Ireland and went to work. Disguised as a beggarman, he set out on a long romantic excursion, mostly afoot, exploring every part of Ireland, talking with hundreds of country people along the way, surveying the field in preparation for applying his Parisian revolutionary education. A Bandon nationalist gave the mysterious wanderer the Gaelic name *seabhac*, "the hawk," and he became known as "Mr. Shook." He found the country both dead and alive. Passing Limerick, he stopped for a short visit with Smith O'Brien and was told that the Irish case was hopeless, that "the respectable people" were "indifferent if not hostile" to the nationalist cause, and that the clergy were an insurmountable obstacle. O'Brien repeated his familiar belief that the people would have risen in '48 "if the priests had not influenced them." Perhaps, said Stephens; but one need not put the blame on others for one's own shortcomings: "Had the leaders come to us in anything like numbers and shown a determined front worthy of the cause they held dear, the priests would have shrunk back. . . ."[3]

Except at the top, Mr. Shook found that the country's political health was not bad. The national sentiment, he concluded, was not a corpse on the dissecting table as Duffy had just announced, but alive and secretly waiting for the next episode to commence: "My three thousand mile walk through Ireland convinced me of one thing—the possibility of organizing a proper movement for the independence of my native land. I found, of course, many circumstances to discourage me throughout my tour: the hostility of the aristocracy, the apathy of the farmers, the pigheadedness of the *bourgeoisie*: but the laborers and tradesmen were on the right track, and the sons of the peasants were very sympathetic."[4]

Two such hard-to-please witnesses as Michael Davitt and John Devoy have ranked Stephens among the very greatest of all Irish leaders, worthy to stand beside Tone, O'Connell, and Davis. He had a gift for moving men. Though Patrick Pearse called him "cold and enigmatical," Stephens exuded confidence not only toward Ireland but also toward his own judgments, a trait that produced a daring and resourceful leader, though dogmatic and uncharitable, too.

He is often set in contrast to John O'Leary. No doubt about it, O'Leary was different, in personality at least; for while all of the other Fenians were enthusiasts, he was not. When he first encountered Stephens in Paris, several years after Lalor's insurrection, O'Leary was still a nationalist in the long view, but the immediate outlook seemed to him totally hopeless. With several hundred a year inherited from his merchant father, he had been sauntering comfortably about since 1849, enjoying his pleasant Bohemian friendships. Theoretically he was a medical student, but he had not bothered to take a degree. More seriously he was a bibliophile, collecting books from here and there, in Dublin, in London, and eventually in Paris, where he surrendered to Stephens' irresistible persuasiveness with "unbounded trust," as his sister Ellen reported. But not without scrutiny. His lifetime discipline was to ask himself daily, what do I really know? An enemy described him not unfairly as "reserved, sententious, almost cynical; keenly observant, sharply critical, full of restrained passion."[5] A hypersensitive care for veracity loaded his speech with caveats and his prose style with the rhetorical device the French call *expoliation*, the nervous mannerism that corrects all its assertions with a qualifying afterthought, "or perhaps I should say . . .," a habit of speech parodied in the "Eumaeus" chapter of *Ulysses*.

But the contrast between Stephens and O'Leary was superficial, merely a contrast of temperaments. Concerning Irish nationalism, their beliefs were identical and shared with all other Fenians. Twice O'Leary formulated the Fenians' credo: at first officially as an editor in 1864–65, and again without essential emendation thirty years later. The two pronouncements serve as a convenient map of the Fenians' ideology. Since their beliefs are commonly misunderstood, largely through Yeats's misapplications, they need to be set out schematically.

II

The first premise of all Fenians was that Ireland was saturated with separatist sentiment, the inevitable end product of the disasters of English rule. Irish disaffection, they believed, had never disappeared and never would disappear short of independence. Sometimes it exploded; otherwise it was just waiting to explode. O'Leary never indulged in gratuitous enthusiasm, and his certainty of the strength of the popular Irish nationalist sentiment represented his most solemn and cautious judgment: ". . . it is the experience of what is now a pretty long life with me that the Fenian spirit is ever present in Ireland, and needs at any time but a little organization to make it burst into renewed activity."[6]

Activated by such a theory, Fenianism was flagrantly illegal, and its foremost enemy was the constabulary. Stephens therefore sketched out a conspiratorial organization resembling the Ribbon lodges and the Carbonari. The larger unit of his secret structure was a "center" commanded by a "head center" who maintained contact with nine subordinates called "As." In the ideal plan, each "A" had contact in turn with nine "Bs," each "B" with nine "Cs," and so on down to the "Ds," the privates of the Fenian army. The

153

sum of all these constituted one full center. To cover all Ireland Stephens envisioned many dozens of centers, all directly responsible to himself. Any one member knew only the one man above him and no more than nine others of his own rank or below. Exposure of any part of the organization would therefore leave the main structure intact, a dismembered starfish. Long after the main body had disappeared, some of the fragments did continue to function, and it was one of these surviving cells that Yeats joined briefly at the turn of the century. To bind the organization together ceremonially, members took some form of an oath in which they usually promised to obey their superiors—except where such obedience would be "contrary to the law of God"—and swore to "preserve inviolate" the confidences with which they had been entrusted.[7]

III

The Fenians "believed in violence." The root of all their behavior was their certainty that England would never surrender dominion over Ireland unless confronted with superior Irish force, ultimately military. The two terms "Fenian" and "physical force" were synonymous, and the notion of many literary commentators that O'Leary belonged to some genteel verbal branch of ethical culture overlooks his essential harsh activism. "England, in the case of Ireland, never yields to any other argument save that of force, in some of its varying forms," he said; ". . . we could get from England nothing but what we could wring from her." O'Connell's nonviolence was in O'Leary's opinion "a doctrine of which it is hard to say whether it is the more foolish or the more base."[8] Yet, Fenians were never lovers of violence qua violence in the hysterical manner of Mitchel, who perpetually cried out: "In God's name, let the storm burst!"[9] They saw in bloodshed no poetic or mystical value, no "lonely impulse of delight . . . somewhere among the clouds above." They thought it simply an ugly pragmatic necessity to the pursuit of Irish goals.

Though committed to physical force as a general principle, the Fenians thought Ballingarry disgraceful altogether. Stephens had been out there, and he could never afterward temper his sarcasm toward those clumsy bunglers, the "rhetorical revolutionaries" of 1848. The people themselves he never doubted, and he located his ultimate authority in the silent will of the Irish mass. O'Leary too, though often stereotyped as an autocrat, honored the populist ideal. "The leaders, naturally, 'cave in' often," he observed, "but the people never."[10] But neither man saw any point in calling together sprawling musters of patriot hordes who first worked themselves into a martial frenzy and then disbanded and all went home. And they believed that Mitchel had been wrong to suppose in 1848 that the nation could propel itself into battle spontaneously, however intense the crisis. Mitchel's reckless trust in spontaneity had echoed Thomas Davis' innocence:

> The troops live not on earth could stand
> The headlong charge of Tipperary.*

This sort of irresponsible talk Stephens would not countenance. "The headlong charge of Tipperary," to be sure; but Meagher had harangued thousands of cheering Tipperary peasants by moonlight on Slievenamon, and where were those same spontaneous fighting men when they were summoned to Ballingarry two weeks later?

The fatal flaw in the 1848 insurrection, Stephens decided, was amateurism. Before the nation could be polarized into a fighting force, it would have to be activated and guided by a disciplined and professional leadership, that is, by Fenians, the "true men" foretold in Young Ireland's fighting songs. Fenian recruiting was therefore selective, and Yeats thought he remembered hearing O'Leary suggest that the fewer their numbers the better, as though he were on the membership committee of the Kildare Street Club. A more cogent purpose of the exclusiveness was explained by O'Leary's friend, Thomas C. Luby: "Far better it were, in a struggle for freedom, to have but 300 true men, on whom you could rely for support to the last drop of their blood—who, if called upon, would conquer or die with you, like the three hundred unforgotten heroes who perished with Leonidas at Thermopylae; better a thousand times such a small band than 50,000 doubters or shams." It was thought wise to disburden the organization of "tea-table revolutionists, who join a cause while danger is remote, who love at once to frighten and fascinate weak girls by tall talk, but who sing small when danger drops on them."[11] When these amateurs had departed, so the theory held, those who remained would be refined into an elite, not weakened by their diminished numbers, but strengthened by the abandonment of the illusion of forces they did not possess. Goodbye therefore to "drawing-room rebels."

IV

Theoretically, Fenian militance strained toward a "pure" nationalism devoid of class orientation. Fenians did not take up Young Ireland's refrain about a combination of all classes because they liked to avoid talking of classes at all. O'Leary was far more spartan than Davis in demanding that every single Irish grievance—except just the one—be set aside. A catalogue was drawn up to list all the peripheral demands being urged by one or

---

* We owe the discovery of these unfortunate lines to Yeats's search.

another Irish group: extension of the franchise, "manufacture-movements," sugar beet cultivation, conciliation of the aristocracy, and so on. All were equally futile, it was said: a hostile Britain stood astride every road toward the amelioration of Ireland's condition. "Let national independence once be reached through manhood's road, the only way it can be reached, and all other blessings will follow as natural results; from narrower regeneration schemes nothing worth having will arise."[12] This position was so forcibly stated and so often reiterated that the inference might easily be drawn that Fenianism not only wanted all grievances postponed, but actually scorned them as such, a thought that later ossified into a fossil and embedded itself in Yeats's attitudes.

As for agrarian grievances, the Fenians thought the peasants' needs no more urgent than anybody else's. This doctrinaire decision to desert the agrarian struggle crippled the rural strength of Fenianism and was undoubtedly a mistake in tactics. It was made in painful bewilderment over the changing rural picture. Since 1847 great numbers of small peasants had taken flight overseas, ten thousand per month, year after year. The neighboring peasants who survived had all the while been accumulating the little plots of land left behind by the fleeing. The "agrarian problem" that Fenianism tabled for the duration was no longer confined strictly to dispossession and starvation. There was now an augmented class of strong farmers and acquisitive "middlemen" who had exterminated their fellow peasants below them and were now turning their thoughts toward exterminating the landlords above. The decision to bypass the agrarian issue was made in part with these "boors in broadcloth" in mind; and the Fenian press did not hesitate to attack them openly as enemies of nationalism, sense, and decency. "As a class," said Kickham, "those men of bullocks are about the worst men in Ireland. They appear to have no more souls than the brutes which they fatten for the tables of our English masters."[13] Naturally, these strictures bore no relevance to the main body of the peasantry, still living on the ragged edge of starvation. But Stephens, Kickham, and O'Leary were not quite sure that the agrarian demands were what was wanted for them, either. The agrarian ideal of a whole nation of strong farmers seemed very foolish. Irish peasants in the mass would always be marginal, they thought, and was heaven to be stormed for no better purpose than to fix Mickey Moran permanently on his miserable ten acres of hillside and bog? Therefore, let the peasants wait for independence like everybody else, and in the meantime be silent.

The classless ideal of Fenianism naturally betrays the lurking bourgeois. Unfortunately for Stephens, the respectability for which he prepared a place had never turned up. Besides the missing peasants, the other faces absent from the movement were the men of substance, middle-class men of the type of Sheil, Woulfe, Davis, Dillon, and Duffy. They did not relish the risk, O'Leary said.

> The middle class, I believe, in Ireland and elsewhere, to be distinctly the lowest class morally—that is, the class influenced by the lowest motives. The prudential virtues it has in abundance; but a regard for your own stomach and skin, or even for the stomachs and skins of your relatives and immediate surroundings, though, no doubt, a more or less commendable thing in itself, is not the stuff of which patriots are made. Your average *bourgeois* may make a very good sort of agitator, for here he can be shown, or at least convinced, that his mere material interests are concerned, and that he may serve them with little or no material risk. A rebel, however, you can rarely make him, for here the risk is certain and immediate, and the advantage, if material advantage there should be, doubtful and distant.[14]

Thus it was that Fenianism, for all its disdain of class, was actually a class organization. By elimination, the "true men" of Ireland had to be found, so Stephens learned, in the bottom strata of the culture, among Tone's "highly respectable class of the community, the men of no property." The gentility were amused by the readiness with which the Fenian brotherhood welcomed laborers and servant girls, O'Leary said. "Let our critics then get such comfort as they can from my confession that our movement was mainly one of the masses, not against the classes, but unfortunately without them."[15] The most numerous Fenian recruits were the "men in the workshops," skilled craftsmen and factory workmen,[16] ranging from poor shoemakers in garrets to superintendents of great engineering works. These artisans turned out to be not only the most militant people about, and the "most intelligent," but very nearly "the most cultivated," too. But if the nationalist impulse was generated only at the bottom, it could seep upward. "It is the *people* who have kept the national faith alive," he said. "Instead of being imbued with the spirit of patriotism by the upper classes, the people impart to them the little of patriotism these upper classes possess."[17] Unfortunately, his famous disciple was not listening when he said that.

Relieved from the "timid breath" of the "merchant and clerk"—Yeats's paraphrase of O'Leary's strictures against the Catholic middle classes—the Fenian cadre was more businesslike than anything Irish nationalism had seen since 1798. O'Connell's strength had consisted of sheer raw numbers, part-time enthusiasts who paid their farthing a week to the parish priest and strolled off casually to the monster meetings to listen to the oratory. Davis had had no organized following at all, just the *Nation*'s subscription list and the Eighty-two Club. The Confederate clubs of 1848 were broad-based but undisciplined. Stephens' conspiracy in contrast possessed a popular base, discipline, mobility, initiative, and numbers. As events proved, these assets were insufficient.

V

A violent breach with the clergy followed naturally from Stephens' projects. If Archbishop Cullen was unable to live in the same country with so gentle a coreligionist as Gavan Duffy, he would certainly not tolerate an "infidel Jacobin" like Stephens. In spite of the rule against the intrusion of sectarianism into Irish nationalism, the Fenians found that collision was unavoidable, for the clergy pressed to the attack with characteristic tenacity and vigor, always startling in its scurrilous inventiveness.

Unless the Fenians were prepared to go out of business, they had to defend themselves against their clerical critics. Their standard tactic was to isolate selected priests and bishops and attack them without restraint, but strictly on political issues. Archbishop Cullen had innocently handed them a weapon when he withdrew the clergy in 1854 from the tenant-right movement. The Fenians now took him at his word and spread his own ideal, "No priests in politics" (a sentiment to which Simon Dedalus adverted repeatedly in Joyce's Christmas-dinner feud). It was a rude slogan but hardly Jacobin, for it suggested approval of the clergy's influence in all spheres except politics. It left a peculiar mark upon the Irish nationalist laity, who fell into the habit of mingling clericalism with anticlericalism, of boldly assaulting Church functionaries (such as "Billy the Lip") without implicating the generalized ideal of Irish piety. In time, the dextrous double attitude became a commonplace of Irish literature: witness Frank O'Connor, Sean O'Faolain, Peadar O'Donnell, and occasionally even Joyce. O'Leary himself rounded out a lifetime of battle against the clergy by returning to the Church just in time to expire in a state of grace.

An alternate line of Fenian defense aimed to outdo the clergy by offering a brand of piety of their own. One outspoken Fenian called "Pagan" O'Leary actually proposed that the Holy Trinity be dispensed with and replaced by a pantheon of the old Gaelic gods and heroes. As a prophet, he was handicapped by a conspicuous hollow in the front of his skull, the result of a kick from a horse; and his idea did not immediately prosper. But neither did it disappear. Unwittingly echoing old "Pagan," Yeats, George Russell, and Joyce were prepared to claim in a later time that their own special brand of immateriality was loftier and more noble than anybody's.

The most impressive Fenian counterpoise to the clergy's spirituality was the ideal of self-immolation. John O'Leary wrote:

> There is a word which should be engraven upon the hearts of all men who struggle for freedom—and that word is self-sacrifice. Not by men who love ease, money, health, or even reputation more than country can it ever be hoped that independence will be won. Pain, poverty, disease, and obloquy have ever been the lot of many of the noblest and purest spirits that have appeared on

this earth, and any and all of these must be faced if we mean that Ireland should be free. . . . to a small number of men in any country, is given . . . large capacity for action and endurance. But the humblest among us can aid in the great work, if only he be willing to immolate self. Time, labor, money, in greater or lesser degree, all men can give, and those the country demands from all; for time, labor, and money must be largely expended before we can ask that great sacrifice—life.[18]

On rereading this declaration thirty years afterward, O'Leary conceded that the phrasing could perhaps have been a bit less "high strung in its pitch," but on the general principle he stood his ground.

His personal interest in the formal code of self-sacrifice seems to have been in part aesthetic. There was a lack of taste, he thought, in a person who assumed the honors that fell to heroism and then complained of their cost. His well-known words to Yeats, that nobody ought to "cry in public," arose in this context, and when his own turn to pay came around, he was glad that he had borne his pain in silence and dignity.

Beyond taste, he proclaimed the redemptive paradox, the sainthood of the patriotic battle casualty. As an Irish poetic idea it was not original, for the theme of patriotic immolation had already been delineated by Tom Moore. Fenianism turned it from a sentiment of the drawing room into action in the streets.

VI

The enmity of the clergy, an inconvenience for any Irish political movement, had the unexpected result of strengthening Fenian power. O'Connell and Duffy had let the clergy do their organizing for them, but the Fenians got no free help. Forced to do everything for themselves, they emerged considerably stronger. Their task not only demanded "rooted men," but found them. Stephens himself was one of the sort, and his head centers had the same gifts. The chief of recruiting in the British regiments, John Devoy, worked with such success that at one time every fourth soldier in the imperial garrison was under Fenian orders. In Munster, Stephens found Kickham, gifted with the common touch and famous for his courage and rectitude. To the west, where "Connaught lay in slumber deep," he assigned Edward Duffy, a melancholic somewhat suggestive of Joyce's "Michael Furey," a saintly consumptive who wore out his life and died in Fenian service.

The most picturesque of Stephens' grass-roots organizers turned up in west Cork. In the late 1850s anyone scanning the bleak Irish scene for some spark of nationalism would have found his eye drawn to Skibbereen and Bantry. There under Stephens' tutelage a young red-haired giant named Jeremiah O'Donovan (O'Donovan Rossa to us) had organized the neighbor youths into the Phoenix National and Literary Society. By day they intoxicated themselves on the *Spirit of the Nation* and in the dark of the evening practiced mock military exercises on the hillside.

Stephens concluded that a corps of full-time organizers like the west Cork men might spread the reborn movement throughout all Ireland, provided somebody chipped in to support them while they were "on their keeping." Famished Skibbereen could spare no money for the purpose, nor all Ireland either. But there was a chance that money might be collected among the Irish émigrés in America. John O'Mahony, now in New York, had recently raised eighty pounds and sent it by courier to Ireland to help launch the new society. Stephens sent him a message that if the Americans would guarantee a regular contribution of a hundred pounds a month for a war chest, he would undertake to organize Ireland for insurrection.

VII

American Fenianism was thus envisaged as the indispensable paymaster for the shock troops at home. While Stephens' projects expanded, the Fenians overseas set about to organize Irish-Americans into a mass auxiliary modeled after O'Connell's peasant agitations, a transplant that blended nicely with native American backwoods political manners. American Fenianism took vigorous root. It soon became a fixture in urban American politics, developing a new mutation altered radically in ambition, if not in vocabulary or accent.[19]

The generous pledge of money was readily forthcoming from America, but not the money itself. O'Mahony was a selfless patriot but not much of a money raiser, and the Fenian command had to take to commuting between Ireland and New York, bringing home funds in driblets to pay for sporadic bursts of organizing activity. From the Dublin point of view, the story of American Fenianism was summed up in St. Paul's perennial complaint: "The collections are not coming in!"

O'Leary, too, sailed in pursuit of some of those "rascally dollars." He boarded ship incognito, a secret agent on a dangerous mission. On the other side, a brass band greeted him at the Battery pier, and he was paraded up Broadway and compelled to make a speech. The Irish-Americans overwhelmed him with picnics and oratory, and in Pittsburgh he listened to a sworn brother deliver as his own composition one of Meagher's best-known oratorical warwhoops. His American adventure forced him to disagree with the opinion of the poet Horace that men who cross seas change only their climate, not their dispositions; yet it pleased him that Irishmen "still, thank God, leave their country with the hatred of England lying deep in their souls."[20] Still, the cash he came for was skimpy.

VIII

While the Fenians' leaders were beating the American bushes for money, their mother chapter in west Cork came to grief. The secret society turned out to be not particularly secret. Early in 1858, a Skibbereen schoolteacher named Daniel Sullivan confessed his membership to the parish priest. The sinner was invited to step into the parlor to repeat his statement outside the secrecy of the confessional. The word was then passed up to the Castle and to the bishop of Kerry, Dr. David Moriarty, who instructed all the priests of the diocese to denounce the new society from the altar. To support that frontal attack, he conceived a flank diversion through a partnership with the *Nation*, hitherto the unsullied emblem of Irish militance and the brave lay adversary of ultramontanism.

Duffy had been three years in Australia by this time, and the *Nation* had just been purchased by Alexander M. Sullivan, a young man of many talents and good impulses, spokesman for a new breed of middle-class Catholic nationalists that had mutated since 1848. He was a west Cork man (with the westerner's pale blue eyes and black curly hair), the son of a Bantry house painter. He had sensed an Irish parliamentary opportunity opening up in the slow British drift toward liberalization of the voting franchise and so, gathering about him three brothers—Donal, Denis, and T. D. (who emerged from Joyce's naming machine as "T. Deum")—besides some cousins, in-laws, descendants, and friends, he created a powerful new clan of politicians, later called "the Bantry band." From 1858 onward they were to be found in the midst of every important episode of Irish history. Sullivan lined up his clan on the moral force side of Irish politics and set himself and the new *Nation* against any future dalliance in military adventure. Without neglecting the old *Nation*'s tradition of fraternity with the nationalist clergy, he was also anxious to bargain with the ultramontanists.

Sullivan soon collided with Stephens. In the summer of 1858 he journeyed home to Bantry for a holiday of yachting on the bay. Stephens' footprints he found everywhere in west Cork and Kerry, and his secrets were everybody's excited talk. Fenianism had won over the youth in the coastal towns and was "creeping inwards." The editor of the new *Nation* was himself sought out by Stephens and invited to join up, an invitation declined with no hard feelings on either side. Sullivan was next sought out, as he tells us, by Bishop Moriarty, His Lordship bearing private information from Dublin Castle that the government was preparing to arrest the Phoenix Society members. Moriarty intimated that if the *Nation* would cause the conspiracy to evaporate before the police could act, there would be a blessed prevention of unnecessary scandal and suffering. It was to give substance to the bishop's logic, Sullivan said, that he composed a long three-column leading article contra Fenianism, a "firm but friendly remonstrance," and published it on October 30, 1858. This small episode, like many seeming trivialities in the Irish chronicle, was found to be laden with signification, and in the end it was magnified to epic stature.

Sullivan's polemic opened with an encomium on Ribbonism. Opposed by fifty thousand soldiers, thirty thousand constabulary, three hundred thousand resident sympathizers, and a host of spies and informers, Ribbonism had "like some enchanted fire" defied all effort "to quench it or discover its source." But for all that, he said in coming to his point, he could not condone the recent activity of a certain new secret society arising in the west of Ireland. The new conspirators proposed to shoulder arms and march against England. To do so would only provoke further repression. That man was an enemy of Ireland who would invite the government to make a "rawhead and bloody-bones scarecrow" of Irish nationalism, whether he acted from ignorance or from more sinister motives, whether "only erringly" or downright "wilfully." The leaders of the new secret society were undoubtedly cowards. They shrank from danger themselves, but they planned to send their "dupes" out to be slaughtered. For his own part, Sullivan would "scorn to connive" at recruiting members to any movement "the dangers of which we were not ready ourselves to share." Further, the leaders were proven liars. By means of "winks, nods, and innuendoes," they claimed to carry the blessing of the heroes of 1848, but without warrant, for he had in his possession a letter from Smith O'Brien stating, "In answer to your inquiry I have no hesitation to say that I do not belong to any secret society." In short, said Sullivan, the watchword for Ireland was—wait. All Europe knew that if it did so, its glorious "time of times" would someday come. To those who had attached themselves to any secret military society, his advice was to get out, not only for their own safety but in the name of patriotism as well.[21]

Then a fresh and more palpable influence against the Phoenix Society introduced itself—the police. A Phoenix informer known as Sullivan-Goulah had been primed and held ready to testify in court. Five weeks after the Nation's article, simultaneous police raids struck the clubs in all the main towns of the southwest. Daniel Sullivan the schoolteacher was the first to be tried, convicted, and jailed. After much behind-the-scenes maneuvering, the other indicted members, including O'Donovan Rossa, were persuaded to plead guilty and to take suspended sentences. Finally all of them, together with the jailed schoolteacher, were given a release subject to good behavior.

The Phoenix victims now turned with unappeasable fury against the Nation. By its own confession, they said, it had confronted Smith O'Brien with a question that no gentleman could ask of another: Do you belong to a certain secret society? Supposing Smith O'Brien did belong, what answer was he permitted in honor to make? Worse yet, the *Nation*'s editorial attack had served as the tip-off to the police. It was the government's hunting dog which pointed the police to their game. Stephens coined the phrase "felon-setter" and fixed it in permanent Irish usage to denote any "firm but friendly remonstrance"—such as denunciation from the altar—that proved serviceable to the police. The charge was false; for as Sullivan proved, two other Dublin newspapers had mentioned the Phoenix Society before the *Nation*'s attack.[22] The Fenians were not pacified. Whether or not he was the first, his attack still carried an unmistakable tone of mischiefmongering, particularly misplaced in the *Nation*, they said. They concluded that he had succumbed to the insidious temptation of impugning in public the motives of the spearhead of his own party in order to commend himself to the enemy. He was henceforth known to all Fenians as "A. M. Sullivan-Goulah," a despicable name borrowed from the government's Skibbereen informer.

The Fenians' hatred of Sullivan, energetically requited, became one of the permanent givens of Irish politics. It survived as one of the miscellaneous hatreds behind the Civil War of 1922–23, sixty years after the "friendly remonstrance." Stephens, O'Leary, and Rossa bore their contempt for Sullivan to the grave, and only John Devoy, softened by extreme old age, brought himself around to pronounce the full formula of forgiveness: "God rest the souls of the Sullivans." Understandably, the old animosity was inherited by Yeats and enlivened by aesthetic considerations. But as we shall see, time was to play interesting tricks with Yeats's testamentary obligation to disdain the Sullivans.

Like O'Connell, Sullivan proposed to drive physical force outside the moral pale in Irish politics. Unlike O'Connell, he failed. The Fenian word of mouth proved more potent than the *Nation*'s pen. Sullivan gave ground, frightened into silence. The *Nation* reported that he had been selected for assassination, but the Fenians laughed at that, for plainly his assassination never took place. With his retreat, physical force stood as an alternative, silent or vocal, to every Irish constitutional move. Its moral stature was never again assailable in Irish nationalist politics, and the argument against it was confined to the consideration of the ordinary logic of expedience.

CHAPTER 11

Fenianism Mobilizes

I

The *Nation* estimated that the physical force impulse was totally extinguished in Ireland by the time O'Donovan Rossa came out of Tralee jail in 1859. A. M. Sullivan felicitated himself on his editorial accomplishment. The Fenians naturally put forward the opposite prediction, and before the year was out James Stephens was back at work in Skibbereen. The story of his reunion with the released prisoners has been preserved in Rossa's childlike prose, telling how half a dozen Phoenix men met him in Bantry: "We went in Denis O'Sullivan's yacht to Glengarriff, where we had dinner. Stephens paid for the dinner. Sailing through Bantry bay, Stephens was smoking a pipe. I remember his taking the pipe in his hand, and saying he would not give the value of that dudeen for the worth of Ireland to England after the death of Queen Victoria; that she, in fact, would be the last English reigning monarch of Ireland."[1]

In prognostication Stephens was not omniscient. Rossa wondered whether he himself believed what he told others: "I do not know did he speak that way that day in Bantry bay, from the strong faith he had in the success of his own movement. Anyway, the way he always spoke to his men seemed to give them confidence that he was able to go successfully through the work that was before him, and before them. That was one of his strong points, as an organizer."[2] Stephens' vision of Ireland's future was too enthusiastic in its timing, yet it was not inaccurate in substance. Victoria herself would never see the end of the Union, but in the midst of the Fenian excitement the future English monarch was born who would. Sullivan's prediction, on the other hand, was absolutely wrong, and he was shortly forced to retract his self-congratulation: "Foolish was the best of our wisdom in thinking this was the end."[3] The Phoenix affair was not the finale of Fenianism, but the overture.

Leaving the Skibbereen veterans to run on their own steam, Stephens now concentrated his energy upon building up the pressure in Dublin. He found the city full of hidden nationalists waiting to be asked, and the serious swearing in of new members quickened. In about a year the organization was ready to demonstrate its strength in public. The issue chosen, the most perfect Ireland could offer, had to do with a wake.

II

Among the seven Young Ireland felons in Van Diemen's Land, the least conspicuous was Terence Bellew MacManus. His history was about the same as Meagher's. After Ballingarry he was captured, tried, convicted, sentenced to death, reprieved, transported, and at last rescued and set ashore a free man in San Francisco, where he settled down in the grocery business. Early in 1861 he died there, still a young man, still unrepentant. Some months afterward a group of San Francisco Fenians hit upon the idea of agitating for the cause by digging up the corpse and shipping it back to Ireland for reburial. Since there was not yet a transcontinental railroad, the project was a considerable undertaking. But a committee formed, money accumulated, and in due course the coffin set forth on its journey. As the Irish nationalist press proudly noted, it was the longest funeral procession attempted in all history, outdistancing by far the return of Napoleon's bones from St. Helena.

The body arrived in Dublin at dawn one Monday and the grand finale was scheduled for the Sunday following. A delegation waited upon Archbishop Cullen requesting him to permit the corpse to lie in state in the Marlborough Street cathedral for the six days before the burial, and also to furnish the same lavish obsequies that had been provided by Archbishop Hughes when the corpse passed through New York. Cullen was trapped in a dilemma. To accede to the Fenian request would sanctify wickedness. But to refuse would desecrate the rigid formalism of the death protocol, offend the flock, and isolate the hierarchy. The troubled archbishop elected the latter choice. The cathedral was closed to the mourners, and the corpse had to be carried down the street to the Mechanics Institute to repose there in state until next Sunday.

Cullen's boycott of the MacManus funeral forced Dublin to declare its allegiance in public. Down to the last hour it was not certain which side it would choose. Luby went to the Mechanics Institute Sunday morning in the rain and was disturbed to find nobody about. After a while a few people wandered in, then some more. In midafternoon, when the procession was ready to start, the brass bands appeared and led out with a funeral march. Luby fell into rank behind the coffin, not certain whether anybody was behind him. The procession moved north up Gardiner Street, and as it turned west into Great Britain Street, he glanced back at the squares along the river where the procession was forming. "Then, indeed, I was overawed," he said. "I saw the whole length of Gardiner Street filled with dense masses of men, and fresh masses, endlessly, as it seemed." Dublin had voted with its feet, and no mistaking its choice. The multitudes that Stephens had promised were really there. The burial of a man almost unknown except as a token of nationality had brought out fifty thousand marchers, more than had followed the coffin of world-famed O'Connell. Onlookers numbered one hundred thousand more. "I could have sobbed and cried," said Luby. "I felt, as I never felt before or since, the grandeur, the magnetism of an immense crowd of human beings, when all are, for the time being, gloriously animated with one and the same noble aspiration and conviction."[4]

From Great Britain Street, where Luby looked back upon the multitudes, the direct route to Glasnevin Cemetery turned right, northward, at Rutland Square. But the funeral procession did not turn. It marched on to the west, veered south, crossed the river upstream, and turned east again. The objective of this detour a couple of miles out of the way was St. Catherine's Church in Thomas Street, before which Robert Emmet had been executed in 1803. At that spot each contingent of the procession stopped for a moment and each marcher bared his head. Then they moved quickly through the College Green and back across the river to Rutland Square again, closing the loop, and at last took the direct road to Glasnevin. It would have been hard to misconstrue the question they had posed: Emmet is to MacManus as MacManus is to—whom?

The "drawing-room rebels" had fixed strong claims on Emmet's memory. They cherished the pathos of Tom Moore's song about his fatal love for Sarah Curran: "She is far from the land where her young hero sleeps"; and they memorized the brave oratory of the doomed patriots' debate against Lord Norbury. But according to Fenian theory, Emmet's courtroom words did not hold all of his meaning. His mode of death, for example, was not congenial to arrangement for voice and pianoforte; yet it contained weighty meanings all the same. The Fenians' line of march to the once-bloody spot in Thomas Street proclaimed that if one cared to stir the embers of Emmet's memory, he should not shrink from its integral horror as a timely political lesson. The languid gentility of Tom Moore's song concealed the ghastly severed head; let it be seen. The street before St. Catherine's Church had run with Emmet's blood, dogs had licked it from the cobbles, and Dublin ladies had shyly dipped their handkerchiefs in it. If O'Connell had not cared for blood, the fact still remained that blood was the pigment with which Irish history had been written—such was the physical force view of the matter.*

* Their point about the inseparability of martyrdom and terror was perhaps well taken, or at least Joyce thought so. He made the same point himself in his collage of the Emmet execution in the "Cyclops" and "Circe" chapters of *Ulysses* with a minute account of the

The MacManus procession did not reach Glasnevin until nightfall. A torch was brought so that the American Fenian who had escorted the body from San Francisco could see to read the manuscript Stephens had prepared. "In order to arrange my ideas the better," the American said, "I have reduced my thoughts to writing." He set to his task "like a Trojan," said Luby, and stumbled only on one word.

Stephens was not Pericles nor Meagher of the Sword, but as O'Leary remarked, the speech "served its purpose fairly well at the time, and that is sufficient to say of most speeches as indeed of most things." That purpose was, first of all, to acknowledge the position just won. Any Irishman not blind could see that the physical force leaders had succeeded in opening an effective revolutionary contact with the Irish people, completing the necessary first step and clearing the barrier where Davis, Mitchel, Smith O'Brien, and Duffy, for two decades past, had all fallen. Stephens was understandably proud of his momentous achievement: "Fellow countrymen, you have accomplished a great as well as a holy work this day, and I congratulate you with all my heart and soul. Why did you ever doubt your capabilities?" As for the transition to the next step, let Irishmen now employ "heart and arm and intellect . . . without noise or bustle," and "the day" for which all Irishmen longed "cannot now be very far off."[5]

III

The MacManus funeral raised the Sullivan-Stephens vendetta to a new stage. Sullivan had "suffered and sacrificed" from the violent recoil of his "friendly remonstrance" and he confessed that a secret revolutionary society is "certainly a terrible power." Looking about for comfort, he first tested the political assets of clericalism. The old *Nation*'s "haughty impartiality" toward sect went under, as Davis' paper turned national-Catholic (and "to my mind," said O'Leary, "much more the last than the first").[6] Increasingly the new *Nation* lifted its eyes to Rome. The story of Pius IX's growing burden of temporal cares filled many columns. "It was not the Pope who desired to have a people to rule but the people who desired to have a Pope rule them," Sullivan said. The *Syllabus Errorum*, that most unecumenical document, received his hearty applause. Modern progress, civilization, free thought—what were they after all? Little more, really, he said, than Bell's

---

hangman's duties, conveyed in the incongruous language of the society page: "On a handsome mahogany table near him were neatly arranged the quartering knife, the various finely tempered disembowelling appliances (specially supplied by the worldfamous firm of cutlers, Messrs John Round and Sons, Sheffield), a terracotta saucepan for the reception of the duodenum, colon, blind intestine and appendix etc when successfully extracted and two commodious milkjugs destined to receive the most precious blood of the most precious victim. The housesteward of the amalgamated cats' and dogs' home was in attendance to convey these vessels when replenished to that beneficent institution." *Ulysses*, pp. 303–4.

Life in London, Renan, Colenso, "lunatic" Garibaldi, and "Joe" Smith (the Mormon).[7] A rival editor complained that Sullivan had taken on board the nationalist movement too many saints, that for himself he was "sick of saints" and "cant about saints."

Sullivan's next step for covering his losses was more original. His Fenian enemies were startled to find that even while the feud raged, their casualties were the object of his studied solicitude. The Skibbereen teacher was hardly behind bars before Sullivan had launched a subscription for the relief of his aged mother, and he wept journalistically for his mortal enemy, O'Donovan Rossa, on his release from Tralee jail: "What a terrible punishment. . . . Jeremiah O'Donovan, once a prosperous trader, a husband, and a father returns to a desolate home, his children beggared!"[8] Sometimes the Fenians spurned his condolences. And yet it was hard to repel his exaltation of their fallen.

At the same time, to fight fire with fire, Sullivan began to accumulate his own private arsenal of bloody symbology. He outdid everybody in the royal welcome he gave the tamed '48 revolutionaries straggling home from Van Diemen's Land. He then exhibited them with their acquiescence as his personal property. When Marshal MacMahon, one of Napoleon III's numerous unattractive generals, won a famous victory in Italy, the *Nation* proved in two columns of small type that his ancestors had indubitably been wild geese. The marshal was presented with a jeweled Irish sword and his glory was also made the Sullivans' private property. Sullivan's most popular book, the *Story of Ireland*, a history for juveniles, offered floods of gore no less than of sentiment, and Emmet's severed head appears in this children's moral force narrative complete with all the details except the ladies' handkerchiefs.

When MacManus' corpse arrived in Dublin, Sullivan took up the challenge contained in the Fenians' implied rhetorical question, Who is the living heir of Emmet and MacManus? and gave the bold answer that he was the heir himself. Archbishop Cullen might disdain the corpse, but he proposed to seize it for his own. He mobilized a moral force flying squadron backed by Father Kenyon and a large, fierce-looking relative of O'Connell's called The O'Donoghue of the Glens (to whom we have already been introduced through Joyce's Donnybrook in *Ulysses*). In six days and nights of intrigue, he fought the Fenians for the select front positions on the obsequies committee, in the procession to Glasnevin, and at the graveside. Holding the advantage of possession, the Fenians beat off his attacks. At the week's close the vanquished retired from the field, leaving behind a rumor that the coffin did not contain MacManus' corpse but only a lot of California rocks.

In strict consistency Sullivan should have had no more use for Mac-Manus' corpse than Archbishop Cullen had, or than O'Connell had for

Wolfe Tone and "the miscreants of 'Ninety-eight." The difficulty was that the consistent moral force position no longer held any allure. Whether Sullivan liked it or not, he was forced to come to terms with the physical force tradition, to attempt a hybrid fusion of bloody sedition and peaceful constitutionalism. So, the fusion was made (a "blend" he called it). He simply referred the bloody face of Irish life to past time and the moral force face to the present and future. With this fine discrimination, his hybrid took root. There was a recklessness about his solution, though, for suppose one's political followers should get their verb tenses confused ?

IV

O'Leary summed up the battle for possession of MacManus' corpse in this way:

> . . . The O'Donoghue and Mr. A. M. Sullivan . . . wished to make the funeral a mere commemoration of the past, having no significance in the present, and affording no lesson for the future. M'Manus had lived and died a rebel. With them all that was a thing of the past. 1848 was dead and gone, a mere thing of memory, and to many of them scarcely among the pleasures of memory. To Stephens, Luby, and their friends and followers, things, however, wore quite another aspect. They felt that they were carrying out the principles of '48 to their legitimate consequences by reverting to that solider and sterner policy of '98. . . .[9]

This old quarrel over the proper ownership of Irish political corpses leaves us with a sensation of *déjà vu*. When the eye picks up O'Leary's catchphrase "dead and gone," we suddenly place the MacManus affair as the original pattern from which Yeats later constructed his second most popular poem, "September 1913," and his refrain, "Romantic Ireland's dead and gone." The parallels are numerous: in both a dead physical force hero, in both a bogus Sullivanite claimant (Yeats's enemy in "September 1913" was a surviving stalwart of the Bantry band, William Martin Murphy), in both an argument for the right of possession based upon the superior nobility of the speaker. Yeats apparently represents himself as the bold Fenian man of 1913, decrying the new age for its cupidity and cowardice. The perfunctory remark is then in order: how little did Yeats guess that in three years Pearse and Connolly would occupy the General Post Office, and so on.

The connections between "September 1913" and the MacManus affair are, I think, overwhelming. It is by no means clear, though, that the conventional conclusion was what Yeats really meant. To begin with, his actual political position in 1913 according to the MacManus parallel was not with, but against, O'Leary's ghost. He was at that time at odds with the IRB,

O'Leary's offspring, and was therefore exploiting that special blend of moral force with bloody ornamentation that O'Leary abominated as belonging by right of discovery to A. M. Sullivan's ghost. The first printing of the poem bore the interesting subtitle, "On reading much of the correspondence against the Art Gallery." The romantic entity buried with O'Leary was thus not primarily his militance, but his taste; and O'Leary's revolutionary name was invoked not to impel Irishmen to shoulder arms rather than live as "slaves that were spat on," but to enforce another demand altogether, very remotely connected—that is, to compel the Dublin Corporation to build Sir Hugh Lane his art gallery astride the Liffey.

In the minds of most Irishmen, though, it was inevitably that other war that O'Leary symbolized, especially when the cues were so unequivocally bloody. When Yeats later deleted the subtitle, the poem seemed to be complaining that O'Leary's heirs were not revolutionary any more, but actually was complaining that they were. We are witness here at the birth of a unique mode of poetic expression, a political double entendre carrying public and private meanings that contradict one another. The device belongs properly to forensic and is rhetorical in the strict and literal sense, perfectly in accord with his advice to Lady Gregory on the morality of equivocal battle: "be secret and exult." We have earlier picked up other traces of the impulse. As we have seen, Yeats's portrait of O'Connell was undoubtedly a debater's sally, using the word "demagogue" with a hidden semantic shift that inverted its normal meaning. His observations on Mitchel and Swift were in the same pattern, and there exist Irishmen so cynical that they can catch a hint of double entendre even in the magnificent "Easter 1916"—the executions brought metaphors for poetry. We will meet it again in his delineation of Parnell.*

* The great enigma of "The Second Coming" may also be traced to this habit, although the forensic masking is more urgent and skillful. It was first published in late 1920 at the peak of the Black and Tan terror, which it was naturally assumed to describe in the most obvious way, with a sphinx added to lend a touch of enigma to the bestial theme. Then an examination of the manuscripts led Richard Ellmann to date its composition in January 1919, many months before the Tans had ever been heard of, and the enigma deepened. Next Jon Stallworthy discovered even earlier manuscripts, written perhaps as early as the summer of 1918 (see *Between the Lines* [Oxford: Clarendon Press, 1963], pp. 16–25). In them he found an allusion to the Treaty of Brest Litovsk; and if the reader will look into the Yeats letters of that time, he will find him deeply absorbed in the hysteria of the Bolshevik scare. With this clue, our enigmatical sphinx gives place to the all-too-recognizable names on the front page of the newspapers. Lenin and Alexander Kerensky are respectively the "mere anarchy" and "the best" who "lack all conviction." But who is the "rough beast"? One would imagine that it would have to be the Bolsheviks, but this will not do, since Lenin is already taken care of. The only possible identification would be the interventionists, Admiral Alexander Kolchak and the English Brigadier General William Edmund Ironside, heralds of the new millenium with Yeats's hearty applause.

But Stallworthy found an even more interesting clue in the canceled line of the manuscripts reading, "And there's no Burke to cry aloud no Pitt." For any Irish nationalist, the

V

With MacManus properly buried, the military question was plainly the next order of Fenian business. During the great wake, Dublin had filled with countrymen ready to be sworn in on the spot. Afterward they scattered to their homes and spread the movement broadcast through Ireland. The Dublin membership tripled in three months. As recruits accumulated, Stephens learned to know the sensation of great power, and he sent O'Mahony in New York instructions to bid farewell to the tedium of postponing Irish action until some English crisis might by chance occur, phrasing his message in his highly individualistic style:

> If there be one thing, in connection with the cause of Ireland, I more cordially detest than any other, it is what scribblers or spouters call "a Crisis." It has been the chronic bane of Ireland—a more fatal bane that famine or any other the enemy have had, to perpetuate their rule. A bane—a scourge—a

name "Pitt" screams out from the page, for it answers "mere anarchy" with the unmistakable threat of '98, with its rich accretion of terroristic paraphernalia. Decoded, Yeats's Irish grievance was thus not against the Tans, but against "incendiary or bigot," against the IRA, whom the Tans were sent into Ireland to destroy; and his message to the IRA said: gentlemen, you have just exhausted my Christian charity. That Yeatsian virtue should wear the mask of the rough beast need not startle. The symbolic structure of "The Second Coming" is a close paraphrase of Standish O'Grady's emotional reaction to the successive phases of the land war, with which we are familiar. Yeats's preface to *Resurrection* remembered the rough beast as rather jolly, "associated with laughing, ecstatic destruction"; and A. Norman Jeffares' annotations of the poem add new testimonials to its virtue and attractiveness. The tone of the symbol also echoes the open threats of the reactionary terrorists of the time and of Yeats himself in 1932.

Stallworthy is inclined to interpret Yeats's tendency to drop off all specific cues as the poem approached final form as being aesthetically motivated, since a symbol too clearly defined "is drained of much of its imaginative potency." But there has probably never been a reader of "The Second Coming" who has not been dissatisfied with its generalities and has not attempted to imagine its natural referents. If my interpretation of the poem is correct, Yeats was very wise to make his readers guess at this or that ambiguity. "The Second Coming" would doubtless have lost some of its enormous authority if the word "Pitt" had by mischance been left in, or if (like "September 1913") it had borne a subtitle that accidentally exposed its secret: an excited longing, far ahead of the crowd, not only for the march on Rome and the beer-hall *Putsch*, but also for the Tans themselves, whose subsequent arrival he (1) deplored in a perfunctory poem later dropped from the canon, and (2) ambiguously linked to the IRA in "Nineteen Hundred and Nineteen" under the sentiment, a plague on both of you weasels.

Yeats's forensic masking casts a sardonic light upon his famous epigram that we make rhetoric out of our quarrel with others but poetry out of our quarrel with ourselves. It also adds a curious footnote to the fierce old battle cry of the 1950s, that every query into intention, single and double entendre alike, is a vulgarism inconsequential to the poem qua poem. "September 1913" and "The Second Coming" appear to make an interesting test of that proposition. And finally, it threatens embarrassment to those who put all their bets on Yeats's myth qua myth, disembodied and historically nonreferential. It would seem difficult to silence the question, What does the mechanism of his mythic "system" mean in *this* concrete setting—for example, in the arrival of the Tans?

disease—a devil's scourge it has been to us. Its best known formula has resolved itself into this: "England's difficulty is Ireland's opportunity." Blind, base and deplorable motto—rallying-cry—motive of action—what you will. May it be accursed, it, its aiders and abettors. Owing to it, and them, the work that should *never* have stood still, has been taken up in feverish fits and starts, and always out of time, to fall into collapse when the "opportunity," predestined to escape them, had slipped through their hands. Ireland's trained and marshalled manhood alone can *ever* make—could have ever made—Ireland's opportunity. And this opportunity, the manhood of Ireland alone, without the aid of any foreign power—without the aid of even our exiled brothers, could have been *made* any time these thirty years; and, whether England was at peace or war, with this manhood alone we could have won our own. . . . Accursed, I say, be the barren, lunatic or knavish clods who raised this dog-souled cry. . . .[10]

Without "even our exiled brothers"? That is, without Irish-American men and money? This was a verbal excess that Stephens could not have meant seriously. Searching for a practical scheme to arm and drill his secret army, he found his answer in the terrible news from America. The Battle of Bull Run had taken place in midsummer 1861 (while MacManus' corpse was at sea), extinguishing the hope for a quick summertime collapse of the rebellion. In the autumn General McClellan began organizing the Army of the Potomac for a prolonged struggle, gathering two hundred thousand recruits for a small first installment. It was noted that thousands of Irish lads were to be found among them. Fenian organizers turned up in Washington to establish centers in the Union army, explaining that this new activity was a roundabout approach to "the day."

Stephens believed that he could rekindle in Virginia and Tennessee the Irish military frame of mind. Long, hard schooling had made Irishmen gun-shy, and a baptism of fire seemed needed to undo the memory of the Penal Laws, the yeoman terror of 1798, and decades of O'Connell's non-violence preachment. A more sophisticated attraction of the war was the opportunity for advanced military training on the American battlefields. While the shooting lasted, it could serve as a school of modern war; when it ended, the Irish pupils would all be graduates, battle-hardened and war-wise. They would (and did) find their way back home and form themselves into a cadre for upgrading the untrained Fenian army already on the scene. The two merged forces were then expected to move in unison to make their own opportunity and settle matters with England.

The cost of Stephens' scheme was to be read in the American casualty lists. Looking on from Richmond, John Mitchel watched the increasing Irish involvement on the Union side and noted sourly that Stephens' program was making a few proficient soldiers and innumerable corpses. One all-Irish brigade, for example, went into action against Lee at Fredericksburg with 1,300 men and straggled out in the evening with only 250 left alive.

In spite of Mitchel's chagrin, the Fenian venture into the American war enhanced the enthusiasm at home. Dr. George Sigerson described the two transatlantic wings of Fenianism as viewing one another "magnified by the sea-mists."[11] Irishmen's servility—"Soft day, sir John, soft day, your honor"—had already been shaken by O'Connell and Young Ireland. The news from American battlefields brought fresh self-esteem. Irish soldiers proved themselves as good as any other, but that was an old story. What was incredible was that large numbers of ordinary Irishmen were actually being commissioned as officers, and not just as second lieutenants. The felon Meagher now wore the stars of a Union general. And Dubliners pondered the case of Mick Corcoran, merely a local peeler until he sailed for New York, who had become General Michael Corcoran and now moved with ease in the circles of the mighty.

Reminding themselves that overseas their comrades were already in arms and would soon take up a place by their side, the Dublin Fenians allowed their optimism to run away with itself, inflating into a fantasy of a formal American invasion with ironclads and the rest of the paraphernalia of easy victory. Overexcitable patriots set a lookout for miraculous American succor, coming like Smith O'Brien's message of hope to the Poles—America to the rescue! A priest of county Queens, one Father Maher, made the salty observation: "The project of the iron-clad ships or by any other scheme of Fenianism is not a whit more ridiculous than if . . . [someone] announced the approach from New York of a fleet of monster sea-gulls, carrying on their backs 100,000 warriors, each with a revolver in his hand and powder and ball and provision for a month in his pocket, to take possession of this isle of ours. . . ."[12]

Those who watched in vain for American salvation were candidates for disenchantment. Echoes of their ancient frustrations persisted down into Joyce's day to sound off in "the citizen's" pronouncement on the American comrades: "We'll put force against force, says the citizen. We have our greater Ireland beyond the sea. . . . But those that came to the land of the free remember the land of bondage. And they will come again and with a vengeance, no cravens, the sons of Granuaile, the champions of Kathleen ni Houlihan."[13] These are history-oriented but highly personal Joycean aversions: a hatred of the 1904 heir of Fenianism, "the citizen," for his Machiavellian ease in inventing lies and his stupidity in believing his own inventions; a hatred also of Irish-Americans as true "cravens," blood brothers of "the citizen" himself. Among Joyce's Americans we recognize our old Phoenix acquaintance from Skibbereen singled out for deflation; for since Joyce knew innumerable Dublin street ballads, he must have known:

> I robbed no man, I spilt no blood, though they sent me to jail;
> Because I was O'Donovan Rossa, and a son of Granuaile.

If the ironclads were not forthcoming, Stephens could still hope for dollars. His home army had the men, but it had no powder and ball. Up to the time of the MacManus funeral, the American Fenians had paid in hardly one-fifth of their 1858 pledge. The first two years of the Civil War saw no improvement. Late in 1863, however, Union victories at Gettysburg and Vicksburg foretold the approaching end of the war and gave hope that Ireland's great day was drawing near. A Fenian convention in Chicago in the autumn of 1863 keynoted a spirit of belligerence and immediacy. After it adjourned, a great burst of generosity swept over the Irish-American community, and in the next twelve months the drought of dollars was broken by a sudden flash flood. Collections increased a hundredfold overnight. By the end of 1864 Stephens was able at last to take action on the one remaining preparatory step for insurrection, the arming of his men.

Dependence on American greenbacks forced Stephens and O'Mahony to throw open the firm to unwelcome partners, the sachems of American Fenianism. Their "shamrock moistened with whisky," the American leaders were inclined toward a hysterical and ignorant style totally foreign to the methods of O'Mahony, Luby, O'Leary, Kickham, or even Mr. Shook himself. There is a quip attributed to O'Faolain:

> Romantic Ireland's dead and gone,
> It's with O'Leary in Chicago.

It was not long before the American subordinates declared themselves to be the principals. The Chicago convention of 1863 stripped O'Mahony of his financial control, transferring it to a "Fenian Senate" composed of Americans. Evidently Stephens was the next on the list. A bystander observed that the Americans told Stephens in effect, "Give us a battle or return our money!"[14] In response to their pressure, he finally fixed "the day," to occur immediately after the cessation of hostilities in America. The year 1865 he named "the year of action."

VI

"The day" was not a close-held secret. Well-armed, the anti-Fenians bestirred themselves to head it off, undertaking a variety of ad hoc countermoves. Their scurrying resembled the activity of the Young Irelanders in 1845 when O'Connell was preparing to cast them out, except that it was now the heirs of Davis who were in the saddle.

Defamation of the Fenian character passed from the *Nation* to other expert hands. The clergy took up A. M. Sullivan's task and augmented his

portrait of the coward patriot with the discovery of new vices, first embezzlement, then "profligacy." The Fenian leaders were charged with squandering in debauchery the pennies wheedled out of poor New York colleens.
Archbishop Cullen issued a pastoral letter pointedly entitled, "Two Letters
to the Catholic Clergy of Dublin, on the Cholera and Other Natural Scour-
ges, and on Orangeism and Fenianism." He represented Stephens and
his lieutenants as "seducers" who skulked "far away from danger, laughing
at the simplicity of their dupes and enjoying the wages of iniquity." And
who might these evil men be? he asked. "Have they been successful in
business? Are they men to whom we would lend money or trust the
management of our property?"[15]

The aging Young Irelanders were asked to save the country from Fenianism. None came to Sullivan's assistance quite as sensationally as Darcy
M'Gee, now transformed into a Canadian spokesman for the empire. On a
return visit to Ireland, he went into Wexford and delivered a speech whose
language was never to be forgiven by Irishmen, and particularly not by one
unbalanced patriot who acted on his own initiative and shot him dead on the
street in Ottawa three years later. M'Gee's speech began with a description
of the American breed of Fenian, then moved by easy transition to the genus
in its totality:

> Their morbid hatred to England has been played upon during the Civil
> War by bounty brokers and recruiting sergeants. . . . They have deluded
> each other, and many of them are ready to betray each other. I have myself
> seen letters from some of the brethren from Chicago, Cincinnati, and other
> places offering their secret minutes and member's rolls for sale; the infamous
> old "stag" business over again; for as sure as filth produces vermin, it is of the
> very nature of such conspiracies as this to breed informers and approvers. . . .
> Men like Thomas Davis and Duffy, and others still living, would have scorned
> to range themselves with these Punch-and-Judy Jacobins, whose sole scheme
> of action seems to be to get their heads broken, and then to squeak out in a
> pitiable treble—"A doctor! ten pounds for a doctor! Send for a doctor!"[16]

The campaign of vituperation necessarily made a cumulative impression
on Irish minds. The Fenian leaders were driven into a characteristic sort of
defensiveness by which they dramatized themselves amid slander as living
proof of the false witness of their traducers. Any Irish public figure was
normally expected to pass through the harrowing of hell, and it was inevitable for Stephens and O'Mahony to be described as monsters of peculation.
For rebuttal, they lived and died in virtual poverty, though both handled
great sums of money. O'Leary's public dramatization of his "old Roman"
probity and stoicism was certainly natural to him, but it was also a specific
answer to M'Gee's Wexford taunt, "Send for a doctor!" flung at him in a

manner that O'Leary took the trouble to describe as "blatant blackguardism" and "corrupt villainy."[17]

The rowdy and scurrilous side of Irish history is familiar to all readers of Irish literature. Irish public controversy often seemed pure madness, yet it did have its decorums. For example, the clergy were permitted vituperation, but rejoinder in kind was disallowed. When O'Leary referred in public to Archbishop Cullen by his naked surname, omitting the deferential "Dr.," he was thought to have outraged civility. Gavan Duffy was simply not himself when he described his clerical opposition in the Tenant League as "the gibbering" of a "horde of busy idiot faces."[18] Even in Joyce's generation, Simon Dedalus' allusion to the "tub of guts up at Armagh" was, in print at least, an astonishing novelty. But as if in recompense for the first rule, the Fenians enjoyed a similar sanctuary in political debate, so that while no limit was set upon the use of personal slander against them, attacks upon their political principles were required to be stated in the name of some patriotism even more noble. T. D. Sullivan complained that "the Fenian leaders were to be free to denounce 'agitation' and 'agitators' to their heart's content"; while "the agitators [i.e., the Sullivans] should not dare to reply, on peril of being held up to opprobrium as aiders, abettors, and informants of the British government."[19] Apart from these two decorums, everybody let his personal spleen be his guide, and naturally all were quick to cry "Foul!" against an opponent. After all, Grattan himself was a virtuoso of vituperation. Those who believe that John O'Leary was incapable of venom would find their opinion shaken by a reading of his attacks upon "A. M. Sullivan-Goulah" in 1863 and 1864. In the same pattern, Yeats's attacks on George Moore, Arthur Griffith, and W. M. Murphy show that he was like everybody else cheerfully at home in the gutter, if there the battle raged.

Not that the Fenians lacked their unique modes of self-expression. After the death of Prince Albert in 1861, the Dublin Corporation announced a plan to erect a memorial statue in College Green. The *Nation* burst into loud protest. The spot where the Volunteers had drilled in '82 could receive only the one fitting memorial, to Henry Grattan. Sullivan called a mass meeting to deplore the insult to Irish honor. Stephens sensed that an agitation of "scribblers and spouters" was afoot, more O'Connellite monster indignation. The Dublin Fenians were called out and given orders to "take over." They jammed the Rotunda, pushed Sullivan and The O'Donoghue of the Glens off the rostrum and out the door of the hall. Sullivan called a second meeting, admission by pass only. The Fenians asked, What kind of a mass meeting is it that requires a pass to get in? Some of them forged passes, but they were exposed by a vigilant doorkeeper in time to prevent a second riot. Disrupted by "England's Allies," as the *Nation* called the Fenians, the agitation over the Albert memorial died.

VII

By 1864 Stephens had thousands of men under his orders in Dublin and Cork, and Kickham had called another fearful hosting on Slievenamon, attended this time by a horde that was disciplined, if still unarmed. In the extreme urgency of the hour, Archbishop Cullen became impatient with the failures of the laity and descended into the arena in person. He announced a new political organization called the National Association of Ireland and summoned the bishops to town to sit with him on the platform of the aggregate meeting. All responded except Archbishop MacHale, whose letter of regret reminded Cullen once more of the firm of Sadleir, Keogh, and Cullen.[20]

The day for launching the association fell not by accident in the same week the news reached Dublin that Sherman had marched into Savannah. On the Rotunda rostrum, raised to extra height to prevent surprise attack by any prowling Fenian scaling party, sat five bishops, six canons, and two priests to represent the rank and file, together with Archbishop Cullen, ready to give the blessing, to deliver the address, to move the first resolution. His speech reviewed the ills of Ireland: depopulation, nearly 40 percent population loss in twenty years; the loss of merchant trade in the county towns; poor farm prices, a compulsive conversation-starter of the strong-farmer class the world around; and general poverty, deepening each year regardless of the emigration. He sketched what seemed to him the causes of these ills: the flooding of Irish rivers, the backwardness of husbandry, the "banishment of manufactures," absenteeism, and the sinful wealth of the Anglican Church of Ireland. When the parliamentary program was presented, it was found to call for only the Ulster tenant right, free sale of improvements, the smallest of the Three Fs. The other two demands were for disestablishment of the Church of Ireland and for a government-funded Catholic college. On the national issue, silence; there was no national program at all.[21]

This was rather a parsimonious counteroffer for an organization hoping to block the Fenian drive toward armed rebellion. Even A. M. Sullivan was dismayed. He would have preferred His Grace to remain behind the scenes where his political obtuseness would be invisible. Stephens and O'Leary barely condescended to assault their new ecclesiastical rival in the field. In Cullen's program they saw O'Connell's old addictions: to beg "a little something for Ireland," to find places for the unemployed Catholic gentility, and to disrupt the projects of the advanced men. The hierarchy, they said, "will be ready to join sham-patriotic movements leading nowhere, such as the Tenant League, the new National League, and others of that stamp; or they will join narrow struggles, tending to promote their own immediate

177

interests; but to a real National movement they will never give their ad-
hesion in good faith."[22] But whatever the triviality of Cullen's response to
the Fenian threat, he had established one momentous precedent. The
"boors in broadcloth" had found a friend in high place; and the Church,
if but ever so timidly, had embarked upon its first agrarian adventure. This
is the inconspicuous seed from which Parnellism later grew.

CHAPTER 12

O'Leary and the Irish People

I

The main trunk of Stephens' revolutionary tree was his secret Irish army, awaiting the issuance of arms. At the peak of Fenian power, this army numbered about eighty thousand civilians, plus fifteen thousand soldiers in the British army, half of them in the Irish garrison regiments and half in northern England. The principal graft upon the trunk was the American brotherhood, an open, legal organization with about forty-five thousand members.[1] To the main stem he had also grafted another branch, an open, agitational, home-soil mass organization called the Brotherhood of St. Patrick. It required no secret oath, hoping to circumvent the Church ban on Carbonari-type organizations, but Cullen simply listed it among the other forbidden fruits and it instantly blighted and dropped off the tree.

The last of Stephens' structural additions to Fenianism was a weekly newspaper, the *Irish People*. Ever since the original quarrel with A. M. Sullivan in 1858, the Fenians had been working closely with a newspaper called the *Irishman*, the *Nation*'s rival weekly. Judging from the abruptness with which it dropped its anti-Fenian stance to take up the terms "felon-setter" and "A. M. Sullivan-Goulah," one can only infer that Stephens had subsidized its publication. This working arrangement was upset by the Fenians' urgent need for money. Luby's arithmetic had led him to imagine that a Fenian newspaper could earn a profit of a thousand pounds a month. Although Stephens believed that a conspiracy ought not to have any newspaper, he was won over by the lure of cash, and on November 28, 1863, the first issue appeared.

Stephens rounded up John O'Leary to help him with the editing; and O'Donovan Rossa, Luby, and Kickham were also added to the staff. Each week after the paper had gone to press, the editors met to relax, like the Young Irelanders in Davis' time. Usually they made their supper of bread and tea, but Kickham remembered a feast that had been sent in as a gift to Rossa by a west Cork patriot:

> After the wild duck and snipe, which had come all the way from Cape Clear . . . there came walnuts and oranges. It is fair to admit that there was also a decanter of what seemed to be the very best Irish whisky, as Luby and O'Leary appreciated a stiff tumbler of whiskey punch. . . . The "Chief Organizer" did not affect the more national beverage, but seemed to have a decided relish for a glass of Guinness's porter. Methinks I see him now—Shakespearian head, flowing auburn beard, lady hand, and all—as he takes his meerschaum from his lips, and pointing with the amber-tipped cherrywood tube to the table, says— "If some people saw that now, what noise there would be about our luxurious habits!"[2]

In three weeks O'Leary was left in full command of the paper. Stephens produced three weighty leading articles and fell back exhausted.[3] With his retirement the paper became O'Leary's entire responsibility, and remained so for the rest of its existence. O'Leary ordinarily wrote only a single article each week, identified as he explained by the scattering of his "perhapses" as contrasted with the "indubitablys" of the other staff contributors. Yet the paper as a whole was really his, since after all he was the editor in chief. If there is a referent for Yeats's epithet "romantic" to describe O'Leary in that well-worn phrase, one should find it in the files of the *Irish People*.

As a money-maker, the *Irish People* was a disappointment. The *Nation* had pre-empted all the more substantial nationalists, so that "there was no public, at least no vocal or literary public, in the least prepared to receive us," O'Leary said. Most of the "talking and writing people" were violently opposed to physical force, and were not absolutely sure of their desire for national independence even if it were free gratis.[4] The *Irish People* thus had very little success in raiding the new *Nation*'s private preserve, and it was T. D. Sullivan's pleasant revenge to be able to say of it in his memoirs, "—and it never paid."[5]

II

As a follower of Davis' teaching, O'Leary felt a special obligation to resurrect Irish cultural nationalism and be once more "racy of the soil." An incorrigible bibliophile, he took up Young Ireland's poetic production at the exact point where it had been interrupted by Davis' death almost twenty years before. Volume one, number one, opened up the literary front with a professional poem by Robert Dwyer Joyce, author of "The Boys of Wexford":

> A stricken plain is good to see,
> When victory crowns the patriot's sword,

> And the gory field seemed fair to me
> Won by our arms at Manning Ford.

This no-nonsense start was approved by the public, for the *Irish People* was immediately deluged with a flood of unsolicited martial verse. O'Leary remarked that "patriotism seems to take a peculiar delight in the manufacture of bad verse, while those who make a good article in this kind are too often not over patriotic." His first editorial job, like Gavan Duffy's on the old *Nation*, was to try to turn back the tide. He cultivated a caustic style, and in the twelfth issue he wrote: "We have received this week such a pile of verses that, though very tired we are tempted to give what we were going to call our poetical contributors a few hints. We confess we do this chiefly to save our own time; for though we are usually told that the authors are hard worked, and only write in the intervals of labor, we are afraid they must have too much time to spare, or rather to waste."[6] There followed a serialized public controversy between O'Leary and the wounded amateur poets. In its course he quoted selections from their works in self-defense, and thus compiled a little anthology of bad patriotic verse along the lines of:

> Sir Hugh O'Neill, a valiant knight,
> Marched toward Armagh with all his might.

Meanwhile he solicited contributions from a number of poets bearing weighty reputations. Many had been original members of Davis' own poetical chorus. Many were women: his sister Ellen, his cousin "Eva of the *Nation*," Parnell's teen-age sister Fanny, Mrs. O'Donovan Rossa, and "Mary of the *Nation*." Besides R. D. Joyce, two more of his poets, T. C. Irwin and John Francis O'Donnell, are remembered in all Irish anthologies. His subeditor Kickham was also a professional, already famous for a song on the emigration theme, which Yeats later anthologized, the tearful "She Lived beside the Anner," and for a popular ballad, "Rory of the Hill":

> "That rake up near the rafters—
> Why leave it there so long ?
> The handle of the best of ash,
> Is smooth, and straight, and strong;
> And, mother, will you tell me
> Why did my father frown,
> When, to make the hay in summer-time,
> I climbed to take it down ?"
> She looked into her husband's eyes,
> While her own with light did fill—
> "You'll shortly know the reason, boy!"
> Said Rory of the Hill.

Back in the 1840s it was noted that when Mangan joined the staff of the old

Nation or Mitchel's *United Irishman*, his poetic inventiveness did not always respond when needed. The *Irish People*'s entire staff of professional poets were a similar disappointment. On assignment, the best Kickham or Irwin could offer was very nearly feeble-minded. In fact, the professional poets were considerably less interesting than the scrappy amateurs. Before the paper was a year old, O'Leary discovered that there was more vitality in naïveté than in talents that were supposed to be proven out. Like Davis, he began to admire the anonymous ballads of the fairs and the casual efforts of a nonpoet, his subeditor O'Donovan Rossa, on the evils of "taking the Queen's shilling":

> I helped to plunder and to slay
> Those tribes of India's sons,
> And I spent many a sultry day
> Blowing Sepoys from our guns.[7]

Although the Fenians, like Young Ireland, put enormous emphasis upon cultural nationalism, they were not very inventive. The single word "Fenian" turned out to be their most striking cultural contribution. (Archbishop Cullen, ignorant of Irish ethnology, guessed that the word must be a corruption of "Phoenician," though it actually referred to the "Fianna," mythical soldiers of Finn MacCumhail, the Gaelic counterpart of British King Arthur.) Even this discovery did not belong to O'Leary's *Irish People*, but to John O'Mahony, interchangeably a Gaelic antiquarian and a Fenian organizer, labors he thought equally important to Irish nationalism. In the patriots' songbook the Fenians made only the one memorable addition, John Casey's "Rising of the Moon," though in their demise they inspired a number of songs and ballads, being, as Plato said, happily more often the subject of encomiums than the authors thereof.

O'Leary meditated on his failure for a long time. In 1886, the year in which he first met Yeats, he was still puzzling over his problem in this fashion: "'Speranza' is certainly *not* entitled to the first place among the delightful warblers of her own sex. 'Mary [of the *Nation*]' is entitled to the first place, 'Eva [of the *Nation*]' to the second. . . ."[8] Eventually he surrendered to reality, and his last statement on the matter was that "the Fenian poets [were] a smaller and weaker band of *littérateurs* than the poets of the *Nation*, but one which accomplished something of note in the domain of practical affairs."[9] We visualize a struggle when O'Leary finally wrote off his poetical auxiliary. In the history of literature, though, his little comedy takes on some significance. Pain had taught him that genuine poetry is somewhat rarer than one would like to suppose. In later times, when this issue became the nub of a controversy between Yeats and Gavan Duffy, his experience on the *Irish People* had readied him to come to Yeats's defense.

III

An essential borrowing from Davis was the *Irish People*'s ferocious non-sectarianism. Its demand for no priests in politics was so insistent as to become at times its sole message. The religious war was conducted mostly by Kickham, the one devout member on O'Leary's staff. His weekly leading article normally took off from a citation of some fresh sally by Cullen, Moriarty, or one of the more ardently loyalist priests, such as a certain Father Burke of Clonmel, who was reported to have made a denunciation from the altar as follows: "The *Irish People* he described as a Government organ, employed to put down the priests first and to sell their dupes after for Government gold. He reminded his hearers that any one reading that paper was excommunicated, and that heads of families allowing it into their houses, or those over whom they had control to read it, were damned. As for the Fenians, they were the scruff of the earth—a wretched rabble; he would ask but two peelers to drive one hundred of them before them, like chaff before the wind."[10]

Well primed by provocation, Kickham's weekly article then turned to Davis' nonsectarian rule: an Irishman was to be judged strictly according to his political behavior, never by his religion. Catholicism and nationality, he reiterated, must never be considered interchangeable terms. A well-known Yeatsian debating point was often asserted, that "nine-tenths of the leading patriots for the last century have been Protestants." But the watchful O'Leary was not satisfied with that formulation. He took pains to correct the simplistic two-way classification, observing that there were not two religious categories in Ireland, but three, the "Protestant patriots" being merely so-called from courtesy, having actually no religion at all.[11] O'Leary's third category clarified a confusion that Yeats never resolved but that Joyce understood well and exploited humorously in the character of Mr. Deasy, his burlesque Orangeman in *Ulysses*, who paradoxically claimed that by being the more bigoted Protestant he was the more genuine patriot.

What must be the feelings in a decent Christian's heart, Kickham asked, when he learns that "the dignitaries of his church, who know not want and nakedness themselves," are the friends of his oppressors? The priests and bishops had slandered devout and unselfish patriots and denied them the sacraments of the Church, he said, but they toadied to every odious impostor; so that "those who would prepare to grapple with the despoiler, and save a suffering people from destruction, are vilified and denounced" while "the base recreant, the place-beggar, the political mountebank, the ermined perjurer [the inevitable Sadleir and Keogh], the very exterminator—all these are courted and smiled upon and blessed." He quoted the seventeenth-century Franciscan, Luke Wadding: "Time was when we had wooden chalices and golden priests, but now we have golden chalices and wooden priests."[12]

The effectiveness of the Fenians' campaign against priests in politics was long debated. T. D. Sullivan thought it had "alarmed and shocked not merely 'the priest'; but multitudes of Catholics in every station in life." O'Leary conceded that the "poison" of Cullen's pastorals was "diffused through a thousand channels through which the refutation can never enter," and that when a parish priest denounced the Fenians from the altar, many parishioners would certainly take him seriously. With his characteristic caution presumably intact, though, he estimated that for each person so influenced, five others turned away from the denouncer in disgust. "We meant to kill clerical dictation," he said in summary, "and we did kill it. If it has come to life again in another generation [i.e., in Parnell's mid-career and fall], the fault is not ours."[13]

IV

But the *Irish People* was not published merely to print martial verses and to exchange insults with the Sullivans and the clergy. Its purpose was to make a revolution. T. D. Sullivan criticized it for letting out the secret every Saturday that an Irish military effort was in preparation. It "ruined the Fenian movement," he said. And O'Leary had to grant that the paper did expose the organization.[14] But necessarily so. It could hardly broadcast the approach of "the day" to unknown Irish friends without the government's buying a paper and eavesdropping. Assuming that the government was bound to know approximately the state of the conspiracy in any case, O'Leary made no secret of the Fenians' generalized methods and objectives. But on timing he offered only enigmas. His battle talk was always stated as innuendo, as though he knew all but would tell nothing. In reality he did not know any more than his readers. And Stephens himself did not know any more than anybody else.

For, when the supposed optimum instant to strike the Fenian blow drew near, Stephens was discovered by his lieutenants to be in deep trouble. His war machine was assembled and poised, but he had neglected to provide it with weapons. There were "no sinews of war," as his enemies wrote in mockery of his prose style. The American branch, suspecting him of lying about his strength, sent their own agents over to Ireland on an inspection. They found the muster and spirit exactly as high as he had claimed—but there were no arms to strike with.

Stephens had some justification for this oversight. For six years he had had no money, and when the money finally arrived from overseas, it could not readily be turned into armament. In 1865 pikes were worse than useless in military combat, as his veteran Civil War advisers explained to him. But pikes were the poetic weapons of Irish insurrection, and lacking anything better, Stephens opened up a pike factory in Dublin with branches in blacksmith shops throughout the country. By midsummer after Appomattox, these constituted the full extent of his armory. As for rifles, he could supply one for each five hundred men. When John Devoy told him the Fenians could not fight without rifles and asked where he proposed to get them, he "received 'The Captain's' assurance that we'd get all we wanted from America,"[15] as though the problem of procuring, shipping, landing, and distributing a hundred thousand contraband rifles was too simple to require discussion.

It is not clear just what Stephens had in mind to do. On the face of it, his talk of American arms already on their way sounded like Father Maher's comical sea gulls. It is likely, though, that he was gambling on the chance that American animosity against England might explode into a diplomatic break, or perhaps that the United States might recognize the Fenians as belligerents, as England had recognized the Confederacy. His thought was not fantasy; in 1865 the relations between the United States and England were very tense over the *Alabama* claims, an American demand to be compensated for the wartime destruction of its merchant marine by the *Alabama* and the other Confederate raiders, in actuality British-built and British-manned warships flying the Confederate flag. Had a break between the two countries occurred, all of Stephens' problems would naturally have vanished. But if he was calculating on such a stroke of luck, he failed like Mitchel to take into account the fact that the existence of his revolutionary organization had made that very contingency unthinkable.

Under Irish-American pressure, as we have seen, Stephens fixed the year 1865 as positively "the year of action." Since his predicament demanded the maximum of delay, the month he chose was December. If, as seemed virtually certain, the midnight bells rang December 31 on a Dublin still at peace, he would have to worry about that when the time came and talk his way out of his embarrassment if he could. But before that time arrived, the initiative passed out of his hands. The government concluded that if 1865 was to be the year of action, it had better take action of its own.

V

A spy had found his way into O'Leary's editorial office. There was in Dublin a Fenian schoolteacher, Pierce Nagle by name, who felt his sensibilities bruised by Stephens' domineering manner. He sailed to New York and called on the British consulate officials to offer his services as a spy. A business arrangement was agreed upon, beginning with the payment of his fare back to Dublin, where he was hired by the *Irish People* as a wrapper in the mail room. He found very little to report to the police for some time, but in September 1865 his opportunity presented itself. A Fenian from Clonmel came to the editorial office bearing a message for "the Captain." Stephens read the message, then entrusted to him an order for the Clonmel centers, warning them to make ready for action. "There is no time to be lost," the message said. "This year must be the year of action. I speak with a knowledge and authority to which no other man could pretend, and I repeat the flag of Ireland—of the Irish Republic—must this year be raised."[16] Stephens also gave the courier some money for a treat. Later in the day the courier returned drunk. Nagle put him to bed on a pressroom bench, and as he did so he removed Stephens' letter from the man's pocket. He took it to the police on the morning of September 15, 1865. That same evening the Dublin detective force appeared at the *Irish People* offices, seized the files, and arrested everybody found there. Luby and Rossa and eight others were picked up before morning. O'Leary returned to his lodging at nine o'clock after supper with a lady and found two detectives waiting for him. While he asked them to please be seated, he poured himself a tumbler of whisky and filled his pipe, and when they were consumed, the three left together for the police station.

The spy Nagle, planted in the *Irish People*'s mail room, represented the third of his kind to surface into Irish history since 1803. The first two, already met along the way, were Kirwan, the Orange *provocateur* of 1848, and Sullivan-Goulah, the Phoenix informer. Nagle was by far the most damaging spy yet to appear, and he made a model for the secret police. Their work made a deep impression on the Irish mind, arousing such resentment that if exposed, few of the spies lived to die a natural death. (Nagle himself was attacked on the street in London many years afterward and died in a hospital from the beating.) But Castle spies aroused a good deal of fear, too, an attitude formulated for literature most notably by Joyce. All readers of *A Portrait of the Artist* remember that one of Stephen Dedalus' prime sources of disenchantment with Ireland was his foreknowledge that every Irish "hurley-stick rebellion" would produce its "indispensable informer." The most distinguished of all the victims of the Castle's informer system was John O'Leary; hence his considered thoughts about the subject carry a sort of authority. "There are something like periodical panics in Ireland on this subject of informers," he said, "but happily the panic is mostly confined to people little likely to risk life or liberty in her cause; neither pressmen nor priests [i.e., the chief disseminators of spy scares], as far as I could ever make out, have succeeded in striking terror into the popular heart."[17]

O'Leary was caught by the spy Nagle but not actually convicted by him. Stephens' message to alert the Clonmel centers did not constitute sufficient evidence against the *Irish People*'s staff, so the attorney general had to fish for what he could catch in wastebaskets and closets. Luby possessed as a common human failing a distaste against throwing anything away. Realizing the danger of this quirk to a practicing revolutionary, he had made up a bundle of all his incriminating papers so that they could be destroyed easily, and a short time before his arrest he took the bundle to the fireplace and burned it. Or so he though; but as it turned out he had by mistake burned his wife's love letters instead. When the police searched his house, they found a prize.

It was a strange letter to the editor written by a journalist, not a Fenian, named Christopher O'Keeffe. Luby and O'Leary both understood that O'Keeffe was half-cracked, and they laughed at an obsession he nursed, that England could be beaten into the dust by a boycott in New York against Belfast linens. But he was a journeyman journalist whose pieces the *Irish People* often bought and printed, after severe editing, under the pen name "Ollamh Fodhla." The letter found in Luby's house was so wild that the *Irish People* would never have printed it, even in part, and Luby had kept it only "as a curiosity." It said: "The French exterminated their aristocracy, and every honest revolution must imitate that of France. We must do the same. But you ask me, 'How are we to get at these men?' My reply is, 'How did the French get at them?' They first wrote them down by the pens of their Voltaires, and then slew them by the hands of the *sansculottes*. We can do as much. . . . the Irish aristocracy must be hounded down by the liberal press and slain afterwards by the hands of an aroused and infuriate people."[18]

VI

Two judges were assigned to the trial—one an ordinary party placeman, the other, Judge William Keogh of the political fellowship of Sadleir and Keogh, a placeman of more note. For the prosecution, the crown was represented by C. R. Barry, Q.C. Resting his case on O'Keeffe's crazy letter, he charged that "the operations of this revolution, as it is called, were to be commenced by an indiscriminate massacre—by the assassination of all those above the lower classes, including the Roman Catholic clergy, against whom their animosity appears, from their writings, to be especially directed."[19] For the defense, the Fenians retained Isaac Butt.

Luby was the first of the prisoners to be convicted. For fear of prejudicing the later cases, he denied himself the luxury of expressing his feelings about the personalities of the court, and confined himself instead to generalities and first principles, stated with exemplary demeanor. "Well, my lords and gentlemen," he said to the court, "I don't think any person present here is surprised at the verdict found against me." But as for the imputation that he had desired to assassinate the priests and landlords, that charge he must declare to be false. Anyone who held such an opinion could never have read the *Irish People*. It had consistently taught reverence for the clergy in their strictly "sacerdotal function," though it had criticized them, vigorously too, when they took unpatriotic political positions not related to their religious vocation. As for the charge of disloyalty at issue, he believed, to be sure, that "nothing can ever save Ireland except Independence." He was naturally unhappy to find himself a victim of British law, but he was pleased to know that the news of his conviction would prove to the world that Ireland could never be lost as long as it contained men prepared "to expose themselves to every difficulty and danger in its service," not excluding, if need be, death itself.[20] Thereupon he was sentenced to twenty years of penal servitude.

O'Leary was the next to be convicted. A. M. Sullivan was present in the courtroom to cover the trial for the *Nation*. "Sad thing, terrible things," he wrote, "have since his arrest and imprisonment been written, uttered, and published of him, and of a brother now no more, by personages whose position forbids much comment at my hands. . . . I pass these statements by." To print a charge so nebulous against one forbidden to reply seemed unforgivable to O'Leary, although the scandal itself was apparently nothing more than that he and his dead brother had left off going to Mass. All the rest of the *Nation*'s news story was on the fulsome side. "His hair is dark, long, and thick," Sullivan's eyewitness description continued, "his moustache and beard are of the same color, the latter flowing profusely over his breast, his prominent Roman nose and deep piercing eye, set beneath fine eyebrows and a noble forehead, gave an air of great command and determination to his countenance. And he not only seems, but *is* a gentleman, in mind, in manner, in education, and in social position. He belongs to one of the most worthy, amiable, and respectable families in Tipperary."[21] Several years later the Sullivan brothers published a lucrative volume called *Speeches from the Dock*, in which O'Leary's heroic colors were still more heightened: "He stepped boldly to the front with a flash of fire in his dark eyes, and a scowl on his features, looking hatred and defiance on judges, lawyers, jurymen, and all the rest of them."[22] The high-flown prose struck O'Leary as being somehow very comical, in spite of his dreadful predicament, and long afterward he liked to quote it for the amusement of his friends.[23]

O'Leary's speech to the court was less courteous than Luby's. Since he was obviously slated for the same sentence, he proposed to speak his mind. He denounced the "foul charge" of plotting assassinations made against him by the prosecutor, "that miserable man Barry." So he had been found guilty of treason ? It was a loathsome crime; Dante put traitors in the ninth circle of hell. But between himself and the court, who was the traitor? "England is not my country," he said to Judge Keogh. "[Algernon] Sidney and Emmet were legal traitors. Jeffreys was a loyal man, and so was Norbury. I leave the matter there."[24] Thereupon he too was sentenced to twenty years of penal servitude.

The court relaxed with a couple of seven- and ten-year-sentence cases, then Rossa was next. His position was hopeless, for in addition to the treason charges arising from his work on the *Irish People*, he also had the old suspended sentence from the Tralee assizes of 1859 hanging over him. He decided to make his downfall as sensational as he could. To save Butt from professional embarrassment, Rossa announced that he would be his own advocate. He had brought into court voluminous files as pertinent evidence, and he opened his defense by reading the printed minutes of the Chicago convention, followed by the files of the *Irish People*. Hours passed, and still he was reading the interminable satires on the "solo trombone of the Pope's Brass Band," the "second Norbury," the "renegade ruffian" and "ermined perjurer." As Rossa's voice and energy began to fail, he suggested several times a brief court recess; Keogh replied, "Proceed, sir." After eight and a half hours he collapsed and surrendered, saying, "There, let the dirty law now take its course." The next day he was found guilty and sentenced to penal servitude for life.[25]

VII

So O'Leary gave up the Bohemian life of a journalist and littérateur to pick oakum in Pentonville prison, from which he later graduated to rock-breaking at Portland. The treatment of the Irish felon had changed greatly since Mitchel used to take coffee and cigars with the lieutenant of the guard at sea and hunt the kangaroo through the Tasmanian bush. The English penal colonies overseas had been dismantled since the days of Young Ireland because of protests from the Australian and South African residents. Now the grim choice of evils was only between hanging and imprisonment. The latter was normally to be preferred, but not greatly. Complaints against "pampering" of criminals had been pressed forward by all of Carlyle's followers, including Mitchel himself, until they were heeded in Whitehall and "pampering" had ceased. After 1865 complaints continued, but they were now directed more against prison sadism, with the Fenian prisoners cited as the most spectacular victims. O'Leary had to bear a systematized cruelty in English prisons, though less than Rossa and many other Fenians experienced. As Yeats often told us, he did not afterward like to relive his prison life and would ordinarily refuse to discuss the subject. "I was in the hands of my enemy," he said. He put aside his reticence only once, to recount, as an instance of British taste, a jail visit from Lady Peel, who opened the flap in his cell door to stare reprovingly at the sinner inside.[26]

Beginning with the *Irish People* trials, the Dublin criminal court became a familiar stage for nationalist dramatic effects. There would be little contrition displayed in the hope of gentlemen's agreements in judges' chambers. The prisoner might be courteous, or he might not, but he would not be repentant. Isaac Butt's final conversion from the *Dublin University Magazine*'s Orangeism followed from his admiration for the astonishing earnestness and self-effacement of Luby, O'Leary, Rossa, and their comrades in the dock. Even the Sullivans were about to revise their opinion of these "Punch-and-Judy Jacobins." The Fenians might in fact be "priest hunters" and "priest burners" and "bad men guided by bad principles." Let that be as it might, said the *Nation*, the phoenix was still, of all the birds that fly, the least likely to be cajoled or blarneyed or "caught with chaff"; and it was ready to confess that it was the Fenians alone who "forget not Israel."[27]

O'Leary's arrest removed him from the Dublin scene just when the excitement commenced. In absolute time the Fenian movement lasted nine years, from 1858 to 1867. He had been in the game through seven innings, so to speak. But the main impact of Fenianism was concentrated in the last two years. O'Leary missed all that and had no special knowledge of it. The events that happened after his arrest are covered in a couple of footnotes to his book on the Fenian movement. Since Yeats was dependent on O'Leary's lead, he lost the Fenian thread at the same point, severing contact with a very lively body of historical folklore. But where he dropped out, other writers came in—especially Joyce, O'Casey, and Brendan Behan.

CHAPTER 13

"*The Year for Action*"

I

The police raids on the *Irish People* failed to catch James Stephens. The most-wanted Fenian bird had flown past those nets. It was generally supposed that he would appear next morning at the head of his men on barricades in College Green, and A. M. Sullivan informed his brother that they would certainly see the signal for a rising "ere twenty-four hours." The Dublin garrison was called out at three in the morning, while artillery and more infantry rushed in from the Cork and Fermoy garrisons. But there was no insurrection that morning nor in the morning that followed. Meanwhile Stephens could not be apprehended. Police searched trains and ships, questioned travelers, investigated every oddity of garment or facial ornament that suggested a disguise. All their leads led nowhere, and they concluded that he must have escaped to America.

All the while Stephens was not exactly under the nose of the police, as the saying is, but was approximately so, being only an easy stroll from Dublin Castle. He was living quietly in Fairfield House, Sandymount, without false whiskers or nun's habit, but simply as himself, though he went under the name of "Mr. Herbert," a keen horticultural enthusiast who was sometimes seen by the neighbors puttering about his greenhouse. On the day after the raids he sent off a letter to O'Mahony in New York reporting correctly that "the enemy is in a rage, and striking like a madman. Like a madman, for, as far as I can yet see, he is much in the dark."[1] He had outsmarted the police, but his exploit had not solved any of his own crushing problems.

Stephens' followers groped in the same dark as his enemy. His membership was awaiting some sort of instructions. The letter to New York reported: "They sent a party in search of me, in order to know what should be done." All he could tell them was just to go home. He had often called Smith O'Brien a clumsy amateur; now in his own first crisis he found professionalism harder than he had supposed. His army had been reduced back to polyps by the sudden disappearance of the solitary center of intelligence and command. Sullivan might think that insurrection was inevitable, but

Stephens knew it was impossible. "Had we been prepared," he wrote O'Mahony, "last night would have marked an epoch in our history. But we were not prepared. . . ."

Stephens stayed in hiding in Sandymount for nearly two months. The proven elusiveness of the mysterious revolutionist caught the fancy of many Irishmen who had avoided all previous traffic with Fenianism. Weird rumors and alarms succeeded one another. Rumor said that Stephens scorned arrest because there was no jail in Ireland strong enough to hold him. Rumor said that O'Leary, Luby, Rossa, and the other prisoners had nothing to fear, for they would soon be wearing the ermine and the wig, while judge and prosecutor would be cringing in the dock. Then the police discovered the hiding place. They surrounded Fairfield House at dawn on November 11, 1865, and captured Stephens in his nightshirt, together with Kickham, Edward Duffy (the tubercular head center for Connaught), two thousand pounds in cash, and large siege stores of food and drink.

A few days after capture, Stephens was brought under heavy guard to the Castle Yard for arraignment before a magistrate. The streets were full of curious Dubliners trying to get a glimpse of the modern Eamonn an Chnuic inside the Sassenachs' prison van. The nobs and their ladies from the Vice-regal Lodge had reserved seats in the courtroom for a close but safe view of their quarry. Stephens listened to the clerk read his incriminating Clonmel letter, and at the phrase that 1865 must be the year of action he commented loudly, to the surprise of his distinguished listeners, "So it may be." Asked if he would enter a plea, he declined because, he said, to do so would recognize British law in Ireland: "Now I deliberately and conscientiously repudiate the existence of that law in Ireland. I defy and despise any punishment it can inflict on me. I have spoken."[2] This little speech was as close as Stephens would ever come to adding his chapter to the impressive genre of Irish jail literature. For his great state trial for treason, which was to scotch the rebellion and send its indispensable leader to prison, never came to pass.

II

Richmond jail was strong enough to hold Stephens exactly two weeks. Among the sworn Fenians in Dublin was a jailer named Daniel Byrne, whose duty it was to patrol the Richmond corridors after midnight. He had a friend, John Breslin, working in the prison hospital as a pharmacist, who was allowed free access to all parts of the jail in order to report on the illness of prisoners and to deliver medicine to the cells. His dispensary duties brought him to Stephens' cell for consultation unusually often. Their subject was not the prisoner's health, but the architecture of the building. Between Stephens and his freedom stood the locked door of his cell, at the end of the main corridor a locked door giving on the stairs that led outside, an inner prison wall, and a very high outside wall. There were also the regular patrols of the night, and as an extra precaution the warden had put a jail-bird in the cell between Stephens and Kickham and provided him with a gong that he was commanded to ring if he heard anything peculiar happening next door. All these difficulties seemed surmountable. The problem of the locked doors was to be solved by making a beeswax imprint of the master keys, from which a Fenian locksmith could file passkeys. The inner wall was to be scaled by a ladder that Byrne would leave negligently nearby. The outer wall required friends on the outside with a rope ladder, one end to be anchored outside, the other end to be tossed on signal over the wall to Stephens.

Every dangerous Irish adventure in modern history intermingled a generous measure of audacity and poise with a residue of bungling. The Fenian who was assigned to bring the beeswax did not respond, and Breslin was forced to run the risk of exposure by buying it himself. Then the keys would not fit. Finally the keys were ready and the rendezvous time set for the dozen-odd outside men, led by John Devoy and Thomas Kelly, the American stand-in for Stephens. That night Byrne treated his fellow patrols to extra porter and, as he hoped, they fell asleep leaning back in their chairs in the corridor. At one in the morning Breslin and Byrne came with the keys and let Stephens out of his cell. The jailbird adjoining, hearing him leave, was too frightened to ring the gong. Then out the locked corridor door by the second pass key, down the steps and into the foreyard. The ladder was there, but when it was put against the inner wall it turned out to be four feet too short to reach the top. Stephens was hidden in an empty sentry box while Breslin and Byrne went back into the jail hospital and brought out two tables. These were placed one on the other with the ladder on top. Stephens climbed up and jumped over, alone now, into the outer court. He threw a bit of gravel over the outer wall; a piece of sod flew back over to him and a duck quacked for reply. His friends were there all right. Nearby they had met a policeman sheltering himself from the cold drizzle under a tree by the canal; but they had given him a friendly stiff drink from a flask of whisky and he had gone his way. They threw the rope ladder over the wall and soon Stephens' head appeared at the top. He looked down; it was eighteen feet to the ground. Nothing for it but to jump. The men below tried to break his fall and were knocked flat in the mud. But the deed was done and one of Devoy's men said to him, "John, we have tonight witnessed the greatest event in history."[3]

At four in the morning Byrne "discovered" the ladder and tables and gave the alarm. As the news broke over the city at breakfast time, the Fenians were unable to disguise their pleasure. A. M. Sullivan remembered afterward that those who had taken the oath exposed their secret to the world by their frank and happy brilliance of eye. The anti-Fenians were also easy to spot. The ones with the hangdog look were the plainclothes detectives; the haggard faces belonged to the Castle officialdom.

The Castle was thrown into total confusion by Stephens' newest disappearance. The very foundation of the state, the bridewell itself, was honeycombed with secret treason. The officials sacked the jail warden, but since he was clearly not the guilty party, they pursued other suspects, especially Byrne. Finding a Fenian oath and pamphlets in his desk, they arrested him; but after two juries failed to convict him, they allowed him to leave the country. Breslin they did not suspect, and he quietly resigned and emigrated a year later, giving a full account of the exploit as soon as he was safely out of reach in America. For Stephens himself they once more looked everywhere. They mobilized the troops and raided houses where he was reported seen, searched the ships in the harbor, and posted placards offering two thousand pounds reward. Neither diligence nor remorse could bring back the twice-flown prisoner; and Stephens was never again to be apprehended, though he remained in Ireland for several months longer.

The more cynical segment of Dubliners argued that the government officials could not conceivably be as stupid as they appeared, and therefore the escape had been made with their connivance for some sinister purpose that would in time reveal itself. Stephens' defiance when arraigned in magistrate court was cited as clinching proof: no wonder he was so self-assured, when his escape was prearranged. Another segment of native Dublin responded to the escape with the most intense delight. All witnesses reported that in surprise, excitement, and popular identification with the object of a hue and cry, Stephens' jailbreak was one of the high emotional peaks of Irish history. The moment did have its solemn side; people reminded themselves that this meant civil war. But the imprisonment of a patriot outlaw was a serious matter, too, and for Stephens to have vanished not once but twice gave to the whole exploit an irresistible picaresque charm.

The Richmond jailbreak appears as such only the one time in Irish literature, in the *Ulysses* leitmotiv of "the man that got away James Stephens." Joyce's interest centered on the accretion of mystery mixed with imposture that grew about the legend itself. "The" man that got away James Stephens, if there must be but one, was John Breslin, long since absorbed into the New York Irish community and dead fifteen years before Joyce's time. But directly involved were a dozen or so other Fenians, the muster of the rescue squad outside Richmond wall. As time passed, this number apparently tended to enlarge, since there was enough secrecy about the affair to encourage bogus claimants to insinuate their way into painless heroism. "The" man thus floats about Joyce's Dublin as a sort of an impostor ghost, embodied first in "the citizen," as cognate with Ireland's champion shot-putter and green chauvinist, and finally alighting upon Mr. Bloom in one of his comic fantasies of mock-heroic grandeur. But Joyce found no place in his structure for any of the more common Dublin responses to the escape. Naturally, he had no sympathy with Dublin Castle. Neither could he see his way to allow the Irish populace—"cute as a fox," in Stephen Dedalus' words—its modest recompense of laughter at the Castle outwitted.

III

Stephens in hiding still held to his assertion that 1865 would be the year for action. His organization was intact, for the loss of the *Irish People* and its staff was not catastrophic. Moreover, the procurement of arms had finally begun. During the summer Colonel Ricard O. Burke, an American Fenian recently demobilized from the Army of the Potomac, had been sent to England to set up a secret purchasing agency for arms. A polyglot of great resourcefulness, he had assumed various poses and Latin-American aliases and got access to the small-arms factories in Birmingham; and he had already taken delivery on two thousand Enfield rifles, which had been shipped to Liverpool and cached there until needed. He had negotiated large additional contracts for arms to be delivered as soon as more funds arrived from America.

At this critical moment the Fenian movement in America split open and began to disintegrate. The American Fenian Senate had fallen under the control of one Colonel William Roberts, a wealthy dry goods merchant. He distrusted Stephens increasingly, and Stephens retorted in kind with recrimination against the senate's parsimony and amateur generalship far from the field of battle. Simultaneously, the relations between Colonel Roberts and O'Mahony also grew more acrimonious. The senate had assumed most of O'Mahony's functions at the Chicago convention in 1863, and at a convention held in Philadelphia in October 1865 most of his remaining powers were taken away, leaving him not much more than the title of president.

O'Mahony's friction with the senate was probably attributable to a hidden source in his own office.[4] He had for a political confidant a voluble master of blarney named "Red Jim" MacDermott, a veteran of the Papal Brigade, which Irishmen organized to save Pio Nono from his democratic enemies. O'Leary and Stephens independently of each other had spotted MacDermott as a possible informer and an undeniable "blackguard." O'Mahony refused to listen to their warnings, and as it turned out, he really was an informer, though the fact was not proved until nearly twenty years later. "Red Jim" was probably the one referred to in Darcy M'Gee's Wexford speech as anxious to sell the membership lists to the Castle. He was a gifted *agent provocateur*; moreover, achieving rare heights of secret-police versatility, he was an accomplished disrupter, carrying malicious tales between O'Mahony and Roberts until their mutual hatred was beyond the cure of any peacemaker. In a bitter reminder of these services, Joyce in *Ulysses* placed him beside the great seventeenth-century Gaelic chieftain, Hugh O'Donnell. In the catalogue of Irish heroes and mock heroes, "Red Hugh" and "Red Jim" paired off as the Siamese twins of Joycean history.

The immediate occasion of the American split was rather petty. O'Mahony, as president of the Fenian Brotherhood, had signed some Fenian warbonds that were supposed to have been signed by somebody else. Hearing of this breach, the senate met in emergency session and fired him from the presidency on December 2, 1865, one week after Stephens' escape from Richmond jail. O'Mahony thereupon pronounced himself the true head of American Fenianism and appealed to Dublin for support. Stephens felt called upon to bring out the heavy artillery of his authority to blast the American dissidents. He wrote O'Mahony a letter that was broadcast through the Irish-American community, characterizing the senators—that is, the holders of his American purse strings—as knaves, cowards, and traitors: "To break with treason and baseness of all kinds, to brand it, smash it—was the policy, and I rejoice at your having made it yours. The manhood of Ireland rejoices at it with me. . . . Cut and hack the rotten branches around you without pity."[5]

The American split naturally brought the flow of dollars into the Irish revolution to a dead halt. The moment chosen by Roberts for his break with O'Mahony could not have fallen at a more sensitive time, since it disrupted the purchase of arms in Birmingham just as Colonel Burke had made a successful opening. Without cash, that door was shut. In the last weeks of December 1865, the year of action, Stephens' Irish centers were still without arms, and without any prospect of arms.

IV

Stephens now showed symptoms of advanced demoralization as his great strength of will began to falter. His short imprisonment had disturbed him, too. Like O'Connell, another illustrious inmate of Richmond jail, he was not quite as self-assured when he came out as when he went in. In the last days of 1865, driven by the logic of the situation to make some kind of explanation to his members, he called in all the head centers one or two at a time and put a peculiar, ambiguous question to them: Could they restrain their members from precipitate action for four weeks or so ? Thus he broke the news of his inability to keep his long-promised date, but at the same time kept their enthusiasm up and drew the sting from his confession of failure. But so stated, the postponement bore a date of expiration, and he was soon back in the same embarrassment again.

The four weeks had passed without any new signs of action. John Devoy, who was in command of all the centers in the garrison regiments, reported to Stephens that a couple of the army units were threatening to start something on their own if he did not give the word. Just then, the British army command caught its first astonished glimpse into the spread of Fenian recruitment among the troops. On February 17, 1866, Lord John Russell, newly returned as prime minister, suspended habeas corpus, rushing the bill through both houses during a single sitting and securing the royal assent the same evening in order to take maximum advantage of surprise. The next morning the police began mass arrests of all outspoken nationalists, together with a swarm of English, Scots, and American Fenians who had gathered in Ireland in large numbers, disguised not very deceptively as tourists. Unless Stephens acted quickly, he would in a very short time have left no organization with which to act.

With his key men disappearing hourly as police caught them on the streets and in their lodging houses, Stephens summoned an unofficial war council of eight advisers, a concession to organizational democracy unprecedented for him. It met on February 20 and 21, 1866, across from the Kildare Street Club in a house belonging to a Mrs. Butler, a society seamstress, subsequently to be ruined when the word of the meeting leaked out and her aristocratic clientele cut her cold. Present at the meeting were Stephens; Thomas Kelly, the American; a second American officer; and the head centers for Athlone, Cork, Limerick, and Ulster; besides John Devoy, whom Patrick Pearse called "the greatest of the Fenians," a twenty-three-year-old military veteran from the French Foreign Legion.[6]

The question debated in Mrs. Butler's dressmaking shop was strictly practical: Were there any avenues open that offered a chance of success for a military assault ? The men present understood perfectly that the success of any bold stroke could never by the nature of things be guaranteed. They understood, too, that to do nothing might be equally dangerous. The discussion therefore confined itself to weighing the reasonable probability against the stubborn fact. Nobody delivered any speeches, said Devoy.

An inventory showed that in all Ireland the Fenians could field only eighteen hundred rifles, most of them in Dublin. But thirty thousand rifles were stored in each of the four provincial army arsenals, and Devoy thought them possibly accessible to Fenian raiders striking by surprise with available forces. The Dublin arsenal at Pigeon House was particularly tempting. This information excited everybody except Stephens. His determination not to fight, though silent, was apparent as the evening wore on, deadening the council until the meeting broke off from fatigue, to meet again after a few hours' sleep.

When the war council reconvened, the atmosphere was more skeptical: how could sixteen hundred Fenians seize a Dublin defended by six thousand regular soldiers? Devoy offered a different arithmetic. The Dublin garrison contained sixteen hundred sworn Fenians, besides another two thousand sympathetic Irishmen. If all these went over to the attack, the score would be fifty-two hundred attackers against twenty-four hundred defenders. Devoy proposed opening the insurrection in the southwest part of the city at Richmond barracks, where two-thirds of the garrison were sworn Fenians and success seemed certain. With the men and rifles picked up at Richmond they could then move toward the heart of the city, gathering momentum as they overwhelmed the barracks along the way, first Island Bridge, then Portobello, then Beggars Bush, until they had sufficient men and rifles to attack the Pigeon House arsenal and the Castle. Kelly and the second American officer were dubious: what if the Fenians in the Dublin garrison would not come over? Devoy was the only man present who knew what they could be expected to do, but the Americans could not be convinced. They thought there should be simultaneous attacks at Richmond and Pigeon House. If they could get the two thousand rifles that Colonel Burke had stored in Liverpool, it would be possible. But that would take several days, and every hour was precious. On that conditional note the meeting trailed off without taking any vote. The result, said Devoy, was that "the last chance for a Rising in that year was thrown away."[7] The most terrible military weapon, the mutiny of Irish troops in the British army, which even Smith O'Brien believed a virtual certainty in 1848, was never to be put to a test in Irish history.

The following day Devoy was arrested. By the end of the week, three thousand Fenians were locked up in jail. Stephens fled the country. It was rumored that he drove secretly through the heart of Dublin disguised as a grand man, lording it in his coach-and-four with liveried grooms before and behind, and that at dusk, when the coach stopped beside the sea beyond Malahide, he was rowed out to a charcoal boat riding at anchor awaiting him. This was A. M. Sullivan's version, romantic enough, said O'Leary, for a police spy's weekly report. Actually, he walked down the landing steps of the Dublin quays into a dory at nine in the evening.

V

Two weeks later Stephens turned up in Paris, en route by leisurely stages to New York to heal the American split. He sent a letter ahead to O'Mahony outlining his intention toward the schismatics: "All these scandals are nearly at an end and only await my appearance, yonder, to die outright, and be forever forgotten. Tell all those dear to us that I go to the States to do such work as shall quicken their frames with joy. I know no such thing as doubt and difficulties must go down before me. . . . I pledge my word that every Irishman who stands in our way shall go down."[8] Father William D'Arcy, the scholar who discovered this document, observes that Stephens was "never one to underestimate his powers." But the Americans were more intractable than expected and wholly absorbed in imaginative projects of their own devising.

For, after the American split, the senate faction had come to the conclusion that it ought to open the battle of Dublin by an attack against Canada, anticipating the Joycean theory that the shortest way to Tara is via Holyhead. Their thought was that if they could seize control of any Canadian seaboard territory, they could use it as a base to fit out Fenian privateers and make holiday hunting down English commerce on the high seas. British Columbia first suggested itself. Then Quebec seemed more convenient. Later they decided to conquer Canada as a whole with a pincers movement from Detroit on the west and Vermont on the east. They received either encouragement or indifferent assent from Secretary Seward's office, for when they began to accumulate rifles and cannon for their highly advertised project, they met with no legal obstacles.

O'Mahony was forgotten in the excitement of preparations for the Canadian war. Then one of his lieutenants designed a new kind of a Canadian venture. In the hope of winning back his accustomed place at the center of Irish-American affairs, O'Mahony, too, rushed into the Canadian game. The possession of Campobello Island—a few hundred yards offshore from Eastport and Lubec, Maine—was in dispute between the United States and England. Therefore O'Mahony assumed it to be a free fish belonging to nobody and available to the Fenians for a homeland and naval base if they cared to occupy it. The prime advantage of the scheme was its speed. The grand strategy of the senate would need all summer to conquer Canada, but the seizure of Campobello could be accomplished next week. The O'Mahony Fenians owned a war-surplus steamship, the *Ocean Spray*. They loaded it with guns and sent it forth by sea toward Passamaquoddy Bay, while troops dressed as civilians converged by railroad on Eastport and Lubec. Kept in touch with the project through reports from "Red Jim" MacDermott, the British embassy protested to Washington against this overt act of war. If

Secretary Seward ever had looked favorably on the adventure, he did so no longer. General George Meade of Gettysburg fame was ordered to Eastport to break up the Fenian assault, an assignment accomplished in a few hours by seizing the *Ocean Spray* and arresting the leaders. The troops then straggled back toward New York, where they found the senate Fenians *en fête* over their ignominy in the great "Eastport fizzle."⁹

It seems not to have occurred to the senate faction that if Secretary Seward had blocked the Canadian adventure of the O'Mahony Fenians, he would do the same for them. On May 31, 1866, six weeks after the collapse at Campobello, with one army poised at Ogdensburg, New York, a second army opened the invasion by striking across the Niagara River from North Buffalo to Fort Erie, Ontario. Two days later, at a place called Limestone Ridge, the invaders clashed with the enemy, a volunteer company of Toronto college boys called "The Queen's Own." After a three-hour battle in which six Fenians and twelve Canadians were killed, The Queen's Own fled, leaving the Fenians in possession of the field of battle. At that moment an American naval gunboat arrived and anchored in the middle of the Niagara River, blocking any further passage of supplies and reinforcements into Canada and forcing the invaders to retreat back to the American shore. At the same time General Meade reached Ogdensburg and once again busied himself with the arrest of leaders and seizure of supplies. By June 3, 1866, the foremost military problem of the hour had become the question of who would pay the railroad fares home for seven thousand stranded Fenian soldiers.¹⁰

VI

Stephens landed in New York just after the first and just before the second of these miserable adventures. His initial act was to listen to O'Mahony's *mea culpa* for squandering the organization's treasury at Campobello, to receive his resignation from office, and to succeed him as president. He called a great mass rally at Jones Wood, where he pledged "war in Ireland and nowhere else" and promised that "as surely as I address you today, we shall take the field in Ireland this very year." He set out on a speaking tour, reiterating his theme at every lecture stop: "We fight for freedom on Irish soil this very year."¹¹ He found himself a general, Gustave Paul Cluseret, a French socialist who had fought with Garibaldi, Fremont, and McClellan, and who would later command the army of the Paris Commune. When Stephens described the Irish as a whole race of men organized by himself into squads, platoons, companies, regiments, and battalions, Cluseret had never before heard of the like. He was attracted by the military potential of such a people. But they had no arms to fight with, Stephens hastened to explain, though this lack would shortly be remedied by aid from America. He guaranteed to supply the arms needed. On that understanding, Cluseret offered to serve as military commander of a striking force of ten thousand men, thought to be sufficient to conquer the country from the British defensive force estimated to be three times greater.

Once more, Stephens was incapable of the performance he had promised. The senate faction was now addicted to schism beyond hope of reformation. Their summer picnics in 1866 featured sham battle re-enactments of the victory at Limestone Ridge, half the picnickers dressing up to represent the hapless Queen's Own. When they held their convention at Troy in September 1866, they showed no interest in unity with Stephens or in Irish insurrection, but spoke of Mexico as the stage for their next patriotic military exploit. Impotence and wounded vanity dissolved all their prime energies into flatulence. "We swear, we swear it to you by the bitter memory of Ireland's woes," said their official organ, "by the gibbets heavy with the martyred bodies of her patriots, by the blood of the braves who fell at Limestone Ridge, by the hopes of her kinsmen waiting, in felon cells, for the roar of the strife that will set them free,—that once again, if you but do your duty to your native land, we will follow the gleam of our unconquered standard to vengeance, victory and liberty."[12]

Stephens' peacemaking consisted in heaping insult upon the senate faction at every opportunity, hoping to separate Roberts from his rank and file. This tactic appears to have had effect, producing backsliders in some quantity. They did not join with Stephens, though; they simply fell away. During the senate's Troy convention, Stephens came to the realization that the unity of the two wings was not to be expected and that, as a result, no more American money would be forthcoming to buy arms. In September 1866 he wrote a friend in Ireland: "It is a question of money with me as well as you. For want of money I have been unable to take the necessary action. For the last month, especially, I could, with the necessary means, have done work to cheer and astound you. But my action has been hampered so that I have been barely able to keep the office open. . . . Sometime this year I shall be again on Irish soil. You can easily understand my reason for not saying what time, but you shall know it ere long."[13]

These were overly familiar turns of phrase, and Stephens' lieutenants became restless and suspicious. General Cluseret described the rising tension: "Stephens, who as it would seem, by no means deceived himself about his material resources, began to blow cold, as he had hitherto blown hot. . . . the moment they [his followers] imagined they saw symptoms of coldness in him . . . they became indignant and enraged."[14] On December 15, 1866, he called his staff together to announce his decision to postpone action, and in his words: ". . . I found that matters were even worse than my apprehensions—we had nothing like what I promised and expected, and the little we had we could not forward." He then proposed to immolate himself in expiation for his failure, "to go to Ireland by the next boat, even though I should be taken and hanged." His staff protested against this proposal, urging that if he were lost, all were lost. Two days later, though, the staff met again and curtly stripped him of his command, putting Kelly in his place. "Colonel Kelly and his backers got up the cry that I had abandoned the cause in despair," said Stephens, "or through cowardice shrunk from the struggle, frightened by the powers I had created." Kelly's public statement was essentially the same, that "Stephens was literally a coward, that he shrank from directing the elements he evoked."[15]

One of Kelly's backers, an impetuous Confederate veteran of Morgan's Raiders named Captain John MacCafferty, put a pistol to Stephens' head and offered to dispose of him then and there. He was restrained, and Stephens was even kept on in charge of nonmilitary Fenian affairs. When the new directory, with Kelly in command, sailed from New York for Ireland on January 12, 1867, Stephens was appointed to go along. But he missed the sailing; and the procrastinator, formerly "the Captain," standing friendless on a Brooklyn pier, closed his accounts with the Irish revolution which he had done more than any other man to make.

CHAPTER 14

The Agony of Fenianism

I

In the twelve months since Stephens fled from Ireland, the balance of forces had altered radically in the Fenians' disfavor. The government was now alert and prepared. The garrison was reinforced. Corroborating Devoy's analysis of the disaffection of the Irish soldiers, the government had removed the Irish regiments and replaced them with safe English and Scottish units. Informers had been successfully planted inside the Fenian high command, both in Ireland and America, so that the English now controlled the element of surprise. Meanwhile the Fenians' absolute strength had diminished. Because of police raids and confiscations the number of available rifles was smaller than it had been a year earlier. The veteran American soldiers who were to provide expert field command were now jailed or deported. The army available to Fenian generals was reduced back to a mass of untrained irregulars, to "men who are insubordinate by temperament, without organization, without any framework," said General Cluseret, who added, "This sort of thing wears out life quickly."[1]

All these facts were general knowledge. At one end of the spectrum, Dr. Cullen, recently made Ireland's first cardinal, wrote an American bishop just at this time: "The Fenians are not all so strong as they were last year."[2] At the opposite end, Devoy, who to the end of his life thought it shameful not to have risen in February 1866, argued that a rising in February 1867 was "foredoomed." The new Fenian directory was not deterred by these judgments, but pressed forward toward immediate insurrection, come what might, and even with the certainty of losing. Devoy in jail got a message from the high command: "The fight will be in about three weeks, but we'll be badly beaten."[3]

"The day" was set for February 12, 1867, then changed to March 5. The countermanding order was intercepted by the police at Cahirciveen, O'Connell's old home village in west Kerry, so that it failed to reach the local centers. There the Fenians rose on the wrong date, captured the police barracks, and in rummaging through the police records, discovered the order to delay action. So instructed, they then returned to their homes, leaving the terrorized gentry, most of them clansmen of the Liberator, barricaded with their silver plate behind sandbags in the hotel. A premature rising was also pressed forward in Chester. Captain MacCafferty had devised a plan to raid the Chester arsenal for rifles, then to seize the ships in the harbor and set sail across the Irish Sea to Dublin. On the incorrect date all his forces converged on Chester Castle as instructed, and MacCafferty set out by train from Manchester to take command of the raid. Along the way his train was sidetracked while one trainload after another filled with troops passed through, also headed for Chester. His adjutant, a long-time Fenian named Corydon, had been discovered by the police to be a homosexual and had been persuaded to turn informer.

On the eve of the correct day for the rising, a blizzard settled down over the British Isles, bringing the heaviest snowfall in memory. In the storm a general insurrection was unthinkable, and only here and there did the centers respond. At Cork four thousand men came out with their fifty rifles and their one American officer, attacked four police barracks, and were repulsed. In Dublin three thousand men attempted to converge at Tallaght, south of the city. A police ambush awaited them there; and as they fled back toward Dublin, hundreds were arrested at the bridges over the canal. Fenians in Limerick, Clare, Louth, and Waterford had local successes. The most vital single spot in the Fenian battle plan was at Limerick Junction near Tipperary. An American named Godfrey Massey was placed in charge of that sector. As he stepped off the train from Cork, he was arrested—by prior arrangement with the police, according to his military superiors. The charge was unproved, though Massey's claims to high rank in the Confederate army were shown to be fraudulent, and he did become the most cooperative witness for the government prosecutor in the Fenian trials that followed. Briefly told, the story of the Fenian insurrection of 1867 was defeat on all fronts and total collapse within forty-eight hours. The amateur Smith O'Brien had been four times longer in the field.

II

The surprise of the insurrection was not that it was so weak, but that it had occurred at all. Why did the leaders call the men out? Why did the men respond? Even if Massey was a *provocateur*, it seems doubtful that provocation was required to set the directory in motion. Captain MacCafferty, for one, needed no urging. He was made of the same stuff as Tolstoy's Dolokhov, a killer never quite himself unless he could smell burning gunpowder. But Kelly, the commander in chief, appears to have believed that the blow on Irish soil would open the way for some form of American diplomatic support. He had stationed men in Washington to call on President Andrew Johnson with a demand for recognition at the cabled news of the first shot, and he was crushed by the report that Johnson had discourteously turned them away.

The dominant motive for the rising was more probably a feeling among the Fenians, both high and low, that the movement could not depart gracefully without some unequivocal gesture to honor its bold promises and to fix its defeated principles unmistakably in the record of history. Like Emmet and Rossa in Green Street Courthouse, they thought it unmanly to go down without a scene. Stephens had talked forevermore about the difference between the "spouters" and the doers, but the difference had never been acted out. Until it was, the Fenians were denounced by their own words as spouters of an especially contemptible breed. If Stephens was not sensitive to that logic, his successors were. Such at least was their reply to Cluseret when he pleaded with them to abandon an enterprise in which there was not one chance in a hundred, or in twenty hundred, of success. "My dear General," he reported them saying, "we are not under the smallest illusion as to what awaits us; but the word of an Irishman, once given, is sacred. Stephens has pledged us to this undertaking without consulting us, but we will keep our word, even though he may not keep his; and the people will know that, if there are some men who deceive them, there are others who know how to die for them."[4]

This explanation might touch the sensibility of many Irishmen, but for Bishop Moriarty, it was only oil on the flames of his wrath. On the subject of his displeasure at the rising in Kerry he preached a sermon that immortalized him. He noted with surprise (and relief) that the rank-and-file revolutionists had observed the rights of persons and private property, leaving untouched all the big houses of the district and giving way to the sin of covetousness only in the single case of Dr. Barry's horse, which some irregular had commandeered and neglected to return. The fear of "rapine and plunder," spread abroad by the clergy—His Lordship of Kerry in the lead—on the authority of O'Keeffe's letter to the *Irish People*, was quite evidently unfounded. About the leaders, though, he could not be so charitable. He took note that they were what would be called today "foreign agitators," proving that even the most inapposite mutations of modern political warfare can be found in the Irish arena. "Thank God, they are not our people," said Moriarty. He was particularly disappointed that the lists of those arrested and awaiting trial for capital crimes did not contain the name of James Stephens, foremost of those "criminals of far deeper guilt—the men who, while they send their dupes into danger, are fattening on the spoil in Paris and New York—the execrable swindlers who care not how many are murdered by the rebel or hanged by the strong arm of the law, provided they can get a supply of dollars either for their pleasures or their wants."

The core of Bishop Moriarty's sermon centered upon the sin of the revolutionary gesture. The fixed policy of the Church, as I have explained, was to condemn all revolutions a priori on the postulated improbability of success. "We are not believers in the chances of rebellion," declared the bishop. But the success of the rising in his diocese was not just improbable, it was absolutely unthinkable. It was unforgivable. To describe the degree of its depravity, he coined the memorable hyperbole known to all readers of Joyce, Sean O'Casey, and Brendan Behan: "I preached to you last Sunday on the eternity of Hell's torments. Human reason is inclined to say—'it is a hard word, and who can bear it?' But when we look down into the fathomless depth of this infamy of the heads of the Fenian conspiracy we must acknowledge that eternity is not long enough nor hell hot enough to punish such miscreants."[5] For these words Lord John Russell, the author of the Ecclesiastical Titles Act, expressed warmest appreciation on the floor of the House. The natural Irish response was anger, and even the anti-Fenians found objections in Moriarty's presuming to slam a theological door that, by first principles, must always remain open. The unkindest criticism came from the least expected source: Cardinal Cullen thought the sermon "foolish and exaggerated" and likely to cause mischief; and he wondered whether Moriarty ought not to be "called to an account for it."[6]

The cardinal's unaccustomed tact and composure was founded in part on his discovery that the Fenians actually had succeeded in driving a wedge between the clergy and the Irish people, as O'Leary claimed. Moriarty's attempt to analyze the Fenian movement into swindlers and their dupes was wishful thinking; Stephens' fall showed the rank and file running ahead of their leaders. The Church would need to exercise diplomacy, understanding, and patience to repair the breach. Cullen also sensed that the Fenian military threat had spent itself, and that he could afford to relax and turn his energies elsewhere for the coming era of peace. If a person calculated according to the regular calendar of Irish rebellions—one every half-century—the next scheduled insurrection date did not fall due until 1917.

III

The obsequies for Fenianism were still somewhat premature. The myth of the American ironclad had never yet materialized, but now it did so. After the collapse of the March 1867 rising, Kelly wrote a frantic letter to New York, pleading for help of some sort, any sort: "What do our countrymen in America want? Will they wait until the last man shall be slaughtered before sending aid? . . . Fit out your privateers."[7] In response, the New York

Fenians got possession through mysterious city-hall channels of a ship called the *Jacmel Packet*, not an ironclad but a brigantine of 138 tons that had been impounded by the port authorities. She was loaded with a great number of piano boxes bearing a Cuban destination but containing in actuality seven thousand rifles for Ireland, leftovers from the Canadian campaigns. Six weeks after the collapse of the March rising, fifty fighting men boarded her secretly at Sandy Hook and she slipped out to sea. She sailed due south for twenty-four hours, then changed her course to east. On Easter Sunday, after two weeks at sea, the captain rechristened the ship *Erin's Hope* and opened sealed orders directing him to proceed with his cargo to Sligo. He ran up the flag of the Republic of Ireland, a golden sunburst on an emerald field, the same flag that the *Ulysses* Sinn Fein "citizen" in a rapture of Joycean pedantry scorned as a historical solecism.

The *Erin's Hope* sailed into Sligo Bay six weeks out of New York. Colonel Burke, the Birmingham arms buyer, had been assigned to meet the ship and direct the unloading, but he failed to make contact. The ship sailed about for two days looking for Burke, and finally two men were put ashore to find him. He was located at last and came aboard with the message that there was no force available to unload the rifles or to use them if they could be unloaded. The crew then fell into dispute as to what should be done. One group recommended that they capture the town of Sligo, whose most famed poetic voice and holiday visitor, at age two, had just been removed by his parents to live at Regents Park, London. Burke was able to persuade the crew to abandon their commando project. Then half the crew decided to go ashore, scatter, and do what they might for Ireland, with the result that all but two were arrested within the day. The rest, after having sailed unmolested up and down the coast of Sligo and Donegal for a full week, turned westward with the seven thousand rifles still aboard and sailed back to New York.

The cruise of the *Erin's Hope* invites the commentator to light ironic effects, for the adventure did have the tone of musical-comedy piracy. It represented a picturesque example of the extravagant headlong squandering of Irish forces—by the leaders and the led with equal good cheer—that gave a certain point to Bishop Moriarty's strictures. But it is not hard to imagine the *Erin's Hope* in another setting where the comedy would vanish. The exploit proved it easy for a Fenian privateer to pass through the Royal Navy patrols off the Irish coast, carrying armament enough to have tipped the balance at some other stage of the war. Seven thousand rifles in hand would have made a great difference in September 1865, at the time of O'Leary's arrest, or after Stephens' jailbreak in November 1865. In 1867 the Cork Fenians were willing to make a try at insurrection with no more than fifty rifles. The *Erin's Hope* was two years too late, something of a marvel of mistiming.

IV

Even after the failure of the *Erin's Hope* mission the Fenians were not silenced. While the organization in Ireland was being battered to pieces by the police, the stragglers retreated into the Irish ghettoes of the English industrial midlands. Kelly called a meeting of the survivors in Manchester in the late summer of 1867 and set about trying to rebuild the organization.

During the Manchester convention three hundred Fenians were able to meet and deliberate in safety; but shortly after it adjourned, Kelly and a companion, Michael Deasy, fell into the hands of the police. The Fenians in Manchester decided that they must attempt a rescue, and Ricard Burke was given the responsibility of devising a plan of attack. Kelly and Deasy had been taken from Manchester jail to court for arraignment, and on their return journey to jail, the police van was attacked at a railroad overpass. The Fenians shot the lead horse to halt the van and then attempted to break open the locked door to free the prisoners. One of the raiding party was supposed to have brought a crowbar but had forgotten, and the door could not be opened. At last another raider shot the lock off with his revolver. In smashing the lock, a bullet penetrated the door and killed a police guard inside, one Sergeant Brett. An infuriated English crowd, closing in around the van, was held off with pistol shots fired over their heads. In the commotion the van door opened, allowing Kelly and Deasy to escape. The Fenians then began to withdraw, the crowd in pursuit. The two prisoners vanished, but the crowd ran down a rear guard of three raiders who lagged behind to delay the hue and cry. At nightfall the streets of Manchester filled with mobs of anti-Irish rioters, and a posse of special constables roamed about arresting hundreds of Irishmen as suspects. The hundreds were in time reduced to twenty-eight, then to five who stood trial and were convicted of murder, and at last to the three of the rear guard—William Allen, Michael Larkin, and Michael O'Brien—who were hanged on November 23, 1867, in front of Salford jail in Manchester.

These young men, the youngest nineteen, are the celebrated Manchester martyrs, one of the crowning exhibits of Irish patriotic symbology. Their apotheosis has puzzled some historians, who see their case as one of ordinary crime and ordinary criminals: the three were guilty of murder and were hanged, so who is to complain? Excellent English scholars put the word "martyrs" in inverted commas, just as they use the same typography for the word "betrayal" in discussions of Keogh and Sadleir. Their point would be, no doubt, that respect for the law is essential to the fabric of order, to preserve society from anarchy. As a matter of fact, Irish legal advocates were more zealous than anyone in their respect for English law, and they particularly honored its decorums and "technicalities" favoring a defendant.

The *causes célèbres* of Irish justice arose when the crown prosecutor, under the pressure of advanced motives of statecraft, found a need to override the troublesome judicial guarantees in order to insure a verdict of guilty. Jury rigging, as in the O'Connell and Mitchel trials, was a familiar experience. In the Manchester case there was a strong presumption that witnesses were suborned, for the defendants were apparently not involved in firing the fatal shot. The mêlée following the attack on the van confused the eye-witnesses, so that the prosecution found itself faced with a paucity of evidence, and treasured any it could get. In any event, the key witnesses were whores and jailbirds, and the prisoners who were convicted had been marked in the jail line-up, apparently for bounty seekers to spot them.

In their zeal for justice, the Manchester police built up a hanging case, also, against one Maguire, a marine of few words and no opinions who happened to possess an Irish name and to be in the neighborhood during the attack on the van. Newspapermen in the courtroom came to the conclusion that he could have had no conceivable connection either with the raid or with Fenianism. They made a representation to the home secretary that Maguire was an innocent man, that is, was convicted on perjured evidence. On their recommendation, he was immediately pardoned and released. Yet the evidence that convicted Maguire was precisely the same evidence that condemned Allen, Larkin, and O'Brien. The implied attitude in the home secretary's discrimination was that Maguire had shown no animosity to the authority of the queen and deserved to live, while the rest took pride in their Irish attitudes and deserved to die. From the home secretary's viewpoint, the defendants seemed to be unduly distressed about the state evidence being tainted, for they openly proclaimed the very treason to which the witnesses, perjured though they might be, had testified.

To be sure, the demeanor of the three condemned men in court was unapologetically Fenian. They sketched out before the courtroom the ethical anatomy of the principle by which one stood his ground: the morality of "the man in the gap," the man who refuses to "sell the gap," the ethic Yeats later formulated in the verses of "The Black Tower":

> . . . he's a lying hound:
> Stand we on guard oath-bound![8]

The first prisoner noted in his closing statement that by being forced to stand in police line-up in irons, he had been marked for the bounty hunters to identify and had therefore been unjustly condemned. But he added, in the Fenian style: "As for myself, I feel the righteousness of my every act with regard to what I have done in defense of my country. I fear not. I am fearless—fearless of the punishment that can be inflicted against me; and with that, my lords, I have done." Michael Larkin, the next man condemned, objected that all the witnesses against him were wanting in respectability, though there were more than a hundred persons present at the raid from whom honorable witnesses ought to have been available to the prosecution. But he was moved to add: "I believe as the old saying is a true one, what is decreed a man in the page of life he has to fulfill, either on the gallows, drowning, a fair death in bed, or on the battlefield." The last man took note that the government tempted witnesses with "blood money," cash rewards for testimony. However that might be, he said, "we have been found guilty, and, as a matter of course, we accept our death as gracefully as possible. We are not afraid to die—at least I am not." And his companions responded, "Nor I," and "Nor I." He concluded: "I have nothing to regret, or to retract, or take back. I can only say, God save Ireland." And again his companions responded, "God save Ireland." A scattering of Irish spectators took up the response and it ran to the back of the courtroom, followed by a second wave murmuring "Amen." The judge then put on his black cap, praised the fairness of the court, declared it his own sincere conviction that Sergeant Brett was murdered by premeditation of the prisoners, and passed sentence.[9]

V

What Englishmen thought the most heinous of crimes—namely, treason— Irishmen looked upon as the loftiest of callings. Irish morality not only exonerated the Manchester three, for they had intended no harm to the unfortunate Sergeant Brett, but it exalted them to the highest glory, just as societies in all ages have honored above other men a rear guard doomed and destroyed. The terror of the Manchester hangings therefore taught Irishmen no lesson in loyalty. Lost on them was the pedagogic message Matthew Arnold sent across the Irish Sea, that "a government which dared not deal with a mob . . . simply opened the floodgates to anarchy." Popular outrage was magnified by the pageantry in which judge and hangman marched them through the ghastly stages to extermination. The day of execution, November 23, became a sort of Irish May Day. P. S. O'Hegarty's Sinn Fein sensibility could never pass that day on the calendar without visualizing the "three Irishmen swinging by their necks in Manchester prison." In seven centuries of the Englishman's rule in Ireland, the Manchester affair was the most damaging miscalculation of statecraft, bar one.

At first, Irishmen could not imagine the Manchester court giving out sentences of more than ten or fifteen years; or, when the death sentences were pronounced, that they would ever be carried out. Then Maguire, the marine, was released, leaving four men under death sentence. A couple of days before the scheduled executions, one of these—the same who had forgotten the crowbar—was reprieved by the intervention of Charles Francis Adams, the American ambassador. Only then did it suddenly occur to the onlookers that the other three could not be saved. On the morning of November 23, crowds stood about the Irish newspaper offices, waiting, as the dispatches came in by telegraph telling first of the arrival of the military with fixed bayonets; then of the gathering of the crowd of Manchester citizens, some curious, some in holiday mood and singing "Rule Britannia"; and at last the somber word itself, followed shortly by the report that the bodies had been buried in quicklime inside the jail yard, an action interpreted throughout Ireland as a calculated religious indignity.

According to the testimony of A. M. Sullivan: "I never knew Ireland to be more deeply moved by mingled feelings of grief and anger."[10] A full-orchestrated nationwide political wake began on the instant. Cardinal Cullen watched while his weeping priests were swept into the national mourning on the next Sunday after the executions. It was the MacManus affair all over again, he said. He dared not block the expression and compromised by issuing an order that all prayers and Masses for the Manchester three must be private in order, as the Sullivans put it, "to ensure that the sacred functions were sought and attended for spiritual considerations, not used merely for illegitimate political purposes."[11]

All over Ireland there were mock funeral processions. In Limerick one-fourth of the population turned out. In Dublin three empty black coffins were labeled "Allen," "Larkin," and "O'Brien" in large white lettering, and brass bands played the funeral march from *Saul* as the procession moved along the MacManus route to Glasnevin. Dr. George Sigerson, a witness, estimated that thirty thousand people marched in the procession. A. M. Sullivan put the number at sixty thousand, larger than the MacManus funeral itself. He was a witness too, and his estimate may have been inflated by self-importance, for at the head of the procession, beside John Martin the old Van Diemen's Land veteran, marched A. M. Sullivan himself. Four days later the viceroy issued a proclamation forbidding funeral processions in Ireland, having discovered, as Dr. Sigerson said, that the government's "strange belief" that the Manchester executions would have "a deterrent effect on the Irish people has not been justified by the result."[12]

VI

A popular ballad appeared, written by T. D. Sullivan, aiming to interpret the Manchester affair and mold it into permanent and universal shape. He took his tune from "Tramp, Tramp, Tramp," as appropriate to the kinship between Fenianism and the American Union soldiers. To get the flavor, the reader must carry the tune:

> Girt around with cruel foes, still their courage proudly rose,
> For they thought of hearts that loved them, far and near,
> Of the millions true and brave, o'er the ocean's swelling wave,
> And the friends in holy Ireland, ever dear.
> "God save Ireland," said they proudly; "God save Ireland," said they all. . . .

Sullivan's ballad seemed to have everything. He had asserted the doctrinaire Fenian formula of the sainthood of the battle casualty. He had caught the running echo of the antiphonal response, "God save Ireland!" that had sent through the court during the prisoners' valedictory speeches "that strange sensation as though the hair of one's head stood up." He had sounded the motif of solidarity, uniting the victims to the millions at home and "o'er the ocean's swelling wave."

Sullivan had also borrowed Michael Larkin's courtroom thoughts about the "page of life." But at the heart of Larkin's words, in the observation that every man has his fate to fulfill "either on the gallows, drowning, a fair death in bed, or on the battlefield"—there Sullivan misconstrued his source. The list of the four chances he reduced back to only two, confusing Larkin's point with another idea alien to it. The refrain concluded:

> . . . "God save Ireland," said they all,
> "Whether on the scaffold high, or the battle-field we die,
> Oh, what matter when for Erin dear we fall!"

Intentionally or from want of clarity, Sullivan's either-or appeared to make patriotic death mandatory. The purpose of the episode was no longer to protect the retreat of the main force at the railroad overpass in Manchester. Now the object was to die for Erin, and as for the forms that death could take, "what matter"? To some observers it seemed odd that the apotheosis of the virtues of physical force should be advanced by the most conspicuous spokesman of the Irish moral force party, and odd, too, that the Fenians' most dogged opponent should be combined in the same person with their poet laureate. But against the background of the Sullivans' intellectual history, his motive could readily be understood as a transformation of Fenian insurrection into a lost cause, most deeply lamented. The Fenians' poet laureate was, more properly speaking, their undertaker.

T. D. Sullivan's song was a full retreat back to the manner of Tom Moore, who "too much loves to weep," as Davis said. It threw a shadow of the death mystique backward over the whole Fenian movement, subduing its cheerful activism under a lugubrious pall. Anyone who reads extensively in the Sullivans' newspapers will sense a family weakness for necrology. A. M. Sullivan published a humorous weekly, called *Zozimus*, where even among the jokes the obituaries were irrepressible, sorrowing for Dickens, for the dead at Metz, for Robert E. Lee, for George Henry Moore, for Charles Lever—"light lie the turf on Lever's grave!" The Fenian dirge bespeaks the same fixation. The Sullivans naturally loved it dearly, and so did countless other Irishmen. It quickly became the most popular of all patriotic songs, and was considered the national hymn. It was congenial to the Fenians, too; they admired it uncritically as great poetry—or well intentioned, at least—and they sang it as earnestly as anybody else. It was not congenial to Fenianism itself, however, for the Fenians never regarded their cause as hopeless nor their military projects as a beautiful suicide, though they clearly understood them to be subject to the ordinary chances of war. Were they deluded in this? Here Sullivan's song breached an Irish historical conundrum: Did the Fenians ever really have a chance?

The automatic answer would seem to be: certainly not. The clergy, the Sullivans, and aging Young Ireland had plainly prognosticated the coming defeat of Fenianism; they told everybody so. In the week when Grant met Lee at Appomattox Courthouse, the *Nation* drew from the event a chilling moral lesson for Ireland, that eight millions with inferior resources can never defeat twenty millions with superior resources.[13] To this argument the wisdom of tautology was added. The cause was lost, therefore it was a lost cause. Years after the event, Archbishop Croke of Cashel, MacHale's successor as the lone episcopal friend and protector of Irish radicals, told John Devoy in New York that the Fenians never "had a ghost of a chance" —although he was almost sorry to say it.[14] From the same perspective, T. D. Sullivan still maintained in 1905 that any other opinion was worthy only "of Jules Verne or Baron Munchausen,"[15] that Fenianism was a lost cause, right enough, a mode of suicide, but thoughtful suicide for the poetic and moral enrichment of Ireland. This is the meaning he had concretized in "God Save Ireland." It was not the only formulation possible, for in an exactly parallel case the old-time Wobbly said, Don't mourn for me, organize.

VII

It goes without saying that Yeats believed "God Save Ireland" unspeakable. In his first youthful battle with the "Irish politicians," he made a scandal by publishing an anthology of Irish nationalist verse from which that most essential of all patriotic effusions had been defiantly dumped. And yet, intent upon the "revolt of the soul against the intellect," he felt on his own part what *Ulysses* calls a "strong weakness" for the same ideal of the death mystique. He hunted it through numerous thematic variations: folkish, in *The Land of Heart's Desire*; philosophical, in *Where There Is Nothing*;

historical, in *Cathleen ni Houlihan*. For this last, he suggested O'Leary as his source, for it was his understanding that if anyone had put to O'Leary the question, Did the Fenians ever really have a chance ? he too would have replied, certainly not.

Yeats put no hedge about his testimony on O'Leary's devotion to lost causes. He had, said Yeats, "as we know" joined the Fenian movement "with no hope of success," but simply because he thought it "good for the moral character of the people."[16] It is not impossible that O'Leary may actually have confided such an opinion to him, though Yeats's witness on such matters was not absolutely trustworthy, especially if one of his emotional vagaries was at issue. Yet when O'Leary was editor of the *Irish People*, he plainly thought the Fenians' chances of success were excellent. After his imprisonment he had the fullest opportunity and motive to re-examine his earlier opinion and to change it if he was so minded. If he ever did, the alteration remained a private secret between himself and W. B. Yeats.

In O'Leary's memoirs these words do appear: ". . . I must candidly confess—judging long after the time, in the coolness of my study and not in the heat and turmoil of action—that I cannot prove that we had any great chance of wresting Ireland from the grasp of England. . . ." But this is not his full sentence; it is preceded by the word "if" and it continues: ". . . [nevertheless] I think I can give strong reasons to show that, under certain contingencies, we might have made a formidable fight, and that, even as it was, we made it manifest to England, or rather to the English ruling classes, that their power in Ireland rested upon somewhat insecure foundations." The discussion he appended to this prologue, running to several pages, consists of a close scrutiny of real contingencies: the possible healing of the Fenian split in America, growing Anglo-American friction over the *Alabama* dispute, and most important of all, the chance of mutiny by Irish soldiers in the British army, which he labeled as not a contingency at all, but an "absolute certainty."[17] He tells us in every page or so of his book that he was not a sanguine man, yet he still appraised the chances and missed opportunities in about the same way as any other sort of Fenian.

The cult of the lost cause is, in fact, to be found in no Fenian utterance. Those Fenians who were expertly versed in the hard realities of their situation found the *Nation*'s prudent Appomattox analogy inapplicable. Devoy, for example, insisted that the Fenians could not possibly have won in February 1867 and therefore should not have tried to; but in February 1866 he pleaded all night long to begin the rising next morning, not because he wanted to immolate himself in a lost cause for the enhancement of Irish spirituality, but because he thought they might just momentarily possess the right combination of forces to win. To the end of his life he regretted that it should have been left to the Boers to capitalize first on the incompetence of the nineteenth-century British army, when the Fenian probes had exposed its soft tissue thirty years earlier.

It cannot be said that the Fenians lacked emotional depth or sensitivity, yet not the slightest interest in the death mystique can be found among any of their statements of purpose. They possessed, not always but often, great courage, a powerful sense of code, a full awareness of mortal danger always near; but they were not addicted to the operatic effect. The Manchester martyrs themselves, addressing the court for the last time, occupied themselves but little in etherealizing their image for posterity, and instead devoted their precious waning life to lecturing judge and jury on the real facts of Irish history: on the misfortune of the American schism, on the ordinary Irishman's alienation from the English law, on Davis' proposition that Ireland ought to support three times its existing population. O'Leary's comment upon them to a lecture audience was grave and lofty: "We cannot all be heroes, but we can all be hero-worshippers. To few of you probably have been given the high heroic qualities of the Manchester Martyrs, and to none of you probably will ever be afforded the supreme opportunity of showing them, but I am happy to feel that you all cherish in your heart of hearts the memory of these simple but sublime men. . . ."[18] This sounded very much like the martyrs themselves, simply stating the old Roman virtues of the man in the gap. "God Save Ireland" he could never stomach, and he was offended when the brass band played it to welcome him home to Tipperary after imprisonment and exile.[19] He seems to have had the Sullivans particularly in mind in the wry twist he put upon his well-known comment on Irish political wakes: It was "clear as the sun at noonday that the heart of the country always goes out to the man who lives and dies an unrepentant rebel. The rebel can reckon upon nothing in life; he is sure to be calumniated, he is likely to be robbed, and may even be murdered, but let him once go out of life, and he is sure of a fine funeral."[20]

There is no literal historical referent for Yeats's "romantic" death-loving Fenian, so that its source must be sought elsewhere. When Yeats assessed the literary work of Young Ireland and discovered in it what seemed to him the imagination of magpies and the rhythms of marching men, he blamed the poetic coarseness upon the poisonous influence of the "good citizen" in Davis' make-up. But as we noted, he had not perceived that his own disembodied Irish spirituality, his "red rose-bordered hem," was another invention of the same "good citizen." When he assessed the Fenian episode in the history of the Irish sensibility, his blind spot recurred. His foremost cultural enemy was still the "good citizen"—positivistic, comfortable, prudent, timid, joyless, pious, and insensitive, the whipping boy of all his verse starting from his apprenticeship in the Irish mode with "The Madness of King Goll." Fifty years later, "The Statues" still carries on the theme, their "filthy modern tide" set against our "proper dark," set against his old affection, the Irish death mystique. But the poet who designed this portentous nebulosity and imprinted it indelibly on the modern Irish mind was of all people, T. D. Sullivan.

Yeats tells how an Irish M.P. once came to a meeting of the Literary Society and recited some kind of dreadful patriotic trash. One felt embarrassed, but was also humbled by the very moving affections of the speaker. It was not impossible that he could find "God Save Ireland" to be an intolerable sentimentalism and yet sense something in it of surpassing attraction. To seize it, to formulate it in his own language, he would naturally remove the blatancy and jingle, but he would hope to preserve the nub. The result would be very much like *Cathleen ni Houlihan*:

> Do not make a great keening
> When the graves have been dug tomorrow.
> Do not call the white-scarfed riders
> To the burying that shall be tomorrow,

and so on; or in philistine language, "what matter when for Erin dear we fall!" And suppose, feeling it unwise to lay on the lugubrious with Tom Moore's too-heavy hand, one had added a few dashing military symbols of proven reliability: " '98," "Killala," "There are ships in the Bay!" and

> O! we'd have pulled down the gallows
> Had it happened in Enniscrone!

These would show that one still kept verbal pace with the advanced men. But like the Sullivans in duress, one would be playing with fire, and if somebody took him at his word and substituted actual for literary death, he might well ask in perplexity:

> Did that play of mine send out
> Certain men the English shot?

In what other imaginable context could those lines have any meaning?

For Yeats to seize upon the Sullivanite affection was a genuine choice, since he had another and considerably better model at hand. We know from the evidence of his borrowing that he had read William Morris' splendid treatment, approximately Fenian in outlook, of the identical theme in *A Dream of John Ball*. But to follow Morris, he would have had to repudiate as Morris did the death mystique; and he would have been left also deprived of his much-cherished theory of tragedy, taken from *Axel,* which insisted that for the tragic protagonist, extermination is simply a wonderful experience.

VIII

Unruffled by the tainted heredity of the Irish death mystique, Yeats handed it on down with his recommendation to the literary movement he founded. There it was admired, embraced, and feverishly practiced. Yeats and Lionel Johnson were alone able to whip it into poetry; for the rest it inspired an appalling number of bad poems, rivaling the output of Irish pepper-pot journalism itself. Here and there it even destroyed a promising talent—in Eva Gore-Booth, for example. Its downfall began one morning in Dublin when George Moore woke up with the feeling that he was about to have a nervous breakdown: in a nightmare he "saw Ireland as a god demanding human sacrifices, and everybody or nearly everybody, crying: Take me, Ireland, take me; I am unworthy, but accept me as a burnt offering." Afterward it disintegrated rapidly, as its substance was discovered to be a figment, a fabrication out of old tunes and wisps of words for oblique motives. O'Casey wrote a war-weary play, *The Plough and the Stars*, to bid it farewell. Most other post-Yeatsians rejected it *in toto* and succeeded in getting it committed as insane. In the end it survived only underground, producing occasional painful oddities like *Pigeon Irish* by Francis Stuart, Yeats's last protégé.

PART IV

Home Rule

CHAPTER 15

The Ballot Box Once More: Isaac Butt

I

Of all the grand episodes of nineteenth-century Irish history, none has been so intensely studied as Home Rule. It was, to be sure, a vast, intricate, and decisive affair. But it was not a new tune, just a variation on the old one. It arose out of the same generalized causes that had brought out a million men to Tara of the Kings. And it sank on the same rock that had wrecked all the previous experiments in the Whig alliance, and that would in due time wreck the last such experiment in John Redmond's alliance with Herbert Asquith.

When Fenianism was in its green youth back in the time of the Mac-Manus funeral, Lord Carlisle was sent over to hold court in the Viceregal Lodge. Belfast was by then the foremost industrial city of Ireland. The huge new shipyard had added a counterbalance of heavy industry to its prosperous light industry in textiles. The middle classes of Dublin, Limerick, and "Rebel Cork" longed excruciatingly for Belfast's good fortune. Said Lord Carlisle, not a chance; except in Ulster, Ireland's true purpose was to be "the fruitful mother of flocks and herds" or as we would now say, to be "bullock-befriending":

> Here we find in the soil and the climate the conditions best suited for pasture. Hence it appears that cattle above all things seem to be the most appropriate stock for Ireland, and the laws of the market to which I refer agree in recommending the source of supply. Corn, you well know, can be brought from one country to another, from a great distance, at rather small freight. It is not so with cattle—hence the great hives of industry in England and Scotland can draw their shiploads of corn from more southern climates, but they must have a constant dependence on Ireland for an abundant supply of meat. . . .

He reminded his listeners of those unsightly mud-walled cabins that were formerly to be seen everywhere in Ireland; eyesores really, they had been "the censure and opprobrium of the country" and the particular condemnation "of commercial travellers." They were, further, a source of constant pain to "those public spirited inhabitants who mourned over a state of things which they were unable, at all events, at once to relieve." Well, he would beg to point out that the census of 1841 had enumerated 491,000 of these cabins, but twenty years later, thanks to the reign of economic progress under the Union, the number had fallen to 125,000. Therefore, he said, "with reference to the general concerns of Ireland, I feel I am justified in speaking to you, upon the whole, in terms of congratulations and hopefulness."[1]

Glory be for the vanished cabin and the great Irish exodus, for the American wake and the emigrant ship, whose pathos was formulated in numerable expressions in the popular culture and treated as a serious literary theme by George Moore, Liam O'Flaherty, and others. Joyce was later to classify these expressions as sentimentalisms:

> I love my country—by herrings I do!
> I wish you could see what tears I weep
> When I think of the emigrant train or ship.[2]

But the lice in Stephen Dedalus' collar and those dreary periodic episodes with the moving van in the Dedalus household—the national "paralysis" for which Joyce was an expert witness—were merely the symptoms of a nation fleeing overseas. O'Leary estimated that Dublin had four hundred barristers but work enough to keep forty of them occupied, and why was this? In 1867 the lord mayor of Dublin tied these threads together: "Emigration is the hemorrhage which drains the life-blood of Ireland away."[3]

II

The executions in Manchester brought the heroic phase of Fenianism to a close. With the organization dismembered and the leaders in jail, systematic action gave place to private adventure. A garrisoned Martello tower near Cork was successfully raided for arms, and several gunsmith shops were cleaned out to the bare walls by Fenians who arrived with primed pistols and large canvas bags to carry off the inventory. During one of these raids a Cincinnati Fenian named William Lomasney was apprehended by a plainclothes detective. As the two men struggled for a revolver, it discharged, giving the officer a nasty leg wound from which he died a week later. Lomasney was tried for murder, but the jury found him not guilty, a verdict that reflected painfully back upon the moral import of the Manchester hangings.

These adventures took on an increasingly frenzied and degenerate mien. A sensational episode in the new style occurred just three weeks after the Manchester hangings. Following the rescue of Kelly and Deasy at Manchester, Colonel Burke himself was soon arrested. He was confined in Clerkenwell House of Detention in mid-London, together with another Fenian, Joseph Casey, Stephens' cousin. A group of London Fenians reasoned that the rescuer ought to be rescued and decided to blast a breach in the jail wall that separated the street outside from the prisoners' exercise yard. The explosion was to be timed for the daily exercise period, when the prisoners were gathered on the opposite side. An informer notified the police that some sort of attempt at rescue would be made, so that Burke and Casey were moved to another part of the jail. The rescuers brought up their explosive in a handcart and in leisurely fashion, watched by idle residents in the nearby houses, they put it in place beside the wall, attached the fuse, lit it, and strolled away. The expert in charge of the operation was said to have been a veteran sapper from the Union army, and no one has ever explained why he used five hundred pounds of black powder, twentyfold too much for the job. The explosion blew out nearly two hundred feet of brick wall and hurled forty tons of masonry across the exercise yard. It would have killed Burke and Casey if they had been there. It shattered every window in the jail, and across the street it demolished a block of tenements, killing twelve persons and maiming a hundred and twenty others.

The theatricality of the Clerkenwell explosion suggested to a few of the more uncomplicated Fenians a model technique for advancing the Irish cause. The old Fenian organization, splitting into fragments, thus formed one small section of "Dynamitards" who made terror against England their purpose in life. Their forays, usually organized out of New York, came in time to be systematized around O'Mahony's colorful assistant, "Red Jim" MacDermott. He recruited groups of youths for this patriotic work, accompanied them overseas as their demonstration leader, and secretly betrayed them to the police; then he returned to New York for another batch. Over the decades the dynamiting passion persisted. Lomasney was among those who followed this work; a gentle terrorist, his ambition was to demolish architectural London without hurting anybody. He died at last by his own dynamite, in the act of placing explosives under the abutment of London Bridge. Another was Tom Clarke, first signatory of the Easter Week Proclamation. Of the next generation was Cathal Brugha, who brought over his little eight-year-old girl to live with him in a London hotel while he studied how to blow up the cinemas. The most literary was Brendan Behan, who as we have seen was still engaged in this misguided occupation in 1939, undismayed by the seventy years of total futility since Clerkenwell had started it all.

The Dynamitards were an embarrassment and sorrow to the other Fenians. Because strict rule forbade the debate of private quarrels within the hearing of the common enemy, the main body of Fenians were reluctant to join a public hue and cry against any fleeing Dynamitard. But in the secret councils terrorism was bitterly attacked. Its effect was to most Fenians painfully obvious: it simply made enemies of their potential friends, since it was not long before bystanders had got more than a surfeit of random explosions. O'Leary was particularly annoyed, and among the concrete meanings of his famous aphorism, "There are things no man should do, even to save a nation," the foremost was that no Irishman should blow up the London theaters in the name of patriotic duty.

III

A quizzical intermingling of revulsion with respect toward terrorism turns up in Joyce's inimitable literary formulation of the Clerkenwell incident in the "Proteus" chapter of *Ulysses*. On his first trip to Paris in 1902 he had taken the trouble to look up a Fenian exile, Joseph Casey, Burke's Clerkenwell cell mate. Richard Ellmann reports that Joyce found the old fellow "a nuisance," but his evidence also shows that first he touched Casey for a small loan, and then made him sit as model for "Kevin Egan of Paris," the Dynamitard, one of the major leitmotivs of *Ulysses*.

Joyce's vignette opens heavy with disgust. The search for Kevin Egan leads down into the squalid Parisian lairs of the exiled and the damned. There he is discovered, "spurned and undespairing," degraded, rapt, an addict of a demented nostalgia for a cause long dead. "The green fairy's fang [of absinthe] thrusting between his lips. Of Ireland, the Dalcassians [i.e., the medieval kings of Thomond from whom Smith O'Brien was descended], of hopes, conspiracies, of Arthur Griffith now. . . . Of lost leaders, the betrayed, wild escapes. Disguises, clutched at, gone not here." His effeminate offspring, Patrice, "son of the wild goose" whose "father's a bird," transforms into an effete socialist surrogate for Christ, whose "father's a bird," too, a pigeon as all Joyceans know. He laps milk instead of the paternal and patriotic "froggreen wormwood," and has learned about the "nature of women" from books, from Michelet, apotheosizer of *la pucelle*, Joan of Arc. Kevin Egan's patriotic compulsion is a symptom of voyeurism, cuckoldry, homosexuality, and nympholepsy; for Joyce wrote in the same pioneer psychoanalytic age that inspired Dr. Ernest Jones's subconsciously English political notation on the hidden meaning of "the Irish problem": those eccentric people who live on lesser islands yearn for a motherland rather than a fatherland.[4] Thus when Kevin Egan dissolved into another of the ghosts that got away James Stephens (not from jail now, but from his hiding place), he disguised Stephens for the occasion as "a young bride, man, veil, orangeblossoms, [and] drove out to the road to Malahide." Joyce's embroidery on A. M. Sullivan's invention about the coach-and-four put in the orange blossoms in order to state a motif he later called "heroticism." Stephens' own testimony on the subject was, "I never donned a female's costume in my life, nor do I intend to."[5]

"Loveless, landless, wifeless," Kevin Egan strains toward a fantasy female vampire: "Maud Gonne, beautiful woman, *La Patrie*, M. Millevoye, Felix Faure, know how he died? Licentious men." Decoded, this astounding concentrate of murderous associations reads: Kevin Egan's patriotic and sexual fantasies interchange with each other as forms of death. Maud Gonne, a hypostatization of Cathleen ni Houlihan, who wears elsewhere in *Ulysses* the poison corsage of potato blossoms, embodies the Irish *patrie*. The real female is as equally inaccessible and merciless as the hypostatized one. While Yeats had been wooing her with those poems of disembodied languid death-longing, she was the licentious bedfellow of M. Millevoye, a henchman of the chauvinist General Boulanger, a man who also combined in his own sensational fashion the morbid trinity of politics, sex, and death. Millevoye, who told Maud Gonne she should seize her destiny in the role of *la pucelle* of Ireland, is associated also with Félix Faure, anti-Dreyfusard president of France. That patriot had interrupted a midafternoon state conference on the Dreyfus crisis to retire to an adjoining private chamber for what the *Encyclopaedia Britannica* once called "an interview" with his own mistress, the wife of the painter Steinheil. Shortly afterward he was heard screaming, and his secretaries rushed in to find him dying of "an apoplexy." Lascivious men, to be sure, but "wars are lost in the same spirit in which they are won," and it takes a lascivious people to expose a lascivious people. And so on: but we must draw breath.

In the middle movement, Kevin Egan, sinister now, lights a "gunpowder" cigarette: "The blue fuse burns deadly between hands and burns clear. Loose tobacco shreds catch fire: a flame and acrid smoke light our corner. Raw facebones under his peep of day boy's hat." Then the explosion, or as it is known in the literary trade, the "apocalyptic vision." "Lover, for her love he prowled with colonel Richard [Ricard] Burke, tanist of his sept, under the walls of Clerkenwell and, crouching, saw a flame of vengeance hurl them upward in the fog. Shattered glass and toppling masonry." All relationships freeze momentarily in primordial space, rescuer and rescued merge in montage lit by a flash as the long sustained strident ignobility is silenced for an instant of the violent, grand, and cosmic. No doubt about it, Joyce, like Yeats and Eliot, found all great loud bangs captivating as having something to do perhaps with History or God. But then another quick twist and Kevin Egan returns in excellent circuitous form to his point of origin, in order that the coda may reiterate the overture:

> In gay Paree he hides, Egan of Paris, unsought by any save by me. . . . He takes me, Napper Tandy, by the hand.
>
> *O, O the boys of Kilkenny* . . .
>
> Weak wasting hand on mine. They have forgotten Kevin Egan, not he them. Remembering thee, O Sion.[6]

IV

The marvelous brilliance of Joyce's Dynamitard is a distraction. In the manner of Dostoevsky's *Possessed*, it spotlighted a small, lurid, half-mad fragment that did exist, right enough, but did not represent anything much but itself. As for the main nondynamiting body of Fenians, nothing so striking could be said of them. They were defunct as a military threat, but not as a nationalist symbol or a body of scattered but like-minded men. The original ganglion that bound Fenianism together was gone with Stephens, but wholesale arrests had provided a new one. Hundreds of Fenian veterans who had originally been tied to the organization only through personal contact with Stephens now met as fellow prisoners and became acquainted for the first time. Then the old question recurred, What next? When one is crushed and can do nothing, what shall he do? According to Swift, that was when Irishmen built a powder magazine. He was a better revolutionist than he imagined. The Fenian answer was similar: then you organize an amnesty agitation.

Irishmen have been often taunted for their murderous factionalism—"great hatred in a little room"—and not without some justice. More remarkable is the contrary trait, an overwhelming urge to draw together in common grief.

The universal compassion of Irishmen for any fellow countryman, friend or foe, held prisoner by the English, was one of the secrets of the political genius of the nation:

> He had done most bitter wrong
> To some who are near my heart,
> Yet I number him in the song.[7]

Hence, the police roundup of Fenians had hardly begun before a popular movement arose to demand reprieves and commutations for the prisoners. The trials that followed Colonel Kelly's rising of March 1867 had handed down a number of death sentences. Immediately an amnesty committee formed, headed by a couple of priests from Cardinal Cullen's National Association. As for Cullen himself, the years had dulled his edge, and he personally intervened in one of the death-sentence cases, that of Colonel Thomas Bourke or Burke (not to be confused with Colonel Ricard Burke of Clerkenwell). After the scaffold had already been built, he drove down to the Castle to make a successful plea for commutation, arguing with the voice of experience that a hanging would "only add fuel to their flames."

The amnesty committee had won all its first round of cases, so that none of the death sentences resulting from the 1867 rising was carried out. One of the Fenians thus saved, James F. X. O'Brien of Cork, was the last man in Great Britain who would ever stand in the dock to hear himself sentenced to be hanged, drawn, and quartered. Shortly afterward the government finally asked itself Swift's unanswerable question: "What needs all this cookery?" and the barbarous old formula was abandoned. As for O'Brien, he was in time released from jail and, mellowing by slow degrees, became at last a decorous and respectable Home Ruler of the anti-Parnellite faction and a particular aversion of W. B. Yeats's.

Then came the amnesty defeat at Manchester and the uproar that followed. A. M. Sullivan, the assistant grand marshal of Dublin's mock funeral for the Manchester martyrs, was shortly in need of amnesty for himself. The *Nation* had taken no care for prudence in its leading articles on the Manchester affair. The term "judicial murder" had been employed. Sullivan was arrested, together with Richard Pigott, the current owner of the one-time Fenian paper, the *Irishman*, who was then just beginning one of the more sensational careers in Irish history. On the day after the Clerkenwell explosion, the police came back to arrest Sullivan again, this time for "conducting a seditious funeral."[8] He was found guilty and went like so many others before and after to serve time, six months as it happened, in Richmond jail.*

For A. M. Sullivan to go to jail on behalf of Fenianism was not a normal expectation, but he had not really succumbed to mental aberration. He knew on the one hand that Fenianism was for the moment crushed. He knew also that, defeated or not, it represented the only popular Irish political mechanism operating in competition against the clergy. When O'Leary told Yeats that in Ireland one must have either the Church or the Fenians on his side, he meant that the two forces were mutually exclusive. Sullivan's idea was that one should combine them together into a "blend."

The Fenians on their own part, unless they wished to take the dynamite road with Rossa and MacCafferty, were pleased to join with anybody interested in amnesty. Fenian prisoners would not be likely to resent an

---

* On his release his friends organized a national Sullivan Tribute and handed him a check for four hundred pounds. He passed the money to the committee for the Grattan statue, and as a result the familiar memorial came into being, poised in College Green with oratorical fingers aloft to receive the toddy cups hung there by Trinity jokers.

agitation, even by "spouters," to free them from jail. With their military ideal reduced to little more than verbal compulsion with a ludicrous remoteness from actuality, they inevitably drifted toward the Sullivans' orbit, though the drift was by inches and with innumerable reservations. And thus it was that in the amnesty movement for the first time "the distinction between Fenian and non-Fenian Nationalists seemed to disappear."[9]

V

The end of the Fenian military threat at the close of 1867 left a great quiet and fatigue in Ireland, like the emptiness that had followed the famine and the collapse of Young Ireland. In such times of Irish political vacuum (and the same again in 1891 and 1923), the Church as the one permanent institution found itself momentarily in possession of a political monopoly, thanks to the extermination of its competitors. Cullen's revival of the Whig alliance might have sounded like comedy to the Fenians in 1864; but in 1868, through sheer survival it had become the dominant and, except for amnesty, the sole Irish political orientation of moment.

Cullen's project had been strengthened by a shift in the English party leadership at Westminster. The retirement at age seventy-five of Lord John Russell, the Whig leader who represented in the Irish mind the famine, coercion, Van Diemen's Land, no-popery riots, and the Manchester hangings, had removed the man who had made the very name "Whig" hateful (a semantic enrichment on which Yeats was later to play his word game about Whigs who were presumed to hate Whiggery). The ugly word, slowly fading out for years past, retired officially with Russell, giving way to the new designation, "Liberal." The old Whig alliance was now called the "Liberal alliance" and was thus purified of some of its unsavory Irish historical memories.

The new Liberal leader replacing Russell was William E. Gladstone, old enough for retirement himself, but still charged with the energy and outlook of a youth of thirty. He had served his apprenticeship as a Tory under Sir Robert Peel, but in the shuffle that followed Corn Law repeal he came out of the scrum wearing the colors of the opposition. In personal life he was more pious than Russell but less bigoted. He had, it is true, resigned from Peel's cabinet in indignation over the Maynooth grants, yet Cardinal Manning was his lifelong friend. His attitudes toward Ireland were as steadfastly English-oriented as Russell's, but his mind was far more astute and supple. Prodded (as he admitted) by the Fenian commotion, he came to believe that it was not a wise English policy toward Ireland to stand upon the old ossified postures and phrases. In the summer of 1868, with Disraeli's ministry collapsing and a new general election near at hand, Gladstone rallied the English Liberals and Irish Whigs into a winning combination around promises to bring "Justice to Ireland" and (not quite the same thing) "to pacify Ireland."

In Cullen's opinion the one thing needed in Ireland was the disestablishment and disendowment of the Church of Ireland. He had not come out unscorched from the Fenian epoch, and he evidently thought that it would be restful to shift the Anglicans into the hot spot. Gladstone brought in a disestablishment bill in haste. Irishmen generally approved the bill as justice three-quarters of a century overdue. Yet the abuses of the Irish established church, if indefensible, were rather superficial compared with the other problems of Irish welfare. As John Mitchel noted at the time, it was not the Anglican vicars who "fling out poor families on the highway in winter."[10] After the bill passed and the Church assets were turned into life annuities for the surplus vicars, everything was about the same as before.

With disestablishment out of the way, the amnesty forces once more took the field. They circulated an amnesty petition, collecting a quarter of a million signatures. They published stories of cruel treatment of Fenian prisoners. Seven had died of exposure, four had committed suicide, four had gone insane. Colonel Ricard Burke, a large muscular man, had shrunk to ninety pounds and turned the color of parchment. Old friends could not recognize him. He claimed that he was being poisoned by the prison doctor, so that it was supposed he too must be insane, though the prison chaplain thought his charges probably true. He then feigned insanity to force the prison officials to transfer him to the shelter of a bedlam. O'Donovan Rossa's treatment was a special scandal. He had been handcuffed with his hands behind his back for thirty-five days; but he was able to prevail on a Highlander prison guard to smuggle out a message about his plight to George Henry Moore, who ventilated the affair on the floor of the House. A select committee of Parliament was set up to investigate the Fenian allegations and found them to be correct.

Gladstone's government then gave its reply to the amnesty movement: releases for half the lesser Fenians and for the ailing Kickham among the leaders, and nothing more. This disposition being only half-satisfactory, the committees set about to heat up their agitation. They called an aggregate meeting in midsummer 1869 to form a permanent Amnesty Association and to elect officers. The board, the first solid substance of the new Irish Nationalist unity, consisted of Father Lavelle, Richard Pigott of the *Irishman*, John Martin, a Fenian called "Amnesty Nolan," and, to be sure, A. M. Sullivan. For president, the association chose the great liberal Tory Protestant, Isaac Butt, who therewith became the new leader of Irish nationalism.

VI

Historical and literary threads in nineteenth-century Ireland often cross in intimate personal relationships: in the intersection of Mitchel with Mangan, of George Henry Moore with *Esther Waters*, of the Dynamitard Casey with James Joyce, of John O'Leary with W. B. Yeats, of the Gregory quarter-acre clause with the Abbey Theatre. Another significant point of intersection centers in Isaac Butt. Until the Yeatses had become famous themselves, he was the family's most prized connection with greatness. He was the life-long friend of grandfather Yeats, the rector of Orange Portadown ("a good man on a horse," but not to be confused with great-grandfather Yeats, the rector of Drumcliff, Sligo). He provided John Butler Yeats, who idolized him, with an unfinished apprenticeship in the law. Yeats *fils* referred to him with offhand ease as "my father's old friend."

For J. B. Yeats, Butt was unique, a man incapable of meanness, acrimony, or calculation: "he could not hate." He spoke often, too, of his warmth, his "naturalness and humanity," and of his artistic sensibility, which had created a romantic novel, the *Dublin University Magazine*, and a personal style. A friend had once found him preparing for some great trial by hiding out in a rural inn to read Milton. He was not one who suffered from dissocation of sensibility, and Yeats *père* recalled the effect of his court arguments on listeners: "I always think a great orator convinces us not by force of reasoning, but simply because he is visibly enjoying the beliefs which he wants us to accept. This is my recollection of Isaac Butt. The cause he was fighting for enshrined itself in him—to follow him seemed health which is another name for happiness."[11] There was none of the repellent "good citizen" in Butt, either—he had been imprisoned for debt; he "loved a lass" like another important Irish politician, rather more scandalously, in fact, maintaining for years separate households for his illegitimate and legitimate ménages, both of whom loved him none the less for it. So be it, Yeats *père* concluded: "The poor muse could only visit him in strange places— in brothels and gaming houses she would meet her son, herself an exile; in those days banished by the respectable poets and Bishops and all the old mumbling bigotries of religion and social hatred. Butt, who loved humanity too much to hate any man, who knew too much of history to hate any opinion—besides how can a self-centered man, with visions to follow, hate? The career of Butt and its disasters is enough to prove the necessity of the Irish poetical movement."[12]

Some of those truths for which Yeats *fils* beat upon the wall were actually more accessible than that, being merely the daily table talk of that wonderful old man, his father. The family idealization of Isaac Butt appears to have served poetry well:

> . . . to be choked with hate
> May well be of all evil chances chief.
> If there's no hatred in a mind
> Assault and battery of the wind
> Can never tear the linnet from the leaf.[13]

Butt's amiability gave the lineaments for the model Yeatsian Irishman, and especially the model Yeatsian politician.

"The Tower" describes an imaginary polity built up by the Irish Protestant:

> Bound neither to Cause nor to State,
> Neither to slaves that were spat on,
> Nor to the tyrants that spat,
> The people of Burke and of Grattan
> That gave, though free to refuse—[14]

Some readers have been troubled by this formulation. Did the heuristics of half rhyme discover for the poet the "spat on" or the "Grattan," or both, each of them misplaced? To suggest that Burke and Grattan were not bound to cause passes into nonsense; if mere paradox is wanted, it would be better to stay with "Love is like the lion's tooth." When one searches for alternative political names that might fit these lines, few possibilities come to mind. Not Tone, a plebeian, nor Emmet nor Lord Edward, who were also bound to cause, and who, incidentally, despised Burke and Grattan. Not Smith O'Brien, driven by his tyrannical evangelical conscience. Perhaps Captain John Shawe-Taylor, Lady Gregory's nephew, for whom Yeats wrote a somewhat eccentric encomium; or perhaps that other ubiquitous nephew, Sir Hugh Lane. The perfect fit would be Isaac Butt, not necessarily the man himself who, as Joseph Hone remarked, "ran after women and was always in debt," but the Yeats family's idealization. And yet the man, too. Any Fenian would have recognized his likeness to Yeats's portrait in the relaxed humanity and, above all, the fine free-handed generosity. When O'Leary and Luby were awaiting trial, their briefs were refused by eminent counsel, and it was Butt who took them up. He spent the greater part of the next four years defending the stream of Fenians who passed through the criminal courts, to finish off the ruin of purse and career. It was also natural to read Butt's assumption of the presidency of the Amnesty Association as a new generosity that he was "free to refuse." That would be in accord with the presence of Father Lavelle and John Martin on the board. But if generosity were all there was to it, what were Richard Pigott and A. M. Sullivan doing there?

VII

Butt's Amnesty Association reacted vigorously to Gladstone's refusal to release all political prisoners. Forty protest meetings were held during the summer of 1869, all pointing up to a grand finale in October, held in an open field at Cabra on the northwest edge of Dublin. According to Butt's guess, two hundred thousand people came out to Cabra to disapprove the continued imprisonment of the forty Fenian leaders and the cruel punishments inflicted on Rossa, Burke and the others who had gone mad or died in prison. Half as many more, Butt said, had jammed the roads solid for a mile back, unable to get through the gates into the meeting, another case of Tara or the MacManus funeral. It is not a common experience for a man to stand in the focus of two hundred thousand pairs of listening ears and watching eyes, and Butt, a literary man in his own right, tried to formulate his feelings. Witnesses of the famine had all said that mere words were futile, and Butt had to fall back upon the same figure:

> There was an awe and a solemnity in the presence of so many living souls. Dense masses of men, outnumbering the armies that decided the fate of Europe on the field of Waterloo, covered a space of ground upon the far-off verge of which their forms were lost in distance. Around that verge the gorgeous banners of a hundred trades' unions, recalling to the mind the noblest glories of the Italian free republics, glistened in the brightness of a clear autumn sun. Words fail to describe—imagination and memory fail in producing—the image of a scene which like the recollections of Venice, is so different from all the incidents of ordinary life, that it seems like the remembrance of a vision or a dream.[15]

The political lesson of the Cabra mass meeting was plain enough to Butt: defeated Fenianism had other attractions besides the romance of a lost cause. This conclusion was demonstrated beyond all doubt several weeks later in a by-election in Tipperary. Somebody in the Amnesty Association thought it would be a good stunt to enter the name of O'Donovan Rossa as a candidate—address, "of Portland Prison, or Pentonville, England." The campaign on his behalf had only one appeal: How would you like to be fettered with your hands behind your back for thirty-five days? It was all that was needed. Rossa was elected, but immediately disqualified by the House of Commons. A couple of weeks later Kickham, just out of prison, campaigned in the same constituency and lost by four votes. The fact that neither of the candidates was eligible to serve only sharpened the point of the voters' intent.*

---

* Rossa told the governor of Chatham prison that he ought to be shipped to Millbank, more convenient to Westminster, so that he could dash back to his cell and "pick a bit of oakum" between parliamentary debates.

With forty years in the House of Commons behind him, Gladstone, too, understood the political meaning of the Cabra and Tipperary occurrences. In February 1870, shortly after the Tipperary by-election, he brought in his land bill. He proposed to make landlords compensate evicted persons for "disturbance," together with the value of the farm improvements they left behind. He hoped thereby to satisfy two of the Three Fs, leaving only fair rent as unfinished business. But fair rent was the key grievance. Sir John Gray, Duffy's old ally and editor of the *Freeman's Journal*, attacked the bill as useless. His judgment of it was not unfair. After it became law, its benefits were overshadowed in the countryside by a new phase of evictions, a new wave of Ribbon violence, and naturally a new coercion bill.

Gladstone's next response was more to the point: at Christmas 1870 he released the rest of the Fenian prisoners, though the leaders were granted only conditional pardons. Their mood was to reject any conditions for release,[16] creating a moral puzzle somewhat like Smith O'Brien's refusal to accept the commutation of his death sentence in 1848. After some negotiations the prisoners agreed to the condition that they leave the British Isles and so walked out of prison more or less free. Devoy and Rossa headed for the United States and never again went home to live. O'Leary settled down for a fifteen-year residence in Paris.

Gladstone's "Justice to Ireland" was exhausted without spectacular accomplishment. Amnesty was a fine thing, but was one expected to thank the Saxon prime minister for releasing one's fellow countryman who should never have been imprisoned in the first place? Disestablishment was in one sense noteworthy; the Irish in teamwork with Gladstone had won in six weeks what the Welsh were going to need thirty-five years to accomplish, for whatever it was worth. The new land act had no Irish defenders except for a few who hoped that it was an entering wedge, but even they admitted that it would be another decade before a better land bill could be passed. From the advanced Irish point of view, the new experiment in the Whig alliance had turned out like the old ones.

VIII

Listening to the rumble of popular restiveness against Gladstone, sensing opportunity, Butt, Martin, and Sullivan decided in the closing days of the debate on the Land Act of 1870 that the time had come once again to reopen the nationalist political offensive along correct lines, the combination of all classes. They persuaded the *Irish Times* to call a meeting of resplendent Irishmen to discuss a new nationalist effort. The meeting, held in the Bilton Hotel on May 19, 1870, was attended by sixty-one persons, including the lord mayor, the ex-lord mayor, the editor of the Tory *Evening Mail*, one

D.D., one M.P., two M.D.'s plus one F.R.C.S.I. (Oscar Wilde's physician father), nine J.P.'s, three P.L.G.'s (Poor Law Guardians), two F.T.C.D.'s (Fellows of Trinity College), two '48 men—John Martin and P. J. Smythe, the man that got away John Mitchel from Van Diemen's Land—one Quaker, one amnestied Fenian in addition to Mr. "Amnesty Nolan," one Q.C. (the *pièce de résistance*, Isaac Butt), besides A. M. Sullivan. There were no priests or bishops. The Committee of Sixty-one asked themselves, said Sullivan, "What can we do for Ireland?" The best answer to arise spontaneously out of the "hereditary passion" voiced from the floor was that H.R.H. the Duke of Connaught ought to be asked to come over and live permanently in the Viceregal Lodge.

Butt was ready with a better answer: not Repeal, since that word was thought too redolent with old unhappy memories for some of the distinguished persons present, but the new coinage, "Home Rule." He explained that there was a difference of meaning in the two words. O'Connell always kept the referent of the word Repeal gloriously vague. Home Rule was not to be vague. It sought an Irish legislature "in the Old House in College Green" for "our own affairs." But it endorsed in advance the wisdom of Westminster to deal for Irishmen on any question affecting the imperial crown, the colonies and dependencies, and "all matters appertaining to the defense and stability of the Empire at large."[17] Let Englishmen have no fears about the integrity of the empire being endangered by Isaac Butt.

In Sullivan's Committee of Sixty-one the reader will recognize the ghost of Young Ireland's Eighty-two Club and a new embodiment of that recurrent longing of middle-class Irish ambition to decorate its adventures with a bit of "the best blood." It was anxious to make clear that Home Rule entailed no excesses, no Jacobinism, no physical force, and none of the new danger just discovered by Butt, English socialism. Normally that meant the clergy would come in to do the legwork, except that they were already attached to Gladstone. But now a new source of popular backing might be available in the rank-and-file remnants of the Fenian movement.

True, the Fenians would not be easy to work with. The first problem, as Butt saw it, was not so much how to make use of them as how to keep them from breaking up meetings. Sullivan had a pained memory of the 1861 riot in the Rotunda when he launched his agitation over the statue of Prince Albert. Nearly a decade had passed since then, and except for the Brotherhood of St. Patrick and the Amnesty Association, both Fenian sponsored, nobody had dared to launch any more Irish moral force agitations. But in the very month of Rossa's Tipperary election, some Limerick farmers determined to try again, and organized a tenant-right mass meeting with a nationalist priest named Father Quaid and also a couple of loyalist priests for the speakers. It was still premature. Two hundred Fenians appeared, and as soon as Father Quaid had finished his speech, they charged the platform and scattered the dignitaries. The Home Rulers' fear of Fenian disruption was realistic, especially in view of the striking limitations of its program, which O'Leary at once described as "perfectly fatuous" and which even the tired '48 men found slightly preposterous, though praiseworthy in its "anxiety to avert revolution and anarchy."[18]

Isaac Butt now came forward to beg the Fenians to reciprocate his generous past favors in the criminal courtroom and the Amnesty Association, and to allow Home Rule a fair hearing. William O'Brien, later to become one of the chief Parnellite lieutenants, attended a banquet given for the first of the Fenians let out of jail in 1869, and he remembered Butt's speech of welcome to the felons:

> Butt's speech was almost wholly a plea to the released Fenian leaders to give him a chance for trying other means. He was argumentative, pathetic, passionate by turns; but the passage that will always live in my memory was that in which, in language actually blazing with the divine fire of eloquence, he declared that, if the conciliatory methods he pleaded for failed, he would not only give way to those who would lead where all nations of the earth had gone before them, but that, old as he was, his arm and his life would be at their service in the venture.[19]

The top Fenian leadership, following rigid doctrine, blasted the idea of collaboration with Butt's moral force nationalism as treason. Apparently, though, Butt and a spokesman for a Fenian splinter group in Limerick, a man named John Daly, arrived at some sort of mutual understanding, perhaps even in writing, since Fenians had a weakness for written instruments of conspiracy. In any case, there was much reference later to an agreed cutoff time that would terminate all further experimentation with moral force methods and with Orange-Tory landlord alliances. Until then, Butt was able to give the illustrious Committee of Sixty-one firm reassurances of personal safety: "As for the men whom misgovernment has driven into revolt, I say for them that if they cannot aid you they will not thwart your experiment. Arise! Be bold! Have faith; have confidence, and you will save Ireland; not Ireland alone, but England also!"[20]

IX

In 1873 Gladstone finally brought in his long-delayed Irish universities bill, a compromise at once both godless and Catholic. Against the advice of Manning, who thought the bill an entering wedge, Cullen condemned it, the Irish members withdrew their support, and it lost by three votes. In a mood of benignity and noticeable relief, Gladstone began to make his plans for retirement to the opposition benches.

His failure to produce a Catholic university provoked some fretfulness among the Irish clergy, dramatized in a series of boisterous by-elections. Occasionally they still stood in a solid phalanx for Gladstone against Home Rule. John Martin, the '48 man, was crushed by the Longford clergy backed by a muscular corps of lay enthusiasts who seized the instruments of the amnesty band sent down by train to help Martin's cause, and afterward paraded through town like Euripides' Bacchae carrying aloft the battered fragments of the bass drum and the trombones for trophies. Because of these excesses, the election was declared void and had to be rerun. Butt next put up his choicest Protestant landlord, the Honorable Edward King-Harman. Once more the Longford clergy rallied to Gladstone and roundly defeated the Home Ruler, this time by means believed to be legal.

In Galway, on the other hand, the clergy were equally partisan toward Home Rule. In a by-election there, the defeated Gladstonite claimed a foul against the priests and demanded that the Home Rule winner be disqualified. The case came up before a well-known personality of the Irish bench, Judge William Keogh, who ruled against the clergy and the Home Rulers and invalidated the election. His decision was in itself nothing out of the ordinary, but his behavior in rendering it was exceptional. He required nine hours to read the decision to the court, with dramatic elocutionary effects—laughing, weeping, shouting, pacing. His speech was a rabid Orange tirade,[21] most singular, since his own career, it will be remembered, was built upon a debt to the Irish ultramontane primate. Nationalists were inclined to treasure Keogh's peculiar denouement for its moral beauty. But he was plainly mad, and a few weeks later, after knifing a serving boy in a Belgian hotel, he died of a stroke.

In a third pattern, the Catholic forces wavered and split among themselves. When John Martin made a second attempt in Meath, the clergy could not reach any unanimity, and so stood aside and backed neither candidate. Martin won, breaking the ice for Home Rule; and the old insurrectionist, treason-felony convict, and Van Diemen's Land veteran took his seat in the House of Commons in January 1871.

In Kerry the wildest of the Home Rule by-elections found the Church rent by mutiny. Bishop Moriarty staked his prestige in a heroic effort to turn back Home Rule. He put up a Catholic Liberal named J. A. Dease and Butt put up a young Protestant landlord, Rowland Ponsonby Blennerhassett. Moriarty raised the slogan, "A Catholic and no souper for North Kerry," but the Kerry clergy refused to follow his command. One priest told Dease he "could not go against the people here, who are all the other way," and another instructed his parishioners to disregard all intimidation, whether it came from "landlord, priest, bishop, or even the Pope himself." The priests won. One of Moriarty's field commanders wrote him the bad news that "the revolutionists aided with the most shameful activity by the priests have scourged the party of order along the whole line in Kerry."[22]

All of this epic by-election warfare in 1871, 1872, and 1873 ended with the clergy, like the rank-and-file Fenians, settled inside the Home Rule camp, but stripped of the dominance they had enjoyed in O'Connell's Repeal Association or Duffy's Tenant League. As the new movement began to gather momentum, they were swept into it, partly by enthusiasm, partly by discouragement with Gladstone, and partly by the absence of any choice but to go with the tide. Their dilemma was exposed in a by-election in Westmeath, which found the same J. A. Dease (now in his third try) pitted against P. J. Smythe, the '48 man. Dease wrote his backers that he did not have "a ghost of a chance" against "the Fenian element," that his own parish priest admitted he was "afraid not to go with the popular demand," and that a local clergyman had begged him to declare for Home Rule "with any kind of mental reservation I pleased." The bishop gave him to understand that he bowed to the popular demand himself only "with bitter shame," knowing that the alternative was the political isolation of the hierarchy.[23] As the Church became more involved in Home Rule, it transferred its educational demands over to its new friends. Butt listened carefully; and casting off the last shreds of Davis' "haughty impartiality" toward sect, he stood for Parliament in Limerick on a platform of Home Rule *cum* denominational education. It was a winning combination, and he went across to join John Martin at Westminster. Some clever Orangeman responded with the new slogan, "Home Rule is Rome rule."

So the ex-Fenians and the lower clergy were tamed, and a token sample of the landed gentry wooed and won. And by whom? The unbroken thread of the *Nation* attested to the continuity of leadership, and the persistent dominance of the *bürgerlich* voice over all others was unmistakable. Home Rule was a creation of the same middle-class stratum of Irish society that had built Young Ireland and the Tenant League. An Irish journalist who covered Home Rule for the press through three decades summed up the least common denominator of its aims: "Well, we could not possibly make a worse mess of Ireland than is being made of it by the Imperial Parliament; and, at any rate, the hands pulling the strings would be Irish."[24] This was not senseless, and yet Davis' heroic ambitions had surrendered to passions that were, by contrast, somewhat paltry.

X

In November 1873 a Home Rule conference assembled in Dublin to enunciate first principles and to design a mode of political action. It ran its smooth and innocuous course until just before adjournment. Then somebody introduced a resolution that future Home Rule M.P.'s ought to operate as a bloc in the House of Commons, not only on the Home Rule motion but on all the business of the House. To support this resolution a delegate from Belfast —Joseph Biggar, a well-to-do meat packer—rose to speak. He was a hunch-backed dwarf with an oversize cranium, a voice like a corn crake's, and a constant leer. These physical misfortunes made him a subject for aristocratic wit, and when he first appeared in the House of Commons, Disraeli is said to have asked, "Is this what you call a leprecaun in your country?"

Butt vigorously opposed Biggar's idea of a bloc, even with a threat to resign. To paraphrase another Irish patriot, he thought there were things no man should do even to save a nation and among them was the formation of a disciplined Irish parliamentary party: "If eighty men by such means could carry Home Rule, eighty men could carry the Permissive Bill or the Inspection of Nunneries." He would be bound neither to cause nor to state; or as he put it himself: ". . . he would betray his own principles, his dignity, his personal honor and personal honesty, if he now gave a pledge that he would submit his future conduct to the absolute control of any tribunal on earth, except his own conscience, and that higher tribunal, his responsibility to God."[25] Overpowered by this moral barrage, Biggar beat a retreat, the resolution was hastily withdrawn, and the Home Rule League came out of its 1873 organizational conference about as amorphous as it went in.

When Gladstone suddenly dissolved Parliament in January 1874, he allowed only three weeks between dissolution and election day, and Home Rule candidates had to be found for more than a hundred constituencies. Somehow Butt rounded up somebody to run in eighty of them, but the ticket that resulted was very loosely put together. Many of Butt's candidates paid lip service to Home Rule as some sort of tiresome political shibboleth, and exercised those mental reservations the clergy of Westmeath had com-mended to the candidate Dease. Still, shibboleth or not, Home Rule proved an exceedingly attractive vote-getting slogan. The Irish Liberal members were reduced from sixty-five seats to ten. Home Rulers, real or pretended, won seats in fifty-nine constituencies, multiplying their parliamentary strength tenfold. Gladstone, musing on Irish ingratitude, settled down for six years of lean kine; and Disraeli, his head filled with dreams of imperial grandeur, became Her delighted Majesty's prime minister.

CHAPTER 16

Parnell and Davitt

I

Isaac Butt's political ideal was proto-Yeatsian. He deplored rancor, party strife, and loose-lipped demagogues. His code of conduct was pure but futile, and he was quickly overwhelmed in the parliamentary jungle. Two months after the 1874 election victory, Butt proposed that the Commons set up a committee to investigate the sources of Irish unhappiness. His motion lost by a vote of 314 to 50. A formal Home Rule motion followed three months later. It lost, 458 to 61. The adverse majority had expanded by a hundred-odd votes since the first try. And everything was going nicely and according to plan, A. M. Sullivan said. The first step toward Home Rule must display factual demonstration before "the mind and conscience of Christendom." Afterward, "this position made good, we shall in due time advance upon another. Courage, men of Ireland! Courage and perseverance!—we have struck the road that leads to liberty."[1]

Butt himself offered a less hearty exhortation and no optimism at all. Home Rulers, he said after one of these brutal parliamentary rebuffs, "could place their views fairly and distinctly before the British House of Commons, and leave to them the responsibility of rejecting the demands of the Irish people. . . ."[2] His defeatism was contagious, and the membership in the Home Rule League proved a "dismal" disappointment.

II

After half a lifetime overseas, John Mitchel now reappeared in Ireland to criticize through precept and example the limitations of Butt's program. He had been put up in absentia for Cork in the election of 1874, but had not won. He now proposed to put his own oar "into the puddle of Irish politics," to campaign in person in Tipperary, famed for its hospitality to revolutionist vote-seekers: "I am savage against that helpless driftless concern called 'Home Rule.' "[3] His campaign promised the voters a new mode of English defiance: if elected, he would refuse to sit, thereby establishing the original model of the great Irish boycotts of Westminster in 1919 and of the Dáil in 1922. He was elected but the House refused to seat him—a disappointment, for until he was seated he could not refuse to sit. He stood a second time, was again elected, and was just being rejected by the House a second time when the commotion was ended by his sudden death at his old boyhood home in Newry, county Down—hence "there's a grave at Newry," as Yeats reported. His brother-in-law John Martin, M.P. for Meath, caught pneumonia at the funeral and ten days later he died too. A by-election was required to fill the Meath vacancy. It was won by Charles Stewart Parnell, twenty-eight years old, a Wicklow Home Ruler, the master of the big house at Avondale, a short stroll from Joyce's favorite non-Dublin topographic feature, Tom Moore's "meeting of the waters."

As a great Protestant landlord, Parnell was considered a lucky find for Home Rule. Barry O'Brien, Parnell's Boswell, met Butt on the street one day looking more cherubic than usual. "My dear boy," Butt said, "we have got a splendid recruit, an historic name, my friend, young Parnell of Wicklow; and unless I am mistaken, the Saxon will find him an ugly customer, though he is a good-looking fellow." Before he could be admitted to the party, the Home Rule council had to sit in judgment. John Martin declared, "I would trust any of the Parnells." A. M. Sullivan said, "Let us see him." The consensus was that they "thought him a nice gentlemanly fellow who would be an ornament but no use,"[4] another handsome front-window display like Edward King-Harman or Rowland Ponsonby Blenner-hassett. The fact that Parnell betrayed this expectation is the starting point for a good deal of biographical speculation. Any landlord of a good Protestant Ascendancy family, so the reasoning runs, should have been a nonentity like the rest of his social class.

To explain how he came to be "a traitor to his class," tradition cites a loathing for Englishmen that he picked up from the chilly hospitality afforded Irishmen at Cambridge. The aversion was said to be reinforced by his mother, an American suffering from an extreme case of Anglophobia inherited from her own parent, Commodore Charles Stewart, Parnell's namesake, the doughty skipper of the frigate *Constitution* in the War of 1812. But Parnell's own Anglophobia was not absolute. For example, he married the sister of a British field marshal. More important, perhaps, Avondale seems to have been less a gentleman's rural seat than a business enterprise, producing lumber and building stone. The American branch of his family, whom he three times visited, was deep in the mania of speculation in railroading and mining in Henry Grady's New South, and his mother was a Wall Street gambler of great determination but indifferent skill. Like Thomas Davis, Parnell was an impassioned mineralogist and prospector. We have met the creative adventurer so often in Irish nationalist politics that Napoleon's *on s'engage* has forced itself upon us as a lietmotiv. Parnell represents the pure type.

Among the Irish landlords, he was one of the few who foresaw that the old land system was essentially played out and that the wisest course was to accommodate to reality and *sauve qui peut*. His rent rolls at Avondale were large; but the universal burden of debt on Irish landed estates made any gross rent figures meaningless. One of his parliamentary colleagues, Frank Hugh O'Donnell, got the impression that he was down at the heels, judging by the shabbiness of his London flat out Gower Street beyond the British Museum. If his appraisal was correct, Parnell found himself in the standard predicament of the British upper-class younger son, forced to bestir himself to make his own way and live up to the family name.

Parnell's personality, like O'Leary's, lies within the domain of belles-lettres as well as of history and must detain us for a brief inventory of its possibilities. Yeats said:

> . . . Parnell was a proud man,
> No prouder trod the ground.[5]

On that point there is universal assent, though most observers give companion traits no less emphasis. He had a mind that was "purely objective," said T. P. O'Connor, adding that "no man has ever been a confidant of Mr. Parnell." To Michael Davitt he was "proud," also "direct"; but "magnanimity and gratitude he had none," for his mind had "few if any generous impulses." Davitt thought of him as an Englishman, really, while Lord Eversley thought him more of an American, "inflexible," "dogged," an engineer with a "turn for mathematics." The journalist Michael MacDonagh found him "coldly impassive," "diffident," and "proud"; and T. D. Sullivan agreed: "He was a proud man, resolute and obstinate." John Morley described him as "a powerful and an extraordinary personality, cold and long-sighted; in clearness of perception of facts he surpassed anyone whom he had been brought into contact with, either in literature or politics. . . . I had been at his side before and after more than one triumphal occasion, and discovered no sign of quickened pulse." None of these sketches is particularly attractive; and William O'Brien, even when still a youthful worshiper, found in Parnell's basic character a somewhat unheroic virtue: "In essence he was an unaffected Irish country gentleman, with a genius for command and for doing Ireland's business"[6]—in short, another "good citizen" like Davis.

III

Among the most censorious of Parnell's critics was John Butler Yeats. I have noted his boundless admiration for Butt; and Parnell and Butt he always paired together as villain and hero. All the Parnell portraits allow the notion of obduracy to creep in beside the praiseworthy "directness" and gift for "doing business." Yeats *père* read the trait as a sort of cruelty or spite: "It was spite to which Parnell appealed when he ousted Butt the statesman. The Irish took to hatred when they deserted the statesman Isaac Butt for the politician Parnell." He thought that what was called pride in Parnell was really hauteur: "Isaac Butt could not hate and so had to resign his leadership to Parnell who had no other qualifications for the task except an immense, unrelenting, inexorable hatred, helped by a theatrical trick of pose and hauteur impressive to simple people. William Pitt treated Lords Castlereagh and Liverpool exactly as Parnell treated his lieutenants T. Healy and Sexton, etc., and Chatham so behaved to the whole House of Commons."[7] John Butler Yeats's word "hauteur" echoes the word "cold" that rises insistently into most of the summaries of Parnell's character.

For Yeats *fils* Parnell was the central figure in a late reshuffling of all his basic antinomical couplings. His father's old animosity against Parnell he turned upside down, making him his hero, tragic Cuchullain disdainful of the ignoble Firbolgs by whom he was dragged down and torn apart. For the sake of symmetry, he might have borrowed his father's pairing of Butt with Parnell, retaining Butt in the dance by converting him to the comic anti-nome. History suggested the role for Butt. Liam O'Flaherty, another spoiled Catholic like Joyce, was inclined to be cynically amused by the professed altruism of Irish Protestants, especially of those who came forward offering generosity "though free to refuse." Hence his portrait of Butt said: "In control of this [Home-Rule] movement . . . there were at the beginning men whom the Americans would call 'morons.' Out of respect for their memory, I refrain from mentioning their names."[8] O'Flaherty's loose-lipped impertinence could not fit at all into Yeats's scheme of Irish values. Besides, he did not need a comedian, for he had found his archetypal Irish fool in the Liberator, whom he set opposite the tragic Parnell, "Ireland's Antiself." We have questioned O'Connell's fitness for the part Yeats cast him in. Now we need to examine his portrayal of Parnell.

IV

Actually, Parnell and O'Connell are better related as identities than as contraries. In the long view their careers were identical exercises in switch-ing the Irish revolution on and off. Parnell's first exploits in the House of Commons would have delighted the old Liberator for their skill in the use of his own weapon of choice, Irish impudence. A well-worn anecdote tells of his parliamentary initiation. He was seated at Westminster April 22, 1875, an important date for a second reason in the history of the Irish parliamentary party. Just that afternoon Joe Biggar had taken up the ex-periment of obstructing the business of the House. The debate was on the perennial Irish coercion bill, introduced a month before and passed smoothly through the first and second readings. Butt promised that the party would "exhaust all the forms of the House" before defeat. When Biggar's turn had come round to speak, he appeared in the House chamber laden with government reports. "Mr. Speaker," he said, "in order to save time I have brought in at once all the authorities to which I propose to refer." He then commenced reading in a droning voice from the documents he had brought. After a couple of hours his voice gave out and he was reminded that the rules of the House required that the honorable member must be audible to the Speaker. He then took his glass of water and books up to the ministerial benches directly beside the Speaker and continued as before. After four hours, "unwilling to detain the House any longer," he surrendered the floor. One of his Home Rule colleagues protested, "I think a man should be a gentleman first and a patriot afterwards."[9]

Parnell joined in with Biggar's sport. For two weeks more, half a dozen Irish members dragged out the coercion debate with factious amendments, repeated divisions on motions to adjourn, and irrelevant palaver. Disraeli complained of the waste of time, but courteously. He was reminded, he said, of a similar Irish fight against the coercion bill in 1843 (the same that sent O'Connell and Duffy to Richmond jail). He was moved almost to applaud the Irish pluck, knowing the effort to be altogether futile. And at last, all their ingenuity exhausted, the disrupters were duly overwhelmed. In the parliamentary sense, they had accomplished nothing, but Irishmen back home had watched the spectacle closely. In a great Trafalgar Square rally for Fenian amnesty held later in the summer of 1875, it was noted that the prince of disrupters, Joe Biggar, drew the loudest cheers.

Butt took pains to dissociate himself from the boorish manners of his troublemakers. After the coercion bill had passed, he made a little speech of appreciation for Disraeli's courtesy: "They had nothing to complain of in the manner in which they had been received by the house, and the manner in which their objections had been met would have some effect in mitigating the effect these coercive measures would have upon the minds of the Irish people." Disraeli graciously returned Butt's compliment; but one of the disrupters objected: "I, for one, will not be a party to accepting from the English government chains, however gilded, or however accompanied by courtesy, politeness, or good manners."[10] On this note of bad temper, and with a record of total Irish failure, Parnell's freshman term came to its end.

V

In his first House session in 1875 Parnell naturally went almost unnoticed. Taking bearings, he quickly realized that Butt's courtly bumbling would never win any Irish advantage. Two projects needed undertaking: first, to build up at home a popular pressure behind the Irish members; and second, to get some sort of discipline into the disorderly Irish parliamentary bloc, to put a stop to the slovenliness exemplified by one member who, when notified by Butt of a caucus, had sent his regrets: "I am desirous of preserving my personal freedom of action."[11] Parnell's conclusion was, "We do not want speakers in the House of Commons, but men who will vote right."[12]

Like Butt and Sullivan, he pondered on the utility of priests and Fenians as vote canvassers back home. The history of the past quarter-century would naturally lead one to hesitate before relying too heavily on the clergy to build a populist movement. Besides, Cardinal Cullen thought Home Rule "a tool in the hands of journalists and adventurers," and he predicted with uncommon foresight that it would all "end in smoke." The Fenians were not ideal collaborators either. Sullivan, as we have seen, thought that the best juncture of the two contradictory supporters would be a blend, but Parnell altered the metaphor. His political movement would use both forward and backward force, one for acceleration, the other for brakes. Barry O'Brien explained the grand strategy: "He was not a son of the Church. He was not a son of the revolution. But he believed profoundly in the power of the one and of the other, and resolved to combine both. This was a herculean labor, but it was not above the stature of Charles Stewart Parnell."[13]

Had a great expert not established that the phoenix was a bird that could not be blarneyed? John Daly, in fact, had just broken up a Home Rule rally in Limerick on the grounds that the agreed time limit for moral force had run out, and where were the results? Parnell surmised that he would never get the active support of Fenians without a substantial offer. For overture he pointed to the Parnell family's radical reputation and to his sister Fanny's poems in O'Leary's *Irish People*. In 1876 he joined the Amnesty Association and made the release of the newest Fenian prisoners his specialty in the House debates. He publicly championed not only the Manchester martyrs —"I wish to say as publicly and as directly as I can that I do not believe, and never shall believe, that any murder was committed at Manchester"[14]— but Clerkenwell also. Irish newspapers took note, and Parnell emerged from anonymity.

VI

Parnell's second parliamentary session (1876) was as empty as his first. A dozen urgent Irish bills were introduced by the Home Rule members, but all were slaughtered somewhere along the legislative path, with a single exception: a bill to empower Irish municipalities to bestow the freedom of the city upon distinguished persons. It actually passed, received the royal assent, and became the law of the land. (Immediately after passage, the freedom of Limerick was bestowed on Isaac Butt.) Stung by the three futile sessions in a row, the left flank of Home Rule went over to open rebellion against Butt's leadership, while the center deliberated whether to desert him.

Spurred on by outcries for more excitement, the Irish obstructionists went into the House session of 1877 prepared to carry out an elaborate sabotage of the proceedings. This was Parnell's third year, and he had risen to joint triumvirate leadership with Biggar and a new member, a very odd one, Frank Hugh O'Donnell. The three were supported by four others, for a total of seven. Setting immediately to work when the session opened in February, they blocked all routine business, then began to talk non-Irish measures to death. These boisterous sessions were an agony of humiliation to Butt, and after three months he wrote letters to Biggar and Parnell asking them to desist, for they were ruining the chances for passage of the Irish measures by offending the English members. And worse: "I am not insensible of that which is higher than all prudence—the duty of maintaining before the civilized world the dignity of the Irish nation and the Irish cause."[15]

In deference to Butt's feelings, Parnell, Biggar, and O'Donnell took a recess from obstruction in the early summer. Six weeks later they burst out again. As the session drew toward its close, the Irish measures were pushed off the House calendar to make way for an important imperial measure, the South Africa bill. The disrupters subjected it to violent attack. Parnell openly proclaimed his purpose to be sabotage, and the *Hansard* stenographer tried to catch his words above the uproar: "The hon. member, who spoke amid much confusion, and who was twice called to Order by the Chairman, was understood to say—As it was with Ireland so it was with the South African Colonies. . . . Therefore as an Irishman, coming from a country which had experienced to the fullest extent the results of English interference in its affairs and the consequences of English cruelty and tyranny, he felt a special satisfaction in preventing and thwarting the intentions of the Government in respect of this bill."[16] After a week of chaos, the government decided to break the filibuster simply by refusing to vote a motion to adjourn until the disturbance had physically exhausted itself.

The bill was taken up at five in the afternoon on July 31, 1877. All night long the obstruction continued, clause by clause: a move to amend, a division on the amendment, a move to adjourn, a division on the motion. At three in the morning Butt appeared on the floor to denounce his Irish colleagues: "If I thought the hon. member for Dungarvin [O'Donnell] represented the Irish party, and the Irish party represented my country— and he does not represent my country—I would retire from Irish politics as from a vulgar brawl. . . ."[17] He was overapologetic, for a sporting spirit had overtaken the English members. At seven o'clock Biggar went into the House library to catch a nap so that he could spell off his exhausted companions in relay. He could not sleep, though, and at eight he was back on the floor with the cheerful announcement, "Mr. Chairman, sir, I am the better able to go on, having had a long sleep and a good breakfast." Late in the morning Parnell left the floor for a rest break, and was still out when the rebellion suddenly collapsed at noon. At two in the afternoon the bill was passed amid prolonged cheers, closing twenty-one hours of sitting, the longest session to date in the history of Parliament.

Why did the government permit Irish obstruction to be carried on when it could—and eventually did—put a stop to it as soon as it was minded to ? One reason, no doubt, was that the rebellion did the government position no real damage. However noisy the new mode of combat, the Irish benefit was still exactly nil. Moreover, Butt and the government both apparently believed that the obstructionists would hang themselves if given enough rope. In this belief they could not have been more mistaken. Obstruction of the House was essentially theater, staged not for London but for Dublin and Cork. There it brought the house down.[18]

VII

So far, Parnell's career followed the biological law that ontogeny recapitulates phylogeny. Parliamentary obstruction was nothing more than O'Connellism brought up to date. The collapse of the all-night rebellion on the 1877 South Africa bill brought Home Rule to the same hard question that O'Connell found himself facing on the Saturday evening before the monster meeting scheduled at Clontarf in 1843. Popular commotion had been excited to the maximum pitch possible under a purely theatrical offensive; so what next ? Unwilling to risk the next step forward for fear of revolution, O'Connell had destroyed himself just here. But after 1843 Irish nationalist political evolution had moved to a new level, and Parnell now had an alternative answer at hand: when he had gone with O'Connell as far as he could, then he might shift over and go a bit of the way with John O'Leary and John Devoy.

The left wing of Home Rule was located in the English branch, called the Home Rule Confederation. Its membership was drawn from expatriated Fenian-oriented industrial workers who were immune from the respectability of the Committee of Sixty-one and impatient with Butt's timidity. Its guiding spirit was John Barry, an English traveling man in linoleum who holds the peculiar distinction in Irish history of belonging simultaneously to the Bantry band (as a Sullivan cousin) and to the IRB. In 1877

Barry gave Butt the honorific title of president of the English confederation, but in 1878 he decided to take it back.

In midsummer the English Home Rule Confederation met for its annual convention in Liverpool. Butt appeared late and spoke briefly. He was hissed on the platform. An hour or so and he was gone. A friend had once told him: "To deal with these obstructives at a public meeting is for a Gentleman to enter into a personal contest with Chimney Sweeps." He felt somewhat the same way himself and was at the moment attempting to avenge himself upon the chimney sweeps by attacks not clearly permissible under the code of a gentleman—to expose Parnell for having appeared on the same platform with the "notorious atheist Bradlaugh," and O'Donnell for having graduated from one of the "godless" Irish colleges.[19] Here was another case of that tedious iterative pattern of Irish politics in which demoralization automatically awakened the lightly slumbering madness of bigotry. Butt's letters were private, but his hostility was open enough. It was a foregone conclusion that the Liverpool convention would repudiate him. In his place, on the nomination of John Barry, it elected Parnell. The date, August 28, 1877, marked the accession of Parnell to the leadership of Irish nationalism.

His public build-up could now begin, following modern lines. At just this stage of his emergence from the chrysalis, the *Nation* acquired a new London correspondent, the famous-infamous Timothy M. Healy. He was another Bantry boy, a nephew of the Sullivans', a cousin of John Barry's. He had been a stenographic clerk on the railroad at Newcastle until Barry found a place for him in the London office of his linoleum firm. By day he worked the commercial line and sat at night in the press gallery of the House of Commons, composing his weekly "London Letter" for his uncle's Dublin journal. His chore was to downgrade Butt and to upgrade Parnell, twin labors undertaken with youthful fanaticism.[20] Everybody knew already about Butt's stumbling, but Healy's study of Parnell's growing mastery on the floor of the House had the force of a creative discovery. He became Parnell's hero-worshiper, the first of the millions. His laudation was not destined to be perpetual; but of all Parnell's close acquaintances, he remained his shrewdest observer. "Parnell's great gift," he once said, "was his faculty of reducing a quarrel to the smallest dimensions,"[21] a talent in which Healy himself was undoubtedly deficient.

Back home, the obstructionists tried to force themselves onto Butt's Dublin executive board. When they failed, Parnell dropped his open factiousness and with charming generosity praised Butt's leadership. He settled down to bide his time until the next general election: "I am young. I can wait." And Butt, not quite understanding the import of the remark, replied, "Hear, hear!"

VIII

Irish members made no scandalous headlines in the next House session. Their parliamentary obstruction was perfunctory and halfhearted. Parnell himself had other projects on his mind. He had moved on from parliamentary vendetta to the next problem, the search for a mechanism to tap the power of Irish militancy. He understood, said John Barry later, that "a Fenian was a man who was ready to go into penal servitude for Ireland." He felt therefore that "the Fenians were the men to drive the ship, but he wanted to steer it himself."[22] After the Liverpool convention, he spent most of his energy for the next two years in a courtship dance with Fenians, now pursuing and now allowing himself to be pursued, a diverting and productive way to bide his time until the Home Rule movement could ripen.

Fenian orthodoxy still permitted no dalliance with "spouters." The question was asked with great solemnity, How can Fenians take the oath of allegiance to their enemy the queen?—a Gordian knot that troubled the philosophical until de Valera cut it in 1927. Kickham thought the Home Rule movement merely another dishonest futility; and the sworn Fenians who took part in it he considered no better than police spies. O'Leary thought it "honest incompetence" and "clever roguery."[23] In New York, Rossa and Devoy attacked the Home Rule Fenians with their normal violence of language.

Still, Parnell was able to penetrate Fenianism's ideological fortress through several important friendships. His House comrade Joe Biggar was a sworn Fenian, joining for the purpose, he said later, of "winning them over to constitutionalism." During the 1877 obstruction circus he was sitting on the IRB supreme council, together with John Barry. But late in that year both men had been censured by the supreme council for parliamentarianism, and when they would neither repent nor resign, they were expelled, cutting Parnell's tie with the Fenian center. But just at this moment, he met Michael Davitt, a Fenian treason-felony convict seven years imprisoned. With several others he was released on ticket of leave at Christmas 1877 thanks to Parnell's agitations through the Amnesty Association. Parnell went out to Kingstown to meet the prisoners as they came off the mail boat and took them all to breakfast at Morrison's Hotel. (At table one of the released convicts fell over dead, giving Parnell a shock that he never forgot.) Davitt and Parnell began to explore the possibilities of joint activity, and in due time they sealed the most explosive political partnership in modern Irish history.

IX

Davitt, like Parnell, was then thirty-one. He was the son of a Mayo Catholic peasant, born near Castlebar during the famine, where Carlyle shortly afterward passed through to inspect the "human swinery." The family survived the starvation, but when Davitt was six, they were evicted during the great postfamine clearances. They migrated to Lancashire, settling down in an Irish-speaking community of cotton-mill hands. The boy went into the mill to earn his own living at age eleven. A year later, he lost his right arm in a machine. Maimed, discarded by the factory, illiterate, he found refuge in a Wesleyan school. The lone Catholic boy was put at ease by all the Methodists, and he concluded that religious bigotry is not inevitably the natural condition of man. He proved a good scholar, and at fifteen was hired as a bookkeeper in a printing shop.

In 1865, Stephens' year for action, he took the Fenian oath, and soon rose to the position of head center. Under orders, he had reported to Chester Castle for MacCafferty's 1867 arms raid. He was unable to shoot off a gun, but was prepared to carry powder and ball to the troops. When Colonel Ricard Burke disappeared off the scene into Clerkenwell, Davitt replaced him as head of Fenian arms procurement in England. In May 1870 he was apprehended by the police in Paddington Station in the act of handing a sack containing fifty revolvers to a Fenian confederate. He was convicted and sentenced to fifteen years imprisonment. Just when O'Leary, Rossa, and Devoy were coming out of prison, he went in—an unlucky chance, for another amnesty could not be expected for a very long time, seven years in his case. From his treatment as a prisoner, he inferred that the government's object was to destroy him by exposure, malnutrition, neglected illness, and insanity. But when Parnell asked him on a train trip what he planned to do, he replied, "I shall rejoin the revolutionary movement, of course."[24]

He saved his sanity during those seven years in Dartmoor by thinking, by trying to locate the missteps that had brought Fenianism to disaster. Something was obviously wrong with Stephens' system, and he was pained to believe that his life was all but wrecked in order to procure firearms simply because dogma asserted that he must, and "without the consolation of knowing that one of them was ever shouldered to smite an enemy of my country."[25] He thought Stephens' great cadre was admirable in many ways. Yet it was rendered too narrow by its scornful refusal to touch any meaningful immediate issue. At the same time it was too broad; for in trying to correct his narrowness, Stephens became intoxicated with big numbers for their own sake and distended his elite corps by mass recruiting until he had enrolled a hundred thousand secret conspirators, an absurdity on the face

249

of it. Irishmen make impossible conspirators anyhow, he said. (This was later to be Joycean doctrine; and it was endorsed by Joyce's friend Sheehy-Skeffington in a biography of Davitt that Joyce is known to have read.[26] Davitt differed with Joyce, though, in tracing the characteristic to an Irish love of making conversation rather than to a genetic urge to betray.) Davitt thought Stephens would have been better off if he had sworn no member into the conspiracy until he could put a rifle in his hand; meanwhile he should have built up a militant, open, mass organization with more animal spirits than Fenianism's anemic orphan, the old Brotherhood of St. Patrick. In any case, some new approach was essential "if Irish revolutionists were ever to accomplish anything beyond wasting themselves in barren conspiracy and in English convict cells."[27]

Davitt hardly knew what the new approach ought to be, but his prison meditations had discovered one new rule on which he felt assured. It was the necessity of "parallel action." Fenianism and parliamentary Home Rule in 1878 must learn to live and work in the same Ireland, he thought, disagreeing at need, but agreeing on the one point that neither would deny the other the right to exist. This was a conclusion Parnell had already reached and incorporated into his actions. Naturally, some criterion would be needed to distinguish a genuine from a bogus nationalist. It could be found in the touchstone question, Do you believe in the necessity for the severance of Ireland from England? Someone asked Parnell the question. Supreme under cross-examination, he replied that when the people were ready, he would be ready. Later, with the same question in mind, he gave the reply carved on his Dublin monument, "No man has a right to fix the boundary of the march of a nation."

If Davitt was determined to climb down out of the thin atmosphere of pure-doctrine Fenianism and take note of the immediate problems of the hour, what issue might command his effort? Irish nationalist sentiment arose out of numberless concrete nodes of deprivation: the empty Dedalus larder, the dung-dodgers at Mrs. Casside's front door, the cold ashes on the Cavan peasant's hearth in Kavanagh's poem, and so on. The points cohered into clusters, "problems," which Yeats in his insulation thought of as "abstractions." To locate these problems one did not have to search under the bushes. The need was rather more one of selection from the *embarras de richesse*. The Fenians had fought off grievances like harpies. Davitt, for himself, started out fresh from prison working with the amnesty agitation and prison reform, but soon he was deep in the problems of the Irish land.

X

In the first few years of the 1870s Irish crops and prices were good, so that rents went up and the tally of agrarian crimes came down. In mid-decade agricultural prices weakened as the United States began to dump cheap wheat from the newly plowed prairies on the European docks. In the late years of the decade the decline of prices accelerated. Gladstone's Land Act of 1870 had not hindered the rise of rents; and now it gave no general immunity against eviction, for tenants in arrears were not protected. The pressures of Irish disaffection were thus rather low at the beginning of the 1870s, but rose to explosive force at the close. Isaac Butt's spirited start and poor finish at the tape were coordinated with this gross materiality.

Davitt went out to his birthplace in Mayo and made a great hit. He was physically impressive in a style opposite to Parnell's. He was striking in coloration, a "black Irishman" of the west, with dark eyes and olive skin. Gauntness, a stoop, heavy facial lines, and the empty sleeve showed him to be a hardened veteran of some new kind of modern war. Mayo welcomed him home with bonfires on the hilltops. Castlebar, like Yeats's "cold Clare rock and Galway rock and thorn," was in the heart of the most miserably poor district of the west. Rack-renting of small tenancies was still the basic Mayo economy, with the potato the staple of life just as in O'Connell's time. For twenty years past, Tipperary and west Cork had been the hotbeds of rural Ireland, and Mayo was the place where Stephens found recruiting all but hopeless. Now the tables were turned: Mayo was awake. Two crop failures in succession had brought back memories of starvation to frighten and anger the western peasantry. Just a month out of prison, Davitt was not quite reoriented, but he could offer the Mayo peasants generalized counsel. He believed that they should not allow another "social suicide" like the one in 1847, when a peasant dutifully paid his rent and said his prayers, then went off and died in the corner simply because he had been told that it was God's will. Something would have to be done. He discussed the problem with Parnell, but not very conclusively.

Six months out of prison, Davitt went to the United States to see his mother, to confer with old Fenian comrades, and to give lectures—for as Sheehy-Skeffington noted, "the American love of lectures is notorious."[28] He found that the foremost Irish-American revolutionary, John Devoy, had suddenly defiled the purity of his Fenianism. He was not only ready to talk "parallel action" with the parliamentarians but had become an enthusiastic Parnellite from having read the headlines in the papers: "All Night Debating," "Speaker in a Fit," and so on, as F. H. O'Donnell humorously parodied them. On the land issue Devoy was ahead of Davitt.[29] The standard agrarian demand of Irish parliamentarians was for the Three Fs, which conceded tenantry to be an immortal institution and hoped only to temper its barbarism. The land bill that Butt presented in the House for the annual slaughter went no further, nor did Parnell's thoughts on the agrarian issue, nor Davitt's either. But in America all the radical Irishmen were afloat on the wave of greenback populism; some were already using Henry George's awesome slogans, "nationalization of the land" and "the single tax"; and all had gone over to the call for the total liquidation of Irish rack-rent tenantry. They would, at the very least, substitute for the Three Fs a demand for a peasant proprietary. Unconcerned with the Jacobin connotation still clinging to that demand, Davitt took it for his main platform, using the more daring slogans of Henry George to give undertone and body to his oratory.

In the autumn of 1878, while Davitt was in Missouri on a lecture tour, Devoy read a news dispatch that led him to conclude—wrongly—that Parnell had seized full control of Home Rule from Butt. On impulse he decided to send Kickham a cable to be handed to Parnell if he was so minded, offering him the support of American Fenianism, conditional upon certain familiar principles: the ultimate goal of national severance, exclusion of all sectarian issues from nationalist politics ("no priests in politics"), the formation of a disciplined Irish parliamentary bloc, and solidarity with "all struggling nationalities in the British empire or elsewhere." Added to the old principles was the important new clause: "vigorous agitation of the land question on the basis of a peasant proprietary, while accepting concessions tending to abolish arbitrary eviction." On receiving the cable, the doctrinaire Kickham did nothing at all. Several days later Devoy published it in the *New York Herald*, which referred editorially to the clause on the land program as "a New Departure," giving it its permanent name in Irish history.

Parnell's biographer once asked Sir Charles Dilke to what he attributed Parnell's success, and Dilke said, "To his aloofness." Later he asked a Fenian, "What was it about Parnell that struck you most?" He got the reply: "His silence. It was extraordinary."[30] When Parnell read Devoy's cable in the newspaper, he put this special talent into practice: he said nothing. But since he might have denounced the offer and did not, his silence could only be interpreted as a vociferous acceptance. Supposing that possibility, all the Fenians on both sides of the Atlantic began an excited debate of the New Departure. In the United States, Devoy's prestige carried the day, supported by an uninhibited Irish-American greenback populist named Patrick Ford, editor of the *Irish World*. The American debates amended the clauses of Devoy's cable slightly. Particularism asserted itself and scratched the clause about Ireland's solidarity with other nationalities in in the British empire. The nonsectarian plank also mysteriously disappeared. In place of the sections dropped, Thomas Davis' program for fostering Irish industries was added, and also a demand for the right to carry arms, fighting the battle of 1865 ten years too late. The agrarian clause stood unaltered.[31]

Everybody was ready to go with the New Departure except the principals.

At the end of 1878 Devoy and Davitt went to Europe to win the assent of the Fenian supreme council on the one hand and of Parnell himself on the other. They took their case first to the IRB. At a Paris meeting in January 1879 the question was argued for four days, and at the end the New Departure was voted down overwhelmingly. John O'Leary, the strongest mind on the supreme council, understood well enough that the Irish land problem had reached a new crisis, but he could not see that any of the proposed solutions had anything to do with Irish nationalism. Henry George he rejected out of hand, and he still thought peasant proprietary unimportant compared to severance from England. And as for the parliamentary half of the New Departure, he believed as strongly as ever that the very atmosphere at Westminster was poison to even the strongest Irish will. He was certain only of his own fallibility. Pure doctrine Fenianism was at the moment undeniably paralyzed, and why should its paralysis be forced on everybody else? He took up an attitude of pessimistic but not unfriendly neutrality to the New Departure; but as for the supreme council of the IRB officially blessing it, he voted no.

The IRB's refusal was naturally unacceptable to Devoy and Davitt. Having already split once when the Dynamitards went their separate way, the Fenian movement now split again. Henceforth there was a pure doctrine wing, called "Old Fenians," represented by O'Leary and Kickham, and a legal-activity-pending-insurrection wing, known as "Ribbon Fenians," represented by Devoy and Davitt. There was a mild scuffle to win the members, but it was not much of a contest really. Richard Pigott's newspaper, the *Irishman*, opted for the Old Fenian wing, but the rank and file mostly went the New Departure way, preferring active pragmatism to stagnant purity. As a result, O'Leary found himself isolated as a kind of a venerable crank during the height of the Parnellite excitement, in that lonely time when Yeats first knew him.

Repelled by the IRB, Davitt and Devoy now turned to their second mission, the assault upon the "cold and enigmatical" Parnell. They invited him to a meeting in Boulogne, together with Biggar and O'Leary. A similar exploratory meeting had been held a year earlier, but to no purpose: Parnell had again exercised his talent for silence and said nothing, but left the meeting with the private remark, "The Fenians want to catch us, but they are not going to."[32] In this next meeting he was more voluble, and Devoy got the impression that he meant business. Three weeks later all met again secretly in Dublin, and Parnell was urged to put himself at the head of the agrarian agitation. This time his reply was, perhaps. Thereupon Davitt went into Mayo to begin organizing hungry tenants.

The agrarians won their first Mayo victory before a month had passed. Davitt tells us of an ugly situation at Irishtown involving the parish priest, one Father Burke, who had just inherited from his brother a property with twenty-two tenants. All were in arrears and Father Burke had taken legal steps to evict the lot of them. The Mayo agrarians called a protest meeting,* and when the scheduled day—Sunday, April 19, 1879—arrived, it was the old story of the monster meetings: Where did all the people come from? Seven thousand tenant farmers arrived on foot, escorted by a bodyguard of five hundred more on horseback. A Ribbon Fenian speaker named Thomas Brennan was rather bold and blunt in his exhortation:

> . . . I have read some history, and I find that several countries have from time to time been afflicted with the same land disease as that under which Ireland is now laboring, and although the political doctors applied many remedies, the one that proved effectual was the tearing out, root and branch, of the class that caused the disease. All right-thinking men would deplore the necessity of having recourse in this country to scenes such as have been enacted in other lands, although I for one will not hold up my hands in holy horror at a movement that gave liberty not only to France but to Europe. If excesses were at that time committed, they must be measured by the depth of slavery and ignorance in which the people had been kept, and I trust Irish landlords will in time recognize the fact that it is better for them at least to have this land question settled after the manner of a Stein or a Hardenberg than wait for the excesses of a Marat or a Robespierre.[33]

Thoroughly cowed, Father Burke surrendered, hastily reducing the rent by one-fourth and dropping his action to evict the laggard tenants. This was big news, and it spread through the western peasantry speedily. The agrarians then moved to the next step, a second tenant mass meeting to be held at Westport in June, with Parnell for the main speaker—if he would come. The oratory at Irishtown had been rather free, even seditious. Parnell asked Butt's legal opinion about the risks in this kind of mass activity and was advised against involving himself in it, since he could be made "responsible for every foolish thing done by the members of the branches." On the other hand, as Devoy made plain to Parnell, the American purse strings would loosen for nothing less than the New Departure. A week before the Westport meeting, Davitt and Devoy met Parnell in Dublin and got his acceptance. Years later Parnell said, "I saw that it was necessary for us to take the risk." He gave his word that he would be at Westport. Immediately Devoy sailed for New York to start raising money.

Cardinal Cullen was gone now, having died during the preceding autumn. He was irreplaceable; but Irish history is rich in examples of the stochastic process that surprises and yet does not. The prelate who took the lead in attacking Davitt was the apologist of Young Ireland, the denouncer of

* Davitt was accidentally detained and did not attend the meeting.

Sadleir and Keogh, the protector of subversive priests—Archbishop MacHale, in whose archdiocese the land war in Mayo was rapidly unfolding. Two days before the Westport meeting, MacHale sent a letter to the *Freeman's Journal* threatening open war if Parnell should dare to appear on behalf of this "occult association" that had been "organized by a few designing men, who, instead of the well-being of the community, seek only to promote their personal interests." Having just emerged from seven years in Dartmoor, Davitt found this last part of MacHale's message particularly marvelous. After reading the letter, some of the scheduled speakers sent Davitt their regrets, and when he went to the hotel in Dublin to meet Parnell for the train trip to the west, he was not sure of his star speaker. "Will I attend?" said Parnell. "Certainly. Why not? I have promised to be there, and you can count upon my keeping that promise."[34] Davitt was overwhelmed with gratitude. The anecdote has fixed itself in Irish history as a token of Parnell's courtly generosity and bravery before the wrath of archbishops. We see the scene also as Shakespearean and the outcome, a deposition. Parnell wanted to steer, said Barry O'Brien, and Davitt was only too glad to leave him in command of the ship.

XI

It was not in MacHale's power to stop the tenant movement. The crowd at Westport was much larger than at Irishtown. Robespierre and Marat were missing from the proceedings, but Davitt hinted that peasant proprietary was within grasp: "Instead of 'Agitate, agitate,' the cry of the present should be 'Organize, organize.' " Parnell met the occasion at Westport head-on. With an incongruity that went unnoticed, he declared that "the maintenance of the class of landlords" must cease, and his speech was best remembered for a fighting phrase: "You must show them [the landlords] that you intend to hold a firm grip of your homesteads and lands. You must not allow yourselves to be dispossessed as your fathers were dispossessed in 1847. You must not allow your small holdings to be consolidated."[35]

Parnell's advice to the Mayo farmers to hold a firm grip of their homesteads was more timely than he thought. The Westport meeting had taken place in the first week of June 1879. It had been a long winter and a wet spring. Heavy rains fell on into midsummer; and six weeks after Parnell's speech, the potato blight suddenly returned with disastrous virulence, destroying the entire crop in Connaught and creating all the natural conditions of 1847. In England the political mood was also reminiscent of 1847. In Ireland, however, the spirit was very different; now "the movement" was rising toward crescendo, not expiring in a dying fall. Hence the cost of the 1878–79 potato blight in human lives would finally add up to zero.

Famines, it appeared, have other causes than the demographic and horti-cultural. Responding to bold leadership, tenants poured into the new organ-ization by the hundreds every day. Within a month of the Westport meeting they had set up the Land League of Mayo. In another six weeks it had burst its bounds and grown to national scope, becoming the Irish National Land League. In October Parnell was elected president to preside over an executive committee made up of Ribbon Fenians, among them Davitt, Thomas Brennan—the "Marat and Robespierre" orator at Irish-town—and Patrick Egan, the treasurer.* A year later the league had set up five hundred local branches and enrolled two hundred thousand members. Its membership overseas grew to equal size. It was, Davitt said, "the most formidable movement that had confronted the English rulers of Ireland in the century."[36]

Just before Christmas 1879, one year to the day from the time Devoy and Davitt had set out from New York to bring the New Departure to Ireland, Parnell sailed from Southampton for the United States to collect a war chest for the collision that lay ahead. His American tour was a "triumphal pro-cession." Lalor's phrase, "the land of Ireland for the people of Ireland," was a constant oratorical effect. Parnell told the Irishmen of Cincinnati that "we shall kill the landlord system" breaking the "last link" of the chain that supported British rule. In Cleveland he greeted the Irish-American militiamen in his guard of honor with the approved Fenian sentiment that "each one of them must wish, with Sarsfield of old, when dying upon a foreign battlefield, 'Oh! that I could carry these arms for Ireland.' " He added, "Well, it may come to that some day or other"; but when he got to Rochester, he warned his listeners that it was "a great responsibility" for any captain to hurl "our unarmed people on the points of British bayonets."[37] He was so swamped with engagements that he cabled Tim Healy in London to hurry across and serve as his private secretary. He had an audi-ence with President Hayes and addressed the Congress. On entering a city he was sometimes greeted with artillery salvos like a chief of state, and when his train came into Montreal at dusk, every house in the city put a lighted candle in the window. In Montreal Healy called him "the uncrowned king of Ireland."

In the midst of his American triumph Parnell received a cable: Parlia-ment dissolved, general election called. Disraeli's dissolution statement declared Ireland to be in a state of rebellion. Escorted by the New York Sixty-ninth Infantry, General Corcoran's old Fenian regiment from the Army of the Potomac, Parnell sailed for Queenstown to plunge into the general-election campaign of March–April 1880.

* Egan's name was later borrowed by Joyce for no discoverable purpose to attach to the milk-drinking "son of the wild goose" in *Ulysses*.

CHAPTER 17

The Land War in Mayo

I

Isaac Butt had died during the excitement of the first 1879 Mayo skirmishes of the Land League and had been replaced as chairman of the Home Rule parliamentary party by a Cork banker, William Shaw, an illustrious relict from the old Committee of Sixty-one whose patriotic fervor reached its most intense moment, caught by an alert historian, when he confessed that he never saw a process-server's cart "without wanting to pull the linch-pin out of it."[1] While Butt's leadership had left much to be desired, the party under Shaw was all but defunct, a condition that Parnell hurrying home from New York hoped soon to remedy.

Parnell's popular appeal in 1880 rested on his identification with the Land League and the Amnesty Association. The New Departure Fenians, Ribbon Fenians, formed the cadre by which his mass power was generated. Unfortunately for him, Wolfe Tone's men of no property were even yet unfranchised. The 1880 electorate of Ireland was still only two hundred thousand in a population of six million, not much changed, in spite of Disraeli's second reform act in 1867, since the Liberator had bargained away the forty-shilling freeholders' franchise back in 1829. But Parnell had also captured the backing of a segment of Irish respectability, those adventuresome middle-class elements represented by the *Freeman's Journal* and the *Nation*, who, in O'Leary's contemptuous sketch, avoided the risk of insurrection but loved to agitate. So much for the accelerator. As for brakes, if the bishops were mostly against him, they were not unanimous, the Land League having won two episcopal friends in Archbishop Croke of Cashel and Bishop Nulty of Meath. The lower clergy were also split, but more favorably. Some of the fiercest Land League fighters were clergymen, and many others came in, like the Kerry clergy in the Blennerhassett election, to avoid being left behind. Their help was not just welcomed by Parnell, but implored. Archbishop Croke reported that Parnell came to him at the time of the Westport meeting and "literally" fell on his knees to beg him to use all his influence "to have the priests join the movement."[2]

257

Disturbed by the flourishing heresy of nationalist collaboration with the clergy, the Old Fenians suddenly became obstreperous. When Parnell walked down the pier at Queenstown on his return from America, a mysterious figure handed him a memorandum warning him to beware, since "the intelligent manhood of the country" had come to the conclusion that his parliamentarianism was "utterly futile." By a freak conjunction the clerical and Fenian anti-Parnellites joined forces for the election at Enniscorthy, county Wexford, the center of the 1798 rising. With a priest directing the battle forces, Fenian rioters tore off one leg of Parnell's trousers, splattered an egg in his beard, and tried to kill him with a black-thorn. One of the rioters coined a striking poetic conceit, "We will show Parnell that the blood of Vinegar Hill is still green." A newspaperman asked Parnell if it was not true that he was opposed by the Fenians and the priests. Mindful of his accelerator and brakes, he replied: "Indeed it is not. I should despair of Ireland if the most active forces in the country arrayed themselves against a movement like this. Individual priests may have con-demned chance indiscretions; individual nationalists have protested that we should lie by while preparations are being made to cope with England by physical force, but that is all."[3]

In England Gladstone was an easy winner in the 1880 elections, return-ing to power with an absolute majority for his second ministry, which was to occupy him from age seventy-one through seventy-six. He chose for his Irish chief secretary the eminent Liberal reformer and businessman, the author of the Education Act of 1870, William E. Forster. In Ireland the voting went very nicely for Parnell. Butt's Home Rule party had elected fifty-nine members in 1874; and in 1880 the count rose to sixty, a net gain of one in six years. But the composition of Home Rule had shifted decisively to the left, and Parnell now had the party majority he had been waiting for. Immediately after the elections, he forced a party vote and defeated Shaw for the chairmanship. A few of Shaw's followers drifted over to Parnell's side, but most of them sank by gentle transition into the two English parties; Blennerhassett reverted to the supine state from which A. M. Sullivan had once hoped to redeem him, while King-Harman became one of the most vocal of the anti-Home Rule partisans, the author of the Orange slogan, "Keep the cartridge in the rifle." With the departure of the Whig Home Rulers, Parnell was surrounded by his congeries of somewhat inharmonious allies, which Conor Cruise O'Brien has illustrated with a map that is rather more revealing than the information that Parnell belongs to Yeats's Phase Ten.[4] Parnell stands in the middle of Cruise O'Brien's diagram like a jug-gler mastering all the separate flying hoops by his fabulous ambidexterity.

II

After Parnell had parted company with Shaw and the last of Butt's Home Rulers, he was left with a nucleus of twenty-three members. He now marshaled these in Westminster to challenge a House of Commons numbering 652 members. The newly elected House was in no amiable mood toward the Lilliputian Irish challenge; and the queen's address on opening Parliament pointedly ignored the distress in Ireland. The immediate danger of mass Irish starvation had in fact slackened since midwinter.[5] In midsummer 1880 a fine harvest began to come in, the first good crop in four years. But prices remained poor and the peasants were still in danger of wholesale dispossession. Parnell's first task as parliamentary leader of the new Irish party was to take bold action against the mounting tide of evictions.

The Irish land dispute in 1880 presented two problems to the peasant. The chronic grievance was the clearances. The landlords, like their predecessors since 1815, still longed to eject the tenants, knock down their cabins, and turn tillage to pasture. The peasant's object was, as always, to hold his ground and to make his removal costly and dangerous. In 1880 an estimated one hundred thousand Irish tenants were in arrears on their rent and hence lived under the threat of summary eviction. The second dispute concerned the amount of the rent. With the world-wide collapse of agricultural prices in the late 1870s, the ordinary Irish tenant could no longer produce the rent at the going scale. He was thus forced to demand a sizable rent reduction, posing a conundrum: what constitutes a fair rent?

When the new House session convened, two parliamentary inquiries into the Irish land problem were already afoot, and it was Gladstone's intention to await the publication of their findings, due in one year, before taking any action. But he was forced by Irish pressure into introducing a modest stopgap measure called the Compensation for Disturbances bill, which proposed to allow those tenants evicted for nonpayment of rent to draw the regular compensation for disturbance—that is, for having to move on—using the money left over from the disestablishment of the Church of Ireland for funding the measure. Parnell subjected the bill to gentle obstruction to dramatize its inadequacy, then supported it on the third reading. It passed the House of Commons at the close of the 1880 session and went to the House of Lords. There it was rejected on August 3, 1880, by a vote of 282 to 51, a gratuitous insolence of the sort that perpetually inspired the murderous sarcasms of Irish Anglophobia.* But the veto was not strictly English. Most of the

* *Ulysses* carefully underscored the word "generous" in the Orangeman Deasy's foolish self-congratulation, "We are a generous people but we must also be just"; and it was Stephen Dedalus' retort to the freehanded Deasy that formulated the lost generation's banner slogan, "I fear those big words which make us so unhappy."

Irish peers also voted to reject the bill. In Yeats's famous phrase, they were "free to refuse," and refuse they did.

The Irish peasant's reply to the House of Lords was the land war in Mayo, "war to the knife" in Joe Biggar's melodramatic language. Directly after House adjournment, the executive of the Land League fanned out into all parts of Ireland to rouse the countryside. Parnell himself went to Ennis, county Clare, and on September 18, 1880 he issued the order of the day. Suppose, he asked his audience, one of you who cannot pay his rent should be evicted; and suppose another tenant should occupy the farm?

"Now what are you going to do to a tenant who bids for a farm from which his neighbor has been evicted?"
Here there was much excitement, and cries of "Kill him!" "Shoot him!" Parnell waited, with his hands clasped behind his back, looking quietly out upon the crowd until the tumult subsided, and then softly resumed: "Now I think I heard somebody say 'Shoot him!'—(A voice: 'Yes, quite right')—but I wish to point out to you a very much better way—a more Christian and a more charitable way, which will give the lost sinner an opportunity of repenting. . . .
"When a man takes a farm from which another has been evicted, you must show him in the streets of the town—(A voice: 'Shun him!')—you must show him at the shop counter, you must show him in the fair and in the market-place, and even in the house of worship, by leaving him severely alone, by putting him into moral Coventry, by isolating him from his kind as if he was a leper of old—you must show him your detestation of the crime he has committed, and you may depend upon it that there will be no man so full of avarice, so lost to shame, as to dare the public opinion of all right-thinking men and to transgress your unwritten code of laws."[6]

Parnell's advice was put into practice without hesitation, producing the famous rout of Captain Boycott.

III

Boycott was the land agent at Lough Mask House for one of the great Irish peers and, on the side, he ran a large herd of beef cattle of his own. George Moore, his neighbor and friend, described him as an accomplished horseman and fox hunter, the best shot with a bird gun in the neighborhood, and a charming host: "Kind in hall and fierce in fray." The tenants on the estate asked for a rent abatement. He refused with more than a touch of old-school curtness. When they retaliated by not paying any rent at all, he went to court; and on the Wednesday following Parnell's Sunday speech at Ennis, the process server arrived to begin ejectment formalities. The tenants met him on the highroad, turned him about, and sent him home with his summonses unserved. Then they hinted to all the servants that they would be wise if they stayed away from work, so that the ladies of Lough Mask House were forced to cook the meals and carry out their own slops. Shopkeepers and blacksmiths "shunned" all members of the household. At harvest time no field hands appeared. Boycott sent out a distress call, and fifty Orangemen from the north volunteered "to save Captain Boycott's praties." But they required police protection, so Forster dispatched two thousand troops supported with field artillery. George Moore saw them camped in their tents among Boycott's flower beds, "amid the rustle of his planted hills." He saw, too, moving through the trees of the park, the anxious captain, armed with a repeating rifle and a pistol on each hip. The harvest lasted two weeks; and when the Orangemen and the army marched away, Boycott fled the country with them. He then began a long and futile correspondence with Gladstone and Forster, demanding further protection on the plea that "the circumstances which compelled me to leave Mayo prevent my return."[7] In the end he ran up the white flag and settled on the league's terms, then returned to Lough Mask to live in amity with his tenants, who bore no grudges and acclaimed him an authentic celebrity of the neighborhood.

A revolutionary crisis grew from the rapid spread of the Land League boycott in October and November 1880. A year earlier Parnell had told his mass meeting audiences: "Stand to your guns, and there is no power on earth which can prevail against the hundreds of thousand of tenant farmers of this country"; and again, "if you are determined, I tell you, you have the game in your hands." As late as the speech at Ennis, he repeated the thought that "if the half million tenant farmers of Ireland struck against the ten thousand landlords," military force could never subdue them.[8] Suddenly all that he had said proved true. The government's most earnest zeal and ingenuity were powerless to wrestle with this amorphous, ubiquitous adversary. Gladstone and Forster began to envy Wellington and Peel the simplicity of facing up to O'Connell's monster meetings, where at least there was somebody to shoot at. "With a political revolution we have ample strength to cope," Gladstone told the House. "But a social revolution is a very different matter." With a note of panic Forster reported, "Unless we can strike down the boycotting weapon Parnell will beat us."[9]

A fascinating government statistical series called "Evictions (Number of Persons)" had registered a fivefold rise between 1877 and 1880. A companion series called "Agrarian Outrages (Number)" showed that outrages accelerated twice as rapidly, multiplying tenfold in the same period. The temptation of the landlords to force clearances was thus overmatched by rising peasant resistance, at first through spontaneous vengeance, but after the Ennis meeting, through boycotts organized by the local branches of the Land League. After two months of the most savage hostilities, the landlords were the first to flinch. The boycott campaign took hold, and the statistic for evictions registered a precipitous decline. The Land League held momentary possession of the field of battle.

The frightful word "anarchy" (without Yeats's loaded qualifier "mere") now sounded out in ministerial memorandums and in newspaper leading articles. To the peasant, though, it was evidently not a word to be afraid of. His economy was already totally atomized, and, such as it was, self-sufficient. Anarchy was the element in which he lived and died. He approved heartily this improved kind of anarchy that dispensed with the unsolicited services of the "middlemen"—the land agent, the process server, the magistrate, and the constable—and gave him firm control of his homestead and land. George Moore testified reluctantly that the peasant's danger was not imaginary nor his means excessive: "I am a landlord today, but I will recognize it as a fact that had not Davitt organized the Land League in '78, a great clearance of peasants would have again been undertaken. . . . For since '49 every good landlord regrets his goodness."[10]

Among those staggered by the prospect that agrarian anarchy would prove the inevitable end result of "moral Coventry" was no other than Parnell himself. Not a month had passed after his speech at Ennis before he showed signs, if not of alarm, of a new sense of caution. A speech at Galway on September 24, 1880, suddenly detached his key motif from the land war and brought it firmly back to his true objective, Home Rule: "I wish to see the tenant farmers prosperous . . . but large and important as this class of tenant farmers is, constituting, as they do, with their wives and families, the majority of the people of the country, I would not have taken off my coat and gone to this work if I had not known that we were laying the foundation in this movement for the regeneration of our legislative independence."[11] He commenced a slow, guarded, and highly circumspect withdrawal back from the dizzy successes of the land war.

In the emergency, the landlords gathered as a semiofficial sort of Second Estate, with Standish O'Grady, an Ascendancy youth of literary bent, for secretary. They "knew the Irish peasant" more intimately than Gladstone or Forster, and were watched in anxious expectation that some brilliant solution to their impasse might issue from their meeting. But they had no novelty or miracle to offer. "They have deliberated, they have spoken," A. M. Sullivan said. "The sum of all their statesmanship, all their counsel, all their reforms, is a bold demand on England for more coercion."[12] They followed the old familiar recipe of their fathers and grandfathers: suspend habeas corpus and send more constabulary. Their crisis behavior in 1880 re-enacted exactly their midfamine crisis behavior of 1847.

The reader has perhaps sensed a tendency toward iteration in Irish history, as it passed through the phases of repetitive attack, defeat, convalescence, and attack once again. The very settings were fixed on a rotating stage. The Rotunda, the monster meeting, the opposition lobby at West-minster, Green Street Courthouse, Richmond jail, Glasnevin Cemetery—these follow one another around and around. It is no marvel that the native writers of a later time were inclined to read the Irish living processes as a monotonously spinning squirrel cage, a contrivance of cycles and recipro-cating buckets in a well. Of the Dublin meeting hall itself it has been in-evitably written: "Gyre O, gyre O, gyrotundo."[13] They were mistaken, though, when they concluded that the cycles were perpetual motion that could not stop.

IV

Gladstone was able to understand, as Englishmen of less intelligence could not, that the Irish problem was not to be solved merely by doubling the constabulary from time to time. He opposed any new Irish coercion until his leisurely gestating land bill could come to birth. But the pressure upon him for immediate coercion grew irresistible as the land war intensified in the autumn of 1880. By the year's end it was clear to most of the Land Leaguers that the time had come when they must prepare to defend them-selves. Davitt had been in the United States raising money since the elec-tion of April 1880, but he returned to Ireland in November and opened a discussion of the dangers under the impending government attack. As things then stood, he felt that the suspension of habeas corpus would des-troy the league within a month, just as it had destroyed Young Ireland and Fenianism. He tried to envision how the work could be carried on if the leaders were all sent to jail. Since the league's prime ammunition consisted of dollars, the American supply line must be protected first of all. The league treasurer, Patrick Egan, therefore prepared to move the cash to Paris for safety. To keep open the channels of money allocation, legal aid, and pro-paganda on the rural fighting front, Davitt organized the Ladies' Land League, headed by Parnell's sisters.

The 1881 session of the House turned, *pro forma*, to pass a businesslike Irish coercion bill. When Forster brought in his bill, he said that he deeply deplored the painful necessities of his position; he regretted even that he had taken a portfolio in Mr. Gladstone's government, but his duty must not be shirked.[14] He was generous but he must be just. Now at last the long-awaited parliamentary moment had come, and the battle lines joined for a final struggle. The same floor scenes that accompanied the House obstruction of the South Africa bill four years earlier were re-enacted, though far more violently. The militant wing of the Irish party now numbered thirty mem-bers instead of seven, so that the government's chance of breaking up resis-tance by physical exhaustion was not good. It was attempted, though. One sitting ran twenty-six hours, and after a day to recuperate, the next ran twice around the clock to forty-six hours. The following day, the Speaker simply terminated the debate and called for a division on the motion. It was the final conflict and no mistake; and Irish parliamentary obstruction was suddenly a thing of the past. The next morning's session, on February 3, 1881, opened with a statement from the home secretary that Michael Davitt had just been sent back to prison for "violation of the ticket-of-leave." In the uproar that greeted this announcement, the entire Home Rule party got itself suspended for the rest of the day. The coercion bill then proceeded smoothly on its way, and it became law four weeks later.

v

Davitt argued afterward that those four weeks squandered the Irish opportunity of the century. The league was presented, he said, with a combination of favorable conjunctions that would never occur again, and just then it lost its boldness. On the day he was rearrested, these conditions prevailed: the anger of the peasants was at its highest pitch; the nationalist sentiment of the towns was inflamed by the state trials and the suspension of the Irish members in the House; the advanced leaders—himself excepted—were still out of jail, but certain not long to remain so; Gladstone's legislation on the land issue was still a vague unknown; the British army had just been defeated in its first skirmish with the Boers; and the Liberal party was not yet rent by the schism that was destined to wreck the future Home Rule bills. There had been talk in the Land League executive about certain counterblows held in reserve against the government's first hostile move. The last resource, the big gun, was to be a nationwide strike against rent. Davitt believed that on February 3, 1881, a general rent strike was feasible and should have been called. He knew that success required nothing less than total peasant support, but his contact with the countryside in the weeks leading up to his rearrest convinced him that the support was poised and ready.

Davitt's observation on the rent strike picked up a recurring pattern in Irish history, a tendency to refuse the bold stroke at the "right" instant, then to follow up with a belated stroke that required even more courage and was certainly hopeless. Like Devoy at the Fenian war council in Mrs. Butler's dressmaking shop, Davitt was in a position to know when the "right" instant was, and his expert judgment is difficult to dismiss out of hand.

Still, he saw the issue of the rent strike with a strong personal bias. When he found himself in handcuffs on a westbound train out of London, presumably to spend the next four years back in Dartmoor prison, he could be forgiven for sharing John Mitchel's dismay at the Dublin North Wall when he had learned that no attempt would be made to rescue him from his fetters and had muttered to himself, "Christ never died for this people." It was a relief to see from the train window that he was bound for Portland prison instead of Dartmoor. His pamphlet against the brutality of English prisons had won him that, in addition to a warm cell and relief from hard labor. He had the special privilege, too, of reading and writing as he wished, and the governor of the prison sent him a blackbird in a cage to share his cell.

VI

Armed with the extraordinary powers of the new coercion act, Forster lost no time in beginning the performance of his unpleasant duty. He had for his chief coercionist a seasoned Castle official, a nephew of Cardinal Wiseman's, Thomas Burke, who had opened his administrative career ten years earlier by ordering the police to charge with batons against one of Isaac Butt's peaceful Sunday afternoon Amnesty Association mass meetings in Phoenix Park. Davitt thought that Burke was Forster's "evil genius": "He personified the Castle system of rule, being an Irishman and a Catholic. He was credited with being the arch-coercionist of the administration, the employer of informers, the active antagonist of all revolutionary movements"[15]—a man to reinforce Forster's evangelical zeal with Irish experience.

Forster explained in the House of Commons that the anarchy in Ireland was caused by the presence in every village of "dissolute ruffians," troublemakers who bullied their fellow villagers into defiance of the law of trespass and ejection. The Irish problem was so simple, he said, that at the instant the "ruffians" were placed behind bars, the unrest of the countryside would cease. He rounded up a couple of hundred men nominated by Thomas Burke and the Royal Irish Constabulary for imprisonment without trial. The first statistical fruit of his rural pacification scheme was, within three months, a sevenfold increase in evictions. Next, the countryside became decidedly less peaceful rather than more. Forster's careful plan, which Gladstone later called "this extraordinary illusion," had in no way solved the problem. Lord Cowper, the lord lieutenant, sent a memorandum to the cabinet protesting that the mass arrests had perhaps removed the wrong parties.[16] The prisoners whom Forster had caught in his net were the Land League branch secretaries, the most earnest, hard-working, and sober leaders in each townland.* These "ruffians" were in fact the restraining

* The reader is familiar with their moral quality through Joyce's Mr. Casey in *A Portrait of the Artist*, modeled upon one of Forster's "ruffians," a rank-and-file Ribbon Fenian, a distant relation whom the Joyces adopted for a short while as a household pet. Forster had sent him to jail in 1881, and Arthur Balfour was about to send him to jail again in 1891 when Joyce was nine years old, apparently for illegal activity in the newest agrarianism.

influences in the countryside, and their imprisonment brought on uncontrolled Ribbon terror.

Under the new wave of agrarian outrages, crimes shaded into a more somber hue. Murder and arson increased, also "firings into dwellings" and "firings at persons," the near-miss shots on which official statistics were solemnly compiled. There was a parallel rise in the maiming of livestock by hocking (hamstringing) and the cutting off of tails.*

When Davitt and the imprisoned Ribbon Fenians had been allowed a month to meditate behind bars, Gladstone paired off his coercion with his conciliation in the classic Peelite manner and presented the House with his new Irish land bill. It was an equivocal measure. On the one hand it appeared to promise a good deal more than had been hoped for. Clean strokes dispensed with the indirection of the Land Act of 1870. Eviction was simply outlawed, except for cause. It also provided that the rent must be a "fair" rent, to be first determined and then frozen for a term of fifteen years by land courts established under the bill. This provision completed the count of the Three Fs, so that Gladstone appeared to have capitulated to the full schedule of the Irish agrarians' pre-Henry George demands.

It needed little study, though, to discover grave shortcomings in the bill. It did not protect the tenants currently in arrears and on the brink of ejection. It offered no definition of a fair rent, and the leading English members of the House had the impression that it meant the present rent. If that were the intent, the bill was simply a fifteen-year guarantee of the landlord's income in a collapsing market. One could not be sure; everything depended on the mysterious mental processes of future land commissioners. Parnell saw that their definition of the word "fair" would not be any sort of a Platonic essence, but a pragmatism that would emerge out of a new season of political warfare. That warfare now commenced.

Parnell's behavior toward the bill oscillated enigmatically between support and attack. At one stage he appeared to be a saboteur but toward the close of debate, the Irish members began an earnest effort to improve the technical details of the bill through expert work on the floor, more than once staving off a defeat for Gladstone. Tim Healy made himself a hero by adding a crucial amendment, necessary for the successful operation of the measure,

---

* This cruel contribution to the war of nerves particularly pained England's poet laureate. His Muse had been silent before the spectacle of the famine, which he had the chance to observe at first hand when he went to Killarney in 1848 to get local color for "The Splendor Falls on Castle Walls." But against the hocking of the Irish landlords' cattle he felt such an inspired wrath that he anticipated by forty years Joyce's pun, "demoncracy": "Celtic Demos rose a Demon, shrieked and slaked the light with blood." Marat and Davitt, both of them Celts, were two of a kind in Tennyson's opinion. This was a popular English sentiment toward the Irish during this terrorist phase of the land war. But anger was accompanied by perplexity and especially by a sense of helplessness.

requiring that the valuation of land for purposes of rent determination could not include the value of improvements "for which the landlord has not paid." But on the bill's third reading, the thirty-five Parnellites ostentatiously walked out without voting, understanding that the bill would pass in any case. It also passed the Lords, much sobered after the catastrophic outcome of their 1880 veto.

The Land League had now to make up its mind whether to boycott the land act or to accept it. Opinion was split and very heated. The Americans sent cables from overseas proclaiming the necessity for revolutionary militancy. "Hold the harvest"—that is, pay no more rent—they said, quoting the title of a song by Fanny Parnell. The clergy on the other hand were strongly for accepting the act as it stood. The deeply troubled rank and file were torn between the fear of binding themselves for fifteen years to a bad bargain and the fear of losing benefits through delay. Parnell came to the league's convention with a solution to the impasse: let the members shun the new land courts until the league could bring "test cases" to "prove the mood" of the land commissioners. The convention accepted his plan unanimously, and Healy set about to find the choicest test cases, involving the most subtle and ambiguous points of interpretation.

VII

While the test cases were being prepared, the countryside became increasingly violent. Forster responded with more severe coercion. He intensified the search for firearms on the peasants' persons and premises. He authorized the constabulary to open fire at discretion, even against unarmed persons. In response to a complaint in the Commons, he announced that in the cause of humanitarianism, the constabulary engaged at close work would henceforth be issued the semideadly buckshot instead of the deadly ball cartridge, an order that earned him the nickname universal among Irishmen, "Buckshot" Forster. Parnell seized upon it, and spoke of "Buckshot" with the same relish that O'Connell had put into his intonation of "Orange Peel." As Forster grew more violent, the peasants replied with more violence still, and the familiar vicious cycle of retaliation against retaliation held the country in a tightening grip.

Parnell felt the sensation of riding a runaway. He effected his escape with striking ingenuity: he deliberately, as many believe, obliged Gladstone to arrest him. He thus forced his enemy into a difficult position. His arrest separated him conveniently from all further responsibility for the violence running out of control in the countryside, and at the same time it inflamed afresh the Irish and Irish-American sense of outrage. The fire would in time burn itself out, he thought, and demonstrate both to his own

267

uncompromising agrarians and to Gladstone the need for a reasonable compromise.

The government was glad to accommodate him if arrest was what he wanted. In the frantic search to find some handle with which to take hold of the crisis, it was persuaded to try out the idea that Parnell must be a sole instigator, the very archetype of a "dissolute ruffian." Gladstone made a speech at Leeds on October 7, 1881, accusing him of inventing the land acts test cases for wanton sabotage, spurning a just law. He threatened unspecified revenge. Parnell replied in a speech the next day not with justification, but with insolence. The "masquerading knight-errant," he said, had claimed as a demand upon Irish gratitude the English nation's "long sustained efforts" on Ireland's behalf. With his best hauteur, he asked Gladstone:

> Long sustained efforts in what? Was it in evicting the two thousand tenants who have been evicted since the first of January last, in putting two hundred brave and noble men into Kilmainham and the other jails of the country; was it in issuing a police circular of a more infamous character than any which has ever been devised by any foreign despot; was it in sending out hundreds of thousands of rounds of ball cartridges and buckshot cartridges to his Bashi Bazouks; was it in sharpening the bayonets of the latest issue of the Royal Irish Constabulary?[17]

The retort might have been made safely in England, where habeas corpus was not suspended. But Parnell chose to go into Wexford to make his provocation, to stay overnight afterward at Morrison's Hotel in Dublin, and to schedule for the next day a repeat performance at Naas. The hotel boots waked him at eight-thirty in the morning to warn that Director John Mallon of the Castle police was downstairs inquiring for him. The boy offered to lead him out by a kitchen exit to escape. Parnell declined, and in a few minutes he was in custody, bound over for a long stay in Kilmainham jail, Richmond jail being regarded as not fully escape-proof. Parnell did not think Kilmainham escape-proof either, and he wrote a friend: "They have let us off very easily. I fully expected that we should have been scattered in different jails through the country as a punishment, but they evidently think no other place safe enough for me. Indeed, this place is not safe, and I can get out whenever I like, but it is probably the best policy to wait to be released."[18]

Parnell had been asked who would take his place if he were arrested. He answered, "Captain Moonlight will take my place." When a reporter from the *Freeman's Journal* came to Kilmainham on the day of his arrest to interview him, Parnell gave him a message to Irishmen: "I shall take it as evidence that the people of the country did not do their duty if I am speedily released,"[19] a transparent directive to step up the pace of rural disturbance. It was an order dutifully obeyed. The statistics on Irish agrarian outrages for January, February, and March in the three consecutive years of the land war were as follows: 294 in 1880, 769 in 1881, and 1,417 in 1882.[20] Meanwhile, the Ladies' Land League marched to battle, distributing relief to the evicted, organizing boycotts against "land grabbers," and carrying on a violent propaganda, with Parnell's sisters in the forefront. Forster naturally read these signs as proof of the need for still more arrests, even of the ladies themselves if it came to that; but Gladstone was beginning to suspect that the remedy lay in the other direction.

The Land League's discipline and unity began to waver under the coercion. The league executive, most of them in Kilmainham with Parnell, debated whether to retaliate with their big weapon, the general strike against rent. There was disagreement. T. D. Sullivan believed it immoral, "against the law of God." John Dillon, who was among the leaders the most violent in public language, thought it a mistake in tactics. Parnell was apparently neutral. But the majority, mostly Ribbon Fenians, were in favor of it. A "No-Rent Manifesto" was therefore drafted inside Kilmainham, smuggled out, and issued to the country. It was an eloquent document in the style of Tom Paine, beginning, "Fellow-countrymen, the hour to try your souls and redeem your pledges has arrived."[21] Its eloquence was not sufficient. The rent strike merely added to the general disorder. But it was either too late or too soon, for it was a total failure.

All in all it was another of Dublin's famous weeks. In the midst of Parnell's arrest and the No-Rent Manifesto, the new land courts opened their doors for business. The weakest link in the boycott of the land act was in Ulster, for the Orange farmers were prompt to appear in the land courts to take what benefits they might. They observed that the new fifteen-year judicial rents always seemed somehow to come out at about four-fifths of the going rate. At last the Land Leaguers themselves stampeded, *sauve qui peut*, and flocked into the land courts without apology or remorse. Except for the Ladies' Land League, the organized agrarian offensive of 1878–81 had expired. Yet the major grievances were still unremedied. Evictions continued, and spontaneous agrarian outrage kept the pace.

With Parnell settled down in Kilmainham, both prisoner and jailer had each won a point: Parnell, in forcing the land courts to declare their hand in the tenants' favor with reduced judicial rents; Gladstone, in destroying the Land League. Yet each adversary was still in the other's power: Parnell was in jail; Gladstone could not cope with rural disorder. So the months passed, while Parnell played chess with the other imprisoned Land Leaguers, and Forster read each morning's Royal Irish Constabulary reports on the fresh outrages.

IX

In April 1882, after six months in jail, Parnell was released with elaborate courtesy for a one-week parole to visit a nephew dying in Paris. Passing through London, he let it be known privately that in his judgment peace negotiations with Gladstone might now commence. The government had made its overture already, selecting for intermediary Captain William O'Shea, the member for Clare, a Home Ruler who seemed some sort of a special friend and confidant of Parnell's. Appearances were deceiving; he was no friend. His surface political coloration was also deceptive. Though nominally a member of Parnell's party, he was actually attached to Joseph Chamberlain, a Liberal minister belonging to the "radical" wing of Gladstone's party. Chamberlain was principally engaged at the time in spinning a great web of personal and imperial dynastic ambition, into which Parnell was in due time to be entangled through the O'Shea connection; but we anticipate.

After Parnell was locked up again in Kilmainham, O'Shea went to work as a courier. Hurrying happily back and forth between Parnell in Dublin and Chamberlain in London, he arranged the armistice known in Irish history as the "Kilmainham treaty." Its major terms were that Gladstone should undertake to put an end to Irish coercion and give relief to the tenants in arrears. Parnell on his part accepted the Land Act of 1881 as approximately the final solution of Irish agrarian grievance and undertook to "slow down the agitation" and withdraw the No-Rent Manifesto. There was an added understanding by Parnell, conditional on the rest of the treaty working out as hoped, "to cooperate cordially for the future with the Liberal party in forwarding Liberal principles." Gladstone, on reading the last clause, exclaimed: "This is a *hors d'oeuvre* which we had no right to expect." The clause was private, but through malice or stupidity O'Shea showed it to Forster, who in due time publicized it on the floor of the House of Commons, to Parnell's intense embarrassment. The reason for the secrecy and for the embarrassment was plain enough: Parnell was fearful that his advanced wing was unready for the hors d'oeuvre, that indefatigable temptation, the Whig alliance.

CHAPTER 18

After Kilmainham: Bakhuninism in Phoenix Park

I

"The thing is done," said Gladstone of the Kilmainham treaty. So it was; but as with any bargain, some of the adversaries held the annoying thought that if they had tried harder, they could have won more. Chief Secretary Forster argued that Parnell was being lavishly rewarded, and for what?— for agreeing to obey the law. He handed in his resignation. His replacement was Lord Frederick Cavendish, a relative of Gladstone's, an amiable and unassuming Liberal politician. His father, the Duke of Devonshire, and his brother, Lord Hartington, were disliked in Ireland, the one for making clearances, the other for enforcing coercion; but Cavendish himself was unknown. Lord Spencer replaced Lord Cowper as lord lieutenant. But Forster's coercionist brigadier during the land war, Thomas Burke, continued in his old assignment. At the finish of his role as the nation's jailer in the epoch of coercion, this well-hated civil servant was now to convert into a benevolent "Antiself" for the new era of good feeling.

When the doors of Kilmainham jail opened on May 2, 1882, Parnell walked out to find his own followers, too, very unhappy with the bargain. Their opposition Parnell set about forthrightly to confound. On May 5 he sent Davitt a letter in Portland prison beginning with the chilly salutation, "My dear Sir." It announced that he and Dillon were journeying to Portland on the day following to greet him on his liberation. During the train ride back to London Parnell gave him the new Kilmainham line bluntly:

> We are on the eve of something like Home Rule. Mr. Gladstone had thrown over coercion and Mr. Forster, and the government will legislate further on the land question. The Tory party are going to advocate land purchase, almost

271

on the lines of the Land League programme, and I see no reason why we should not soon obtain all we are looking for in the league movement. The No-Rent Manifesto had failed, and was withdrawn. A frightful condition of things prevailed in Ireland during the last six months, culminating in several brutal murders, moonlighting outrages, and alarming violence generally.[1]

Davitt was as irritated by the news as Forster had been on hearing it from his own chief.

II

Parnell's prime fear was of the Irish "secret societies." In the Kilmainham negotiations Chamberlain had made it clear that any hopes of "something like Home Rule" were contingent upon the restoration of Irish quiescence. Yet the ancient Ribbon reflex was well known to be stubborn. In America the Dynamitard Fenians were vocal and munificent. O'Donovan Rossa and Patrick Ford had caught the fever, collecting a generous "Skirmishing Fund" to finance terror against England on a grand scale. Native Irish terrorist impulses took new reinforcement from emanations of Bakhuninism arising out of Spain and Italy and from the nationalist movement inside the Austrian empire. Anarchist terror assassinated Tsar Alexander II and President Garfield just at the climax of the Irish land war. For the more impatient Irish patriot, there was a timely charm in the thought that he too could "strike a match and blow," following the teaching of "Red Jim" Mac-Dermott's jingle:

> Not a cent for blatherskite,
> But every dollar for dynamite.

On the same Saturday that Parnell greeted Davitt at the gates of Portland prison, the Irish terrorists let their existence be unmistakably known. In Dublin the day had been devoted to festivity honoring the installation of the new reform chief secretary, Lord Frederick Cavendish. Following the ceremony, he left the Castle for his official residence in the compound at the Viceregal Lodge. On his way across Phoenix Park he fell in with the permanent undersecretary, Thomas Burke. The two dismissed their carriages and bodyguards and set out to stroll together arm in arm the quarter-mile or so home. Along the path they encountered a band of men walking together; and as they passed, one of the men seized Burke and stabbed him to death with a knife held, as one rumor put it, "between the third and fourth fingers." When Cavendish tried to rescue his companion, he too was stabbed to death. As the bodies lay in the grass, one of the band cut their throats. Some of the assailants then climbed into a cab and the others into a jaunting car and fled from the park at top speed in opposite directions, the cab back toward town, the car westward toward Chapelizod. Cards dropped secretly into the mailboxes of newspaper offices announced that the assassinations were the work of "The Invincibles." Two days afterward a printed apologia appeared on the streets signed "Executive of the I.R.B.," but it was immediately disowned by Kickham and O'Leary.*

Parnell, as his biographer tells us, was at first "profoundly moved by the event," then "collapsed utterly." Mrs. O'Shea was with him at Blackheath surburban railway station when he bought the Sunday *Observer* carrying the news: "I noticed a curious rigidity about his arms. He stood so absolutely still that I was suddenly frightened, horribly, sickeningly afraid—of I knew not what, and, leaning forward, called out, 'King, what is it?'" His first thought was that the object of the assassinations was to ruin him politically, and he said to Davitt, "I am stabbed in the back." He called on Joseph Chamberlain at home and proposed to resign, but was dissuaded. He then wrote a note to Gladstone repeating the offer. "I was much touched," said Gladstone. "He wrote evidently under strong emotion." And he wrote him in reply that his resignation "would do no good; on the contrary would do harm." Put at ease, Parnell, together with Davitt and Dillon, sat down on Sunday afternoon to compose a manifesto "To the Irish People" condemning the murders. A final sentence, appended by A. M. Sullivan to add a tone of sincerity, expressed particular shame over the violation of Irish hospitality in the "cowardly and unprovoked assassination of a friendly stranger," that is, of Cavendish, and trusted that his murderers (and Burke's too, for that matter) would be brought speedily to justice.[2]

Parnell's panic was brief. The assassinations gave no signal for catastrophe. The danger lay in England, and his manifesto to the Irish people was more particularly for Englishmen. The Irish members walking about the London streets were momentarily nervous about the possibility of being lynched in another mass outburst like the Cheshire no-popery riots of 1850. Gladstone let these opportunities pass unexploited, being of a larger mold of statesman than Lord John Russell and Lord Derby, and thinking perhaps also of Parnell's proffered hors d'oeuvre. Englishmen did not come out into the streets in reaction to the Phoenix Park murders, but they did not forget them either.

At the same time Gladstone charged a stiff political price for the murders. He renounced the section of the Kilmainham treaty that promised a rapid relaxation of Irish coercion and shortly introduced a brand new coercion bill far more repressive than the expiring act. It provided not only for

---

* It contained among the usual nationalist pronouncements a paragraph on import duties that must be unique in the anthology of Black Hand literature: "We are convinced that no true prosperity can exist in Ireland so long as England possesses her customhouses, these allowing her manufactures to pass into Ireland duty free, thereby leaving our Irish mechanics unemployed. . . ." See P. J. P. Tynan, *Irish National Invincibles*, p. 273.

arbitrary arrest but also for conviction and imprisonment without jury trial in some types of Irish crimes. But along with his new Crimes Act, he forced through the House under urgent pressure the conciliatory new Rent Arrears Act drafted by Parnell and Healy in Kilmainham. Though strained, the Kilmainham treaty thus survived the Phoenix Park crisis.

III

The Irish reaction to the Phoenix Park murders is difficult to reconstruct. Historians sometimes assert that Dubliners were "angry" and "deeply shocked," conventional phrases not conveniently documented. Forster reported in the House of Commons that Irishmen were "incensed," but not nearly as much as they "ought to be." But he was no longer an eyewitness. Another witness, though very untrustworthy, described Dublin more credibly as "perplexed" and "greatly excited."[3] No doubt the murders were deplored as a lunacy, pointless at best. But after that had been conceded, no nationalist was likely to weep over the demise of Thomas Burke; and while many were sorry for "poor Cavendish," they could console themselves with the reflection that his death, like Sergeant Brett's in the police van at Manchester, was an accident such as one must expect in war. Life was cheap in Ireland, and in 1882 especially so. Any Irishman could have named off a dozen of the year's homicide victims. The affair in Phoenix Park was special because political assassination, unlike agrarian outrage, was hitherto unknown in Ireland and because the social elevation of the victims and the novelty of the bloody details lent to the murders a distinctive fillip. Irishmen did remember the crime vividly, and its extraordinary sequel no less.

Charged with the duty of solving the murder mystery, Director Mallon of the Castle police was for a time baffled. To generate a spirit of healthy rivalry in the detective branch, the Castle appointed a second investigator, John Curran. He was baffled too. Many months passed and still no suspect had been brought to trial. Everybody was speculating about who the culprits might, and especially might not, be. Kickham declared that they were certainly not Old Fenians, but could well be Ribbon Fenians. Davitt was equally certain that they were not, pointing out that the Land League had celebrated the Kilmainham treaty with a triumphal torchlight victory procession not twenty-four hours before the murders. He wondered whether the assassins were even Irishmen: "There is not one instance in the long list of outrages in Ireland where the dagger was used. The shot-gun and the stick have always been the weapons employed."[4] If swinging the shillelagh and shooting behind the shrubbery were ruled out, he thought an Irishman would choose next the blackjack, not the foreign bowie knife or stiletto, a morsel of minor particularist wisdom that found its way eventually into the cab-shelter conversation in the "Eumaeus" chapter of *Ulysses*. But he was inclined finally to think that the culprits must be Irish after all, probably a secret extermination squad of "Emergency Men," organized among the more reckless Ascendancy landlords to make sure there would be no interruption in the continuity of Irish coercion.

Davitt's and Kickham's guesses were off the mark. The Invincibles were not landlords, peasants, Texans, or Sicilians. They were ordinary Dublin "artisans," and not very secretive about their exploit. Confident that witnesses would not be anxious to appear in court against them, they felt tempted to drop dreadful hints into their conversation with friends. Detectives listening in the public houses and operating "after the manner in which the police often receive valuable information"[5] were thus able to get some names on a list. One was a twenty-two-year-old stonemason named Joe Brady, a barrel-chested fellow of solemn mien and prodigious strength. Another was a master carpenter named Daniel Curley, a strong family man with numerous children at home. Another was a tavern keeper named Mullet, a hunchback whose physical resemblance to Joseph Biggar, M.P., was not overlooked by the English press. Another was a smalltime building contractor named James Carey, who had started life a hod carrier, achieved a rude respectability, and blossomed into a slum landlord, a town councilor, and a paragon of piety. Mallon arrested these men and many others, but everybody denied everything and all the suspects had to be released.

Immediately there followed a new wave of street assaults, political in motive. A juror who had voted for the guilty verdict in a political trial was set upon by men with knives and a sword cane and left for dead in the gutter. An informer was found murdered. A man was caught in an attempt to shoot an unpopular judge outside the Kildare Street Club. In each case police picked up small bits of new evidence and got fresh names on their list. At last, fishing with the standard police method of simulated omniscience, Inspector Curran hooked one of the minor suspects, a young man named Robert Farrell: "I put certain questions assuming all my suspected facts to have been proved. Farrell appeared to be very much surprised. . . . he was sure that someone had turned traitor and had given us information which had led to my questions. He further said that he did not intend to be left in when others were turning informers, and then made a statement which he signed."[6] Farrell had not been in on the Phoenix Park affair, having been unable to get off work that day, but his deposition was a full description of Invincible personnel and operations. With his information in hand, police suddenly rearrested the suspects, twenty-seven in all counting Farrell. This was in January 1883, eight months after the crime.

Mallon's next step was to find an approver who had actually been in

Phoenix Park. Farrell had identified the two cabbies: the driver of the jaunting car was named Kavanagh, and the driver of the four-wheeled cab, a man named Fitzharris, better known as "Skin-the-Goat." Since the two seemed to be enemies, Mallon told each that the other was about to inform against him unless he informed first. Fitzharris was adamant, qualifying thereby as a genuine Dublin folk hero; but Kavanagh was frightened into giving evidence. He swore that the name of the other driver was "Skin," causing Fitzharris to shout from the dock: "Begone, you scorpion! Don't call me nicknames."[7] He swore that he had driven Joe Brady and three other Invincibles in his car to Phoenix Park late in the morning on the sixth of May. About sunset, whipping his horse at "furious breakneck speed," he took the same persons away from Phoenix Park on a long semicircuitous route, racing westward on the Palmerston road to Chapelizod and beyond, then south through Inchicore and Roundtown, then back into the city again, past Harolds Cross and Ranelagh, stopping at last at Davis' public house in Leeson Park, where Brady paid him three pounds for his rather full afternoon's service.*

Kavanagh's immortal travelogue from Phoenix Park to Davis' pub completed the structure of evidence ordinarily needed by the government to get guilty verdicts against the prime murder suspects. Mallon was not satisfied at that. The political climate for the Invincible trials now being prepared bore a resemblance to that of the Manchester trials. In both cases "everybody knew" that the accused had really done the deed, right enough. However thickheaded, the Invincibles pursued motives that were undeniably political rather than avaricious, just as at Manchester. The prosecution was thus put on notice to adhere to strictest protocol in the game of winning guilty verdicts. A failure of scrupulosity had won the government case in Manchester, but the victory had backfired in a catastrophic Irish political recoil. The same danger lurked in the Invincible trials. English law wisely stipulated that the testimony of approvers must be independently corroborated by other witnesses, a requirement not always convenient for the Castle detectives to honor without a bit of well-meant perjury here and there, as in the embarrassing conviction of the marine Maguire, the innocent bystander in the Manchester case. Mallon's intention was to buttress his evidence, not only with copious corroborators but above all with more and better approvers.

* Kavanagh's itinerary forms the basis for a familiar passage in the windy newspaper office of *Ulysses*, in which the cub reporter Ignatius Gallaher achieved a world-paralyzing news scoop by cabling to the *New York World* on the afternoon of the sixth of May the entire story of the Phoenix Park murders. As Robert M. Adams has pointed out, Joyce's low opinion of the newspapers as a guide to truth is hidden in the slip-ups in his yarn. See Robert M. Adams, *Surface and Symbol* (New York: Oxford University Press, 1962), pp. 162–63.

He considered it urgent to catch a new Invincible witness more weighty than Farrell and Kavanagh. Curley and Carey were two of the choicest suspects, and Mallon began to try pressure on their families. Rumors began to circulate in the Dublin neighborhoods that first the one, then the other was about to turn informer, rumors reaching even as far as the English press. The terrorized wives held anxious jail conferences with their husbands. The Curleys could not be broken, but the Careys showed some promise. Then the hearings featured one of Carey's slum tenants testifying that during the summer he had slipped into an old cockloft where Carey had often been seen to go and found there two very wicked-looking knives. A witness swore that, yes, such knives could possibly have made the fatal wounds. Another witness testified that he had chatted with Carey on a bench in Phoenix Park toward sundown on the sixth of May. Holding these trumps, Mallon drew up a second Kilmainham treaty; and Carey concurred.

IV

A debate now arose in the Castle between Mallon and Curran as to whether Carey's services were acceptable. Curran thought not; let him hang, was his feeling. Tempting rewards for evidence, "blood money," had been posted from the start, though for a long time there were no takers. But as soon as all the suspects had been jailed, witnesses suddenly found their tongues. Curran thought that he had already a redundancy of hanging evidence against all the Invincibles, including Carey, without any need of Mallon's bargain. But Mallon argued a couple of particular uses for Carey, and Curran was overruled by Lord Spencer. "Counsel for the Crown took a different view—I do not say wrongly," said Curran. "They were of opinion that the fact of a man of Carey's position turning . . . [queen's] evidence would be a warning to all who might in future engage in similar conspiracies."[8] Attorney General A. M. Porter underscored the didactic motif: "This case should teach one lesson—that there could be no honor among members of such a society. When, as in this case, the light was let in, when there was the faintest hint of knowledge known to those outside, the whole miserable union dissolved and the people were only too ready to come forward to save themselves at the expense of the wretched society which they had joined."[9] Disloyalty to Her Majesty and betrayal to the hangman by fellow rebels were, in the government's presentations, an inseparable pair of events.

On February 17, 1883, Carey came into the preliminary-hearing room at Kilmainham, greeted his comrades warmly, then moved over and "took the witness table" instead of entering the dock. As theater, the moment stands with O'Connell's shattering of Davis in Conciliation Hall, or the Richmond jailbreak, or the defendants' speeches at Manchester. Those newspapermen who thought that Dublin was "stunned" and "infuriated" by the assassination itself had fired off their hyperboles prematurely. In the trials that followed, crime and punishment were only the official business; betrayal was the great theme. The prosecution highlighted the star witness' perfidy in the charge, the defense repeated it in the cross-examination. Carey was put on exhibition over and over, always the star actor, always in the one role, a leader who had enticed men into the movement, set them their task, then destroyed them. Led by the same Castle officials who had broken him, a chorus of indignation fixed him in Irish history as "the prince of informers," as the man who saved "his own life at the expense of his accomplices."[10] In the unrelenting Irish hue and cry that pursued him, all danger of another Manchester fiasco for the government naturally vanished.

Backed by his impresarios—Attorney General Porter for the prosecution and A. M. Sullivan and his brother Donal for the defense—Carey made a permanent mark on the Irish imagination. It is not surprising that James Joyce, the foremost expert on the Judas theme in Irish history, should have found him an attractive literary morsel. *Ulysses* formulates Carey's signification with notable insistence. Mr. Bloom is our informant. Carey breaks into Bloom's thoughts three times in the course of his day. The first time, in the "Lotus-Eaters" chapter, Bloom ponders on the ostentatiously pious Carey as a contradiction or "Antiself": "That fellow that turned queen's evidence on the invincibles he used to receive the, Carey was his name, the communion every morning. This very church. . . . Wife and six children at home. And plotting that murder all the time."[11] Carey's mixture of piety with perfidy was a subject that never became tedious, either, to the Castle officials, who were grateful for all examples of what Mallon's admiring biographer called "the extraordinary mass of contradictions there is to be found in Ireland's wrongdoers."[12] The second time *Ulysses* brings Carey onstage, in the bread-and-butter "Lestrygonians" chapter (p. 161), Mr. Bloom sounds the betrayal note in its richest inveracity, straight out of the attorney general's courtroom sermon and *A Portrait of the Artist*: "Like that Peter or Denis or James Carey that blew the gaff on the invincibles. Member of the corporation too. Egging raw youths on to get in the know. All the time drawing secret service pay from the castle."

But the third time Carey appears in *Ulysses*, in the "Eumaeus" chapter (p. 626), Mr. Bloom both asserts and blasts his homiletic use, expressing himself (as the chapter requires) in imaginative solecism and platitude:

> [There is always] the offchance of a Dannyman coming forward and turning queen's evidence—or king's now—like Denis or Peter Carey, an idea he utterly repudiated. Quite apart from that, he disliked those careers of wrongdoing and crime on principle. Yet, though such criminal propensities had never been an inmate of his bosom in any shape or form, he certainly did feel,

and no denying it (while inwardly remaining what he was), a certain kind of admiration for a man who had actually brandished a knife, cold steel, with the courage of his political convictions though, personally, he would never be a party to any such thing, off the same bat as those love vendettas of the south—have her or swing for her. . . .

Joyce's psychoanalytic reduction of Irish nationalism to "heroticism" we have seen in operation before. We have already noted, too, that one eye-witness definitively described Dublin's reaction to the Phoenix Park case as "perplexed."

Carey explained at the witness table that the Invincibles consisted of about fifteen members recruited from ex-Fenians, dropouts unable to share O'Leary's low opinion of terrorism. The purpose of the band was "to make history by removing tyrants." The organizer and commandant was called "Number One." The first Number One came from London to set up the shop in December 1881, after Parnell had been a couple of months in jail. The formation of the Invincibles thus added another crosscurrent in the general Irish turbulence during Forster's last months as chief secretary. The original Number One was shortly replaced by Captain MacCafferty, lately in command of the attempted arms raid on Chester Castle. The third, his name unknown to Carey, was tentatively identified by some witnesses as Patrick Tynan, a small shopkeeper in Kingstown. Carey told that the first task of the Invincibles was to "remove" Forster, but he lived a magic life and strolled untouched through twenty-odd ambushes. The final try had been set up on the Kingstown boat train after he had resigned, but he had gone on ahead on an early train. The task then shifted to the removal of Thomas Burke, a project suggested by an observation in the *Freeman's Journal* that with the change of Irish policy after the Kilmainham treaty, Burke "ought to be removed."

Carey stated that he was not in command on May sixth, however much the government cared to insinuate that he was. He was under orders from Dan Curley, and was scolded once during the afternoon for watching a polo game instead of attending to business. His assignment was to identify Burke when he entered the park. This he did by waving a white handkerchief to alert the killers and sending word up ahead that Burke was the man in the gray suit. He said that the assassins who met Burke and Cavendish on the path were seven, that Joe Brady wielded the knife, and that Burke's companion was unnoticed until he counterattacked Brady with his umbrella, then he too was murdered.

So then the juridical profession took its inning. The accused were tried separately and hanged separately, the same shattering iterative method that was revived for a similar purpose in 1916. The grinding occupied nearly four months. Joe Brady was the first to be convicted. On the morning of his execution, many hundreds gathered spontaneously outside Kilmainham, kneeling in the street to weep and pray; and when the black flag went up, a great keening wail arose from the crowd. Other gatherings were permitted for each execution; but when the mourners organized a mock funeral procession to Glasnevin bearing an empty coffin labeled "Daniel Curley," their demonstration was broken up by the police. After three quick convictions, the fourth trial ended in a hung jury. Two days later the case was retried with the same outcome. In another two days an unprecedented third trial found the defendant guilty. The next to be tried was Skin-the-Goat, described in the newspapers as "looking like Father Christmas" with his white whiskers and ruddy nose. His defense lawyer's plea consisted in an invidious comparison between James Carey, who had waved a fatal white handkerchief in Phoenix Park, and the prisoner in the dock, who had merely driven a cab there following his mode of livelihood. Then came a great surrise: the prisoner was found not guilty. The jury panel was by now extremely jumpy. A fine of one hundred pounds was assessed against any man who refused a call to jury duty, and in the fourth trial the fine had to be levied against seventy-six thin-skinned panelists. After five death sentences, five of life imprisonment, and four more of long penal servitude, the government decided that it had made its point, and rested.

V

The Phoenix Park affair seemed closed. But not quite. Emigrating with his family to South Africa in disguise and under an assumed name, Carey was recognized on shipboard by a Donegal peasant named Patrick O'Donnell. With a pistol he shot Carey dead. For that unlawful act he was arrested and shipped back to London for trial. His defense was conducted by A. M. Sullivan, who gave the court a full description of James Carey's failings and a learned argument that under admiralty law it lacked jurisdiction. The jury and court were equally unmoved. O'Donnell was found guilty and hanged. With that, the total cost in lives taken by the Phoenix Park episode reached nine, the score standing at three for the civilians and six for the law. Many Irishmen were ready for a recess. But in the meantime Rossa's and "Red Jim" MacDermott's dynamite war had opened on a large scale in England. "Strike away!" said Rossa. "Keep striking till England is on her knees." English newspapers carried each day two equally sensational Irish columns side by side: one from Liverpool telling of the busy Merseyside projects of the Dynamitards; the other from Dublin on the extermination of the Invincibles by the hangman Marwood, a businesslike personage, familiar to many but admired by few, the model for Joyce's memorable hangman, Horace Rumbold.

And long after that, even, the Phoenix Park actors living and dead still came back to disturb the equanimity of Dubliners. "Like actresses," Mr. Bloom complained, "always farewell—positively last performance, then come up smiling again."[13] Patrick Tynan fled to New York and made a life's career as "the mysterious Number One." The Irish-Americans shunned him as a bore, and his claim, though possibly genuine, was universally disbelieved. The slight injured his self-esteem. He wrote a book that contains much random information and, in addition, twelve appendixes setting forth the documentary evidence for his claim. It also contains purple passages that sound as though they were secretly composed in Dublin Castle to undermine the Irish nationalist movement: "And Mr. Torquemada Curran stroked his beard in his inquisitorial chair in the Castle, and began to dream of a judgeship in the near future. And the detective chief Mallon licked his lips with satisfaction, and purred his song of pleasure at the result of his labours. . . ."[14] The statement is not factually inaccurate, but something is wrong in the tone. Later he wrote another book on the "great Irish Transvaal conspiracy," illustrated with facsimiles proving his own complicity therein. He became another of those dubious Irish hero-claimants, floating in limbo between imposture and honor, like Joyce's ghosts who may (or may not) have "got away James Stephens."

VI

Found not guilty of murder, Skin-the-Goat was rearrested in the courtroom and charged with conspiracy. Under Gladstone's new Crimes Act, he was tried without a jury, convicted, and sentenced to prison for life. After many years his release was won by the Amnesty Association, that branch of Irish nationalism that never lacked for an issue. Joyce exhibits him at length in the "Eumaeus" chapter of *Ulysses*. He is "said to be" the famous Invincible, but Mr. Bloom "wouldn't vouch for the actual facts" and is forced merely to assume "that he was he." The historical Skin-the-Goat was not deficient in statuesque solidity, but this portrait is, once again, of a man like Tynan who is not quite real. Skin-the-Goat's style of patriotism in *Ulysses* repeats exactly that of the Fenian, "the citizen," in the earlier "Cyclops" chapter. That Joyce felt compelled to rerun an effect already made suggests that his repellent Irish patriot had passed beyond disciplined artistic control into a gentle phobia.*

* Among Skin-the-Goat's twice-told banalities lies hidden one startling new formulation: "Brummagem England was toppling already, and her downfall would be Ireland, her Achilles heel, which he explained to them about the vulnerable point of Achilles, the Greek hero—a point his auditors at once seized as he completely gripped their attention by showing the tendon referred to on his boot." Richard M. Kain once noted that Joyce's farcical fanatic appears to have augured the future with a more astute vision than his gifted

VII

The most vividly remembered of the hanged Invincibles was Joe Brady. He was fabulous, a youth of "almost Herculean strength" as the attorney general described him. To some he was a hero, for in staking his life he had had nothing to gain. He knew how to "keep his mouth sealed," he had the bad luck to pick the wrong experiment, and so on. And yet the martyr's crown and the hero's oak-leaf garland looked somewhat grotesque on a cut-throat. Well-intentioned or not, he initiated a long chain of Irish mischief, and his chief accomplishment was his demonstration that every other politi-cal methodology was superior to his own. He was dead or alive an equivoca-tion. Joyce's eye caught this trait and found it useful.

Who else but Joyce could have discovered for us that the word "corpse" contains the anagram "cropse"? Like Yeats, he had a literary journeyman's specialized interest in the accumulated store of Irish transfiguration tropes. Indifference on his part would have spared him much pain, for he was un-happy with them all. He too was distressed at the success with which T. D. Sullivan's "God Save Ireland" had swept the popular field, and he gave it the full quota of three satiric barbs that *Ulysses* allots to the standard patrio-tic symbols. A rival for national anthem, "The Croppy Boy," a lugubrious song about the yeoman terror of 1798, pleased him no better. Rendered in bass by Ben Dollard in the "Sirens" chapter, it highlights the impromptu lunchtime musicale at the Ormond Hotel bar. ("They know it all by heart," says the nonjuring Mr. Bloom. "The thrill they itch for.") For himself, the ballad brings on, first, a spell of lascivious fantasy (by the formula that Irish nationalism is a type of sexual mischief); then prudential caution ("All the same he must have been a bit of a natural not to see it was a yeoman's cap"); and finally Joyce's unrivaled closure of the subject.[15]

In preparation for Joe Brady's appearance, *Ulysses* assails Robert Emmet's exalted place in Irish symbology with two savage ironies. Mr. Kernan, the frock-coated drummer in the "Wandering Rocks" chapter, humming "The Croppy Boy," passes down James Street toward St. Catherine's Church and responds parrotlike to the cue of Emmet's place of execution seen ahead in Thomas Street. ("Down there Emmet was hanged, drawn and quartered. Greasy black rope. Dogs licking the blood off the street when the lord lieutenant's wife drove by in her noddy.") But Kernan's real errand is to reach a corner on the quays where he can see at close hand Lord Lieutenant Dudley pass with his entourage. ("His excellency! Too bad! Just missed by a hair. Damn it! What a pity!")—a variation on a theme borrowed from Yeats's "September 1913." The recapitulation of these motifs in "musical

creator. See Joyce, *Ulysses*, pp. 605, 624–25; and Kain, *Fabulous Voyager* (Chicago: University of Chicago Press, 1959), p. 176.

statement" provides the comic denouement of the "Sirens" chapter. Suffering flatulence blown up to critical pressure by the festival of patriotic song at the Ormond bar, Mr. Bloom flees to the street, then lets his mind drift back on the tune of "The Memory of the Dead," another contender for national anthem. He sees an engraving of Emmet in an antique-shop window and recites his two farewell sentences with the blessed relief of crepitus marking each punctuation point.[16]

Into this medley of Emmet, croppy boy, and "who fears to speak of ninety-eight?" Joyce inserted as necessary to the composite Irish political martyr Joe Brady's fifteen stone of muscle. He first appears in the "Cyclops" chapter, which Joyce instructed Stuart Gilbert to classify on his chart as follows:

Organ: Muscle
Art: Politics
Symbol: Fenian[17]

"The citizen," Skin-the-Goat, and Joe Brady hold equally valid credentials under this scheme. To particularize Brady, Joyce invented an account of his hanging and the "consequent scission of the spinal cord" by which *"per diminutionem capitis"* his corpse generated a striking tumescence *"in articulo mortis."* As with the story of James Stephens' escape at Malahide in orange blossoms, another Joycean signature too good to be true, Joyce cited folk-lore for the source of his imaginary prodigy.

Later, in the "Circe" chapter, "the citizen" has chanted a lyrical maledictive prayer:

> To slit the throat
> Of the English dogs
> That hanged our Irish leaders.

Enters the croppy boy, fused with Parnell's 1798 Wicklow peasant who was flogged to death across the belly at the cart's tail. He wears "the rope around his neck" and "gripes in his issuing bowels with both hands," singing, "I bear no hate to a living thing." Hangman Rumbold advances with a "gladstone" bag to do his "fell but necessary office." Strangled on the gallows, the croppy boy expires and is transformed into Joe Brady the Invincible: "A violent erection of the hanged sends gouts of sperm through his death clothes to the cobblestones." Three women in the crowd "rush forward with their handkerchiefs to sop it up." The ladies who conserve the regenerative treasure in this considerate manner recall those who actually did dip their handkerchiefs in Emmet's blood flowing down the cobbles of Thomas Street. Joyce gives them names. They are Mrs. Bellingham, Mrs Yelverton Barry, and the Honorable Mrs Mervyn Talboys,[18] three fantasy Anglo-Irish females in Lord Dudley's set who, a short while before were surrealistically flagellating Mr. Bloom. As the ultimate consumers of the pure essence of national rebirth, they sharpen Joyce's critique of the standard patriotic transfigurations (such as Yeats's "Rose Tree") in which the bloody visceral component of the death mystique is, in his opinion, too softly sounded.

VIII

A late-Victorian visitor to Madame Tussaud's wax museum might see a tableau of the Phoenix Park murders displaying the true jaunting car purchased from the informer Kavanagh and, of special interest, a pair of "long dissecting or amputating knives" bought from the London surgical supply house that had sold the murder weapons themselves. The famous dissecting knives intruded into the case late, for the bowie knife or stiletto theory had served adequately up to the time of the Invincible trials. Offhand the new detail might seem unimportant; if Joe Brady had been armed with a pair of seamstress' scissors, the result could hardly have been different.

When the Castle detectives were bargaining for Carey's life, they originally intended to exhibit him as proof to Irishmen of what Stephen Dedalus called "the indispensable informer" in the ranks. A second object, not featured in the genial memoirs of the detectives but clearly stated in the newspapers, was to try to establish a connection between Carey and the Land League, or even bigger game. Asked in court about the Invincibles' source of money, Carey replied that "everybody assumed" that it could "only have come from the Land League," a statement legally worthless but valuable for other purposes.

The dissecting knives were first heard of in public on February 3, 1883, when Carey's tenant testified to seeing them the previous August in the cockloft. And two weeks later, when Carey turned queen's evidence, the knives made an exciting ornamentation to his testimony, for he swore that he received them from a Mrs. Frank Byrne, who had brought them to Dublin from London secreted "in her petticoats." And who was her husband, Mr. Frank Byrne? Beyond question he was an official of the Land League, and the newspapers identified him further, with enthusiasm but not with accuracy, as "Mr. Parnell's private secretary." Captivated by this thread of evidence, the English public was alerted to expect that it would shortly receive news that "a member of Parliament was at the head of the conspiracy."[19] Here we find the first trace of the grandiose dream that fixated English political ambitions for many years to come, to "solve the Irish problem" by proving Parnell implicated in the Phoenix Park murders. At the outset the project got off to a bad start. Moved by some remnant of morality, Carey failed to cooperate as expected, perhaps as promised. For when Mrs. Byrne was brought before him, he swore that he could not identify her.[20]

In the House of Commons the deposed Irish chief secretary, William E. Forster, rose to fill in the sketch outlined by the questions being put to James Carey in Dublin. "Probably no more serious charge was ever made by any member of the House of Commons against another member," he said in prologue, and he proceeded to incriminate Parnell as the guilty agent of the Phoenix Park murders, which were nothing more than "the natural outcome" of his policy of boycott: "It is not that he himself directly planned or perpetrated outrages or murders, but that he either connived at them, or when warned [Here Parnell interrupted, "It is a lie."] . . . he determined to remain in ignorance." He addressed to Parnell the parliamentary question, "how far the hon. member inquired into the actions of those with whom he was associated." The question was expected to force Parnell into a dilemma: either he would have to denounce his left support and, with that, scuttle the policy of parallel action that for five years past had been so galling to the English dominion in Ireland; or he would have to denounce the witch hunters and, with that, stigmatize himself as an assassin.

Parnell's reply at the next day's session brought out a full gallery, with the Prince of Wales and Cardinal Manning among them. He was at his most disdainful: Who was Forster but a failure, cashiered in disgrace? By what right did Forster presume to question him? Forster's evidence for his lurid insinuations was contemptible: he and Carey made a pair, two imaginative police informers together, though that "miserable creature" in Dublin had the better excuse of trying to save his life. As for the Irish ultras, he did not endorse the particular opinions of Patrick Ford as they had been reported to him, for he himself did not read the New York *Irish World*. And Patrick Ford did not endorse the policies for which he stood. At the same time, he did not propose to serve as England's policeman. Nor would he applaud the police work of others. The dismissed chief secretary's first words on hearing of the assassination of Burke and Cavendish had been, "They find the pressure taken off."[21] And his first act was to send word to Gladstone that he was ready to return to duty on the next Irish express out of Euston Station. Perhaps, said Parnell, the issue might be clearer if Gladstone had accepted this presumptuous offer, if Ireland were still subject to the power of this "seasoned politician now in disgrace. Call him back to his post; send him to look after the secret negotiations of Dublin Castle [a veiled accusation that perjured evidence had been demanded in the bargain with Carey]; send him to superintend the payment of blood money; send him to distribute the taxes which an unfortunate and starving peasantry have to pay for crimes not committed by them. All this would be congenial work to the right hon. gentleman. Send your ablest and best men to push forward the work of misgoverning Ireland!"[22] Then turning deftly back to the spirit of the Kilmainham treaty, he offered the prediction that all like Forster whose single idea was coercion of a brave, generous, and impulsive people would shortly be disowned by Englishmen themselves.

English members who heard the debate complained of Parnell's "evasiveness." In beginning his speech, he had warned them that nothing he could say would "have the slightest effect upon the public opinion of this House or upon the public opinion of this country [England]." But he was accustomed to expect their incomprehension, he said, and to "rely instead upon the public opinion of those whom I have desired to help, and with whose aid I have worked for the prosperity and freedom of Ireland." The confidence was generously reciprocated. The Irish members greeted his speech with prolonged cheers, and Davitt thought it "the best and noblest speech an Irish leader ever spoke in any English parliament."[23] At home his supporters had recently launched a Parnell Tribute to help him out of a financial difficulty—he was about to lose Avondale through foreclosure, thanks to parliamentary reforms for which he was himself responsible. The tribute now took on the enthusiasm of an agitation, and money poured in. Gladstone sent an English Catholic as special emissary to Rome to persuade Leo XIII that the Irish clergy should be forbidden from participating. A papal rescript against the Parnell Tribute went forth, but it was immediately identified as English-inspired. The money then flowed in more copiously than ever. In December 1883, a few months after the finish of the Invincible hangings, Parnell was invited to a great mass meeting in the Rotunda to be handed a check, a free gift of the people of Ireland, for thirty-seven thousand pounds. He pocketed the check without comment. His listeners, somewhat disappointed, thought that for so large a sum they were entitled to just a bit of effusiveness.

CHAPTER 19

After Kilmainham: Davitt and Standish O'Grady Take Stock

I

The essence of Parnell's reply to Forster was that the Phoenix Park affair was not an issue of substance for Irishmen—a correct tactical position. And yet he was himself suddenly apprehensive of terror, and even militance. When he turned to carry out his own Kilmainham promise to calm down the land agitation, his fear of the irrepressibles reinforced his habitual scrupulousness in honoring a commitment. Davitt's first question on being told of the new Kilmainham line was, what did Parnell propose to do with the other family enterprise, the Ladies' Land League? He touched a tender spot. Toward his agrarian sisters Parnell felt no chivalry and no gratitude, negative attitudes he shared with others, Cardinal MacCabe for one, and also Mrs. O'Shea, who considered their actions "crass folly" and "criminality" and applauded her influential good friend's displeasure with "this wild army of mercenaries" and "fanatics."[1] Parnell's answer to Davitt's question was: "I fear they have done much harm" and "they have expended an enormous sum of money." He added that "they"—presumably his sisters— had told him that Ireland would have been better off if he had stayed in Kilmainham.

In Parnell's irritation can be seen the birth of the theme of the frenzied Irish amazon, of whom the Maud Gonne of Yeats's verse is the most resplendent and indefatigable example. The parentage was explicitly acknowledged by some of the more insistent voices of the myth. St. John Ervine, Belfast's unique contribution to Yeats's Irish literary movement, enthusiastically seconded Mrs. O'Shea's critique: the fanaticism of Irish women was "almost inhuman."[2] Liam O'Flaherty, too, felt drawn to sympathy

THE POLITICS OF IRISH LITERATURE

with Parnell's aversion against his female auxiliary: "There was a women's organization called the Ladies's Land League, which did as much harm by thoughtless statements and actions as the organizations of political women among us in Ireland nowadays"[3]—a reference to Mesdames MacBride, Markiewicz, and MacSwiney. On this particular theme he wrote a novel, *The Martyr*. It was not one of his best; like some other Irish literary historicisms, this one is not weather-tight. Listening to Parnell's attack, Davitt remembered that it was the ladies after all who had finally toppled Forster, and he replied, "It appears to me that they have given good value for the money which was contributed to give the landlords and the Castle all possible trouble." However that might be, Parnell silenced the ladies' agrarianism without ado simply by cutting off their money. His habit of diplomacy was missing from the transaction, and his sisters never spoke to him again.

The Land League itself was the next to go. Davitt, Brennan, and Dillon were summoned to Avondale for discussions in September 1882, immediately after House passage of the twin bill for Ireland, the coercive Crimes Act and the conciliatory Arrears Act. The meeting was tense, for the Kilmainham treaty was not working well. Great numbers of peasants were barred from benefits under the new reform and were threatened with eviction. And as soon as the new Crimes Act became law, evictions began once again to soar. The league militants went out to Avondale to argue that Parnell had betrayed the neediest strata of the peasantry and written them off for extermination. They urged that the old Land League be reactivated and the land war reopened with the full vigor of November-December 1880.

By standing pat on the Kilmainham treaty, Parnell opened up the familiar vista of the Irish schism. Schism did not occur, though. The one was victorious over the three, but not, as John Butler Yeats thought, by the exercise of hauteur and insolence. Parnell never "governed with the iron hand," said Davitt. "No leader was ever more indulgent in the exercise of power or interfered less with his followers or gave a wider field for discussion or criticism. . . ."[4] Still, he did prevail; which is to say that the other three, who had it in their power to tear the movement apart if they chose, chose not to. They submitted, and so it was that an agreement to bury the land agitation, "the Avondale treaty," was reached. A new political mass organization was announced, to be called the "National League," cleansed of the offensive word "Land." Its platform was, first of all, Home Rule; incidentally it also advocated "land reform" and the stimulation of Irish industry. By a revision of the old Land League constitution, the moderate Irish M.P.'s assumed the dominant voice in its affairs; and in 1884 local priests were co-opted into every branch as ex officio members. Soon the organization that two years earlier was the de facto government of rural Ireland had mutated into an O'Connellite vote-getting machine for the Irish parliamentary party. It welcomed the old land-war generals to membership, if they cared to come along, but most of them quietly drifted away. Dillon went to Colorado for his lungs; Egan settled down in Lincoln, Nebraska; Davitt accepted a place on the new board, and even journeyed to the United States to pacify the discontented Irish-American sponsors. But he remained critical, with Lancashire gradually replacing Ireland at the center of his thought and effort.

To defend himself against the charge of premature demobilization, Parnell argued that the land-war resurgence was now an exhausted force. He believed that it would be a foolish general who would overextend his pursuit without pause to catch breath. He believed that he had already achieved, in Yeatsian language, "of all things not impossible, the most difficult." Reversing Lalor's 1848 program, he proposed to kennel the wolf dog, or to alter the metaphor, to unhitch the economic issue from the political, to sidetrack agrarianism and to highball down the line with Home Rule. He believed that the great mass of his Irish followers approved his decision: "I believe that the Irish People have very moderate ideas as to the improvement of their condition. . . ." He thought that men like Davitt, Dillon, and Egan who would push on with the land war regardless would soon find that they had no followers at their backs, and his order of the day was above all else to strengthen the Irish parliamentary party.[5]

In Davitt's opinion, on the other hand, Parnell's peace treaty broke a rising revolutionary wave and instituted a "counterrevolution." He believed that the agrarian upsurge of 1880 had bought precious little with its prodigal expenditure of heroic energy. As we have seen, he thought the No-Rent Manifesto had come too late; but he also believed it premature. Since Parnell had refused his chance to call the rent strike on that angry day when his ticket of leave was canceled and all the Irish members were suspended from the House, he thought he ought to have waited until some future time when he could mobilize the entire peasantry. Then the chief secretary might well study whether he could evict half a million farmers and dig potatoes with bayonets. Until the Kilmainham treaty had undermined its fighting strength, the old league was, he thought, competent to deliver a knockout blow to landlordism.[6]

In this old argument, Davitt's contention had its point. He saw that if the force of the agrarian offensive was waning, none was so weary of it as "the Chief" himself. Parnell had once remarked that imprisonment would drive him mad if he ever had to endure it for long, and Davitt surmised that claustrophobia was his prime motive for the Kilmainham treaty. Long afterward, Mrs. O'Shea's publication of Parnell's prison letters threw a different light on Davitt's suspicions. One letter written on the day after his arrest was anything but claustrophobic. It said: "Politically it is a fortunate thing for me that I have been arrested, as the movement is breaking fast, and all will be quiet in a few months, when I shall be released." But the expected rural quiet did not descend, and on February 14, 1882, with five months of jail behind him, he wrote Mrs. O'Shea: "I am very glad that the days of platform speeches have gone by and are not likely to return. I cannot describe to you the disgust I always felt with those meetings, knowing as I did how hollow and wanting in solidity everything connected with the movement was. When I was arrested I did not think the movement would have survived a month, but this wretched Government have such a fashion of doing things by halves that it has managed to keep things going in several of the counties up till now."[7] It is hard to read these letters as anything other than a wish for Forster to move in on the league and its ladies' auxiliary speedily and with his most efficient constraints.

Davitt's critique of the Kilmainham treaty raised a general alarm that the national revolution stood in danger of being stunted before its full growth. He thus anticipated a major anxiety for thoughtful Irishmen of a later time and broached the most repetitive if not the most perspicuous of all political fixations in later Irish literature—the disenchantment-with-Ireland theme. When the Treaty of 1921 finally arrived, it bore an incongruity between effort and achievement that would fascinate astringent bystanders, and imperialistic Englishmen particularly would be anxious to vociferate over the nonappearance of the Gaelic utopia (though they were more prone to a hurt silence, like Lady Peel on her visit to O'Leary). But Irishmen too, and even the Free State leaders themselves, felt twinges of embarrassment. When forced to make some kind of a statement on his program in 1922, Michael Collins announced unheroically: "The keynote to the economic revival must be development of Irish resources by Irish capital for the benefit of the Irish consumer in such a way that the people have steady work at just remuneration and their own share of control. How are we to develop Irish resources? The earth is our bountiful mother. Upon free access to it depends not only agriculture, but all other trades and industries."[8] Davitt early caught hints that banality was an Irish historical potential; and he feared that Parnell had made it possible that an Irish revolution might sometime be fought, as Dubliners later heard it said perhaps excessively, to paint the royal-red pillar boxes a patriotic green. But it was Davitt himself who beckoned Parnell into the revolutionary leadership at Westport; and very happy he was that day when Parnell's courtesy relieved him of his revolutionary responsibility.

Davitt thought it possible to outwit the forces that would stunt the Irish revolution, if agrarianism could be kept in team with the other prepotent Irish objectives. Henry George gave him one kind of program: to "nationalize the land" by government purchase, the "economic rent" to be then collected by the government and used for amortization of the purchase debt, with the leftover cash used to defray the expenses of government.[9] This slogan made no appeal to Irishmen. Davitt dreamed, too, of a union of Irish agrarianism with English socialism, and at one stage he started a newspaper in London, the *Labor World*, with a mixed trade-union, socialist, and agrarian orientation. Studying these shifts of his thought, his old Fenian comrades suspected that his brain was becoming addled. O'Leary concluded that he was not a nationalist any more, but "some sort of an internationalist and socialist." But to the modern observer, it is plain that he was groping toward the same fusion of land and urban grievance that was destined to ignite all of the major social revolutions of the twentieth century. He was notably lacking, though, in any theoretical grasp of either goals or methods. While Ireland in 1880 possessed all the ingredients for an explosion of the twentieth-century type, it is impossible to imagine that Michael Davitt was a man to weld them into a striking force, or supposing some initial success, that he could have organized a holding action to survive the fury of the inevitable counterattack. His program receded into the mists, to be superseded after a couple of decades by the forthright Marxism of James Connolly, Jim Larkin, and Sean O'Casey.

More self-commanding and more sensitive to the immediate actualities of the Irish and English balance of forces, Parnell curtly overrode Davitt's position, knocking down his ideas seriatim. The alliance with Henry George he disposed of by reminding the Irish peasant of his peasant human nature: "The desire to acquire land is everywhere one of the strongest instincts of human nature." He dispelled Davitt's scheme for an alliance with English socialism by pointing out that such an ally did not actually exist. Scorning the vague, half-militant, half-utopian tone of Davitt's language, he observed that there were but two ways by which the Irish peasant could possess the land—he could fight for it or he could buy it. The first of the alternatives, he said, "I say nothing about"; the total absence of any Irish army, arms, allies, or opportunity spoke for itself. The other alternative was at best not painless, but he warned the land-hungry that they would perhaps finally have to go on being land-hungry. Constitutional agitation had no magic solution for peasant frustration; it could at most "whittle down the price that the landlord asks for his land, but it must be paid" in the end.[10]

II

Parnell's decision to cut free of Irish agrarianism for unfettered adventures in parliamentarianism entailed the dangers of stagnation in the same doldrums that becalmed O'Connell in 1842 and Butt in 1875. But without waiting for any prompting by Parnell, the Irish land issue was propelled by its own self-motion to trace out a new mutation not clearly foreseen by Gladstone, Davitt, or Parnell either.

The novelist George Moore wrote a series of naturalistic sketches of the land war for *Le Figaro*, later reprinted as *Parnell and His Island*. He had been living as an absentee landlord in high decadent style in Montmartre when the reverberations of Parnell's Ennis speech penetrated even so far and called him back home. In 1880 he was forced to meet with delegations of Moore Hall tenants, a task for which he was almost too enlightened. In Mayo, he wrote, no landlord could hide the naked essence of his privilege to collect rent—it was simple extortion: ". . . in Ireland there is nothing but the land; with the exception of a few distillers or brewers in Dublin, who live upon the drunkenness of the people, there is no way in Ireland of getting money except through the peasant. . . . in Ireland rent is a tribute and nothing else."[11] His own "tribute," mailed to him regularly in Paris until it suddenly stopped altogether, had been exacted by virtue of the right of arbitrary eviction. But with the new peasant discipline and organization superior to the landlords' own, the arbitrary evictions and the tribute had vanished together.

Boycott's flight from Lough Mask House had demonstrated the impotence of both courts and military. Negotiating with his Land League tenants, Moore probed their minds to find what lingering power to threaten might still be left to him. Affecting indifference, he suggested that he had half a mind to sell out to some Englishman:

> "An Englishman here," cries a peasant. "He would go back quicker than he came."
>
> "Maybe he wouldn't go back at all," cries another, chuckling. "We would make an Irishman of him forever."
>
> "Begad! we would make him wear the green in great earnest, and a fine sod it would be," shouted a third.[12]

Reaching for weapons Moore suddenly found he had none. He was ready to understand why Forster concluded that there was no effective counter-measure against the boycott, and why Parnell had said to the peasants at Ennis, "You have the game in your hands."

The surprise result of this disturbance of old relationships was that the outcry for a peasant proprietary, formerly linked with Jacobinism and jacquerie, once shelved by Thomas Davis as too dangerous, and lately fixed by Parnell as the daring limit beyond which he would never venture, was suddenly taken up seriously by Irish landlords themselves. They foresaw a long sloping fall of agricultural prices resulting in an interminable agrarian warfare that they could never hope finally to win. They concluded that it would be wise to turn their dubious land values into sterling, to sell out to the tenants, and to betake themselves to England or the colonies. Not too hurriedly, though. They were disheartened, but not so much that they could be panicked when Davitt threatened that they "did not deserve in the way of compensation the price of their tickets to Holyhead."[13] Parnell had spoken of whittling down the price. They settled back to wait him out. The conclusion came leisurely. It reaches beyond the limits of this study, but it should be sketched briefly in order to give a bearing on the sweeping cultural changes implicit in Gladstone's Land Act of 1881.

III

For many years landlord and peasant haggled, unable to agree on price or terms. Tory ministries sponsored new Irish land acts in 1885, 1887, 1891, and 1896, each containing schemes for peasant land-purchase, but none ever passed beyond pilot experiment. Then the Boer War rudely disturbed the English sense of imperial security. More portentous still, the German naval threat broke through the traditional encrustations of British ministerial thinking. To check the German advance, the Entente Cordiale with France was hastily concluded. At the same time and apparently in the same mood of military forethought, Arthur Balfour, the Tory prime minister (whom the Irish with their affection for nicknames called "Bloody" Balfour), and George Wyndham, his Irish chief secretary, determined to foreclose the danger of an Irish peasant explosion in the British rear and to bring to completion the agrarian solution left half-finished by Gladstone.

In 1903 a Connaught landlord named Captain John Shawe-Taylor, one of Lady Gregory's nephews, took it upon himself to call a meeting between the Irish agrarian leaders and the landlords to discover whether they might finally strike a bargain. The discussions resulted in a proposal: let the British government pay from the exchequer the difference between the asking and the offering price and advance one hundred million pounds to buy up the peasants' land-purchase debt, enabling the landlords to cash in at once and depart. Balfour and Wyndham were informed that on these terms the bargain could be sealed. In a memorial to Shawe-Taylor, Yeats later spoke of this episode as "so entirely unmixed with any personal calculation" that it seemed a "miracle," probably originating in "the communion of the soul with God"; and he garlanded Shawe-Taylor with the lines of Tennyson:

> My strength is as the strength of ten,
> Because my heart is pure.[14]

When asked to pay the unprecedented sum necessary to close the land transaction, Balfour and Wyndham doubtless saw Shawe-Taylor's motives in a less mystical light. They decided, though, that the result would be worth even so high a price. Parliament that year passed the Wyndham Land Act, which promised the Irish peasant that when he had completed sixty-two and one-half years of installment payments, the farm would really be his.[15]

Joint beneficiaries with their former landlords of the "fall of feudalism in Ireland," the Irish peasants were indubitably better off after the Wyndham Land Act guaranteed them against eviction, rack-rents, and famine. It has been said that the Irish countryman now consumes more home-grown calories than his counterpart anywhere else in Europe. Stability he has won, too. Yet in the midst of one of the most favored farming areas of the world, his per capita income is still among Europe's lowest. The massive enclosure of the land that followed the famine was permanent: by and large, the graziers held the choicest land and the small holders kept the fringes and the leftovers. Ireland was thus no more able to support its population after the agrarian reforms than before. One result, already noted, was that the unique Irish custom of postponed marriage was practiced to grotesque excess. And even so, the huge net emigration that had begun in 1847 persisted without a single year's pause for half a century beyond Wyndham's time. The land reforms were naturally better late than never. But if Thomas Davis' demands for a peasant proprietary could have been enforced in 1842 instead of sixty years later, Ireland today might resemble Greece and Spain less and Norway and Denmark more.

IV

The era of the agrarian reforms altered in a substantial way the "human nature" of the Irish peasant. With security, his old servile deference faded out altogether, carrying to completion O'Connell's campaign to resuscitate Irish self-respect. The shift of peasant manners was noted by George Moore when he unveiled the new liberated Moore Hall tenant with his genial threat of homicide. Moore was one of those to whom the traditional deference was owing, yet he recorded its disappearance without the slightest sense of injury. With Yeats it was otherwise. His relationship to Irish peasants was abstract and literary rather than immediate and personal, and his knowledge of Irish historical motion, the source of both the servility and the loss of servility, was not merely inferior to Moore's, but minimal by any standard. Yet he decried the passing of the old paternalism with a violence that recalls Carlyle's extermination of the "Repale" advocate he met on the Kildare railroad in 1848. In the revised *Countess Cathleen* he inserted a speech by the old household servant, declaring the proper norm:

> . . . my old fathers served your fathers, lady,
> Longer than books can tell. . . .[16]

This attractive pristine servile state, Yeats insisted, was the condition genetically appropriate to the Irish lower classes and the condition really preferred by them, though momentarily perverted by John Locke's materialism and native loose-lipped demagogues.

In his rise out of starvation, the Irish peasant acquired a new sense of prudence and parsimony. Demonic recklessness faded into respectability. In literature, mad peasants like Yeats's Red Hanrahan and Synge's Playboy were transformed into cunning money-makers like the protagonist of Padraic Colum's play, *The Land*, or Somerville and Ross's incomparable Mr. Canty in "The Holy Island," with his copious potato pancakes, his snug farm, his substantial publican brother, his easy familiarity with the bishop himself. Stability encouraged literacy. The new Irish peasant drifted slowly free from the spirituality associated with his bronze-age belief in *sowlths* and changelings. Almost a propertied man, he threatened after the Land Act of 1881 to turn as materialistic as Maupassant's Normandy peasants or Dostoevsky's kulaks. To try to counter that threat, the Irish literary movement in its opening phase unmuzzled its spiritual wolf dogs. George Russell, the editor of the farm journal that Stephen Dedalus called "the pig's paper," fought peasant materialism on its own ground, insinuating spiritualized poetry in among the columns of livestock market quotations and advice to Irish beekeepers. Yeats converted himself into a Savonarola (a "Torquemada," Moore said) with the one text: materialism does not pay.

Politically, the post-Kilmainham land reforms drew the Irish countryside slowly out of its land-war belligerence into relative docility. Wyndham's fiscal gamble had turned a brilliant stroke in neutralizing the political pressure of Irish agrarianism. One Irish historian, Michael Tierney, even advanced the paradox that the Irish peasants had never been nationalist at all, leaving unexplained the question of where O'Connell's million listeners at Tara had come from. In 1916 the peasant did not rise, or even think about rising, to support his urban relatives in the Dublin insurrection; and de Valera is said to have complained in an unintentional but fascinating double entendre: "If only you'd come out with knives and forks!" Patrick Hogan, the first Free State minister for agriculture, found that English land legislation had worked over the ground so thoroughly that his ministry was left without any particular functions to perform, and he was forced either to contrive some duties or do without. Arming himself with the powers granted him under the Free State Egg Act, he struck with "ruthless" force against some twenty-three Irish farmers who had shipped eggs to London "externally dirty."[17] Such was the initiative left for Irish agrarian reform after Wyndham completed the steps begun by Gladstone's Land Act of 1881.

The English stratagem, to disconnect colonial agrarian grievance from colonial political radicalism—it was Parnell's late strategy, too—became a standard counterrevolutionary technique in the course of the twentieth century. For all that, it did not forestall the Irish revolution for national independence. It bought only the neutrality of the Irish peasants, not their affection; and it ignored the historical fact that the spark of Irish revolutionary sentiment since 1847 had been first struck in the cities.

V

George Moore cast his literary observations on the land war into the Balzacian mode;* appropriately so, since the urge to get money or to keep money was the undisguised passion of the historical episode. Later, other Irish writers would also use Balzac's mode with striking success, as in Patrick Kavanagh's *Tarry Flynn* (1948) or in Somerville and Ross's great novel, *The Real Charlotte* (1894). But alternative literary modes were available. Standish O'Grady chose to do his literary stocktaking of the land war in the mode of Thomas Carlyle. This, too, was appropriate, since Carlyle's voice had already been officially adapted to Irish usage through the prose of John Mitchel.

O'Grady was Anglican, Trinity educated, the nephew of a peer, and as I have noted, the secretary of the landlord's convention called to act upon the crisis of 1881. Like Mitchell in the same post a generation earlier, he too came away crushed from listening to landlords exposing their incompetence and triviality. He wrote a gloomy pamphlet called *The Crisis in Ireland* (1882), reflecting the same mood of surrender that had overcome Moore in Mayo: "The 'No-Rent' movement, if the people voluntarily or through terrorism go out rather than pay, constitutes a difficulty which is, so far as I can see, insurmountable." The certain result would be "the complete destruction of the Irish landlords as a class." The Ascendancy was destined to be "turned adrift upon the world, ruined, hopeless, and homeless, many of them middle-aged and old," and bedeviled with a "more immediate and perhaps more terrible danger," that of Davitt's and Patrick Ford's socialism.[18]

After the threat of outright land confiscation vanished, O'Grady overcame his first fright and issued a second pamphlet, *Toryism and the Tory Democracy* (1886), dropped his pathos for a session of recrimination against his class, guilty he thought of behavior "recreant" and "resourceless" in its "day of trial." Mitchel had harbored the same thoughts at the landlords' convention in 1847. But at the point where Mitchel had appealed to the

---

* Moore's Dublin-society novel called *A Drama in Muslin* (1886) depicts the languid fatalism of the Ascendancy after 1880, seen through the eyes of debutantes watching passionlessly the withering of their marriage prospects. For chorus to their pathos, a procession of duns from the unpaid moneylenders and dressmakers passes through the scene.

Irish people to rise up and let him see "a hundred thousand pikes flashing gloriously in the sun," here O'Grady turned aside to follow an ideological path of his own. For he believed that the most noxious flaw in the Irish landlords' behavior, more deadly than their totem worship of the horse or their recourse to England's "rotten staff," was their willingness to parley with the "anarchic *canaille*," the "scum." Woe to those landlords who bowed to "the people at large"; they were "traitors to their class," these "foolish and cowardly," "silly and ignoble" men, so craven as to "pay Danegeld to their enemies." They would brainlessly loose "the unchained, masterless democracy," surrendering Ireland to "this waste, dark, howling mass of colliding interests, mad about the main chance—the pence-counting shopkeeper; the publican; the isolated, crafty farmer; the laborer tied to his toil, or tramping perhaps to the polling booth, as an enfranchised citizen, a member of the sovereign people, a ruler in the land, with the wolf on his right hand, and the poor house on the left, and in front, at his *disposal*, the whole property of the island."[19]

Not that the Irish demos lacked great reserves of "noble qualities." Its "spiritual" assets were substantial: foremost among them was "poverty," augmented by "simplicity, religion, including respect for priests and bishops, and perhaps, above all, the pursuit of one ideal, which is not material interest—national independence." But their good impulses were never obedient to "moral suasion." They answered only to the summons of pitiless discipline: "For as sure as the earth under law rolls, so surely do all men need control, and most of all the poor laborer. . . . It is a tameless people, this, none on the earth's surface in such need of the whip and rein, having, indeed, much of the wild ass in its composition."[20] Luckily, though, Irish laborers respected the whip and the rein and the superior man's "will to chastise." Luckily, as Yeats said later, their "backs ached for the lash."[21]

And where was this master to be found? Not among the "Cat-Heads," for O'Grady at that time read no emblem of charisma in either Parnell's or Davitt's countenance. He wrote: "This land-leaguing democracy has no representative, not even a Tyler or Cade, anywhen back to the dim days of the Cat-Head [Cairbre Cat-Head, the Irish Spartacus], let them rave as they please of Silken Thomas or Red Hugh, or any worthy they please to choose and dub him theirs. Red Hugh, I think, would have offered but a short shrift to a committee of modern patriots going down to organize his tenantry on National-League principles." But among the scattered heroic fragments of the landlord class itself the savior would be found waiting. "Of you as a class, as a body of men, I can entertain not the least hope; who, indeed, can?" Yet, "you are still the best class we have, and so far better than the rest that there is none fit to mention as the next best." Who else could sense the measureless superiority of nobility over equality? Some lonely aristocrat hero of "the right mettle and the right calibre" stood ready, listening for the call. "To you, here and there over Ireland, or outside Ireland, and though but one, or two, or three I would now address myself, and especially to the young. . . . Ireland and her destinies hang upon you, literally so. Either you will re-fashion her, moulding us anew after some human and heroic pattern, or we plunge downwards into roaring revolutionary anarchies, where no road or path is any longer visible at all. And, dear friend, a word at parting: Make haste."[22] This sounded like a requisition for Coriolanus, and it is a disappointment to learn that the redeemer on whom O'Grady finally settled his affection was Coriolanus' "Antiself," not even an Irish horseman, but that merry cynic and demagogue, Lord Randolph Churchill.

VI

All this overheated opinionation will, I think, sound familiar to many readers. For O'Grady was mentor and elder friend to W. B. Yeats, who reverberated sympathetically to the main features of his thought—attachment to oligarchy, belief that the end of the Irish gentry foretold the end of the world, yearning for the solitary redeemer, condescension to the Irish populace when its mood was obsequious, and hysteria against its more up-to-date moods.

A memorial for O'Grady written by his son informs us, inevitably, that these attitudes suggest Swift. "The scathing invective which he here hurls forth reminds one forcibly of Swift. Those who wish to realize what depths of scorn and heights of enthusiasm can be expressed by language should study its pages."[23] It will be remembered that the prestigious Swift was once invoked also to praise John Mitchel's defense of slavery against the "cant" of Henry Ward Beecher. Yeats, too, freely borrowed Swift's name to ornament his borrowings from O'Grady's Irish visions. He once advanced the theory that Swift chose celibacy out of a dreadful half-mad foreknowledge that the seizure of the eighteenth-century historic process by "intellect" and "mechanism" would shortly "beget the sans-culottes of Marat."[24] The idea is arresting, but displeasure against Marat need not be fetched from so far back. In embracing O'Grady's social polity, Yeats's thinking traces more clearly from Cheyne Row in Chelsea than from the deanery of St. Patrick's. For Carlyle was O'Grady's prophet and writing master. Yeats admired O'Grady's pamphleteering prose and even praised it surprisingly for freedom from "rancor." The source itself, Carlyle's own prose, was not admired—that "vast popular rhetoric" derived from "preachers and angry ignorant congregations," with "no sentence not of coarse humor that clings to the memory"—another case of the Liberator

298

grinning through the horse-collar.[25] Perhaps. But all the same, the frenetic attitudes Yeats dignified with the stately phrase *saeva indignatio* from Swift's epitaph had themselves been derived through the middleman Standish O'Grady from "Shooting Niagara" and "On the Nigger Question."

One of the strands running through O'Grady's thought is easily identified as the Carlyle-Froude critique of the Irish gentry for its incompetence in scourging the restive canaille. The full force of O'Grady's anger against his class was a prodigy of nature. Set beside it, Grattan's rascals standing "in the sphere of their own infamy," Davis' "criminal dandies," and Mitchel's "genteel dastards" seem restrained. The landlords of Ireland, O'Grady said, were boys with a "boyish devotion to boyish amusement," attached only to their quadrupeds. They deserted their own wounded. They hid their ineffectuality in "anile and fatuous vituperation." They were "the sorriest and most ovine set of men that the encircling sun looks down upon today." History had no example to show of "an aristocracy so rotten in its seeming strength," so stupid, degenerate, outworn, effete, and so on.[26] Naturally this profusion of enthusiastic self-critical maledictions did not pass into Yeats's thought, for they are directed against the "lovers of horses and of women," the Irish Protestant gentry, his favorite social class.

The reader may judge for himself whether the actual record of Irish history brings support to Yeats's position. The class that had no defenders found a friend in W. B. Yeats, through chivalry, and through eccentricity too, almost as though he had contrived an Oscarian paradox for the sport of it:

> O what am I that I should not seem
> For the song's sake a fool ?[27]

But it was not quite that either; he was in earnest right enough. Lady Gregory stands in our line of vision here. The effeminate tone of Yeats's class pride—for example, in his attack on George Henry Moore[28]—suggests a source in the Persse girls' "bitter Protestant" disdain for the Catholic gentility of the neighborhood; and "A Prayer for My Daughter" is well recognized to be more at home in its matter than "A Prayer for My Son." But the same lifelong need to "bend mediaeval knees" dominates *Countess Cathleen*, drafted eight years before Lady Gregory took him under her wing. For further explanation we are thrown back on John Butler Yeats's warm personal satisfaction—"vicarious" in the literal sense—in observing the theatrical leisure of the Irish aristocracy. "After this war a struggle will come between the haves and have-nots," he said during the First World War, "and though I know that the people are always right because always for justice, yet I will be against them because they would persecute and hunt like wolves and mad dogs the people who like to idle."[29] Which came first, the father or the son ?

299

Whatever the source, W. B. Yeats's infatuation was total. It obscured not only the vices of his model, but the virtues no less. Outside the literary orbit, the Irish Protestant gentry will never be widely acclaimed for its generosity "though free to refuse"; nor for its "planted lawns" (the grounds at Lissadell, Avondale, and Moore Hall resembled barracks parade yards); nor for its Italianate patronage of the arts ("Christ save us!" O'Grady said. "You read nothing, know nothing."[30]); nor for its "tragic gaiety," for there was no tragedy. The Irish gentry will be remembered instead for its cheerful non-Yeatsian Benthamite good sense, since it provides history with its solitary example of a social class that took solid money in exchange for its privileges and went away quietly.

CHAPTER 20

The Irish Party in Maneuver

I

By the end of 1883 Parnell began to look unbeatable. He had precipitated the "fall of feudalism in Ireland," demoralized the gentry, driven "Buck-shot" Forster out of office, tamed Davitt and Dillon, silenced his maenad sisters, hurried Gladstone and the Liberal party off to conduct private debates on the hidden virtue of Home Rule, confounded a hostile papal rescript, and ridden out safely both the Phoenix Park assassinations and James Carey's garrulousness at the witness table. His lifelong enemy, the London *Times*, confessed itself mastered: "The Irishman has played his cards well, and is making a golden harvest. He has beaten a legion of landlords, lawyers, and encumbrances of all sorts out of the field, driving them into workhouses. He has baffled the greatest of legislators, and outflanked the largest of British armies in getting what he thinks his due."[1] Parnell himself noted dryly that his power already exceeded O'Connell's and was still rising. That power he now diverted into his single-minded post-Kilmainham objective: to force Parliament to make Ireland a free gift of her independence.

Parnell's first move under his revised offensive was to start up his own newspaper. Drawing from the American funds, he bought up Richard Pigott's printing presses and commenced publication of a weekly called *United Ireland* (not to be confused with various newspapers of similar name conducted by John Mitchel, Arthur Griffith, and General O'Duffy). Nobody could have said that the newspaper shared in Parnell's own qualities of silence and coldness. For editor he selected a young reporter from Cork named William O'Brien, another Irishman in possession of a fearful word hoard. Once when he was in jail he wrote a novel called *When We Were Boys* (1890). He apologized for its epic excesses; if he had had a shorter jail sentence, he said, he could have been more economical in his verbal effects. It is by no means an imperishable work of art, but it has a striking verbal energy. In writing for *United Ireland*, O'Brien developed a talent to sting and to rally that rivaled Mitchel's. Putting aside the sedate and learned journalistic style developed by the *Nation* under Duffy and the Sullivans and practiced, too, by O'Leary on the *Irish People*, he brought to perfection the Irish newspaper mannerism that Yeats called "pepper-pot."

A passage from O'Brien's leading article on the Kilmainham treaty will suggest the free and easy belligerence of *United Ireland*: ". . . the money it [the Castle] spends and the favors it distributes, and the foul toads who use it as a cistern to knot and gender in it, are just the things which make the harmless travesty of Vice-Royalty an offence and scorn to Irishmen. The toads are the gang of alien officials who nestle in the snuggeries of the Castle like as many asps in the bosom of their country. Down with the whole bundle of rottenness and imposture!" This stirring message went to press on Thursday, May 4, 1882, and appeared on the Saturday of the Phoenix Park murders. English members suggested in the House that O'Brien's prose style had inspired the murders.[2] The next Saturday his hysteria against the assassins outscreamed the English press itself.

This frenzy was the antithesis of Parnell's self-control, but Parnell liked O'Brien the better for that. He raised no objections to *United Ireland* (though he did not read it himself), and cheered O'Brien on, freeing the paper from any league executive veto and guaranteeing him whatever financial support he needed to fight off his multiplying brood of libel litigations. Later O'Brien argued that his verbal fury was never intended to be taken seriously: "Violence is the only way of insuring a hearing for moderation."[3] This stratagem obviously embodied incompatibilities, and they troubled him. He once told Wilfred Blunt, "I sometimes think of Joe Brady and O'Donovan Rossa, and my mind misgives me whether they may not all this while have been right and we the botchers."[4] The time-honored anodyne for the pains of political contradictions was the cultivation of the national mystique, and O'Brien welcomed it back affectionately from its long vacation during the hardheaded materialistic epochs of Fenianism, parliamentary obstruction, and the land war.

He could invoke without effort all the standardized, or Sullivanite, forms of sanctimonious political spirituality. The hero in his novel exclaimed: "Woe's the day [when] this high-strung Irish race of ours gives up its faith! It is to us what purity is to a woman. Without mystery, without the supernatural, both in religion and in politics, every fruit we care for turns to ashes upon Irish lips." Like Patrick Pearse he repeopled the countryside with barefoot saints "governed by the harp and the Angelus bell." The stoical Old Fenian exaltation of the man in the gap he transposed into pure maudlin. In one of the scenes of his novel the hero is on trial in Green Street

Courthouse for treason. He meets another defendant called "the poet" coming from the courtroom: " 'What luck ?' Ken whispered, as they clasped hands. The poet's large, melancholy eyes filled with a luminous glow, and the sweetest smile came over the deep-dug lines that curved from his nostrils around the corners of his mouth. 'The best of all luck—death for Ireland!' "[5] T. D. Sullivan naturally interpreted Parnell's newspaper venture as a raid into his private poetic property. As I have noted, he once belittled John O'Leary's newspaper competition with the taunt, "and it never paid." He could not say the same for *United Ireland*. O'Brien's sensationalism sent his circulation soaring to one hundred thousand, stealing away the *Nation*'s subscribers until its net worth sank toward zero.

II

To transform Irish political activity after Kilmainham into a serious parliamentary threat demanded a more disciplined Irish party than then existed. Vestiges of Butt's old oratorical society gave place to the mechanisms of the modern political machine. Like O'Connell and Stephens, Parnell ran a one-man show. He took full personal command of the party treasury, the choice of candidates, the tactics at Westminster, and all major policy decisions. He named the party's vice-chairman to suit himself, picking Justin M'Carthy, a literary man believed unlikely to be troublesome.

The old phrase, "pledge-bound Irish party," loosely used since the days of the Tenant League, now took on meaning; and the Irish members for the first time in history dared not miss a division of the House. Parnell's boldest innovation was the practice of sending Irishmen without private incomes into the House of Commons. Since the members drew no salary, he simply paid them a living allowance out of the American funds. Needless to say the scheme tightened party discipline, but shock waves followed. Frank Hugh O'Donnell resigned in protest against the plebian contamination of a society of gentlemen under the new "Tammany centralism," and Captain O'Shea expressed his grave displeasure that "the worst features of American politics had been introduced into our country by filthy swine like Parnell and his crew."[6] George Moore's book on the land war devotes a special chapter to the new Irish member as a type. A bogtrotter made drunken on the scents of Mayfair, a ruffian ignorant of Baudelaire and Wagner, he hides the tainted sources of the income that keeps him at Westminster by pretending to be an inventor or a journalist. This solemn anxiety lingered on into the last days of the Irish party, giving an added touch of contempt to the literary stereotype of the Irish politician; and one particularly hears its echo in the abstraction of those who "put party above nation."

303

III

The finished design for the heroic Parnell, the Irish colossus, the Chief, was now roughed out for the casting. He was perfectly congruent in the lofty role. His superb talent for command had overcome all the Irish competition. He excelled all his Irish comrades in his coolness under fire, drawing upon incomparable inner reserves of tranquillity and self-assurance. None of his comrades could match his disdain for every attractive public mask of English imperial motive. On the floor of the House he was in his very element: there he was not only unrivalled among the Irish members, but was conceded to be next only to Gladstone himself, the most formidable parliamentarian of the age.

It must not be supposed from Parnell's ample gifts that he was a self-created leader raised up by some act of sheer Nietzschean will. The political energy behind his succession of dazzling victories had sprung directly, unmistakably, out of the swarming social-revolutionary impulse of the Irish nation. Beginning at Westport, the revolution polarized around him. He had counseled militance; and victorious militance carried him on its shoulders for its emblem. The agrarians and Home Rulers named themselves "Parnellites," feeling the strength that they had given him flowing back upon themselves as a strength that he seemed to have given them. In Bertolt Brecht's impressive words applied to a parallel case, he became "*der Lehrer des Volkes der von den Volk gelernt hat.*" That was his secret: The teacher of the people, by the the people taught.

After Kilmainham the tonic interaction between the leader and the led slowly weakened. Parnell's authority took on increasingly the quality of sleight of hand, of regal mannerisms in a staged atmosphere. Tim Healy explained: "We created Parnell and Parnell created us." The pattern of reciprocity envisioned in his image was, unhappily, fast losing its creative force. A claque formed among the young lieutenants. Davitt thought he saw rising up a "cult of personal worship." He protested that there was too much of the "high-flown" in this new Parnell, this "Moses of the Irish race,"[7] this "Leader destined by Providence to carry them to the Goal of the National Aspirations."[8] In reply, the young lieutenants labeled Davitt a crank and commanded him to be silent.

The Parnellite cult of personal worship with its fabulous Parnell, endowed openly with supernatural attributes, fixed itself in the minds of most Irishmen. The old victories of the land war seemed through the haze of time to have been Parnell's personal magic, even to those like Joyce's Mr. Casey who had gone to jail to help win them.

> Whatever good a farmer's got
> He brought it all to pass.[9]

The "cult of personal worship" made an attractive Carlylean design out of Irish history, recasting it as the biography of the Chief, a self-moved mover with cosmic contacts. The fervor of this tribute to Parnell is altogether understandable, but it does not supply a particularly penetrating insight into the substance of Irish history.

While Parnell's private will was winning total control of the Irish party, he grew more magisterial, mysterious, inaccessible. Weeks would pass without his appearing on the floor of the House. Once Gladstone sent him an urgent message but he could not be found. There was fear that he might have been accidentally injured or killed. Pursuing every clue to the mystery, Justin M'Carthy finally felt it necessary to open his mail in search of an address. In this way the party's inner circle picked up a hint that pointed to the Kent suburb of Eltham, to the residence of Mrs. Katherine O'Shea, where he had established himself secretly but substantially, with his gold-assay laboratory set up in the basement. His romatic elusiveness was partly explained by a natural preference for the company of Mrs. O'Shea over that of T. D. Sullivan and Joe Biggar. It was later learned also that he had been critically ill and that Mrs. O'Shea's nursing care had perhaps saved his life. But an overruling motive in his disappearance was political. He understood that inertia is as essential to political warfare as spasms of energy. From 1882 to 1884 he mostly sat out the performance, waiting, surrendering the public arena to his young fighters.

IV

The Parnellite party's new discipline and centralization of leadership greatly enhanced its freedom to maneuver. James Fintan Lalor had warned the parliamentarians in 1847: "You lie helpless on the highway before the great English parties and they will trample you to death." Irish history offered ample evidence to support his contention. Melbourne, Russell, Aberdeen, and Gladstone all had thrived on their Irish alliances, but the junior partner always ended up with a headache. Parnell felt that the success of his new program depended upon his ability to avoid the old trap. Naturally, it would be necessary for him to philander, especially with the Liberals, but always short of matrimony in order not to chill the ardor of the rival suitor. For the way to Irish success at Westminster lay in the "independence of the Irish party," that is, in playing off the one English party against the other.

Parnell's Irish party of 1884, a little band now grown to thirty-odd, was still not very impressive among six hundred hostile members. It held promise, though, of great strength soon, if it could bide its time. Gladstone had decided that the Liberal party must penetrate the bottom strata of

British society in search of votes, and he had put into the legislative works a daring new extension of the franchise to include all householders. For Ireland, the bill promised to enfranchise the "mud-cabin vote," expanding the existing electorate from one-quarter million to three-quarters of a million voters. Late in 1884 the new voting reform became law. Shortly afterward a second act was passed leaving the Irish House apportionment unchanged at 103 members, even though the population had drastically declined since the number of Irish members was last fixed. Immediately the recluse of Eltham was once more in the midst of the whirl. Without waiting for formal certification by the next general election, Parnell began to demonstrate what "the independence of the Irish party" meant in practice. When Gladstone brought in a bill to extend the life of the old Crimes Act of 1882, the skeleton left behind by the Phoenix Park murders, Parnell led the Irish members into the Tory opposition lobby and defeated the government. In June 1885 Gladstone resigned and joined William E. Forster as another of the distinguished company who had been driven from office by the uncrowned king of Ireland.

A season of busy Irish political intrigue set in, as the two parties came forward to play in Parnell's game, bidding for the new Irish votes. The Tories held power only on his sufferance and were amiability itself. Lord Salisbury, the new prime minister, courteously neglected to re-enact Gladstone's Crimes Act. He also sponsored a land-purchase act. His lord lieutenant of Ireland, Lord Carnarvon, designer of the semi-independent government of Canada, solicited an interview with Parnell. The two met in a Mayfair mansion closed for the summer; and among the rolled-up carpets and covered furniture Parnell distinctly heard his host intone the magical words "Home Rule." Lord Randolph Churchill gave Parnell to believe that a Tory like himself was "as likely" to take up Home Rule "as any other Englishman": "The policy of the late government so exasperated Irishmen— maddened and irritated that imaginative and warm-hearted race—that I firmly believe that had the late government remained in office no amount of bayonets or military would have prevented outbreaks in Ireland."[10]

On behalf of the Liberal party, there came wooing Joseph Chamberlain, leader of the "radical" wing. Through his courier, Captain O'Shea, he offered Parnell a large measure of Irish municipal autonomy short of legislative independence. Parnell welcomed the bid, receptive to any concession he could get; but he refused to consider it a substitute for Home Rule. Chamberlain seems to have dreamed of himself as the next prime minister, for he also offered the Irish chief secretary's post to O'Shea, and he in turn passed along to Mrs. O'Shea the happy news that she and "the chicks" (Parnell's "chicks") were about to occupy the Viceregal Lodge.

Gladstone opened the general-election campaign of 1885 with a plea to English voters to give him an absolute majority in Parliament so that he could form a government free of Irish encumbrance. As well as Parnell could judge, there was a danger of a Liberal sweep following the new extension of the franchise. But it was believed to be to the Irish party's advantage to hold the House representation of the two English parties in near balance. Parnell therefore considered it tactically proper to attack Gladstone in *United Ireland* (naturally with great violence) and to campaign in the English Midlands, where the Irish vote was sizable, with a "Vote-Tory Manifesto" and the slogan, "Remember Gladstone and Coercion!"

Thanks to Gladstone's election reforms, the Irish party won 86 out of the 103 Irish contests, the celebrated "86 in '86." In Mayo the mud cabins swamped the big houses at the polls by a ratio of one hundred to one. The Irish party even held a majority of seats in Ulster, and it won every contest outside Ulster except for two learned Tories returned for Trinity College. Until the rise of Sinn Fein thirty years later, there would henceforth be no political party in Leinster, Munster, and Connaught other than the Irish nationalist party.

The 1885 elections gave the Liberals 334 seats and the Tories 250, so that the difference between the two was almost exactly equal to the number of Irish members. The Irish party could veto any Liberal ministry by voting with the Tories, but it could not form a stable Tory coalition government. In concert with the Liberals, however, it could make up a sound working majority; or so it seemed. By Gladstone's estimate, Parnell's vote-Tory manifesto had swung fifteen seats from Liberal to Tory. It had thus served its purpose to block the Liberals from forming a government without an Irish voice. The Irish members congratulated themselves on the wisdom of their independent course.

Gladstone's son threw Ireland and England into great excitement on December 15, 1885, with a statement to the newspapers, known to history as "the Hawarden kite" or trial balloon, launched from Gladstone's home near Chester. He suggested that his father might be ripe for conversion to Home Rule. The announcement immediately transformed the relationship of all the parliamentary parties. Gladstone offered Lord Salisbury the Liberal party's blessing if he would introduce a Tory Home Rule bill, and he delayed driving the defeated ministry out of office in the hope that he might consent. Salisbury rejected the proposal outright. He thought Gladstone was trying to split his party. He preferred to split Gladstone's party. He had a vision that Home Rule might smash the Liberals and the Parnellites together. When Parnell told an American reporter that he "expected" that Gladstone would be the one who would bring Ireland her independence, Salisbury and Lord Randolph Churchill professed themselves personally offended, withdrew Carnarvon's half-offer and denied even that any substantive conversation with Parnell had ever taken place. Without any pain Churchill was able to break off his friendship with those "imaginative and warm-hearted" Irish people, and went into Belfast to agitate the Protestants for a holy war. "Ulster will fight, and Ulster will be right," his inflammatory slogan proclaimed as he played the Tory trump, "the Orange card." He predicted hopefully that Parnell's following would disintegrate from its own contradictions: "Personall jealousies, government influences, Davitt, Fenian intrigue will all be at work, and the bishops who in their heart of hearts hate Parnell and don't care a scrap for home rule will complete the rout."[11]

For a crowning insult to the Irish party, Salisbury reintroduced Gladstone's Crimes Act as his own measure. With this declaration of war, the Tories proclaimed themselves no longer available to be "played off against the Liberals" for the Irish party's benefit. Parnell's vote-Tory manifesto in the 1885 general election seemed to have been a gamble that failed (since it had channeled votes into the party that had now become his mortal enemy). But the alternative gamble that he had declined, to keep hands off and allow Gladstone's party to win an absolute House of Commons majority, would have failed equally (since no Liberal cabinet in history would ever sponsor a Home Rule bill unless its life depended on Irish votes). Parnell's freedom of maneuver was at an end. The Irish party and the Liberal party were forced into an unhappy, sterile, and indissoluble partnership until their simultaneous deaths did them part at the close of the First World War.

v

When Gladstone finally replaced Salisbury as prime minister in February 1886, the Tories had the pleasure of watching the Home Rule issue disintegrate the Liberal party according to plan. The spoiler was Joseph Chamberlain, the "gray eminence of the Kilmainham treaty." Following the libertarian English tradition, he had begun his career in Parliament as a partisan of "Justice to Ireland," and he was still ornamented with that reputation. But the youthful disciple of John Stuart Mill would grow into the elderly caricature of a Kipling-Kitchener chauvinist, and the year 1886 was the turning point of his career. The fissure opened on an Irish tour he undertook to test for himself the sentiment of the clergy toward his scheme for municipal autonomy in lieu of Home Rule.[12] Omitting the thousand welcomes of Irish legend, Healy and O'Brien attacked him as a contemptible busybody, a "radical," and perhaps even an infidel. To broadcast their particularist anathemas, they used *United Ireland*, Parnell's newspaper. In great anger, Chamberlain cut short his tour and returned to England bent upon vengeance. He then took a portfolio in Gladstone's new cabinet, but occupied himself full-time with undercutting the prime minister. To be honest about it, he said, he was forced to re-examine certain details of Home Rule; in some respects the proposal went too far, in others not far enough, and so on.

In March 1886 Chamberlain openly broke from Gladstone, resigned from the ministry, declared war against Home Rule, and split the Liberal party. To join him in rebellion he led out of the party a good sampling of Gladstone's Whigs, including Lord Hartington, the brother of "poor Cavendish," besides many radicals. His rump of Liberal dissidents mustered in at the division on the Home Rule bill with ninety-three members. They made up something of a parliamentary party on their own, larger than Parnell's, and they gave themselves the distinctive name of "Unionist" Liberals. By slow digestion they were gradually absorbed inside the Tory party. The one-time "Danton of West Birmingham" made himself comfortable in the new home and built a nursery there for his sons Neville and Austen, famous politicians of a later time.

VI

Chamberlain's fear of Home Rule was based on his slowly maturing opinion that if England allowed Ireland any impetus toward self-government, it would be a prelude to an armed insurrection seeking total separation, a familiar line of thought later echoed by the Orange catch phrase, "Not an inch!" Gladstone was equally passionate in his own abhorrence of Irish separatism. He sponsored Home Rule to forestall separation, believing that strategic reforms at the edges of the problem could protect the imperial center. His Home Rule bill was therefore especially striking for the self-control it placed on generosity. It proposed a Dublin legislature, right enough, but forbade it to meddle with the crown, foreign affairs, the army and navy, the customs, trade, treason, titles of dignity, coinage, post office, or constabulary. After these exclusions, the Dublin parliament was to be left in control of the land, the schools, the courts, and any balance in the exchequer after paying Whitehall a levy equal to 7 percent of the total imperial budget. The "age of Burke and of Grattan" had done considerably better by Ireland. For a brief moment Parnell debated with himself whether he could support a scheme so meager.

The momentous debate on Home Rule occupied Parliament for two full months in the late spring of 1886. At the close, Parnell's speech hinted at a danger of civil war if the bill were defeated. Gladstone's last speech told off Chamberlain's opportunism: "He has trimmed his vessel and he has touched his rudder in such a masterly way that in whichever direction the

winds of heaven may blow they must fill his sails." He then made his case
for "Justice to Ireland":

> Go into the length and breadth of the world, ransack the literature of all
> countries, find, if you can, a single voice, a single book—find, I would say, as
> much as a single newspaper article, unless the product of the day, in which the
> conduct of England towards Ireland is anywhere treated except with profound
> and bitter condemnation. Are these the traditions by which we are exhorted
> to stand? No; they are a sad exception to the glory of our country. They are a
> broad and black spot upon the pages of its history. . . .

But the bill was already lost, as he knew. His closing admonition to the
House was to think well and wisely of the future of England no less than of
Ireland "before you reject this bill."[13] The vote taken late in the night on
June 7, 1886, stood at 313 for, 343 against.

Gladstone's comment on the vote was a line from "Chevy Chase": "The
child that is unborn shall rue the hunting of that day." Barry O'Brien
searched through the corridors and found Parnell in the House smoking
room, looking crushed and ill. But many were the joyful hearers of the news.
The Conservative and Unionist benches were in pandemonium and outside
the crowds sang "God Save the Queen."[14] Matthew Arnold, touring in
America, had thought Gladstone a madman, a "desperado burning his
ship," to introduce the Home Rule bill. When he read of the vote in the
Germantown, Pennsylvania, newspaper, he wrote home, "A load is taken
off my spirit."

CHAPTER 21

Enter: W. B. Yeats

I

In the general election that followed the defeat of the first Home Rule bill, the strength of the Irish party stood unchanged. Gladstone's personal stature was also undiminished, but in only six months since the Liberal victory of 1885, his party's popularity had collapsed. In England, 144 constituencies fell away from Gladstone and swung over to the opposition, giving the Tory-Unionist coalition a flat majority of 118 over Gladstone and Parnell combined. Gladstone resigned. Salisbury had recently imagined that he must wait six years before he could try again, but he was back in as many months. The Tories concluded that the Home Rule issue was a gift sent from heaven, and Chamberlain told John Morley that he "quaked" for fear the Liberal party might some day jettison Home Rule and reappear as a serious political rival.

The Tory intellectual J. A. Froude once philosophized in Carlylese that what Ireland really needed was half a century of "government that governed": "We have professed to govern, and we have not governed." Probing for that corner of the Victorian mind where caning was revered as proper pedagogy, Salisbury now proposed also a government that governed, though for a more modest twenty-year term: "My alternative policy [to Home Rule] is that parliament should enable the government of England to govern Ireland. Apply that receipt honestly, continuously, and resolutely for twenty years, and at the end of that time you will find that Ireland will be fit to accept any gifts in the way of local government or repeal of coercion laws that you may wish to give her. What she wants is government—government that she cannot hope to beat down by agitation at Westminster. . . ."[1] The most generous interpretation to put on Salisbury's Irish blueprint is contained in the phrase, "killing Home Rule with kindness." The kindness, as we have seen, was among other things a willingness to convey the great Irish estates to the peasantry at the asking price. The barb in the catch phrase is somewhat hidden, but Salisbury did propose to "kill" Home Rule, with or without the kindness of a land-purchasing scheme, by refusing to countenance any further Irish boisterousness.

Parnellites and Liberals were hypnotized by the success of the Tory verbal formulas. Attempting to neutralize the jingo magic in the word "Unionism," they invented a counter slogan, proposing the "Union of Hearts" between the two "sister Kingdoms," and they spoke warmly of the virtue of an exchange of good cheer, courtesy, and culture across the Irish Sea. Irish party wags were put on the speakers' list for all Liberal party rallies in England and displayed as living specimens of the Union of Hearts. A wave of Irish good feeling addressed itself to Englishmen, and the Irish love of moderation was stressed. Gladstone's photograph appeared on the wall in Irish nationalist homes beside the engravings of Emmet and the Chief, and William O'Brien's prose beatified the Grand Old Man "with a face like a benediction and a voice like an Archangel's."[2]

II

In the autumn of 1885 fell the twentieth anniversary of the day when John O'Leary had stood in Green Street Courthouse to hear his sentence pronounced and to pay his respects to Judge Keogh and the prosecutor Mr. Barry (now Lord Justice Barry), "that miserable man." His twenty years were up and his exile over. Wearing Rip van Winkle's beard, back he came to Ireland, bringing with him innumerable crates of books. The Dublin of 1885–86 remembered him well and respected him as always. But gripped by the Home Rule fever, Dublin was slow to seek O'Leary's out-of-style opinions. After a rousing welcome home he was shortly forgotten. He reminded himself that after waiting twenty years, he would now have to wait still longer. Parnellism, he said, must have time to "play itself out."[3]

In his habitual unparanoid manner, O'Leary still wished Parnell well, but was skeptical as always of what he could accomplish with heretical non-Fenian tactics. He had discounted each of the stages of Parnell's development since the breakup of the New Departure conferences of 1879. At homecoming, he was still unchanged. We pick up a trace of his 1886 thoughts in a conversation between Barry O'Brien and the famous English radical, John Bright, discussing a letter written by the most honored of the Old Fenians, that is, by O'Leary. The interview proceeded as follows:

> *Mr. Bright.* I am not afraid that Home Rule would lead to separation. We are too strong for that. But I think that there are certain men in Ireland who would make an effort to obtain separation. I mean what you call Old Fenians. I saw a letter from one of those men a few days ago—he does not know I saw it—a very long letter. I was much interested in it. I should like to know what you are going to do with him. He is an upright, honorable man, ready, I can quite believe, to risk anything for his country. Now, he wants separation, and he wants to obtain it in regular warfare. He is mad, but a madman with a conscience is sometimes dangerous. I should think that he could appeal to the

young men of the country, young fellows full of sentiment and enthusiasm—(a pause)—fools; but they might make themselves troublesome to your Irish parliament. Now, what will you do with —— ? Will he be content with an Irish parliament of any sort?

[*Mr. O'Brien.*] Well, Mr. Bright, I am in a good position to answer that question. I saw —— last night. I asked him if he would accept an Irish parliament and an Irish executive which would have the fullest control of Irish affairs—the connection with England, of course, to be preserved.

Mr. Bright. Yes; and what did he say?

[*Mr. O'Brien.*] He said, "I would take an oath of allegiance to an Irish parliament; I will never take it to an English parliament. I would enter an Irish parliament; I would give it a fair trial—."

Mr. Bright. Well, you surprise me. This is certainly a new light. The man is quite honorable. He will do what he says. Well, but does your friend think that you will get a Home Rule parliament?

[*Mr. O'Brien.*] No. He thinks that we are living in a fool's paradise, and that his turn will come again.[4]

Settled down once again in Dublin to wait until his turn would come again, O'Leary looked about him and found that he did not care at all for Parnell's "stalwart lieutenants." The political prosperity of the Bantry band necessarily dismayed him, though unrecorded are his thoughts upon T. D. Sullivan's elevation to lord mayor of Dublin, that honored post which would in due time make him eligible for coded listing in *Finnegans Wake*. Nor did he take a reading of Healy's personal horoscope. His general objections to "a certain sort of people going into parliament" cited Thomas Sexton as his bad example.[5] Willy O'Brien and John Dillon he thought a pair of clowns. O'Brien's nine trips to jail did not seem to him much of a martyrdom. He was appalled that the Irish parliamentary party had scrapped the Fenians' principle of no priests in politics and surrendered the ancient nonsectarian redoubt.

The Union of Hearts O'Leary particularly condemned. He had once warned Parnell that Irish members could not long resist the corruption of Westminster, and now he thought he saw their corruption manifest. Irishmen had no cause to love the Gladstone of the Hawarden kite, he said; it was the same Gladstone who had sent Parnell to jail. English generosity was merely a healthy respect for Irish force. "If Mr. Gladstone, for his own ends, choose to come a certain way in our direction, well and good. But that is quite his concern."[6] The fixed base of Irish political behavior seemed to him as simple and clear and as true for 1886 as it had been for 1865: "We hear constantly of the diminution of disaffection in Ireland, and even of late we have been hearing of the growth of affection, but all that is very idle talk. Disaffected we have been, disaffected we are, and disaffected we shall remain, till the English let go their grip of us."[7]

313

O'Leary's automatic impulse was to start organizing. Lectures delivered at Cork in February 1886 and at Newcastle-on-Tyne in December 1886, one just before and one just after the defeat of the first Home Rule bill, sounded like the Old Fenian editor, as though the twenty years of absence had been merely the time before next Saturday's issue of the *Irish People*. He set about to resuscitate a dormant network of Young Ireland clubs by recruiting, according to an authoritative witness, from "clerks" and "farmers' sons"[8] in the manner of the old Confederate clubs of 1848. Rowing against the Home Rule tide, he made only modest headway. His reported remark to Yeats that he possessed (and sought) no more than "two or three" disciples suggests an attempt to put the best face on an enterprise not thriving.

O'Leary found already in existence a Gaelic Athletic Association, fiercely anticricket and prohurling. Its cantankerous founder was Michael Cusack, known to readers of Joyce as "the citizen" of *Ulysses* and under his proper name in *Stephen Hero* and *A Portrait*. Cusack had made enemies, who then dethroned him, and the association passed under the patronage of Archbishop Croke, a keen sportsman.[9] O'Leary believed that Irish sport needed Fenian guidance more than ecclesiastical sanction. IRB men moved in and took control of the GAA, and O'Leary became one of the editors of the *Gael*, the organ of revolutionary anticricket athleticism.

III

Unquestionably, O'Leary's most spectacular national-cultural enterprise was literary. Everybody knows that shortly after he came home from exile, he made the acquaintance of W. B. Yeats, a newborn infant when the convict first entered prison in England; and that the providential conjunction of the two extraordinary minds marks the point of origin of the modern Irish literary movement. As an actor in Irish history in his own right, Yeats now appears *in situ* in our narrative for the first time since he was hurried out of Sligo in his crib during the Fenian troubles.

At the Dublin Cosmopolitan Club, an intellectual-discussion society where the two first met, O'Leary startled the assembled members (all but the one) with the pronouncement that the young poet, then twenty-one, was the only person in the room "who will ever be reckoned a genius."[10] No other Fenian had that percipience. When genius is up for bid, one cannot be pedantic about inconsequentials, but genius apart, Yeats was not the perfect nationalist recruit. His great-grandfather and grandfather had been Anglican rectors serving "the enemy," the Ascendancy pales in Sligo and Down. His father, a gentle, loquacious bohemian, could discern that the Irish nationalists were not outright lunatics, though his sympathies were aloof and critical. Yeats's mother's family, the Pollexfens of Sligo, were loyalist businessmen, "hucksters" in the common if not in the Yeatsian usage of that term. According to John Butler Yeats, the Pollexfens were not readily distinguishable from ordinary Orangemen in the narrowness of their outlook, an opinion not contradicted in Yeats's memoirs and poems. Yeats was hardly Irish even in the geographical sense. He had been born in Dublin, but the family moved to England when he was two. Except for holidays in Sligo, he had grown up a Londoner. In the early 1880s the Yeatses were back in Dublin again and were living there when the meeting with O'Leary took place, but shortly afterward they left for London once more, this time for good.

Irishmen nursed a persistent suspicion that the convert Yeats was not really converted, and that on social and political issues, at least, the rebirth had failed to take. Yeats's Unionist biographer Joseph Hone was puzzled that O'Leary's raid could ever have succeeded at all. "I never quite understood, nor did he ever fully explain, what brought him into the Irish movement," he said, adding that all Dublin Unionists were naturally expected to grouse about the Union and to invent sarcasms at the Englishman's expense, but that actually to associate with "papists" and separatists was carrying criticism too far—the old syndrome of Grattan's Parliament once more.[11] Yeats himself once said musingly of O'Leary, "I often wonder why he gave me his friendship."[12]

If Yeats's Irish bond was somewhat spongy by and large, it made a sturdy knit along the literary branch. When he met O'Leary, his poetic imagination was unattached. The localized English affections he would never find attractive. Decades of physical residence in Chiswick, Bloomsbury, and Oxford, from childhood to old age, were to leave not the slightest trace of English mannerism upon his work. As for English letters, he came on the scene to find them at dead end as the great line of romantic poetry petered out in "the tragic generation" and expired in the eccentricities of Swinburne, Wilde, and Symons. The family's distinguished friend William Morris was searching for a fresh poetic elixir even as far as the mists of Iceland. Yeats at age twenty-one was searching, too, groping to find his path in Clapham orientalism, in imitations of Shelley and Spenser, in an art school. Just then O'Leary appeared. He told him to forget the art school—he was a poet. He gave him armloads of books by Irish authors unknown in London and disdained as subliterature in Edward Dowden's and Sir John Mahaffy's Dublin drawing rooms.*

* At the same moment that Yeats received O'Leary's Irish books, he found A. P. Sinnett's *Esoteric Buddhism*. Irish nationalism and the occult thus came to occupy the center of his life simultaneously. O'Leary railed at the rival, but Yeats held firm. He reasoned that magic was simply another spirituality like Ireland itself. To take a stroll to Soho for an afternoon with a medium was precisely equivalent to a journey into Sligo "to sit at turf fires" and, as time passed, a good deal more convenient.

Among O'Leary's Irish writers (besides Mitchel, Davis, and Mangan, whom we have already met) there was Ulster-born William Allingham, latterly a friend of Tennyson's and a colleague of J. A. Froude's on *Fraser's Magazine*. In Fenian times he had written an authentic Irish classic, a volume of couplets on the agrarian problem in the style of George Crabbe, called *Laurence Bloomfield in Ireland*.* O'Leary had praised it highly in the *Irish People* and printed lengthy excerpts to save his impecunious subscribers the purchase price. It was an impressive work, and it is impressive yet, but Yeats had no interest in grievances and passed it by. He studied carefully, though, a number of Allingham's short nostalgic lyrics that, in Yeats's phrase, wedded race to Ballyshannon's "hill and wood"; and he was especially excited when the poet got around to the fairies.

Then there were the works of Samuel Ferguson, who died at a venerable age in the same year that Yeats and O'Leary met. Since his youthful exploits on the *Dublin University Magazine*, where we last saw him, he had settled into a knighthood, a rich marriage, and a government sinecure. Along the way he had written a farce called *Father Tom and the Pope*, a lampoon against Catholic illiteracy, which he attributed to the priests' sabotage of the national schools on the grounds that "ignorance is the thrue mother of piety." It is the solitary literary masterpiece of Orangeism as such, an honor so ambiguous that he kept his authorship a secret to his dying day. In the year of the monster meetings he had toyed with Davis' nationalism. The residue was an elegy on Davis and a testy farewell to Davis' heirs:

> I do not care a button for Young Ireland, or Old Ireland;
> But as between the two, I rather like old Dan,
> And I wish the *Nation* would let the agitation
> Die a humbug as it first began!

But all the while he remained a poet in after hours, pursuing his old hobby of trying to adapt Irish prosody to English verse. A lifetime of patient work never surpassed a single happy impulse in his twenty-third year:

> They're glancing through the glimmer of the quiet eve,
> Away in milky wavings of neck and ankle bare;
> The heavy-sliding stream in its sleepy song they leave,
> And the crags in the ghostly air.

Many years later George Russell told Austin Clarke that he and Yeats had taken their "twilight hue" and their "vowel music" from these Gaelic "internal assonances" in "The Fairy Thorn,"[13] a more convincing explanation than T. S. Eliot's stereotyped attribution to "the pre-Raphaelite mode."

Every romantic, Yeats among them, carried an identical emotional set

* It stand beside *When We Were Boys* in Bloom's extraordinary Eccles Street library

against the new nineteenth-century urban jungle, against William Cobbett's "Great Wen"; and each found cherished affections in primitivism, the obverse of the coin. Out of the variety of experience was engendered a variety of primitivisms. Cobbett himself exalted the Wiltshire yeoman who brewed his own ale; Morris, the medieval handicraftsman; Synge, the endlessly fresh individuality of the Aranman whose world had not yet been fractured by "the division of labor." Ferguson has singled out the Ulster peasant's tenacious piety toward his pre-Christian superstitions. When the fairies and assonances joined in Ferguson's harmonious combination, they overwhelmed Yeats. To London and Dublin he proclaimed his finding: Ferguson was "the greatest poet Ireland has produced," and he seconded O'Leary's judgment that this Belfast Orangeman had served the Irish nation better than the Old Fenian veteran himself.

Yeats's youthful discovery of Allingham and Ferguson provided the base for his unique contribution to Irish thought, the proposition that Ireland's purest essence was located in the peasants' primitive belief in holy wells and fairy thorns and in those supernatural "pale windy people" who dwelt with "white lillies among dim shadows, [in] windy twilights over grey sands." His great find possessed substantial virtues. It was militantly anti-philistine. It was courteously anticlerical. It destroyed the old stage Irishman, setting a new one in his place. It was not a fantasy primitivism: the base was "really there," and hence it was almost populist. It was literally inexhaustible, so that when the folklore commission set out after the Treaty to gather up all the riches, it found itself in possession of a billion words more or less, endless iterations of Yeats's *Celtic Twilight*. Moreover, it actually generated poetry, filling a special and unique little niche in the English literary canon. But it also invited Yeats and more particularly his imitators, his "fleas," to the artistic vice of quaintness. Among the Irish ethnic traits that presented themselves to an observer in 1886, the belief in fairy thorns was undoubtedly one. But to insist that it was the sole trait of importance was bound eventually to outrage good sense, as Yeats himself concluded at last.

Ferguson's antiquarianism had also stumbled upon the Irish sagas and had begun to exploit them. One adaptation in an epic called *Congal* constitutes his major work. Yeats paid it formal deference but complained of its length, always a suspicious criticism, although its fourteen-syllable line (compelling a mental accompaniment to the tune of "The Wearing of the Green") does give a physical sensation of taskwork:

> And southward still to where the weird De Danaan kings lie hid,
> High over Boyne, in cavern'd cairn and mountain pyramid.[14]

And yet the reader will catch in the internal half-ryhmes a stunt with which

Ferguson's young imitator would ornament his fame. In point of fact, *Congal* is the best example we have of a successful exercise in the mode with which James Macpherson's *Ossian* failed. Ferguson also wrote several shorter versions of the sagas, including the Deirdre story. Another, called "Conary," a very free Victorianized translation of "The Raid on Da Derga's Hostel," Yeats occasionally nominated, though not convincingly, as the best poem ever produced in Ireland.

Ferguson had broken open the main storehouse of the Irish saga, but the choicest exhibit, the hero Cuchullain, the Irish Achilles, he left almost untouched. By right of discovery this priceless claim fell to Standish O'Grady. In 1878 O'Grady had published a prose translation of the Cuchullain myth treated as an objective record in the history of Ireland, his intuition having told him that it could not be other than true. Like his model, the "historian" James Macpherson, he released himself from the "curb of history" and was thus free to "give full expression to the feelings that arose within."[15] A special flamboyance colors O'Grady's epic style. It was not taken from Carlyle now, but from Macpherson spiced with Lang, Leaf, and Myers' familiar unloved translation of the *Iliad*. While his distressing prose mannerism was later to be ridiculed by James Joyce and Flann O'Brien, there were some (George Russell, for example) who loved it; and his pages delineated the original outline of Yeats's Irish mythology.

The sensation of a sudden burst of splendor was common among the Irish writers at this moment in their careers. O'Grady had no hesitation in asserting that his bonanza was "incomparably higher in intrinsic worth than the corresponding ages of Greece."[16] George Moore's metaphor for rediscovered Ireland was "The Untilled Field," and Yeats (momentarily matter of fact) wrote to Katherine Tynan, "I think you will be right to make your ballad Irish, you will be so much more original—one should have a specialty."[17] Latecomers would find difficulty in rekindling the pioneer's mood. Joyce, for example, could see nothing in the old Irish literary tradition worth his time, and he pronounced Lady Gregory's folklore "sorrowful and senile." But in the beginning everything was golden and morning-fresh, and Yeats recaptured Davis' emotion when he had cried out under a very different stimulus, "Arigna must be pierced with shafts." Yeats set everybody an example of courage, said Moore. He also set an example of solid and uninterrupted literary accomplishment, starting from the moment when the suddenly released flood of his Irish poems and essays burst into the press in 1887 (see the bibliographical listing of his first publications in chronological order in Allan Wade, *A Bibliography of the Writings of W. B. Yeats* [London: R. Hart-Davis, 1951]). "In the presence of his theme," he became overnight not just a poet, but a very good poet. With O'Leary rounding up patrons to pay the printer, he published at age twenty-three

The Wanderings of Usheen, the finest sustained apprentice poem to appear in the English language in half a century.

IV

The Parnell-Gladstone Union of Hearts soon escaped out of its strict political environment to operate as an aesthetic influence. For poets, the moral issue it raised was to be painful and complicated, and no final stability of attitude toward it could ever be found. The greater audience for Irish writers was always to be among Englishmen, less spontaneously poetical than Irishmen but more dutiful in the actual cash purchase of printed pages. It was therefore thought wise not to outrage English feelings, as Yeats's delicacy in withholding "Easter 1916" and *The Dreaming of the Bones* from publication during wartime showed. But there was very little impulse to flatter English opinion, either; and the stance of the "West Briton" was altogether unthinkable. "She had no right to call him a West Briton before people," said Gabriel Conroy in Joyce's "The Dead." Deference to England carried social stigmata, disaffection being the norm. It also carried occasionally pangs of private guilt. Above all, it was a heavy weight upon the imagination. Anybody with an urge (like Anthony Trollope) to conceive a West Briton novel was quite certain to give birth to an aesthetic cretin, and Yeats was moved more than once to state in public his contempt for all the belles-lettres ever composed in the penumbra of Trinity College loyalism.

O'Leary's advice on this quandary of the sensibility was unclear. He insisted that Irishmen should be Irish, like Ferguson's "kindly Irish of the Irish, neither English nor Italian." Still, the noisy Irish pothouse patriot was no less distressing to him than he would later be to Joyce and Yeats: "Abuse of England is too often but the mere stock-in-trade of canting agitators, frequently the imperfect utterance of the illiterate." And he proposed the paradox that the Union of Hearts and the "abuse of England" were identities: "Queerly enough, the canting agitator has changed his stock-in-trade since. Now he sings the praise of the Saxon. He is all for the Union of Hearts and full of faith in the English democracy. But 'tis only the Englishman who believes him, and in him [the Englishman] is only listening to the echo of his . . . own unwisdom."[18] There was perhaps a valid point here; but if one was not permitted either to praise or to abuse England, one would naturally be puzzled to know just what attitude was allowed.

A popular solution to this aesthetic impasse was to be found in Matthew Arnold's essay, "The Study of Celtic Literature" (1867). This work had been published in the year of the Fenian rising, a time when it was not a dissociation of ideas for earnest Englishmen, when thinking of the Irish, to wish "to fairly unite, if possible in one people with them." According to Arnold's ethnology, the Teutonic and the Celtic temperaments are polarities: the one masculine, energetic, and heavy; the other feminine, artistic, and incompetent. The Celt and the Saxon harmonized sweetly when joined together, though in isolation each was a cacophony. The Victorian personality he thought enriched by a partial "commingling" of the two polarities, and he cited the authority of John Morley, a future chief secretary for Ireland, for the opinion that except for "the lively Celtic wit," infused through the Celtic "blood" of the Norman, "Germanic England would not have produced a Shakespeare." But as Arnold saw it, the fusion of the two creative opposites was still incomplete.

It seems transparent that Arnold was offering, besides an ethnopoetic theory, topical advice on "the Irish problem." He declared the Union of Great Britain to be a natural organic unity: Saxon *cum* Celt. The racial mission of any Saxon was to command the practical world of politics and business, encircling the world with "doors that open, windows that shut, locks that turn, razors that shave, coats that wear, watches that go." Yet who could deny it?

> For dullness, the creeping Saxons,
> For beauty and amorousness, the Gaedhils.

The Celt too was indispensable and his racial mission, like that of Evelyn Waugh's Welshman—just to sing.

Some critics thought from the start that the ethnicism of Arnold's Celtic essay was nonsense. Their dour scientism did not prevent it from building up an enormous influence.[19] It has always held interest for Irishmen, in part, no doubt, because of the novelty that a distinguished Englishman could find any virtue at all, even of a secondary sort, in the Irish temperament. Irish poets have particularly cherished the essay, for it said in effect that their imagination was the sole thing of importance in Ireland and it commanded English readers to pay it the honor it deserved.[20] Every Irish writer, from Yeats's first beginnings down to Frank O'Connor's valedictory eighty years later, has felt an urge to work within Arnold's categories, though not always toward Arnold's conclusions.

The simplest Irish adaptation of Arnold's ethnicism was to take it as it stood. William O'Brien, a partisan of the Union of Hearts, expropriated the idea complete with all its parts. In his novel the good priest explains the theory to an Irish miller: "Do you know, Myles, whenever I look at your fire I never despair of a union between Ireland and England! The coal has the staying power, the body; give me the turf for the poetry, the glow, and the soul of the thing; but the two make a capital blend."[21] Such literal-minded plagiarism from Arnold was rare, though George Russell's peculiar dualistic combination of aether and animal husbandry somewhat resembled it.

Yeats's own adaptation of Arnold held fast to his appraisal of the poetics of the Celt, leaving intact all the listed virtues: sentiment, magic, poetry, titanism, melancholy, style, and intensity. He also preserved Arnold's dualism, but he made the two halves discordant instead of complementary. His poetic imagination declared a holy war against a paraphernalia of trigonometry, Newton, economic grievance, George Eliot, "the good citizen," logic, adding-machine religion, social leveling, and the anti-poetry of doors that open and windows that shut. At first he gave this cluster of vices no specific ethnic designation. Arnold's complement of Saxon and Celt emerged from Yeats's mind as an antithesis, formulated in the well-known battle standard: "the war of the soul against the intellect." "The soul" was Celtic, just as Arnold had said. But Arnold's creeping Saxon dropped out of the dualism, supplanted in the beginning by faceless abstract international philistines, of no fixed address, but gradually localized as Irishmen who "hated the *Playboy*," and old "Paudeen of the fumbling wits."

v

O'Leary could hardly have anticipated that his disciple would honor the injunction against the "canting abuse of England" with such high scrupulousness. One might suppose that the word "England" would be indispensable to speech in a great corpus of verse whose governing theme was modern Ireland. Yet for the first thirty years of his career Yeats succeeded in banning it from his poetry absolutely. During the next twenty years, the word got into the poems once, in "Easter 1916":

> For England may keep faith
> For all that is done and said.

It also got into the plays once, in the *Dreaming of the Bones*, subversively as Yeats thought, in the phrase "English robbers," which he immediately corrected with the chivalrous concession:

> In the late Rising
> I think there was no man of us but hated
> To fire at soldiers who but did their duty
> And were not of our race. . . .[22]

So a half-century of his career had passed. Meanwhile the First World War had come and gone, giving him occasion to scold Pearse for being a "pro-German," though one entitled to the benefits of "the truce of the Muses," and to berate Mitchel, normally his favorite, for having "exalted the hatred of England above the love of Ireland." The "gaping harpies" that are "on our rooftree now" he blamed upon Mitchel, the main event taking place as he wrote being the opening battles of the First World War.[23] A few years before he died the tabooed word appeared again in the famous conundrum from "The Man and the Echo":

> Did that play of mine send out
> Certain men the English shot?

There was one additional appearance. But otherwise Ireland's colonial condition, the root fact of Irish history, was represented in the verses of Ireland's national poet by an almost total blank.

In the last year of his life, Yeats broke this silence with a poem called "The Ghost of Roger Casement," a sarcasm on the Chamberlain family's imperial chickens come home to roost, reinforced with indignation against the willingness of the English government to use the frame-up as an instrument of statecraft if and when necessary:

> O what has made that sudden noise?
> What on the threshold stands?
> It never crossed the sea because
> John Bull and the sea are friends;
> But this is not the old sea
> Nor this the old seashore.
> What gave that roar of mockery,
> That roar in the sea's roar?
> *The ghost of Roger Casement*
> *Is beating on the door.*[24]

Sub specie aeternitatis this is piercing satire. But how odd that Yeats should have taken up his theme at that tardy hour after a lifetime of shying away from it. When we turn to Yeats's letters, we find on February 11, 1937, a letter to Ethel Mannin offering a gloss on the poem as follows: "I am an old Fenian and I think the old Fenian in me would rejoice if a Fascist nation or government controlled Spain, because that would weaken the British empire, force England to be civil to Indians, perhaps to set them free and loosen the hand of English finance in the East of which I hear occasionally."[25] I assume that the non sequitur of Yeats's rejoicing for India upon Franco's victory needs no elucidation. Less obvious is the peculiarity of his timing. The elementary message that Davis, Mitchel, Gavan Duffy, and Pearse could not put through to him in half a century of iteration had come instantaneously by way of Joseph Goebbels and Wyndham Lewis—just when it was no longer apposite to Ireland. The unspoken burden of his song is: *Wir fahren gegen Engelland!* (We are marching against England!). Sir Roger Casement's function in the poem is to signify that if he could come back to Wilhelmstrasse in 1938 he would find Unity of Being there, not the cynical decadence that greeted him in 1916. One could no doubt search and find Old Fenians who might have said that (though many more probably would not). One difference between them and Yeats was that at least they had been saying it all their lives.

The Casement poem is something special and unique. Mostly the Union of Hearts governed Yeats's imagination. He occasionally argued that even *Cathleen ni Houlihan* was—if the truth were known—really nonpolitical, a startling contention at variance with his original dedication (quickly dropped) "To the Memory of William Rooney," a proto-Sinn Feiner whose patriotic frenzy made Arthur Griffith's seem tepid. Still, it is true that the word "England" is missing from the play, too, its place filled by "strangers" who had got possession of the Old Woman's "four beautiful green fields," it does not say how. The Irishman of the play is about to be translated into eternity in the passive voice, but no agent is actually going to kill him. The Abbey audience was undoubtedly in on the secret of who the "strangers" might be, but when the play was staged in Stockholm during Yeats's Nobel-award festivities, the point was lost. Not recognizing the "strangers" and never having heard of "Killala" before, the Swedish producer was forced to depart from the Abbey's classic direction for acting the play. Yeats reported that the Swede's alterations were most agreeable to him, since the play was really "symbolic,"[26] that is, nonreferential—and as relevant to any random time and place as to Mayo-Sligo in 1798. This was stretching credibility thin, but had O'Leary himself not disapproved of the "canting abuse of England"?

There was a price exacted for this accommodation to the Union of Hearts. It cost him a measure of emotional severance from those Irishmen who were incapable of his impartiality. It led him into a mare's nest of historical confusions. It brought him around to a sort of inverted Union of Hearts in which the Celtism of the Celt rather than the Saxonism of the Saxons was blamed for all the trouble, even back to the fall of man. His best-known formulation of the Irishman's human nature says:

> Out of Ireland have we come.
> Great hatred, little room,
> Maimed us at the start.
> I carry from my mother's womb
> A fanatic heart.[27]

Evidently, the original sin of Ireland is unmotivated fanaticism, "mere anarchy." And that being the case, the poet is doomed with the rest, and he proposes to enjoy his sinful tantrums to the full limit, *fág an bealach !* clear the road!

For all that, Yeats's Union of Hearts stratagem had immeasurable pragmatic value unappreciated by those fellow countrymen of his who were always asking him to show them some results. In the nationalist division of labor, he made the most winning of all the Irish ambassadors-at-large. His historical task was not militance at home but diplomacy abroad; and it would be hard to find fault with George Russell's statement on the Abbey's twenty-fifth birthday that "it was our literature more than our political activities which created outside Ireland a true image of our nationality." By breaking through the Englishman's guard and surging in on him with the winsome qualities that Arnold thought the Celt's "special charm and power," Yeats undoubtedly helped to soften the imperial bond. He led hostile Englishmen gently toward the difficult new idea that if Ireland should ever finally succeed in forcing a separation, they need not panic. The infant nation could be expected to flow abundantly with Celtic sentiment, magic, poetry, titanism, melancholy, style, and intensity.

For Joyce a Union of Hearts between himself and the "brutish empire" never tempted in any guise. Both *A Portrait* and *Ulysses* explicitly state their contempt for the Union of Hearts.* The sodden Saxon vices depicted in Arnold's essay Joyce endorsed in full, adding his own embellishments, "beer, beef, bibles, bulldogs, battleships, buggery and bishops." All his Englishmen are clowns and scoundrels, barring only Shakespeare and Dr. Newman. The Saxon delegation in *Ulysses* is particularly rich in comic monsters: Haines, the Oxford dilettante; Orangeman Deasy; the hangman Horace Rumbold of Liverpool; Private Carr and Private Compton; Lieutenant Colonel Tompkins-Maxwell ffrenchmullan Tomlinson of Limehouse; the flagellating Mrs. Mervyn Talboys; and Edward VII, who brings onstage in the "Circe" chapter a bucket with the label *défense*

---

* From *Ulysses* on the Union of Hearts:

"Prove that he [Bloom] had loved rectitude from his earliest youth. . . .

"In 1885 he had publicly expressed his adherence to the collective and national economic programme advocated by James Fintan Lalor, John Fisher Murray, John Mitchel, J. F. X. O'Brien and others, the agrarian policy of Michael Davitt, the constitutional agitation of Charles Stuart Parnell (M.P. for Cork City), the programme of peace, retrenchment and reform of William Ewart Gladstone (M.P. for Midlothian, N.B.) and, in support of his political convictions, had climbed up into a secure position amid the ramifications of a tree on Northumberland road to see the entrance (2 February 1888) into the capital of a demonstrative torchlight procession of 20,000 torchbearers, divided into 120 trade corporations, bearing 2,000 torches in escort of the marquess of Ripon and John Morley."

The last two persons on this list were Gladstone's lieutenants, a category for which Joyce's contempt was boundless. See *Ulysses*, p. 701; also Joyce, *Critical Writings*, pp. 197–200 and 209–13 for an extension of remarks on Ripon, Rosebery, and Morley. On Gladstone, see also *A Portrait*, pp. 249–50.

d'uriner. He dances "slowly, solemnly, rattling his bucket" and sings "with soft contentment":

> On coronation day, on coronation day,
> O, won't we have a merry time,
> Drinking whisky, beer and wine![28]

These fine forays speak of affections that Joyce's fellow countrymen could fully share, for to say of an Irishman that he is Anglophobic is not to communicate anything very astonishing. When Yeats's good offices got Joyce put on the British pension list, it could not be said that his benefactors got any reciprocal value whatever, other than the strictly aesthetical.

CHAPTER 22

Catastrophe

I

The Union of Hearts surrendered the momentum of the Parnellite resurgence. Under the newest Whig alliance, the field command of Irish affairs passed out of Parnell's hands and into Gladstone's. Within his natural limitations, Gladstone made a superb Irish general; and yet—who could deny it?—it was an incongruous role for even the friendliest Englishman. Meanwhile, the breathing spell that resulted from the Union of Hearts allowed the Unionists time to venture out with their own potent weapons: divide and rule and counterattack.

After the defeat of the first Home Rule bill Parnell fell ill of rheumatic fever. He was bedridden for a long time, and Tim Healy thought he might die. When he had recovered, he kept in seclusion. As he saw it, his task was once again to wait. In six years or perhaps sooner, there would be another general election, and if Gladstone should be returned, Home Rule would once more come alive. His seclusion was troubled, though, for his enemies decided to smoke him out.

The agrarian issue flared up again. The fifteen-year term for the judicial freeze of rents proved too long. Agricultural prices after 1881 continued to decline, then in 1886 they suddenly plunged 30 percent. Judicial rents had once more become rack-rents, just like old times. Parnell introduced a new land bill in the summer of 1886, and when it was duly defeated by the Salisbury government, the Irish party lieutenants went into action on their own responsibility. William O'Brien and John Dillon reignited the land war with a new offensive, the "Plan of Campaign."[1] Under this scheme, distressed peasants were to offer the landlord what they considered a fair adjusted rent. If he refused the offer, they would pay him what they had offered, and would deposit the difference in a general war chest to be used to fight evictions. Parnell said later that he was not consulted or even informed until the Plan of Campaign had been in operation for some months. He disapproved, he said. In his opinion, every action that did not directly advance Home Rule was improper, and he declared, "If I had been in a position to advise about it, I candidly admit to you that I should have advised against it."[2]

Salisbury replied to the Plan of Campaign with the unoriginal formula, conciliation plus coercion. Parnell's land bill was copied, reintroduced as a ministerial measure, and passed. Simultaneously, Arthur Balfour, the new Irish chief secretary, introduced a coercion bill containing all the advanced modern features of Gladstone's Crimes Act of 1882—suspension of habeas corpus and trial by magistrate instead of by jury, plus a novel feature, perpetuity. So extreme a measure was not expected to be wholly palatable even to the English public. In the midst of the House debate on Balfour's bill, the London *Times* in a spirit of helpfulness began a series of feature articles entitled "Parnellism and Crime," stirring the misty memories of battle alarms in the Mayo land war. The series reached a climax on April 18, 1887, timed to the second reading of the crimes bill, in a sensational document, a facsimile of a letter signed "Chas. S. Parnell," stating that his public denunciation of the Phoenix Park murders was not sincerely intended and approving the murder of Thomas Burke as "no more than his deserts." One of Barry O'Brien's friends in the Liberal party picked up the *Times* that morning on his breakfast table. "The first thing which met my eye was that infernal letter," he said. "Well, I did not much care about my breakfast after reading it. 'There goes Home Rule,' said I, 'and the Liberal Party too.'"[3]

A casual glance at the facsimile suggests imposture. It was written in two different styles of penmanship. With the sheet folded in the middle to make four pages in the way of old-fashioned letter writers, it carried the message on page one and the signature isolated on page four. The *Times* explained that this oddity was "an obvious precaution" by which "the half-sheet might if necessary be torn off and the letter disclaimed." It also directed the reader's attention especially to two scratched out words as "undesigned proof of authenticity." In anticipation of Parnell's denial of authorship, the *Times* said ominously: "We possess several samples of the member for Cork's undoubted handwriting and signature," i.e., other incriminating letters. It dared him to bring suit for libel.

The letter really was a forgery, a fact about which Parnell naturally felt well assured in his own mind. He said to Mrs. O'Shea in that unfortunate private language of the Eltham household that she later made the world's property: "Wouldn't you hide your head with shame if your King were so stupid as that, my Queen?"[4] He was troubled, however, about proving the forgery to the public. Although botched, its cleverness was striking, too.

It was plainly the work of some imaginative person, some miscast novelist who was at the same time intimate with Irish generalship in the land war. Hence, the letter had the quality that one of the conspirators later called "intrinsic probability"; that is, it sounded exactly the way Parnell's enemies thought he ought to sound.

Parnell refused the *Times*'s invitation to sue, and there the matter rested. A year passed, and in June 1888 Frank Hugh O'Donnell emerged out of retirement in Germany and instituted the lawsuit that Parnell had avoided. The motive is a mystery, for his stated explanation is decidedly unhelpful: ". . . the attacks of the *Times* upon the Parnellites had the unexpected result of forcing me to bring an action for libel against the mighty newspaper."[5] Parnellites have always suspected that he must have been working for Chamberlain. But no conclusive evidence is at hand, and Healy's explanation of the motive was about as good as any: O'Donnell was "off his nut."

If Chamberlain were not the Machiavelli behind O'Donnell's lawsuit, he was, temporarily at least, the chief gainer by it. The *Times* retained the attorney general, a member of Salisbury's government, as its defense counsel. Snubbing the plaintiff and ignoring his absurd litigation, he turned the courtroom into a Unionist political rally against Parnellism and crime. For *pièce de résistance* he introduced into evidence a packet of brand new incriminating letters, some purportedly by Parnell, others by Patrick Egan. Among them was this letter dated from Kilmainham jail and addressed to Egan:

DEAR E.

What are these fellows waiting for? This inaction is inexcusable; our best men are in prison and nothing is being done.

Let there be an end to this hesitency. Prompt action is called for.

You undertook to make it hot for old Forster and Co. Let us have some evidence of your power to do so.

My health is good, thanks.

Yours very truly,
CHARLES S. PARNELL

This forgery was a good deal less imaginative than the *Times*'s first. There was also a marked orthographic degeneration to be seen in the word "hesitency."

The augmented scandal now demanded some sort of action by the House of Commons. A special commission was set up to examine evidence on the Parnellite charge of forgery, and in addition, to study the history of Ireland and its multitudinous troubles. The Parnellites instituted a desperate search to find the forger. They suspected two men. One was Captain O'Shea. The other was Richard Pigott, former publisher of the Old Fenian newspaper, the *Irishman*. Pigott had once attempted to extort money out of Egan, and later the two had corresponded about the sale of his printing presses to the Land League. When Egan read in a newspaper in Nebraska the text of the newest forgeries, he took out his file of correspondence and discovered in it Pigott's misspelling of "hesitency." He wrote at once to the Parnellites, "Dick Pigott is the forger." In October 1888 Pigott was lured to a house in London where Parnell was waiting to confront him. He cheerfully admitted everything but he refused to disown his forgeries in public. He had been promised a fee of five thousand pounds, he said, to serve as the *Times*'s witness, and he had no way of knowing what Parnell's side might want to offer.

The special commission went to work. After five months spent in grilling Parnell, Davitt, Sexton, O'Brien, and miscellaneous Land Leaguers, after proving that Davitt had been a Fenian, that Parnell was Land League president, and that there had been a land war, after hearing O'Shea's assurances that the *Times* letters were genuine, it finally got around to Pigott himself in February 1889. He went to the witness table gaily enough, but was quickly trapped not by his misspelling, but by the introduction of a blackmail letter he had written to William Walsh, archbishop of Dublin, just before the publication of the first forged letter in April 1887. He had reported to the archbishop that a sinister plot involving spurious documents and endangering the future of Ireland was about to be perpetrated, and could he have the privilege of a private conference with His Grace on this matter? He could not explain this letter. He could not explain why Parnell and Egan had written each other in the same handwriting though with different signatures (traced from genuine autographs held against a window pane). At last he could not explain anything. After three days of tortured testimony he vanished and was traced to Madrid. When arrested for extradition on a perjury charge, he excused himself to the Spanish police, went into the hotel bedroom, and put a bullet through his brain.

When the House of Commons met in session the next day, Parnell's entrance was greeted with a standing ovation, an honor that had not been accorded a fellow member for a hundred years. Gladstone invited him to Hawarden Castle as house guest. The *Times* apologized and prepared to defend itself as best it could against his action for damages, for he had at last accepted its invitation to sue. There were mutterings that Salisbury's resignation and a dissolution of Parliament were in order. The ministry was implicated in the scandal through the attorney general and also the home secretary, who had cooperated in the conspiracy by giving Pigott leave to contact the convicted Irish Dynamitards in English prisons with an offer of a free pardon if they would corroborate the forged letters in court. (He got no takers.) Salisbury's ministry did not have clean hands; but unlike the guilty French ministry in the Dreyfus case, it was wise enough not to double its bets on the frame-up. The special commission was not disposed to protect the government's jackal Pigott but it did protect the government itself, refusing to allow the Parnellites to subpoena the membership list of the Unionist conspiratorial organization that had financed Pigott's activities. A few names came to light accidentally—Gladstone's former chief whip, for one, and for another, a name familiar here, Sir Rowland Ponsonby Blennerhassett. None of these names held any embarrassment for the prime minister. There was no dissolution, no new election. Salisbury, like Gladstone and Parnell, took up the waiting game himself, hoping that the embarrassments from the Pigott scandal would fade away with normal public forgetfulness. The Tory ministry survived the forgery crisis nicely, and nought was lost save honor.

III

With Richard Pigott we are back once more on the Judas theme in Irish history, and once more we find Joyce in the thick of it. While everybody in Dublin had known for years that Pigott was a scoundrel, he was ostensibly a nationalist, almost an Old Fenian; and what better proof that Ireland is the old sow that eats her farrow? The episode also bore an added attraction in its Joycean rummaging for clues among verbal slips. Joyce simplified Pigott's career into a detective story turning on a fatal misspelled word. The word "hesitency," accompanied by its doublet "hesitancy" thus replicates merrily through *Finnegans Wake*, and Mrs. Adaline Glasheen, who discovered the referent for the word, has given us her assurance that whenever "hesitency" occurs, "somebody is lying."

Yeats's letters show that he was not only aware of the Pigott episode, but watched it closely. During the week in which Pigott killed himself Yeats wrote to Katharine Tynan: "Poor Pigott! One really got to like him, there was something so frank about his lies. They were so completely matters of business, not of malice. There was something pathetic too in the hopeless way the squalid latter-day Erinyes ran him down. The poor domestic-minded swindler."[6] Noteworthy is the phrase about the "squalid latter-day Erinyes." Leading the actual Erinyes were the Irish House members, including Parnell himself, all inclined to be less philosophical about poor Pigott's frame-up than the Irish poet of Bedford Park, Chiswick.* Among

---

* A generation later, Yeats's play *The Dreaming of the Bones* made atonement for this singular response to the Pigott frame-up. The Easter Week executions had freed Maud Gonne from her estranged husband, John MacBride; and Yeats, after a decent interval for mourning, set forth in 1917 for her home in Normandy to propose marriage. The play gave expression to his last self-conscious nationalist effort and contains his last and loveliest

the Erinyes were numbered, too, all the rest of the Irish nationalists of every degree; for in Dublin, Pigott's was the most warmly applauded suicide since John Sadleir, M.P., drank his dram of prussic acid on Hampstead Heath thirty years since.

IV

While Parnell moved from triumph to triumph, nobody could deny that a measure of domestic ambiguity prevailed in the O'Sheas' arrangements at Eltham. Captain O'Shea, for himself, had never cared particularly for Eltham, or for Mrs. O'Shea either. Long before she ever met Parnell he had moved out and taken quarters downtown in order to pursue his private pleasures. In twenty-three years of married life, he had spent a total of one year at home. In his absence, Parnell and Mrs. O'Shea had lived for a decade at Eltham, happily and without interruption except for his seven months in Kilmainham jail in 1881–82. Mrs. O'Shea had thought often of divorce but she was prevented by another fatal family complication, her millionaire aunt, Mrs. Wood, an opinionated old lady who deplored scandal. She subsidized Captain and Mrs. O'Shea on separate allowances, and with good behavior both of them had great expectations from her estate, which God willing would soon be their own, for she was already eighty-eight when Mrs. O'Shea and Parnell first met in 1880.

Captain and Mrs. O'Shea each hated the other, but neither one cared to sever their connection while old Mrs. Wood was still alive. A general untidiness of sexual relations resulted. Mrs. O'Shea, with three children already, gave birth to three more while she was living with Parnell; and O'Shea claimed that he had excellent reason to suppose they were his own. Meanwhile, so it was charged, he was carrying on his own adulterous affair with Mrs. O'Shea's sister. Yet as early as 1881 he had challenged Parnell to

---

Celtic-twilight lyric; it thus seems clearly a courtship gift. It is built around the Judas theme, but in neither the "poor Pigott" nor the Joycean mode. Joyce's proposition was that anybody who stood by Ireland would be betrayed; Yeats's, that anybody who betrayed Ireland would not be forgiven in seven hundred years. For good intentions the play wins the biscuit, as Lynch once said; and the strain of his effort (which included some imaginary atrocities) exudes from the text. Yeats sustained his interest by trying out two new poetical inventions. One was the "dreaming back" of the past, the unwinding of the bobbin, a vehicle that so precisely fit his theme that he understandably believed this the best of his Noh plays. The other innovation was the Spenglerian apocalypse, the parting cry of the "cat-headed bird" and the herald of dawn by the "red bird of March": "Up with the neck and clap the wing, Red cock, and crow!" Since Irish mythology deciphers the "cat-head" as the Demos (Cairbre Cat-Head being, as I have said, the Irish Spartacus), this innovation runs counter to the play's theme: Pearse and Connolly did not barricade themselves in the General Post Office in order to crush a slave rebellion. The contradiction generates an artificial enigma; see my comment on "The Second Coming," pp. 170–71.

a duel after discovering his luggage in a closet at Eltham. (Parnell's un-romantic response was: What did you do with my luggage?) O'Shea knew at the time of the Kilmainham negotiations in 1882 that Parnell was living with Mrs. O'Shea at Eltham, though what construction he put on the information is unclear. Historians are unable to discern the precise points of alternation between the deceived and the compliant, extortionist husband, but all are agreed that his role virtually throughout was that of a parasite and adventurer.

A few months after Pigott's suicide, Captain O'Shea brought suit for divorce against his wife, naming Parnell as corespondent. The Parnellite historian Henry Harrison, Yeats's friend, carried on research for many years hoping to prove that Chamberlain was, once again, the clever brain behind this last blow against Parnell. His contention undoubtedly has "intrinsic probability." The Unionists had long pondered on the possible political yield from Parnell's love affair. O'Shea thoroughly understood that the divorce action had political significance. As brazen as Pigott himself, he delivered a prompt demand upon Balfour for services rendered by the divorce proceeding. But another motivation was also sufficient to have set him off.[7] For, just at the time of Pigott's suicide, old Mrs. Wood died at age ninety-seven. O'Shea's living allowance immediately stopped; worse yet, he got nothing in her will. Penniless, chagrined by the collapse of his hopes for revenge from the forged letters, brooding even over the old Parnell Tribute of 1883 which he somehow felt had rightly belonged to him, he had many grievances besides the one on which his divorce suit rested, and no further restraints. He was ready "to hit back a stunner."

The divorce trial did not follow for almost a year. During all this time there was little public reaction. Parnell gave the Irish party his assurance that all was well, that the divorce suit would amount to nothing, that "if this case is ever fully gone into, a matter which is exceedingly doubtful, you may rest assured that it will be shown that the dishonor and discredit have not been upon my side."[8] His confidence seems to have been based in part on his feeling that his own behavior had been honorable; and in part on an understanding that all O'Shea wanted was money, and that twenty-five thousand pounds from Mrs. Wood's estate would pacify him. If he really was relying on O'Shea's cupidity, he had not allowed for the unlucky chance that the old lady's will was going to be legally contested. Mrs. O'Shea could not get her hands on the money needed to buy O'Shea off, and the defendants realized before the trial that O'Shea would come into court fighting.

Parnell's reaction was, so be it. He wanted a quick divorce so that he could marry Mrs. O'Shea and legitimize his children. Hence he decided on his own impulse that the suit must not be contested. But a slip-up occurred in legal tactics. Mrs. O'Shea entered counterallegations against O'Shea without preparing to follow them up. This technical blunder allowed O'Shea to take the witness stand and disport himself with an eye to the newspaper headlines through two days of uninhibited commentary on his enemy, depicted to the court in the role of the treacherous friend who skulked in the background under the aliases of "Mr. Fox" and "Mr. Preston," seduced his wife, and wrecked his happy home. It allowed him to introduce into evidence a fatal letter from Parnell to Mrs. O'Shea in which Tim Healy was referred to as a "chimney sweep." It allowed him to bring in for collaborating witness Mrs. Caroline Pethers, a one-time cook of Mrs. O'Shea's who testified that Captain O'Shea's unannounced homecoming had "three or four times" routed Parnell out of the family living room and forced him to flee by a knotted rope fire escape.[9] After a few minutes, she testified, he would then present himself as a casual social caller at the front door. This strange story of defenestration was not subjected to cross-examination and it sounded believable to the judge. O'Shea got his decree and the custody of somebody else's children; and the judge pronounced Parnell to be one "who takes advantage of the hospitality offered him by the husband in order to debauch his wife."[10]

V

Who does not know of the "thunderclap"—Gladstone's metaphor—that burst from the divorce decree? Dublin lived on melodrama, but it had never heard the like of the storm that moved down on Ireland out of London, where the *Freeman's Journal* sent a whole corps of reporters to transmit every precious word, up to twenty-four columns in a single day. Yeats said later: "I cannot . . . look upon Captain O'Shea as merely amusing. I am not sufficiently unselfish. He has endangered the future of Irish dramatic literature by making melodrama too easy. . . ."[11]

It will be remembered that the health of Gladstone's party after 1886 was not robust. It had already split once over Home Rule, which had cost it the control of the Commons and the defection of most of its young leaders. It still derived strength from Gladstone's incomparable personal grandeur. But he was over the threshold of his eightieth year, and so solitary in distinction inside his party that he could be said to be without either lieutenants or heirs. His political base lay among the Wesleyans of the industrial English towns; and it was there that the outcry against Parnell's sexual unconventionality first swelled, led by a violent London revivalist preacher named Hugh Hughes. The divorce decree was handed down on a Monday and by the next Saturday a convention of the Liberal party in Sheffield was in full cry after Parnell's resignation. On Sunday Gladstone showed signs of great perturbation over the threat of a second Liberal party split. On

Monday he took the decisive step of writing a letter to John Morley stating that in view of the displeasure of the "Nonconformist conscience" of the north, Parnell's continuance at the head of the Irish party would "render my retention of the leadership of the Liberal party, based as it has been mainly upon the presentation of the Irish cause, almost a nullity." Justin M'Carthy was then called in, shown the letter, and asked to communicate its message to Parnell and the party. He was briefed by Gladstone: ". . . he told me very sadly that his [Parnell's] remaining in the leadership now means the loss of the next elections and the putting off of Home Rule until the time when he [Gladstone] will no longer be able to bear a hand in the great struggle to which he has devoted the later years of his life."[12] The letter gave the Irish party the harsh alternative either to drop Parnell or say farewell to Home Rule. If one understands that Gladstone was an English statesman and not an Irish patriot, one can hardly conceive of his behaving otherwise.

In Ireland, meanwhile, all was quiescence and solidarity. The moral issue, though now thoroughly exposed, was passed over as being a mere insignificance. The clergy and the bishops maintained silence. Dublin's first formal expression on the crisis came on the day after the divorce decree, as the National League put itself on record unanimously in Parnell's support. The *Freeman's Journal* followed suit with a message proclaiming in somewhat overwrought diction that all was well. A cable came in from America to express support for Parnell, signed by a money-raising expeditionary force, including O'Brien, Dillon, and T. P. Gill.*

Davitt was the first to crack the solid Irish front. He was one of the few who had worried about O'Shea's attack; and he alone had faced up to Parnell to ask whether there were political dangers in his domestic quarrel with O'Shea. Parnell had changed the conversation: "Before we talk on that subject, there is a matter I want to speak to you about. I don't approve of your labor organization in the South of Ireland; it will lead to mischief and can do no good. . . . What is trades-unionism but a landlordism of labor? I would not tolerate, if I were at the head of a government, such bodies as trades-unions. They are opposed to individual liberty and should be kept down, as Bismarck keeps them under in Germany."[13] On that other painful subject, Davitt misunderstood him to say that he was not living with Mrs. O'Shea. When the divorce decree proved otherwise, he published in his newspaper *Labor World* his opinion that Parnell should step down from leadership, should "efface himself for a brief period," not for violation of the seventh commandment, but simply in order not to "disintegrate the forces behind the Home Rule cause in Britain."

* Gill is a key figure in Moore's *Hail and Farewell*, a farcical bureaucrat with an Henri Quatre beard.

The day after Davitt's attack a mass meeting in Leinster Hall, Dublin, declared its loyalty. Healy crossed in a winter storm to speak at the meeting. He berated Davitt for deserting Parnell. He was reminded, he said, of Charles II's comment to his brother James: "No, no, Jamie, no one will kill me to make you king." It was his opinion that if the Irish people "were so frivolous and light hearted" as to desert Mr. Parnell over the pretext of "this wretched and unfortunate [divorce] case," sensationalized by the hysteria of "Wesleyan chapels," then "the Irish nation would be my nation no more."[14] In a storm at sea, he said, "you are requested not to speak to the man at the wheel."

On Tuesday of the second week, in preparation for the opening of Parliament the following day, the Irish party met in a caucus and unanimously re-elected Parnell chairman. To this meeting Justin M'Carthy brought Gladstone's ultimatum. Being one who disliked scenes, he neglected to mention it to the assembled members. He did, however, inform Parnell about Gladstone's stipulation and asked him whether he planned to resign. Parnell said no; he would "stand by his guns." As soon as Gladstone learned that the Irish party had failed to meet his demand, he handed the Morley letter to the newspapers for the morning editions of Wednesday, November 25, 1890. With its publication "the Split," usually spelled in Irish history with the portentous capital letter, became a fact. By midday an anti-Parnell faction had crystallized around John Barry, the same man who had first beckoned Parnell into Irish leadership. He accused Parnell of trickery and asked him to convoke a new meeting of the party. Parnell refused. Barry then circulated a petition call and got enough signatures to summon the party back into session the next day, the meeting to take place in an empty caucus room in the parliament building, Committee Room Fifteen.

VI

Barry, it will be remembered, belonged to the Bantry band. In addition to him, the band was composed of two Sullivan brothers, T. D. and Donal (A. M. Sullivan had died several years before the Split); their two Healy nephews, Tim and Maurice; and another county Cork relation, William Martin Murphy, who was later to win Dublin notoriety during the years just before the First World War as the employers' strong man who locked out and broke Jim Larkin's dockers' union and inspired Yeats's most celebrated lampoon, "September 1913." The natural leader of the band by the test of capability was Tim Healy. Unembarrassed by his declarations of loyalty in Leinster Hall the week before, he now took command of the Sullivan wing of the Irish party with full determination to destroy Parnell, to

335

"drive him into the grave or into the lunatic asylum," as tradition quotes him. All the Irish party needed now, he said, was "the tomahawk and the sweeping-brush."

The quick turnabout was made in such pain that weeping was a daily occurrence in Committee Room Fifteen. But reasoning contra Parnell was compelling, not only to Healy and Barry but to many other members not warm in their affection for the Bantry band. The Irish party, it was noted, had maximized its strength by 1886. It would never have many more than eighty-six members, or many fewer either. This achievement was admittedly owing to Parnell's guidance, a cue for tears. But with party strength now firmly established on a plateau, Parnell was no longer indispensable. The indispensable man now was Ireland's English benefactor, for the party could never prevail at Westminster except as the protégé of Gladstone and the Liberal party. Therefore, if one must choose, one must choose Gladstone. When Gladstone said that Parnell must go, then go he must.

Parnell thought otherwise, and came out fighting. He seized the initiative first off. He sent the newspapers an extraordinary document, a manifesto "To the People of Ireland," aiming to smash the Liberal alliance forever and to cut all connections with Gladstone, now suddenly transformed into an "arch coercionist" and "unrivalled sophist." The manifesto charged Gladstone with "wirepulling" to "sap and destroy" the "independence of the Irish party" by assuming the right to veto its decisions. Parnell added a detailed account of his secret negotiations at Hawarden; the sum of it was that Gladstone was ready to surrender to the Unionists and landlords in drafting the new Home Rule bill.

This astonishing manifesto was directed simultaneously to the extremes on both the left and right. In emotional appeal, the language was boldly Fenian. But at the same time it seemed addressed to Salisbury, and in effect proposed that the Tories buy a continuation in office at the Irish price. This interpretation, if true, implies an eclipse of Parnell's astuteness, for the Tories made no attempt to disguise their happy expectation that the divorce scandal had smashed Gladstone and opened their road to glory. Though a scion of the ancient Cecil family's "spreading laurel tree," Salisbury could not restrain his pleasure in another gentleman's embarrassment, and he offered the public a variant upon the fire-escape story as told by Mrs. Pethers, not a member of his social class. Having "recovered in the divorce court what they had lost in the Special Commission," the Tories were almost certainly confident enough of their final victory against Home Rule to refuse any further transaction with Parnell, and even to welcome a short respite from office in order to allow Gladstone scope to work out his own destruction. But one is uncertain, and Cecil Rhodes's curious friendship with Parnell in the late 1880s suggests that some sort of scheme for an accommodation between Home Rule and overseas imperialism may not have been as farfetched as it seems.

The instantaneous effect of the manifesto was catastrophic for Parnell. His whimsical recasting of Gladstone's Irish role from Grand Old Man into "grand old spider" alienated most of the Plan of Campaign agrarians. They were already angry over his lofty indifference to the Plan of Campaign. And they thought that if Gladstone was really as evil as Parnell now reported, they should have been told so as soon as he first learned of it at Hawarden, not a year later. Thus O'Brien and Dillon, who might have stood between the Sullivans and the Parnellites and rescued the situation from total disintegration, were drawn into Healy's orbit, taking with them the party's balance of power.

The unrestrained language of the manifesto made retreat unthinkable. Nobody was left in any doubt about Parnell's contempt for Davitt's naïve suggestion that he could trustfully "efface himself for a brief period" and then come back as though nothing had ever happened. He intended to stay put, even if it meant the "postponement," as his euphemism put it, of Home Rule. To this sporting resolve Parnell's later fame owes an extra measure of bounteousness. It was Emmet's and O'Donovan Rossa's performance all over again. Even Healy was forced to admire:

> The deposed leader was a magnificent fighter where his own concerns were at stake, and after the split he was suddenly stirred up to a display of energy which, if it had been exerted earlier, must have brought down the Tory Government. Even in the evil dispute which the divorce case produced, his combative qualities won the admiration of the Celtic temperament. In truth, he came so gallantly to the charge
> That even the ranks of Tuscany
> Could scarce forbear to cheer.[15]

This was written years afterward, when Healy could afford to be big about it all. At the time, the Sullivans were thrown into unrestrained wrath. Healy said that the Parnellites were "appealing to the hillside men."[16] T. D. Sullivan said, "The 'anti-Parnellites' saw at a glance what this meant —it was civil war in Ireland in the near future."[17] To this chronic Sullivanite fear of revolution was added an acute chagrin. Parnell had spoken about "the Promised Land." It was close enough to reach out and touch, and the Sullivans had come a long way. They were sons of a Bantry house painter, yet three of them had already gone to Westminster and one to the Mansion House as well. Sullivan sons would be Q.C.'s. Nephew Healy had risen from a railway clerk to great wealth, acquired out of land-court retainer fees.* Why might they not all envision themselves as lord chancellors,

* In *Ulysses* Healy is no longer the "cowardly little scoundrel" of Committee Room Fifteen, but a vaguely grand financier, a trustee for the Trinity College endowments.

ministers, prime ministers? And Parnell talked of postponement yet. Their fury in contemplating the wreck of their ambitions was well conveyed by J. F. X. O'Brien, the same man we once saw standing long ago in the Cork courthouse dock to hear death sentence passed: "For myself, this is the most anxious moment of my political life of over forty years. Twenty-three years ago I stood face to face with Judge Keogh in the dock at Cork. I can tell you that on that occasion my pulse was not stirred in the slightest. I cannot say that now. This is the most wretched moment of my life, for I see shattered by you, who brought us to a splendid position, all the hopes of Ireland."[18]

The formal session in Committee Room Fifteen convened on Monday, December 1, 1890, just two weeks after the divorce decree. It was prepared to decapitate Parnell with one clean blow. Easier said that done. "Mr. Fox" was not inexperienced in the parliamentary arts. As chairman of the session he simply ruled all hostile motions out of order, so that the moralistic re-criminations on sex and sin rehearsed and ready to be flung in his face had no context in which to issue. He then took over. He assigned a loyal fol-lower to introduce a motion that the deliberations be transferred from West-minster to Dublin, where advanced nationalists could challenge Healy's representativeness, watch over his shoulder, and perhaps join in the debate.

It took two days in Committee Room Fifteen for the session to vote down the motion to go to Dublin, 44 to 29. Parnell's ingenuity in politicalizing the issue next produced an arresting query: Suppose you drive me from my post, he asked, what assurance have you that Gladstone will stand by Home Rule? Nobody could answer the question, and Parnell pursued it. After all, he said, "you are dealing with a man who is an unrivalled sophist." With amiable irony he offered the observation that Joyce somewhat oversolemnly seized upon for the elaboration of his favorite theme in Irish history: "Don't sell me for nothing. If you get my value you may change [exchange] me tomorrow. . . . And if I surrender to him, if I give up my position to him—if you throw me to him, I say, gentlemen, that it is your bounden duty to see that you secure value for the sacrifice."[19] And so a delegation led by Sexton went forth to ask Gladstone what assurance he might care to offer as a token of his good faith and veracity.[20] Naturally they got no answer to such a singular inquiry. But in this way three more days passed; the debates had now lasted five days. On the sixth and last day, the Sullivans attempted once more to introduce a motion to depose Parnell, and once more he refused to recognize the motion. With that, forty-five members led by M'Carthy got up and left the room, walked down the corridor to another room, and caucused as the anti-Parnellite party. Parnell had fifteen members left with him. The Split was now institutional.

VII

It was understood on both sides that the last appeal would be made back to the Irish people. Healy offered a metaphor to clarify the issue: "We are the representatives of the people. Place an iron bar in a coil and electrize that coil and the iron bar becomes magnetic. This party was that electric action. There [pointing to Parnell] stood the iron bar. The electricity is gone and the magnetism with it, when our support had passed away." Parnell challenged Healy's claim by saying it remained to be seen who had the electricity. And Healy declared, "The knives are out."

So far the debate for and against Parnell had been held to real political issues, which were not obscure. William O'Brien stated the anti-Parnellite position in the plainest language: "That issue is whether it is humanly possible to win the general election [in England] under Mr. Parnell's leadership."[21] Parnell's position, put with equal clarity in the manifesto "To the People of Ireland" was: "Ireland considers the independence of her party as her only safeguard within the constitution, and above and beyond all other considerations whatsoever." Strictly on these issues, judged by common sense, Parnell did not stand on strong ground. His phrase "beyond all other considerations whatsoever" clearly meant that Ireland could be well lost for love, a highly controversial point. One imagines that on that issue he must have lost in any high-level campaign. As it turned out, it was a low-level campaign that was actually fought. In the closing hours of the debate in Committee Room Fifteen, after the knives came out, Healy gave notice that when he got back to Ireland, he was not going to pay much attention to Parnell's instructions that the members "keep their mouths sealed" about his private life. Ireland could look forward to hearing a good deal about "the stench of the divorce court" in the battles that lay ahead.

Listening to the daily mounting pitch of Healy's vituperation in Committee Room Fifteen, Parnell at last interrupted to tax him with ingratitude: "Mr. Healy has been trained in this warfare. Who trained him? Who saw his genius? Who telegraphed to him from America to come to him?"[22] Healy's "poisoned tongue" was a spectacle all its own, setting a standard for skill in wounding that his enemies could never match. In memory of this trait, Irish history has set him in a special niche to which few admirers come. "Tiger Tim" he had been in the land war. After the Split he was "Healy the Hound." His savagery was a gift of personality, but it was also representative.

As soon as Healy took the field, the contest speedily degenerated into a vendetta, pitiless on both sides. The Parnellites might never be able to rival him in scurrility, but they could try. The pain arising out of wrecked

339

ambition was not all confined to the Sullivan side. In the Joyce family, for example, the Split meant catastrophe on the bread-and-butter level. Richard Ellmann has noted that "for John Joyce the fall of Parnell, closely synchronized with a fall in his own fortunes, was the dividing line between the stale present and the good old days."[23] Yeats described John Joyce as essentially a minor Parnellite canvasser. That was not much of a career, living like the characters in "Ivy Day in the Committee Room." But Parnell's ascendancy beckoned to "the Promised Land" and seemed certain to arrest his downward drift, hopeless otherwise, from the petty *rentier* with property in Cork and a son in Clongowes Wood to the rummy cadge of later life. He had "been among the first to greet the rising star of Parnell," said Stanislaus Joyce.[24] He backed the favorite, staking everything. Soon the Chief was to be Ireland's prime minister; then all the English placemen would be sent home and the patriots would be summoned to staff the posts of Irish government. Unfortunately, there was this sound of "shattered glass and toppling masonry."

VIII

Among those appalled by the Parnell–O'Shea thunderclap was William Walsh, archbishop of Dublin. His considered thought was that the Church would do well to do nothing. He proposed to "stand by"; and for several days he held to his heroic caution against intense counterpressures. Again, Davitt was the first to speak out publicly, when *Labor World* chided the Church for its silence on the "moral issue" and for leaving to the "sturdy dissenters of Great Britain" the task of guarding the sanctity of the marriage tie. Unknown to Davitt, Manning was already busy. From the start the Sassenach cardinal was well abreast of the "sturdy dissenter," the Reverend Hugh Hughes. He had gone instantly into action with a personal message to Gladstone advising him to do what he in fact did do, that is, to demand Parnell's resignation. Next, representing himself as spokesman for the pope, he took up Davitt's bullying tone toward Archbishop Walsh. Before the first week of the crisis had passed, he sent to Dublin one of the most piquant of all the unguarded comments elicited by the heated atmosphere of the passing days. He told Walsh: ". . . if ten years ago the bishops and priests had spoken and acted together, the movement would not have fallen into the hands of laymen. There is now both in Ireland and in Rome the opportunity of your regaining the lead and direction." The Irish bishops fell into step with Manning. Archbishop Croke of Cashel, Davitt's friend the "Land League archbishop," wrote a letter that, were he not a great dignitary of the Church, might be thought vengeful:

I have flung him [Parnell] away from me forever. His bust which for some time held a prominent place in my hall I threw out yesterday. And as for "the party" generally, I go with you entirely in thinking that they made small, or no, account of the bishops and priests now, as independent agents, and only value them as money gatherers and useful auxiliaries in the agitation. This I have noticed for a considerable time past, and I believe we shall have to let them see and feel unmistakably that, without us, they would be simply nowhere and nobodies.[25]

After dragging his feet for a week, Walsh finally convoked a council of the Irish bishops to take a position on the crisis. On the Wednesday following the day when Parnell lost the test vote in Committee Room Fifteen, he wired their decision to his courier William Martin Murphy, one of the Bantry band: "Important you and members should know bishops issue unqualified pronouncement. Mr. Parnell unfit for leadership, first of all on moral grounds, social and personal discredit as result of divorce court proceedings, also in view of inevitable disruption, with defeat at elections, wreck of Home-Rule hopes and sacrifice of tenants' interests."[26] True to the political animal instinctive in every Irishman, he counseled Murphy on the urgency for "more and yet more local organization" to counter the Parnellites at the parish level. It is unclear whether the sexual or the political outrage was the more obnoxious, but in any case, the clergy were in the thick of it from then on. And thus it was that the same prelate whose testimony to the special commission destroyed Pigott is fixed in literature by Simon Dedalus' "Billy the Lip" and the pasquinade of Joyce's "Gas from a Burner." In the end Parnell retained the loyalty of two priests, the same magic number who had stood by Smith O'Brien in 1846, Gavan Duffy in 1852, and James Stephens in 1865.[27]

IX

Their stark transaction in Committee Room Fifteen completed, the parliamentary belligerents set out for North Kilkenny, where a by-election was to be fought out on December 22, 1890. Dublin was always the strongest Parnellite base, and now the city welcomed the troubled Chief with cheering crowds and brass bands. His first task was to recapture *United Ireland* from the enemy. When William O'Brien passed over to the anti-Parnellites, he cabled from New York to Matthias Bodkin, the editor, instructing him to switch the paper's line. Parnell marched directly from the railroad station into Lower Abbey Street to storm the editorial offices, ejecting the incumbents and installing his own men while the police looked on. The raiders disposed of Bodkin's resistance easily: "Matty, will you walk out or would you like to be thrown out?"[28] That evening, while the Parnellites were all off cheering the Chief at a mass meeting in the Rotunda, Healy led a stealthy expedition against the undefended newspaper office and recon-quered it. Early next morning, on the way from the hotel back to the station to take the train for Kilkenny, Parnell's traveling party detoured past the *United Ireland* office and once more overwhelmed the enemy after forcing the doors with crowbars.*

Originally, North Kilkenny was to have one candidate running un-opposed. He had been endorsed by Parnell just before the Split, but now he suddenly denounced Parnell. A new Parnellite candidate was then brought forward and entered in the poll, and the battle was on—Parnell on one side, Healy and Davitt on the other, backed by seventy Irish M.P.'s who had con-verged on Kilkenny. They stated and restated the true issues earnestly; but the Kilkenny by-election is best remembered for the magnificence of its red herrings.[29]

Physical violence, not unknown in Irish elections, was advanced as an argument by both sides, and all three field generals were to report in as minor casualties. Somebody hit Davitt (a one-armed man, as the reader will remember) on the side of the head with a stick. Healy arrived in Dublin on the same boat train with Parnell and was shoved about at Westland Row by the crowd of welcoming Parnellites; and later on in Cork he was struck across the face, his front teeth and his glasses broken by the blow. A frag-ment of glass entered one eyeball but was removed without causing per-manent damage. Pallid and cadaverous and looking, as Barry O'Brien thought, "like a dying man,"[30] Parnell was hit in the eye with a rock at Castlecomer and showered with some kind of white dust, whether flour or stone or quicklime was disputed;[31] but in any case the injury was irritating rather than serious.

The most striking novelty in the North Kilkenny campaign was Healy's deadly utilization of the O'Shea case. To him we owe the currency of Mrs. O'Shea's sporting name of "Kitty," now used the world around in forgetfulness of its original connotation (carefully observed by Joyce) of a prostitute. Once Healy spoke of her as "a convicted British prostitute," an excess anticipating Joyce's Skin-the-Goat: "That bitch, that English whore, did for him. . . . She put the first nail in his coffin." Healy used the Eltham fire escape for an ornament in every speech. One day the stenogra-pher picked up this oratorical effect: Parnell, he said, had made a new law, "and the law he had made was that whilst they had his name upon their lips, there was one name that they must not mention at all, and that was the name of a precious personage who was more dear to Mr. Parnell than

* The commotion attracted a crowd of curious Dubliners, and as told in the "Eumaeus" chapter of *Ulysses*, one among them is Mr. Bloom. He witnesses the uncrowned king truly uncrowned as his silk hat is knocked off in the scuffle. Mr. Bloom rescues it and returns it, giving occasion for the Chief to utter "with perfect *aplomb*" the deathless words, "*Thank you, sir.*"

342

Ireland itself." And from the crowd came the antiphonal response, "Kitty O'Shea!"[32] As Yeats's friend Katharine Tynan said darkly, when an Irish peasant is coarse, he is truly coarse.

The hosting of the clergy for election duty at North Kilkenny was less novel, yet it had been a long while since their exuberance in a task had been so tonic. It was as though they felt with Cardinal Manning some need to make up for lost time. Court evidence on the by-elections, reinforced by hearsay and legend, repeated the details familiar to those Irishmen who remembered the past field campaigns—the withholding of sacraments, incitement to riot, scurrility, and in one case (one only) a threat to turn an unrepentant Parnellite into a goat. In New York, John Devoy got word on the state of affairs from J. J. O'Kelly, through whom he usually communicated with Parnell: "The priests have smashed the movement."[33] Barry O'Brien, who was at Parnell's side throughout the Kilkenny campaign, drew the same conclusion: ". . . the priests, and the priests alone, influenced and dominated the electors of North Kilkenny." Two historians, Francis Sheehy-Skeffington and Emile Strauss, have sensed a note of poetic justice here, since it was Parnell who had recruited the clergy into the movement, though naturally for other purposes than this one.[34]

A Fenian in Kilkenny told Barry O'Brien what O'Leary once told Yeats: "The only power in Ireland that can stand up to Parnell is the Church, and the only power that can stand up to the Church is Fenianism."[35] His back against the wall, Parnell called out to Fenianism for help. He found an enthusiastic response. John Devoy had already cabled during the opening phase of the divorce crisis: "If Parnell yields to English clamor will destroy American movement. No other man or men can keep it together. Retirement means chaos, leaving Ireland at mercy of English whims and Irish cranks."[36] This support was expected of an old ally like Devoy. But Rossa had fought Parnell with dynamite throughout the eighties, and now he too came around to his support. James Stephens, settled peacefully in Dublin again and believed harmless, wrote the newspapers supporting Parnell immediately after the publication of the manifesto "To the People of Ireland." The three Fenian fragments thus reunited for the first time to defend Parnell against the multitude of his enemies. John O'Leary was more deliberate. With fifteen years in Paris behind him, he never could grasp the "moral issue" at all, and he told Katharine Tynan, "Good God in Heaven, you can't depose a man for gallantry."[37] Of the unwisdom of Parnell's politics, he remained confident. But when the clergy moved into Kilkenny, he declared himself: "The question is where are we going, and not whom are we following; and if Mr. Parnell were dead tomorrow, I and men like me, who are above and before all things Irish nationalists, should never dream of following the party of clerical intimidation and compromise with England. We go with Mr. Parnell as long as he goes and, insofar as he goes, for Irish freedom."[38]

Davitt, no less than Healy, blasted Parnell for "appealing in his desperato the hillside men and the Fenian sentiment of the country to face the might of England in the field."[39] The curiosity in Davitt's charge was that it borrowed the Chief's own often-repeated words. An element of opportunism undoubtedly stood among Parnell's motives for his sudden Fenian turn. There was even more opportunism in a later appeal, an "impudent attempt" the *Times* called it, to win English labor support with left-wing rhetoric, and Davitt found it amusing that the man who admired Bismarck's repression of trade-unionism in 1890 was plagiarizing the *Labor World*'s socialism in 1891.

It is tempting to overstate the cynicism in Parnell's new position. In point of fact, his pledge in the Kilkenny campaign holds well up enough under scrutiny. He was, he said, a constitutionalist, just as he had always been. He still believed that the potential energy in moral force must be used to exhaustion. But suppose that were done, he asked, and it were then discovered to be a futility? At that point, but not before, he would cease to be an Irish constitutionalist while remaining an Irish nationalist:

> But when it appears to me that it is impossible to obtain Home Rule for Ireland by constitutional means, I have said this—and this in the extent and limit of my pledge, that is the pledge which has been accepted by the young men of Ireland, whom Michael Davitt in his derision calls the hillside men—I have said that when it is clear to me that I can no longer hope to obtain our constitution by constitutional and parliamentary means, I will in a moment so declare it to the people of Ireland, and, returning at the head of my party, I will take counsel with you as to the next step.[40]

These were words that the "advanced men" of Irish nationalism wanted to hear, and for them they forgave him everything.

Kilkenny was not Dublin, and Parnell could not find enough Fenians there to rescue him. His candidate lost by about two to one. He then announced himself ready for a compromise with the party majority and entered into negotiations at Boulogne toward "effacing himself" and turning the chairmanship over to William O'Brien. But a dispute arose over who would then hold the actual power, and the negotiations collapsed. In the early spring of 1891 the battle moved into Sligo. He got an old-time welcome at Ballina, but Sligo town was so hostile that he kept away. His candidate lost again. In July 1891 a by-election at Carlow went almost three to one for the anti-Parnellite. The *Freeman's Journal* deserted him, and J. J. O'Kelly, his closest confidant, gave up the struggle. Now certain of victory, the opposition became more insolent. Parnell came into the House one day

344

to find that a junior Irish member had appropriated his seat, and he had to find a place on the Liberal benches. In June 1891 the Sullivans' newspaper, the *National Press*, published under the headline "Stop Thief!" a sensational charge that Parnell had embezzled great sums from "the Paris funds," the Land League war chest, to support his licentious love life. The author was either Healy or T. D. Sullivan's brother Donal, known as "the silent Sullivan," famed for never making a speech or missing a division in a lifetime spent in the House of Commons. It said: "If Mr. Parnell debauched Mrs. O'Shea, one of the commandments delivered to us by Moses called this 'adultery.' If he appropriated the moneys left in trust with him—and we are prepared to prove that he did—the same old fashioned law-giver called that 'theft.'"[41] In midsummer, when the divorce decree became final, he married Mrs. O'Shea. To the clergy this action only added the sin of polygamy to the sin of adultery, and the bishop of Raphoe denounced the marriage as a "climax of brazen horrors."

As his political position deteriorated, Parnell responded with more tortured effort. To a reporter from the *Freeman's Journal* who asked him what message he had for the Irish people he replied, "Tell them I will fight to the end."[42] Before 1890 he often let a year or more pass without visiting Ireland. Though ailing, he now went across every weekend to give two, sometimes three, even four speeches before setting out again on the long and wearing journey back to Brighton, where the couple had moved after leaving Eltham. "I am weary," he wrote his mother, "weary unto death." His wife noticed that he looked increasingly exhausted as the autumn came on and became alarmed at the deepening of "tired gray shadows" about the lines of his face. She consulted their London physician about her fears for him, but she could not persuade him to go for an examination.

At the end of September 1891 he set out for his regular stint of weekend speech-making. Arriving in Dublin, he suffered a severe attack of rheumatism in the left arm. His Dublin doctor advised him to cancel his speaking appointments and to stay in Dublin for rest. He disregarded the advice and appeared on schedule in the village of Cleggs, county Roscommon, on Sunday, standing bareheaded in a driving rain, his arm in a sling to ease the pain. He had difficulty articulating his words. Back in Dublin he felt better, and he spent the first half of the week working on the problems of financing a new daily newspaper, made necessary by the defection of the *Freeman's Journal*. On Wednesday he was ill again with pain and fever, and the doctor tried to persuade him not to travel home, again without success. Between trains in London he took a Turkish bath to relieve his pains. When he reached home at Brighton on Thursday he had a severe chill and was slightly confused in his mind. Next morning he could not walk; in a couple of days he could scarcely move an arm or a finger without unbearable pain.

345

Saturday evening his mind wandered, turning to tales of the famine he had heard as a boy in Wicklow. Monday night his fever mounted out of control. He was last heard trying to say something about "the Conservative party"; then he fell unconscious. Shortly after midnight he died, on October 6, 1891, at age forty-five.[43]

X

The attending physician assigned the cause of death to "rheumatic fever with hyperpyrexis," or excessive bodily temperature, and "failure of the heart's action." Another physician mentioned fatigue from overwork as a contributing cause. Because of the high fever, the tissues began to decompose very rapidly. No death mask could be made, and the body was hurriedly sealed up in a lead coffin. A couple of the young Parnellite Irish members went to Brighton and persuaded Mrs. Parnell to allow the body to be sent for burial to Dublin, famous for funerals. She did not accompany the body; and in the end, although she twice stood ready for the call to become the grand hostess at the Viceregal Lodge, she died without ever having set foot in Ireland.

The reader will require no argument to be persuaded that for creative imagination in organizing a political funeral, the Fenians were without a peer. At Parnell's death their opportunity was particularly choice, since the normal struggle for the corpse did not occur. Out of delicacy the agrarians and the Sullivans had been forced to step back from their chief mourners' post at the national obsequies. The IRB came out of hiding and took charge.[44] There was a seeming incongruity in the Fenians' new hero. Physical force and moral force were reasonably distinct entities, and in the ordinary use of language Parnell must be thought to belong in the second category rather than the first. But O'Leary looked upon Parnell's ideological agility in 1891 as amends for the heresies that had separated them in 1879. Whether he overestimated Parnell's deathbed Fenianism was a matter of opinion. By default the other claimants permitted him to appropriate Parnell's name and fame, momentarily disvalued and free-floating, and to pronounce its true meaning to be—physical force. Those fifteen years of parliamentarianism, what were they but an irrelevance, a husk to be discarded leaving the clean grain, Parnell the Fenian martyr?

United Ireland editorialized on the day of the funeral:

> They have killed him. Under God today we do solemnly believe that they have killed him. . . . Murdered he has been as certainly as if the gang of conspirators had surrounded him and hacked him to pieces. . . . And the leprous traitors who talk of morality with a lie in their hearts—*they* may rejoice today that their purpose has been accomplished. Is Mr. John Dillon

satisfied now? Is Mr. William O'Brien—dead Caesar's Brutus? Are they as happy as Mr. Thomas Sexton, who plotted the Great Betrayal of November last? . . . Shall this fatal perfidy, this slow torture of our beloved Leader go unavenged?[45]

The count of mourners who marched in the procession to the Glasnevin grave was estimated at from 100,000 to 150,000, depending on the political bias of the witness. In the procession, walking abreast and just behind the lord mayor's carriage, were James Stephens and John O'Leary, each conspicuous in his seditious badge, the Fenian's wide-awake hat. As Yeats told us more than once, O'Leary's philosophy was the old Persian, to pull the bow and speak the truth. In his honest opinion, there was never any funeral to outtop Terence Bellow MacManus', though next to it, he conceded, came Léon Gambetta's and Parnell's in a dead heat.[46]

CHAPTER 23

Poetry Defends the Gap: Yeats and Hyde

I

Parnell's relicts on the parliamentary side of his political family, his faithful few, took for their new leader young John Redmond. The inheritance from the fallen Chief was not a great ballot box asset just then, and for a time it seemed that the heirs would be totally eliminated from Irish politics. The Sullivans naturally expected to inherit the mantle of party leadership as their reward for Healy's extermination of Parnell. They were challenged, though, by rivals equally willing to lead and substantially stronger, the anti-Parnellite agrarians Dillon, O'Brien, and Davitt. The old discipline and unity—once the envy of Westminster—broke into a loose and snarling anarchy divided behind the three feudists Redmond, Healy, and Dillon. Later on Dillon and O'Brien also fell out, and then the factions were four. Everybody has always deplored this dissension among Parnell's lieutenants, the lieutenants themselves most of all. The censure is understandable, but it is hard to discover how it made any particular difference in the parliamentary struggle, strictly regarded.

We have said a good deal about the "first," or 1886, Home Rule bill. There was a "second," or 1893, Home Rule bill too, not as well known, but in some ways more interesting. Unlike the first, it actually passed the Commons. Parnell's grave in Glasnevin was still fresh when Salisbury's second ministry ran to the end of its six-year term. In the general elections of 1892, Redmond's Parnellite party just barely survived with nine seats. By contrast, the anti-Parnellites of varied descriptions won seventy-two. The total Irish parliamentary strength was therefore eighty-one.* The real

* These were the electoral statistics that fixed themselves in Joyce's mind as the tell-tale of Irish ignobility, and he allowed Mr. Bloom to quote them for his thoughts "of seventy-two of eighty-odd constituencies that ratted at the time of the split and chiefly the belauded peasant class, probably the selfsame evicted tenants he had put in their holdings."

significance of these figures lay not in Redmond's poor showing, but in the size of the Irish total, approximately the same as in glorious 1886. The broken heads and the dead Chief had hardly touched the overall strength of the Irish parliamentary party.

All Irish eyes turned, then, upon England, Scotland, and Wales. In the new elections of 1892, Home Rule was again the big issue. Lord Salisbury's campaign adverted to the Irish cockpit with upturned eyeballs and despaired at the prospect that the ruffian quarrel inside the Irish party might be transferred to the floor of an infant Irish parliament. Gladstone, in turn, campaigned once again on "Justice to Ireland." In the voting Home Rule won him back 80 of the 114 seats it had cost him in 1886. With the backing of the 81 Irish members, he had a majority of 40 seats, enough to form a government. Gladstone introduced his second Home Rule bill, and the theory of Parnell's expendability was holding up well.

Gladstone had just passed his eighty-fourth birthday when the new Home Rule battle opened. His general staff was perhaps less treacherous than in 1886, but his new ministers were publicly unenthusiastic for Home Rule, and privately they would have been glad to hear the last of it.[1] The seven years since 1886 had also multiplied Gladstone's difficulties in Ulster. At the critical instant in the Home Rule debate, Belfast Unionists staged the largest protest rally the north had ever seen. A Presbyterian preacher named Robert Lynd gave them fresh spiritual guidance to go with Lord Randolph Churchill's "Ulster will fight," the old watchword of 1886. "We say of Home Rule as Lord Macaulay said of O'Connell's demand for Repeal," Lynd said, "—never! never! never!"[2]

These were trying problems. Still, Gladstone had the votes. When he called the third reading, his bill passed, 301 to 267. And so the seven-hundred-year-old story of Irish troubles ended happily after all. Great Irish rejoicing. But there was one last barrier to clear: the House of Lords. The Commons had spent eighty-four days in careful debate before passage. The Lords debated the bill for less than a week, then divided—41 for to 419 against. Fatigued and despairing, Gladstone resigned. The queen, without consulting him about his successor, appointed Lord Rosebery prime minister. Rosebery struggled along for another year before he, too, collapsed. Parliament was mercifully dissolved and a new general election called. The Tory-Unionists came in with a majority of 152 seats, making the most one-sided House of Commons in sixty years.[3] For the Irish moral force nationalists, it was the darkest day since 1801. Some flaw seemed to have developed in the logic by which Parnell was expended in order to clear the road for Home Rule.

II

The mandate that Salisbury had once asked for was now given him. He became a fixture in office, standing upon the Union at home; and, with Chamberlain now in the colonial office, upon the promise of imperial glory overseas. During the two decades following the 1886 Home Rule election, Salisbury or his nephew Arthur Balfour was to be prime minister for seventeen years. A whole historical epoch was dominated by the Tory-Unionist ascendancy, with the bedraggled Irish parliamentary party absorbed into the impotent Liberal opposition. A youth like Joyce, aged eleven at the second defeat of Home Rule, could grow up and leave the country without ever knowing any other Ireland than Salisbury's and Balfour's.

Those who read in the opening words of Joyce's *Dubliners* an Irish historical allegory may be somewhat simplistic, but they are probably not far off the mark. Father Flynn is dying: "There was no hope for him this time: it was the third stroke." This is Balfour's Ireland right enough, a perfect likeness. But it was unwise to generalize any more broadly than that. Joyce's paralyzed priest was not the ultimate Irish emblem. We know him well, for we have met him constantly in our excursion through nineteenth-century Irish history: he was Gavan Duffy's corpse on the dissecting table. Balfour's Irish government was not for perpetuity—it only seemed so; and Duffy's corpse was never a very trustworthy corpse. It was always rising up again, like the one at the end of Synge's play who pops out of his coffin ready to fight: "You'll see the thing I'll give you will follow you on the back mountains when the wind is high."

III

The Tory-Unionist victory of 1895 closed the last act of the Parnell affair, four years after his death. All the boxers' postures taken by his political heirs were frozen by the posthumous catastrophe. The anti-Parnellites interpreted their defeat as the necessary result of Parnell's perverse passion to rule or ruin. They saw the nation wrecked by a monomaniac obsessed with private objectives utterly inimical to statecraft. He had destroyed the Irish party, they said, destroyed the English Liberal party, and for good measure destroyed himself, too.

As for remorse, they had none, for they agreed with Healy when he said with less originality than usual: "The wine was drawn and it must be drunk." Unlike Matty Bodkin, Parnell would not go quietly. Some who would object to Healy's sponsorship might prefer Davitt's formulation: these "uncrowned kings" make splendid leaders, and for all that, they can wreck everything too.

350

Over in the Redmondite corner, the defeat of the second Home Rule bill was seen as a just vengeance upon the party Judases, a cosmic sarcasm to match Parnell's quip in Committee Room Fifteen: if you sell me, get my price. He had been sold for Home Rule, but there was no Home Rule. Gladstone the swindler* had finished off the betrayal begun when Healy, O'Brien, and Sexton "surrounded Parnell and hacked him to pieces." Redmond taunted his enemies with the contention that the party would have won through somehow if the Chief were still alive and at the helm. Many believed him, and many believe him to this day.

IV

The Old Fenians stood amid the wreckage of Home Rule the most successful Irish ideological speculators on the catastrophe. The outcome held no surprises for John O'Leary, hardened by forty years of Irish political experience. Had he not predicted that Parnellism must at last "work itself out"?

Proven prophetic power and the ownership of Parnell's corpse put Fenianism back in business once more, with insurrection again the order of the day. But its new efforts were frosted by bad news on the American wing. Unexpectedly the Clan-na-Gael fell apart. A Chicago Fenian named Alexander Sullivan (not to be confused with the Bantry Sullivans) formed an Irish-American junta called "The Triangle," seized control of the organization, and pushed John Devoy to the sidelines. The dispute was at first political, arising when Devoy criticized Sullivan's diversion of Clan-na-Gael money into dynamiting. Then the differences got out of control. Devoy and Sullivan took to carrying pistols for protection against one another, and at one Irish-American gathering the two stood face to face in such anger that the bystanders expected each man to draw and fire.

Devoy's Chicago ally in the feud was a fellow Fenian, a physician named P. H. Cronin. One afternoon in 1889 just before the Parnell divorce case broke, he went out on a house call and never came back. Some weeks later his beaten and butchered body was fished out of a Chicago sewer. The murder suspects were Alexander Sullivan himself and another Triangle Fenian known as "Sullivan the Iceman." Sullivan's defence was the claim that Dr. Cronin was not dead at all, that the body found in the sewer belonged to somebody else, and that the supposed victim would turn up in

---

* Joyce seems to have believed that Gladstone had actually connived wickedly with the Lords to kill the second Home Rule bill. This would naturally be an interesting fact, if true. It is almost certainly untrue. Still, his biographer J. L. Hammond speaks of his last effort as "hopeless," since the slaughter by the Lords was "certain," and his own Liberal cabinet was in rebellion against him. The suggestion of window dressing in the whole 1893 parliamentary transaction is rather strong.

London in due time and reveal himself as a British spy. The awaited reappearance never took place, and the taint of murder for private revenge settled on the Clan-na-Gael. The lurid scandal disintegrated American Fenianism, and by Devoy's estimate, set Irish nationalism back fifteen years in its work.[4]

Archbishop Croke read the burial service over Irish nationalism: "The hope of attaining a legislature for our country within measurable time is no longer entertained by reasoning men," because "what one set of Irish politicians proposed for the common weal would, almost of a surety, be derided, denounced, and scornfully rejected by another."[5] But according to the standard Irish rule, the nadir of one political cycle marked the start of the next cycle. The moment to start rebuilding was at hand. O'Leary's most successful nationalist enterprise was, as we have seen, his literary movement. At the final defeat of Home Rule it was a fine healthy seven-year-old with real achievements behind it and many hyperactive minds already involved. It now subdivided and began to proliferate like yeast.

V

With the Tory election landslide of 1895, my formal history ends. In the past all literary commentators used to pause just here—where Ireland lay once more a corpse on the dissecting table—to admire Yeats's poetic "revulsion against Irish politics." But recently this aesthetic piety has been jolted by Conor Cruise O'Brien's study of Yeats's politics in the 1930s, which demonstrates that his embarrassing ideological "flirtations" were not flirtations at all but the real thing, and that his tendency "to write off all politics with a kind of contempt, a plague-on-both-your-houses air,"[6] can be taken at face value only at great peril to the truth. It we surrender up the theory of the nonpolitical Yeats, we must say good-by as well to the touching old image of the Irish muse of the early 1890s lifting her skirts to avoid being soiled by ruffian mudslinging.

While the Fenians set great value by the Glasnevin Parnell as a symbol of defiance against prime ministers and priests, they had no further use for the concrete issues on which he fought his last campaign. They repelled Redmond automatically. Those like Devoy who lived to witness the logical end of Redmond's leadership in 1914—when he renounced the Irish demand for immediate Home Rule *because* England was in extremity—were entitled to claim that they had predicted it all a quarter of a century before, if that were any solace. The Fenians' post-Parnell line, memorably stated by Maud Gonne, noted that Dr. Cronin was dead and that "you cannot bring him back to life," and that Parnell and Home Rule were dead, too. But she added, "the British Empire is not dead yet." As for the parliamentarians' great purpose in life: "Home Rule was the carrot dangled before the donkey's nose to keep the donkey quietly trotting along in the harness of the British Empire." And the meaning of the Split was simply that "Redmond and Dillon were quarrelling over who should hold the carrot."[7] The order of the day was to go over the heads of all the factionalists, Parnellite and anti-Parnellite equally, in order to get on with the work of the Irish revolution.

The first of the Fenians' tasks was to try to tranquilize the Split. They now brought forward those nationalist projects that were by nature most immune from factionalism and most likely to penetrate to the Irish people directly. Immediately after Parnell's funeral, Yeats pressed O'Leary to suggest something for Maud Gonne to do: "What she needs is some work," he said.[8] O'Leary set her to resuscitating the old Amnesty Association, the ideal nationalist activity for the nadir phase. As with the Ladies' Land League, there was no defense against a maenad in fury, and in record time she won the release of the generation of Dynamitard prisoners.

VI

The literary movement too was estimated to hold promise for undercutting the Split. Parnell was no more than buried before the established Irish literary societies, the Southwark Literary Club in London and the Pan-Celtic movement in Dublin, began to simmer. Yeats took command, calling a hosting of all the literary Celts of London on December 28, 1891, a couple of months after Parnell's funeral, at his father's house in Chiswick. The official historian of the movement has left us a memorial of the celebrated moment. He reported: "The house seemed 'beyant the beyants,' as we say in Ireland, but when reached at last we had our reward, for it was in every sense a meet haunt for a poet or an artist. We soon forgot the taunts and rebuffs of old Boreas, wafted as we were by the associations and the conversation to the dreamland of an Irish Olympus. Yeats was full of schemes and projects: and I cannot say that the Southwark element was wanting in enthusiasm." The schemes Yeats had in mind were: (1) to open an intense cultural agitation centered around weekly concerts, lectures, discussion, and poetry readings; (2) to set up a network of nationalist reading rooms throughout the country; and (3) to organize the mass distribution of a series of new nationalist books. These proposals were adopted as the official program of the accelerated poetical movement. In addition, Yeats planned to organize a national theater that would stroll through the countryside performing at the cart's tail before peasant audiences. Douglas Hyde sat in at the Chiswick launching of Yeats's movement, but shortly afterward wandered away to pursue his own ambition in defiance of Yeats's advice, to revive the Irish language through the organization of the Gaelic League.

The reader will recognize that Yeats and Hyde had lifted the machinery for the new Irish cultural movement bodily from Young Ireland's literary organization of 1843, which Thomas Davis had contrived originally as an instrument to challenge O'Connell's monopoly upon the peasants' sources of political guidance. While it would be incorrect to say that the 1843 and the 1891 cultural movements were not aesthetic, they were certainly political as well. The new unity slogan, "Parnell is dead," did bear an ambiguity, though. In the process of transmission, Hyde and Yeats altered the original Fenian stratagem, and the cultural movement was carried through mutations even more bizarre than the student of Irish history is accustomed to expect.

On the language-revival side the confusion was impossible to conceal. Hyde's speech stated his object in this way:

It is a fact, and we must face it as a fact, that although they adopt English habits and copy England in every way, the great bulk of Irishmen and Irishwomen over the whole world are known to be filled with a dull, ever-abiding animosity against her, and—right or wrong—to grieve when she prospers, and joy when she is hurt. Such movements as Young Irelandism, Fenianism, Land Leagueism, and Parliamentary obstruction seem always to gain their sympathy and support. It is just because there appears no earthly chance of their becoming good members of the Empire that I urge that they should not remain in the anomalous position they are in, but since they absolutely refuse to become the one thing, that they become the other; cultivate what they have rejected, and build up an Irish nation on Irish lines.

No ambiguity here; this is good strong political language. And even further, he chose an exciting political simile to describe how his object was to be carried out: ". . . nothing less than a house-to-house visitation and exhortation of the people themselves will do, something . . . analogous to the procedure that James Stephens adopted throughout Ireland when he found her like a corpse on the dissecting table."[9] This is also plain speaking. But he quickly added the qualification that the house-to-house canvass would be "with a very different purpose" than Stephens'. Now his listeners were forced to wonder what he was driving at, for it was very late in the evening to claim nonpolitical purity, though afterward he did so, vociferously. The question unanswered was what kind of politics did Hyde have.

The reader will remember that Thomas Davis' nationalist activity followed twin guidelines: one, that "Arigna must be pierced with shafts and Bonmahon flaming with smelting houses," the other, that Irishmen must "reach at what is above and beyond it all . . . [in order to] extricate the lightning flash from the black cloud that bound it." Hyde hit upon the thought that if Davis' purpose was to create a spiritual nation, why need

354

Irish political aspiration pursue the old methods that were so roundabout, agonized, and foredoomed ? If one simply walked off and forgot Arigna and Bonmahon, and Home Rule, and poverty, the spiritual nation was already at hand. There it was, waiting to be seized—provided Irishmen could be induced to revive the dying language.

Hyde's recruiting campaign led off with the familiar Irish dilemma of Esau and the mess of pottage: Let us suppose, he said, that there should arise in England a corps of "able administrators" and "careful rulers" who succeeded in "making Ireland a land of wealth and factories," until all were "fat, wealthy, and prosperous," but at the cost of the extinction of the "O's" and the "Mac's" of Irish names and the obliteration of Irish history— would Irishmen accept this bargain ? "Nine Englishmen out of ten would jump to make the exchange, and I as firmly believe that nine Irishmen out of ten would indignantly refuse it."[10] Put bluntly, Irish spirituality and Irish poverty were pronounced a natural harmony. Along with his genuine nationalism, Hyde felt a temptation toward collaboration derived from the presumption that Salisbury and Balfour were permanent fixtures in Downing Street. But the Gaelic League, like the old Land League, spread like fire and among the tens of thousands of new members there were many who had no desire for collaboration. The league thereupon took on a peculiar double life. Joyce seems to have thought of it as a repressive clerical institution and he nominated satirically "Soggarth Eoghan O'Growney," the San Francisco priest who wrote little Gaelic League primers, among the nation's mock heroes. But his contemporary, W. P. Ryan, charged that the clergy had sabotaged the league's work from fear of revolution. And Patrick Pearse was able to harbor two contradictory opinions: first, that "the Gaelic League was no Messiah . . . the Gaelic League, as the Gaelic League, is a spent force"; and three months later that "the Gaelic League will be recognized in history as the most revolutionary influence that has ever come into Ireland."[11] After the Treaty, the language movement was still torn by the same confusion, and while the government enshrined it officially among the nation's schoolroom pieties, in daily practice it was thrown into the hopeless struggle against English and told in effect to survive if it could.

VII

On Yeats's side of the movement, a parallel equivocation developed, fogged over by the normal mysticism of his critical utterance. His first mid-crisis experiment in formulating a rationale plucked at Davis' spiritual string:

> Amid the clash of party against party we have tried to put forward a nationality that is above party, and amid the oncoming roar of a general election we have tried to assert those everlasting principles of love of truth

and love of country that speak to men in solitide and in the silence of the night. So far all has gone well with us, for men who are saddened and disgusted with the turn public affairs have taken have sought in our society occasion to do work for Ireland that will bring about assured good, whether that good be great or small.[12]

Standing not merely "above party" but "in the silence of the night," Yeats's purity was altogether ethereal. On a second look, however, his claim seemed somewhat presumptuous, and it was so interpreted by his contemporaries. For, while one might with great mental effort imagine a league of nonpolitical Gaelic-speakers, a society of nonpolitical Irish poets is simply unthinkable. Nonpolitical poets do not form societies; they abhor societies. Hence with Yeats as with Hyde the question that lingered was: What kind of politics is it?

The charter objective of the new literary movement was revealed in its decision to co-opt all the warring parliamentary leaders of the Split as vice-presidents. Except for a strong dislike of Healy, the society did not have much serious preference for any one of the parliamentarians over another. It was therefore an occasion for rejoicing when it succeeded in recruiting as literary comrades to Old Fenians, to poets, and to one another, the august political personages who were said to have just hacked Parnell to pieces: T. D. Sullivan, Justin M'Carthy, and the agrarian William O'Brien, a true friend who was still sponsoring Yeats's literary movement down into the old age of the Abbey Theatre.

Anti-Split sentiment poured out profusely. "During this evening at least, we are disarmed"—this was the peace message of the opening address delivered by the Anglo-Irish littérateur, the Reverend Stopford A. Brooke. "We speak together pleasantly, as French and English did in the Peninsula, when beside the brook in the evening they drew water for the armies that in the morning were to renew the battle." And feeling called on for the highest spiritual effort, he added lugubriously: "As the dead who were enemies are reconciled at last when they lie together in some great church like Westminster, so living foes are reconciled at last when they lie together in the great Temple of their country's literature."[13]

VIII

The special sorrows of the Irish poets as compared to the Gaelic linguists are nicely formulated in Yeats's poem to Hyde beginning, "Dear Craoibhin Aoibhin, look into our case," a humorous plaint against the impossibility of making poetic peace with Dublin's taste. The Irish Literary Society opened up its work of unifying the nation with a grand cat-and-dog fight. In the name of amity, the presidency was offered to the most illustrious living patriot, the aged veteran of 1843, Gavan Duffy, now Sir Charles Gavan Duffy. After his departure from Australia he had retired to Nice, at the right distance to cheer on the Parnellite offensive without incurring any partisan stigmata. Sir Charles accepted the new honor gladly. Yeats had already made publication arrangements for the new Irish library with T. Fisher Unwin in London, and with courteous firmness he sent Duffy his instructions, giving the scheduled date of the first Dublin meeting and adding:

> Perhaps you will be in Dublin then and will be so kind as to take the chair. The young men wish greatly that you would. . . . P.S. It seems to Mr. O'Leary and myself that it would be a good step towards ensuring circulation to fix as soon as possible upon the first 3 volumes of the proposed library. Mr. O'Leary and myself think that a good first volume would be a life of Wolfe Tone. . . . Mr. O'Leary thinks that my "Ballad Chronicle" would make a good second volume. For the third volume he suggests that Lady Wilde be asked to take up again the book on Sarsfield that had been projected for her. We of course wish to know if you think this a good selection or if you have anything to say in opposition or in modification.[14]

It turned out that Sir Charles had something, had much, to say in opposition. He held very strong opinions of his own, not one of them in accord with "Mr. O'Leary and myself."

Half a lifetime in Australia had obliterated from Duffy's brain most of the vestiges of the old *Nation*'s mystique. As soon as he had "kindly" taken the chair and commenced his oration to the assembled poets, he made it clear that his mind was now wholly captive to Arigna and Bonmahon. His keynote was challenging: "When I met in France, Italy, and Eygpt the marmalade manufactured at Dundee, I felt it like a silent reproach"; and to let his listeners share his reproach he added the further superfluous information, "Oranges do not grow in Dundee." One could hardly misconstrue his meaning, and he drove home his thought with insistent blows on the one theme: "Good books make us wiser, manlier, more honest, and what is less than any of these, more prosperous."[15] (He did say "less," an atavism.) He then announced that the first title for the new library venture would be an unpublished manuscript by Thomas Davis called "The Patriot Parliament" describing the constitution of James II's Dublin government-in-exile of 1689. It would be followed by anthologies of important but forgotten patriotic effusions taken from the Irish magazines of the decades just before and after the Act of Union. As for publishing the literature currently being written in Ireland, that was totally out of the question. "Who is W. B. Yeats?" he asked. He canceled Yeats's publishing arrangement with T. Fisher Unwin and replaced it with a contract of his own.

To a bystander, Duffy would seem to have invented problems where no problems were, setting up a senseless publication dilemma between Yeats's poetry and Davis' history. Anybody ought to have seen that what the situation called for was not either-or, but both. The celebrated Girondist habit of seeking the middle way had somehow failed Duffy, through vanity or ignorance resulting from residing too long abroad, a disability later to be experienced also by his fellow countryman, Joyce. To Yeats the fact that Duffy was a great untouchable fifty years his senior meant nothing. What only concerned him was that his projected "Ballad Chronicle" was dead and the *Countess Cathleen* had lost the society's sponsorship, forfeiting an estimated sale of ten thousand copies. He counterattacked furiously, supported by John O'Leary and the anti-old-fogey youth.

It was "on both sides" that "hard words were spoken." The fighting turned dirty all around and in the thick of it was Yeats, discovering for the first time his redoubtable gift for public controversy. The citizens of Dublin learned from his polemics contra Duffy that it would be unpatriotic to direct the Irish National Library project from distant Nice; also, that forty years earlier Duffy had destroyed William Carleton's talent by enticing him to didacticism in the anti-Ribbon novel, *Rody the Rover*. Aged Mitchelites turned out and disrupted one of Duffy's meetings with catcalls, "Remember Newry" and "There's a grave there." Though indebted to these graybeard ruffians, his unsummoned champions, Yeats offered Duffy formal apologies. In his memoirs he added further angry embellishments drawn from afterthoughts: that Duffy "so lacked rancor" that he was barren of personality; that he had hired a boy to read to him in the evenings from Carlyle's *Heroes and Hero Worship*; that he had brought to town a Carleton manuscript "into the center of which he had dropped a hot coal, so that nothing remained but the borders of every page" (an anecdote suggested by the actual fate at the Yeats fireside of an unsolicited manuscript from a young poetess).[16] When he used "a bad argument," O'Leary withdrew his support[17]—a caprice, Yeats said, because "one cannot fight a battle in whispers." Suddenly he was drawn to the joyful wisdom that "strife is better than loneliness," an opinion that was to furnish Dublin with a succession of poetic crises through the rest of his life.

IX

The *casus belli*—should Davis or Yeats take precedence in the new Irish library scheme?—was immediately obscured by other contentions. When attacked, Duffy invoked his authority as the possessor of the Young Irelanders' patriotic mantle. Yeats thereupon attacked Young Ireland, declaring its poetry worthless as poetry, mere doggerel and flatulence. Outraged, Duffy stood on his dignity and white hairs and attempted to defend the dubious position that the Young Irelanders were the supreme masters of the poetic art. Yeats thus succeeded in getting the issue into the most convenient form for his purpose. He brought over from Fleet Street the poet Lionel Johnson, an English aesthete–convert to Catholicism, to lend a touch of holiness to the poetic attack. Against the venerable Duffy he pitted the venerable John O'Leary, whose ancient difficulties with the poetry page of the *Irish People* had slowly and painfully forced him out of Duffy's position and into Yeats's. Yeats lost the battle but won the war. Duffy lacked the wit to retreat to a stronger position, so he held his ground and let himself be slaughtered. "Old fogeyism" in literature went down to defeat and Yeats established himself as a fearful champion of Irish poetry, a position he occupied permanently. "Oh yes, Shakespeare?" said Stephen Dedalus. "You mean that chap that writes like Synge."

It would have been fortunate for Ireland if all her quandaries were so easily dissolved. But under the aesthetic battle smoke there had opened a cluster of other pressing issues where Yeats's natural advantage was considerably weaker. Like an embattled Shakespearean king, he was in every corner of the field searching for Duffy. Duffy lifted an idea from his old enemy Cardinal Cullen and hinted at mortal sin lurking in any literary effort sympathetic to the French, those "godless scoffers." He quoted with approval the position taken by Father Hogan of Maynooth urging the Church to take a leading part in the Literary Society in order to give weight to "our denunciations of dangerous books, and especially of light and licentious reading" or of "what is either silly or debased."[18] At the crucial vote in the society, he defeated Yeats by letting it be known that he carried in his pocket a letter offering the support of Archbishop Walsh, but only on the condition of the poet's good behavior. Yeats's memoirs say that it "warned that after his [Duffy's] death the [publishing] company would fall under a dangerous influence."[19]

Duffy having enlisted the clergy on his side, Yeats set himself against the clergy. But his inherited Anglicanism was not so reckless as to suggest a frontal attack, for somebody had taught him his basic nonsectarian lesson well. Before the Split he had made the clergy a peace offering in those marvelous ballads on the two priests O'Hart and Gilligan. After Archbishop Walsh and Duffy joined forces, there were no more of these clerical offerings, but only stern and stubborn opposition. Nerve and good spirits served him well, and he was ready to defend himself as required. Eventually Frank Hugh O'Donnell, a familiar acquaintance of ours out of Irish history, turned up in town and set about to destroy Yeats by the same time-tried treatment he had once given "the atheist Bradlaugh" in the House of Commons. He wrote a pamphlet attacking *Countess Cathleen* on various grounds, but especially for an incredibility—an Irish woman "unfaithful to her marriage vows"—and for a blasphemy—a scene where "good old Father John, in spite of his prayers and his breviary, [is] killed by the devil in the shape of a brown pig! How Irish! How exquixitely Celtic!"[20] Yeats was fully competent to handle O'Donnell at any time without resort to "removal" of O'Donnell in the "manly way," as one of his somewhat credulous biographers tells us was seriously urged by his patriot comrades.

Yeats challenged the clergy to a gentlemanly duel on fair terms, the spirituality of the *sidhe* to be pitted against the holiness of the saints, and let the best man win. His first literary response to the Split was to hasten to Sligo for spiritual reinforcements: "I went down into Connaught to sit at turf fires," he said—or more precisely, to write down from the dictation of Mary Battle, the Pollexfens' cook, her rendition of the "ancient tradition" of pre-Christian Irish supernatural belief. His first post-Split publication, *The Celtic Twilight*, was built from Mary Battle's responses; his second was the sensational spirituality of *The Land of Heart's Desire*; his third, the 1895 *Poems* containing the collected *sidhe* poems that had been fed into W. E. Henley's London journals at a steady pace since the fight with Duffy. He intensified his London occult involvement. Out of these sources he constructed a complete new Irish national mystique, and not very long after, he was able to claim: "The arts are, I believe, about to take upon their shoulders the burdens that have lain upon the shoulders of priests, and to lead us back upon our journey by filling our thoughts with essences of things, and not with things."[21]

Yeats's critique charged that the Catholic clergy was positivistic, concerned merely "with things"; and in a later time his metaphorical "greasy till" for Irish prayers reached print one year ahead of Joyce's cash register accounting system in heaven. But naturally nobody could be quite as positivistic as positivists themselves. Duffy advocated economic progress and Yeats set himself against economic progress with an astonishing dogmatism. In the midst of the Duffy fracas he sent the *Boston Pilot* a sketch of the scene inside the Dublin library. "At my left hand is a man reading some registers for civil service and other examinations; opposite me an ungainly young man with a puzzled face is turning over the pages of a trigonometry work," he wrote in disgust.[22] No man doth live by bread alone, and what Ireland wanted was not progress but poetry. Before O'Connell disturbed the Irish peasants, their normal outlook was poetic, and they could "still remember the dawn of the world," following a dream that "has never been tangled by reality." From "their unbroken religious faith, and from their traditional beliefs, and from the hardness of their lives" they had learned "that this world is nothing, and that a spiritual world, where all dreams come true, is everything,"[23] a thought that harmonized precisely with Dr.

Cullen's own homily on poverty at Thurles. Naturally the life of the Irish poor was "somewhat inhospitable," but it was beautiful, because "little had changed since Adam delved and Eve span." In the peasants' world "everything was so old that it was steeped in the heart, and every powerful emotion found at once noble types and symbols for its expression."[24] Catholic Emancipation was the peasants' first big mistake, he said, and the tithe war was the second. Afterward they had been led astray by the bog lights of mechanistic and abstract economic and political grievances.

X

One of Duffy's contentions was that Irishmen could better employ their time in the study of the Irish past than in the reading of contemporary poetry. Yeats enthusiastically accepted this either-or challenge, either Davis or Yeats, either history or poetry. Against the advice of Edward Garnett, Unwin's reader, he turned it around and opened fire against Davis' "tractate" (the manuscript competing for publication against *The Countess Cathleen*). To show that he meant business, he offered a list of the "Thirty Best Books" for the proposed new lending libraries, and filled the section called "History" mostly with historical effusions by Standish O'Grady.[25] (His list of poets, masters at "the banquet of the moods," consisted of Allingham, Ferguson, Hyde, and also Katharine Tynan, of whom he had recently written truthfully in a London review that her lyrics were superior to those of "Eva of the *Nation*.") His stunt aroused widespread indignation, and in a revision he did add as a conciliatory gesture the *Jail Journal* and Wolfe Tone's *Autobiography* to stand beside O'Grady. But when he was attacked for his "ignorance" of Irish history, he made the startling reply that ignorance is a superior state of being; far better to be, as he later said, "ignorant and wanton as the dawn." He put his curse on all "argument, theory, erudition, observation," quoting Blake for his authority. What was wanted in history was not records, but revelations, not "illusions of our visible passing life," but service to "the moods," lacking which "we have no part in eternity."[26]

Extreme historical subjectivism was not new with Yeats, for his well-known banner inscription, "Words alone are certain good," dated back to 1885. His predilection had no doubt been reinforced by his reading of O'Grady's subjective historiography in the mid-1880s. The fight with Duffy did not weaken it. After 1892 he was permanently committed to the proposition that truth is the passionate conviction of just such a person as himself. But other people's passionate convictions—Constance Markiewicz's, for example—were "abstractions." As a theatricality, his opinion flaunted an arresting impudence like Wilde's epigram, "Nature imitates Art." But

361

Yeats's version asks to be much more solemnly intoned than Wilde's. Everybody quotes the sonorous lines in "An Acre of Grass":

> Grant me an old man's frenzy,
> Myself must I remake
> Till I am Timon and Lear
> Or that William Blake
> Who beat upon the wall
> Till Truth obeyed his call.[27]

So what does it mean? If the reader will stare at it long enough, he will discover that the word "obeyed" will finally stare back at him. It is a simple solipsism, the view that the world is generated in the angry vision of W. B. Yeats. Solipsism is the content, too, of his oracle that "man can embody truth but he cannot know it," which interpreted means, among other things, that history is not records but revelations.

Irish records in particular. As Thomas R. Whitaker's very thorough investigation of Yeats has put it: "If, as Yeats' occult tradition had also maintained, the will is transcendental and the world is its mirror or shadow, the poet who interprets such unconscious manifestations may be an ideal historian."[28] The view carries some authority, for did not Keats say (in part) that Beauty is Truth? Yeats's fellow countrymen necessarily held the opposite view: "We Irishmen think otherwise." They sometimes felt Yeats's flamboyant ignorance a nuisance, believing that if they might be permitted to think so, Irish history was not merely a neo-Kantian construct in the minds of poets, but was a public reality to which any symbolic invention could properly be asked to make some sort of reference.

Yeats's further elaborations of his theory explained that valid Irish history must seek only to create "strangeness" and "personality": contradictions of character must be highlighted, and the depiction of Irish history as "a mystery-play of devils and angels" must be abandoned forthwith,[29] even though "there really had been," as he explained later, "villain and victim" in some mysterious form not specified. His general historical directive was: find an irony! By this stipulation he seemed to mean that all important historical personages ought as a usual thing to be projected as Hamlets. We have already remarked on his portrait of O'Leary in the role. Somewhat more outrageously, he subjected Davitt to the same transformation, meaning it for high commendation. But Davitt's companion J. F. X. O'Brien (our old acquaintance from the Cork courtroom), whom he disdained as a Sullivanite, he refused to transform into Hamlet because he "did not care whether he used a good or a bad argument, whether he seemed a fool or a clever man, so that he carried his point."[30] Patrick Sarsfield's biographer must emphasize, he said, that his hero had married for money and was lax in his discipline of pillagers. Major Sirr, the murderer of Lord Edward Fitzgerald, must be admired by Irish historians for his love of children and painters. In projecting Daniel O'Connell's personality, the big point was that he was unchaste and had once said, "the verdict's *the* thing." The rule seems a powerful truth instrument, very modern-American-academic. One discovered, though, that it was difficult to apply, for when George Moore in *Hail and Farewell* told how Sir Hugh Lane had exhibited himself to the guests at Coole Park in one of his Aunt Augusta's frocks,[31] Yeats found in the anecdote no ironic discovery of personality or strangeness at all, but only a dastardly slander by "an old foul mouth."

Anyone familiar with Irish history will understand that Yeats's free-ranging counterattacks invited trouble. William Martin Murphy's newspaper, the *Independent*, supported later by D. P. Moran's weekly *Leader*, replied with untiring rebuttal against the Celtic twilight, somewhat in the style of Joyce's celebrated pun. Yeats's normal self-defense should have turned for support to the Fenians. But they too were offended by the oddities in his onslaught, so that when the sides were chosen, they went mostly over with Duffy, creating a spasmodic unity of all shades of nationalists against him. Hence his political commentary afterward tended to obliterate the differentiation between Fenian and Sullivan, between John MacBride and W. M. Martin, blurring a distinction necessary to comprehend modern Irish history and literature.

XI

The advanced nationalists could see Yeats's genius right enough, but they were somewhat repelled by the manner at once chilling and frenetic, or in his phrase, "cold and passionate." In the Wade letters one picks up a thread of his waywardness on July 25, 1889, where he is found plunging head first into the murk of the Cronin murder case. There appeared in London Mrs. Alexander Sullivan, the wife of the head of the Chicago Triangle. A couple of months after the "poor Pigott" letter, Yeats wrote to Katharine Tynan:

> I have seen such a good deal of Mrs. Alexander Sullivan. She is looking much better than when I wrote last and seems to have quite recovered her spirits. She is coming this evening to meet York Powell, Sydney Hall and Miss Purser. I wrote an article for her a day or two ago—something about Dr. Cronin. She is not yet sure that he is dead at all. He seems to have been great rascal. It was really a very becoming thing to remove him—if he be dead and the man found in Chicago be not someone else. A Spy has no rights.[32]

Yeats's biographers have told us wrongly that he "had a sensible impatience of internecine quarrels." His haste to follow Mrs. Sullivan's invitation to entangle himself in a blood feud in far-off Chicago looks instead like adolescent adventurism for no conceivable object. The escapade naturally made him new enemies. He alienated the Dublin Fenians, all anti-Triangle and pro-Devoy. He also alienated John Devoy himself, the last man that any Irishman would want to choose at random for his enemy. Another believer in the theory that "one cannot fight a battle in whispers," Devoy counter-attacked Yeats through his poetry, and all of O'Leary's efforts failed to make peace between them. Devoy's files contained a courteous solicitation from Yeats for an interview in New York dated 1903. His answer has not survived, but as late as 1911 his enmity was still lively, for in that year John Butler Yeats watched him writhing at an Abbey performance of the *Playboy* in New York and muttering, "Son of a bitch, that's not Ireland." For further expressions of his tenacious vengeance, the reader may consult the *Gaelic American*'s vituperative stories about the Abbey's American tour which were gathered by Lady Gregory.[33]

XII

One's eye is drawn next to a couple of startling letters from Yeats to O'Leary dated July 1892. The first recounts Yeats's private negotiations with S. L. MacGregor Mathers, an adept, magician, and translator of *Kabbala Unveiled*, a hysteric whose mind ran on "streets running with blood" as a necessary prelude to the conversion of the world to occultism. He is the magician in Yeats's essay called "Magic" and the subject of the line, "I thought him half a lunatic, half knave." The letter says:

> Dear Mr. O'Leary, I wrote to Mathers but found that he is as I feared in Paris. He has written me a long letter going into the question of organization. I would send it on to you but he had mixed up with it some occult matters which are of course private. He would be glad to meet any one who came from us, and would go carefully into the whole question. . . . He is strong for an immediate commencement on the ground of the length of time such things take. I am writing to him an explanation of my own position in the matter and the reasons I see for some delay. My own occult art (though I cannot expect you to accept the evidences) has again and again for a longish time now been telling me of many curious coming events and as some have come true (all that have had time) I rather expect the others to follow suit and the time for his plan among the rest.[34]

One would have to infer from this mysterious message that Yeats had on his own responsibility committed "us"—O'Leary and himself—to undertaking joint political adventures of a sensational but unspecified nature with the "half a lunatic" occultist. O'Leary's reply we lack, but its content can be reconstructed. He apparently reprimanded Yeats for proposing any political adventure whatever with Mathers and for seeking his political guidance in Mathers' magic incantations. Yeats's second letter, replying to O'Leary's missing reprimand, first gave excuses for his negotiations with Mathers, then said: "Now as to Magic. It is surely absurd to hold me 'weak' or otherwise because I chose to persist in a study which I decided deliberately four or five years ago to make, next to my poetry, the most important pursuit of my life. Whether it be, or be not, bad for my health can only be decided by one who knows what magic is and not at all by any amateur." He then accused O'Leary of conspiring with John Butler Yeats against him, and concluded with a defiance of O'Leary's "reproving postcard": "If I had not made magic my constant study I could not have written a single word of my Blake book, nor would *The Countess Cathleen* have ever come to exist. . . . I have always considered myself a voice of what I believe to be a greater renaissance—the revolt of the soul against the intellect—now beginning in the world."[35]

If this second letter on the Mathers affair could be isolated from the first, it would look like a plucky *Defense of Poesie* against a brutal political encroachment, and it is universally so interpreted. But when poetry is not under attack, can it be said to be defended? The issue raised is not the integrity of poetry, but political adventurism, those "curious coming events" of which Yeats and Mathers had second-sight prior notice.

Yeats's tantalizing, mysterious language in the two letters to O'Leary was clarified thirty years later in his autobiography (see "The Tragic Generation," part 18). MacGregor Mathers, it turns out, was a literalist. He believed in the "power" of magic, and by power he meant just that. As Yeats's recollections tell us, his dream was "doubtless vague," but however that might be, he got himself a sword and "imagined a Napoleonic role for himself, a Europe transformed according to his fancy." Like Joseph Chamberlain in 1886, he further occupied himself in passing out prospective ministerial appointments "to unlikely people." Unfortunately, a scholar has no choice but to read the same literalism back into Yeats's two letters. The coming "revolt" of soul against intellect was apparently envisioned as military. Inflamed by Mathers' "lunacy," Yeats's dreams had apparently forecast the imminence of Armageddon, after which the blessed state that he later called Unity of Being would be imposed on Ireland. But what about the "sinews of war"? They would consist in the invocation of vast and terrible magical images, ready to "move of themselves with some powerful, even turbulent life, like those painted horses that trampled the rice-fields of Japan." Naturally, the imminent Irish revolution would be directed by adepts and occult poets; for it is Mathers' dubious distinction in political science to have invented a polity more repulsive even than theocracy.[36] Offhand, Yeats's overexcited state of mind might seem charmingly youthful and Shelleyan. But it needed only another crisis and the comrades in Sam Browne belts to produce the unamusing adventurism of 1932, when he set out with General O'Duffy to make certain that "Europe belongs to Dante and the Witches's Sabbath, not to Newton."[37] In any case, O'Leary and John Butler Yeats read his letter and stood appalled. They thought he must be losing his "health," that is to say, his mind. He thought them fools, mere positivists, an opinion easily extended to their less brilliant compatriots in the mass.

This extraordinary exchange of letters on Mathers closed the creative phase of the Yeats–O'Leary relationship. They continued to correspond, mostly about the repayment of a trifling debt Yeats owed O'Leary. Yeats now took all pains to stress his independence. Mathers came once again into the correspondence. Yeats wrote, enclosing a bit of cash, that he was off to Paris and could be reached at a certain address—care of S. L. Mathers. Responding to O'Leary's offer of Parisian introductions, he added that besides Mathers he wanted to see nobody else in Paris except Verlaine and Mallarmé, "for just now I want a quiet dream with the holy Kabbala and naught else, for I am tired—tired."[38] Let O'Leary put that in his dudeen and smoke it. Eventually Yeats made a public declaration of his independence in a *Bookman* review of O'Leary's long-awaited book, *Recollections of Fenians and Fenianism*. The review praised O'Leary for "abstract" moral courage, which he contrasted to the "loose-lipped, emotional, sympathetic, impressionable Irishman." O'Leary believed, he added, that there are things a man should not do even to save a nation. But his book he found to be "ill arranged" (it is chronological), "rambling," and, an afterthought added, "unreadable." As for himself he preferred "the history of the soul" to any "history of things."[39] With these remarks, the Yeats-O'Leary correspondence terminated except for a few strays, requests by Yeats for some favor, always amiably granted. The severance was perhaps overdue. O'Leary was drawing toward his seventieth year, and the designation "Old Fenian" was finally becoming literally accurate. And after reading the letters about Mathers, one is surprised to make the calculation of Yeats's age and find that it comes out at thirty years.

The friendly separation from O'Leary left Yeats in much more complete command of the new national literary activity than Hyde could ever build on his side of the fence. In marvelous self-contradictory style, the poetic movement flew Fenian colors but (by Yeats's revision of the anti-Split slogan) officially disdained politics. Yeats operated henceforth upon the hidden premise that no urgent Irish problem remained on the list of unfinished national business except the correction of Irish taste. His subsequent behavior in nearly all its details can be referred back to this base, both in its hits and in its misses. I have spoken a good deal about the misses;

among the hits, the most wonderful was naturally the Irish literary movement itself, which proliferated with such energy, and composed so many poems, plays, essays, short stories, and novels that some misanthropic onlookers began to complain of overproduction. In wrestling with the enigma of Parnell's rise and fall, I quoted earlier Brecht's great epigram about the ideal leader, political or cultural: the teacher of the people, by the people taught. Yeats's last serious attempt to honor the principle was his projected multivolumed treatise on the Irish fairies, which he finally aborted as a monster of pedantry and tedium. Afterward, he fell into a habit that can only be described by the phrase of a well-known sociologist of Victorian times, "the fetishism of commodities," the commodities being works like *The Shadowy Waters* and *At the Hawk's Well*. The inevitable concomitant was resistance and in turn the burgeoning of his two dominant last themes: alienation from those who refused to be taught, and the method that Herbert Howarth has called "the story of the making of the work made."

To replace O'Leary Yeats chose for his new political guides his fellow occultists, among whom Armageddon was a subject for daily breakfast-table conversation. His memoirs, in mysterious language, recall these years as a time when he was driven by fear of democratic excess into personal fanaticism, attributed unchivalrously to Maud Gonne's example. We are indebted to Richard Ellmann for finding a letter by Stuart Merrill describing a talk with Yeats in 1896: "Yeats, who has a very clear idea of social questions, and who sees them from a lofty level, favors a union of superior forces for revolutionary action. He envisages revolution after an impending European war, like us all. He has even collected the prophecies of various countries on this subject, and all are agreed that the war will be unleashed in these next few years."[40] Merrill's words "prophecies," "superior," and "lofty" were not carelessly chosen, and this conversation can hardly be what Ellmann had in mind when he described Yeats's behavior of the time to be essentially struggles against extremists.

XIII

Fenians were thoroughly familiar with the phenomenon of the verbal revolutionary, called a "spouter" and believed dangerous. Yeats thought it singular that his young nationalist acquaintances were constantly scrutinizing one another to estimate how much each "would be willing to sacrifice for Ireland." He failed to grasp what their question meant because his own case was naturally special: an acknowledged genius is not to be confused with the public-house warriors of "Slattery's Mounted Fut." Yet Irishmen sensed in Yeats, beginning at the Duffy fight, a reserve, even a contempt, lurking in the great sensibility, and a feeling that he had strayed among

367

them (as he later confessed) much as "one might choose a side upon the football field."[41]

The formal public face of his patriotism was dull enough, consisting mostly of exhumed slogans out of the Irish past. He deplored the rancors of class, thinking of the Coopers and the Gore-Booths of Sligo. Acting from a sense of aristocratic obligation to art, those great Ascendancy families had condescended to recognize socially the poet nephew of their bourgeois neighbor Pollexfen; and Yeats in gratitude took up his enemy Duffy's old ideal of "a combination of all classes." Not understanding the unpopular reception accorded Lord Carlisle's consignment of Ireland to be forever the "mother of flocks and herds," he offered his audience the same bucolic future, predicting that "Ireland will always be a country where men plow and sow and reap."[42] He occasionally said something, though very little, about certain political differences existing between Ireland and England. Prosperity he rejected on behalf of his countrymen, as he spoke a very great deal about Ireland's preference for "visions of unfulfilled desire" over English materialism and the "sordid compromise of success."[43] All this added up to an elaborate endorsement of Douglas Hyde's retreat to the proposition that Irish spirituality and Irish poverty were two sides of the one priceless coin. Yeats and Hyde—like Arnold—were both ready to settle for a strictly poetic solution of Irish national ambitions. There was an important difference, though, between them. The gentle Hyde, angry at no living soul, thought his object could be achieved peacefully. But Yeats anticipated a need for physical force. He could not draw his mind from Mathers' bloody apocalypse, from overheated meditations on "The Valley of the Black Pig." There, as prologue to the soul's reconquest of the world,

> the clash of fallen horsemen and the cries
> Of unknown perishing armies beat about my ears.[44]

Looking at the anemia of his social ideals, his fellow countrymen were entitled to wonder why, if his Ireland was never actually going anywhere, his melodrama was so very pressing.

Many times in later life Yeats suggested that the smashup of Parnellism signaled the great moment for Irish poetic release: "A couple of years* before the death of Parnell, I had wound up my introduction to those selections from the Irish novelists with the prophecy of an intellectual movement at the first lull in politics, and now I wished to fulfil my prophecy. I did not put it in that way, for I preferred to think that the sudden emotion that now came to me, the sudden certainty that Ireland was to be like soft

* The phrase "a couple of years" is inaccurate; "a couple of months" would be closer. The introduction mentioned was written during the frenzy of the North Kilkenny by-election. The effect of the slip of the memory is to smear the glories of Parnellism at the height of its power with the shame of the Split.

368

wax for years to come, was a moment of supernatural insight."[45] The statement is puzzling, for Ireland already had "an intellectual movement." The six years before Parnell's death were as happy and creative as any in Yeats's whole life. That "Ireland was to be like soft wax for years to come" is curious too; it refers not only to Mathers' schemes for a takeover, but to more humble ambitions as well, to the need of normal literary acclaim. He had passionate hopes for his projected Unity of Image. His hopes were at least in part a futility. For that he could rightly blame the senility of Sir Charles Gavan Duffy. He could rightly blame himself, too, though he did not do so.

Irishmen might be hostile, but Oscar Wilde turned up one night in London after the theater and praised all of Yeats's work extravagantly. By definition that was the epitome of success, and it added to his bitterness over Irish troubles. In March 1894 he published a strange, rancorous story, "The Crucifixion of the Outcast," in which monks torture and then crucify an Irish "gleeman," a poet like himself. They hate him for his imagination. The story has a marked paranoid tone, like Stephen Dedalus' uneasiness over "the archons of Sinn Fein and their noggin of hemlock"; and thus was born a new literary recipe, the theme of the crucifixion of the Irish outcast-poet.

On bidding farewell to O'Leary, Yeats chose for his new literary mentor a poet of "the tragic generation," Arthur Symons. Through Symons he met George Moore and in turn, Moore's cousin, the Galway landlord and littérateur Edward Martyn, the hero of *Hail and Farewell*. Martyn invited Yeats and Symons to visit him at his Victorian-Gothic castle in Galway. They went and there met Martyn's regal neighbor from Coole Park, the widowed Lady Gregory, who had a marble bust of Maecenas in her garden and an incipient literary organizing ability second only to that of Yeats himself. She saw in Yeats a rare and delicate talent in process of destroying himself with madness and bad company, and a genius competent to restore the tarnished luster of her social class. A "witch," said Symons; "he could tell from her 'terrible' eye that she would 'get Willy.'"[46] Get him she did, if that is the right phrase, for in her he saw "the best blood," ceremonial stability, understanding, convalescence, and the promise of being pampered with custard and hot-water bottles. Ring out the old, ring in the new.

Lady Gregory's new phase of Irish literature prepared to recapitulate the old struggle against Duffy. To narrate these wars in full would range far beyond the limits of my study, for an intense conflict occupied the next thirty years, the *Playboy* fracas itself forming merely one skirmish. The dispute never was finally adjudicated. It can be said in brief that over the years many telling points were scored on both sides. Yeats established three facts incontrovertibly. (1) The author of "God Save Ireland" was not "one of the greatest poets who ever moved the heart of man."[47] (2) ". . . It is extremely easy to be less great than Mangan or Carleton; it is not impossible to be greater; but to *be* Mangan, to *be* Carleton, is a clear impossibility"—in short, if you have no individuality of style and theme you have no literature.[48] (3) No one would dare say "that Irish literature had not a greater name in the world" than it had had when he first came forth fighting.[49] Yeats's opposition established their three points with equal clarity. (1) It was incongruous for Ireland's national poet to assert, or even to think privately, that *The Shadowy Waters* "is a wild mystical thing carefully arranged to be an insult to the regular theatre-goer who is hated by [myself and Florence Farr]."[50] (2) Abstractly considered as poetry, Yeats's work was undeniably beautiful, but as nationalism it was noteworthy for his laughable alienation from the Irish nation, past or present. (3) While any audience must grant "the postulate of freedom for the dramatist," still, in a theater called national it must "reserve the right to judge" for itself "whether these dramas are national," since all "art must be judged by the actual results the artist submits to our criticism" and not by the author's "intention."[51] This last argument undoubtedly sensed that the reciprocating creative cycle of poet and people was seriously disturbed, if not ruptured. Yeats's respectful rebuttal stated that while all valid art is certainly national, criticism must always "be international." His adversaries translated "international" to read "English," and there the issue joined and the battle lines formed for the contention that continues to this day.[52]

CHAPTER 24

Literary Parnellism

I

In Irish literary tradition, in Yeats, in Joyce, in O'Casey, an operatic finale is obligatory for Parnell. The strains of Siegfried's funeral march ascend fittingly out of the denouement, for the Wagnerian effect was "really there." We must remind ourselves, though, that the story had a beginning and middle as well as an end, and that the end itself was equivocal. As we watch the curtain call of all the dramatis personae, naturally the leading man will come first to the footlights, followed by Captain and Mrs. O'Shea, by Gladstone and the Nonconformist English voter, by Archbishop Croke and the mob at Castlecomer, by Healy and the Bantry band—all of them stars with a top billing. But then come the other actors more quickly forgotten: Pigott and his accomplices, the *Times*, the attorney general, the home secretary, and Sir Rowland Ponsonby Blennerhassett (some find it very hard to keep in mind the frame-up); followed by "the hillside men," whose unexpected entry into the last scene when Parnell called them to his side suddenly set afire Healy's previous indifference to the sexual scandal; and at last Lalor and O'Leary, who had repeatedly said for two generations that the English party system and the circumambient air of Westminster would corrupt any Irish patriot and blunt any Irish parliamentary assault.

As I have pointed out, the Fenians were pleased to magnify the revolutionary nationalism embodied in Parnell's name, while they simultaneously combated the destructive factionalism that fed at the same source. Their campaign against the "nine years's vituperation" of the Split gradually took hold of Irish politics. Yeats himself became in time almost mellow toward Tim Healy, and he looked with an adulation that some think excessive upon the most formidable champion of the "Sullivan gang" (his own phrase), T. D. Sullivan's grandson, the "pitiless" Kevin O'Higgins. The Sullivan gang, in reciprocity, made Yeats a senator of the Irish Free State. When the homicidal face of the Split had passed into slow eclipse, the Fenian slogan, "Parnell is dead," came true at last. In literature, though, Parnell was patently anything but dead. Parnellism as a literary phenomenon enjoyed a vigorous life history of its own, with many surprises.

The first literary reaction to Parnell was not adulatory. George Moore and Lady Gregory begrudged him more than the minimum of formal respect that was due to his power to injure them as great Irish landlords. I have described how George Moore, indulging his Balzacian impulse to record clinically the nerve spasms of his panic-stricken fellow landlords, had meanwhile held himself ready for the surrender. Lady Gregory was less public in articulating her attitudes, and they have to be reconstructed.

While still Miss Augusta Persse she had watched the opening of the land war from her family's great estate at Roxborough, county Galway. In March 1880 at age twenty-eight she married a neighboring sexagenarian landlord and colonial administrator, Sir William Gregory, and moved over to Coole Park. It too was under Land League siege. Her biographer tells that the Gregory family did not carry firearms for protection, explaining that they had no reason for fear because "Coole was on the side of the people" always.[1] This explanation credits Sir William's genial urbanity, but it forgets the Gregory clause and the famine clearances. Sir William had been a governor of Ceylon, but he was apparently an unorthodox colonialist, for in visiting Egypt he and Lady Gregory expressed open sympathy for the native revolutionists. Their liberality to the Egyptian fellahin did not extend to Ireland. During the debate on the first Home Rule bill in 1886, Wilfred Blunt recorded a conversation with Lady Gregory about the Irish crisis:

> Called on Lady Gregory, who is growing very bitter against my politics, if not against me. It is curious that she, who could see so clearly in Egypt when it was a case between the Circassian Pashas and the Arab fellahin, should be blind now that the case is between English landlords and Irish tenants in Galway. But property blinds all eyes, and it is easier for a camel to pass through the eye of a needle, than for an Irish landlord to enter into the kingdom of Home Rule. She comes of a family, too, who are "bitter protestants," and has surrounded herself with people of her class from Ireland, so that there is no longer room for me in her house.[2]

This attitude was certainly not final, but it does chart her point of origin in "bitter" Protestantism and in eyes "blinded" by ownership of a house shaken, as Yeats's indignant poem said, by the land agitation.

Each of these two wounded Connaught landlords felt an understandable urge to write off Ireland and go away. Lady Gregory described herself as an emigrant and set up a London salon. After she was widowed in 1892, she put her son in Harrow and took up professional editorial work in England, preparing her late husband's family archives for publication. Meanwhile, Moore systematically eradicated his Irish past and proclaimed himself more

English than Dickens, citing the British success of his new novel *Esther Waters* as proof. It was not until some years later that W. B. Yeats, acting as a talent scout for the Irish literary movement, discovered him and Lady Gregory, found them work to do, and ordered them home.

II

The first literary writer to sense the literary potential of the Parnell story was Standish O'Grady. To the discoverer of Cuchullain thus belongs the second and equal honor, the discovery of Parnell. Socially oriented like Moore and Lady Gregory, he too had been wrathful in the beginning, as we have seen. But afterward a chance meeting with the dying Chief moved him to pity. The violent clerical explosion that accompanied the Split had stirred him to feel almost fellowship with the hard-pressed fellow Anglican. He suspected, too, that Parnell was harmless, "no out-and-out revolutionist," and that he must all along have "planned out ways and means for preserving the Irish gentry, not at the cost of the Irish peasant but at the cost of the Imperial Treasury,"[3] envisioning Wyndham's Land Act two decades ahead of the event.

O'Grady had attended the Rotunda mass meeting after the close of the sessions in Committee Room Fifteen, and he noted that Parnell was "ill-dressed, his hair was long and untrimmed, he was nearly bald, the rigid back and upright carriage were gone, he was bowed in the shoulders, his face was emaciated, he looked like a man who would not last long." A few weeks later he met him driving along a country road in Wicklow. It was a cold day and Parnell, he said, was "muffled in the most copious manner [with] quite a hill of rags, cloaks, and shawls." The two men talked for ten minutes, or rather Parnell talked, "talked almost altogether about his mines and quarries, on that subject he was almost cracked." In tune with Thomas Davis, Parnell had ordered Avondale to be "pierced with shafts" and told O'Grady "he believed that at last he had struck iron, and was going to do great things in the bowels of the earth." Again O'Grady noted the "pallor of death" on his "worn and hollow face."[4]

After Parnell had fulfilled these prognostications and died, O'Grady remembered him fondly. A little book of historical essays called *The Story of Ireland*, published just in time to catch the disaster of the second Home Rule bill, is packed with a miscellany of sharp new paradoxes. He admired the "cheerful, careless" rapacity with which the Viking raiders had gutted the Irish tombs of their treasure; he admired Cromwell; he admired the yeoman militia who crushed the rebellion of 1798.[5] He also admired the dead Parnell. Concerning the scandal, he predicted that history would reverse the verdict of the hysterical passing moment:

The offense which led to his overthrow and then to his death will not militate against his reputation in history. The Muse of history loves best her imperfect heroes. That is curious, but a fact, and the imperfection found in Parnell is just that which, instead of showing as a blot, becomes, when seen through softening mists of time and memory, something that radiates a pathetic beauty. This too is curious, but a fact. Posterity will easily forgive Parnell and like him probably all the better for his weakness.[6]

This was a bold and original interpretation, the first sketch of literary Parnellism.

O'Grady concluded his Parnell vignette with a second originality, pitched in a more exalted tone. Always a student of heavenly melodrama, he described the graveside scene at Glasnevin in the falling October dusk:

Again I state a fact; it was witnessed by thousands. While his followers were committing Charles Parnell's remains to the earth, the sky was bright with strange lights and flames. Only a coincidence, possibly; and yet persons not superstitious have maintained that there is some mysterious sympathy between the human soul and the elements, and that storms and other elemental disturbances have too often succeeded or accompanied great battles to be regarded as only fortuitous. Truly the souls of men were widely and deeply troubled that night, electrical and high-wrought in the extreme.[7]

Modern Yeatsists will instantly recognize O'Grady's words; his eschatological meteorology was destined to see hard literary service. Not for a long time to come, though.

III

In the beginning Yeats watched Parnellism remotely, a casual and mildly interested spectator. His aloofness is not surprising, since O'Leary himself did not become a Parnellite until December 1890. The Sligo Pollexfen clan was naturally anti-Parnell; and John Butler Yeats was another Irishman to be called home by the outburst of the land war in 1880, threatened with poverty at the loss of his Kildare rents. Yeats *fils* at age fifteen was too young to comprehend the land war itself, but he had reached seventeen and eighteen at the time of the imprisonment of Parnell, the Kilmainham treaty, the Phoenix Park murders, and the hanging of the Invincibles. The Yeatses were living in Roundtown that year, and if young Willy had been on the roadway one May evening after teatime he could have seen the cabby Kavanagh drive by at high speed with Joe Brady clinging to his outside car. On all this passionate historical drama his published writings are totally silent.

In 1885, as we have noted, Yeats began his study of Young Ireland and stood "in the presence of his theme." Two years later, after seven years in

Ireland, the Yeatses moved back to London again, at first briefly to South Kensington and afterward to Bedford Park, Chiswick, for a long residence. Yeats now meditated his theme in the British Museum. He composed Irish verse, anthologized Irish fiction, and assembled from published folklore a book about Irish fairies. Meanwhile Irish history continued as always to produce its regular quota of startling episodes. The *Times* facsimile and the Plan of Campaign came to pass, and the special commission set up shop. Though Yeats was pleased to write at this time, "with Irish literature and Irish thought alone have I to do,"[8] he allowed these events also to pass him by unperceived, or at least, unrecorded in the published letters.

Up to the moment of the Split, Yeats's letters show an attitude toward the living Parnell that can only be called indifferent. Through O'Leary's recommendation, he became literary correspondent for the *Boston Pilot*, published by John Boyle O'Reilly, a Fenian alumnus of English prisons. In the three years beginning with 1889, nineteen letters were sent forth and printed under the by-line, "The Celt in London." In all these pieces, which combined to make a book of modest length, the very term "Home Rule" was taboo, and Parnell's name appeared but twice, once in a list of the pre-publication subscribers to O'Leary's book on Fenianism, once again in a simple notation of passing time, in the phrase, "down to the death of Parnell."[9] Yeats's private letters are equally indifferent. As soon as the family moved back to London in 1887, he told of hurrying to the House of Commons in order to listen to the Irish oratory. He was particularly taken with Tim Healy's "rugged, passionate speech," denoting "a good earth power."[10] The one trip was seemingly all he required. The first appearance of Parnell's name in the Wade collection of letters does not occur until four years later, after the Split and the North Kilkenny by-election, in a letter to John O'Leary dated January 22, 1891. It restates approximately O'Leary's own position of the time, and while acute, it also carries a toneless quality of ventriloquism. Yeats said:

> It seems as though Parnell's chances had greatly improved these latter weeks. His last two speeches were wonderfully good. I wish I was over in Ireland to see and hear how things are going. The Hartlepool victory should help him by showing that his action has not injured the cause over here as much as people say. [Hartlepool was the Liberal party's first English by-election victory after the Split.] My father is bitterly opposed to Parnell on the ground chiefly, now, of his attacks on his followers. To me, if all other reasons were absent, it would seem plain that a combination of priests with the "Sullivan gang" is not likely to have on its side in political matters divine justice. The whole business will do this good anyway. The Liberals will have now to pass a good measure if any measure at all—at least so I read the matter.[11]

Richard Ellmann quotes a similar expression of this sentiment in another letter to O'Leary not in Wade, presumably written at about the same time.[12]

While the Parnellite storm mounted to its final fury, Yeats relapsed once more into silence, which lasted nine months. Late in the summer of 1891 he went to Ireland on occult and literary errands. He had by then established a London publishing connection with W. E. Henley's journals, an unsatisfactory outlet because both English and "ninetyish," two poetic themes he already judged to be nullities. He looked to "Ireland alone," but he had no Irish publisher. He had been rebuffed by the *Nation*, apparently because he was identified with O'Leary. T. D. Sullivan had featured a clerical attack against the godlessness of his anthology of scenes from Carleton. Probing for new Irish outlets more distinguished than the *Vegetarian* or the organ of the Gaelic Athletic Association (defunct), he called at the *United Ireland* editorial office in Dublin. The welcome he received was effusive, for in August 1891 the future of Parnellism was not so sanguine that *United Ireland* could afford to slight any opportunity of extending its list of friends. Yeats wrote to O'Leary that the editors were "ready for articles" and to Katharine Tynan he upgraded the phrase to "anxious for literary articles."[13] For Parnell's paper he wrote twenty articles with his normal taboo still virtually intact, except for one statement of the anti-Split line and one attack on Healy.

His silence on Parnell was broken by a sudden, brief, and resounding burst. The same angry black-bordered Saturday issue of *United Ireland* that demanded revenge upon Sexton, O'Brien, and Healy for the murder of the Chief contained dirges for the occasion written by poets of O'Leary's group, now banded into the Young Ireland League. Katharine Tynan and Lionel Johnson were represented. Among them too was W. B. Yeats, who offered a poem entitled "Mourn—and Then Onward," a doctrinaire statement of the Fenian line. He thereupon disowned it. He never reprinted it, justifying himself no doubt with the knowledge that it is not a good poem, though he did reprint other occasional pieces equally flat (for example, "Shepherd and Goatherd"). And he never attempted to strengthen it with the revisions that reclaimed other unripe efforts.

On Sunday, the very next day after "Mourn—and Then Onward," Parnell's corpse arrived in a sealed lead casket at Kingstown at six in the morning. His poet-encomiast happened to be on the Kingstown pier. "I was expecting a friend [Maud Gonne], but met what I thought much less of at the time, the body of Parnell." Yeats did not go to the funeral, for (at age twenty-six) "being in my sensitive and timid youth, I hated crowds," besides hating "what crowds implied,"[14] and thus to his later chagrin he missed the cosmic skyrockets. He seems to have watched the procession, however, for on the same Sunday he wrote his sister Lily a colorful report:

I send you a copy of *United Ireland* with a poem of mine on Parnell, written the day he died to be in time for the press that evening. It has been a success.

The Funeral is just over. The people are breathing fire and slaughter. The wreaths have such inscriptions as "Murdered by the Priests" and a number of Wexford men were heard by [a] man I know promising to remove a Bishop and seven priests before next Sunday. Tomorrow will bring them cooler heads I doubt not.

Meanwhile Healy is in Paris and the people hunt for his gore in vain. Dillon and he are at feud and the feud is being fought out by the *Freeman* and *National Press* in diverse indirect fashions.

Tell Jack I have no more fairy articles at present but will get some done soon.[15]

This occurrence of Parnell's name is the second to appear in Wade's edition of the Yeats letters, and the last occurrence of substance. His little youthful flurry of Parnellism he had now put behind him. Two months later, Parnell's name occurred a third time when he reported to O'Leary that he had written to a certain Lavelle about stirring up the Young Ireland League and that he had received the reply—"they were waiting until things had settled down after Parnell's death." To find the fourth occurrence in his letters, we must skip ten years forward.

It was no effort for Yeats to embrace the Fenians anti-Split line proclaiming that "Parnell is dead" and "you cannot bring him back to life," Fenian slogans that aimed to cool down the popular debate whether Parnell had or had not been "hacked to pieces" by his stalwart lieutenants. At the first appearance of O'Grady's new line on Parnellism, it was Yeats himself who took the trouble to scold him for trouble mongering:

The Story of Ireland [is] an impressionist narrative of Irish affairs from the coming of the gods to the death of Parnell, which has aroused acrimonious controversy, and is still something of a byword, for Ireland is hardly ready for impressionism, above all for a whimsical impressionism which respects no traditional hatred or reverence, which exalts Cromwell and denounces the saints, and is almost persuaded that when Parnell was buried, as when Columba died, "the sky was alight with strange lights and flames."[16]

O'Grady might be ready to be "almost persuaded" about the heavenly portents, but plainly Yeats was not. His Parnellism still lay in the remote future.

Years passed, and toward the turn of the century he is found condemning Parnell for his materialism. Parnell's great effort, he said, was really un-Irish and utilitarian: "the Celt, never having been meant for utilitarianism, has made a poor business of it. . . ."[17] The literary movement's initial Dublin theater successes led him to speculate that Parnell's death might be the work of an all-wise but devious Providence bent on creating an Irish theater: "Our [dramatic] utterance was so necessary that it seems as if the hand that broke the ball of glass, [i.e., destroyed Home Rule] that now lies in fragments full of a new iridescent life, obeyed some impulse from beyond its wild and capricious will."[18] If the reader will turn back now and reread Yeats's stirring public message on Irish history that I used for the epigraph of this volume, he will be in a position to learn what his private understanding of the "important destiny" of Ireland was: it was his completion of the manuscript of *The Shadowy Waters*.

In 1900 Redmond announced that he had the cash in hand to build the great Parnell monument in Rutland Square. The project carried no political interest for Yeats. But one day he read in the papers that the lord mayor had gone to America to shop for a Parnell statue, and he was seized by the reasonable fear that the new memorial would prove to be another in the sculptural taste of A. M. Sullivan and in the style of Father Mathew's marble effigy on O'Connell Street. He wrote a letter to the press demanding that a commission of artists be made responsible for the artistic design. Dubliners were read a lecture, strictly aesthetic: "The good sculptor, poet, painter or musician pleases other men in the long run because he has first pleased himself. Work done to please others is conventional or flashy and, as time passes, becomes a weariness or a disgust. Yours truly W. B. Yeats."[19] Thereupon his silence on the subject of Parnell once again descended, lasting this time for more than a decade.

IV

Without prologue there suddenly appeared in Dublin the most daring addition to literary Parnellism since O'Grady's original discovery fifteen years before: Lady Gregory found Parnell's tomb empty, so to speak. In 1911 the Abbey Theatre produced her one-act play, *The Deliverer*, about the Egyptian captivity of the chosen people. When the first Israelite speaker opens with, "I'm near starved with the hunger," the Kiltartan dialect bespeaks an Irish allegory. With study, the modern reader will discern that one of the peasant characters represents Dillon, that another carries the loose-lipped name of "Dan," that another one is sufficiently revolting to stand for Healy (who had just donated five pounds to the Abbey endowment fund), and that a fourth, called "Malachi," is some sort of a poetical Parnellite.

After a leisurely dramaturgical preparation, enters on stage Moses-Parnell, called "The King's Nurseling" because of his favored position in Pharaoh's household. On overhearing a conversation that reveals his parentage to be Israelite instead of Egyptian, he "then and there" resolves to set his captive people free: "What way could I have an easy mind in it, and my own people being under cruelty and torment? It is along with you I will stop." As his scheme for flight matures, Healy and Dillon are at first effusively appreciative, relishing especially the coarse materialistic pleasures to come: "Quality fish it would be easy to be eating. The bones of them will melt away in the fire. The smiths do be forging gold the same as iron. . . . We will lift him up on our shoulders passing every bad spot on the road! We'll have a terrible illumination for him the day we will come to our own! We will, and put out shouts for him through the whole of the seven parishes! His name will be more lasting than the cry of the plover on the bog!"

But after a few more lines of dialogue they turn suspicious and resentful. He had neglected to give them a "red halfpenny" to drink his health with, and "according to what I'm told, he's a regular Pagan." So they stone him to death and throw his body to "the King's cats"—"They'll have the face ate off him ere morning." These sacred carnivores, kept to honor some mysterious superstition, appear to have arisen out of Lady Gregory's bitter Protestant imagination; and Malachi moralizes in a speech marked for sardonic delivery: "They [the Egyptians] were said to give him learning and it is bad learning they gave him. That young man to have read history he would not have come to our help."

Then a prodigy happens. Bleeding and lame, Moses-Parnell rises up and crosses the stage while Malachi delivers the curtain speech: "Wandering, wandering I see, through a score and through two score years. Boggy places will be in it and stony places and splashes—and no man will see the body is put in the grave. A strange thing to get the goal, and the lad of the goal being dead. (*Another screech of the cats. He laughs.*) I wouldn't wonder at all he to bring back cross money to shoot the cats. He will get satisfaction on the cats (*Curtain*)." An appendix to the published play explains that ten years earlier Lady Gregory and Yeats had heard an old man chanting an incantation in Gaelic which was translated for them: "He is living, he is living," meaning Parnell. When they inquired of a policeman what he meant, they were told: "There are many say that. And after all no one ever saw the body that was buried."[20]

By chance, *The Deliverer* was the first Abbey play to experiment with the revolutionary new scenery and stage lighting freshly imported from Moscow by Gordon Craig. The audience response dwelt mostly on the scenery, so that Lady Gregory's message about the risen Parnell did not get through. The contemporary press reports pasted in William Henderson's scrapbook at the National Library pronounced the allegory unfathomable. The *Freeman's Journal* concluded that it intended "an application wider than the actual historical one" but it did not speculate what it might be. The *Daily Express* said it was "somewhat peculiar"; the *Irish Times*, being unfamiliar with Cairbre Cat-Head, said it was "unclear." The sour and compulsive playgoer Joseph Holloway, after condemning Craig's "freak scenery and lighting," condemned the play as well: "The audience looked on in wonder during the progress of *The Deliverer*, all wondering what it was about and why all the Egyptians spoke Kiltartan, like the natives of the region of Lady Gregory's [home]." It was all in all "beneath contempt," he said, and he enthusiastically seconded the actress Sara Allgood's characterization of it as "tripe."[21]

From this point of vantage it seems plain that Lady Gregory's object in *The Deliverer* was to borrow Parnell's luster to refurbish the image of her social class. Since history clearly identified him with agrarianism, the "contrary" of the Protestant landlord, her claim might be supposed a daring adventure into paradox. In military metaphor her stratagem would be called turning the enemy's flank; or in the language of the man in the street, confusing the issue. But the little play happened to be devoid of literary force and so it sank into oblivion, message and all; and more years passed.

Yeats had not forgotten it, though. Among the poems of *Responsibilities* (1914) appeared his first Parnellite poem since 1891, "To a Shade," an occasional piece. The occasion was not at all Parnellite, but an encore on the adventures of Sir Hugh Lane, Lady Gregory's nephew. I ask the reader's pardon for one last mention of his offer to donate paintings to the Dublin Corporation, and of its rejection when the would-be benefactor and his proffered gift were enthusiastically denounced by the philistine "pack" gathered around William Martin Murphy. The poem advises Parnell's "shade," if it should return to Dublin, to visit only the harbor:

> drink of that salt breath out of the sea
> When grey gulls flit about instead of men,

for in the town "they"—the Sullivans (not yet Yeats's friends)—"are at their old tricks yet."

Following up Yeats's discovery in "To a Shade," the device of the *revenant ironique* expanded into an Irish literary fad. In 1916 George Moore used it in *The Brook Kerith*, not upon Parnell but Christ. Lennox Robinson in *The Lost Leader* (1918) took Christ out and put Parnell back in again, working from Moore's model and with Moore's hearty applause. Like Moore's Christ, Robinson's Parnell is not dead, only hiding; and what a rare setting for soliloquy when he re-emerges to comment upon the contemporary scene: ". . . I feel there is in Ireland a vague passion, an objectless desire. It's the great moment that comes but once or twice in a nation's history, it's when the water stirs, it's when the mind of a nation is broken up, is ready to be moulded, is soft clay, warm wax. That moment has come now. . . ."[22] The soft wax was evidently a canonical metaphor.

380

Responsibilities also put on display for the first time, beside "To a Shade," Yeats's personal trademark of "coldness," of morning light "the hour before dawn." The theme proliferated in *Wild Swans at Coole* (1917) in "The Fisherman," to whom he would like to write one poem "cold and passionate as the dawn." The fisherman is said to be "a man who does not exist." But as everybody knows, coldness was Parnell's trademark as well as Yeats's. The coincidence was not yet noted, though the two drew steadily toward a moment of dramatic impact and cross-fertilization.

During the Black and Tan War Yeats was busy composing his auto-biography. In 1921 he published a section called *Four Years: 1887–1891*, years when Parnell was the solitary actor on the Irish stage. Not on Yeats's stage, though; during those years he had been preoccupied with Chiswick, Morris, Blake, Madame Blavatsky, and the British Museum. Parnell gets into his volume briefly and abstractly, but in the important new role of O'Connell's contrary, the "solitary and proud" against "bragging rhetoric and gregarious humor." In the next few months there was a violent shift in the balance of Irish politics. The Treaty was signed, the Civil War began, and Yeats was drawn into closest comradeship with the "Sullivan gang," culminating in his appointment as a Free State senator in September 1922. As soon as he put on the statesman's mantle, his Parnell "changed mask" and became so abstractly tragic that he could never pain the new comrades. Yeats borrowed from Mrs. O'Shea's book her scene from *Axel*, when Parnell had proposed a double suicide on Brighton pier, and an anecdote of Parnell's bloody hands, torn by his own nails, when he finished his reply to "Foster" in the House of Commons. He added a family remembrance: uncle Pollexfen, though anti-Parnellite, did Parnell some courtesy in the disastrous 1891 Sligo by-election. He then talked with Parnell for a few moments, proving that the family had seen him plain. (Yeats was not attentive when he gave out the content of the conversation—not the stag dragged down by dogs nor the iron-ore prospects at Avondale, but a detail jarring to the emerging literary Parnell—the unspeakable perfidy of Gladstone.[23]) In *A Vision* (1925), the domestic tragedy is still dominant, and Parnell is consigned to the Tenth Phase, reserved for all those prone "to some woman's tragic love almost certainly."

v

In 1932 we reach a new twist in the long road. Yeats was now no longer a senator. The Free State saw no more use for his services and had taken back his seat. On his own part, he had been outraged by the Dáil's enactment of sectarian censorship and divorce laws; he felt, too, that Mr. Cosgrave had not been sufficiently ruthless in the extermination of his ex-comrades of the left. His political gloom was deepened by the appearance of portents, not confined to those gifted with second sight, of the approaching election victory of the surviving remnants of those same ex-comrades, organized behind de Valera in the Fianna Fail party. Mere anarchy was about to be loosed upon Ireland, and Yeats believed that it would be necessary to forbid the election: "If any government or party undertake this work it will need force, marching men (the logic of fanaticism, whether in a woman [those amazons once more] or a mob is drawn from a premise protected by ignorance and therefore irrefutable); it will promise, not this or that measure but a discipline, a way of life; that sacred drama must to all native eyes and ears become the greatest of the parables." The "sacred drama" he explained, would project a Unity of Image which would beget Unity of Culture. "A nation should be like an audience in some great theatre," he said, and he quoted Victor Hugo: "In the theatre the mob becomes a people."[24] Therewith, he threw the prestige of his genius, of the Nobel Prize, and of the senate of a sovereign republic behind the Blue Shirt champions of Unity of Culture, General O'Duffy and his adjutant Captain MacManus, who was even then gestating a book on Irish fairies.

Parnell's induction into the "sacred drama" occurred in the opening months of de Valera's year of victory, in an unnamed, unattached stanza beginning, "An age is the reversal of an age." It said that when "strangers" had murdered Emmet, Fitzgerald, and Tone, Irishmen were only spectators: "It had not touched our lives." But the death of Parnell threw the cones into reverse gear:

> . . . But popular rage,
> *Hysterica passio* dragged this quarry down.
> None shared our guilt; nor did we play a part
> Upon a painted stage when we devoured his heart.[25]

What happened to poor Pigott, the Nonconformist English voter, and "the hillside men"? As history this is plainly ludicrous, but as an expression of private hatred, it is powerful, if enigmatical. The fact that more than two more years passed before he released the poem in its augmented and definitive form suggests difficulty in composition. Two of the new verses expand on the phrase "devoured his heart." Yeats had written in 1927 the splendid lyrics, "Two Songs from a Play," a statement of the myth of Dionysus— his murder, the ingestion of his heart by his murderer, and his perpetual rebirth. He now felt an understandable temptation to repeat his success, as Joyce had done in bringing back the "citizen" as Skin-the-Goat, "positively last performance." He resurrected Standish O'Grady's old meteor portent at Parnell's graveside ("What shudders run through all that animal blood?") and then reworked the Dionysus lyrics as an embellishment for Parnell.

Next, the old 1931 stanza was set into final place, "An age is the reversal of an age," and so on. He now named the poem "Parnell's Funeral."

These stanzas would make a conventional base for a rebirth trope transfiguring Parnell's death. But the spooky ritual leads nowhere; there is no rebirth, and the poem trails off into a stridency equating Parnell with Swift, more an atavism than a rebirth. Was the reborn savior first assigned to General O'Duffy, his horoscope then in the ascendant? If so, Yeats's roster of "true Irish people" possessing "the best blood" would have read: "Berkeley, Swift, Burke, Grattan, Parnell, Augusta Gregory, Synge," and then—not "Kevin O'Higgins" the Irish Mussolini, the name actually listed in *On the Boiler*[26]—but an even more incongruous name, General O'Duffy. Perhaps it was unfortunate for the unity of "Parnell's Funeral" that the Blue Shirts had faded in the two years between. As Conor Cruise O'Brien said, "O'Duffy proved a flop,"[27] and in the end he had to be left out of any hero role and with only modest moral ascendancy set down at last between de Valera and Cosgrave as another of the unregenerate who had been a grave disappointment to Yeats.

If this were the whole poem, it would be notable mainly for its fanciful insolence. But there is a fourth stanza in Part I, the most arresting, added just after the old 1931 nucleus, as follows:

> Come, fix upon me that accusing eye.
> I thirst for accusation. All that was sung,
> All that was said in Ireland is a lie
> Bred out of the contagion of the throng,
> Saving the rhyme rats hear before they die.
> Leave nothing but the nothings that belong
> To this bare soul, let all men judge that can
> Whether it be an animal or a man.[28]

Now, this stanza is not instantly clear, since the antecedents of "that," "this," and "it" in lines 1, 7, and 8, respectively, are open and conjectural. Where there are equivocations there will be variant readings, and for myself I take the "that" to refer to the "animal blood" of the first stanza and the "popular rage" in the third stanza, the "this" and the "it" both to refer to Yeats's "bare" or disemboweled soul ("Where there is nothing, there is God" was one of Yeats's early exercises in paradox). So read, the effect of the stanza would be to place Yeats beside Parnell as another sacrificial victim, another proud and lonely man dragged down by Irish dogs. An impulse of a similar sort had arisen at the beginning of his career in "The Crucifixion of the Outcast" and it was reiterated in the early plays, most clearly in *The King's Threshold*. Line for line, this last version of his theme is by far the most resonant, but as a whole it adds up to the same story as forty years before: Irishmen spurn Unity of Culture; I am crucified; mad

Ireland hurts me into poetry. The outcry seems rather disproportionate to the grievance.

Over the years the literary image of Parnell had been enlarged through a series of identifications. First came Moses, then Christ. "Parnell's Funeral" added Swift and Dionysus. Yeats's last play added Cuchullain. And still he was not through. One of his last poems, called "Parnell," identifies him with Coriolanus. It says *in toto*:

> Parnell came down the road, he said to a cheering man:
> "Ireland shall get her freedom and you still break stone."

One senses here a dull malignancy, and rejoinder comes instantaneously: Who ever supposed otherwise? Yeats told Dorothy Wellesley that the poem is "an actual saying of Parnell's,"[29] though indefatigable scholars have not found when or where. Whether it belongs to the historical Parnell or not, it undoubtedly pleased Yeats's fancy. To the cluster of Parnell-Moses-Christ-Swift-Dionysus-Cuchullain-Coriolanus we must therefore add W. B. Yeats himself. As if we did not already know of the identity from the limestone slab in the graveyard in county Sligo—"Cast a cold eye"—"Parnell's Funeral" makes it explicit. The man he called by the name of the most spectacular Irish statesman of the nineteenth century refers to somebody else, to the poet as a demoralized but eloquent old man.

One need not look further for the source of the paradox that the national poet of Ireland is not without honor save in his own country. "Parnell" and "Parnell's Funeral" demand for their poetic effect not only a Yeatsian "ignorance," but ignorance of the ordinary sort. Remembering that a reading of Joyce is impoverished by ignorance, not enriched by it, one would judge Yeats's contrary arrangement not the best conceivable. Possibly it is to be grieved over. From *Countess Cathleen* to *Purgatory*, one is again and again struck by the incongruous match of dazzling verbal energy to fables that miscarry and to attitudes that, for excellent reason, he dared not state with total candor. There is little benefit, though, in brooding on the point: as Maud Gonne had said, Parnell is dead, Dr. Cronin is dead, and "the British Empire is not dead yet." Yeats is dead, and it is hard to imagine that he could have been other than he was.

Still, yesterday's determination is today's free, enlightened option. Yeats's practice demonstrated with resounding finality the untruth of his theory that whatever is well said must be so. Like his precursor John Mitchel, he almost lacked the capability to write an uninteresting sentence. But on the question whether what he wrote would wear—that we would have to see about, and have to judge according to Flaubert's principle that beauty is the splendor of truth. We would not want to go on forever praising him for his vices and his virtues indifferently.

VI

In the Joyce family, as I have explained, Parnellism was not an abstract exercise in ethics, but one of those realities that politicians call a "gut issue," old John Joyce's last hope for rescue from his dismal downward journey in life. In the Split he maintained a ferocious loyalty to the Chief, and we are told that he once accosted Tim Healy in a theater and made him feel the sting of his tongue. James Joyce's experience of Parnellism was thus more concrete than Yeats's and his literary exploitation of it far more substantial and wide-ranging. He began, like Yeats, with a funeral dirge. Aged nine at the Split, young Jimmy exercised his precocity in the composition of an occasional poem called "Et Tu, Healy," now lost. A quarter of a century later, he opened *A Portrait of the Artist* with a Parnellite fantasy, the delirium of the feverish child at Clongowes Wood who sees the Kafkaesque death ship entering Kingstown harbor in the dark of night and the people kneeling and wailing: "He is dead. We saw him lying upon the catafalque." This was the same scene that Yeats saw at six o'clock in the morning and remembered with very different affections.

Since time did not stop with the Chief's death, the faithful few of 1891 were forced to move along with history and to choose one of the two alternate paths that Parnell himself had opened. They might on the one hand follow the path of least resistance with the Irish parliamentary party. In Joyce's college days, the Split had healed. John Redmond, who had once rallied the Parnellite remnant at the brink, finally made a fusion with O'Brien and the Sullivans in a new party which he headed. Joyce rejected this choice with contempt. *Dubliners* demolishes Redmondism in "Ivy Day in the Committee Room," Joyce's first experiment in mock epic and by intention one of the most mercilessly dreary episodes ever put on record. A careful reading of the story reveals that the tragic flaw in Redmondism is its lack of patronage, though much emphasis is put also on Irish ignorance, ignobility, and catarrh. By coincidence the election of an alderman falls on the anniversary of Parnell's death, and the miserable ward headquarters of the party bears the name, if not the number, of the fateful caucus room at Westminster. One of the ward canvassers in the story generates enough phlegm in his throat to douse the fire with his spit, and the petulant whine of Parnell's heirs is punctuated by the one sort of cannonade appropriate to the craven and verminous, the pop of stout-bottle corks warmed on the hob.

On the other hand, Joyce had also open before him Parnell's own last Fenian turn, moving with John O'Leary down the path that led in good time to Easter Week. He felt a certain remote respect for this alternative. Among the Irish heroes whom he spared from his lampoons, O'Leary is one of the fortunate few. It is Fenianism that exalts the world-famous Christmas

385

dinner in *A Portrait*. When the Ribbon Fenian Casey and the devout Catholic Dante re-enact the Split over the turkey and dressing, has any reader ever been known to feel that Dante got the better of the argument? But Joyce did not take the Fenian road either. Maud Gonne's epithet for Skin-the-Goat—"brave Fitzharris"—will not be found in his works. His sense receptors had reported that Fenianism was a lost cause; that the khaki power of Private Carr and Private Compton in the "Circe" chapter of *Ulysses* was fixed for all time and impregnable; and that with the terminal defeat of Gladstone, Ireland belonged absolutely to Balfour and Chamberlain: "Who fears to speak of nineteen four?" His estimate of the "power structure" was naturally not groundless, and among the life models for the college boys in *A Portrait* (whom Stephen Dedalus twitted for conspiring to make a "hurley-stick rebellion"), two of them did meet their death from British bullets. Reality has been harsh, however, in its silent critique of Joyce's elaborate, lovingly ornamented theme of Irish revolutionary perversion, betrayal, and futility.

To remain a pious Parnellite and yet to be neither Redmondite nor Fenian was not easy. Joyce's expatriation undoubtedly made it simpler. He accomplished the feat intellectually by freezing history at the instant of the Parnellite disaster, like the Lisbon clocks that stopped at the first shock wave of the earthquake. He cherished and savored the rancors of the Split forever. Twenty years after the funeral he was explaining to Italians that Irishmen had honored Parnell's appeal not to throw him to the wolves— instead, "they tore him to pieces themselves":

> 'Twas Irish humor, wet or dry
> Flung quicklime into Parnell's eye.[30]

Even in the last months of his life, fleeing before the advancing Nazi armies after the fall of France, he rejected the suggestion that he should seek safety in Ireland, and the quicklime rumor of half a century earlier was cited as a sufficient reason. Some might think he was living in the past.

The Christmas dinner of *A Portrait* generates the most empathic formulation in all literature of the sheer ecstasy of factional and sectarian rancor, a gob of spit in a harridan's eye. Its nationalism is therefore antinational, a paradox well known to the Fenians, who feared the allure of just this addiction above all other political pitfalls. Joyce's scene is so powerfully remembered and wrought that it has constituted for the ordinary reader— and for the literary expert as well—a gloss to explain all Irish history. When the aging Yeats entered his last period of political fanaticism, he turned back to it for meditation and inspiration. Even so careful a scholar as Adaline Glasheen speaks impulsively of the "traditional faithlessness of the Irish people." Thus old John Joyce's chagrin at the collapse of his job prospects is monumentalized as though it were some universal truth rather than for what it is, a dramatized instant of impassioned self-contradiction. Mr. Casey's touching words hide an equivocation, and Dante (if she had stopped screaming) might have trapped him with the question, Do you go with John Redmond or with Tom Clarke?

Joyce's literary vehicles for Parnellism include elegy, fantasy, mock epic, verse pasquinade, public lecture, and Balzacian realism. The list is completed by a rich addition: farce. Among the high comic successes of *Ulysses*, one of the chief is a passage in the "Eumaeus" chapter, where Mr. Bloom cogitates with clichés and mixed metaphors upon Parnell and the meaning of his life.[31] The old Joycean venom lingers. "Friend cabby" in Skin-the-Goat's shelter offers an incoherent catalogue of the popular theories about Parnell, then asserts: "Dead he wasn't. Simply absconded somewhere. The coffin they brought over was full of stones." These words provoke Bloom into a long chain of thought. He was surprised that any Irishman had remembered Parnell, for though in the beginning "in nine cases out of ten it was a case of tarbarrels, and not singly but in their thousands," still, in a short while it was "complete oblivion." Corroborating Joyce's lecture to the Italians, Bloom decided that "evidently something riled them in his death." It was the fact that "they were distressed to find the job was taken out of their hands" by natural death owing "to his having neglected to change his boots and clothes after a wetting when a cold resulted and failing to consult a specialist he being confined to his room till he eventually died of it amid widespread regret before a fortnight was at an end."

As for Parnell's return from the dead, the positivistic Bloom thought it "highly unlikely." All the same, his "whereabouts" were always "decidedly of the *Alice, where art thou* variety"; therefore it was "within the bounds of possibility" that he really might be somewhere in hiding. If so, he would not be happy at the state of Irish affairs. "Naturally, then, it would prey on his mind as a born leader of men, which undoubtedly he was, and a commanding figure, a six-footer or at any rate five feet ten or eleven in his stockinged feet, whereas Messrs So-and-So who, though they weren't even a patch on the former man, ruled the roost after their redeeming features were very few and far between." Natural or supernatural, any Joycean Irish *revenant* would necessarily have to be *ironique*, and now Bloom's thoughts recall Yeats's "To a Shade," though with a blessed loss of solemnity. "As regards return," it would be wise in his opinion to "sound the lie of the land" beforehand, and "you were a lucky dog if they didn't set the terrier at you directly you got back."

Bloom's silent thoughts are disturbed by a remark from Skin-the-Goat, questioning Captain O'Shea's masculine sufficiency. All laugh except Bloom,

O'Shea's counterpart in a different triangle. "Without the faintest suspicion of a smile" he begins to pass through his mind the elements of Parnell's domestic catastrophe. The mode being farce, Bloom cannot assume the tragic manner of Yeats's suicide scene on Brighton pier, or of Henry Harrison's dictum that the Parnell-O'Shea case was one of the world's greatest love stories. He must deflate, and there follows a new addition to literary Parnellism:

> A magnificent specimen of manhood he was truly, augmented obviously by gifts of a high order as compared with the other military supernumerary, that is (who was just the usual everyday *farewell, my gallant captain* kind of an individual in the light dragoons, the 18th hussars to be accurate), and inflammable doubtless (the fallen leader, that is, not the other) in his own peculiar way which she of course, woman, quickly perceived as highly likely to carve his way to fame, which he almost bid fair to do till the priests and ministers of the gospels as a whole, his erstwhile staunch adherents and his beloved evicted tenants for whom he had done yeoman service in the rural parts of the country by taking up the cudgels on their behalf in a way that exceeded their most sanguine expectations, very effectually cooked his matrimonial goose, thereby heaping coals of fire on his head, much in the same way as the fabled ass's kick. . . . it was just the wellknown case of hot passion, pure and simple, upsetting the applecart with a vengeance and just bore out the very thing he was saying, as she also was Spanish or half so, types that wouldn't do things by halves, passionate abandon of the south, casting every shred of decency to the winds.[32]

The effect of Bloom's spate of inexact yet lucid verbiage is to transform the Chief, the uncrowned king, the proud and solitary, the august Moses-Christ-Swift-Dionysus-Cuchullain-Coriolanus-Yeats, into a humbled suffering specimen of Homo sapiens, much like Bloom himself. "She also was Spanish," said Bloom, sensing an identity of Molly with Mrs. O'Shea, and in turn of Parnell with himself. With this observation, Bloom had come back to Standish O'Grady's first formulation thirty years before, when he pitied the seedy and spectral invalid he met on the frozen road in Wicklow. O'Grady had said that the time would come when history would admire Parnell for his very weakness, and Joyce thought him correct. Thus the two branches of literary Parnellism both belonged to O'Grady: first Yeats's portentous Dionysus, whose signal is a shooting star; and now Joyce's poor forked radish, who has been "carried away by a wave of folly," and "for the millionth time" encounters "the usual sequel, to bask in the loved one's smiles." While the literary Parnellism of Mr. Casey's tearful "My dead king!" was a political self-contradiction, Bloom's newest variety was not, having bypassed the political issue altogether. To someone now proposing the question, What kind of a Parnellite are you? Bloom could cheerfully reply: *humani nihil a me alienum puto*. This is a resounding disposition of the

Parnell case. But we must not get our categories mixed; and a last rebuttal must still be made to Joyce's solution: this *homo humanus* was not exactly an ordinary citizen.

VII

Bloom's great discovery has run like spring sap through all the branches of modern Irish literature. At Henry Harrison's urging, Yeats wrote a Parnellite poem without any shooting stars and with only a touch of Coriolanus' acerbity. One of the nighttown people in Skin-the-Goat's shebeen remarks to Bloom: "A fine lump of a woman, all the same," and Yeats's rendition of 1937 goes:

> But stories that live longest
> Are sung above the glass,
> And Parnell loved his country,
> And Parnell loved his lass.[33]

Conor Cruise O'Brien has shown that a Parnellism like Bloom's forms the dominant theme in the work of Sean O'Faolain,[34] and from that cue one is led to see it dominating also Frank O'Connor, F. R. Higgins, Austin Clarke, Liam O'Flaherty, Brendan Behan, and all the profusion of wonders contained in O'Faolain's old literary journal, the *Bell*. Where did Bloom get it? At a source that antedates literary Parnellism. His immediate model is Stephen Dedalus' "profane joy" in the choice "to live, to err, to fall, to triumph." But before that, it had permeated all the work of James Stephens, all of Synge except the two tragedies, and all of George Moore's Irish work. And before that?

The theme summed up in Stephen Dedalus' "Welcome, O life!" suggested a formidable contrary at hand. If we start far back up the chain of historical events, the reader will remember that we first encountered a singular Irish habit of mind in the factionalism of the O'Connells, when they attacked Young Ireland's "indecent" song about a young man infatuated with a "cloistered nun." Then it was Gavan Duffy, a younger man in those days, who anticipated Joyce's point. Later we met the stance again in Archbishop Cullen's stern synodical sermon at Thurles. There was no reply to the Thurles doctrine. The decades pass; the fifties, the sixties, the seventies, fall in silence. But in the eighties the silence is suddenly ruptured by a partnership between a young poet and a middle-aged Irish revolutionist:

> My singing sang me fever free,
>   My singing fades, the strings are torn,
> I must away by wood and sea
>   And lilt a ululu forlorn,
> Or fling my laughter to the sun
>   —For my remembering hour is done.[35]

This is not a very good try. It survives only a couple of printings before it is replaced by another stanza. After all, the boy is hardly twenty-two. But the tone is bold, the aim is right. Next year, at twenty-three, he will fix the theme in its permanent form, out of which countless glories of Irish literature will arise. For if an issue turns on nothing more complicated than Irish puritanism, who could match W. B. Yeats's blasts, then or ever? Oisin and St. Patrick are in colloquy about the Fenians in hell:

> *Oisin.* Ah me! to be shaken with coughing and broken with old age and pain,
> Without laughter, a show unto children, alone with remembrance and fear;
> All emptied of purple hours as a beggar's cloak in the rain,
> As a hay-cock out on the flood, or a wolf sucked under a weir.
>
> It were sad to gaze on the blessed and no man I loved of old there;
> I throw down the chain of small stones! when life in my body has ceased,
> I will go to Caoilte, and Conon, and Bran, Sceolan, Lomair,
> And dwell in the house of the Fenians, be they in flames or at feast.[36]

NOTES

CHAPTER I

1. Darrell Figgis, *The Economic Case for Irish Independence* (Dublin: Maunsel and Co., 1920), pp. 2–10.
2. Sir Charles Gavan Duffy, *Young Ireland: A Fragment of Irish History, 1840–1850* (New York, 1881), p. 89.
3. G. Locker Lampson, *A Consideration of the State of Ireland in the Nineteenth Century* (London: Arnold Constable and Co., 1907), p. 664.
4. John Mitchel, *A History of Ireland* (New York, [1868]), p. v.
5. Frank O'Connor, *The Big Fellow: A Life of Michael Collins* (New York: T. Nelson and Sons, 1937), pp. 210–21.
6. P. S. O'Hegarty, *John Mitchel: An Appreciation* (Dublin: Maunsel and Co., 1917), p. 35.
7. John O'Leary, *What Irishmen Should Know* (Cork, 1886), p. 8.
8. W. B. Yeats, *The Variorum Edition of the Poems of W. B. Yeats*, ed. Peter Allt and Russell K. Alspach (New York: Macmillan Co., 1957), p. 836.
9. W. B. Yeats, *Autobiographies* (New York: Macmillan Co., 1953), p. 62.
10. See Michael Adams, *Censorship: The Irish Experience* (University: University of Alabama Press, 1968).
11. Quoted in Lady Gregory, ed., *Ideals in Ireland* (London: Unicorn Press, 1901), p. 6.
12. Frank O'Connor, *A Short History of Irish Literature* (New York: G. P. Putnam's Sons, 1967), p. 165.
13. Duffy, *Young Ireland*, p. 123.
14. W. B. Yeats, *Autobiographies*, p. 124.

CHAPTER 2

1. Quoted in James Connolly, *Labor in Irish History* (Dublin: Maunsel and Co., 1934), pp. 65–66.
2. See Benedict Kiely, *The Poor Scholar: A Study of the Works and Days of William Carleton* (New York: Sheed and Ward, 1946).
3. Quoted in John Mitchel, *The Last Conquest of Ireland (Perhaps)* (New York, 1876), p. 75.
4. James Joyce, *Ulysses* (New York: Modern Library, 1942), pp. 582–83.
5. Quoted in J. H. Whyte, *The Independent Irish Party* (Oxford: Oxford University Press, 1958), p. 80.
6. W. E. H. Lecky, *A History of Ireland in the Eighteenth Century*, 5 vols. (New York, 1893), 3:10.
7. See Hereward Senior, *Orangeism in Ireland and Britain, 1795–1836* (London: Routledge and Kegan Paul, 1965), pp. 277 ff.

8. See Lawrence J. McCaffrey, *Daniel O'Connell and the Repeal Year* (Lexington: University of Kentucky Press, 1966), p. 29.

CHAPTER 3

1. See Angus Macintyre, *The Liberator: Daniel O'Connell and the Irish Party, 1830–1847* (New York: Macmillan Co., 1965), pp. 1–20.
2. *Nation*, September 16, 1843.
3. Sean O'Faolain, *King of the Beggars* (New York: Viking Press, 1938), p. 39.
4. *Nation*, April 1, 1843.
5. Ibid., September 14, 1843.
6. Denis Gwynn, *Daniel O'Connell* (Cork: Cork University Press, 1947), p. 227.
7. Quoted in the *Nation*, September 16, 1842.
8. Augustin Thierry, "Sur l'esprit national des Irlandais," *Censeur européen*, November 24, 1819, reprinted in Camille Jullian, *Extraits des historiens français du XIXe siècle* (Paris, 1913), pp. 24–26.
9. *Nation*, April 5, 1845.
10. Thomas Davis, *Essays Literary and Historical*, ed. D. J. O'Donoghue (Dundalk: Dundalgan Press, 1914), pp. 52–90.
11. Ibid., p. 75.
12. Ibid., pp. 73–74.
13. Duffy, *Young Ireland*, p. 357.
14. *Nation*, June 15, 1844.
15. Ibid., August 17, 1844.
16. Ibid., April 5, 1845.
17. Ibid., July 1, 1843.
18. Ibid., October 8, 1842.
19. Ibid., December 3, 1842.
20. Joseph Hone, *Thomas Davis* (Dublin: Talbot Press, 1934), p. 96.
21. Duffy, *Young Ireland*, pp. 777–78.
22. Ibid., p. 778.
23. Sir Charles Gavan Duffy, *Thomas Davis: The Memoirs of an Irish Patriot, 1840–1846* (London, 1890), p. 99.
24. Duffy, *Young Ireland*, pp. 662–63.
25. W. B. Yeats, "The Literary Movement in Ireland," in Lady Gregory, ed., *Ideals in Ireland*, p. 99.

CHAPTER 4

1. *Nation*, April 1, 1843.
2. Ibid., February 18, 1843.
3. Quoted in Donal O'Sullivan, *Irish Folk Music and Song* (Dublin: Colm O'Lochlainn, 1952), p. 5.

4. Duffy, *Thomas Davis*, p. 109.

5. *Nation*, November 16 and 30, 1844.

6. Duffy, *Young Ireland*, p. 182. Davis' "Lament" did not appear in the *Nation* for many months, however.

7. *Nation*, February 11, 1843.

8. Ibid., December 9, 1843.

9. W. B. Yeats, *Variorum Edition of the Poems*, p. 779. Yeats also cast this verse away, raising an interesting problem in logic.

10. W. B. Yeats, *A Tribute to Thomas Davis* (Oxford: B. H. Blackwell, 1947), p.13.

11. W. B. Yeats, *A Book of Irish Verse* (rev. ed.; London: Methuen, 1900), p. xviii.

12. Duffy, *Young Ireland*, pp. 288–89.

13. Mitchel, *Last Conquest of Ireland*, p. 44.

14. *Nation*, July 13, 1844.

15. Duffy, *Young Ireland*, p. 64.

16. Ibid., p. 184.

17. *Nation*, October 15, 1842.

18. Ibid., December 28, 1844.

19. Ibid., February 4, 1843.

20. John O'Leary, *Recollections of Fenians and Fenianism*, 2 vols. (London, 1896), 1:2.

21. Duffy, *Thomas Davis*, pp. 156–58.

22. *Nation*, August 5, 1843.

23. Ibid., September 23, 1843.

24. Duffy, *Young Ireland*, p. 274.

25. Ibid., p. 349.

26. *Nation*, August 19, 1863.

27. Duffy, *Young Ireland*, p. 382.

28. *Nation*, October 7, 1843.

29. Mitchel, *Last Conquest of Ireland*, p. 43.

30. Duffy, *Young Ireland*, p. 349.

31. Thomas Davis, *The Poems of Thomas Davis*, ed. John Mitchel (New York, 1854), p. iii.

32. Duffy, *Young Ireland*, p. 66.

CHAPTER 5

1. Mitchel, *Last Conquest of Ireland*, pp. 54–56.

2. *Nation*, September 14, 1844.

3. Duffy, *Young Ireland*, p. 349.

4. *Nation*, September 30, 1843.

5. Ibid., October 14, 1843.

6. Sir Charles Gavan Duffy, *Four Years of Irish History: 1845–1849* (London 1883), p. 58.

7. *Nation*, December 10, 1842.

8. Ibid., September 21, 1844.

9. Ibid.

10. Duffy, *Young Ireland*, p. 508.

11. Ibid., p. 657.

12. *Nation*, January 16, 1845.

13. Duffy, *Young Ireland*, p. 661.

14. See R. B. McDowell, *Public Opinion and Government Policy in Ireland: 1801–1846* (London: Faber and Faber, 1952), p. 248.

15. *Nation*, October 18, 1845.

16. Duffy, *Young Ireland*, p. 299.

17. Ibid., p. 300.

18. W. B. Yeats, "Literary Movement in Ireland," p. 102.

19. Duffy, *Thomas Davis*, p. 99.

20. W. E. H. Lecky, *Leaders of Public Opinion in Ireland*, 2 vols. (New York: Appleton, 1903), 2:64.

21. Duffy, *Four Years of Irish History*, p. 104.

22. *Nation*, February 25, 1843.

23. Ibid.

24. Ibid., September 23, 1843.

25. Ibid., May 31, 1845.

26. Ibid., September 27, 1845.

27. W. B. Yeats, *Tribute to Thomas Davis*, p. 17.

CHAPTER 6

1. *Nation*, February 1, 1845.

2. Ibid., November 8, 1845.

3. William Dillon, *Life of John Mitchel*, 2 vols. (London, 1888), 1:37, 111.

4. *Nation*, November 22, 1845.

5. Denis Gwynn, *Young Ireland and 1848* (Oxford: Cork University Press, 1949), p. 58.

6. *Nation*, January 10, 1846.

7. Ibid., November 1, 1845.

8. Ibid., November 8, 1845.

9. Ibid., January 24, 1846.

10. Ibid., April 16, May 23, 1846.

11. Ibid., April 16, 1846.

12. Ibid., May 16, 1846.

13. Ibid., June 13, 1846.

14. Ibid., July 18, 1846.
15. Ibid., December 5, August 8, 1846.
16. Gwynn, *Young Ireland and 1848*, p. 69,
17. Joyce, *Ulysses*, p. 141.
18. W. B. Yeats, *Tribute to Thomas Davis*, p. 15.
19. *Nation*, August 1, 1846.
20. Ibid., January 2, 1847.
21. Ibid., June 5, 1847.
22. Duffy, *Four Years of Irish History*, pp. 494–95.
23. Ibid., p. 405.
24. Sir William Gregory, *An Autobiography*, ed. Lady Gregory (London, 1894), pp. 133–36.

CHAPTER 7

1. James Fintan Lalor, *The Writings of James Fintan Lalor*, ed. John O'Leary (Dublin, 1895), pp. 2, 6, 11, 31, 69.
2. *United Irishman*, May 20, 1848.
3. P. S. O'Hegarty, *A History of Ireland under the Union* (London: Methuen, 1952), p. 318.
4. Mitchel, *Last Conquest of Ireland*, p. 219.
5. Ibid., p. 131.
6. W. B. Yeats, *Autobiographies*, p. 128.
7. Mitchel, *Last Conquest of Ireland*, p. 116.
8. Dillon, *Life of John Mitchel*, 1:224–25.
9. *United Irishman*, April 29, 1848.
10. Mitchel, *History of Ireland*, p. 574.
11. *Nation*, January 1, February 8, 1848.
12. Duffy, *Four Years of Irish History*, p. 551.
13. *Nation*, February 26, 1848.
14. Duffy, *Four Years of Irish History*, p. 543. The same extraordinary letter naturally appears in the Smith papers too, and is reprinted in Gwynn, *Young Ireland and 1848*, pp. 158–59.
15. Gwynn, *Young Ireland and 1848*, p. 160.
16. *United Irishman*, May 13, 1848.
17. Gwynn, *Young Ireland and 1848*, p. 206.
18. Mitchel, *Last Conquest of Ireland*, p. 186.
19. Ibid., p. 191.
20. Gwynn, *Young Ireland and 1848*, pp. 246, 296.
21. *Nation*, April 29, July 29, 1848.
22. Desmond Ryan, "Stephens, Devoy, Tom Clarke," in *The Shaping of Modern Ireland*, ed. Conor Cruise O'Brien (London: Routledge and Kegan Paul, 1960), p. 27.

23. *Nation*, July 29, 1848.

24. A. M. Sullivan, *New Ireland* (Philadelphia, 1878), p. 122.

25. Gwynn, *Young Ireland and 1848*, p. 206.

26. Sir Charles Gavan Duffy, *My Life in Two Hemispheres*, 2 vols. (London: T. Fisher Unwin, 1903), 1:291.

27. W. B. Yeats, *Autobiographies*, p. 293.

28. Kevin B. Nowlan, *The Politics of Repeal* (London: Routledge and Kegan Paul, 1965), p. 215.

29. Gwynn, *Young Ireland and 1848*, pp. 277–78, 256–58, 268.

30. *Nation*, January 25, 1851.

CHAPTER 8

1. Sir William P. MacArthur, "Medical History of the Famine," in *The Great Famine*, ed. R. Dudley Edwards and T. Desmond Williams (Dublin: Browne and Nolan, 1957), p. 312.

2. W. B. Yeats, *Variorum Edition of the Poems*, p. 130.

3. MacArthur, "Medical History of the Famine," p. 315.

4. Thomas Carlyle, *Reminiscences of My Irish Journey in 1849* (London, 1882), p. v.

5. Ibid., pp. 140, 204, 260, 130.

6. Ibid., pp. 202–3.

7. Ibid., p. 79.

8. Sir Charles Gavan Duffy, *Conversations with Carlyle* (New York, 1892), p. 184.

9. *Nation*, September 1, 1849.

10. Ibid.

11. Carlyle, *Reminiscences of my Irish Journey*, p. 199.

12. *Nation*, September 8, 1849.

13. Ibid., October 13, 1849.

14. Ibid., September 22, October 6, 1849.

15. Whyte, *Independent Irish Party*, pp. 6–13.

16. Ibid., p. 13.

17. Duffy, *My Life*, 2:115.

18. Reproduced in E. R. Norman, *The Catholic Church and Ireland in the Age of Rebellion, 1859–1873* (Ithaca, N.Y.: Cornell University Press, 1965), p. 196.

19. Fergal McGrath, S. J., *Newman's University* (New York: Longmans, Green, and Co., 1951), p. 95.

20. Whyte, *Irish Independent Party*, p. 115.

21. *Nation*, August 24, 1850.

22. Ibid., September 21, 1850.

23. Ibid.

24. O'Leary, *Recollections of Fenians and Fenianism*, 2:69. Cullen's enemies naturally seized upon this statement, and I take my citation from them.

25. T. P. O'Connor, *The Parnell Movement* (London, 1886), p. 146.

26. Whyte, *Independent Irish Party*, p. 113.

27. Duffy, *My Life*, 2:97.

28. Sir Charles Gavan Duffy, *The League of the North and South: An Episode in Irish History, 1850–1854* (London, 1886), p. 308.

29. Ibid., p. 364.

30. Norman, *Catholic Church and Ireland*, p. 1.

CHAPTER 9

1. Peadar MacSuibhne, *Paul Cullen and His Contemporaries*, 3 vols. (Kildare: Leinster Leader, 1961–65), 1:386.

2. O'Leary, *Recollections of Fenians and Fenianism*, 1:7–8.

3. Gwynn, *Young Ireland and 1848*, p. 206.

4. Smith O'Brien, *Lecture on Poland* (Dublin, 1863), p. 25.

5. O'Hegarty, *John Mitchel*, p. 121.

6. W. B. Yeats, *Autobiographies*, p. 137.

7. John Mitchel, "Introduction," in James Clarence Mangan, *Poems* (Dublin: O'Donoghue, 1903), p. xxxv.

8. John Mitchel, *Jail Journal* (Dublin: M. H. Gill and Son, 1921), pp. 72, 93.

9. Ibid., p. 278.

10. See W. B. Yeats, *Autobiographies*, p. 137.

11. Mitchel, *Jail Journal*, p. 4.

12. Ibid., p. 89.

13. John Mitchel, *The Last Conquest of Ireland (Perhaps)* (London, 1876), p. 206; see also Mitchel, *Jail Journal*, p. 220.

14. Mitchel, *Jail Journal*, pp. 141, 145.

15. Ibid., p. 204.

16. Dillon, *Life of John Mitchel*, 2:218.

17. Mitchel, *Jail Journal*, p. 154.

18. *Citizen*, September 2, 1854.

19. *Citizen*, January 14, 1854.

20. Mitchel, *Jail Journal*, p. 386.

21. *Irishman*, January 25, February 1, 1862.

22. *New York Times*, June 27, 1865.

23. Dillon, *Life of John Mitchel*, 2:236–37.

24. Ibid., p. 219.

25. Ibid., p. 46.

26. Arthur Griffith, "John Mitchel: A Biographical Sketch," in Mitchel, *Jail Journal*, p. 458.

27. *Citizen*, January 28, May 20, 1854.

28. Dillon, *Life of John Mitchel*, 2:103–6.

29. Michael Davitt, *The Fall of Feudalism in Ireland* (New York: Harper and Brothers, 1904), p. 53.

30. W. B. Yeats, *The Variorum Edition of the Plays*, ed. Russell K. Alspach (London: Macmillan and Co., 1966), p. 16.

31. Joyce, *Ulysses*, p. 324.

32. E. R. R. Green, "Agriculture," in *The Great Famine*, ed. Edwards and Williams, p. 124.

33. Thomas P. O'Neill, "The Administration of Relief," ibid., pp. 244, 257.

34. Cecil Woodham-Smith, *The Great Hunger* (New York: Harper and Row, 1964), p. 375.

35. Dillon, *Life of John Mitchel*, 2:250.

36. Brian Inglis, *The Story of Ireland* (London: Faber and Faber, 1956), p. 140.

37. W. B. Yeats, *Variorum Edition of the Poems*, p. 638.

CHAPTER 10

1. Desmond Ryan, *The Fenian Chief: A Biography of James Stephens* (Dublin: M. H. Gill and Son, 1967), p. 62.

2. O'Leary, *Recollections of Fenians and Fenianism*, 1:242.

3. Ryan, *Fenian Chief*, pp. 70–72.

4. Ibid., p. 80.

5. A. M. Sullivan, *New Ireland*, p. 320.

6. O'Leary, *Recollections of Fenians and Fenianism*, 1:148; see also 2:10.

7. See E. J. Hobsbawm, *Primitive Rebels* (New York: W. W. Norton and Co., 1959), pp. 165–66.

8. O'Leary, *Recollections of Fenians and Fenianism*, 1:56, 57; 2:183n.

9. *United Irishman*, February 28, 1848, p. 11.

10. O'Leary, *Recollections of Fenians and Fenianism*, 2:130.

11. Ibid., pp. 57, 56.

12. O'Hegarty, *History of Ireland under the Union*, p. 431.

13. O'Leary, *Recollections of Fenians and Fenianism*, 2:44.

14. Ibid., 1:31.

15. Ibid., 2:239.

16. Ibid., p. 148.

17. *Irish People*, January 23, 1864.

18. Ibid., December 19, 1865.

19. See Thomas N. Brown, *Irish-American Nationalism* (Philadelphia: Lippincott and Co., 1966), and Edward M. Levine, *The Irish and Irish Politicians* (Notre Dame, Ind.: University of Notre Dame Press, 1966).

20. O'Leary, *Recollections of Fenians and Fenianism*, 2:39.

21. *Nation*, October 30, 1858.
22. A. M. Sullivan, *The Phoenix Society in Ireland and America* (Dublin, 1862).

CHAPTER 11

1. O'Donovan Rossa, *Rossa's Recollections* (Mariner's Harbor, N.Y., 1898), p. 235.
2. Ibid., p. 234.
3. A. M. Sullivan, *New Ireland*, p. 279.
4. O'Leary, *Recollections of Fenians and Fenianism*, 1:162.
5. Ibid., pp. 168–69.
6. Ibid., 2:177n.
7. *Nation*, July 9, 1859; January 28, 1865.
8. Ibid., July 30, 1859.
9. O'Leary, *Recollections of Fenians and Fenianism*, 1:156.
10. O'Donovan Rossa, *Recollections*, pp. 284–85.
11. "An Ulsterman" [George Sigerson], *Modern Ireland* (London, 1868), pp. 20 ff.
12. *Nation*, August 26, 1865.
13. Joyce, *Ulysees*, p. 324.
14. Gustave Paul Cluseret, "My Connection with Fenianism," *Littell's Living Age*, 114 (1872): 364.
15. MacSuibhne, *Cullen and His Contemporaries*, 1:398–409.
16. *Nation*, May 20, 1865.
17. O'Leary, *Recollections of Fenians and Fenianism*, 2:22n.
18. *Nation*, August 9, 1851.
19. T. D. Sullivan, *A. M. Sullivan: A Memoir* (Dublin, 1885), p. 65.
20. Norman, *Catholic Church and Ireland*, p. 141.
21. *Nation*, January 7, 1865.
22. *Irish People*, June 4, 1864.

CHAPTER 12

1. William D'Arcy, *The Fenian Movement in the United States, 1858–1886* (Washington, D.C.: Catholic University of America Press, 1947), p. 181.
2. James Maher, comp. and ed., *The Valley near Slievenamon* (Mullinahone, 1941), p. 186.
3. O'Leary, *Recollections of Fenians and Fenianism*, 1:247.
4. Ibid., 1:258–59; 2:177.
5. T. D. Sullivan, *Recollections of Troubled Times in Irish Politics* (Dublin: M. H. Gill and Son, 1905), p. 50.
6. *Irish People*, February 13, 1864.
7. Ibid., December 26, 1863.

8. "Historicus," *The Best Hundred Irish Books* (Dublin, 1886), p. 28.

9. Stopford A. Brooke and T. W. Rolleston, eds., *A Treasury of Irish Poetry in the English Tongue* (New York: Macmillan Co., 1900), p. 199.

10. O'Leary, *Recollections of Fenians and Fenianism*, 2:67.

11. Ibid., p. 66.

12. Ibid., pp. 13–14, 58.

13. Ibid., pp. 50, 53.

14. Ibid., p. 2.

15. John Devoy, *Recollections of an Irish Rebel* (New York: Charles P. Young, 1929), p. 56.

16. O'Hegarty, *History of Ireland under the Union*, p. 449.

17. O'Leary, *Recollections of Fenians and Fenianism*, 1:236.

18. T. D. Sullivan, *Recollections of Troubled Times in Irish Politics*, p. 60.

19. Ibid.

20. Devoy, *Recollections of an Irish Rebel*, pp. 301–2.

21. *Nation*, December 9, 1865.

22. T. D., A. M., and D. B. Sullivan, *Speeches from the Dock* (Dublin, n.d.), p. 173.

23. O'Leary, *Recollections of Fenians and Fenianism*, 2:219.

24. Devoy, *Recollections of an Irish Rebel*, p. 287.

25. Ibid., pp. 324–25; O'Donovan Rossa, *My Years in English Jails*, ed. Sean Ua Cearnaigh (Tralee: Anvil Books, 1967), p. 50.

26. O'Leary, *Recollections of Fenians and Fenianism*, 2:218.

27. *Nation*, February 11, 1865.

CHAPTER 13

1. D'Arcy, *Fenian Movement in the United States*, p. 76.

2. A. M. Sullivan, *New Ireland*, pp. 357–61; Devoy, *Recollections of an Irish Rebel*, p. 72.

3. Devoy, *Recollections of an Irish Rebel*, chap. 13.

4. Ibid., p. 269.

5. D'Arcy, *Fenian Movement in the United States*, pp. 105–6.

6. Devoy, *Recollections of an Irish Rebel*, chaps. 15–16.

7. Ibid., p. 111.

8. D'Arcy, *Fenian Movement in the United States*, p. 151.

9. Ibid., pp. 135–40.

10. Ibid., pp. 154–71.

11. Ibid., pp. 151, 191.

12. Ibid., pp. 197, 217.

13. Ibid., p. 213.

14. Cluseret, "My Connection with Fenianism," p. 357.

15. D'Arcy, *Fenian Movement in the United States*, pp. 219–20, 224.

CHAPTER 14

1. Cluseret, "My Connection with Fenianism," p. 361.
2. D'Arcy, *Fenian Movement in the United States*, p. 220n.
3. Devoy, *Recollections of an Irish Rebel*, p. 187.
4. Cluseret, "My Connection with Fenianism," p. 359.
5. T. D. Sullivan, *Recollections of Troubled Times in Irish Politics*, p. 84.
6. Norman, *Catholic Church and Ireland*, pp. 117–19.
7. D'Arcy, *Fenian Movement in the United States*, p. 243.
8. W. B. Yeats, *Variorum Edition of the Poems*, p. 635.
9. T. D., A. M., and D. B. Sullivan, *Speeches from the Dock*, pp. 264–72.
10. A. M. Sullivan, *New Ireland*, p. 395.
11. T. D., A. M., and D. B. Sullivan, *Speeches from the Dock*, pp. 325–26.
12. [Sigerson], *Modern Ireland*, pp. 20 ff.
13. *Nation*, May 20, 1865.
14. Devoy, *Recollections of an Irish Rebel*, p. 317.
15. T. D. Sullivan, *Recollections of Troubled Times in Irish Politics*, p. 90.
16. W. B. Yeats, *Essays and Introductions* (New York: Macmillan Co., 1961), pp. 246–47.
17. O'Leary, *Recollections of Fenians and Fenianism*, 2:228, 23.
18. John O'Leary, *What Irishmen Should Feel* (Dublin, 1886), p. 11.
19. Marcus Bourke, *John O'Leary: A Study in Irish Separatism* (Tralee: Anvil Books, 1967), p. 154.
20. O'Leary, *Recollections of Fenians and Fenianism*, 1:152n.

CHAPTER 15

1. *Nation*, February 12, 1865.
2. James Joyce, *Critical Writings*, ed. Ellsworth Mason and Richard Ellmann (New York: Viking Press, 1959), p. 245.
3. Isaac Butt, *The Irish People and the Irish Land* (Dublin, 1867), p. 142.
4. Ernest Jones, "Die Insel Irland," in *Psychoanalytische Bewegung*, 1 (1929): 103–14.
5. Ryan, *Fenian Chief*, p. 42.
6. Joyce, *Ulysses*, pp. 43–45.
7. W. B. Yeats, *Variorum Edition of the Poems*, p. 393.
8. T. D., A. M., and D. B. Sullivan, *Speeches from the Dock*, p. 358.
9. A. M. Sullivan, *New Ireland*, p. 395.
10. David Thornley, *Isaac Butt and Home Rule* (London: MacGibbon and Kee, 1964), p. 65.
11. John Butler Yeats, *Letters to His Son, W. B. Yeats and Others, 1869–1922*, ed. Joseph Hone (London: Faber and Faber, 1944), p. 126.

12. Terence De Vere White, *The Road of Excess* (Dublin: Browne and Nolan, 1945), pp. 287–88.
13. W. B. Yeats, *Variorum Edition of the Poems,* p. 405.
14. Ibid., p. 414.
15. White, *Road of Excess,* pp. 245–46.
16. John Devoy, *Devoy's Post Bag,* ed. William O'Brien and Desmond Ryan, 2 vols. (Dublin: Fallon Press, 1948–53), 1:2.
17. A. M. Sullivan, *New Ireland,* p. 466.
18. Thornley, *Isaac Butt and Home Rule,* p. 107. The words were John Martin's.
19. Ibid., p. 88.
20. A. M. Sullivan, *New Ireland,* p. 465.
21. White, *Road of Excess,* p. 271.
22. Thornley, *Isaac Butt and Home Rule,* p. 127; Norman, *Catholic Church and Ireland,* p. 430.
23. Thornley, *Isaac Butt and Home Rule,* p. 118.
24. Michael MacDonagh, *The Home Rule Movement* (Dublin: Talbot Press, 1920), p. 26.
25. Thornley, *Isaac Butt and Home Rule,* pp. 167–68.

CHAPTER 16

1. Thornley, *Isaac Butt and Home Rule,* p. 234.
2. Ibid., p. 239.
3. Ibid., p. 251.
4. R. Barry O'Brien, *The Life of Charles Stewart Parnell* (popular ed. London: Thomas Nelson and Sons, n.d.), pp. 63–64.
5. W. B. Yeats, *Variorum Edition of the Poems,* p. 587.
6. O'Connor, *The Parnell Movement,* p. 254; Davitt, *Fall of Feudalism in Ireland,* p. 658; Lord Eversley, *Gladstone and Ireland* (London: Methuen, 1912), p. 70; T. D. Sullivan, *Recollections of Troubled Times in Irish Politics,* p. 313; Henry Harrison, *Parnell Vindicated* (London: Constable and Co., 1931), pp. 72–73; William O'Brien, *The Parnell of Real Life* (London: T. Fisher Unwin, 1926), pp. 10, 119.
7. J. B. Yeats, *Letters to His Son,* pp. 210, 219; John Butler Yeats, *Further Letters of John Butler Yeats,* ed. Lennox Robinson (Dundrum: Cuala Press, 1920), pp. 69–70.
8. Liam O'Flaherty, *The Life of Tim Healy* (New York: Harcourt, Brace and Co., 1927), p. 46.
9. Thornley, *Isaac Butt and Home Rule,* pp. 255–59.
10. Ibid., p. 258.
11. Ibid., p. 272.
12. R. B. O'Brien, *Life of Parnell,* p. 72.

13. Ibid., p. 86.

14. *Hansard's Parliamentary Debates*, 230 (1876): 808.

15. R. B. O'Brien, *Life of Parnell*, p. 96.

16. *Hansard*, 235 (1877): 1809.

17. Ibid., 236 (1877): 271.

18. F. Hugh O'Donnell, *A History of the Irish Parliamentary Party*, 2 vols. (London: Longmans, Green, and Co., 1910), 1: 213–14.

19. Thornley, *Isaac Butt and Home Rule*, p. 333.

20. Conor Cruise O'Brien, *Parnell and His Party, 1880–90* (Oxford: Clarendon Press, 1957), p. 10.

21. R. B. O'Brien, *Life of Parnell*, p. 86.

22. Ibid., p. 117.

23. Bourke, *John O'Leary*, p. 143.

24. Davitt, *Fall of Feudalism in Ireland*, p. 111.

25. T. W. Moody, "The New Departure in Irish Politics," in *Essays in British and Irish History in Honor of James E. Todd*, ed. H. A. Cronne et al. (London: F. Muller, 1949), p. 323.

26. Francis Sheehy-Skeffington, *Michael Davitt* (London: T. Fisher Unwin, 1908), p. 16; Clive Hart, *Structure and Motif in Finnegans Wake* (Evanston, Ill.: Northwestern University Press, 1962), p. 250.

27. Davitt, *Fall of Feudalism in Ireland*, p. 129.

28. Sheehy-Skeffington, *Davitt*, p. 77.

29. Brown, *Irish-American Nationalism*, p. 89.

30. R. B. O'Brien, *Life of Parnell*, pp. 111, 177.

31. Quoted in O'Hegarty, *History of Ireland under the Union*, p. 480.

32. O'Donnell, *History of the Irish Parliamentary Party*, 1: 282.

33. Davitt, *Fall of Feudalism in Ireland*, pp. 148–49.

34. Ibid., p. 153.

35. Ibid., pp. 154–55.

36. Ibid., p. 301.

37. R. B. O'Brien, *Life of Parnell*, pp. 159–62.

CHAPTER 17

1. C. Cruise O'Brien, *Parnell and His Party*, p. 25.

2. Ibid., p. 68.

3. R. B. O'Brien, *Life of Parnell*, pp. 168, 174, 175.

4. C. Cruise O'Brien, *Parnell and His Party*, p. 37.

5. John E. Pomfret, *The Struggle for Land in Ireland* (Princeton: Princeton University Press, 1930), pp. 134–36.

6. R. B. O'Brien, *Life of Parnell*, pp. 185–86.

7. Norman Dunbar Palmer, *The Irish Land League Crisis* (New Haven, Conn.: Yale University Press, 1940), p. 211.

8. R. B. O'Brien, *Life of Parnell*, p. 153.

9. Davitt, *Fall of Feudalism in Ireland*, pp. 339, 349.

10. George Moore, *Parnell and His Island* (London, 1887), p. 89.

11. R. B. O'Brien, *Life of Parnell*, p. 188.

12. Palmer, *Irish Land League Crisis*, p. 224.

13. James Joyce, *Finnegans Wake* (New York: Viking Press, 1939), p. 295.

14. *Hansard*, 258 (1881): 174–82.

15. Davitt, *Fall of Feudalism in Ireland*, pp. 359–60.

16. R. B. O'Brien, *Life of Parnell*, p. 223.

17. O'Hegarty, *History of Ireland under the Union*, pp. 503–4.

18. Katharine O'Shea, *Charles Stewart Parnell: His Love Story and Political Life*, 2 vols. (London: Cassell and Co., 1914), 1:213.

19. R. B. O'Brien, *Life of Parnell*, pp. 241, 245.

20. Harrison, *Parnell Vindicated*, p. 333.

21. Palmer, *Irish Land League Crisis*, p. 297.

CHAPTER 18

1. Davitt, *Fall of Feudalism in Ireland*, p. 356.

2. R. B. O'Brien, *Life of Parnell*, pp. 273–75; O'Shea, *Parnell*, 1:262–63; Davitt, *Fall of Feudalism in Ireland*, p. 359.

3. Patrick J. P. Tynan, *The Irish National Invincibles and Their Times* (London, 1894), p. 265.

4. D. B. Cashman, *The Life of Michael Davitt* (London, 1882), p. 238.

5. John Adye Curran, *Reminiscences* (London: Edward Arnold, 1915), p. 153.

6. Ibid., p. 164.

7. *Manchester Guardian*, February 12, 1883, p. 6.

8. Curran, *Reminiscences*, p. 181.

9. P. J. P. Tynan, *Irish National Invincibles*, p. 319; *Manchester Guardian*, April 12, 1883, p. 6.

10. Curran, *Reminiscences*, pp. 193, 194.

11. Joyce, *Ulysses*, p. 80.

12. Frederick Moir Bussy, *Irish Conspiracies* (London: Everett and Co., 1910), p. 157.

13. Ibid., p. 626.

14. P. J. P. Tynan, *Irish National Invincibles*, p. 316.

15. Joyce, *Ulysses*, pp. 281, 285.

16. Ibid., pp. 237–38, 286.

17. Stuart Gilbert, *James Joyce's Ulysses* (New York: Alfred A. Knopf, 1952), p. 254.

18. Joyce, *Ulysses*, pp. 299, 578.

19. *Manchester Guardian*, February 19, 1883.

20. Tom Corfe, *The Phoenix-Park Murders* (London: Hodder and Stoughton, 1968), p. 248.

21. T. W. Reid, *Life of the Right Honorable W. E. Forster* (London, 1889), pp. 573–74.

22. *Hansard*, 276 (1883): 627–28; 716–25.

23. Davitt, *Fall of Feudalism in Ireland*, p. 461.

CHAPTER 19

1. O'Shea, *Parnell*, 1:261.

2. St. John Ervine, *Parnell* (Boston: Little, Brown and Co., 1925), p. 199.

3. O'Flaherty, *Life of Tim Healy*, p. 86.

4. Davitt, *Fall of Feudalism in Ireland*, p. 379.

5. O'Hegarty, *History of Ireland under the Union*, pp. 521, 522.

6. Cashman, *Life of Michael Davitt*, p. 229.

7. O'Shea, *Parnell*, 1:207, 235–36.

8. Michael Collins, *The Path to Freedom* (Dublin: Talbot Press, 1922), p. 130.

9. Sheehy-Skeffington, *Life of Michael Davitt*, p. 229.

10. R. B. O'Brien, *Life of Parnell*, pp. 315–16.

11. Moore, *Parnell and His Island*, pp. 6, 8.

12. Ibid., pp. 65–66.

13. Standish O'Grady, *Toryism and Tory Democracy* (London, 1886), p. 225.

14. W. B. Yeats, *Essays and Introductions*, pp. 344–45.

15. See Emile Strauss, *Irish Nationalism and British Democracy* (London: Methuen, 1951), pp. 198–99 for a summary of the effects of the post-Gladstone Irish land reforms.

16. W. B. Yeats, *Variorum Edition of the Plays*, p. 19.

17. Denis Gwynn, *The Irish Free State* (London: Macmillan and Co., 1928), p. 293.

18. Standish O'Grady, *The Crisis in Ireland* (Dublin, 1882), pp. 13, 14, 16, 19.

19. O'Grady, *Toryism and Tory Democracy*, pp. 216, 218, 238, 241, 243, 289–90.

20. Standish O'Grady, *Selected Essays and Passages*, ed. Ernest A. Boyd (Dublin: Phoenix Publishing Co., [1918]), pp. 167, 169, 231.

21. A. Norman Jeffares, *W. B. Yeats* (New York: Barnes and Noble, 1966), p. 278.

22. O'Grady, *Selected Essays and Passages*, pp. 167, 169, 265.

23. Hugh Art O'Grady, *Standish James O'Grady: The Man and the Writer* (Dublin: Talbot Press, 1929), pp. 40–41.

24. W. B. Yeats, *Wheels and Butterflies* (New York: Macmillan Co., 1935), pp. 26–27.

25. W. B. Yeats, *A Vision* (New York: Macmillan Co., 1961), p. 176.

26. O'Grady, *Toryism and Tory Democracy*, pp. 211–12, 239.

27. W. B. Yeats, *Variorum Edition of the Poems*, p. 553.
28. W. B. Yeats, *Autobiographies*, pp. 243–44.
29. J. B. Yeats, *Further Letters*, p. 59.
30. O'Grady, *Toryism and Tory Democracy*, p. 240.

CHAPTER 20

1. O'Hegarty, *History of Ireland under the Union*, p. 517.
2. Michael MacDonagh, *The Life of William O'Brien* (London: E. Benn, 1928), pp. 59, 60.
3. Ibid., p. 82.
4. Wilfred Scawen Blunt, *The Land War in Ireland* (London: Stephen Swift and Co., 1912), p. 417.
5. William O'Brien, *When We Were Boys* (London, 1890), pp. 136, 536.
6. Harrison, *Parnell Vindicated*, p. 272.
7. Davitt, *Fall of Feudalism in Ireland*, p. 467.
8. C. Cruise O'Brien, *Parnell and His Party*, pp. 10, 183.
9. W. B. Yeats, *Variorum Edition of the Poems*, p. 586.
10. R. B. O'Brien, *Life of Parnell*, pp. 322, 326.
11. C. Cruise O'Brien, *Parnell and His Party*, p. 104.
12. Michael Hurst, *Parnell and Irish Nationalism* (Toronto: University of Toronto Press, 1968), p. 80.
13. *Hansard*, 306 (1886): 1233, 1239.
14. L. P. Curtis, Jr., *Coercion and Conciliation in Ireland* (Princeton, N.J.: Princeton University Press, 1963), p. 106.

CHAPTER 21

1. O'Hegarty, *History of Ireland under the Union*, p. 563.
2. C. Cruise O'Brien, *Parnell and His Party*, p. 193.
3. Devoy, *Devoy's Post Bag*, 2:237–38.
4. R. B. O'Brien, *Life of Parnell*, p. 401.
5. Devoy, *Devoy's Post Bag*, 2:237–38.
6. Mark F. Ryan, *Fenian Memories* (Dublin: M. H. Gill and Son, 1946), p. 149.
7. O'Leary, *Recollections of Fenians and Fenianism*, 2:10.
8. W. B. Yeats, *Representative Irish Tales*, 2 vols. (New York, [1891]), 1:16.
9. David Greene, "Michael Cusack and the Rise of the G.A.A.," in *Shaping of Modern Ireland*, ed. C. Cruise O'Brien, pp. 74–84.
10. Mary M. Macken, "John O'Leary, W. B. Yeats, and the Contemporary Club," *Studies*, 28 (March 1939): 136–42.
11. Joseph Hone, "Yeats as a Political Philosopher," *London Mercury*, 29 (March 1935): 492.
12. W. B. Yeats, *Autobiographies*, p. 129.

13. Samuel Ferguson, "To Clarence Mangan," *Dublin University Magazine*, May 1847, p. 623; Austin Clarke, *Poetry in Modern Ireland* (Dublin: Colm O'Lochlainn, 1951), p. 15.

14. Sir Samuel Ferguson, *Congal* (Dublin, 1897), p. 20.

15. Standish O'Grady, *History of Ireland*, 2 vols. (London, 1878–81), 2:46.

16. Ibid., p. 201.

17. W. B. Yeats, *Letters*, ed. Allan Wade (New York: Macmillan Co., 1955), p. 71.

18. O'Leary, *Recollections of Fenians and Fenianism*, 2:141.

19. Frederic E. Faverty, *Matthew Arnold the Ethnologist* (Evanston, Ill.: Northwestern University Press, 1951), pp. 223–24.

20. John V. Kelleher, "Arnold and the Celtic Revival," in *Perspectives of Criticism*, ed. Harry Levin (Cambridge, Mass.: Harvard University Press, 1950), pp. 218–19.

21. W. O'Brien, *When We Were Boys*, p. 123.

22. W. B. Yeats, *Variorum Edition of the Plays*, p. 765.

23. W. B. Yeats, *Tribute to Thomas Davis*, pp. 12, 18.

24. W. B. Yeats, *Variorum Edition of the Poems*, p. 583.

25. W. B. Yeats, *Letters*, p. 881.

26. W. B. Yeats, *Autobiographies*, pp. 338–39.

27. W. B. Yeats, *Variorum Edition of the Poems*, p. 506.

28. Joyce, *Ulysses*, p. 575.

CHAPTER 22

1. F. S. L. Lyons, *John Dillon* (London: Routledge and Kegan Paul, 1968), pp. 82–90.

2. R. B. O'Brien, *Life of Parnell*, p. 431.

3. Ibid., p. 436.

4. O'Shea, *Parnell*, 2:130.

5. O'Donnell, *History of the Irish Parliamentary Party*, 2:225, 251.

6. W. B. Yeats, *Letters*, pp. 112–13.

7. F. S. L. Lyons, *The Fall of Parnell* (London: Routledge and Kegan Paul, 1960), p. 67.

8. C. Cruise O'Brien, *Parnell and His Party*, p. 280.

9. Harrison, *Parnell Vindicated*, p. 299.

10. Curtis, *Coercion and Conciliation in Ireland*, pp. 312–13.

11. W B. Yeats, *Essays and Introductions*, p. 488.

12. Lyons, *Fall of Parnell*, p. 86.

13. Davitt, *Fall of Feudalism in Ireland*, p. 636.

14. O'Flaherty, *Life of Tim Healy*, pp. 125, 143.

15. Ibid., p. 151.

16. Ibid., pp. 135, 139.

17. T. D. Sullivan, *Recollections of Troubled Times in Irish Politics*, p. 287.

18. Ibid., p. 289.

19. R. B. O'Brien, *Life of Parnell*, pp. 496, 498.

20. T. D. Sullivan, *Recollections of Troubled Times in Irish Politics*, p. 291.

21. Lyons, *Fall of Parnell*, p. 182.

22. O'Flaherty, *Life of Tim Healy*, p. 135.

23. Richard Ellmann, *James Joyce* (New York: Oxford University Press, 1959), p. 32.

24. Stanislaus Joyce, *My Brother's Keeper: James Joyce's Early Years*, ed. Richard Ellmann (New York: Viking Press, 1958), p. 28.

25. Emmet Larkin, *The Roman Catholic Hierarchy and the Fall of Parnell* (Cambridge, Mass.: Massachusetts Institute of Technology Publications in Humanities, 1962), pp. 5, 7, 17; C. Cruise O'Brien, *Parnell and His Party*, pp. 286, 291.

26. C. Cruise O'Brien, *Parnell and His Party*, pp. 314, 335.

27. Lyons, *Fall of Parnell*, pp. 155, 172.

28. Ibid., p. 157; R. B. O'Brien, *Life of Parnell*, p. 506.

29. Lyons, *Fall of Parnell*, p. 163; R. B. O'Brien, *Life of Parnell*, p. 502.

30. R. B. O'Brien, *Life of Parnell*, p. 513.

31. Lyons, *Fall of Parnell*, pp. 167–68.

32. Ervine, *Parnell*, pp. 307–8.

33. Devoy, *Devoy's Post Bag*, 2:317–18.

34. Sheehy-Skeffington, *Michael Davitt*, p. 187; and Strauss, *Irish Nationalism and British Democracy*, p. 209.

35. R. B. O'Brien, *Life of Parnell*, p. 517.

36. Devoy, *Devoy's Post Bag*, 2:316.

37. Katharine Tynan, *Twenty-five Years* (London: Smith, Elder, and Co., 1913), p. 195.

38. M. F. Ryan, *Fenian Memories*, p. 149.

39. R. B. O'Brien, *Life of Parnell*, p. 516.

40. Ibid.

41. Lyons, *Fall of Parnell*, pp. 272–74; Jules Abels, *The Parnell Tragedy* (New York: Macmillan Co., 1966), p. 368.

42. R. B. O'Brien, *Life of Parnell*, p. 505.

43. Lyons, *Fall of Parnell*, pp. 304–7; R. B. O'Brien, *Life of Parnell*, pp. 549–51.

44. Bourke, *John O'Leary*, p. 206.

45. T. D. Sullivan, *Recollections of Troubled Times in Irish Politics*, pp. 316–17.

46. O'Leary, *Recollections of Fenians and Fenianism*, 1:170.

CHAPTER 23

1. John Morley, *The Life of William Ewart Gladstone*, 3 vols. (London: Macmillan and Co., 1903), 3:493.

2. *Annual Register for the Year 1892* (London, 1893), p. 101.

3. J. L. Hammond, *Gladstone and the Irish Nation* (London: Longmans, Green, and Co., 1938), pp. 690–93.

4. Devoy, *Devoy's Post Bag*, 2:233.

5. James Carty, *Bibliography of Irish History* (Dublin: James Carty, 1940), p. xv.

6. Conor Cruise O'Brien, "Passion and Cunning: Essay on the Politics of W. B. Yeats," in *In Excited Reverie*, ed. A. Norman Jeffares and K. G. W. Cross (New York: Macmillan Co., 1965), p. 264.

7. Maud Gonne MacBride, *A Servant of the Queen* (London: V. Gollancz, 1938), pp. 198, 200.

8. W. B. Yeats, *Letters*, p. 181.

9. Douglas Hyde, "The Necessity for De-Anglicizing Ireland," in Sir Charles Gavan Duffy, *The Revival of Irish Literature* (London, 1894), pp. 120, 138.

10. Ibid., p. 122.

11. Dorothy Macardle, *The Irish Republic* (London: V. Gollancz, 1965), p. 61; Patrick Pearse, *Political Writings and Speeches* (Dublin: Phoenix Publishing Co., [1922]), p. 91.

12. W. B. Yeats, *Letters to the New Island*, ed. Horace Reynolds (Cambridge, Mass.: Harvard University Press, 1934), p. 157.

13. Stopford A. Brooke, *The Need and Use of Getting Irish Literature into the English Tongue* (London, 1893), pp. 15–16.

14. W. B. Yeats, *Letters*, p. 212.

15. Duffy, *Revival of Irish Literature*, pp. 17, 19.

16. See W. B. Yeats, *Letters*, p. 103.

17. W. B. Yeats, *Autobiographies*, pp. 136–38.

18. Duffy, *Revival of Irish Literature*, pp. 20, 51.

19. W. B. Yeats, *Autobiographies*, p. 138.

20. Frank Hugh O'Donnell, *Souls for Gold! Pseudo-Celtic Drama in Dublin* (London, 1899).

21. W. B. Yeats, *Essays and Introductions*, p. 193.

22. W. B. Yeats, *Letters to the New Island*, p. 154.

23. W. B. Yeats, "Literary Movement in Ireland," pp. 93–94.

24. W. B. Yeats, in *Bookman*, October 1893, p. 20.

25. W. B. Yeats, *Letters*, p. 247.

26. W. B. Yeats, in *Bookman*, August 1895, p. 138.

27. W. B. Yeats, *Variorum Edition of the Poems*, p. 576.

28. Thomas R. Whitaker, *Swan and Shadow* (Chapel Hill: University of North Carolina Press, 1964), p. 79.

29. W. B. Yeats, in *Bookman*, November 1895, pp. 59–60.

30. W. B. Yeats, *Autobiographies*, pp. 125, 213.

31. George Moore, *Hail and Farewell*, 2 vols. (New York: D. Appleton and Co., 1925), 2:261.

32. W. B. Yeats, *Letters*, p. 131.

33. Lady Gregory, *Our Irish Theatre* (New York: G. P. Putnam's Sons, 1965), pp. 280, 304–5.

34. W. B. Yeats, *Letters*, pp. 208–9.

35. Ibid., pp. 210–11.

36. W. B. Yeats, *Autobiographies*, pp. 119, 202–3.

37. Joseph Hone, *W. B. Yeats* (New York: Macmillan Co., 1943), p. 434.

38. W. B. Yeats, *Letters*, p. 230.

39. W. B. Yeats, in *Bookman*, February 1897, p. 147.

40. Richard Ellmann, *Yeats: The Man and the Masks* (New York: Macmillan Co., 1958), pp. 97, 112.

41. W. B. Yeats, *Autobiographies*, p. 142.

42. Ellmann, *Yeats*, pp. 112–13.

43. Lady Gregory, ed., *Ideals in Ireland*, p. 101.

44. W. B. Yeats, *Autobiographies*, pp. 202–3.

45. Ibid., p. 120.

46. Hone, *W. B. Yeats*, p. 131.

47. W. B. Yeats, *A Book of Irish Verse* (London: Methuen, 1920), p. xxvi.

48. W. B. Yeats and Lionel Johnson, *Poetry and Ireland* (Dundrum: Cuala Press, 1907), p. 41. The epigram is Johnson's, dated 1894.

49. W. B. Yeats, in *United Irishman*, October 10, 1903.

50. Joseph Holloway, *Joseph Holloway's Abbey Theatre*, ed. Robert Hogan and Michael J. O'Neill (Carbondale: Southern Illinois University Press, 1967), p. 106. The statement appeared in a letter to O'Leary that escaped into the public domain at O'Leary's death.

51. James Connolly, in *United Irishman*, October 24, 1903.

52. A very full chronicle of Yeats's wars in the 1890s is presented in Phillip L. Marcus, *Yeats and the Beginning of the Irish Renaissance* (Ithaca: Cornell University Press, 1970).

CHAPTER 24

1. Elizabeth Coxhead, *Lady Gregory* (London: Secker and Warburg, 1961), p. 30.

2. Blunt, *Land War in Ireland*, p. 146.

3. Standish O'Grady, *The Story of Ireland* (London, 1894), p. 210.

4. Ibid., pp. 203–5.

5. Ibid., pp. 74, 181, 182.

6. Ibid., p. 211.

7. Ibid., pp. 211–12.

8. W. B. Yeats, *Letters to the New Island*, pp. 137–38.

9. Ibid., pp. 112, 153.

10. W. B. Yeats, *Letters*, p. 35.
11. Ibid., pp. 163–64.
12. Ellmann, *Yeats*, p. 100.
13. W. B. Yeats, *Letters*, p. 177.
14. W. B. Yeats, *Variorum Edition of the Poems*, p. 834.
15. W. B. Yeats, *Letters*, pp. 179–80.
16. W. B. Yeats, "Irish National Literature," *Bookman*, August 1895, p. 139.
17. Ellmann, *Yeats*, p. 111.
18. W. B. Yeats, "Literary Movement in Ireland," p. 88.
19. W. B. Yeats, *Letters*, p. 333.
20. Lady Gregory, *Irish Folk-History Plays*, second series (New York: G. P. Putnam's Sons, 1912), pp. 161, 169, 172, 181, 182, 183, 195.
21. Holloway, *Holloway's Abbey Theatre*, p. 148.
22. Michael J. O'Neill, *Lennox Robinson* (New York: Twayne Publishers, 1964), pp. 83, 85.
23. W. B. Yeats, *Autobiographies*, pp. 141, 155.
24. W. B. Yeats, *The King of the Great Clock Tower* (London: Macmillan and Co., 1935), pp. 37–38.
25. W. B. Yeats, *Variorum Edition of the Poems*, p. 542.
26. W. B. Yeats, *On the Boiler* (Dublin: Cuala Press, 1938), p. 30.
27. C. Cruise O'Brien, "Passion and Cunning," p. 257.
28. W. B. Yeats, *Variorum Edition of the Poems*, p. 542.
29. W. B. Yeats, *Letters on Poetry to Dorothy Wellesley* (London: Oxford University Press, 1964), p. 123.
30. Joyce, *Critical Writings*, pp. 228, 243.
31. Joyce, *Ulysses*, pp. 633–36.
32. Ibid., p. 635.
33. W. B. Yeats, *Variorum Edition of the Poems*, p. 587.
34. Conor Cruise O'Brien, *Maria Cross* (London: Chatto and Windus, 1963), pp. 87–109.
35. W. B. Yeats, *Variorum Edition of the Poems*, p. 86.
36. Ibid., p. 63.

BIBLIOGRAPHICAL NOTE

Concerning Irish literature, I have assumed my readers to be already more or less familiar with its standard fare. A person could not possibly avoid contact at some time with W. B. Yeats and James Joyce, and also with their gifted fellow countrymen: J. M. Synge, George Moore, Sean O'Casey, George Russell, Frank O'Connor, Sean O'Faolain, Liam O'Flaherty, Brendan Behan, Patrick Kavanagh, and many more, including the celebrated Victorian trinity, Thomas Davis, James Clarence Mangan, Samuel Ferguson. The full corpus of modern Irish literature is so extremely vast and popular that I feel no call to present here even an informal bibliography of the field.

Concerning Irish history, these specialized studies are particularly illuminating for the period I have covered:

Beckett, J. C. *The Making of Modern Ireland*. New York: Alfred A. Knopf, 1966.

Bourke, Marcus. *John O'Leary: A Study in Irish Separatism*. Tralee: Anvil Books, 1967.

Cruise O'Brien, Conor. *Parnell and His Party, 1880–90*. Oxford: Clarendon Press, 1957.

Curtis, L. P., Jr. *Coercion and Conciliation in Ireland*. Princeton, N.J.: Princeton University Press, 1963.

D'Arcy, William. *The Fenian Movement in the United States, 1858–1886*. Washington, D.C.: Catholic University of America Press, 1947.

Edwards, R. Dudley, and Williams, T. Desmond, eds. *The Great Famine*. Dublin: Browne and Nolan, 1957.

Gwynn, Denis. *Daniel O'Connell*. Cork: Cork University Press, 1947.

———. *Young Ireland and 1848*. Oxford: Cork University Press, 1949.

Larkin, Emmet. *The Roman Catholic Hierarchy and the Fall of Parnell*. Cambridge, Mass.: Massachusetts Institute of Technology Publications in Humanities, 1962.

Lyons, F. S. L. *The Fall of Parnell*. London: Routledge and Kegan Paul, 1960.

———. *John Dillon*. London: Routledge and Kegan Paul, 1968

McCaffrey, Lawrence J. *Daniel O'Connell and the Repeal Year*. Lexington: University of Kentucky Press, 1966.

Moody, T. W., ed. *The Fenian Movement*. Cork: Mercier Press, 1968.

Norman, E. R. *The Catholic Church and Ireland in the Age of Rebellion: 1859–1873*. Ithaca, N.Y.: Cornell University Press, 1965.

Nowlan, Kevin B. *The Politics of Repeal*. London: Routledge and Kegan Paul, 1965.

Palmer, Norman Dunbar. *The Irish Land League Crisis*. New Haven, Conn.: Yale University Press, 1940.

Ryan, Desmond. *The Fenian Chief: A Biography of James Stephens*. Dublin: M. H. Gill and Son, 1967.

Thornley, David. *Isaac Butt and Home Rule*. London: MacGibbon and Kee, 1964.

Whyte, J. H. *The Independent Irish Party*. Oxford: Oxford University Press, 1958.

Woodham-Smith, Cecil. *The Great Hunger*. New York: Harper and Row, 1964.

The primary historical materials accessible to me were, first of all, the files of the Irish revolutionary journals of the nineteenth century: the *United Irishman* under John Mitchel; the *Irish People* under John O'Leary; the *Irishman* under Denis Holland and Richard Pigott; and the *Nation* under Thomas Davis, John Mitchel, Gavan Duffy, and A. M. and T. D. Sullivan. Second, the following published memoirs, manifestoes, and pamphlets of the Irish historical actors and eyewitness observers were also of value:

Blunt, Wilfred Scawen. *The Land War in Ireland*. London: Stephen Swift and Co., 1912.

Davitt, Michael. *The Fall of Feudalism in Ireland*. New York: Harper and Brothers, 1904.

Devoy, John. *Devoy's Post Bag*. Edited by William O'Brien and Desmond Ryan. Dublin: Fallon Press, 1948.

———. *Recollections of an Irish Rebel*. New York: Charles P. Young, 1929.

Duffy, Sir Charles Gavan. *Young Ireland: A Fragment of Irish History, 1840–1850*. New York, 1881.

Harrison, Henry. *Parnell Vindicated*. London: Constable and Co., 1931.

Lalor, James Fintan. *The Writings of James Fintan Lalor*. Edited by John O'Leary. Dublin, 1895.

MacBride, Maud Gonne. *A Servant of the Queen*. London: V. Gollancz, 1938.

Mitchel, John. *Jail Journal*, Dublin: M. H. Gill and Son, 1921.

———. *The Last Conquest of Ireland (Perhaps)*. New York, 1876.

O'Brien, R. Barry. *The Life of Charles Stewart Parnell*. Popular ed. London: Thomas Nelson and Sons, n.d.

O'Donnell, F. Hugh. *A History of the Irish Parliamentary Party*. 2 vols. London: Longmans, Green, and Co., 1910.

O'Grady, Standish. *The Crisis in Ireland*. Dublin, 1882.

———. *Toryism and Tory Democracy*. London, 1886.

O'Leary, John *Recollections of Fenians and Fenianism*. 2 vols. London, 1896.

O'Shea, Katharine. *Charles Stewart Parnell: His Love Story and Political Life*. 2 vols. London: Cassell and Co., 1914.

Sullivan, A. M. *New Ireland*. Philadelphia, 1878.

Sullivan, T. D. *Recollections of Troubled Times in Irish Politics*. Dublin: M. H. Gill and Son, 1905.

Irish histories divide into two classes: the deliberative or critical and the partisan. These ought to complement each other, since it is equally pointless to deliberate upon inanity or to champion paranoid hallucinations. Like any science, deliberative history is cumulative, and the newest is likely to be the best. As it happens, the last work out is F. S. L. Lyons' *Ireland since the Famine* (New York: Scribners, 1971), a massive job that not only synthesizes a whole generation of brilliant research into nineteenth-century Irish history, but also bravely opens up the hitherto tabooed field of post-Treaty history. As for partisan history, I cannot commend the sanctimonious and lugubrious genre represented by A. M. Sullivan's *The Story of Ireland*. I myself lean upon these works: Giovanni Costigan, *A History of Modern Ireland* (New York: Pegasus, 1969); P. S. O'Hegarty, *A History of Ireland under the Union* (London: Methuen, 1952); Emile Strauss, *Irish Nationalism and British Democracy* (London: Methuen, 1951); and T. A. Jackson, *Ireland Her Own* (London: Cobbett Press, 1946)—which Frank O'Connor once praised as the best book on Ireland that any Englishman would ever be able to write.

All of these volumes are anti-imperialist, for except among Yeatsist disciples, Froude has not survived as an intellectual influence in the twentieth century. All are lively in the best Irish cultural tradition, so much so that the O'Hegarty has been called "worthless" and the Strauss "cocksure," in the courtly language of the academic cloisters.

Literary commentators have long shown a partiality for T. R. Henn's fine nostalgic chapter on the big houses of Sligo in his book on Yeats called *The Lonely Tower* (London: Methuen, 1966). I can perhaps helpfully add a list of other essays very different from Henn's, but all short enough to be read without fatigue: (1) The opening chapter of Daniel Corkery's *The Hidden Ireland* (Dublin: M. H. Gill and Son, 1925). (2) Benedict Kiely's little book on William Carleton, *The Poor Scholar: A Study of the Works and Days of William Carleton* (New York: Sheed and Ward, 1946). (3) The opening chapter of Carleton's *Rody the Rover*, and chapter 9 of his *Valentine M'Clutchy*, in *The Works of William Carleton*, 2 vols. (Freeport, N.Y.: Books for Libraries Press, 1970), vol. 1. (4) Yvor Winters' pamphlet, also on Yeats's Sligo background, *The Poetry of W. B. Yeats* (Denver: Alan Swallow, 1960). (5) Conor Cruise O'Brien's essay on the Dublin poetico-political cockpit, "Passion and Cunning: Essay on the Politics of W. B. Yeats," in *In Excited Reverie*, ed. A. Norman Jeffares and K. G. W. Cross (New York: Macmillan Co., 1965). (6) The last chapter of Herbert Howarth's *The Irish Writers, 1880–1940* (London: Rockliff, 1958). (7) James Connolly's pamphlet, *Labor in Irish History* (Dublin: Maunsel and Co.,

1934). (8) The chapter called "The Sword of Light" in Sean O'Casey's *Pictures in the Hallway* (New York: Macmillan Co., 1960).

For readers less hurried, I must commend the most important single literary work ever written by a leading Irish revolutionist, Charles J. Kickham's *Knocknagow* (rhymes with "snow"). This expert panorama of the Irish rural scene in the age of Isaac Butt provides the sharpest possible image of the forces that moved Irish history. It is also remarkable for what it is not. Totally devoid of rancor, vague in all its action lines, and so prolix that its leisureliness is actually charming, it is the precise Antiself of the rabid novel we would be led to expect from Yeats's late aspersions on it. (He earlier borrowed from it with gratitude the literary idea for his fine ballad on the dying fox hunter.) Its literary ancestor is *Adam Bede* rather than "A Modest Proposal," and its perennial popularity in Ireland is weighty evidence for both Irish good taste and Irish good sense.

Concerning the interaction between Irish history and Irish poetry, several bibliographical items not usually met in the ordinary Yeats-Joyce critical literature need to be mentioned:

Brooke, Stopford A. *The Need and Use of Getting Irish Literature into the English Tongue*. London, 1893.

Duffy, Sir Charles Gavan. *The Revival of Irish Literature*. London, 1894. This book also contains Douglas Hyde's address, "The Necessity for De-Anglicizing Ireland."

———. *Thomas Davis: The Memoirs of an Irish Patriot, 1840–1846*. London, 1890.

O'Grady, Standish. *The Story of Ireland*. London, 1894.

Gregory, Lady, ed. *Ideals in Ireland*. London: Unicorn Press, 1901. This volume contains essays by W. B. Yeats, George Moore, George Russell, Standish O'Grady, and D. P. Moran.

Yeats, W. B. *Letters to the New Island*. Edited by Horace Reynolds. Cambridge, Mass.: Harvard University Press, 1934.

———. *A Tribute to Thomas Davis*. Oxford: B. H. Blackwell, 1947.

———. *Uncollected Prose*. Vol. 1. Edited by John P. Frayne. New York: Columbia University Press, 1970. This volume contains miscellaneous pieces that appeared in *Bookman* (London) between 1890 and 1896.

Index

Butler, Mrs. (dressmaker), 197, 264
Butt, Isaac, viii, 33, 56, 189–90, 235,
241, 244–46, 251, 257–58, 265, 291;
founder of *Dublin University Magazine*, 59–60; champions Orange Order,
60; debates O'Connell, 68; on famine
causes, 104–5; defends Smith O'Brien,
115; defends Fenians, 189–90, 231;
founder of Amnesty Association, 229,
232; friendship with Yeats family,
230–31; Yeats's ideal politician, 231;
founder of Home Rule, 233–34;
affection for British empire, 234;
abandons nonsectarian political strategy, 237; believes party discipline
immoral, 237, 243, 245–46; parliamentary disasters of, 239; discovers
Parnell, 240; O'Flaherty on, 242
Byrne, Daniel, 192–94
Byrne, Mr. and Mrs. Frank, 284–85
Byron, George Gordon, Lord, 63

Cairbre Cat-Head, 297, 331n, 379
Calvin, John, 138
Cambridge, Duke of, 90–91
Campbell, Thomas: "Hohenlinden,"
63
Carbonari, 179
Carey, James, 275–80, 284–85, 381
Carleton, William, 24, 65, 81, 92, 140,
370, 376
The Black Prophet, 92
Rody the Rover, 113, 358, 414
"Tubber Derg," 92
Valentine M'Clutchy, 65, 414
Carlisle, George William Frederick, 7th
earl of, 221–22, 368
Carlyle, Thomas, 15, 30, 117–20, 138,
249, 298, 308
Chartism, 117–18, 142
French Revolution, 86
Heroes and Hero Worship, 358
Latter Day Pamphlets, 142
"On the Nigger Question," 299
Past and Present, 47
"Shooting Niagara," 299
Carnarvon, Henry Howard Molyneux
Herbert, 4th earl of, 306
Carnot, Lazare, 72
Casement, Sir Roger, 322–23

Casey, John: "The Rising of the Moon,"
182
Casey, Joseph, 223–24, 230
Catholic Church, 30–33, 77, 113–14,
228; puritanism of, 126–27, 359; feud
with Fenians, 174–75; supports Home
Rule, 237, 257; ex-officio members of
National League, 288; role in Parnell
Split, 340–41, 343
Catholic Defense Association, 130
Catholic Emancipation, 23, 45, 360
Castlereagh, Robert Stewart, 2nd vis-
count, 131, 242
Cavendish, Lord Frederick, 271–72,
279, 285, 309
Cavour, Camillo, 123
Celtic Twilight, 51, 217, 330–31n
Censorship, Irish, 11, 126–27
Chamberlain, Sir Austen, 309
Chamberlain, Joseph, 270, 272–73, 306,
308–9, 311, 328, 350, 365, 386
Chamberlain, Neville, 309, 322
Chartism, 35–36
Churchill, Lord Randolph, 298, 307–8
Churchill, Sir Winston, 55–56
Civil War (1922–23), 57, 381
Clan-na-Gael, 7, 351–52
Clarendon, George William Frederick
Villiers, 4th earl of, 105, 108, 112, 118
Clarke, Austin, 11, 316, 389
Clarke, Thomas, 223
Claverhouse, John Graham of, 34
Clerkenwell explosion, 223–25, 244
Cluseret, Gen. Paul, 200–1, 203, 205
Cobbett, William, 48, 142, 317
Coercion, legal, 74, 110, 119, 263, 274,
306, 308
Colenso, Bishop John, 165
Collins, Michael, 42, 290
Colum, Padraic, 9, 14; *The Land*, 295
"Combination of all Irish classes," 52–
53, 104, 147, 368
Committee of Sixty-one, 233–35, 257
Connaught, Arthur William Patrick
Albert, duke of, 234
Conner, William, 69
Connolly, James, 55, 57, 291, 331n
Conway (Repealer), 82
Cooper family, 368
Corcoran, Gen. Michael, 173, 256